POWER
IN AND AROUND
ORGANIZATIONS

Henry Mintzberg

McGill University

PRENTICE-HALL, INC., Englewood Cliffs, N.J. 07632

Library of Congress Cataloging in Publication Data

MINTZBERG, HENRY.
    Power in and around organizations.

    (The Theory of management policy series)
    Bibliography: p.
    Includes index.
        1. Organization.   2.–Power (Social sciences)
    3. Corporations–United States.   I. Title. II. Series:
    Mintzberg, Henry.   Theory of management policy series.
    HD38.M4865 1983   302.3'5   82-12296
    ISBN 0-13-686857-6

Editorial/production supervision
and interior design by Esther S. Koehn
Cover design by Celine A. Brandes
Manufacturing buyer: Ed O'Dougherty

To Mom and Dad
. . . from your puddinghead

The Theory of Management Policy Series
Henry Mintzberg, Editor

©1983 by Prentice-Hall, Inc., Englewood Cliffs, N.J. 07632

Printed in the United States of America

10 9 8 7 6 5 4 3 2

ISBN 0-13-686857-6

Prentice-Hall International, Inc., *London*
Prentice-Hall of Australia Pty. Limited, *Sydney*
Editora Prentice-Hall do Brasil, Ltda., *Rio de Janeiro*
Prentice-Hall Canada Inc., *Toronto*
Prentice-Hall of India Private Limited, *New Delhi*
Prentice-Hall of Japan, Inc., *Tokyo*
Prentice-Hall of Southeast Asia Pte. Ltd., *Singapore*
Whitehall Books Limited, *Wellington, New Zealand*

Contents

Foreword

The Theory of Management Policy Series

Management Policy has long been the stepchild of the management school. It had to be taught—the issues it dealt with were too important to ignore—yet it never quite attained the status of other fields, such as management science, organizational behavior, and marketing. The reason for this seems quite clear. While the other fields were developing substantial theoretical content throughout the 1960s and 1970s, Management Policy—having shed its long-standing "principles" orientation—was focusing its attention on the teaching of cases. Theory—systematic knowledge—was, and often remains, unwelcome in the Policy course.

I had the good fortune to study for a doctorate in Policy at a management school (the MIT Sloan School) that had no Policy area, not even a Policy professor. That enabled me to explore the field from a different perspective. Cases had no special place at MIT. Theory had. So my exploration became a search for Policy theory—specifically descriptive theory based on empirical research. And that search convinced me of one thing: that there in fact existed a large and relevant body of such theory, sufficient to put the field on a solid theoretical foundation. But that theory was to be found in no one place—no one textbook, for example; indeed a great deal of it was not recognized as Policy-related theory per se. In other words, the field lacked synthesis, even compendium—the bringing together of the useful theoretical materials. So by the time I completed my Ph.D. at the Sloan School in 1968, I had made up my mind to write a book called *The Theory of Management Policy*.

Ten years were spent paying the price of that decision. What began as files on each chapter quickly became boxes, and then the boxes began to overflow, in some cases two and even three times. Convinced that the field needed a thorough publication, I let the chapters run to their natural lengths. In two cases, that came to over 400 pages of text! Hence this series.

The original outline of *The Theory of Management Policy* called for eleven chapters, eight of which are shown on the accompanying figure. Two (not shown) were introductory. The first, entitled "The Study of Management Policy," traced the development of the field, from its principles and case study traditions to contemporary approaches based on grand planning, eclectic and descriptive theory. This chapter concluded that the field should be built on descriptive theory, that this theory should be based on inductive research of the policy-making process and and be supported by research in underlying fields such as cognitive psychology, organizational sociology, and political science, and that the policy-making research should be rich in real-world description and not obsessed with rigor. The second chapter, "An Underlying Theory for Management Policy," combined the general systems theory of Ludwig von Bertalanffy with the decision theory of Herbert Simon to develop a framework in which to integrate the different topics of Management Policy. These two chapters actually exist as chapters, and may one day see the light of day in a single synthesized book. In the meantime, parts of them have been published as "Policy as a Field of Management Theory" (in the *Academy of Management Review* of January, 1977), a paper that outlines my general views on the field.

Five chapters made up the core of the book—the descriptive theory. These will form this series, as it is presently conceived. The first three—the "policy elements"—were designed to synthesize the empirical research on three topics (generally considered in "organization theory") that I believe underlie the study

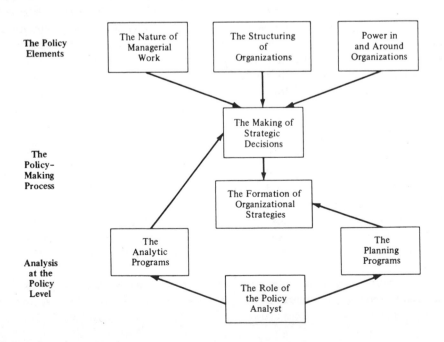

of policy making—managerial work, organizational structure, and organizational power. *The Nature of Managerial Work*, based on my own doctoral research as well as related empirical literature, was originally published in 1973 and was reproduced in this series in 1980. *The Structuring of Organizations: A Synthesis of the Research*, is the original Chapter 3 having run a little long, and appeared as the first book in this series in 1979. And this book, *Power In and Around Organizations*, is Chapter 5 having run even longer. Like the *Structuring* book, this one is based on the study of a large body of (mostly empirical) literature.

The two chapters on the "policy-making process" were intended to focus on the central core of the field of Management Policy. *The Making of Strategic Decisions* currently exists as a (not unreasonably) large Chapter 6; it will be expanded into a (not unreasonably) small volume four (or five). Like the volume on managerial work, it combines a synthesis of the empirical literature with our own research, carried out at McGill University (and published in article form as "The Structure of 'Unstructured' Decision Processes," together with Duru Raisinghani and Andre Théorêt, in the *Administrative Science Quarterly* of June, 1976). This volume considers the question of how organizations actually make single strategic decisions. The final volume, *The Formation of Organization Strategies*, is designed to look at how organizations combine such decisions over time to form strategies. This is the one book in the series that does not yet exist (although it has begun to take shape in a number of articles including, "Strategy Making in Three Modes," published in the *California Management Review* in the winter of 1973, "Patterns in Strategy Formation," published in the May, 1978 issue of *Management Science*, and "Tracking Strategy in an Entrepreneurial Firm," with James A. Waters, published in the *Academy of Management Journal* of September, 1982). Here again, the empirical literature will be combined with our own research, except that in both cases the dimensions are much larger—four boxes of published materials coupled with the results of a decade of research.

The prescriptive section of *The Theory of Management Policy*—three chapters on "analysis at the policy level" and a fourth on the future for Management Policy—remains a project on a dim horizon. A number of shorter items have been published on policy analysis (such as "Impediments to the Use of Management Information," a 1975 monograph by the National Association of Accountants and the Society of Industrial Accountants of Canada, "The Planning Dilemma" with James S. Hekimian in the May, 1968 issue of the *Management Review*, and especially "Beyond Implementation: An Analysis of the Resistance to Policy Analysis" in K. B. Haley [ed.] *Operational Research '78*, North Holland, 1979). Perhaps these will one day be drawn together into a sixth volume on policy analysis, but more likely that volume will focus on the broader issue of organizational effectiveness.

And what of *The Theory of Managment Policy?* In the not too distant future, I hope to draw the central concepts of all the books and articles into a single volume, a textbook along the lines of the original conception.

A few words about the title of the series are in order. "The" is meant to signify "the body" of theory in Management Policy, not "the one" theory of Management Policy. In fact, if one central theme runs through the series, it is an attempt to synthesize by seeking reconciliation among conflicting theories. The approach is essentially a contingency one—not which theory is correct, but under what conditions does each apply. Not planning *versus* muddling through, but *when* planning, *when* muddling through; not maximizing *versus* satisfying, but *where* maximizing, *where* satisfying.

"Theory" signifies that the series seeks to build conceptual frameworks. Theories are useful because they shortcut the need to store masses of data. One need not remember all the details one has learned about a phenomenon. Instead, one stores a theory, and abstraction that explains many of them. The level of that abstraction can vary widely. These volumes seek to present theory that is "middle range." In this sense, the series seeks to position itself between— and in so doing to reject both—Policy's case study tradition, which never sought to develop conceptual interpretation of its lower-range (concrete) descriptions, and Policy's principles tradition, whose high-range abstractions lost touch with the descriptive reality.

The attempt throughout this series is also to present theory that is "grounded"—that is rooted in data, that grows inductively out of systematic investigation of how organizations behave. I am firmly convinced that the best route to more effective policy making is better knowledge in the mind of the practitioner of the world he or she actually faces. This means that I take my role as researcher and writer to be the generation and dissemination of the best *descriptive* theory possible. I believe it is the job of the practitioner—line manager, staff analyst, consultant (including myself when in that role)—to prescribe, to find better approaches to policy making. In other words, I believe that the best prescription comes from the application of conceptual knowledge about a phenomenon *in a specific and familiar context*. To me, good descriptive theory in the right hands *is* a prescriptive tool, perhaps the most powerful one we have.

I use the word "Management," instead of the more common "Business," as the adjective for Policy to indicate that this series is about all kinds of organizations—not only automobile companies, banks, and consulting firms, but also cultural centers, penitentiaries, and space agencies. It is the focus on process rather than content—strategy making rather than strategies, the flow of power rather than the resulting goals—that enables us to take this broad perspective.

Finally the word "Policy," one that has been used in all kinds of ways. A government "policy" can range from having to use black ink on Form F6 to refusing aid to nonaligned nations. Here the word is used strictly as a label for a field of study—that one concerned with the management of the total organization, with particular emphasis on its decisional behavior. (I prefer Management Policy to Strategic Management—a term popular in parts of the field—because the latter seems to me to have a narrower and more prescriptive orientation.)

I shall save specific acknowledgements for each of the volumes, with one exception. I began work on *The Theory of Management Policy* when I first taught the MBA Policy course at McGill University in 1968, doing the original detailed draft of its outline for my first students in that course. Over the years, nearly a thousand McGill MBAs have worked through various versions of this work, most of them too long. These students can take some solace in the fact that this series has benefited enormously from their inputs. Specifically, using the theory as the basis to study Montreal organizations, the students have applied, elaborated, modified, and rejected various parts of the theory, thereby grounding and enriching it as no other inputs could possibly have. I owe these students a large thank you. I can only hope that they learned something along the way.

HENRY MINTZBERG

(From the Foreword to the Series, first published in *The Structuring of Organizations*, with minor changes.)

"The fox knows many things, but the hedgehog knows one big thing." This quotation, dating back to ancient Greek times, has always intrigued me, probably because I have never been quite sure what it means. What I do know is that my first two books, both published in this series—*The Nature of Managerial Work* and *The Structuring of Organizations*—were hedgehog books. Each knew one big thing—the first, that managerial work was not what almost a century of writings had made it out to be, the second, that a confusing and disparate body of research about organizations could be synthesized around the concept of configuration. The third book in the "Theory of Management Policy Series" is a fox book. It knows many things. It knows that an even more disparate literature on power can be synthesized around the concept of configuration (elaborated and extended from the *Structuring* book). It knows, moreover, that power is not what a great deal of the writings has made it out to be. Power is, at the same time, less complicated than the abstractions of much of the theoretical literature and more intricate than the ready interpretations of much of the popular literature (on subjects such as social responsibility, boards of directors, corporate democracy, and the setting of objectives). It also knows, to cite a few sections:

> —how "outsiders" try to control the behavior of organizations (Chapter 4), how they sometimes succeed (Chapter 18), but why they often fail (Chapter 19)
>
> —how ideologies develop in organizations (Chapter 11) and sometimes capture them for better as well as worse (Chapter 21)

—how politics develops in organizations (Chapter 13) and sometimes captures them for better as well as worse (Chapter 23)

—how organizations reconcile conflicting goals and what it means for some to be able to maximize a single goal (in Chapter 15)

—why efficiency is a dirty word and how it as well as other "systems" goals (survival, control, growth) have managed to displace mission as a goal in large organizations over the last two hundred years (in Chapter 16)

—why unions that arise because of dysfunctions in professional organizations render them even more dysfunctional (Chapter 22)

—how the destructive forces intrinsic to each of a number of power configurations tend to give rise to a pattern of life cycles of organizations, and how these have boxed us into a society of self-serving and politicized monoliths (Chapter 24)

—who wants to control the corporation, why, and how (Chapters 26–33), and what we should do about it (Chapter 34)

The fox is the right symbol for this book because power is a sly and elusive phenomenon. Even when you have it cornered, you can never be sure it won't slip away. And a 700-page fox is no ordinary fox. It seems to me (on July 2, 1982) that I have been writing this book for most of my career. In fact, I wrote it first in the form of a chapter—which I thought would be about goals—around 1971, hid it for four years and then began to rewrite it in a quiet post-sabbatical sabbatical year in Aix-en-Provence, France, largely free of organizational commitments and power relationships. By 1976 I had two large printed volumes. I put the manuscript aside for a couple of years to finish my *Structuring* book, and then returned to it around 1978 to clean it up for publication. I rewrote it, then rewrote it, and rewrote it again. When my secretary, Cynthia Derynck, sent me the last chapter of what was to be the final draft while I was on vacation in France in the summer of 1980, she wrote, "Now all I have to look forward to is the index!" I came home and rewrote it again. A year later, on July 18, 1981, I finished revising that revision—the final one—eight hours before boarding a plane for another vacation in France.

What made completing this book so difficult? For one thing, it turned out to be so long that every time I finished revising Chapter 34, I had to go back and rewrite Chapter 1 (a 700-page fox chasing its tail). More important, though, is the nature of the phenomenon. The literature on power is so disparate, the concepts so elusive, and the issues so complicated that I was never satisfied with the drafts I read after they were typed, and so I continually insisted on rewriting them.

Despite all this, I feel the final result is successful. The book is long and in places it is difficult. It does not achieve the same integration as my *Structuring* book or the straightforwardness of my *Managerial Work* book, nor what I feel is the consistency of both. I strove for integration and I feel I achieved it, but not to the degree of my second book. The ground to be covered was vast, and the phenomenon to be discussed complex. Power in and around organizations is a subject which interests all kinds of scholars—management theorists, sociologists, political scientists, economists, lawyers, philosophers, anthropologists—not to mention the practitioners themselves who work in organizations. The reviewer can go to no one place—no tightly knit set of journals, no definitive textbook with a comprehensive bibliography, in any of the subareas let alone the whole area of organizational power. Sources as different as the *American Journal of Sociology* on mass movements in organizations and the *Harvard Business Review* on corporate social responsibility had not only to be reviewed but also reconciled. I spent two long periods tracking down hundreds of references, and I know there is a great deal more that I missed, hidden in obscure pockets. Consistency was hampered by huge gaps in this literature (particularly the research literature, with the purely theoretical literature often too abstract to be of any real use). The result is that some sections are simply not as strong as others.

Yet I believe the book is successful, simply because I learned a great deal about power in and around organizations (and, unexpectedly, about why organizations impact on our lives as they do), and because I feel that this learning is also available to the patient reader. Some of it is contained in the central thread that runs throughout the book, and some in the various notes and asides tucked away here and there.

This learning will lead me (and already has) into some new issues. I am neither a sociologist nor a political scientist, and while I used a good deal of the literature of the former and some of the latter, I did not set out to comment on government per se (as opposed to organizations that happen to be contained within government), and certainly not on society as such. My perspective was organizational. But, increasingly, we live in a world of organizations, indeed of giant organizations. And in such a world, the organization theorist has much to offer in understanding government and society. Today's government seems less like a legislative process than a collection of large organizations; likewise the economy and other spheres of activity seem more like networks of giant organizations that negotiate with each other politically than systems of numerous small ones that adjust to general economic and social forces. Organization theorists may have more to tell us about such a society than political scientists and economists, and so should be drawn into commenting on it.

Thus a central, if unintended, theme of this book is the examination of power as a social issue in our society of organizations. This theme appears throughout, sometimes indirectly (as in the discussion of the "external means of influence" in Chapter 4, which amounts to society's ways of controlling its organizations), sometimes directly but peripherally (as in the mention of the government equivalents of each of the power configurations discussed in Part IV), and sometimes centrally (as in the whole of Part V on "who should control the corporation"). It is this theme that leads me to believe that, although this book may be more difficult than my other two, it may ultimately prove more significant. This theme may contain the book's one big message. The fox may prove to be a hedgehog after all.

Any book, but especially a large one, requires many favors, much biting of lips, a great deal of undeserved consideration. Agreeable throughout were Cynthia Derynck, who did more drafts than she or I care to remember; Elise Beauregard, who did two drafts, and Janet Rose, who somehow managed to find the most obscure references and contributed as my research assistant in numerous other ways. In New Jersey, Esther Koehn was always ready to help during the production of the book. We have lived through this three times and are still good friends, thanks to her good nature. A deep-felt thank you to all of you.

Thanks to the Institut d'Administration des Entreprises in Aix-en-Provence, France, I had quiet time to write the first draft of the book. Quieter still were the summers on Mme. Bost's farm in the Perigord region of France, where the world of organizations seems to remote, so unreal, (and so unnecessary?). Perhaps it is only by getting so totally away from that world that one can begin to see inside of it.

A number of my colleagues commented on parts or all of the manuscript. Maurice Boisvert, whose untimely death was a loss to all of us, was generous with his comments on the first draft, as was Michel Paquin. Amittai Niv commented extensively on the Missionary chapter, Jean Pasquero, Rene Reeves, and Jim Waters provided useful feedback on "who should control the corporation," as did Don Armstrong on "restore it" and Ned Bowman on "ignore it"—although I did not always take their good advice. The family—Yvette, Susie, Lisa—bore with me through all my concerns; somehow we manage to grow closer through all the madness.

Last as well as least, I should like to thank a mule somewhere in Corsica, whose shoe (see p. 529) proved just the right size for getting a grip on who should control the corporation.

HENRY MINTZBERG

A Note to the Reader

In the note to the reader in *The Structuring of Organizations*, the companion volume to this one, I drew an analogy with a banquet, commenting not on the quality of the offerings but on the order in which they were to be taken. Well, if Structure is a banquet, then Power is a play. In our society, power in and around organizations is a kind of tragicomedy; we would like to laugh, and sometimes do, but there is also much to cry about.

Again, the offerings are meant to be taken in their given order. Like a mystery, this is a play that builds up to a climax. To weave the story requires the introduction of a great many clues and other details. Some clues are clearly important, others more subtle, some may seem trivial. But the audience can never be sure which is which until the climax is reached, or perhaps later, after reflection.

This is not a light play. It is long and its pace varies. The best parts, in my opinion, are interspersed in no special order. The play opens with a three-chapter overture, followed by the essence of the presentation in four parts comprising 21 chapters—four acts of 21 scenes, if you like—with the climax coming in the last one. A final part with ten chapters serves as a kind of epilogue.

To be specific, we begin with three introductory chapters, which set the stage for power as treated in this book. The first chapter establishes the tone and presents—or, perhaps more exactly, dismisses—the necessary terms and definitions. The second looks back on the literature of organizational power—a theatre in its own right—as it emerged from that of goals. And the third introduces the cast of players. We then move into the four central parts of this play on power.

Parts I, II, and III describe the basic elements of power in and around organizations. Part I looks at power around the organization: who seeks it, why, and, particularly, how—how people outside organizations try to influence what organizations do. Such people are described as forming three basic "coalitions" of external power—a first in which one (or a consensus of them) dominates, a second in which they divide external power, and a third in which all of them remain effectively passive. Part II then looks at power inside the organization— again, at who seeks it, why, and how. Five systems of internal influence are introduced—personal control, bureaucratic control, ideology, expertise, and politics—and each, when dominant, is described as giving rise to a different basic coalition of internal power. Part III considers the consequences of the play of power in and around the organization—specifically the kinds of goal systems organizations seem to use and some specific goals they appear to pursue as systems.

All of these elements are combined into a single synthesis in Part IV. This is presented in terms of six basic "configurations" of power derived by considering how the three types of coalitions of power around the organization might combine naturally with the five types of coalitions of power inside the organization. Each configuration is characterized in the terms of the theatre: the *Instrument* is described as "a command performance in two acts"; the *Closed System*, "a private showing in one act"; the *Autocracy*, "a solo performance"; the *Missionary*, "a passion play"; the *Meritocracy*, "a talent show in many acts," and the *Political Arena*, "a circus, with many rings." By then considering the various possible transitions among these configurations in Chapter 24, a life-cycle model of stages of organizational development emerges; this serves as the climax to our play about organizational power.

A final section of the book—Part V, referred to earlier as an epilogue— might be viewed as an appendix, or as an illustration of the theory of the book, or as a necessary finale to the questions of power in and around contemporary organizations. It considers who should control the corporation in terms of eight positions around a "conceptual horseshoe."

In *The Structuring of Organizations*, I used sentences in **boldface type** to summarize all the discussion, so that the reader could get the gist of the entire book by reading those sentences. I use this type here too, but in a different way. **Boldface type is used in various places to highlight major propositions; the sum total of this type serves not to summarize the main line of argument, but simply to emphasize certain points of interest.** The reader who wishes to get a rough summary of the general line of argument should read Chapters 1 and 3 for introductory material, Chapter 7 (which integrates Part I), the introductory material of Chapter 8 and all of Chapter 14 (which introduce and integrate Part II), and Chapter 17 and the last section of Chapter 24 on stages (which introduce and integrate Part IV—although all the chapters of Part IV are strongly recommended since this part synthesizes the materials of the first three parts of the book). Part V, which stands by itself, is introduced in Chapter 15 and partly summarized in Chapter 34.

So there you have it. Curtains, please!

1

Power

An expert has been defined as someone with no elementary knowledge. Power seems to require a good deal of elementary knowledge. That is perhaps why everybody seems to know what it is except the experts. They debate definitions of power endlessly, and how it differs from influence, control, authority, etc., etc. Yet ordinary people seem to have no trouble with the concept. They know what it means to have power and they can sense who has it. Salancik and Pfeffer (1977) asked ten department managers in an insurance company to rank twenty-one of their colleagues as to their influence in the organization, and all but one got right on with the task. "Only one person bothered to ask, 'What do you mean by influence?' When told 'power,' he responded, 'Oh,' and went on" (p. 4). The ten ranked their colleagues in remarkably similar ways.

This book opens with the premise that we too can get on with it, that what is of interest in the study of power in and around organizations is who gets it, when, how, and why, not what it is. If you don't know what power is, then perhaps you should read another book.

Why bother to study power? Why spend time on what one writer has called a "bottomless swamp," another, "the messiest problem of all" (Dahl 1957, p. 201; Perrow 1970, p. ix). The answer is that although there are many other, more tangible forces out there that affect what organizations do—such as the buying habits of clients, the invention of a new machine, an upturn in the economy—power is a major factor, one that cannot be ignored by anyone interested in understanding how organizations work and end up doing what they do. If we are to improve the functioning of our organizations from within, and to gain control of them from without to ensure that they act in our best interests, then we must understand the power relationships that surround and infuse them.

For those who decided to read another book, the choice is vast. It runs the gamut from studies of individuals in organizations to studies of societies of organizations, and it comes from the pens of people who call themselves sociologists and management or organization theorists, as well as political scientists, economists, psychologists, anthropologists, and a sprinkling of others. Everyone seems to be interested in questions of organizational power. But to date, that literature has not been focussed in any one place. And so the primary intention of this book is to synthesize the writings of authors who do not usually speak to each other, writers who concern themselves with the social responsibility of businessmen and the power of attendants in mental hospitals, with "distinctive" colleges and conglomerate corporations, with the building of empires inside organizations and the destroying from the outside of the empires that organizations build. In other words, this book is based on a reading of the literature that seems to shed the most light on questions of power in and around organizations. But at the outset, my biases in selecting that literature should perhaps be made clear.

A good part of the literature, as noted, is more concerned with abstractions of what power is than with the realities of how it gets used. Thus we are told that John R. P. French, Jr., defines "the power of A over B (with respect to a given opinion) [to be] equal to the maximum force which A can induce on B minus the maximum resisting force which B can mobilize in the opposite direction" (Dahl 1957, p. 202). Our concerns here are more parochial: with whether company presidents listen to the shareholders, or hospital directors to the orderlies, with what the right of workers to elect directors does to the power of the plant manager, with how Ralph Nader was able to get General Motors to say "uncle" so often while thousands of government bureaucrats seem unable to change hospitals or school systems very much.

As for the more tangible literature, probably the greatest part of it deals with power from the perspective of the individual—with what kind of person seeks power and with how, as an individual, he or she gets it, rather than with how that search for power affects processes in organizations. And at the other extreme, another body of literature—smaller but growing—concerns itself with the interplay of power between organizations. Its perspective is societal, or at least interorganizational, and it too sets aside questions of internal organizational process. This book positions itself between these two bodies of literature, seeking to cover neither the individual nor the societal perspective, but rather the perspective of the organization itself.[1] In other words, this is a book about the structure and the flow of power in and around organizations.

[1]The interorganizational perspective is well reviewed in Pfeffer and Salancik (1978). Toward the end of this book, our analysis does lead us into a number of statements about the social consequences of organizational power.

We seek first to understand the basic elements of that game called organizational power—specifically who are its players, or *influencers*, what are the *means* or *systems of influence* they use to gain power, and what are the *goals* and *goal systems* that result from their efforts; then to draw these elements together to describe various basic "configurations" of organizational power; and finally to see how we can use these configurations to better understand the behavior of organizations. Taking the organizational, rather than the individual or societal perspective, however, is not to say that this book is always necessarily pro-organization. We certainly live in a world of organizations—and shall continue to do so—and so must learn to live with them. But at a number of points in our discussion the reader will be asked to question whether we are in fact always blessed with our organizations.

In my selection of the literature that takes an organizational perspective, I have expressed further biases. Specifically, I have tried to favor the more applied works, especially those based on direct empirical study of organizations. This bias, unfortunately, narrows down the literature substantially—in some areas to virtually nothing—for there has long been considerable hesitation to go out and study the issues of power directly. And so I could not always satisfy this particular bias, having to resort primarily to nonempirical literature in places.[2] Until recently, power—in organizations if not governments, especially in the United States—was not quite a respectable topic for research. Few researchers were inclined to knock on the organization's door and announce: "I'm here to find out who has the power in this place." So the field was left mostly to sociologists, who tended to take a societal rather than an organizational perspective, and to study organizational power from without, at a distance. A few exceptions certainly stand out—such as Selznick's (1966) detailed analysis of the Tennessee Valley Authority and Dalton's (1959) firsthand observations of a factory—but most students of power tended to stand back or to stay away and abstract.

In one sense, this situation has changed dramatically since about 1975, especially in the field of management. Today everybody seems to be investigating questions of power in and around organizations. It has become respectable, indeed faddish. But some distance still remains between most researchers and the organizations they claim to study. Even in the field of management, there is a tendency in studying power to view the organization from the outside, apart from its functioning. In the words of one of my colleagues,[3] these researchers

---

[2]The companion volume in this series—*The Structuring of Organizations* (Mintzberg 1979a), which seeks to draw together the literature on organizational structuring—was subtitled *A Synthesis of the Research* because the conclusions were based largely on the results of empirical research. In this book, because in many places I was forced to draw on purely conceptual works in the absence of relevant empirical findings, I could not in good conscience use that subtitle, although that was my original intention.

[3]James A. Waters, in personal communication.

seem to lack a place to stand, which leaves their theories in mid-air. If I may be forgiven the extension of the metaphor, I like to believe that in taking the perspective it does, this book tries to bring this research down to earth.

To summarize, this book presents a theory of power in and around organizations, which has been developed to synthesize the literature of a practical and, where possible, empirical nature, from a number of different fields. After two other brief introductory chapters—one which traces the evolution of theory on power and goals and the other which introduces the power game and the players—we move into the heart of the book. The book contains five parts in all. The first three introduce the elements of our theory of organizational power, and the last two seek to synthesize and use these elements. Part I looks at power *around* the organization, investigating who are the *external* influencers and how they—in effect, how society in its various forms—seek to control what the organization does, through such means of influence as laws, pressure campaigns, and membership on the board of directors. Part II then looks at power *in* the organization, at the *internal* influencers on the receiving end of these pressures, and how they affect outcomes through the use of their own means of influence—personal and bureaucratic systems of control, ideology, expertise, and politics. In Part III we turn briefly to the question of goals, looking first at different systems of goals, and then at specific goals common to many organizations. In Part IV we then seek to pull all of the material of these first three parts together in describing six basic types or "configurations" of organizational power. We call these the Instrument, the Closed System, the Autocracy, the Missionary, the Meritocracy, and the Political Arena. Finally, Part V uses many of our findings to try to answer an important question in our society: Who should control the corporation? This part is like an appendix, except that in applying so much of the theory of the book, it serves to illustrate and to summarize it.

A NOTE ON DEFINITIONS (NEVERTHELESS)

If you have read this far—have not gone off in search of another book—yet are still bothered by definitions, this brief note is intended to tell you where I stand vis-à-vis other writers on the subject.

Essentially I stand for trying to simplify the problem as much as possible to avoid debating abstractions. **Power is defined in this book simply as the capacity to effect (or affect) organizational outcomes.** The French word "pouvoir" stands for both the noun "power" and the verb "to be able." To have power is to be able to get desired things done, to effect outcomes—actions and the decisions that precede them.[4]

---

[4]Since a decision is a commitment to action, power can sometimes be exercised between decision and action. This means that effecting the decision is sometimes not good enough; it is effecting the action that matters. We shall return to this issue in Chapter 8.

"Power" and "to be able" may be treated as synonymous in French, but not always in English. Dahl (1957, p. 202) may be right when he says that the problem with the word "power" in English is that it lacks a convenient verb form. We are forced to talk of "influencing" or "controlling" instead, and all kinds of semantic problems arise as a result. In any event, we are not alone in treating power as "to be able": Bertrand Russell defines power as "the production of intended effects" (1938, p. 35), and to Rosabeth Moss Kanter, "Power is the ability to *do* [later "to mobilize resources"], in the classic physical usage of power as energy" (1977, pp. 166, [247]). But a more widely used definition treats power as the capacity to affect the behavior of other people. Dahl's definition is probably the most frequently quoted: "A has power over B to the extent that he can get B to do something that B would otherwise not do" (1957, pp. 202–3). This second definition is, however, narrower than the first, since power as changing someone's behavior is a subset of power as effecting outcomes. Behavior needn't always be changed to get things done, nor must behavior necessarily be changed to have "power," as the term is popularly used. By Dahl's definition, the hermit who can grow a field of corn has no power, nor has the leader who is followed by people who would otherwise follow someone else.

Defining power exclusively in terms of one's ability to change behavior seems to deflect attention from outcome toward manipulation. Power would appear to become synonymous with politics. What matters is not what gets done, but who is convinced. The focus ends up on power for its own sake, as McCall says, on the "imposition" of will (1979, p. 186). In using the first definition here, we view **politics** as a subset of power, treating it (as we shall see at greater length in Chapter 13) as **informal power, illegitimate in nature.** Likewise we also treat **authority** as a subset of power, but in this case **formal** power, **the power vested in office,** the capacity to get things done by virtue of the position held.

Influence is another word that receives a good deal of attention in the literature, a number of writers distinguishing it in terms of enactment versus potential. Again I join a minority of writers, such as Kanter (1977) and McCall (1979), in finding this distinction of little help in the study of power. "It is an unrealistic separation of the phenomenon to consider the power a person has separately from the power (s)he actually uses" (McCall, p. 188). Hence influence will be treated as a synonym of power in this book, with the two words used interchangeably throughout.[5]

And then goal. We shall get to it in some detail in Chapters 15 and 16. Suffice it at this point to define **goals** as **the intentions behind decisions or actions,** the states of mind that drive individuals or collectivities of individuals

[5]It might be noted that the Webster's Student Dictionary defines power as, among other things, "The possession of control, authority, or influence," and influence, among other things, as "power to affect others."

called organizations to do what they do. But as we shall soon see, this is rather more complicated than it seems. In contrast to goal, **mission describes the organization's basic function in society, in terms of the products and services it produces for its clients.** Thus, the mission of a publishing company is to put books on the market, although one of its goals, perhaps, is to put profits in the pocket of its owner. The mission of a union is to represent its members in dealing with their employers, but its overriding goal may be to bring down— or alternatively to prop up—the existing political order. Is mission not one kind of goal? That seems to depend. Both the gourmet chef and the hamburger franchisee run restaurants; thus their missions are identical—to feed their clients. But their goals differ. For the gourmet chef, goal and mission usually coincide. He prepares his meals to satisfy both himself and his client. His goal—the intention behind his actions—is to perform his mission well. Not necessarily so for the franchisee. He typically prepares his meals to make money (or to make friends, or whatever). If he could make more money selling fanbelts, he probably would; the gourmet chef would not.

    An objective is a goal expressed in a form by which its attainment can be measured.[6] And **an operational goal is one that lends itself to such expression.** The operational goal is to cut costs, the objective to reduce the budget by 5 percent. A *nonoperational* goal does not lend itself to measurement, that is, cannot be easily "operationalized," as in "the aim of this university is to seek truth" or "love they neighbor as thyself." Thus we have, from "the Diary of a Lady":

Long-Range Goals:
    1. Health—more leisure.
    2. Money.
    3. Write book (play?)—fame////??
    4. India.

Immediate [objectives?]
    Pick up pattern at Hilda's.
    Change faucets—call plumber (who?)
    Try yoghurt?

(Quoted from *The New Yorker* by Ansoff 1965, p. 43)

    Organizations, too, can have trouble operationalizing their lofty goals, with the result that their *official* goals—what they claim to be their goals—

---

[6]Unfortunately some of the literature defines goal and objective in exactly the opposite way. Ackoff writes: "States or outcomes of behaviors that are desired are objectives.... *Goals* are objectives whose attainment is desired by a specified time within the period covered by the plan..." (1970, pp. 23–24). But everyday usage seems to favor the other definitions; for example, "management by objectives" means management by measurable results. It might also be noted that Richards usefully calls objectives (by the definition we are using) closed goals, ones that are "achievable and 'closed' when met" (1978, p. 6).

often do not correspond with the ends they actually seem to pursue. Sometimes, of course, the official goals are merely for public consumption, not for internal decision making. Thus Zald found that institutions treating juvenile delinquents stressed the goal of rehabilitation and denied those of punishment and containment, no matter how they really acted, because the former were more "conducive to public support" (1963, p. 214). And Warringer concluded that, in general, official statements of organizational purpose "must be treated as fictions produced by an organization to account for, explain, or rationalize its existence to particular audiences. . . ." (1965, p. 141). In other words, goals do not have lives of their own, independent of actions. Hence, in this book, we are safer talking about power than about goals, a point we shall develop in the next chapter. It is only through studying power as manifested in actual decisions and actions that we come to understand goals.

But enough of definitions. Let us trace briefly in the next chapter the shift in management theory from a focus on goals to one on power, and then get on with the study of power.

2

The Management Literature: From Goals to Power

Management theory, in particular the theory about the goals of the business firm, has done a complete about-face in the last three decades or so, from a reliance on classical economic theory to an increasing attention to newer sociological themes, from the notion of given organizational goals to that of fluid power in and around the organization with no set goals, from an organization devoid of influencers to one in which virtually everyone is an influencer, from the view of the organization as society's instrument to that of it as a political arena. As we shall soon see, four major assumptions which served as the pillars of this theory at the outset have one by one been shaken loose, proposals having been made to replace each by a diametrically opposed assumption. Tracing these changes briefly in this chapter—in terms of four basic stages—can serve to "unfreeze" certain notions about how power is traditionally thought to flow in organizations. This will set the stage for introducing our theory of power in and around organizations.

ONE ACTOR/ONE GOAL

Early economic theory depicted the organization as synonymous with the single entrepreneur— in effect, the owner-manager—who functioned in a system of purely competitive market forces. Only those firms that maximized their profits survived. In essence, four assumptions supported this view of organizations.

1. There is only one actor in the organizational power system, that is, one person who makes decisions.
2. The organization can in fact be said to have goals, specifically, one goal.
3. That goal is the quest for profits.
4. That goal is maximized.

Figure 2–1 shows schematically the notion of one actor and one goal.

Figure 2–1.   *One Actor, One Goal (Classical Economic Theory)*

Allison (1971) has appropriately referred to this as the "rational actor model." The organization was viewed as one individual who acted "rationally," which to the economist meant he took every action to satisfy one given goal. Indeed, in some sense even that actor was not a true influencer, since the entrepreneur merely responded to economic pressures, making the decisions he had to, not those he wanted to. Profit maximization was a behavior necessary for survival. As such, the study of organizational power was irrelevant. The organization, as Adam Smith (1937) pointed out so clearly, although the agent of the entrepreneur, was unwittingly the *instrument* of the economy.

What the early economists did (and classical economists continue to do) was to provide management theory with both a point of departure and a straw man. For, one by one, each of their assumptions came into question. First to encounter problems was the assumption of maximization of profits. Three major questions were asked.

First, is profit the goal that is maximized? Why profit? Why not some other goal? Robert Gordon (1945) and then William Baumol (1959) put forth the convincing argument that many firms maximized sales subject to a profit constraint. In other words, so long as profit was acceptable, they pursued growth instead.

> Surely it is common experience that, when one asks an executive, "How's business?", he will answer that his *sales* have been increasing (or decreasing), and talk about his profit only as an afterthought, if at all. . . .
>   Almost every time I have come across a case of conflict between profits and sales the businessmen with whom I worked left little doubt as to where their hearts lay. It is not unusual to find a profitable firm, in which some segment of

> its sales can be shown to be highly unprofitable.... When such a case is pointed out to management, it is usually quite reluctant to abandon its unprofitable markets. (Baumol 1959, pp. 47–48)

Other writers suggested that the firm maximized different goals, for example, "managerial welfare" or even "the period of [its own] existence" (Williamson 1963; Easterbrooke, cited in Papandreou 1952, p. 216).

In essence, this first attack on profit maximization called the third assumption into question, that profit is *the* goal of the organization. But it left the other assumptions, especially that of maximization, intact. Even sociologists of the period, whose attack on profit maximization centered on the clash between public and private goals, did not really question the assumption of, in Talcott Parsons' words, the "primacy of orientation to the attainment of a specific goal" (1960, p. 17). In viewing the firm as society's instrument, they merely substituted a public goal for the private one.

> A firm can thus be defined as a social system organized toward the pursuit of a particular goal: economic production...profit being the secondary goal. The pursuit of the principal goal is also the accomplishment of a specific function for the general social system which is society. (Sales 1972, p. 234)

Second, is maximization possible? This criticism struck closer to the roots of classical economic theory, attacking the notion of *one* goal directly. The question was raised, How is profit maximization to be operationalized? What kind of profit, for whom, and when? The economists' answer was that the entrepreneur simply set marginal revenue equal to marginal cost so as to gain the largest possible surplus. Unfortunately this simple prescription never quite worked in practice. Accountants could never figure out how to measure marginal revenues, although they made some progress with marginal costs. In the words of one of their best-known writers, "This is a fantastically difficult task, so difficult that it is rarely attempted in practice. All studies of actual practice that I am aware of testify to its rarity. Who can accurately estimate the demand for a product at even one price?" (Anthony 1960, p. 129).

In lieu of the traditional economic measure, theorists in finance argued that firms could maximize profit by choosing all and only those capital projects whose returns on investment exceed their cost of capital. But problems remained; for example, the prediction of returns in uncertain markets (as all are). In fact, there was evidence that uncertainty could introduce a great deal of distortion in such investment calculations (e.g., Cyert and March 1963, p. 81).

Basically, the arguments against the possibility of maximization seemed to boil down to four in number:

1. The problems inherent in choosing a time frame: Should profits be maximized in the short run or the long run? Should the entrepreneur exploit

a sellers' market by charging "what the market will bear," or instead consider long-term customer sentiment and hold prices down? The economist Andreas Papandreou commented: "In the absence of knowledge concerning entrepreneurial horizon and expectations the profit-maximization construction becomes an empirically irrelevant tautology" (1952, p. 208).

2.   The problem of dealing with uncertainty, since "there is no generally accepted criterion used under these conditions" (Feldman and Kanter 1965, p. 631). How is one to know which of a number of actions to take when their consequences remain a mystery?

3.   Demands on human cognition which simply cannot be met. In simple terms, it was claimed that no person, no organization could be smart enough to maximize anything. "Even the fastest, largest computing system cannot make the calculations required by a maximizing strategy" (Feldman and Kanter 1965, p. 631). Even in the simplified game of chess, no computer can handle the quantity of information needed to select the "best" move. In the far more complex world of business, the calculation of marginal revenue requires a level of knowledge—the future buying behavior of consumers—far beyond even the most sophisticated market research team.

4.   An unrealistic one-dimensionality: People (even entrepreneurs and economists) sleep, eat, sometimes play golf; tradeoffs are part of their everyday lives. While it is true that one goal may be favored over others (thus, some of us live to eat while others eat to live), no human being can allow a single goal to dominate his or her every working action.

To conclude this second argument, maximization, particularly, profit maximization as expressed in economic theory, was simply dismissed as a nonoperational concept. In a real world with time marching on, with uncertainty, and with human beings both cognitively limited and multidimensionally motivated, the assumption of maximization seemed to collapse.

Third, is profit maximization responsible? The third argument against profit maximization led to the same conclusion as the second, but by a different route. Here the point was not that organizations *could not* maximize profits but that they *should not*.

> Profit maximization requires the businessman to use every trick he can think of to keep wages and fringe benefits down, to extract the last possible dollar from the consumer, to sell as low quality merchandise as he can legally hoodwink the customer into buying, to use income solely for the benefits of the stockholder, to disclaim any responsibility to the community, to finagle the lowest possible price from his vendors regardless of its effect on them, and so on.
>
> The profit maximizers . . . deny the existence of a businessman's conscience, and they exclude ethical considerations as being irrelevant to the subject. (Anthony 1960, p. 132)

Instead, it was argued that business firms should, and usually do, seek a *reasonable* profit. This point of view found expression beginning in the 1950s among a number of liberal and pragmatic management theorists, notably Joel Dean. In his classic book, *Managerial Economics,* Dean commented:

> "This trend" [towards a reformulation of the concept of profit-maximization] reflects a growing realization by theorists that many firms, and particularly the big ones, do not operate on the principle of profit maximizing in terms of marginal costs and revenues, but rather set standards or targets of reasonable profits. (1951, p. 28)

The effect of all three arguments against profit maximization—that it is not profit that is maximized, and that the maximization of profits is either impossible or irresponsible—was to set up the argument for an organization with multiple goals. The assumption of one goal was eliminated from the theory. But a new question faced management theorists: How does the organization reconcile conflicting goals?

ONE ACTOR/MULTIPLE GOALS

PAPANDREOU'S MODIFICATION   Andreas Papandreou was one of the first economists to see clearly the problem facing his discipline. If classical economic theory was to be salvaged, then the assumptions of maximization and of one actor would have to be retained even if the assumption of a single goal was dropped. Papandreou's solution published in an important paper in 1952, was to view the organization as a system upon which multiple goals were imposed from the outside, all passing through a single actor, whom Papandreou called the *peak coordinator.* This actor in turn reconciled these goals into a single *preference function* which was then maximized. This is shown symbolically in Figure 2–2.

Figure 2–2.   *One Actor, Multiple Goals (Papandreou)*

The effect of Papandreou's paper was to open up the organization, in theory, to influencers other than the principal actor or entrepreneur.

External *influence* and authority may be exercised over a firm by: (a) the government (in its sovereign aspects); (b) groups earning income by contributing factor services to the cooperative system (i.e., owner-stockholders, lenders of money, suppliers of goods on lease, operative labor, executive and professional labor); (c) buyers of the firm's product; (d) sellers of products and services to the firm; (e) competitors in the factor and product markets; (f) other persons, groups, or organizations which take interest in its operations. (p. 193)

But within the firm, in Papandreou's proposal, while the goals were multiple, the assumption of maximization remained, as did the assumption of one actor. Only that person could comprehend the totality:

It is a major thesis of this essay that the preference function maximized by the peak coordinator is itself a resultant of the influences which are exerted upon the firm. The Peak Coordinator is conceived as performing the integrating function; he is conceived as formulating the preference system of the enterprise. He does so, however, under the "weight" of the unconscious and conscious influences exerted upon him. (p. 211)

Meanwhile, in the theory of sociology, the view of the single actor who expressed the goals of the organization was also prevalent. As Zald commented in 1963, "Usually the sociologist considers goals to be determined outside of the organization but internalized via the top executives, those who have legitimate authority" (p. 209).

Papandreou's contribution was to introduce parties external to the organization to the process of goal formation, and to introduce the notion of a top management serving as the target of their attempts to influence the organization's goals. But problems remained with his proposal, although Papandreou was the first to recognize at least one of them:

This formulation contains one disturbing possibility. It must be evident that if influence takes the form of authority, and if authority is simultaneously exercised by two or more interest groups in a contradictory manner, the peak coordinator will not be able to formulate a consistent preference system. (p. 211)

Critics of utility theory questioned further whether the notion of a utility or preference function was feasible in a world of changing preferences, and whether individuals were capable of expressing such functions. Thus, in a handbook review article in which they sought to reconcile the conflicting theories of psychology and economics, Simon and Stedry asked whether a utility scale "'exists' at all," whether behavior could be consistent over time and choices sufficiently transitive to make the concept of utility meaningful in practice (1968;

p. 273). Their review of laboratory studies provided them with a negative answer: In situations of any complexity (and even in rather simple ones) subjects could not express accurately the weights they claimed to use in their decisions, and, more importantly, did not even behave to suggest the presence of consistent weights. In the final analysis, utility theory proved useless, ultimately, as Stigler had noted in 1948, a tautology.

> The statement that a person seeks to maximize utility is (in many versions) a tautology: it is impossible to conceive of an observational phenomenon that contradicts it. . . . any contradiction of a theorem derived from utility theory can always be attributed to a change of tastes, rather than to an error or postulates in the logic of the theory. (pp. 603, 604)

ENTER SIMON, EXIT MAXIMIZATION Papandreou recognized the existence of multiple goals, but his method of reconciling them proved untenable. Then along came Herbert Simon in 1964 with a key paper entitled "On the Concept of Organization Goal," in which he suggested that the assumption of maximization should be dropped altogether in favor of treating all goals as constraints, levels of satisfaction to be attained. The organization, to use Simon's earlier term, "satisficed" rather than maximized. Simon's organization faced a whole host of constraints; for each decision, some were evoked while others remained dormant. For example, in building a new factory, a firm might be concerned with maintaining a return of ten percent on its investment, presenting a modern image in its facilities, not exceeding a capital cost of $3,000,000, and ensuring safe working conditions in the plant design. With this formulation, Simon seemed to do away with the problem of reconciling conflicting goals. As his colleagues Cyert and March noted: "Each goal enters [decision making] as a simple constraint. All of the goals taken together define a space of acceptable solutions" (1963, p. 10).

In his 1964 paper, Simon did not discuss the notion of a peak coordinator directly. But in his other works (1957; March and Simon 1958), he depicted the organization as a top-down hierarchy of means and ends, in which goals emanated from the top and were elaborated and differentiated by units or departments as they flowed down, as shown in Figure 2-3. Thus did the organization deal with the cognitive limitations of its members: "Each part of the organization can . . . be given a goal such that if all goals are satisfied, the organization's problem is solved . . ." (Feldman and Kanter 1965, p. 35). But with all these goals "given" from a single center, the assumption of one actor—or more exactly, one center of power—was retained in Simon's theory. The organization remained essentially a rational actor.

> . . . in the very act of trying to destroy the old theory of the perfectly rational decision-maker, Simon contributed to the creation of another notion which has greatly attracted the disciples of "rational" planning techniques, namely that a

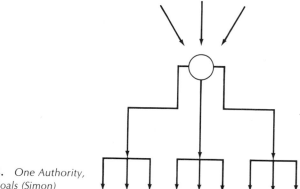

Figure 2-3. *One Authority,*
Multiple Goals (Simon)

planning problem can be solved by a rational partitioning of the whole issue into ends and means, ordered in a hierarchy.

Thus, despite his observations, Simon does not really abandon the rationality model altogether. Instead he is content to make modifications and extensions within its existing framework. (Normann and Rhenman 1975, p. 13)

MEANWHILE BACK AT BARNARD   On a related front, in 1938 Chester Barnard had introduced what came to be known as "equilibrium theory," the notion that those involved in the organization's functioning had to be offered *inducements* in return for their *contributions.* An organization could function effectively only when some kind of balance was achieved between the contributions of and the inducements to the different participants. In effect, Barnard introduced the notion that the participants accepted the organization's goals not automatically but for a price: They too were now given some power in the system.

Barnard's theory was elaborated by Simon and his colleagues in various publications. In a chapter entitled "Motivational Constraints: The Decision To Participate," March and Simon (1968) discussed five major classes of participants in the organization: employees, investors, suppliers, distributors, and consumers. Each sought inducements in return for their contributions; for example, employees contributed work in return for wages and other gratuities, investors contributed funds in return for financial returns and certain levels of security. However, management—Papandreou's peak coordinator—remained in charge: "Ordinarily, it is the group of participants called the 'management' or the 'administrators' who take responsibility for the adjustment..." (p. 109). As Feldman and Kanter noted, the other participants, "by joining...agreed to accept the authority of some managing group or individual over a certain part of their lives" (1965, p. 637).

Thus, although equilibrium theory ultimately retained the assumption of a single center of power—at least formal power (authority)—it did introduce a fundamental crack in that assumption. The central authority retained control, but was subject to the demands of others. That is, groups such as employees had goals of their own, distinct from organizational goals, which they sought to operationalize through their participation in the organization. The peak coordinator remained in charge, but to achieve organizational goals he had to negotiate with these groups. They too were on their way to becoming actors in the system, even influencers. Figure 2–4 shows this modification.

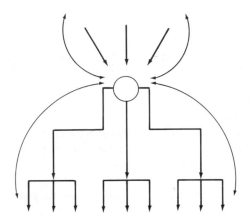

Figure 2–4.   *One Authority, Multiple Goals, Negotiation (Barnard)*

MULTIPLE ACTORS/MULTIPLE GOALS

CYERT AND MARCH'S COALITION   The scene was now set for the full relaxation of another assumption, namely, that of the single actor or center of power. At about the time that Simon was elaborating his theory of organizational goals as constraints, his colleagues Cyert and March (1963), in their attempt to reconcile economic and behavioral theory in management, were presenting a theory wherein a *coalition* of individuals bargained among themselves to determine the organization's goals. What the Cyert and March theory effectively did, as shown in Figure 2–5, was to replace one authority at the center of power with multiple authorities. The participants who were previously shown outside of the decision-making system, negotiating individually with the peak coordinator for inducements in return for contributions, now became actors inside of it who bargained to determine outcomes and thereby to establish the organization's goals.

But how did such an organization reconcile conflicts among the different goals? And how did it deal with the dynamics—shifting participants, shifting needs, shifting power within the coalition? Cyert and March introduced an ingenious concept to explain how organizations dealt with inconsistent and dynamic demands. They attended to them sequentially: "...the business firm

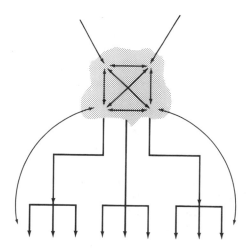

Figure 2–5. *Multiple Actors, Multiple Goals (Cyert and March)*

is likely to resolve conflicting pressures to 'smooth production' and 'satisfy customers' by first doing one and then the other" (p. 118).

Of course, this raised the question of logical inconsistencies in behavior. But this presented a problem neither to Cyert and March nor to the organization they described. The assumption of "rationality," at least as described by the economists, simply did not hold up in practice.

> The sequential attention to goals is a simple mechanism. A consequence of the mechanism is that organizations ignore many conditions that outside observers see as direct contradictions. They are contradictions only if we imagine well-established, joint preference ordering or omniscient bargaining. Neither condition exists in an organization. (p. 36)

And in the Cyert and March theory, the firm no longer functioned in a top-down manner. The employees took their place alongside others in the coalition, indeed in roles no less important than, say, those of the owners. Earlier theories had in effect told the employees: "If you don't like it, leave." Cyert and March now said: "You can stay and complain, change things." No longer was it "What can I do for the organization?"—now it became "What can the organization do for me?" Power was there for whoever could seize it in the bargaining:

> To what extent is it arbitrary, in conventional accounting procedures, that we call wage payments "costs" and dividend payments "profit" rather than the other way around? Why is it that in our quasigenetic moments we are inclined to say that in the beginning there was a manager and he recruited workers and capital? . . . ultimately it makes only slightly more sense to say that the goal of a business organization is to maximize profit than to say that its goal is to maximize the salary of Sam Smith, Assistant to the Janitor. (p. 30)

As Cyert and March described it, "the bargaining process goes on more or less continuously, turning out a long series of commitments..." (p. 32). From the participants' point of view, these commitments consisted of "side payments," taking a variety of forms—money, personal treatment, and, most importantly, policy promises—for example, to introduce a new product line that the salesmen wish to sell. This notion of commitments of a policy nature led to a fundamental break with equilibrium theory. There the organizational goals were given a priori; bargaining then took place to induce the employees to contribute to the attainment of them. For Cyert and March, however, goals were not given in advance; they came directly out of the bargaining process itself. "Side payments, far from being the incidental distribution of a fixed, transferable booty, represent the central process of goal specification" (p. 30). Thus, in the Cyert and March theory, goal formation became a power game in which multiple actors vied for personal benefits.

But it is important to note that in the Cyert and March theory goals still did come out of the bargaining process, operationalized in the form of agreed-upon budgets, standard operating procedures, and the like, to be elaborated through the organizational structure. These goals may not have been neat or consistent, but they were nevertheless, in Cyert and March's view, somewhat stable. That is, they did not change radically from one time period to the next but rather evolved gradually based on how the organization learned and set precedents: "...individuals in the coalition are strongly motivated to accept the precedents as binding....they remove from conscious consideration many agreements, decisions, and commitments that might well be subject to renegotiation in an organization without a memory" (p. 33).

Thus, in destroying so many of the assumptions of the classical theory, Cyert and March still managed to retain one of them: that organizations do indeed have goals.

MULTIPLE ACTORS/NO GOALS

The logical finale to our story—logical at least in terms of the evolution of goal theory if not perhaps in how organizations actually behave—is that organizations consist of multiple actors but have *no* goals. In effect, management theory was now ready for an onslaught from the theory of sociology, which, unencumbered with a managerial perspective, had been coming around to this particular point of view. Petro Georgiou, among others, obliged in a 1973 article in which he took the final leap that Cyert and March avoided. Georgiou argued that organizations are, in effect, purely political arenas, with no goals of their own. They are "arbitrary focusses of interests, marketplaces whose structures and processes are the outcomes of the complex accommodations made by actors exchanging a variety of incentives and pursuing a diversity of goals" (p. 291).

Thus, to Georgiou organizations were not the instruments of their owners, nor even places where the bargaining among different actors eventually expressed itself in the form of stable goals. In terms which, ironically, rung of the dogmatic tone of the classical economists, Georgiou stated that:

> Organizational analysts have been unable to cope with the reality of organizations because their vision is monopolized by an image of the organization as a whole; an entity not merely greater than the sum of its parts, but so superior that it is effectively divorced from the influence of the parts. The whole is regarded not as the product of interaction between the parts, but as determining them. The organization is endowed with a personality while the individuals constituting it are depersonalized, role players in the service of the organization's goals. (p. 299)

In place of this, Georgiou offered three basic points: (1) that "the concept of organization must be recognized as an arbitrarily defined focus of interest" (p. 304), (2) that "the basic strategic factor in organization is the individual" (p. 305), with the organization's behavior only understandable in terms of the rewards these individuals pursue, and (3) that the organization is a "marketplace in which incentives are exchanged" (p. 306). Figure 2–6 shows this view schematically, with inputs to a bargaining process in the form of the goals of the actors—employees and others indistinguishable—but no outputs in terms of common goals.

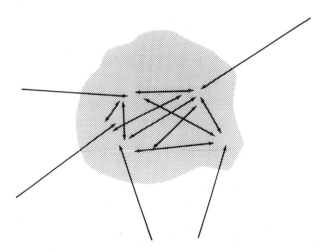

Figure 2–6. *Multiple Actors, No Goals (Georgiou)*

Thus the literature has gone full cycle, from a classical theory of organizational goals with a number of rigid, closed assumptions, through a series of changes that loosened up each of these, to a final logical ending point as a theory of organizational power that, ironically, seems to be just as rigid and as closed as the classical theory. The organization has been changed from a system of one actor to a system of many, from a system with a single goal to one having so many that it has none, from a maximizing device to a satisficing device, from a given instrument with fixed ends and no conflict to an arbitrary political arena with no ends and consumed by conflict.

THE FUNDAMENTAL QUESTIONS

Four fundamental questions emerge from this review, which this book has been written to address:

First, *how does the organization deal with multiple goals, or conflicting pressures?* Does one dominate, leading it to maximizing behavior? If so, how does the concept of maximization become operational? Or if multiple goals must coexist, how are the conflicts reconciled? By a weighting system? By treating goals as constraints? By attending to them sequentially?

Second, are goals independent variables? In other words, *is the organization the* **instrument** *of some group—owners, society, another group—which imposes goals on it, or is the organization a* **political arena** *in which individuals vie for power? Or is it perhaps a* **system** *unto itself, with its own intrinsic goals,* as another group of theorists, in sociology, have argued? To put these important questions in yet another way, for whom does the organization exist? For its own sake? For its official owners? For society? For its clients? For its workers? For its administrators? For all of them? For none of them?

Third, *can organizations be said to have goals at all, or only their participants?* Bearing in mind our definition of goal—the intention behind a decision or action—can the organization as an entity be said to have a "collective intent"? Or can we say no more than that the individual actors have intentions which get translated into organizational actions? Is there, in other words, a common intent as distinguished from the sum of individual intents? Is the organization endowed with a "life" separate from its actors, a consistent system of goals separate from theirs?

Fourth, and the overriding question, *how do all of the personal goals, values, intentions, needs, and expectations, of the individual actors get translated into organizational decisions and actions?* In other words, how is power operationalized? What takes us from individual need to organizational action? This, above all, is the question addressed in this book: How are the needs and power of the individual actors linked to organizational actions?

The different points of view in the literature on goals all hint at answers to these questions, but none really probes deeply enough into reality of power.[1] Let us therefore turn to the evidence from the literature on power.

[1]Even the sophisticated views of Simon and Cyert and March leave much unanswered in the views of some theorists:

> . . .Simon's conceptualization merely shifts the need for definition from the term "goal" to the term "constraint." We have no rule for determining what is or is not a constraint. . . (Mohr 1973, p. 472)

> . . .although Cyert and March. . .discuss conflict they are never specific about its determinants. They offer only vague discussions of sub-goal identification. Their model of coalition formation, while smacking of realism, lacks depth of presentation. There is no mention of the organizational structure of the firm, nor therefore of the membership of the bargaining subgroups in the coalition. Little attention is given to how and why coalitions are formed and changed, or to the generation of support and how the structure of the organization might limit such a process. (Pettigrew 1973, p. 22)

3

The Power Game and the Players

The core of this book is devoted to the discussion of a theory of organizational power. It is built on the premise that organizational behavior is a power game in which various players, called *influencers,* seek to control the organization's decisions and actions. The organization first comes into being when an initial group of influencers join together to pursue a common mission. Other influencers are subsequently attracted to the organization as a vehicle for satisfying some of their needs. Since the needs of influencers vary, each tries to use his or her own levers of power—*means* or *systems of influence*—to control decisions and actions. How they succeed determines what configuration of organizational power emerges. Thus, to understand the behavior of the organization, it is necessary to understand which influencers are present, what needs each seeks to fulfill in the organization, and how each is able to exercise power to fulfill them.

Of course, much more than power determines what an organization does. But our perspective in this book is that power is what matters, and that, if you like, everyone exhibits a lust for power (an assumption, by the way, that I do not personally favor, but that proves useful for the purposes of this book). When our conclusions here are coupled with those of the first book in this series, *The Structuring of Organizations* (Mintzberg 1979a, which will subsequently be referred to as the *Structuring* book), a more complete picture of the behavior of organizations emerges.

THE EXERCISE OF POWER

Hirschman (1970) notes in a small but provocative book entitled *Exit, Voice, and Loyalty*, that the participant in any system has three basic options:

- To stay and contribute as expected, which Hirschman calls *loyalty* (in the vernacular, "Shut up and deal")
- To leave, which Hirschman calls *exit* ("Take my marbles and go")
- To stay and try to change the system, which Hirschman refers to as *voice* ("I'd rather fight than switch")

Should he or she choose voice, the participant becomes what we call an influencer.[1] Those who exit—such as the client who stops buying or the employee who seeks work elsewhere—cease to be influencers, while those who choose loyalty over voice—the client who buys without question at the going rate, the employees who do whatever they are told quietly—choose not to participate as active influencers (other than to support implicitly the existing power structure).

> To resort to voice, rather than exit, is for the customer or member to make an attempt at changing the practices, policies, and outputs of the firm from which one buys or of the organization to which one belongs. Voice is here defined as any attempt at all to change, rather than to escape from, an objectionable state of affairs . . . (Hirschman 1970, p. 30)[2]

For those who stay and fight, what gives power to their voice? Essentially **the influencer requires (1) some source or basis of power, coupled with (2) the expenditure of energy in a (3) politically skillful way when necessary.** These are the three basic conditions for the exercise of power. In Allison's concise words,

---

[1]Some writers call the influencer a "stakeholder," since he or she maintains a stake in the organization the way a shareholder maintains shares. Others use the term "claimant," in that he or she has a claim on the organization's benefits. Both these terms, however, would include those who express loyalty as well as voice.

[2]There are some interesting linkages among these three options, as Hirschman points out. Exit is sometimes a last resort for frustrated voice, or in the case of a strike (temporary exit), a means to supplement voice. The effect of exit can be "galvanizing" when voice is the norm, or vice versa, as in the case of Ralph Nader who showed consumers how to use voice instead of exit against the automobile companies (p. 125). Of course, an inability to exit forces the disgruntled individual to turn to voice. Hirschman also makes the intriguing point that exit belongs to the study of economics, voice to that of political science. In economic theory, the customer or employee dissatisfied with one firm is supposed to shift to another: ". . . one either exits or one does not; it is impersonal" (p. 15). In contrast, voice is "a far more 'messy' concept because it can be graduated, all the way from faint grumbling to violent protest . . . voice is political action par excellence" (p. 16). But students of political science also have a "blind spot": ". . . exit has often been branded as *criminal*, for it has been labelled desertion, defection, and treason" (p. 17).

"Power . . .is an elusive blend of . . .bargaining advantages, skill and will in using bargaining advantages. . ." (1971, p. 168).

THE GENERAL BASES OF POWER   In the most basic sense, the power of the individual in or over the organization reflects some *dependency* that it has—some gap in its own power as a system, in Crozier's view, an "uncertainty" that the organization faces (Crozier 1964; also Crozier and Friedberg 1977). This is especially true of three of the five bases of power we describe here.[3] **Three prime bases of power are control of (1) a resource, (2) a technical skill, or (3) a body of knowledge, any one critical to the organization.** For example, a monopolist may control the raw material supply to an organization, while an expert may control the repair of important and highly complex machinery. To serve as a basis of power, a resource, skill or body of knowledge must first of all be *essential* to the functioning of the organization. Second, it must be *concentrated*, in short supply or else in the hands of one person or a small number of people who cooperate to some extent. And third it must be *nonsubstitutable*, in other words irreplaceable. These three characteristics create the dependency—the organization needs something, and it can get it only from the few people who have it.

A fourth general basis of power stems from legal prerogatives—exclusive rights or privileges to impose choices. Society, through its governments and judicial system, creates a whole set of legal prerogatives which grant power—*formal* power—to various influencers. In the first place, governments reserve for themselves the power to authorize the creation of the organization and thereafter impose regulations of various sorts on it. They also vest owners and/or the directors of the organization with certain powers, usually including the right to hire and fire the top executives. And these executives, in turn, usually have the power to hire and perhaps fire the rest of the employees, and to issue orders to them, tempered by other legal prerogatives which grant power to employees and their associations.

The fifth general basis of power derives simply from access to those who can rely on the other four. That access may be personal. For example, the spouses and friends of government regulators and of chief executives have power by virtue of having the ear of those who exercise legal prerogatives. The control of an important constituency which itself has influence—the customers who buy or the accountants who control costs—can also be an important basis for power. Likewise power flows to those who can sway other influencers through the mass media—newspaper editors, TV commentators, and the like.

Sometimes access stems from favors traded: Friends and partners grant each other influence over their respective activities. In this case, power stems not from dependency but from *reciprocity*, the gaining of power in one sphere by the giving up of power in another. As we shall see in many examples in this

---

[3]Related discussions of bases of power can be found in Allison (1971), Crozier and Friedberg (1977), Jacobs (1974), Kipnis (1974), Mechanic (1962), and Pfeffer and Salancik (1978).

book, the organizational power game is characterized as much by reciprocal as by dependency—one-sided, or "asymmetrical"—relationships.[4]

WILL AND SKILL   But having a basis for power is not enough. The individual must act in order to become an influencer, he or she must expend energy, use the basis for power. When the basis is formal, little effort would seem to be required to use it. But many a government has passed legislation that has never been respected, in many cases because it did not bother to establish an agency strong enough to enforce it. Likewise managers often find that their power to give orders means little when not backed up by the effort to ensure that these are in fact carried out. On the other hand, when the basis of power is informal, much effort would seem to be required to use it. If orders cannot be given, battles will have to be won. Yet here too, sometimes the reverse is true. In universities, for example, power often flows to those who take the trouble to serve on the committees. As two researchers noted in one study: "Since few people were involved and those who were involved wandered in and out, someone who was willing to spend time being present could often become influential" (March and Romelaer 1976, p.272). In the game of power, it is often the squeaky wheel that gets the grease.

In effect, the requirement that energy be expended to achieve outcomes, and the fact that those with the important bases of power have only so much personal energy to expend, means that power gets distributed more widely than our discussion of the bases of power would suggest. Thus, one article shows how the attendants in a mental hospital, at the bottom of the formal hierarchy, could block policy initiatives from the top because collectively they were willing and able to exert far more effort than could the administrators and doctors (Scheff 1961, discussed at greater length in Chapter 13). What this means is that influencers pick and choose their issues, concentrating their efforts on the ones most important to them, and, of course, those they think they can win. Thus Patchen (1974) finds that each influencer stakes out those areas that affect him or her most, deferring elsewhere to other influencers.

Finally, the influencer must not only have some basis for power and expend some energy, but often he or she must also do it in a clever manner, with political skill. Much informal and even formal power backed by great effort has come to naught because of political ineptness. Managers, by exploiting those over whom they have formal power, have often provoked resistance and even mutiny; experts regularly lose reasonable issues in meetings because they fail to

---

[4]French and Raven's (1959) five categories of power, as perhaps the most widely quoted typology of power, should be related to these five bases of power. Their "reward" and "coercive" power are used formally by those with legal prerogatives and may be used informally by those who control critical resources, skills, or knowledge (for example, to coerce by holding these back). Their "legitimate" power corresponds most closely to our legal prerogatives and their "expert" power to our critical skills and knowledge. Their fifth category, "referent" power, is discussed below in our section on political skill.

marshall adequate support. Political skill means the ability to use the bases of power effectively—to convince those to whom one has access, to use one's resources, information, and technical skills to their fullest in bargaining, to exercise formal power with a sensitivity to the feelings of others, to know where to concentrate one's energies, to sense what is possible, to organize the necessary alliances.

Related to political skill is a set of intrinsic leadership characteristics—charm, physical strength, attractiveness, what Kipnis calls "personal resources" (1974, p.88). *Charisma* is the label for that mystical quality that attracts followers to an individual. Some people become powerful simply because others support them; the followers pledge loyalty to a single voice.

Thus power derives from some basis for it coupled with the efforts and the abilities to use the basis. We shall assume this in the rest of the book, and look more concretely at the channels through which power is exercised, what we call the *means* and *the systems of influence*—the specific instruments influencers are able to use to effect outcomes.

THE CAST OF PLAYERS
IN ORDER OF APPEARANCE

Who are these influencers to whom we have referred? We can first distinguish *internal* from *external* influencers. **The internal influencers are the full-time employees who use voice, those people charged with making the decision and taking the actions on a permanent, regular basis; it is they who determine the outcomes, which express the goals pursued by the organization. The external influencers are nonemployees who use their bases of influence to try to affect the behavior of the employees.**[5] The first two sections of our theory, on the elements of power, describe respectively the *External Coalition*, formed by the external influencers, and the *Internal Coalition*, formed by the internal influencers.

(As the word *coalition* was retained in this book only after a good deal of consideration, it is worth explaining here why it was chosen. In general, an attempt was made to avoid jargon whenever it was felt to be possible—for example, employing "chief executive officer" instead of "peak coordinator." "Coalition" proved to be a necessary exception. Because there are no common labels—popular or otherwise—to distinguish the power in from that around the

[5]As we shall soon see, there are some circumstances in which external influencers can impose decisions directly on the organization, and other in which full-time employees acting in concert through their associations behave as external influencers by trying to affect the behavior of the senior managers. As Pfeffer and Salancik (1978, p. 30) point out, actors can be part of the organization as well its environment. Nevertheless, the distinction between full-time employees—those individuals with an intensive and regular commitment to the organization—and others will prove to be a useful and important one in all that follows.

organization, one had to be selected. But why "coalition"? Because it seems to fit best, even though it may be misleading to the reader at first. The word coalition is normally used for a group of people who band together to win some issue. As the Hickson research team at the University of Bradford notes, it has the connotation of "engineered agreements and alliances" (Astley et al. 1980, p. 21). Ostensibly, we are not using the word in this sense, at least not at first. We use it more in the sense that Cyert and March (1963) introduced it, as a set of people who bargain among themselves to determine a certain distribution of organizational power. But as we proceed in our discussion, the reader will find the two meanings growing increasingly similar. For one thing, in the External or Internal Coalition, the various influencers band together around or within the same organization to satisfy their needs. They do form some sort of "coalition." As Hickson et al. note in an earlier publication, "it is their coaltion of interests that sustains (or destroys) [the] organization" (1976, p.9).[6] More importantly, we shall see that the external and internal influencers each typically form rather stable systems of power, usually focussed in nature. These become semipermanent means to distribute benefits, and so resemble coalitions in the usual meaning of the term.)

Our power play includes ten groups of possible influencers, listed below in order of appearance. The first four are found in the External Coalition:

*   First are the *owners,* who hold legal title to the organization. Some of them perhaps conceived the idea of founding the organization in the first place and served as brokers to bring the initial influencers together.

*   Second are the *associates,* the suppliers of the organization's input resources, the clients for its output products and services, as well as its trading partners and competitors. It should be noted that only those associates who resort to voice—for example, who engage in contacts of other than a purely economic nature—are counted as influencers in the External Coalition.

*   Third are the *employee associations,* that is, unions and professional associations. Again these are included as influencers to the extent that they seek to influence the organization in other than purely economic ways, that is, to use voice to affect decisions and actions directly. Such employee associations see themselves as representatives of more than simple suppliers of labor resources. Note that employee associations are themselves considered *external* influencers, even though they represent people who can be internal influencers. Acting collectively, through their representatives, the employees choose to exert their influence on the organization from outside of its regular decision-making and action-taking channels, much as do owners and clients. (Singly, or even collectively but in different ways, the employees can of course bring their influence to

---

[6]It might be noted that the Hickson group in the 1980 publication cited earlier (as Astley et al.) decided to replace the word "coalition" by "constellation." That was tried in this book, but dropped as not having quite the right ring to it.

bear directly on these processes, as internal influencers. Later we shall in fact see that it is typically their impotence in the Internal Coalition that causes them to act collectively in the External Coalition.)

    * A fourth category comprises the organization's various *publics*, groups representing special or general interests of the public at large. We can divide these into three: (1) such general groups as families, opinion leaders, and the like; (2) special interest groups such as conservation movements or local community institutions; and (3) government in all of its forms—national, regional, local, departments and ministries, regulatory agencies, and so on.

    * Another group of influencers, which is really made up of representatives from among the other four, as well as from the internal influencers, are the *directors* of the organization. These constitute a kind of "formal coalition." This group stands at the interface of the External and Internal Coalitions, but because it meets only intermittently, and for other reasons we shall discuss in Chapter 6, it is treated as part of the External Coalition.

The Internal Coalition comprises six groups of influencers:

    * First is the top or general management of the organization, Papandreou's peak coordinator. We shall refer to this by the single individual at the top of the hierarchy of authority, in standard American terminology, the *chief executive officer*, or CEO.[7]

    * Second are the *operators*, those workers who actually produce the products and services, or who provide the direct support to them, such as the machine operators in the manufacturing plant or the doctors and nurses in the hospital.

    * Third are the managers who stand in the hierarchy of line authority from the CEO down to the first-line supervisors to whom the operators formally report. We shall refer to these simply as the *line managers*.

    * Fourth are the *analysts of the technostructure*, those staff specialists who concern themselves with the design and operation of the systems for planning and for formal control, people such as work study analysts, cost accountants, and long-range planners.

    * Fifth is the *support staff*, comprising those staff specialists who provide indirect support to the operators and the rest of the organization, in a business firm, for example, the mailroom staff, the chef in the cafeteria, the researchers, the public relation officers, and the legal counsel.[8]

---

[7]An alternate term which appears frequently in the more recent literature is "dominant coalition." But we have no wish to prejudice the discussion of the power of one of our groups of influencers by the choice of its title.

[8]For a more elaborate description of each of these five groups as well as clarification of the differences between technocratic and support staff and of line and staff in general, see Chapter 2 of the *Structuring* book.

* Finally, there is an eleventh actor in the organizational power system, one that is technically inanimate but in fact shows every indication of having a life of its own, namely the *ideology* of the organization—the set of beliefs shared by its internal influencers that distinguishes it from other organizations.

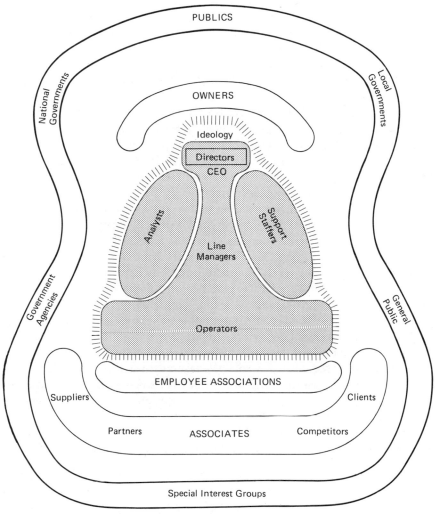

Figure 3-1. *The Cast of Players*

Figure 3-1 shows the position of each of these eleven groups schematically. The Internal Coalition is shown in the center, with the Chief Executive Officer at the top, followed, according to the formal hierarchy of authority, by the line managers and then the operators. (In some parts of the discussion, we shall accept these notions of formal authority, in others, we shall not. For now, we retain them.) Shown at either side to represent their roles as staff members are the analysts and the support staff. Above the CEO is shown the board of directors to which the CEO formally reports. And emanating from the organization is a kind of aura to represent its ideology. Surrounding all this are the various groups of the External Coalition. The owners are shown closest to the top of the hierarchy, and to the board of directors, where they are often inclined to exert their influence. The associates are shown surrounding the operating core where the operators work, the suppliers on the left (input) side and the clients on the right (output) side, with the partners and competitors in between. The employee associations are shown closest to the operators, whom they represent, while the various publics are shown to form a ring around the entire power system, in effect influencing every part of it. Thus the organization of Figure 3–1 can be seen to exist in a complex field of influencer forces.

Each of these eleven groups of players in the organizational power game will be discussed in turn, together with the means of influence they have at their disposal. We assume in this discussion that each is driven by the needs inherent in the roles they play. For example, owners will be described as owners, not as fathers, or Episcopalians, or power-hungry devils. People are of course driven by a variety of needs—by intrinsic values such as the need for control or autonomy, or in Maslow's (1954) needs hierarchy theory, by physiological, safety, love, esteem, and self-actualization needs; by the values instilled in them as children or developed later through socialization and various identifications; by the need to exploit fully whatever skills and abilities they happen to have; by their desire to avoid repetition of painful experiences or to repeat successful ones; by opportunism, the drive to exploit whatever opportunities happen to present themselves. All of these needs contribute to the makeup of each influencer and lead to an infinite variety of behaviors. All are, therefore, important to understand. But they are beyond the scope of this book. Here we focus on those behaviors that are dictated strictly by role. We assume throughout that each group discussed above is driven to gain power in or over the organization—in other words, is an influencer; our discussion then focusses on what ends each seeks to attain, what means or systems of influence each has at its disposal, and how much power each tends to end up with by virtue of the role it plays in the power coalition to which it happens to belong. This is the point of departure for the discussion of our theory.

PART I

THE EXTERNAL COALITION

We begin our discussion of the elements of the theory of power in and around organizations with the External Coalition, made up of those influencers with less than a full-time commitment to the organization—those *around* rather than in it. Chapter 4 introduces the four main groups of external influencers—owners, associates, employee associations, and the various publics that surround them all. Chapter 5 then looks at the various means of influence these external influencers have at their disposal, given that they must work through the internal influencers to affect organizational outcomes. These means include social norms, formal constraints, pressure campaigns, and a variety of direct controls. A fifth external means of influence, as well as our final group of external influencers, is reserved for more detailed consideration in Chapter 6—membership on the board of directors. And finally in Chapter 7 we seek to pull some of the material of this section together in discussing three basic types of External Coalitions—Dominated, Divided, and Passive.

4

The External Influencers

Four groups of external influencers constitute the External Coalition of the organization. These are the owners of the organization, the associates who deal with it, the associations that represent its employees, and the various publics that surround all of them. We discuss each in turn in this chapter.

THE OWNERS

The owners are those influencers who hold legal title to the organization. Ownership may take a variety of forms—from the shopkeeper who retains sole proprietorship of his store to the millions of shareholders who jointly own the giant corporation, from that corporation itself with respect to its own subsidiaries to the government which "owns" the postal system or the regulatory agency.

The owners contribute in two ways to the organization. First, some of them typically create the organization in the first place, in many cases hiring the management to set up the structure. And it is they who usually provide the organization with its initial capital to get started, and perhaps with further funds subsequently to maintain its viability. In return, the owners expect perhaps a monetary return on their investment, perhaps some influence over specific actions that the organization takes.

We can formally distinguish at least five different ownership patterns. First is *personal* ownership, where one or a few identifiable individuals own the organization personally. In the case of proprietorships or partnerships, the owners, sometimes called entrepreneurs, actually manage their own organizations. In many cases, this traditional type of ownership has given way to a second, more complicated form, which can be called *institutional* ownership. Here one organization owns another, as in the case of a corporation with its subsidiary, a religious order with its school, a government with its post office.

Third is *dispersed* ownership, where many individuals own an organization together, as in the case of American Telephone and Telegraph which had over 3 million shareholders at the start of 1980. One special case of dispersed ownership is distinguished as our fourth group, called *cooperative* ownership. Here another group of influencers—employees or clients or suppliers—owns the organization. In the farmers' cooperative, the suppliers own their marketing agency; in the retail cooperative, it is the clients who own the organization that supplies them; in the factories of Yugoslavia, the workers own the organizations that employ them. Evers et al. (1976) point out that about half of all the families in the United States own investments or shares in cooperative organizations, far more than in publicly held, profit-making corporations. And this does not include all the volunteer organizations—clubs, political parties, unions, trade associations—that are in effect cooperatively owned by their members.

Finally there are certain organizations with *no* legal ownership. Private universities, charity campaigns, and the like, are typically not owned by any identifiable group; rather, charters to establish them are granted by governments to self-perpetuating boards of directors.

Leaving this fifth type aside, what the other four suggest are two prime dimensions of ownership. First is *involvement*, distinguishing owners who play other roles in or around the organization from those who are detached—who are exclusively owners. In the case of client or supplier cooperatives, as well as subsidiaries vertically integrated with their parents (that is, supplied by or suppliers to them), the owners have some natural if indirect involvement in the organization's daily actions. In the case of proprietorships, partnerships, and employee cooperatives, the owners are involved directly and intimately with the day-to-day actions of the organization. Detached owners, in contrast, are totally removed from the decisions and actions of the organization; to become influencers in the power system requires greater effort on their part.

The second dimension is *dispersal* (or its opposite, *concentration*) of ownership. Organizations can be "closely held" or "widely held," with ownership ranging from a single individual to the 3 million shareholders of AT&T. Concentration can help to overcome the problem of detachment, since a single owner can develop a close rapport with the management. In contrast, dispersal can defeat the advantages of involvement, since thousands of employees, clients, or suppliers cannot easily maintain close contact with a central management.

Combining these two dimensions gives us the following two-by-two matrix:

	Concentrated Ownership	Dispersed Ownership
Detached Ownership	closely held businesses, conglomerate subsidiaries and agencies	widely held corporations
Involved Ownership	proprietorships, partnerships, vertically integrated subsidiaries and agencies	cooperatives

A central question in the study of organizational power, especially of the large, widely held corporation, is whether the owners can be said to control the organization. Legally the answer has traditionally been yes. But even legal prerogatives are giving way in the face of the demands of other "claimants." German law, for example, grants the employees as many seats on the boards of directors of major corporations as the owners.

But more interesting is the question of de facto control: Can the owners in fact control the decisions and actions of the organizations they own? In the context of our theory, the answer clearly depends not on their legal title but on the influence they can wield in the power game we are describing. And in terms of our two dimensions, we can propose the following proposition: **The more involved the owners, and the more concentrated their ownership, the greater their power in the External Coalition.** In other words, referring to our matrix, proprietorships, partnerships, and vertically integrated subsidiaries and agencies should be most tightly controlled by their owners, and widely held corporations, the least tightly controlled.

This point has in fact been addressed in heated debate about control over the giant American corporation. A concluding section of this book entitled "Who Should Control the Corporation?" will take up the issue in some detail; at this point we need only introduce it. The issue came sharply into the focus of the American consciousness with the publication in 1932 of a controversial book by Adolf Berle and Gardiner Means entitled *The Modern Corporation and Private Property.* In it the authors presented a continuum of five kinds of ownership of the corporation, with increasing separation from actual control:

1.   *Control through almost complete ownership:* ". . . a single individual or small group of associates own all or practically all the outstanding stock. They are presumably in a position of control . . . being [able] to elect and dominate the management" (p. 67).

2.   *Majority control:* ". . . ownership of a majority of the stock by a single individual or small group [which] gives to this group virtually all the legal powers

of control which would be held by a sole owner of the enterprise..." (p. 67).

3. *Minority control:* "...an individual or small group hold a sufficient stock interest to be in a position to dominate a corporation through their stock interest. Such a group is often said to have 'working control' of the company...[based] upon their ability to attract from scattered owners proxies sufficient when combined with their substantial minority interest to control a majority of the votes at the annual elections.... The larger the company and the wider the distribution of its stock, the more difficult it appears to be to dislodge a controlling minority" (p. 75). Berle and Means note, however, that should management challenge the minority shareholders, with the proxy voting machinery in management's hands, the minority group "has only the expensive recourse of sending out a duplicate set of proxies and bidding for the stockholder's support in opposition to the management" (p. 76).

4. *Control through a legal device:* The case of "pyramiding" by which an individual or group is able to parley relatively modest minority holdings into a control of a large system of corporations. The authors recount the story of the van Swerangen Brothers who in 1930 pyramided a $20 million investment into control of eight railroads with combined assets of over $2 billion. Although pyramiding is now outlawed in the United States, other similar possibilities still exist. For example, mutual and pension funds and life insurance companies have enormous potential power through the huge blocks of shares they buy on behalf of their clients, although they have steadfastly refused to exercise it.

5. *Management control:* The case "in which ownership is so widely distributed that no individual or small group has even a minority interest large enough to dominate the affairs of the company" (p. 77), with the result that, according to Berle and Means, power passes to the top management (that is, into the Internal Coalition). These researchers cite a number of illustrations of management controlled corporations, for example, the Pennsylvania Railroad in which, for the year 1929, the largest shareholder held one-third of 1 percent of the outstanding shares, and in which all of the shareholders combined who held more than five hundred shares—236 of them—did not hold 5 percent of all the stock.

Assuming a minimum ownership of 20 percent of the shares to ensure minority over management control, Berle and Means found, as shown in Table 4-1, that in 1929, of the 200 largest American corporations (industrials, railroads, and utilities), 44 percent were controlled by management, 44 percent by minority shareholders (including those using legal devices), and 11 percent by majority or complete owners. A follow-up study in 1963 using a 10 percent cutoff point for minimum minority control found these respective figures to be 84.5 percent, 13 percent, and 2.5 percent. These figures created considerable controversy in the world of finance and economics, and a number of studies have sought to show (a) that even the 10 percent figure is too high, minority control being effected at far lower figures, and (b) that a much greater percentage of large American corporations are in fact controlled directly by minority shareholders. Thus, Eisenberg (1974) cites one study which suggests that in about a third of the 520 largest United States industrial corporations, an individual or a single family owned at least 10 percent of the stock; he cites a second study which showed evidence of more concentrated ownership in smaller corporations. Zald (1969) cites another study, "impressionistic but historically rich" (p. 101), which indicated that about two-thirds of the 200 largest corporations have "large" family holdings.

TABLE 4-1. Owner Control of Large American Corporations (Industrials, Railroads, and Utilities)

	Percentage of the 200 Largest Corporations	
	1929	*1963*
Private Ownership	6	0
Majority Ownership	5	2.5
Minority Control	23	9
Legal Device	21	4
Management Control	44	84.5

Figures adapted from Berle and Means (1968, p. 358). The 1929 figures come from the first edition of the Berle and Means study, published in 1932 (note that 1 percent of the firms were recorded as being in receivership), while the 1963 figures come from a study by R. J. Larner entitled "Ownership and Control in the 200 Largest Non-financial Corporations, 1929 and 1963," *The American Economic Review* (1966, pp. 781 ff.). Note that the 1929 study used 20 percent ownership as the cutoff figure for management control while the 1963 study used 10 percent. Used with permission.

While these debates have served to indicate that as members of the External Coalition of at least some large corporations, the owners are not dead yet, they have not dampened enthusiasm for the increasingly popular hypothesis that effective control of the large corporations has shifted increasingly from the owners to the managers. In fact, later we shall see evidence that most of the widely dispersed shareholders of the large corporations cannot be considered influencers at all. More and more they look like detached suppliers of capital, in a purely economic relationship with the corporation. They did not create the organization in the first place, and they exhibit little serious commitment to it. When they become dissatisfied with the behavior of the operation, they typically sell their stock. In other words, their choice is almost always exit over voice. (The same has held true, as we shall see, for pension funds, mutual funds, and insurance companies. We shall also see equivalent evidence for the dispersed owners of many cooperatives.)

Thus, the answer to our question—does the ownership of an organization constitute control over its behavior?—must be, at the very least, "not necessarily."

THE ASSOCIATES

If the last section indicates that the owners, who are supposed to play a key role in the External Coalition, can become detached associates, outside the power system, then this section shows that associates, who are supposed to play a purely economic role outside of the power system, can in fact become influencers within the External Coalition.

As noted in Chapter 3, an associate of the organization—a supplier, client, partner, or competitor—who engages in a purely economic relationship with the organization, that is, who trades for goods or services with no intention of influencing any of its behavior directly, is not considered to be part of the External Coalition. In the pure market relationship, the associates buy or sell when the price and the product are right, otherwise they go elsewhere. They raise no voice, bring no special influence to bear on the organization.

This is behavior typical of a great many associates, especially where markets approach pure competition. The supplier of soap to a prison has little interest in how its inmates are treated; the client of a barbershop cares little whether it pursues growth or profit.

But just as not all markets are competitive, so not all associates are disinterested. A variety of factors encourage some of them to wield greater influence over the actions of the organization than traditional economic theory would have us believe. One such factor is economic concentration, which creates dependencies. A supplier or a client who controls the marketplace—a monopolist or a monopsonist—can wield power over the organization, and so extract certain advantages.

David Jacobs (1974) probes into this issue in a paper called "Dependency and Vulnerability: An Exchange Approach to the Control of Organizations." He identifies five points at which organizations are dependent on their environments: input acquisition, output disposal, capital acquisition, acquisition of production factors, and acquisition of a labor force. Jacobs identifies two conditions necessary for a dependence relationship, the essentiability of the item received in the exchange and its availability from alternate sources. Thus, organizations are dependent where essential inputs are available from few suppliers, as in the case of a service station that must buy all of its gasoline from a given oil company.

But dependency can be counteracted by effort: vulnerable suppliers or clients may seek ways into the External Coalition of their associates to control their actions directly. As Hirschman notes, "the role of voice would increase as the opportunities for exit decline" (1970, p. 34), to the point where the associate who cannot exit from an economic relationship must rely only on voice. Thus, parents who feel dependent on the school system that educates their children, and who worry about the quality of education, vie for positions on the school board to influence its behavior.

Jacobs also discusses the dispersal of associates: "To the degree that buyers of an organization's products are fractionated and widely dispersed, they will be less able to exercise close control over the organization" (p. 55). Sufficiently aroused by the actions of the organization, however, dispersed associates can also exert the effort needed to offset the power imbalance: They can organize into a unified and concentrated force to pressure the organization. Jacobs cites the case of the refusal of Jewish consumers to buy Ford automobiles during the 1930s because of Henry Ford's anti-semitic behavior. And Richards (1978, p. 77) discusses the IBM customers who organized to request the creation of certain software packages, and the apartment tenants whose associations have collected and withheld rents to pressure landlords into improving services. In these cases, we have groups of associates, ostensibly in purely economic relationships with organizations and therefore outside their External Coalitions, in fact using their collective market power to enter these coalitions to try to influence the organizations' behaviors directly.

Thus we have three key factors—*essentiability, substitutability,* and *concentration*—that lead to dependency or power relationships between the associates and the organization. These can be expressed in terms of the following propositions: **The more essential the resource supplied to the organization, the more power the supplier has in the External Coalition;** furthermore, **the more concentrated the suppliers or clients, the greater their power in the External Coalition; and the more dependent the clients or suppliers on the organization, the more effort they exert to gain a place in its External Coalition.**

A fourth factor that leads to associate power is access, or *intimacy.* **The longer and more intimate the relationship between the organization and an associate, the more power the latter is likely to have in the External Coalition.** For example, we would expect transient patients of a general hospital to have less influence on its decisions than the chronic patients of a tuberculosis hospital (Hall 1972, p. 77). Likewise in a typical manufacturing firm, we would expect those associates with standing orders to have more influence than those buying or selling on an ad hoc basis; those who buy or supply custom-made products, more than those buying or selling from stock, and those who negotiate individually, more than those bidding on tenders.[1]

Let us now look briefly at the contribution to the organization of each of the associates and the ways in which each may seek to influence its behavior directly.

---

[1]For an example of a research study that sought to operationalize various means of dependency and intimacy between the organization and its associates, as well as its owners, see Pugh et al. (1968).

SUPPLIERS   Suppliers provide the organization with its inputs; in return, under traditional economic conditions, they demand only financial payments. But when there is some kind of dependency or intimacy, they may seek more than remuneration. They may, for example, try to guarantee the markets for their products and even try to encourage the organization to buy more than it needs. Thus, the manufacturer of military aircraft seeks access to the decision makers of government, to influence directly the decisions they make about the kinds and numbers of airplanes to buy. Suppliers on whom the organization is dependent may also extract a variety of special considerations from it. At a number of points in our discussion, we shall be presenting illustrations of power relationships from studies carried out by management students in the author's courses at McGill University. In one, the students found an interesting dependency between a racetrack and the suppliers of its horses:

> There are not enough horses in the. . .surroundings to really present the top kind of horses the public would like to see. This gives the horsemen a privileged word in the horse racing business. . . . [The racetrack] managers do everything they can to attract and keep the good horses around. [They admit to] consulting with the horsemen before any change is planned on or around the track. . . .when the government threatened to pursue the horse buyers who did not pay the provincial sales tax on the horses they bought, the horse owners and breeders delegated the [race-track vice-president] to settle the matter with the government.[2]

A critical influencer in any External Coalition can be the financial institution that supplies the organization with capital. Small firms in particular are often notoriously short of cash and therefore dependent on their bankers. Furthermore, the relationship with financiers is often an intimate one, maintained on a face-to-face, day-to-day basis. To keep this relationship a purely economic one is almost impossible. Just the capacity of a conservative banker to withdraw a loan (that is, potential exit rather than exit itself) is often enough to influence an entrepreneur's propensity to take risks (Papandreou 1952, pp. 199–200).

CLIENTS   Clients are supposed to buy the products and services of the organization according to price, design, quality, delivery conditions, and so on, in return for financial payments. But again dependency and intimacy complicate matters considerably. For example, the clients of monopolies such as power utilities and telephone companies do everything they can to control the prices of these services.

It is an interesting fact of the organizational goal system that, of all the influencers, it is the clients who are often most predisposed to treat the mission of the organization as its primary goal. Indeed, it is not uncommon for the

[2]From a paper submitted to the author in Management Policy 701, McGill University, 1969, by Claude Rinfret, Peter Ross, Myron Wolfe, and Conrad Sabourin.

owners and managers of a business organization to focus on goals such as profit and growth, showing little concern for the mission by changing the products and services at will, while the clients fight within the External Coalition to preserve the mission. When the railroads proposed to close down money-losing passenger services, it was the clients—notably the dependent ones, who lacked alternate means of transportation—who sought to block the actions.

Sometimes associates are both suppliers and clients of the same organization, and thereby are able to develop a more intimate relationship with it, to the advantage of their power in the External Coalition. Banks often find themselves in this position, in the sense that they loan funds to the organization as well as accept its deposits and provide it with financial services. Such situations can lead to a condition formally called "reciprocity," which is known informally, as Perrow notes, as "kickbacks" or "back scratching":

> Large, diversified firms have numerous opportunities for exercising reciprocity; one division has a contract for armored aluminum personnel carriers, for which a large amount of aluminum plate must be purchased, while another division makes soda ash and caustic, which are used to make alumina. The man who exploits these opportunities is called the trade-relations man; now such specialists even have a professional association. (1970, p. 121)

Perrow points out that 60 percent of the five hundred largest American industrial corporations have such trade-relations specialists, which he sees as a manifestation of the increasing centralization of economic power in the United States due to the conglomerate merger movements.

PARTNERS   Partners join the organization in cooperative undertakings, as when a television network and an electronics company team up to develop a new broadcasting technology. This gives them a special intimacy with the organization, which can in turn lead to their playing a role in its External Coalition.

COMPETITORS   Finally there is the case of the competitors. Again classical economic theory puts them clearly outside the External Coalition. They are supposed to compete with the organization in a detached, purely economic manner. But that assumption, like so many others, is often violated. Competitors are often significantly affected by the actions of the organization—that makes them in a sense dependent on it—and so they too often seek to enter its External Coalition. Intimacy is often a factor here as well: Different competitors share the same markets, often for long periods of time. They get to know each other. And they learn to live with each other, in other words, to develop cooperative, mutually beneficial arrangements. This naturally tempers their enthusiasm for cutthroat competition. Perrow (1970, pp. 124–25) tells the story of the box factory that, six weeks after it was destroyed by fire, was back in normal operation, thanks in part to competitors who diverted to it $600,000 of new machinery that they had on order. Perrow attributes this behavior to "strong norms about taking advantage of a respected competitor under certain circumstances" (p. 124). An extreme form of competitor cooperation is the cartel, an agreement—in some countries legal, in others clandestine—to set prices and divide up markets.

More subtle are the activities of trade associations which often serve not only to encourage communication among competitors but also to define common stands on issues—social, political, economic—and then to police member behavior. Such associations are of course not restricted to industry; some of the most active in policing pricing behavior are those of professional organizations. Should a member of one of these "clubs" break the rules—by charging too little as well as too much—social pressures can bring it back in line.

THE EMPLOYEE ASSOCIATIONS

So far we have seen that the owners, with legal title to the organization, can become, in effect, suppliers outside of the External Coalition, and that the associates, who are supposed to play a purely economic role, can become important influencers within it. Now we shall see that the operating employees, who usually constitute the majority of the internal influencers, often choose to exert their influence from outside the organization, and sometimes even do so in a purely economic relationship that renders them associates not part of the External Coalition. They do so through two types of associations: unions that typically represent the less skilled operators of specific organizations (and sometimes also unskilled members of their staff and even the lower line), and professional societies that represent more highly trained operators and staff experts across organizations.

Why do operators and other employees choose to exercise their power in the *External* Coalition? First it should be noted that *as individuals* many of them also exercise power in the Internal Coalition, that is, in the making of decisions and the taking of actions. But their associations, although functioning outside of the operating processes of the organization, enable workers to act collectively, that is, to bring their combined power to bear on the organization. The association can face the management as an equal partner at the bargaining table, what Galbraith (1952) has called a "countervailing power." The individual operator cannot.

Indeed, in the case of unions the very reason the operators typically join is because they find themselves relatively powerless as individuals in the Internal Coalition. Typically they hold routine jobs in highly bureaucratic operations; this means that, despite their roles as action takers, they work according to strict standards, or rules, that leave them little discretion as individuals to affect outcomes. Collectively, however, they have the power to change things.

Professionals, on the other hand, because their work is highly skilled, typically have more power as individuals in the Internal Coalition. But that power is supported in good part by the presence of professional societies. The professionals, too, work according to standards, but in their case the standards are based on skills and bodies of knowledge. Many of these, in fact, derive from the prejob training received by the professionals, which itself is under the control of the professional societies. In effect, these societies serve as key influencing agents in determining how the work of their members gets done.[3]

European unions have tended to act as external influencers in the full sense of the term. They have sought to influence a host of organizational decisions, ranging from working conditions to major strategic moves by corporations. In recent years, many have pushed strongly for "co-determination," or formal representation on the boards of directors of corporations, alongside the owners. Later we shall investigate the results of these efforts.

The tradition in the American union movement, however, has been to stay outside of the External Coalition, that is, to negotiate in a purely economic sense as a supplier of labor and to leave the decision making to management. When asked what the unions wanted, the great leader of the early American union movement, Samuel Gompers, replied simply: "More." By that he meant more financial inducements for labor's contributions. And "unions have persevered in being . . . largely instruments for protecting and enhancing the immediate economic interests of members. This purpose has been achieved largely (although not exclusively) through collective bargaining with management" (Tannenbaum 1965, p. 717).

But American unions have also moved, especially in more recent years, to have their members treated as more than "factors of production." For example, they have sought to bargain about safety equipment on the job, layoff policies, and promotion by seniority. By so seeking to influence specific decisions directly, the union enters the External Coalition of the organization, as we have defined it. And the evidence suggests that despite a long tradition against this, it will inevitably spread. The reason, again, is dependency, in the relationship between worker and management. The acceptance of employment commits an individual to an organization and makes him or her dependent on it. Employees do not take and quit jobs the way merchants buy and sell wheat on a grain exchange. The decision to accept a new job is typically a major one for individuals. They commit about one-third of their waking hours to it; taking it may involve the uprooting of a family; promotional systems based on

---

[3]Recently, the professionals of some specific organizations have unionized as well. Later we shall see that they seem to do so when treated by the administrators like unskilled workers (i.e., as relatively powerless), but that the effect of unionization is to encourage more of such treatment.

seniority, or even on personal contact, as well as pension plans and the like, even habit, serve to lock them into that job, to make them view it as a long-term commitment. If they become disatisfied with something the organization does, it may make more sense to try to change the behavior of the organization than to change the job. Thus it is natural for individuals to seek some control over the decisions and actions of the organization, at least those that impinge on them directly. And if they cannot do so as members of the Internal Coalition, then they join a union and try to do so as members of the External Coalition.

This suggests an ironic twist in the assumptions of classical economic theory, for now it is the employee of the organization who emerges as immobile, who stays to influence it, while the owner is the one who more often leaves the organization when dissatisfied, that is, who sells the stock rather than staying to influence the behavior. The employees use voice, while their ostensible employers, the owners, exit.

Earlier it was noted that the client may be the member of the External Coalition who most favors the organization's mission as its goal. The union, in contrast, may be the one that favors it least. Workers often join unions because they are alienated from their workplace. Their tasks may be dull and are probably beyond their control, and they themselves are socially isolated from the higher status levels of the hierarchy. It becomes natural for them to have little commitment to the actual work they do, less to its final product, which they may never even see, and even less to the clients—faceless creatures with whom they may have no contact. Under these conditions, it stands to reason that the unions would take stands on issues related to the conditions of the work and its remuneration, not on those related to the mission of the organization. This often puts the unions in positions diametrically opposed to the interests of the clients. Indeed, it is not uncommon for labor negotiations to pit a union looking after the interests of its members against management and the owners concerned with profits and growth, while the interests of the client go unattended. In a marketplace that lacks competition, the only recourse the client has is to seek power in the External Coalition.

THE PUBLICS

The final group of external influencers are technically the most detached from the organization. They neither own it, work for it, supply it, nor purchase from it. But they nevertheless feel sufficiently affected by its actions to try to influence it. These will be referred to as the various *publics* of the organization.

What right do these publics, not being in any formal exchange relationship with the organization, have in its External Coalition? There are a variety of viewpoints here. One classical line of sociological theory, usually identified with Talcott Parsons (1960), views the organization as an instrument of society, with its mission as its prime goal. In other words, each organization exists to fulfill some societal purpose—the automobile company to provide means of transportation, the hospital to care for society's sick, and so on. As such, society has every right to worry about the behavior of every one of *its* organizations.

Another general view, more in line with a laissez-faire political philosophy, views the legitimate role of the publics as seeking to control the *externalities* of the organization, leaving everything else to management and other more involved influencers. Externalities are inadvertent byproducts of the organization's activities, of concern not to it but to others, such as the downstream pollution from a pulp mill. The organization, in effect, incurs certain costs, but is not charged for them. In this example, it is a distant local community, not the suppliers, customers, owners, or employees, who are most affected, and their losses justify their entry into the External Coalition.

Both these views postulate some kind of legitimacy for the public influencer—that the organization is responsible to society at large or elements of it affected by its actions. A third view dismisses legitimacy altogether, and sees the issue as a pure power game. The organization should be controlled by whoever can amass the power to control it. This need no more be the owners than the payroll clerks or the local civil rights society. And so any public that can gain power has every right to do so.

What gives a public group power over the organization? One factor, again, is access, or intimacy. Family and friends close to a manager may be able to influence his or her decisions just because they have regular contact with the manager. Another is the ability to disrupt the organization, to interfere with the flow of resources or to raise questions of legitimacy. Thus, the townspeople downstream may threaten to expose the organization in the press as a polluter, and thereby hurt its image. Or failing that, they might walk into the headquarters one day and spill river sludge on the carpets of the senior executives, a tactic that has already been used with notable success. High-status individuals, whom sociologists call "elites," can resort to more refined tactics of disruption, as when a government leader calls a steel company president to tell him that if his firm does not roll back a price increase, his company will be nationalized.

Who are the publics that seek to influence organizations? Roughly, these can be grouped into three categories. One may be referred to as the general purveyors of the *public interest*, the newspaper editorialists, priests, teachers, friends, spouses, children, and so on. All are influencers—members of the External Coalition—to the extent that they seek to influence some specific behavior of the organization.

A second group of publics are the *governments* in their various forms faced by the organization. Governments have special power over all organizations because, first, they represent the ultimate legitimate authority of the society, and second, they establish the rules—the laws and regulations—within which every organization must function. A most important set of rules covers the granting of the charter by which the organization came into existence in the first place. So some government ultimately controls the legitimacy of every formal organization. Governments employ "moral suasion" and, failing that, specific legislation to control the behavior of organizations, especially those deemed "affected with the public interest." Indeed, the vacuum in the External Coalition of the giant corporations caused by the loss of power of the shareholders has to an increasing extent been filled by governments.

But government no more provides to the organization a clear definition of the public interest than do the variety of general purveyors of it. In place of one government speaking with one voice, organizations face a variety of governments at various levels and within each a myriad of different voices. Local governments worry about employment and sourcing, pollution, and so on, while national governments concern themselves with broader economic issues, hiring policies, training of workers, research and development, major price increases, foreign ownership, and so on. There are even calls for stronger world government to curb the habit of multinational corporations of playing national governments off against each other, for example by building their plants in those countries that offer the longest tax holidays or the most tolerant pollution laws. And each government is fractionated into a host of departments and quasi-autonomous agencies, each with its own interpretation of the public interest, these frequently in direct contradiction with each other.

The third set of publics the organization faces are the *special interest groups.* These are organized groups, outside of government, that seek to represent some kind of special interest in the External Coalition. In some cases, groups that already exist turn their attention to new organizations, as when a black group becomes interested in the employment practices of a large corporation. In other cases, groups form around a particular issue in one organization, as when the townspeople downstream create a vigilante group to carry the sludge up to the executive offices. Special interest groups may act out of private interests, or they may take it upon themselves to represent what they believe to be the public interest, especially when they believe that government is too slow or too conservative or not properly representative. The best-known example of this in recent times is Ralph Nader's so-called "Raiders," a group of Davids who have on numerous occasions brought corporate and government Goliaths to their knees. The list of special interest groups is long indeed, representing conservation, science in every conceivable form, students, blacks, Jews, airport residents, parents, and many others. In England there is even a "Society to Clothe Animals" (if my memory of the title serves me correctly), an influencer no doubt in the External Coalitions of the circuses that tour the British countryside!

Thus organizations exist in potentially intricate fields of influencer forces. These forces come from a great variety of groups—owners, suppliers, clients, partners, competitors, unions, professional societies, newspaper editors, family and friends, governments at different levels, including a myriad of departments and agencies, and a wide range of special interest groups. Each has its own set of distinct needs to be satisfied by the organization. But perhaps more interesting than their needs is how they are able to bring their external basis of power to bear on the organization, that is, how they are able to evoke the outcomes they desire when they must function from outside the regular decision-making and action-taking processes of the organization. We turn to this issue next.

5

External Means of Influence

The question posed at the end of the last chapter can be stated in a much more fundamental way, namely, How does society control its organizations? It can also be reversed for our purposes in this chapter: How does the organization feel the pressures of the external influencers? To arrive at an answer, it will be helpful to isolate a number of dimensions of external influence.

First, an act of influence can be *regular* or *episodic*. At one extreme, an owner demands a certain level of sales every month; at the other, a conservation group challenges a paper company to close down a facility that has been polluting for twenty years. Second, an act of influence can be *general* or *focussed*, in one case directed at all organizations of a certain class, in the other, directed at one specific organization. Thus, a government may bring in legislation to reduce the spending of all public hospitals, or it may intervene to cut the budget of a single one. Moreover, within one specific organization, an outsider can seek to influence a range of different actions, a single type of action, or a single action. To continue with our example, the government may reduce the hospital's budget across the board; it may concern itself with the equipment budget, for one year or many; or, it may disallow the purchase of one specific x-ray machine. Third, an act of influence can be *detached* or *personal*. For example, a strip mining company may be attacked in the press, from a distance, or its executives may be subjected to personal approaches from members of the affected community. Fourth, an act of influence can be of an *initiative* or *obstructive* nature, that is, designed to provoke the organization to do something new, as when customers pressure a firm to introduce a new product line, or else to block it from carrying a proposed or existing activity, as when a government refuses to grant an export license to a uranium mine or when conservationists seek to reduce the pollution from a company's smokestacks. And finally, an act of influence can be *formal* or *informal*, that is, sent through official channels based on legal prerogatives or else pursued by unofficial means, using control of critical resources, skills, knowledge, or access to people who control them. Thus the government can use its formal power to revoke licenses as a means to reduce pollution while the conservation group must resort to informal pressures on the company (unless, of course, it can fall back on formal antipollution laws).

These dimensions give us some idea about the characteristics of acts of external influence, but they do not tell us what they are. What we require is a categorization of the actual means that can be used by external influencers to change organization behavior. I have found no such categorization scheme in the literature. What does appear, however, are many anecdotes about acts of influence, and these have been used to construct the following categorization of five means of external influence. These five form a rough continuum, from the most regular, general, and detached—in effect, the least direct and forceful—to the most episodic, focussed, and personal—the most direct and powerful. They are listed below and then discussed at greater length.

1. *Social norms* cover the overall system of general norms and ethics within which all organizations must function; this means of influence is rather general and regular in nature, in a sense a permanent atmosphere around the organization; it is informal, and can be either detached or personal; and it would seem to be obstructive more often than initiative, in the sense that it defines minimum levels of acceptable behavior below which the organization should not fall.

2. *Formal constraints* are specific impositions on the organization; this means of influence is usually obstructive because it, too, sets limits on behavior, but of a more precise kind; it is formal in nature, regular (once in place), often detached, and usually focussed on specific types of actions; sometimes formal constraints apply to all organizations, other times to organizations in specific groups or even to single organizations.

3. *Pressure campaigns* are informal episodes of focussed influence carried out by specific groups; these campaigns may be personal or detached, and they generally apply to specific organizations or specific groups of organizations; they are usually focussed on single types of actions or even single actions, and they may be either initiative or obstructive.

4. *Direct controls* include a whole range of direct and personal means of influence brought to bear on specific organizations, including the use of direct access, the inclusion of a participant in an internal decision process, the implantation of the representative of an external influencer in the Internal Coalition, and the authorization or even the imposition of specific decisions; these controls are often episodic, but may be regular as well, sometimes focussed on

specific decisions or actions and sometimes on types of them or even on organizational behaviors in general; they may be either formal or informal, and they are used both to initiate and to obstruct organizational actions.

　　5.　*Membership on boards of directors* is a personal, focussed and formal means of influence; as we shall see, it turns out to be episodic in nature and used more often to obstruct than to initiate, when it is used at all.

　　All of these five are *external* means of influence in that they are the devices at the disposal of those with power in the External Coalition when they wish to influence organizational behavior. However, only the first three are clearly separate from the decision-making and action-taking processes, that is, indirect. The fourth means of influence—direct controls—enters the grey area between the External and Internal Coalitions, for although the influencers are outside the organization, their acts of influence take them close to or even inside actual decision-making processes. And the final means of influence—membership on the board of directors—stands squarely between the External and Internal Coalitions, for the board is the vehicle—formally at least—through which external influencers are supposed to be represented in organizational decision-making processes. But as we shall see in the next chapter—where we discuss this last external means of influence in some detail—it clearly falls into the External Coalition, not the Internal Coalition. Now let us look at each of the first four external means of influence in greater detail.

SOCIAL NORMS

　　The most general of the external means of influence are the various social norms, or generally accepted standards of conduct, that surround every organization. Social norms range from the very broad values or ethics ("thou shalt not steal") to the rather specific (hospitals should release patient information to relatives first). But they are not, by definition, formal; rather they are accepted implicitly in a certain social context and are reinforced through social sanctions such as ostracism.

　　Social norms filter into the activities of an organization through every participant. Each was instilled with a set of social values in his or her youth, by parents, teachers, and others; in adulthood, these are reinforced continually through all kinds of activities—exposure to the media, chance encounters, the reading of books, personal observations, comments of influential friends. Furthermore, all the employees of the organization play a series of other roles wherein they develop allegiances and subscribe to various sets of norms. They are fathers, sisters, Masons, mountain climbers, Spaniards. The norms internalized in each role underlie the ways in which the employee decides and acts. The message an employee hears in church influences the charitable donations he or she chooses to make on behalf of the organization; the comment by a spouse at home may alter a manager's attitude toward labelling a product; an article in the local newspaper may change one's feelings about employing workers from the city's slums. Every decision and action taken in the organization is so influenced.

Every society or culture contains a whole set of social norms, based on its particular history, religions, philosophies, and the nature of its people and the problems they have faced. Thus, in an ancient society of more than 100 million people crowded into a chain of small island, Japanese ethics emphasize collective responsibility and loyalty to the group, while in a younger American society with its fresh memories of a frontier past and with almost twenty times the land area for each citizen, individualism, property rights, and competition have traditionally been favored.

> The most lauded activities of Japanese business are related to the "humane" nature of their organizational structure and personnel policies, emphasis on internal harmony, guaranteed employment, no layoffs, and a wage structure geared to the workers' needs. . . .
> Japanese companies do not pursue their humane policies for altruistic reasons. They do so because the nature of Japanese society is such that they could not behave any other way and expect to survive as viable entities. (Sethi 1975, p. 60)

While social norms may appear to remain stable being based on long traditions, in fact they are in a continual state of evolution. Periodically, behaviors that were previously unacceptable pass into respectability, as in the case of money lending in the Middle Ages or abortion earlier in the twentieth century, while other previously acceptable behaviors become unacceptable, as in the case of slavery in nineteenth-century America or industrial pollution in the twentieth century.

> What was greeted with praise yesterday may be tolerated today and considered reprehensible tomorrow. Thus, one firm has a mural of one of its plants in the corporate foyer. Until 1972 smoke belched proudly from the smoke stacks. The smoke has now been painted out. (Ackerman 1975, p.32)

Thus do values change as new issues move into the public consciousness, and then become accepted and internalized as social norms. Yesterday American society felt strongly about child labor, sweatshops, and corporate trusts. Today, the issues are pollution, labelling, and the quality of working life. Some of tomorrow's issues, it now appears, are likely to be democracy within the organization and public control over it.

Changes in social norms, of course, have a more profound effect on the behavior of the organization than simply forcing it to paint out clouds of smoke. In a paper entitled "Business and the Changing Society,"[1] George Lodge (1974*a*) argues that the traditional norms of American society have recently undergone a major shift, with profound implications for American business. He sees these norms as having been based on

> ...five great ideas that first came to America in the eighteenth century, having been set down in seventeenth century England as "natural" laws by John Locke, among others. These ideas found a particularly fertile soil in the vast, under-populated wilderness of America and served us well for a hundred years or so. They are now in an advanced state of erosion. (p. 62)

Lodge identifies these ideas as individualism, property rights, competition, limited government, and scientific specialization and fragmentation. He discusses some "powerful American myths associated with these ideas: John Wayne as the frontiersman; Rags to Riches with Horatio Alger; and, most fundamentally, the myth of material growth and progress" (p. 63). Lodge believes that these ideas are in the process of being replaced by the following ones:

> 1. Individual fulfillment occurs through participation in an organic social process.
> 2. Rights of membership are overshadowing property rights.
> 3. Community need to satisfy consumer desires is replacing competition as a means for controlling the uses of property.
> 4. The role of government is inevitably expanding.
> 5. Reality now requires perception of whole systems, not only parts. (pp. 63-67)

Lodge then shows how these changes have affected such aspects of American business as advertising, employee motivation, public attitudes towards its ownership and legitimacy, competition, government control of it, and attitudes toward its growth.

One of the problems organizations face is that different influencers often press different and contradictory norms on them, especially, as in the case Lodge describes, when one set of norms is in the process of being replaced by another. For example, should the American corporation favor individual competition or group participation in its promotion policies? Were norms clearly defined and articulated, the organization might be able to figure out the necessary tradeoffs. But they never are. Leys (1962) discusses six basic human values that he believes are at the root of social norms—happiness, lawfulness, harmony, survival, integrity, and loyalty. He then shows how even these can come into direct conflict with one another, for example, in the case of integrity and loyalty: "When he detects malfeasance in a superior, should [the employee] tip

---

[1]Lodge's points were elaborated in a book entitled *The New American Ideology* (Lodge 1975).

off an opposition senator (the Teapot Dome Case)? Or when he sees that racial integration might proceed a bit faster than the courts require, should he stick his neck out?" (p. 91).

But no matter how vague, contradictory, and unstable, the fact is that each organization encounters in its society a set of norms that defines a kind of multidimensional box outside of which it ventures at its own risk. The exact location of the walls may be vague, but there is no doubt that they exist. A major issue, which we shall address near the end of this book, is where organizations should operate within that box: at the walls, treating social norms as constraints, minimum limits of acceptable behavior, or near the center, treating them as goals to initiate positive action to serve society.

FORMAL CONSTRAINTS

In one sense, formal constraints are social norms made official. When social norms do not evoke the behavior desired of the organization by some group of external influencers, they may seek instead to impose formal constraints on it. These differ from social norms in four fundamentals ways:

1. They are formally (legally) imposed by some external influencers.
2. They are defined more clearly and explicitly.
3. They are usually coupled with some official sanction (such as the system of justice in the case of a law imposed by a government).
4. They more likely obstruct actions rather than initiate them.

A formal constraint may apply to one organization, to many in a class, or even to all organizations in a society (as in the case of a minimum wage law). It may apply to a variety of decisions and actions, although it tends to focus on single types of them (as in the above example, which applies only to wage decisions). However, by definition, it never applies to a single decision or action on an ad hoc basis; that would make it a direct control. Formal constraints apply impersonally to all decisions and actions of a given type.

Any external influencer may impose formal constraints on the organization. A union can negotiate to establish a grievance procedure or a safety rule, while a college of surgeons may specify minimum rates of remuneration for hospitals. Owners, if they are sufficiently concentrated, can impose formal constraints, as when they fix a dividend rate. Even associates can get into the act, notably when the organization is dependent on them. Thus, there are automobile companies that impose sales quotas on the independent dealers they supply with cars, even though the dealers are their customers. Through their trade association, competitors too impose constraints. The parity committee—an association of small employers and employees—in the Montreal food store trade sets wage levels and the annual number of statutory holidays.

But of all the external influencers, it would seem to be the government that relies most on formal constraints as a means of influence in the External Coalition. This stands to reason, since formal constraints stem directly from legal prerogatives, and ultimately it is the government that controls all such prerogatives. Government constraints tend to develop, in the form of laws and regulations, around those social norms that require strict enforcement, for example, safety requirements for the production of food or the flying of airplanes. Governments have been active in this field for a long time, at least back to 2000 B.C. when the code of Hammurabi set guidelines for merchants and peddlers (Kast and Rosenzweig 1974, p. 28). As we shall see in Chapter 28, government regulation in America only became a factor late in the last century, although it has increased dramatically since that time. Today, legislation restricts price fixing, establishes packaging and labelling standards, sets minimum wages, specifies where and how buildings can and cannot be built, defines financial reporting conventions, specifies safety standards, determines how money can leave the country, establishes the temperature of heat in warehouses, and specifies who can be a private detective, not to mention determining what share of corporate profits the government itself will take in taxes.

When the regulations are numerous, the stakes high, and enforcement complicated, the government will tend to set up a "regulatory agency." In the United States, the Food and Drug Administration regulates the production of foodstuffs, the Federal Aviation Authority imposes safety standards in the skies, the Interstate Commerce Commission sets common carrier rates on the ground, the Securities and Exchange Commission regulates stockmarket trading, and the Federal Power Commission sets natural gas prices.

To conclude our discussion of formal constraints as the second external means of influence, we note that these constraints put the organization into a second, smaller and better-defined multidimensional box—what Hill calls a "feasibility polygon" (1969, p. 207). Here the walls can be more easily, if still not perfectly, discerned. Formal constraints do not typically motivate the organization to act, but they do indicate rather clearly some limits on the actions it can choose to take.

PRESSURE CAMPAIGNS

When neither social norms nor formal constraints elicit the behavior desired by certain external influencers, they may take matters into their own hands by bringing a concerted campaign of pressure to bear directly on the organization. Such a campaign is generally directed at one specific issue, such as the pollution from a factory, or even at one specific decision, such as that to construct the factory itself.

THE STEPS IN THE CAMPAIGN   The typical pressure campaign seems to develop in steps, as follows:

*   First, there exists outside the organization a group of people who have hitherto been relatively passive, at least on the issue in question. The group may already have been in existence, or it may be what Elbing (1970, p. 288) calls a "latent group," that is, a set of unaffiliated individuals who are ready to coalesce around some issue.

*   Second, the members of the group become disturbed by some behavior of the organization, typically a sensitive and rather well-defined issue that they consider vital to their concerns.

*   Third, the group perceives itself as being outside the formal power system of the organization, that is, unable to impose decisions or constraints directly. Furthermore, it believes that those inside that system have not given adequate consideration to its concerns, and will not. In many cases, the belief is that government did not impose the necessary regulations or that the board of directors is not sufficiently representative. Here is how Father Leonard Dubi, an activist catholic priest in Chicago, described his role in the External Coalition of a giant electric utility:

> I have no vote on the board of directors of Commonwealth Edison. I count for absolutely nothing. But that company is polluting my environment, is shaping my life, is limiting it and the chances of the kids at St. Daniel's parish. It's killing me as a person, as life in the steel mill is killing my father. I have to fight back. (quoted in Terkel 1972, p. 564)

*   Fourth, with the usual means of external influence—social norms and formal constraints—closed to the members of the group, their frustrations begin to mount. At some point, typically signalled by a single event or action by the organization, the situation erupts. The group coalesces and mobilizes for action. In West Virginia, a community long angered by safety conditions in the local mine mobilized for action when an explosion killed some if its kinfolk. In order to draw the attention of the decision makers of the organization, the group must act in a dramatic way. And once it has done so—succeeded in overcoming the inertia that characterizes all stationary bodies—it can move quickly indeed. The result is a pressure campaign, an intense, unofficial, focussed, direct episode of pressure exerted on the organization.

Thus pressure campaigns do not start easily, appearances notwithstanding. What the public sees, and the organization experiences—the sudden coalescing of a group at the drop of a hat, with an outpouring of emotions, seemingly coming from nowhere—is often just the first public manifestation of deep-rooted frustrations that have developed over a long period of time. Change is considered by the activists to be long past due. New social norms or expectations have arisen but have not been satisfied by what appears to the activists as an intransigent organization, and formal constraints believed necessary have not been forthcoming from anyone else in the External Coalition. So an impassioned group seeks a more dramatic means to express its will.

WHO CAMPAIGNS   All organizations are surrounded by a multitude of dormant and latent pressure groups, any one of which can flare up unexpectedly. Such groups may include any of the external influencers dissatisfied with some behavior of the organization. Clients from a minority group may boycott the products of a firm it perceives to be racist. Likewise, suppliers may refuse to sell to it and even some owners may join in, as happened when certain church groups sold their shares of corporations operating in South Africa. Unions, too, mount pressure campaigns, in the form of work slowdowns and strikes. Even governments use this means of influence, as for example, when the Kennedy administration publicly confronted U. S. Steel in 1962 and forced the rollback of certain price increases. But the main user of the pressure campaign is, of course, the special interest group, since it is outside the organization's usual trading and communication relationships, with the other means of external influence least accessible to it. The pressure campaign is its most natural way into the External Coalition of the organization.

HOW THE ACTIVISTS CAMPAIGN   The pressure campaign these groups mount can take a great variety of forms. Indeed, since the object is to outsmart the management, the more unexpected the form of campaign, the more likely it is to succeed. Some old tricks are well known: press attacks, demonstrations, boycotts, strikes, even sabotage.[2] But each year brings newer, more imaginative, or, depending on your point of view, more jaded, ones. For the American corporation, the late 1960s and 1970s were activist years which saw the introduction of all kinds of new special interest groups using new harrassments techniques. Students battled Dow Chemical recruiters on campuses to stop the production of napalm for Vietnam, conservationists sat down in front of bulldozers to block construction projects, activists disrupted annual meetings of corporations they believed were producing unsafe products. Here is

---

[2]Pressure campaigns seem often to sit on the border line between exit and voice. A common pressure campaign tactic is to use voice to threaten exit, or to go one step beyond and boycott or strike—in other words, to exit temporarily with the promise to return when changes are made (Hirschman 1970, p. 86). Of course, the special interest group has nothing from which to exit, so its approach is often to disrupt operations, to threaten to do so, or simply to embarrass the organization.

how Father Dubi describes the encounter his group had with Commonwealth Edison:

> The most exciting moment in my life? Picture this. It's the annual meeting of the shareholders of Commonwealth Edison, one of the largest public utilities in the entire country. The chairman of the board and all the directors are up on the stage. We have about two thousand people in the lobby. It was like a festival—people dancing. About twenty of us entered the hall. The chairman heads for the podium and is about to gavel the meeting to order. We walk down the aisle. Here is the symbol of the establishment of the United States—the annual meeting of a large corporation. I look up at the chairman and I tell him, "We're here to find out what you're going to do about pollution. You have a half-hour to give us your answer." People were on their feet: What is this priest doing here, disrupting this meeting? We did it. . . .
>
> A half-hour later we came into the hall again. . . . I faced the chairman again and asked for his answer. There was no answer. He threatened to adjourn the meeting. I said, "Okay, here's *our* answer. You won't listen to the people, but we're not gonna take it. We're gonna go to city hall and force this issue through law". . . .
>
> At the city council we forced them to pass one of the strongest air pollution ordinances in the country. We tangled with the all-powerful Commonwealth Edison and forced them to purchase six million tons of low sulphur coal. They've retired much of their antiquated equipment. It's not over yet. There's a lot of struggle ahead. But we've had a touch of victory and it's sweet. (quoted in Terkel, pp. 563–64)

Some pressure campaigns are intended to obstruct existing or proposed actions while others are designed to initiate action—to get the organization to do something it has never done. For example, many of the conservation campaigns are intended to stop polluting practices, while a number of Ralph Nader's attacks on General Motors have been aimed at initiating activity in the area of safety. Since the pressure campaign generally pits a weak, temporary group against a powerful, established organization, the obstructive campaign may seem to work better than the initiative one: "Limited power is most effective when used negatively to veto or deny some specific outcome" (Deutsch 1969, p. 260). Thus, a mouse can stop an elephant in its tracks, or at least deflect its course significantly. On the other hand, it can also get the elephant moving. It is amazing how much activity a tiny special interest group can generate in a giant corporation, especially a corporation that is sensitive to adverse publicity. Later, in Chapter 29, we shall see how a handful of young lawyers holding 12 of its 286,000,000 outstanding shares caused significant changes in the world's largest corporation through an activity they called "Campaign GM."

Of course, it is not always the Davids that attack the Goliaths. Brager (1969) recounts how Mobilization for Youth (MFY), a deliquency and antipoverty project in New York's Lower East Side, was subjected to a two-pronged pressure campaign, first, repeated attacks for harboring communists and fomenting strikes and racial disorders, and then investigations by city, state, and federal officials. Here was the reverse of Campaign GM—a fragile organization under attack by society's establishment. When we return to this story later we shall see how this small organization, with its back up against the wall, threw its beliefs to the wind and opted for accommodation and survival.

In essence, the pressure campaign represents an attempt to realign the External Coalition of the organization, either temporarily on one issue or permanently on many. An outsider may seek entry into the External Coalition for the first time, or an existing member may set out to increase his or her influence. In the process, the whole power equilibrium of the organization is called into question, which results in emotional responses both inside the organization as well as elsewhere in its External Coalition. As Brager concludes in his study of the MFY: "One consequence of a public attack is that it upsets the equilibrium with which the organization has in the past accommodated to [its] varying publics. Actions invisible in the past now become observable, and formerly uninterested groups now become concerned" (pp. 166–67).

THE PRESSURE CAMPAIGN AS AN AGENT OF CHANGE   The pressure campaign is one of society's prime ways of changing the behavior of its organizations. Outmoded activities that organizations insist on perpetuating as well as desirable new ones that they refuse to adopt can be influenced by the pressure campaign. Social norms are often too vague and contradictory to evoke the desired behavior, while formal constraints are often too rigid, limited to rather well-defined behaviors, and obstructive rather than initiative. Moreover, formal constraints specify only minimally acceptable levels of behaviors, and, because they are formal, they are slow to be changed, often following rather than preceding changes in social norms: "...laws tend primarily to codify socially acceptable behavior and seldom lead to social change" (Sethi 1975, p. 61). The pressure campaign, in contrast, is highly flexible and provides the effect often needed to shock a myopic organization into realizing that shifts to which it must respond have taken place in its environment. Thus, after one of its factories was destroyed during the Watts rioting of 1965, the president of a large national corporation commented:

> Suddenly I saw we could close our eyes to this issue no longer. I went out and saw the ghetto, not because I had never been there, but because circumstances forced me to really *look* at what before I had only seen. It was appalling. If we do not straighten this matter out, we will be in an awful mess. We are going to get on board of the civil rights thing—and seriously. I will be the first to admit that we have been blind to the Negro problem in our company. It is because *I* have been blind. Well, that is over. We are going to do our part. If we do not, we will all go under. (quoted in Levitt 1968, p. 88)

The comments of the last paragraph suggest that the pressure campaign can be used *in lieu* of social norms and formal constraints, that is, where the latter do not work. But the pressure campaign may also be coupled with these other external means of influence. Looked at in this context, the pressure campaign, while it may be directed at one specific issue or decision, really becomes part of a broader process of social change.

Figure 5–1 shows a number of possible patterns among these three external means of influence.

Pattern A: Social Issue Life Cycle   Pattern A begins with the pressure campaign. An issue first enters the public consciousness through such a campaign, which seeks to block or initiate a particular example of some behavior, such as the pollution of the atmosphere. Gradually, as the public comes to accept the importance of the issue, its formal institutions introduce formal constraints to limit the behavior more broadly and systematically. In fact, as the issue becomes fully internalized in the public consciousness, it emerges as a social norm which guides behavior implicitly. Then even the formal constraints

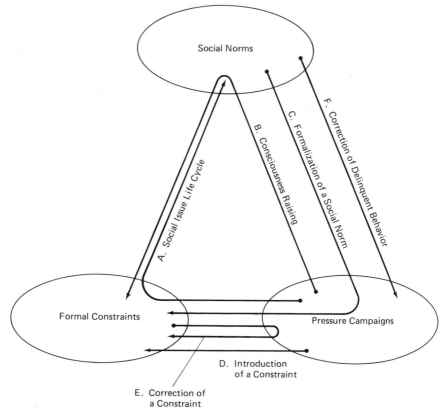

Figure 5–1. *Patterns Among Social Norms, Formal Contstraints, and Pressure Campaigns*

may no longer be necessary. This is the pattern described by Ackerman (1975) as the "social issue life cycle."

> Most social issues follow patterns that, in retrospect, appear to be quite predictable. There was typically a time in which the issue was unthought of or unthinkable. . . . However, should interest develop and be sustained, the issue passes through a period of increasing awareness, expectations, demands for action and ultimately enforcement. At the end of this period, probably measured in decades, it may cease to be a matter of active public concern. New standards of behavior may then have become so ingrained in the normal conduct of affairs that to behave otherwise would bring the social and economic sanctions formerly reserved for the contrary behavior. Thus, like the product life cycle, there is an analogous social issue life cycle. (p. 31)

Ackerman cites a number of examples. The right to collective bargaining which, although in 1890 "would have been viewed as folly, if not openly subversive to the American way of life" (p. 31), after a series of traumatic confrontations in the 1930s was written into U.S. law so that "by the 1970s, the union-management relationship, while not always amicable, had become an integral part of doing business" (p. 32). Similarly in the case of ecology, when a research institute estimated in 1913 that air pollution cost the people of Pittsburgh $10 million per year, nothing happened; ". . .ecology had no constituency in those days. 'Smoke means jobs' so the saying went" (p. 33). That constituency formed in the 1960s: "Prompted by such accounts as Rachel Carson's *Silent Spring*, public awareness of the social costs of environmental degradation increased and was gradually converted into legislation at the federal level aimed at controlling air and water pollution" (pp. 34–35). Today the issue is moving more firmly into the realm of social norms.

Pattern B: Consciousness Raising   Pattern B takes a slightly different view of the same phenomenon. It sees the pressure campaign, not as directed at evoking tangible change through the imposition of formal constraints, but as a kind of publicity event that seeks to change the social norms of the public in general. That in turn is expected to prompt government to enact formal constraints to reflect the popular will. Thus, Campaign GM could be viewed as a form of consciousness raising, an attempt to show the public that the giant corporation is a system closed to external influence and therefore requiring change through legislation.

Pattern C: Formalization of a Social Norm   Pattern C sees the pressure campaign as the intermediate step by which a social norm becomes formalized as a specific constraint. Here, society changes first, before the organization does, even before there are pressure campaigns. New norms become accepted, but organizational behavior lags. Then come the pressure campaigns aimed at specific organizational actions in order to bring the unacceptable behavior to the attention of society. These in turn lead to formal constraints, designed to bring organizational behavior into line with the new social norms. For example, norms in America appear to have changed with respect to the treatment of migrant workers on farms. Yet old patterns of behavior persisted in California in contravention of these norms. And so pressure campaigns were carried out in the 1970s, including strikes, demonstrations, and boycotts, to publicize the issue so as to bring about new rules by which these workers would be treated.

Pattern D: Introduction of a Constraint   In Pattern D, a pressure campaign is used to introduce a formal constraint directly. For example, if the consumers desire representation on the board of directors of an organization, they may boycott its products until its constitution is so changed; if the unions wish to have safety conditions included in their collective agreement, they may strike the organization until they get it.

Pattern E: Correction of a Constraint   In Pattern E, because an existing formal constraint is being circumvented by a group of organizations, a pressure campaign against one of them is undertaken to bring the problem to the attention of the public and thereby to correct the problem. For example, if steel mills are ignoring existing pollution legislation, a publicity campaign against a major polluter can raise the attention of the government, which may then tighten the regulations.

The five patterns so far discussed all treat the pressure campaign as an intermediate step toward longer-lasting change, that is, toward changes in social norms or formal constraints. (Another way to put this is that none of the arrows of patterns A to E in Figure 5-1, end up in pressure campaigns.) Although the pressure campaign is always focussed on particular issues or actions, it is above all a means to effect change in a broader class of organizational behaviors. Indeed, by showing no single arrow between social norms and formal constraints, independent of pressure campaigns, in Figure 5-1, we mean to imply that pressure campaigns are generally a necessary element in social change, needed to focus the attention of the rule makers, or the public, on the requirement for the change. In changing themselves, therefore, societies would appear to proceed inductively, from the single tangible case to the general condition.

Pattern F: Correction of Delinquent Behavior   In our final pattern the pressure campaign is viewed as the end in itself. Where existing social norms are violated by an organization, a pressure campaign may be undertaken to correct the delinquent behavior in that one organization. For example, if an American firm in Europe, in contradiction of local practice, lays off its workers each time the market for its products dips, the local government may use a campaign of moral suasion—informal, personal pressure, perhaps linked with threats of legislation—to change its behavior. Of course, should the firm persist in violating the norm, then legislation may be enacted, for example requiring union consent or three months notice to lay off workers. When this happens, as in Pattern C, the pressure campaign becomes the specific means to expose the general problem, an intermediate step on the way to the enactment of a formal constraint.

DIRECT CONTROLS

Social norms are very general: The external influencer can only hope that they will evoke the desired behavior. Formal constraints focus more decisively, with penalties for noncompliance, but specify only minimally acceptable levels of behavior. They typically block rather than initiate behavior, and they are detached from the specific behaviors of specific organizations and so are often easy to circumvent. Furthermore, much behavior cannot be so constrained, especially in the case of the one-time strategic decision. Yet these are often the very ones that external influencers most wish to control. Pressure campaigns can be aimed at such decisions, but they are apart from the orgainzation's action taking; the external influencer can only hope that sufficient pressure will force the organization into responding. Thus all three means of external influence are rather indirect and only marginally effective to the external influencer who has the power and the will to control closely specific behaviors of the organization.

These influencers have two means to get them more directly into the organizational decision-making processes. One is to attain a seat on the board of directors, the body that formally controls the organization; the other is to bypass that body altogether and seek to control internal decision making more directly. In one of the most important studies of power processes in organizations, entitled *TVA and The Grass Roots*, Philip Selznick (1966) discusses under the term "cooptation" various means that were used to exert influence over the government-owned Tennessee Valley Authority. Selznick defines cooptation as "the process of absorbing new elements into the leadership or policy-determining structure of an organization as a means of averting threats to its stability or existence" (p. 13). He distinguishes two basic kinds of cooptation, which correspond roughly to our two remaining means of external influence:

> Cooptation in administration is a process whereby either power or the burdens of power, or both, are shared. On the one hand, the actual center of authority and decision may be shifted or made more inclusive, with or without any public recognition of the change; on the other hand, public responsibility for and participation in the exercise of authority may be shared with new elements, with or without the actual redistribution of power itself. (pp. 259–60)

Selznick refers to the public sharing of power as *formal* cooptation, which corresponds to what we here refer to as membership on the board of directors (although Selznick includes all "formerly ordered relationships" (p. 13)—other official positions, contracts, and so on). And what Selznick calls *informal* cooptation—the actual sharing of decision-making power—is more closely related to what we refer to here as the direct controls. Selznick describes informal cooptation as a reciprocal influencing process. On one hand, the decision-making behavior of the organization is opened up to the external influencer. On the other hand, that influencer is in turn "coopted" by the organization, in other words, comes to identify with it, appreciate its needs, and therefore to give it his or her support.

The direct controls—focussed in a personal way on specific organizations and often on specific decisions by these organizations—are generally reserved for those who have significant bases of power in the External Coalition. Five kinds of direct controls are discussed here, which may be considered to fall on a continuum of increasing influence. These are (1) accessing decision makers directly, (2) being included in an organizational decision-making process, (3) planting a representative in the Internal Coalition, (4) having the power to authorize one or more of the organization's decisions, and (5) actually imposing one or more of the organization's decisions on it directly.

DIRECT ACCESS   In the first case, the external influencer is not quite inside organizational processes, but he or she has a direct line to it. By virtue of their direct access to internal influencers, the external influencers are able to communicate personally with decision makers about those issues that concern them. Here the line between consultation and control can be very thin, for communication is often tantamount to control. As Sayer and Kaufman note about interest groups around the government of the City of New York:

> . . . the inner core of each group develops close relationships with one, or at most, a few agencies. In some particular segment of officialdom, leaders of each group are usually received whenever they request an audience, their advice considered seriously when offered and often incorporated in official decisions, their views canvassed when not volunteered. In a manner of speaking, many group leaders become intimate parts of the city's machinery of governmental decision in certain spheres. They are nongovernmental in the sense that they cannot *promulgate* binding orders and rules the ways officeholders clothed with public authority can, but they often have as much to say about what officeholders promulgate as the officeholders themselves. . . . (quoted in Lindblom 1965, p. 111)

Figure 5–2 shows various routes of direct access by external influencers to a church-owned convalescent hospital studied by one of the McGill student groups. A number of departments of the provincial government, which funded the hospital, had regular contact with the chief executive, the nurses, and the director of finance (for example, in budget negotiations); the union had access to the personnel department and, of course, the workers; the church congregation to the chief executive; the creditors to the chief executive as well as members of

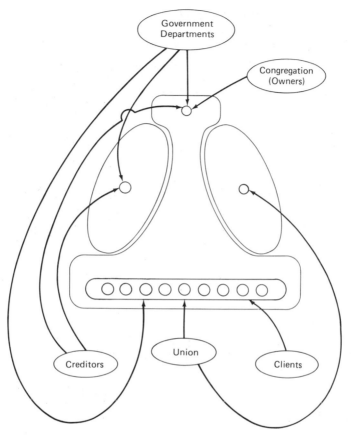

Figure 5-2. *Direct Access to a Convalescent Hospital*

the financial department; and the clients (patients) to the nursing staff.[3]

INCLUSION IN A DECISION PROCESS   Here, an external influencer becomes a temporary member of the Internal Coalition, joining a team or committee of insiders to work on some decision process. For example, a customer may be invited to send one of its engineers to join in a product development team, or a local community may be invited by a state agency to name someone to participate in an urban development project. The external influencer cannot dictate choices, but his presence gives him a good deal of influence in what is finally decided.

[3]Adapted from a report submitted to the author in Management 422, McGill University, 1970, by Jean Côté, Robert Gendron, and Michel Pellerin.

IMPLANTATION OF A FULL-TIME REPRESENTATIVE   In the third type of direct control, the external influencer gets to plant one of his own representatives right inside the Internal Coalition as a full-time member. Although the implanted individual is liable to be coopted by the organization, he nevertheless maintains some allegiance to the external group that named him and that can remove him. This is shown symbolically in Figure 5–3.

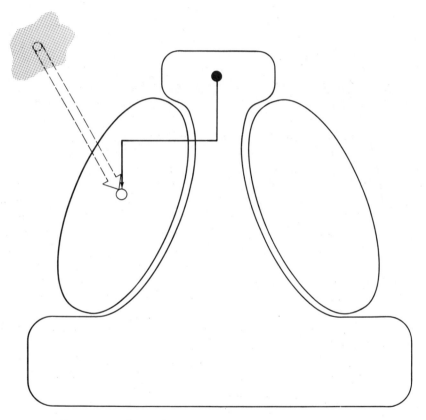

Figure 5–3. *The Implantation of a Representative in the Internal Coalition*

Selznick found this to be one of the principal forms of informal cooptation in the TVA. To deflect the goals of the Authority toward their own, certain important external influencers—who charged it with being socialistic and unfairly competitive with private enterprise—forced it to accept staff members who represented them. In this way the TVA set up by the Roosevelt administration to help the poor and black farmer, became an instrument of the wealthy white.

The literature presents a number of other examples of the implantation of a full-time representative. For example, Frank (1958) notes that in Soviet companies, "The chief accountant in each enterprise is appointed directly by the manager's superior. . .and is charged with reporting financial irregularities to that superior" (p. 9). Dalton (1959, pp. 24–25) describes the same occurence in the United States (in fact, a common one in divisionalized firms). This involved a factory whose accountant, although officially reporting to the factory manager, in fact retained his allegiances to the head office, which appointed him to his position.[4]

AUTHORIZATION OF DECISIONS   An external influencer with an important basis of power may be able to ensure that he or she can authorize certain of the organization's decisions before they are executed. This means of influence may be formal or informal. Earlier we noted the case of the racetrack that informally consulted the horsemen—owners of a scarce and vital resource—on major decisions. Formally, an organization may be required by law or by its own constitution to seek authorization from an external influencer before taking certain kinds of actions. Thus, regulatory agencies must approve certain major decisions of the organizations they regulate—the Canadian Radio and Television Commission, for example, must accept all changes in station ownership. Similarly, a corporation may require that it approve all senior executive appointments in its subsidiaries.

This means of external influence should be clearly distinguished from the imposition of a formal constraint. The latter constitutes a specific guideline that applies to a whole class of decisions. In contrast, authorization as a form of direct control pertains to individual decisions, with no guidelines. In other words, the external influencer can act arbitrarily if he so chooses, approving one decision and rejecting another without giving any reasons. This gives him significant power—albeit with the expenditure of a certain amount of energy—not only to block decisions at will but also to initiate change in them to make the outcome more to his liking. Thus a city can refuse to grant a building permit until changes are introduced into the design to make it more attractive.

IMPOSITION OF A DECISION   Finally, an external influencer possesses the most powerful form of direct control when he or she can make the organization's decision in the first place. In this case, power over the decision process passes outside of the Internal Coalition altogether; it is merely informed of the result—what action it must take. For example, a parent organization might impose a budget, perhaps even deciding on its allocation by departments. Lourenço and Glidewell (1975) describe how a network controlled the local television station

---

[4]Dalton's example is drawn from within an organization, Frank's ostensibly from the relationship between an External and Internal Coalition. But as noted in the *Structuring* book (Chapter 20), the dividing line between a Soviet government controlling various businesses and an American headquarters controlling various divisions (or in this case even plants) can be thin.

that it owned, notably by deciding what prime time shows it could broadcast. And suppliers in monopolistic situations sometimes dictate to their customers what products they will buy, in what quantities, and on what delivery schedules.

Of course, enough of this and the organization cease to be an autonomous entity. Regardless of legal distinctions, the external influencer who imposes many important decisions becomes the de facto chief executive, or else the Internal Coalition folds into the External Coalition as the organization emerges as a unit or department of some other organization. The local television station becomes merely a broadcasting arm of the network. Likewise the notion of an airline as an autonomous government corporation fades as the government tells it what planes to buy and where to fly them.

To conclude, our first three means of external influence—social norms, formal constraints, and pressure campaigns—maintain a clear distinction between environment and organization. By using any of the three, an External Coalition seeks to control the behavior of a distinct Internal Coalition. The pressure campaign, for example, acknowledges the internal decision makers' rights to make choices—it is used merely to influence what those choices will be. Our discussion of the various forms of direct control, in contrast, shows the increasingly close linkages that can grow up between an organization and its environment. As these linkages tighten, the Internal Coalition surrenders more and more power to the External Coalition until it can disappear within it. On the other hand, the more involved are the external influencers in the organization's decision-making processes, the more they come to identify with the organization and to be coopted by its needs. Eventually it is they who may disappear within the Internal Coalition. Once again the issue of reciprocity appears in the play of power.

This completes our discussion of four of the external means of influence in the organizational power system. We now turn to the fifth, and the most formal, of the means used by the external influencers to try to control the behavior of the organization.

6

The Board of Directors

Between the organization's Internal Coalition and External Coalition—that is, between those who actually make the decisions and take the actions and those who seek to influence them—stands a kind of "formal coalition" known as the board of directors (or trustees, governors, regents, etc.). To this "governing" board, as it is sometimes called, is designated various official representatives, typically both insiders and outsiders.

The board is the one place where different external influencers of the organization meet regularly, on a face-to-face basis with each other and with the managers, to discuss and ostensibly control the decisions and actions of the organization. As an external means of influence, therefore, the board seems to be the most formal, not to mention the most regular, focussed, and personal of the five we discuss. It should, therefore, serve as the prime means of influence for those members of the External Coalition fortunate enough to gain representation on it. The central issue we shall be addressing in this chapter, in looking at the various roles the board plays, is whether or not this is in fact true, that is, to what extent can the board really control the behavior of the organization. We begin with a discussion of the board as legal entity, and then outline a number of roles that it seems to play in the organization. We then conclude the chapter with a description of three different postures boards seem to adopt depending on which of these roles they emphasize.

THE BOARD IN LAW

The notion of a governing board is related to the concept of the "corporation." General corporation law in the United States states that "The business of a corporation shall be managed by a board of at least three directors." The corporation first developed in the Middle Ages as "an instrument for self-governance for groups carrying on a common activity" (Bell 1971, p. 29). The first ones were in fact religious orders (Zald 1969, p. 97), and the classic case that defined the corporation as a legal entity in the United States, separate from its particular constituents, dealt with Dartmouth College in 1819. But popular usage today has restricted the term to business firms incorporated by law, particularly the largest of these (that is how the term shall be used in this book), although by virtue of being legally incorporated and having a governing board, many other organizations utilize the corporate form of organizing as well. Indeed, almost all complex organizations do, from welfare agencies and private schools to hospitals and semi-autonomous government agencies.

As Zald (1969) notes, the corporate form was created as an entity that could outlive any of its members, to assure the accomplishment of tasks beyond the capacity of individuals. And its board was established in law as the vehicle to ensure its continuity—"to fix a locus of responsibility for [its] control" (p. 99). But three important ambiguities arose, and remain, in the legal definition of the governing board: First, who has the right to membership on it? Second, whose interests is the board supposed to represent? and, Third, how can the board exercise its powers of control?

Who has the right to gain entry to the board of directors? Private hospitals and universities have no owners per se, yet they have boards. Business corporations do have owners, yet a survey of the 5,995 directors of the Fortune 500 in 1977 showed that only 1.6 percent of them represented major outside shareholders (that is, ones who held more than 5 percent of the stock). Another 9 percent represented other investors or were professional directors, 6 percent were commercial bankers, 3 percent investment bankers, 5 percent lawyers, 25 percent other businessmen, 7 percent nonbusinessmen, 39 percent active managers and 4 percent retired ones of the corporations themselves (Smith 1978, p. 152). The fact is that the membership of the board is not usually specified by law, with the result that any influencer can be found on it, or excluded from it. So in the absence of legal specification, this first ambiguity is handled empirically: **membership on the board is a matter of influence and negotiation.**

The second ambiguity in the law concerns whose interests the board is supposed to represent. A 1967 report of the Conference Board claimed that "The basic legal responsibility of the board is to manage the company in the interests of the stockholders. In carrying out this task, the directors must exercise 'reasonable business judgement' and be 'loyal to the interests of the corporation'" (National Industrial Conference Board 1967, p. ii). But even in this short quotation there is an important ambiguity. Should the board be loyal to the corporation or responsible to the shareholders, for example, should it vote to liquidate the corporation when that is in the interest of the shareholders? In other words, once appointed, do the directors have external constituencies—owners, clients, employees, or whoever—in which case the board can become an arena for face-to-face bargaining among the influencers? Or are the directors responsible for the organization as a system separate from all of its influencers? Maniha and Perrow (1965–66) discuss a city Youth Commission whose key directors initially saw their role as protecting well-defined constituencies. For the YMCA chief and high school principal, it was the protection of the reputations of their institutions. Then a physician with no constituency was appointed chairman, and he took a different stand. Referring to the two other directors, he claimed: "They have difficulty separating their roles as YMCA chief and principal from their roles as Commission members. They often speak and act in terms of their own organizations and not the Commission" (p. 248). So here again, the solution is an empirical one. In the absence of legal definition, **the directors can protect whomever they choose to—organization or external constituency—depending on their own needs and the pressures to which they are subjected.**

The third ambiguity is the most interesting for our purposes. The law gives the board the formal power to control the organization, but it provides no *specific* means to do so. Rather, it implicitly provides *every* means. The board has the right to make or overturn every single organizational decision. But organizations have managers—sometimes thousands of them—to make decisions, and the board clearly cannot approve, let alone make, any significant number of them. Thus it is recognized that the board must appoint its own "trustee" to run the organization—the chief executive officer. This person then develops a system of management by which the decisions get made. But surely the board must do more than simply appoint a trustee. And so a literature has developed, much of it in the constitutions of organizations themselves, to describe the functions of the board. For example, the Conference Board report mentioned above lists seven functions of the board of the business corporation:

> (1) To establish basic objectives and broad policies of the company; (2) to elect the corporate officers, advise them, approve their actions, and audit their performance; (3) to safeguard, and to approve changes in, the corporation assets; (4) to approve important financial decisions and actions, and to see that proper reports are given to the stockholders; (5) to delegate special powers to others on matters requiring board approval; (6) to maintain, revise, and enforce the corporate charter and by-laws; (7) to ensure maintenance of a sound board. (p. 2)

But again, the words of job descriptions and journal articles notwithstanding, the issue of how the board is to control the organization is an empirical one—that is, one decided on the basis of power and practice.

Thus we have the definitions and functions of the board in law and in theory. Now for some facts.

THE BOARD IN PRACTICE: CONTROL ROLES

Those who have researched the behavior of boards of directors have assumed neither that the board represents a single group, such as the owners, nor that it necessarily controls the organization. Rather they have started with the premise that its membership as well as its influence are dictated by the circumstances of power in and around the organization. The results of this research have been rather interesting. First, as we have seen, they show that a wide variety of influencers can join this formal coalition. Indeed, they find that membership is determined not only by the power an individual holds in the External Coalition but also by what that individual can offer *to* the organization. In other words, while some directors represent external influencers, others represent no one: they are appointed to *serve* the organization. Second, in keeping with this first result, researchers have found that while some boards do indeed control their organizations (and some intend to but do not succeed), others neither do nor intend to. Thus, apparently, the board can play various roles, some related to control and others to service of one kind or another. We begin our review of the results of empirical research with a discussion of three roles the board plays in a control capacity, and then, after summarizing the real power of the board, we turn to the roles of a service nature.

ROLE 1: SELECTING THE CHIEF EXECUTIVE OFFICER   The most tangible function of the board is the selection of the chief executive officer of the organization. This is the one decision the board can never fully delegate (except, of course, to one of its members, who might in fact be the outgoing chief executive). And the power to appoint of course constitutes the power to dismiss as well. Were the board to possess no power other than this one—and truly to possess this one—then it would be a potent force indeed in the organizational power system. For in the nature of the chain of authority of formal organizations, as we shall see in Part II, the chief executive is inevitably a powerful individual. So power over that individual constitutes an important source of power over the organization.

We might then ask, Do boards indeed fully exercise this power to select and dismiss chief executives? And the answer suggested by the research seems to lie over a wide range, from "not really" to "yes, certainly." Some of the literature demonstrates unquestioned board control over the choice of chief executive. Consider the following anecdote:

> In one instance [a] trustee-director, discouraged by the declining sales and profits of the company, arranged with the president to have a two-day session at the company headquarters. . . . Shortly after these conferences he said: "I had no idea how badly off this company is. It has lost its market share in its traditional businesses, and the recently acquired ventures are not panning out at all. There are unex-

posed and undisclosed liabilities, and implicit obligations to throw good money after bad in these ventures. These facts have not been communicated to the board at all. I spent fifteen hours with the president, and during that time he dodged, ducked, and came up with the most unresponsive answers you have ever heard. I am the trustee of a family trust that owns 5 percent of this company, and I cannot stand by and watch it go down the drain because of the shortcomings of an incompetent president."

The trustee-director then called the other outside directors, expressed his concern, and arranged a meeting to discuss what should be done. All nine outside directors of a board of fifteen were present, and after a three-hour discussion they agreed to direct the chairman to ask the president for his resignation. A few days later the usual form announcement was made: "The chairman of the XYZ Company announced today that Mr. John Jones, president, has resigned because of policy differences with the board. The chairman will assume the office of president and chief executive officer. Mr. Jones was not available for comment." (Mace 1971, p. 63)

But in other cases, to say that the final "decision" rests with the board is to conceal a complex set of power relationships that can precede the last step in any strategic decision process. In an interesting paper entitled "Who Shall Rule? A Political Analysis of Succession in a Large Welfare Agency," Myer Zald (1965) details the play of power between a polarized board and a biased retiring chief executive in the choice of one of two candidates as his successor. Was it the board that made the decision? Consider the events:

Mr. Heis, the chief executive, originally wished to have his successor chosen six months before his retirement, but since the candidate he favored had been interviewed for a similar job in another city, he asked that the decision be put forward by one year. The head of the board of directors in consultation with Mr. Heis agreed to have an enlarged executive committee of the board consider the issue, and he recommended this course of action to the full board. Of the two candidates, Mr. Leaf was younger and more innovative; although he had the strong backing of Heis, his supporters on the board did not seem to be in control of it. Mr. Maddy, older and representing a traditional perspective of the organization, also "had a long association with many of the more 'substantial men,' as Heis called them, on the Board of Directors—the powerful bankers, investment brokers, and other more conservative members of the Board" (p. 56). Whereas Maddy upheld "the preventative and middle class orientation of the organization," Leaf "strongly identified with social welfare and liberal points of view" (p. 50).

The board chairman and the chief executive agreed on a process that implicitly favored Leaf, one that allowed "full discussion of the directions the board wanted the organization to take and a full analysis of the candidates" (p. 50). Each of seven potential candidates were to be interviewed by the executive committee on their views on three questions, dealing with the organization's future, its competition from other agencies, and its capacity for expanding its services.

> The process of election worked against Maddy in several ways. First, it broke up the expectation pattern in which Maddy was seen as the likely successor. The longer the debate went on, the more an alternative was possible. Second, it exposed Leaf to a group of men with whom he had had little previous contact. At least two of the more important members of the Board consciously abstained in judgment until they had had more contact with Leaf. Third, in any systematic discussion of program and directions of change, Leaf would clearly emerge as the more far-sighted and forward-looking, for he was the more articulate of the two and the three questions were, in effect, loaded in favor of him. (p. 57)

As Leaf emerged as a more serious contender, one of the older, more traditional board members accused Leaf of being unfit as an administrator. Heis was called to comment, and "presented to the executive committee evidence from annual ratings of executive personnel which disproved the charges" (p. 57). At this point, asked by an important board member for his opinion, Heis explicitly backed Leaf. "The committee voted to nominate Leaf" (p.57).

> Throughout the discussion, the [Chairman of the board] did not take an assertive role, essentially serving as a discussion leader rather than as a prime mover. But he did use his power as chairman of the executive committee at the last meeting preceding the announcement of the executive committee's nomination to the full Board. At this time the Board member who had questioned Leaf's administrative abilities tried to reopen the question. The [Chairman] strongly asserted his role and argued that the process had been a fair one and that all relevant considerations had been discussed, thus cutting off further debate. (p. 57)

Who then made the decision? Zald's description shows very clearly how complex such a question really is. On the surface, the board did, but below it the chief executive had considerable influence. If Leaf had no support to start with, the Board would likely have chosen Maddy no matter what Heis thought; alternately, had Heis been totally neutral, or had he fallen out of favor with the Board, it would again likely have chosen Maddy. Here we have the first of many instances reported in this book that show the dangers of drawing simple conclusions about the complex game of organizational power.

In his paper, Zald also discusses the vital importance of the CEO succession decision for organizations, typically the most and often the only important decision in which boards are frequently involved. Zald notes that it is at the time of choosing a successor for the top executive that the power of the board is most highly mobilized. Despite the apolitical appearance of the succession decision—"a transfer of power without politics" (p. 53)—and despite its infrequent or "episodic" occurrence, in fact that decision often proves critical. Not only does the decision process itself provide "an opportunity for a general examination of goals and policy" (p. 53), but the choice also gives a new individual great power to change the behavior of the organization. In fact, Zald discusses how the welfare agency changed significantly under Leaf's directions, becoming more innovative and liberal, and reorienting its programs toward its neediest clients.

In his study of the boards of business corporations, Mace lists "selecting the president" as one of the tasks that typical boards do *not* do. He argues that the outgoing president "knows the key members of his organization better than anyone else" while "board members with relatively brief exposure to company executives—whether on the board or not—base their appraisals necessarily on very inadequate evidence" (1971, p. 189). Thus, in spite of the appearance of "careful evaluation" by board committees, "in most cases the decision as to who should succeed the president is made by the president himself" (p. 189).

How can we reconcile this conclusion of Mace with that of Zald? It must be remembered that these two researchers studied very different kinds of organizations.[1] Zald looked at a welfare agency where the board did have considerable influence; for the most part, Mace surveyed large, "widely held" business corporations, whose directors represented no serious shareholder interests, and were in effect, according to his own findings, selected by the chief executive himself. (Indeed, in those cases where directors did represent important shareholder interests—as in his example cited earlier of the director whose investigation lead to the dismissal of the president—Mace was prepared to reverse his conclusion.)

Thus the evidence suggests that the power associated with this first role of the board can range widely depending on a number of factors. It also suggests that true control over the succession decision constitutes one important means to influence the behavior of the organization. But that decision, it should be noted, happens infrequently. Chief executives retire or die only occasionally, and no organization can afford to have its chief executive dismissed frequently by a board of directors intent on consolidating its own power base. So if the board is to have more significant, and more regular, control over the organization, its power must extend beyond this one decision.

ROLE 2: EXERCISING DIRECT CONTROL DURING PERIODS OF CRISIS   In his analysis, Mace is prepared to accept two conditions under which boards of directors of widely held corporations may in fact take control of their organizations. First is when "a president dies suddenly or becomes incapacitated," and second is when "leadership and performance of the president are so unsatisfactory that a change must be made" (p. 182). Mace emphasizes in both cases the importance of selecting a successor quickly to ensure continuity. But in the second case especially, he adds that the board members may also take direct control of the organization, devoting "more than casual amounts of time to the company in distress" (p. 184). To use Drucker's colorful terminology, the board serves as a "'stand-by' in case there is a 'power failure'" (1973, p. 634).

---

[1]And they studied them very differently, Zald probing deeply into one succession decision, while Mace surveyed many organizations more generally.

In another, more general paper on the boards of directors Zald goes further than Mace in describing this second role of the board. He notes that "board power is most likely to be asserted" during the handling of "major phase problems, or strategic decision points" (1969, p. 107)—in addition to times of executive succession, during the raising of funds, the expansion of facilities, and transitions in the organization's life cycle. As we shall see in the discussion immediately following, during these strategic decision points, boards may in fact be more inclined to review management's decisions carefully than to actually make the decisions themselves, so long, of course, as they retain confidence in that management. But when the issue involves the management itself, there seems little doubt that boards are prepared to move into positions of direct control.

ROLE 3: REVIEWING MANAGERIAL DECISIONS AND PERFORMANCE   The final role of a control nature involves the right of the board to pass judgment on managerial activities—to review and if necessary reject certain specific managerial decisions as well as to review and pass judgment on managerial performance in general.

We can, in fact, discuss a whole continuum of control here. At one extreme—really beyond review per se—would be those decisions boards make themselves without any managerial initiative. But there seems to be only one such decision consistently made by boards, and that is not a very important one—the setting of the compensation of the chief executive, and perhaps other senior managers as well. And the reason for making this decision is obvious: It simply looks bad for senior managers of public corporations to be setting their own salaries.

In virtually all other cases—save decisions to replace and sometimes to select the top management, as already discussed—boards seem at most to restrict themselves to reviewing the decisions proposed by the management. The nature of such review can vary widely. It may involve close scrutiny followed by formal authorization, so that the board specifically sanctions managerial actions or, alternately, rejects or modifies them. In this case, the initiative rests with the board. A milder form of review has the management merely informing members of the board of proposed actions. Here the initiative rests with the management; unless the board objects, management will proceed. The approval is tacit. A distinction should be made here—although it can be a subtle one—between the board serving in a control versus an advisory capacity (the latter related to a role to be discussed later). On one hand, the board is informed in order to provide it with the opportunity to block the action if it so chooses; on the other hand, it is informed so that management can benefit from the wisdom of the board members. Of course, a chief executive who wishes to sound out the board can always ask advice; later if the action is questioned, he can claim that board members had a chance to discuss it and express their concerns.

Finally, at the other extreme, is the board that simply rubber-stamps managerial decisions. Ostensibly it authorizes; in fact, that authorization is only for appearances. In the case of some decisions, board authorization is required by law.

A variety of decisions can be reviewed by boards, for serious authorization, tacit approval, or rubber-stamping. Most common, of course, are those of a strategic nature—the introduction of new products or services, the initiation of large capital projects (such as the building of new facilities or the purchase of expensive machinery), decisions related to the acquisition, merger, or divestment of businesses, the raising of capital, and the reorganization of structure. Other decisions of a less strategic nature but commonly reviewed by boards—at least in business corporations—are those related to dividends, charitable contributions, and employee benefit plans (Clendenin 1972; Mace 1971; Bacon and Brown 1975). Board approval would seem to add a touch of legitimacy to these sensitive decisions.

Mace (1971) discusses in detail one of these types of decisions in the large corporation—the approval of capital projects. Most corporations require that projects above a certain cost be submitted for board approval. But Mace found a few cases where boards were never even advised, let alone consulted. Said one president: "I would never take a capital appropriation request to the board. What in the world would they know about it!" (p. 44). Indeed, one director of three corporations told Mace that, in a number of cases, "I learned about a major acquisition by one of my companies when I read it in the paper" (p. 48). Typically, however, the boards were involved. But they "never, ever" (to use the words of one president) disapproved of an expenditure. They simply lacked the information needed to question the decision. As one president remarked, "the board is in no position, and doesn't undertake to be in a position, to challenge or question the specific capital appropriation recommendations of management" (p. 46). Instead, to quote another "I would say that directors tend to read the capital appropriation requests in which they have some experience or some interest, and they pay very little attention to all the rest—they just thumb through them, look at the front page so they know what is being talked about" (p. 46). This last comment brings to mind the famous story C. Northcote Parkinson (1957, pp. 25–32) tells of an apocryphal board meeting. Feeling somewhat self-conscious about having just approved, in two and a half minutes with no questions, the funding of a $10-million nuclear reactor, the directors seize on the next item, which they happen to know something about—the project for a $2,350 bicycle shed—and discuss it for three quarters of an hour.

The board can review—in a cursory or serious manner—not only specific decisions of managers but also whole sets of them together, before or after they are executed. Before the fact, the board may review the plans of management—its objectives, intended strategies, operating plans, budgets. And after the fact, it can review or monitor managerial performance—the sum total of its decisions—how well management did vis-à-vis its own plans, its competitors' performance, or simply the expectations of the directors.

Boulton (1977, 1978) suggests in his research that board review of performance can take place on three levels, what he calls "legitimizing," a ritual involving the minimum that is necessary by law; "auditing," involving the review of financial reports to be published; and "directing," entailing a much more intensive search for all kinds of information by which the true performance of management can be assessed. As might be expected, Mace found that the boards he studied were at Boulton's lowest level:

> I have concluded that generally boards of directors do not do an effective job of evaluating or measuring the performance of the president. Rarely are standards or criteria established and agreed upon by which the president can be measured other than the usual general test of corporate profitability, and it is surprising how slow some directors are to respond to years of steadily declining profitability....Directors base their appraisals largely on data and reports provided by the president himself. Also, top executives serving as outside directors, being exceedingly busy men, typically do not devote the time to pursue [their concerns]....(pp. 182–83)[2]

But since Mace's study, the auditing level has become much more common, encouraged by a New York Stock Exchange requirement that all of its member companies set up "audit committees" of their boards. And Boulton found in his more recent study that boards were sometimes prepared to undertake third-level directing review when performance declined or major new commitments were undertaken.

Nevertheless even cursory review—of general performance or specific decisions—can have its effect, as Zald points out in his study of the succession decision. It is not what the board *does* in this role of review so much as what it *can* do that may influence management's behavior. A board can temper the actions of management implicitly, much as bees in the vicinity temper the actions of someone picking flowers. As long as the directors or the bees are not disturbed, one proceeds unimpeded. But upsetting them can have disastrous consequences. Thus behavior is influenced.

THE REAL POWER OF THE BOARD   Before proceeding to discuss other roles of the board, we stop at this point to address the issue of what real power these three control roles give to the board.

It will be helpful to return to our analogy of the bee. For if the bee does indeed choose to attack, it gets to sting only once. And the same is true more or less for the board of directors.

[2]Here Mace receives the support of Clendenin (1972) who also interviewed the presidents of large business corporations: "Few boards make an exhaustive evaluation of operating performance unless the need for such an evaluation is precipitated by a crisis. Many chief executives stated that the board's review of operating performance is rather superficial" (p. 63).

The United States General Corporation law notwithstanding, the business of the corporation is not managed by its board of directors. It is managed by its full-time managers, in the first instance by its chief executive officer.[3] The board intervenes only when something disturbs it, such as a crisis, the loss of an executive, the grave deterioration of performance. In terms of our discussion of the last chapter, as an external means of influence, the board of directors is episodic though it appears regular, obstructive though it may seem initiative, and less focussed and personal than appearances suggest. Its real power, like that of the bee, lies in its sting, which it gets to use only infrequently, if ever.

Why is this so? All the evidence points to one simple reason. Directors outside the Internal Coalition—that is, outside the day-to-day decision-making processes of the organization—simply lack the information needed to make decisions. There are exceptions: external issues outside the management's area of expertise (such as special fund raising), directors who used to work for the organization, or organizations that are small and simple to understand (Zald 1969). But for the most part, the part-time directors simply know much less than the full-time managers.

> The determination of a company's objectives, strategies, and direction requires considerable study of the organization's strengths and weaknesses and its place in the competitive environment, careful, time-consuming, penetrating analysis of market opportunities, and a matching of the organizational capacities to meet and serve the changing requirements of the market....The typical outside director does not have time to make the kinds of studies needed to establish company objectives and strategies. At most he can approve positions taken by management, and this approval is based on scanty facts...(Mace 1971, p. 185)

Mace claims that directors do not even ask "discerning questions" at board meetings. "Many board members cited their lack of understanding of the problems and the implications of topics that are presented to the board by the president, and to avoid 'looking like idiots' they refrain from questions or comments.... In most companies it would be possible to write the minutes of a board meeting in advance" (pp. 187–88).

Thus, even the board that is intent on control chooses its top management—presumably one that reflects its general values—and then lets it manage the organization. The board cannot continually look over management's shoulder to do that for it. It may reserve the right to review carefully certain major decisions—especially during times of crisis and transition—and occasionally it may overturn one. That can have the healthy effect of keeping the management on its toes. And, of course, the clever chief executive knows what may upset the board, and so avoids broaching such issues. In some other cases,

---

[3]A number of states have in fact replaced "managed by," or added to it, "managed under the direction of" (Estes 1977, p. 21).

when the chief executive is unsure of a major decision, when he or she feels that the board has more knowledge (say in the case of dividend policy), or when the board is intent on deciding for itself (as in the setting of senior management salaries), the chief executive may choose not to go to the board with a commited stand but instead to leave the choice to it. But such situations need to remain rare. Too many decisions deferred to the board raises questions about the ability of the top management to run the organization. And too many decisions overturned by the board raises questions about its confidence in the top management. And so **board approval of management decisions and performance under normal circumstances tends to be a foregone conclusion.** Even the board that has doubts about a proposal will not usually buck a management in which it otherwise has confidence. The one exception to this, as we shall see more clearly, later in this book, can be the board so caught up in its own conflicts that it becomes an arena wherein directors vie with each other for power. Management emerges as a kind of innocent bystander (or, more likely, just another influencer in the bargaining).

Thus, Mace lists among the functions that boards do *not* perform, "establishing objectives, strategies, and policies" (1971, p. 185). And Clendenin (1972) concurs, with his finding that "two-thirds of the executives interviewed stated that the board discussed important issues of policy and strategy only occasionally," and that a further one quarter claimed that they were not involved "at all" (p. 62). The same thing can be seen in nonprofit organizations, as in the comments of an executive of a family service agency:

> . . . we tell [the directors] how to vote and they vote and we call that process "the Board sets the policies of the agency. . . ." I can frankly cite very few instances when Board opinion has influenced my judgment about policy and practices during the (many) years I have been Executive of this agency, although the Board has made every important policy decision and has been "informed" ad nauseum before every decision. (quoted in Zald 1969, p. 98)

The effect of these conclusions is to collapse the third role of the board into the first: decisions and performance are reviewed primarily in the context of replacing the chief executive. And, as we saw earlier, the second role—exercising direct control during periods of crisis—is also associated with problems of succession and performance. We can conclude, therefore, that, **when a board does indeed have control, its real power amounts to the capacity to dismiss and appoint the chief executive officer—and to the CEO's knowledge of that fact.** That is all.[4]

[4]Thus a board without the power to name the chief executive is truly impotent. In 1966, taking a leaf straight out of an Orwellian novel, the French government in Paris created "le Port Autonome de Marseille." Autonomy for the Port of Marseille meant a representative board (five members from the national government, seven from the Chamber of Commerce of Marseille and one from that of Arles, seven users of the Port and two of its employees), but no power to name the chief executive. That right, as befits traditional French government ideas about decentralization, remained in Paris.

This conclusion raises a fundamental dilemma for the board of directors. As long as its members are part-timers, outside the Internal Coalition, they cannot possibly gain the knowledge of the organization needed to match that of management. How can individuals, many of them executives running their own organizations, who by Clendenin's estimate typically spend twenty hours or less in board meetings per year, possibly match wits with the full-time managers in the thick of things? How can they even know enough to decide when to replace the chief executive, given their main channel of information into the organization is typically through that very same chief executive? How then can the directors control the organization? The fact is, as we have seen, that they do not control it on a regular basis at all; they do not even pass judgment on most of its individual actions. Under normal conditions, they sit back passively, being fed their information by the top management, to all intents and purposes, subject to its guidance. Indeed, when something does go wrong, it is not uncommon for the directors to be the last to learn about it, "always" the case, according to Peter Drucker, "in the great business catastrophies of this century" (1973, p. 628).

The solution to the problem seems obvious: to appoint full-time directors. They would have time to inform themselves properly and so to ensure some kind of control over the organization. But that does not solve the real problem at all; it merely introduces the other side of the dilemma. The real problem is the need for *external* control of the organization, control independent of the management. It is not control by the board per se that matters, but control by the External Coalition, the board being merely the formal manifestation of it. But if the directors work full-time on the board, they shift their allegiances from the External to the Internal Coalition. They become, in effect, employees of the organization, and their outside roles become secondary. The price of their intimacy with the organization is their cooptation by it. And to the extent that this happens, they cease to represent *external* influencers. More significantly, the dividing line between authorizing decisions and making them disappears at the margin. As the highest-ranking authorities of the organization, the full-time directors inevitably get deeply involved in decision making; they become, not the controllers of the management, but the de facto managers themselves. What is called the board of directors thus becomes in effect the executive committee, and its chairman becomes the organization's chief executive officer, with the other directors his subordinates. The organization ceases to have a real board, in the sense of a body detached from those who run the organization, able to exercise control on behalf of the external influencers. The full-time board may control the organization, but the External Coalition does not control the board.

Two manifestations of this can be seen clearly in the large American business corporation. First, the role of chairman has gradually changed from that of a part-time individual, at one time a representative of the owners, to that of a full-time chief executive officer who runs the organization much as the president once did. And second, there has appeared the so-called "inside board," where all the directors are full-time managers, so that members of the External Coalition—including the shareholders—have no seats whatsoever. It is curious to hear the arguments used to justify the inside board. Under questioning at a symposium of directors of large American corporations, at a time when Standard Oil of New Jersey (Exxon) had an inside board, one of its director-managers made the case that inside directors are better informed than outside ones. His position was summarized as follows:

> . . . the philosophy behind the advocacy of the full-time director is that the meaningful discharge of a director's responsibilities requires a more extensive knowledge of corporate operations than can be acquired through part-time contact. Especially in the large corporation, some of the panel felt, directing is a full-time job, requiring substantial work on the part of individual directors between board meetings, to understand the full range of the business' affairs. (Brown and Smith 1957, p. 91)

But the price of being so informed is a rather high one—the exclusion of external influencers, including shareholders, from one of their key means of influence, and the loss of the one possibly objective means to review the performance of management. That review is left to the management itself, the directors being expected to sit in judgment on the chairman, their boss. Thus, Chandler, in a *Harvard Business Review* article entitled "It's Time to Clean up the Boardroom," writes:

> An insider board is an absurdity. Subordinates are in no position to determine fairly the CEO's compensation, nor can a strong CEO get frank opinions from them. . . .
> You hear the argument that the CEO needs the insider's advice. That they have knowledge of the business which outsiders lack is true but irrelevant. . . . The place to get informed input from officers, former officers, and company lawyers, however, is not in the boardroom, but in the CEO's office before the board meeting. (1975, p. 75)

These kinds of arguments must have touched a nerve—they certainly exposed the absence of any semblance of formal external control over many large corporations—because the inside board is now becoming a relic of the past (at least in the United States although apparently not in Britain). The proportion of inside directors on the Fortune 500 declined by 19 percent from 1967 to 1977 (Smith 1978). And with the New York Stock Exchange now requiring that boards have audit committees staffed exclusively with outside directors, the pure inside board has disappeared from its listed companies. (Even the chairmanship has in recent years shown signs of swinging back to a part-time position.)

Thus the external influencers wishing to use the board as a serious means of influence are left with the dilemma of choosing part-time directors who lack the information necessary to control the management or full-time directors who lack the will necessary to represent the external influencers. Obviously given the choice they would opt for the former, that is, for inadequate control over no control.

A number of commentors on the roles of the board of directors in the large American corporation have sought solutions to this dilemma. One proposal, put forward by Mace and Clendenin among others, is to use "professional directors," properly paid and supported individuals who can devote all of their time to serving on the boards of a handful of organizations. This middle ground position would enable the directors to retain their independence yet would grant them time and resources to inform themselves adequately. Although some prestigious individuals—including two former presidents of the New York Stock Exchange—"proudly" refer to themselves as professional directors (Smith 1978, p. 168), the idea has not yet caught on, a reflection perhaps of the fact that management prefers the weak board to the professional board.

To conclude our discussion of the control roles of the board, while potentially, at least, the board has some power over the organization, that power is less than generally imagined,[5] and necessarily exercised infrequently. It amounts at best to the right to replace the chief executive, and what effect the chief executive's knowledge of this fact has on his behavior. The part-time board clearly functions outside the Internal Coalition of the organization, and, all things considered, while not wholly impotent, neither is it the most important of the external means of influence.

But if the board as a device to control the organization turns out to be weaker than is generally imagined, as a device to serve the organization, it turns out to be more useful. The next five roles describe this aspect of the board of directors.

THE BOARD IN PRACTICE: SERVICE ROLES

We have seen that some boards exercise a kind of indirect control of management, while others do not do even that. But in either case, there are other roles that boards can play, specifically by including members who can render a variety of services to the organization. We can distinguish at least four of these services: (1) the coopting of external influencers, (2) the establishing of contacts (and the raising of funds), (3) the enhancing of the organization's reputation, and (4) the giving of advice to it. We shall first discuss each of these service role briefly, showing how they are distinct from one another in principle. But then, in discussing some of the research related to them, we shall see how

---

[5] In a study of perceived power in universities ("Who makes the big decisions?"), Gross found that faculty and administrators scored the regents (directors) as second after the president. "Some persons may be surprised that the regents score as high as they do (regents themselves usually were) since they rarely do more than rubber-stamp the decisions of the president. But they do select the president and are often perceived as a rather shadowy, mysterious group" (1968, pp. 537–38).

difficult it has been to disentangle them, partly because directors are often appointed for more than one reason and partly, as we shall see, because of the nature of the research itself.

   ROLE 4: COOPTING EXTERNAL INFLUENCERS   The fact that the board of directors cannot easily be used by the external influencers to gain direct control over the management does not preclude the management from trying to use the board to gain some kind of control over external influencers. Here we come to Selznick's "formal cooptation," the first of the four roles that see the board as a tool of the organization rather than as a vehicle by which power is gained over it. The difference between cooptation and the other roles of the board is that here a power relationship continues to exist between the directors and the organization, except that it flows the other way. Power is not a central issue in the other service roles, while in the control roles it of course is, but there it is the directors who seek to exercise it. In this fourth role of the board of directors, the organization tries to use membership on it to win the direct support of important outside individuals.

   The organization may try to diffuse the power of an important external influencer by providing that person the status of a seat on the board. As Selznick (1966) describes it, granting membership on the board of directors is one possible means by which an organization can give up the trappings of power without giving up any real power. An external influencer can content himself with status instead of a serious say in decision making. Or else, the organization may try to elicit the support of an influential individual who might otherwise ignore it, as when a private hospital or university offers a board seat to a wealthy potential donor (or to an existing donor, to ensure that his or her generosity will continue). The seat buys the donation (or, sometimes, vice versa). Of course, the organization does not always get away that easily; the price of cooptation can in fact be the giving up of some real power. As Perrow notes in the case of hospital directors who forced a reluctant team of medical researchers to release information prematurely on a new technique, "publicity is what the large donors buy with their donations" (1970, p. 114). But the point of formal cooptation is that it is largely the trappings of power that satisfy the influencer; the organization gains a good deal more than it surrenders.

   ROLE 5: ESTABLISHING CONTACTS (AND RAISING FUNDS) FOR THE ORGANIZATION
In this case, we move beyond direct power relationships, describing the role of the board as the establishment of contacts for the organization. Directors are appointed for the people they know, the contacts they can establish. They themselves neither control nor are coopted. They merely open doors. Thus, on the board of many an American corporation that deals extensively with the Pentagon sits a retired military officer. He no longer has any formal power in the Pentagon, but does retain his contacts with those who do. Likewise one study found that "hospitals operating with relatively more government money . . . tended to place more importance on selecting board members for their

political connections" (Pfeffer 1973, p. 358). Indeed, in this study, the growth of the hospitals—in facilities and programs, number of beds, and size of budget—correlated positively with the extent to which board members were chosen for their political connections and *negatively* with the extent to which they were chosen for their knowledge of hospital administration. The contacts role seemed to take precedence over the advising one in these institutions.

An important subrole here—really beyond just making contacts—is to help the organization raise funds. Not-for-profit organizations—hospitals, universities, private welfare agencies—often choose as their directors people who can raise funds by virtue of their contacts. Returning to the hospital study, Pfeffer predicted and then confirmed that

> . . . the larger the proportion of the capital expenditure budget obtained from private donations, the more important will be fund raising as a board function and the ability to raise money as a consideration in the selection of directors. Conversely, the larger the proportion of the budget obtained from the government, the less important will be fund raising as a board of directors function. (1973, p. 352)

In return for the prestige of the board membership, directors are expected to tap their contacts to bring in money. A similar situation, though perhaps less direct, takes place when business corporations put bankers, investment counsellors, and the like on their board to help them float stock and bond issues.

This role of establishing contacts, or raising funds, can also be described as a form of *indirect* cooptation, in that the board member is used as an intermediary to help elicit the support of important influencers. Indeed, a number of researchers include it under the label of cooptation. We do not, because strictly speaking it is not the director who is being coopted. That person is not an influencer—he or she represents no interests, no constituency. The relationship is more one of reciprocity than dependency. The director is simply hired to perform a service—providing contacts, raising funds, or whatever—in return for the status, or the money, of the directorship.

ROLE 6: ENHANCING THE ORGANIZATION'S REPUTATION   The sixth role of the board is also akin to cooptation in a way—in fact, Selznick includes it in his use of the term. But again we maintain a distinction. Here the board serves as a vehicle to enhance or maintain the general reputation of the organization, to legitimize it. To draw on Selznick, when the formal authority lacks "a sense of historical legitimacy," or is "unable to mobilize the community for action," "it may not be necessary actually to share power"; rather the "creation of a 'front'" may suffice to develop "an aura of respectability" (1966, pp. 259–60). High-status individuals are invited to join the board for their public relations value. As one director commented:

> I don't think there's the slightest doubt in my mind that a great many shareholders have a feeling of satisfaction when they see the names of some very prominent

people on their board of directors. I have a feeling also that they place a great deal more confidence in the contribution the big name people make to the company than is justified. ...they would like to see, oh, President Eisenhower on the board. It just makes them feel good to have those kinds of people. (quoted in Brown and Smith 1957, p. 83)

It may be true that as prestigious individuals, the directors themselves are in a sense coopted—drawn in to supporting the organization. But in a broader sense the phenomenon is not really one of cooptation so much as, again, service for a fee. As in the fifth role of establishing contacts, the directors are not influencers with their own constituencies to represent. Indeed, they are not even appointed to gain the support of specific individuals, but rather of the public in general. And so they are even less likely to try to exert power over the organization. To cite one poignant example of our times, when a corporation names an astronaut to its board of directors, it is fairly safe in assuming that he will mind his own business, not its.

Mace finds that "presidents in selecting directors for their companies regard the titles and prestige of candidates as of primary importance" (1971, 195). As a result, "newly elected company presidents and newly elected university presidents and deans of graduate schools...were surprised by the sudden influx of invitations they received to become board members of large and prestigious companies" (p. 196). Mace notes further that corporations are careful to match the titles of the new directors with those of the old—for example, by naming no vice-presidents or presidents of small firms to boards with presidents of large corporations—presumably so as not to dilute the status of the board.

The same thing goes on in the not-for-profit sector. Zald notes in the case of welfare agencies that "students of these organizations suggest that there is a correlation between the prestige of the boards of agencies and their likelihood of having a request granted a respectful hearing. Auerbach...suggests that the settlement house serving a slum neighborhood but having an unknown board is less likely than the middle-class agency having a prestige...board to receive a favorable hearing" (1969, p. 103). In his own study of the thirty-four YMCA departments in Chicago, Zald (1967–68) found that the central office rated as highest on scales of level of efficiency, program quality, and board strength itself, those departments with the highest percentage of well-to-do business leaders on their boards. (The correlation coefficients were .67, .48 and .42.) Of course, direct cooptation also could have been a factor, because these board members also contributed substantially to their departments. In other words, these departments might have come out best on the performance measures because the prestige of their boards actually helped them to function more effectively (or at least convinced the central office personnel doing the rating that they were so functioning) or else because they simply had more money—donated by their board members—to do things better.

ROLE 7: GIVING ADVICE TO THE ORGANIZATION   As Bacon and Brown note, the "chief executive occupies a lonesome post; from time to time he must resolve matters in which he needs counsel, yet he may be reluctant to discuss these matters with subordinates" (1975, p. 18). The board of directors becomes his "sounding board." In fact, one of the three functions that Mace believes the boards of widely held corporations *do* do is provide "advice and counsel."

> It was found that most presidents and outside board members agree that the role of directors is largely advisory and not of a decision-making nature. Management manages the company, and board members serve as sources of advice and counsel to the management. (1971, p. 179)

In his study of Norwegian corporate boards, Gustavsen (1975) found that the chief executives rated the importance of directors as highest on financial matters, followed by economic analysis, legal aspects, and then relationships with other enterprises. They rated them lowest on issues related to managerial techniques, internal organization, and technical innovation, in effect those very areas where management is best informed. This probably best explains why bankers and lawyers are prized as board members. (The survey by Bacon [1973] of 855 corporations found that 41 percent of all outside directors were bankers, lawyers, investment house dealers, or consultants.) They are experts on the very issues which concern organizations at their highest levels, and on which inside expertise is often the most limited—raising capital, working out acquisition contracts, dealing with regulatory agencies, handling issues of social responsibility. As Dooley notes: "Stock and bond issues, mergers and acquisitions, and other questions of high finance require expert counsel. Such questions are not the daily business of the salaried executives of nonfinancial corporations. . . ." (1969, p. 322).

Of course, we can explain the presence of these people in terms of other roles too, for example, in the case of bankers, to establish links with other financial houses to help float financial issues (contacts or fund-raising role), to ensure the continued financial support of their own banks (cooptation role), even to look after the investments of these banks (the control roles). And even when the directors' roles are ostensible only the service ones, again as we saw in the case of the cooptation of wealthy donors, the organization may still have to pay some price in control over its own decisions. As Chandler notes, "Even if the CEO says to pay no attention [to the affiliation of directors], the purchasing department can't help being aware of the relationship" (p. 70). Thus Mace notes that the banker-director "serves as a signal to the outside world that a firm-client relationship exists": other bankers are discouraged from approaching "the apparently captive company" (p. 201). And so, notwithstanding the denials of some presidents and bankers, Mace found that the company with a banker-director generally bought its investment services only from his firm. What these comments suggest, as a bridge to our next discussion, is that while the different roles of the board can easily be distinguished in principle, distinguishing them in practice is another matter.

UNTANGLING THE ROLES
OF THE DIRECTORS IN PRACTICE

In principle we have been able to distinguish the four service roles of the board from each other and from the three control roles. Efforts to exercise power can flow into the organization from directors intent on controlling it, out of the organization to the directors it tries to coopt, or in neither direction as directors are simply engaged to serve the organization by developing contacts or raising funds for it, helping to enhance its reputation, or providing it with advice. But in practice, how is one to know which role is really operative? Indeed, how can one distinguish, say, control from cooptation, or advice from contacts, when two or more roles can very well operate concurrently? In other words, at the margins the real purposes of the directors can be very subtly intertwined, discernible if at all only through intensive study of the actual behavior of board members.

But the research on boards of directors has for the most part been of a survey rather than of an intensive nature. Indeed, this area lends itself to survey research, because one prime body of data—the number, names, and affiliations of directors—has always been readily available. It is published in the organizations' annual reports, which are typically in the public domain. Here we look at two sets of such studies with some interesting results, but also, in the final analysis, a number of difficulties of interpretation.

In his research, Jeffrey Pfeffer sought to make the case that "board size and composition are not random or independent factors, but...rational organizational responses to the conditions of the external environment" (1972, p. 226). Specifically he sought to demonstrate that it was the service roles, especially cooptation and the establishing of contacts as well as the raising of funds (all of which Pfeffer includes under the term cooptation), that best explain the selection of directors. In two studies based on a wide sample of organizations in business (1972) and in the hospital sector (1973), Pfeffer amassed some interesting evidence (some of which we have already cited). His premise was that since the typical board is controlled by management, its members can be selected to the organization's advantage.

Pfeffer's study of eighty business corporations supported the following relationships (with the levels of statistical significance shown in parentheses): the larger the capital requirements of the organization, the greater the percentage of directors from financial institutions (.04); the greater the organization's need for access to external capital markets, the larger the number of directors (.05) as well as the proportion of outside directors (.001) and the proportion of lawyers (.05); organizations in regulated industries have more outside directors (.002), and those regulated nationally, more lawyers (.05); and the larger the organization, the greater the total number of directors (.001), in Pfeffer's view because large size means more segments in the environment in need of cooptation and more of a need to coopt them. All of these results still left a good deal of the variance unexplained, so Pfeffer proposed a final, more ambitious hypothesis, namely, that "organizations that deviate relatively more from a preferred inside-outside director orientation should be relatively less successful when compared to industry standards than those that deviate less from a preferred board composition" (p. 225). Using two different measures of performance—net income to sales and net income to shareholders' equity—Pfeffer found correlation coefficients of about .30 with levels of significance of the order of .005.

In his second study, Pfeffer (1973) tested some of the same relationships on fifty-seven hospitals. He hypothesized that larger boards serve to coopt, while smaller ones act to control. The larger boards were believed necessary to raise large quantities of funds, especially in private hospitals reliant on donations (compared with public ones that could rely on government grants or those that were funded by religious orders). Among his findings:

> The size of the hospital boards, as predicted, tended to be larger the larger the hospital budget, the larger the proportion of funds obtained from private donations, and the more important influence in the community and fund raising were a criteria for selecting board members. . . . the board was smaller, the larger the proportion of funds obtained from the federal government and the more important hospital administration was as a board function. In general, the data support the argument that the more the hospital requires linkage to the local environment for fund raising and support, the larger the board; while the less that linkage is needed, and the more hospital management is emphasized as a board function, the smaller the board is. (pp. 358–59)

Thus, Pfeffer produces a set of impressive results concerning the board of directors. But caution in interpretating some of them might be in order. First, power—whether cooptation or control—may not be a factor in many board appointments. As we saw, bankers may typically be asked to join corporate boards, not to exercise any power with financial institutions, but simply to provide financial advice to the management. Likewise, lawyers may have no ax to grind as directors of regulated companies; after all they represent no apparent constituency. They may be there simply to share their knowledge of regulation with the management. And second, even assuming a power relationship, the question remains: Which way does it flow? Do these findings about boards reflect the organization's ability to coopt external influencers or do they reflect the ability of these influencers to gain power over the organization by the use of the board as a means of influence? Correlational analysis only indicates the relationship between two variables; it is Pfeffer who infers the causation. Lawyer-directors may have no ax to grind, but some bankers may. They could have investments to watch over. Indeed, that too could explain Pfeffer's performance result, since bankers may be more interested in the profitability of the corporation than other directors or even the managers themselves (who, as we shall see in Chapter 9, tend to favor growth over profit as a goal).

In the case of board size, the cooptation argument is likely stronger than the control one, at least in the light of the finding in a study of a bank reported by James (1951) that the average size of action-taking groups among officers and directors was 6.5 while that of nonaction groups was 14. The implication is that the larger the board, the less likely it will be able to exercise control over the management. This is corroborated by Clendenin who was told by many of the chief executives he interviewed that "large boards...are unmanageable" (1972, p. 62). What better way to keep a board passive than to make it unmanageable! But that still does not mean large boards are used for cooptation. They may be required for other service roles. For example, large organizations or those having special funding needs may also have greater needs for advice, and so appoint more directors. Where many of the directors are donors themselves (or fund raisers)—as was probably the case in Pfeffer's private hospitals—then the cooptation explanation (direct or indirect) would seem to hold. But where the directors are not for the most part directly associated with fund raising—quite possible in many of the business corporations of Pfeffer's first study—then the cooptation argument would seem to be more tenuous.

The cooptation (or control) explanation of board membership can be extended to whole networks of boards, through their common membership—a phenomenon known as "interlocking" directorships. This leads to a kind of conspiracy view of power, that interlocks represent efforts to build giant power networks to circumvent free market forces. This view was no doubt viable in the days of the giant trusts, when the so-called captains of industry controlled their holdings through their captive bankers and lawyers. As Louis Brandeis, adviser to President Wilson on trust problems and later Supreme Court Justice, wrote in 1914:

> The practice of interlocking directorates is the root of many evils. It offends laws human and divine. Applied to rival corporations, it tends to the suppression of competition and to violation of the Sherman law. Applied to corporations which deal with each other, it tends to disloyalty and to violation of the fundamental law that no man can serve two masters. In either event it leads to inefficiency; for it removes incentive and destroys soundness of judgment. (quoted in Dooley 1969, p. 314)

Whether this same conclusion can be drawn about present-day interlocking directorships is another matter. Let us look at the results of two studies—those of Levine (1972) and Dooley (1969). This phenomenon makes for tidy research, since as noted earlier, the data is accessible and easily quantified. One simply finds the annual reports of the corporations in question, extracts the lists of directors, and looks for interlocks. (What complicates things, however, is the need to include large numbers of organizations in the research sample, and so to analyze involved chains of interlocks.) In his study, using some fancy statistics, Levine found, literally, a sphere of influence. "This is a strong result. Eighty-four corporations with 150 links, and 703 non-links, have obligingly arranged themselves in a sphere" (1972, p. 22). There was no corporation at the center, but rather, jetting out from different radii were clusters or sectors with banks at the center of each. Levine describes a Morgan sector, a Chase-Manhattan sector, a Mellon sector.

Dooley's research was richer if less elegant. In an analysis of the 250 largest U.S. corporations (industrial, merchandising, transportation, utility, and financial) in 1965, he found director interlocks among all but twelve of them, with the finance corporations interlocking most frequently (16.1 times on average for the fifty firms compared with 9.9 for the whole sample). In seeking to explain the causes of these interlocks, Dooley addresses five findings.

1.   The larger the firm, the more the interlocks. Dooley offers three possible explanations for this: that the directors of the large corporations are most in demand because they are smartest, that they can open the doors to trading with big organizations, or that their contacts are inherently the best.

2.   The more inside directors, the fewer the interlocks. Presumably corporations with many inside directors are inward looking and reluctant to share their power; correspondingly, their own executives stay at home.

3.   The nonfinancial corporations had about one-third of their interlocks with financial corporations; specifically, 200 of them interlocked 616 times with the 50 banks and insurance companies. Dooley believes that power was a key factor here; he found that interlocks increased as the nonfinancial corporation became less solvent and as its assets increased. It was perhaps to the advantage of both parties—one needing capital, the other needing customers—to establish close relationships (although again, these nonfinancial corporations may simply have had greater need for financial advice).

4.   One interlock in eight involved competitors. Dooley suggests this might have been a means to restrict competition, although here service would seem to be a valid explanation as well: they needed the same contacts and expertise.

5.   The most prevalent interlocks involved companies with head offices in the same commercial center. In a result similar to that of Levine, Dooley found that by virtue of networks of interlocking directorships, almost half of the 250 firms fell into one of fifteen clearly identifiable local interest groups, for example, a New York group, a Chicago group, a San Francisco group. Again, like Levine, Dooley found banks or life insurance companies at the center of the groups, with the greatest number of interlocks. Utilities formed a second ring, and on the outside, with the least number of interlocks, were the manufacturing, merchandising, and transportation companies that did the major portion of their business near the city in question.

This last point, about the effect of physical proximity on interlocks, can be interpreted in terms of the contacts or even the advising role of the board. Because interactions among executives tend to be personal in nature, based on oral, face-to-face encounters (Mintzberg 1973), it would seem logical for interlocks to cluster on a geographical basis, among executives easily accessible to one another. Bank and insurance company executives, because they have the widest number of connections and the easiest access to other companies in their regions, would logically be favored as directors to establish contacts. Moreover, companies in need of financial expertise would naturally favor the experts who reside in their region. As Mace notes in his research, "investment bankers, through exposure to many different companies in many different industries and regions, bring to company presidents and company boards of directors what one president described as 'a treasury of information'"—they are the "great pollenizers" (1971, p. 200), for both contacts and information.

Further support for the service over the power or conspiracy explanation of interlocks comes from studies that investigated the persistence of interlocks over time. A series of recent studies (Ornstein 1980; Koenig et al. 1979; Palmer 1980) have looked at what happens to an interlock when the director in question dies or retires. Seldom is the tie retained (in Palmer's study, only 14 percent of the time). This indicates strongly that power—whether control in one direction or cooptation in the other—is not a factor in the choice of directors. And Dooley compared his results on interest groups with those of a similar study done in 1935. That one found eight groups, but only three related to location. The other five clustered around well-known families (Morgan, Rockefeller, Kuhn-Loeb, Mellon, and DuPont). In contrast all fifteen of Dooley's 1965 groups had geographical locations, and only one was, in addition, dominated by a family (the Mellons of the Pittsburgh group). So whereas power may have played a more important role in 1935, physical proximity and, presumably, contacts and advice seemed to be more significant in 1965. This would correspond to the demise of the trusts in the U.S. economy. As large corporations became more autonomous, power relationships in their boards diminished, and the boards came more to serve organizations than to control them.

Our discussion seems to lead us to the conclusion that while many of the roles of directors cannot be disentangled—especially the different service roles, as we saw in the case of bankers—in a gross way, we can distinguish boards that exist primarily to exercise some kind of control over the organization from those that are designed primarily to serve the organization. And then, of course, as implied in our earlier discussion, are those boards that do nothing: they exist merely because of legal requirements. Hence we conclude our discussion by presenting three basic kinds of boards.

THE BOARD AS CONTROL DEVICE, TOOL, OR FACADE

While directors may play many different roles on a particular board, the studies discussed in this chapter suggest that many boards typically favor one of three postures—they see their primary function as exercising a certain control over the management, as serving the organization, or as neither of these.

1.   **The board as a control device really seeks to act as a vehicle for external control of the organization, sometimes on behalf of some dominant external influencer.** Mace, for example, exempts from his general line of argument the corporation with a sizeable minority of its shares in the hands of one individual or family. Here he finds directors who really seek to exercise their control function, notably by closely monitoring managerial performance. "It was found that many directors who own, or represent the ownership of, substantial numbers of shares of stock spend considerable time in learning the business, and insist on being involved in major company decisions" (1971, p. 191). As noted earlier, however, even the board as control device does not manage the organization. But it does review managerial activities closely enough to ensure that decisions reflect external interests (or organizational ones broader than those of the managers themselves.) And management knows this. So long as the directors perceive the direction of the organization to be appropriate, management retains an ostensible autonomy. But as soon as that perception changes, out goes the management.

2.   **As a tool of the organization, the board serves it by coopting external influencers, establishing contacts and raising funds for it, enhancing its reputation, and/or providing it with advice.** Here the board does not play an important role in controlling the organization; external influencers in search of power bypass it completely. In effect, the directors of this second type of board are selected to deal with tangible problems of the organization, such as its need for funds or government connections, its precarious status in society, a gap in its knowledge base. Here we can imagine a whole array of possible boards—*prestige board, liaison board, coopting board, advising board, fund-raising board.* In the research literature, it is Pfeffer who makes the strongest case for the board as a tool of the organization, even offering evidence that organizations able to so use their boards achieve performance superior to those that do not.

3.   **Finally, the board as a facade appears where some individual or group, such as top management or the sole owner of a business firm, has full control**

of the organization and chooses to exploit the board neither as a controlling device nor as a tool. The real power system again bypasses the board—it exists only as a legal formality. "A few presidents regarded their board as an unnecessary legal appendage and board meetings as bothersome interruptions of their busy day-to-day management of the company" (Mace 1971, p. 193). Mace quotes an executive vice-president of a large southern company about such a board:

> The old man has exactly the kind of a board he wants. They all live here in the city, and they just don't do a damn thing as directors. The old man thinks it is a great board, and from his point of view he is probably right. From my point of view they are a big glob of nothing. Not that there aren't some extremely able outsiders on the board—there are. But as board members, they know who is in control and they will never cross the old man. (p. 79)

These are the boards where the chief executive chooses and dismisses the directors, holding them accountable to him, not vice versa. "In short, he selects his appraisers" (Bacon and Brown 1975, p. 12). The inside board must be considered a special case of the board as facade, not because it is powerless but because it precludes external control of the organization, and does not even provide for outside blood to serve the organization.

But the board as facade—whether composed of insiders or outsiders—may in fact be in the process of disappearing, at least for the larger organizations. For one thing, with the service roles becoming more evident—and with research such as that of Pfeffer indicating that it may pay to so use the board—organizations whose boards do not try to control them will be naturally inclined to try to use their boards to serve them. Why waste board memberships? And second, recent events have put limits on how much of a facade the board of the public corporation can be. The Penn Central debacle, among others, resulted in legal attacks on directors for shirking their responsibilities to monitor the performance of the management. The threat of legal liability has sent shivers through the spines of many passive directors, causing them to reassess their roles and even their memberships. And that has made some increase in the reviewing role inevitable. It also seems to have resulted in a decrease in the number of associates as directors, in order to avoid accusations of conflict of interest. Moreover, the New York Stock Exchange ruling requiring audit committees of outside directors has done away with totally inside boards among its companies, and has given the proportion of outside directors an important boost.

All of this is supported in a *Fortune* survey reported by Smith (1978) of all 5,995 directors of the Fortune 500 in 1977.[6] Compared to a 1967 survey,

---

[6]The NYSE ruling on audit committees actually came into effect on June 30, 1978, after this survey was completed, although the Smith article notes that they had already become "almost universal" (p. 162).

outside directors were up 12.7 percent and current managers down 18.7 percent. (Retired managers were down 18.1 percent). Commercial bankers diminished by 8.2 percent, investment bankers by 32.2 percent, and lawyers by 6.7 percent. (Note that major shareholders also diminished by 23.2 percent, while independent businessmen rose by 24.0 percent, "other investors and professional directors" by 11.4 percent, and nonbusinessmen directors by 101.5 percent, although the actual proportion of the latter, at 6.9 percent, remained small. Also the ten firms with the fewest outside directors showed lower average return on equity than those with the most—11.7 percent versus 16.8 percent.[7]) Bowman (1979), citing a study by a consulting firm for the year 1979, presents supporting data. The average board of the large American corporation had thirteen directors of whom nine were outsiders. And these directors were busier than ever (reportedly spending an average of eighty-nine hours annually in each directorship, including eight board meetings). Bankers and lawyers were becoming less numerous on these boards, and, in general, more distance was being put between board members and the chief executive officer. "To overstate the case, [the increased prevalence of board nominating committees] would make the corporate situation more analogous to that of the public university in which the next board member may be essentially a stranger to the president at the time of appointment/election" (p. 105). Moreover, this study found greater concern among board members with managerial succession and financial results. In general, the new pressures have caused corporations to be more selective in their choices of directors, and the directors themselves more careful in the performance of their duties. But as Bacon and Brown note, the courts have not been prone to convict derelict directors, and so the changes have been "gradual": There has not been "any major upheaval"; "the boardroom is still something of a club" (1975, p. 1).

One major question remains: Under what conditions do boards emerge as controlling devices, tools, or facades? In Part IV of the book, we shall seek to answer this question more fully. But here we can review some of the factors suggested by our discussion, most of which are also covered in Zald's (1969) paper, "The Power and Functions of Board of Directors: A Theoretical Synthesis."

1. Concentrated ownership: Ownership of a concentrated nature enables directors representing these interests to exercise the control function (Zald, p. 100), although the owners may of course choose to bypass the board altogether as a means of influence and deal with the management directly.

2. Dependency, especially need for financial support: When the organization is dependent on the directors themselves for financial support, the board may emerge as a controlling device (Zald, p. 102), unless, of course, formal cooptation works—that is, the directors are satisfied with the trappings of office. When the organization requires mass campaigns and community drives

[7]Even though one money loser was excluded from the former.

for financial support, the board will presumably tend to adopt the posture of a tool of the organization. Likewise, organizations in need of external advice or contacts, of the support of external influencers, or of social legitimacy in general, will try to use the board as a tool where it can be of help. And organizations with a minimum of external dependencies of any kind might be those most likely to have boards as facades.

3. *Knowledge of the operations:* The more the directors know about the organization, the better they are able to control it. And so we expect that the smaller the organization, the less complex its operations, and the greater the personal experience of its directors with these operations, the greater the control of it by the directors.

4. *Crises and transitions:* Loss of a chief executive, deteriorating performance, periods of major transition, all should drive the board toward a control posture, at least temporarily.

These factors help to put into perspective the range of behaviors we have seen in our discussion of the board of directors as the organization's formal coalition. For example, Mace focussed on large, well-established business organizations, with widely dispersed shareholders, in many cases able to generate much of their needed capital through retained earnings. Every one of these factors points to a weak board. In contrast, the not-for-profit organizations discussed by Zald and others were often smaller, sometimes simpler for the outsider to understand, more dependent on directors for fund raising and legitimacy. More of a control posture was to be expected. Similarly, Sukel notes that the directors of artistic-cultural organizations "seem to become more involved in what, by business standards, might be considered 'picayune' matters" (1978, p. 351). Everyone is an expert on these matters! Pfeffer's hospitals were complex organizations, difficult for the outsider to understand, and their need for fund-raising help varied. We would expect relatively little control, but service to the extent that directors were needed to help raise money. While Pfeffer did not really address the role of the boards in trying to control the hospitals, he did emphasize their use as tools of the organizations in the presence of resource dependencies. He made the same case for the business corporations he studied.

To conclude, the board may be an influential or a powerless body, an agent for control of the management or a tool that can be used by that management, or simply a facade. To the extent that an organization is autonomous, relatively independent of its environment, it can perhaps afford the board as facade. But to the extent that it is dependent on its environment, the composition of its board must be designed accordingly. Both sides in our power play—the External and Internal Coalitions—seek to turn the board to their own advantage. The Internal Coalition—notable the management—wishes to use the board as its tool while surrendering a minimum amount of control. It succeeds to the degree that its dependency is not extensive or concentrated—for example, based on the need for legitimacy in society in general but not the cooptation of certain influencers in particular. Where that dependency is extensive and concentrated, and the organization simple enough to understand, the power can flow the other way: The board emerges as the control device of external influencers. But even the controlling board does not manage the organization. It remains in the External Coalition, retaining the power to realign the Internal Coalition—a power it can exercise only infrequently. In the final analysis, the board of directors—this formal coalition—may not be the most important field for the external influencer in search of considerable power over the organization, but it remains nevertheless an important one.

7

Three Basic External Coalitions

What has emerged from our discussion of the board of directors is an indication that it can vary substantially in the control that it exercises over the organization. This in fact underlies a broader conclusion: that the External Coalition itself can wield a wide range of power with respect to the Internal Coalition. This range can be expressed neatly in terms of three basic types of External Coalitions. Forming a continuum from the most powerful to the least, these will be referred to as the *Dominated EC*, the *Divided EC*, and the *Passive EC*. In the first type, a single external influencer (or a number that cooperate) dominates the External Coalition, and thereby controls the Internal Coalition.[1] In the second, a few competing groups of external influencers divide the power of the External Coalition, which tends, as we shall see later in the book, to politicize the Internal Coalition. And in the third type, the number of external influencers grows so large, and, as a result, their power becomes so dispersed, that the External Coalition becomes impotent, or passive, and all of the power passes into the Internal Coalition, where, as we shall see later, it tends to concentrate in one of a number of ways.

The continuum of these three types of External Coalitions is shown in Figure 7–1. In fact it is U-shaped, since the Passive EC is really a special case of

[1]As the word "Dominated" has frequently caused confusion in verbal presentations, its use should be clarified here. In this book, by definition all of the external influencers together are said to make up a single coalition, called the External Coalition. Thus, "Dominated" means that the External Coalition is itself dominated by a single individual or group. A dominant coalition would refer to one coalition that dominates others. (James D. Thompson, [1967; p. 128], uses the term in this way.) Within a Dominated EC, one external influencer or group is dominant.

domination except that here the dominating force is inside the organization. In mathematical terms, we can say that **as the number of independent external influencers increases from one to infinity, the External Coalition tends to metamorphose from the Dominated to the Divided and then to the Passive form.** As we shall see below, this simple continuum helps us to understand a good deal of the power-related behavior that takes place around organizations, and enables us to summarize our findings of this first section of the book.

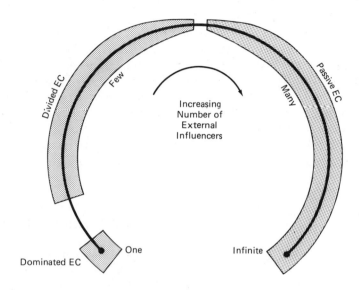

Figure 7-1. *Three Basic Types of External Coalitions*

THE DOMINATED EC

Where one external influencer—or a set of external influencers acting in concert—holds most of the power around the organization, the External Coalition can be said to be dominated. Furthermore, since the power of this influencer can be direct, focussed, and personal—he or she can easily develop personal access to the top managers and gain the power to replace them or block any of their decisions—this dominant influencer typically controls the Internal Coalition as well. Of course, these powers need not be exercised continuously; management knows where the real power lies, and is careful to stay within bounds acceptable to the key influencer.

Under these conditions, the board of directors may be used as the device to exercise control: The dominant influencer takes his or her seat on it (presumably as its chairman) and uses this formal committee as the means to control the management. However, as we noted in the last chapter, the board is a formal body with limited powers, and it is probably more likely that the dominant influencer will bypass it and control management directly, behind the scenes, particularly through formal constraints and direct access, supplemented perhaps by the authorization or imposition of specific decisions. In this case, the board could be used as a tool of the organization, or, given the absence of power in the rest of the External Coalition, it may simply be a facade.

When the dominant influencer speaks with a clear voice, the organization must typically follow suit with a consistent set of goals. Thus, in their article on the city Youth Commission as a "reluctant organization," introduced in the last chapter, Maniha and Perrow (1965-66) show how in its first year the Commission came to be dominated by two members acting in concert—the high school principal and the YMCA director. Both reflected the same conservative, don't-rock-the-boat philosophy, because of their sensitivity to criticism about the activities of the youth under their own direction. The high school principal "set the tone of cautious procedure," while the YMCA director "took on the role of seeing that no one was misquoted, misinterpreted or otherwise compromised in dealing with the press" (p. 273). And the behavior of the organization followed suit. A charter to "appraise, evaluate and recommend" became in practice only to appraise:

> During the first year several formal and informal attempts by relatively weak groups were made to enlist the help of the Commission in meeting problems related to youth. The Commission resisted these attempts on the grounds of the no-action policy made explicit by the two dominant members and shared by others. For example, a local Protestant minister tried to get the Commission interested in doing something about all-night parties after the senior prom at the high school. The minister was referred to the PTA, since his proposal was "beyond the role of the Commission, because we are not an action group." (pp. 246-47)

What causes one influencer to emerge as dominant? In the Youth Commission, it may have been simply a matter of status or personality or even effort expended. But more commonly, dominance seems to stem from a dependency relationship. The organization dependent on a single client or supplier may have to yield considerable power to it. In one of his early papers, Charles Perrow (1961) traces the shift in the power coalitions of private hospitals as a result of changing dependency relationships. When donations were critical, and medical expertise less developed, the donors and fund raisers came to dominate the hospital boards of trustees and emerged as centers of power. For example, they imposed conservative financial policies and opposed large financial outlays for equipment, research, and education. In such hospitals, Perrow found that the administrators had little power, prestige, or responsibility. Perrow believes that such dominance was common at the turn of the century. But as medical technology developed, the hospital became increasingly dependent on a technical competence that the trustees did not possess. Thus, power gradually passed from the External Coalition into the Internal one as the trustees were forced to yield to the medical staff. As a result, the goals of technical excellence and professional development emerged as central. More recently, with hospitals facing increasingly difficult tasks of coordinating the work of the medical specialists, Perrow believes that the hospital administrators, as the people most capable of dealing with this critical dependency, have established themselves as the dominant members of the power system.[2]

These hospitals had no owners. But in the case of corporations and other organizations that are owned, it is the owners that can emerge as the dominant members of an External Coalition. We saw in the last chapter that, while widely held corporations tend to have Passive ECs, those whose shareholdings are concentrated—to the degree, some believe, of as little as 5 percent of the total in single hands—tend to be externally controlled. Small firms are especially susceptible to dominated External Coalitions, unless of course, they are owner-managed. Their size and their markets, which are typically competitive, mean that they draw little attention from governments and special interest groups; small size also tends to restrict associates and unions to purely economic relationships. That leaves the owners, who are typically few—often one individual has total or majority control. When that individual has no management position, the External Coalition can be described as dominated. When that individual is also the chief executive—as in the case of the entrepreneurial firm, probably the more common occurrence—then the External Coalition can be described as passive and the Internal Coalition as dominated by the chief executive.

Ownership of an impersonal nature—when one organization owns another—can lead to a hierarchy of coalitions. Thus, a widely held corporation, with its own Passive External Coalition, may itself dominate the External Coalition of its subsidiaries through tight direct controls. The result is that the parent firm has much more freedom of action than its subsidiary. Figure 7–2 shows how one McGill student group chose to depict the External Coalition of the Canadian subsidiary of a well-known producer of consumer goods, whose American parent dominated it through various planning and control systems as well as the imposition of specific strategies and decisions.

All of the External Coalitions so far discussed are *individually* dominated, in the sense that a single individual or specific group holds the power. However, an External Coalition can also be concensus dominated. Here different groups of external influencers coalesce around a single point of view and so impose uniform demands on the organization. In effect, the External Coalition is

---

[2]This last conclusion of Perrow was not accepted in the *Structuring* book (see especially Chapter 19), based on the argument that the coordination necessary in hospitals comes primarily from the standardization of the professionals' skills and perhaps some mutual adjustment among them, not from administrative intervention.

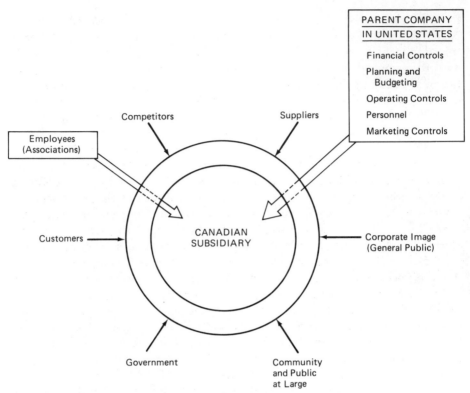

Figure 7–2. *The Dominated External Coalition of a Canadian Sub-sidiary (from a paper submitted to the author by A. Kalhok, R. Melville, P. Heitner, and L. Clark, Management Policy 701, McGill University, 1968)*

dominated not by a single individual or group but by a single *theme*. By acting in concert, different members of the External Coalition are able to control the Internal Coalition. Cressey discusses a classic case of this, the prison with a custodial (as opposed to a treatment) orientation:

> . . .the significant external groups of the custodially-oriented institution were police, judges, prosecuting attorneys, and other groups having custodial goals. This prison's "public," thus, was made up principally of groups emphasizing the institution's job of protecting society from criminals. (1958, p. 46)

THE DIVIDED EC

As soon as one influencer, or a number of them acting in concert, ceases to dominate the External Coalition, the power system of the organization changes fundamentally. With power in the External Coalition divided among independent influencers, the organization is pushed in different directions, to respond to conflicting demands.

How many different influencers does it take to make an External Coalition divided? Two seems to be enough. So long as there is a rough balance of power between two conflicting external influencers, the External Coalition will be divided. Thus, Stagner contrast the conflict in Belgium between the Flemish and the Walloons, "a good example of almost perfect balance of power," with the racial situation in South Africa where, at least at the time of his writing, "all power seems to be concentrated on the side of the whites" (1967, p. 158). And as the number of conflicting external influencers increases beyond two, the External Coalition remains divided so long as no one influencer dominates the others yet each retains some significant power over the organization. Some organizations, such as political parties, are able to identify literally dozens of important groups that significantly influence their behavior.

The various external influencers of the Divided EC use all the means of influence at their command, for example, pressure campaigns, formal constraints, and sometimes direct controls. Since each group of influencers normally concerns itself with only a few special issues, the tendency is to pressure the organization only sporadically, focussing the pressure on the insiders directly. In this way, different external groups seldom lock horns with each other, and the true power situation in the External Coalition is defined only vaguely.

But there is one exception to this—the board of directors, the one place where the external influencers can meet each other in face-to-face bargaining. In the case of the Dominated EC, as we have seen, it makes little difference whether or not the dominant influencer chooses to exercise power through the board; everyone knows where the real power lies in any event. Not so in the case of the Divided EC. Because the distribution of power is always vague and fluid, every means of influence becomes a battleground for control. And that includes the board, where power is formally distributed (in terms of seats). Despite the weaknesses of the board as a means of influence, it has great symbolic meaning. And so especially those groups more intimately involved with the organization, across a whole range of issues, try to define their power formally by seeking representation on the board of directors. In fact, a major issue in the organization with a Divided EC is whether the de facto power distribution of the External Coalition corresponds with the de jure power distribution of the board. When it does not, political battles often ensue over the distribution of the seats.

Thus, the design of the board tends to be a sensitive issue in those organizations with no apparent dominant influencer. In Maniha and Perrow's Youth Commission, the mayor sought to achieve a balanced representation by appointing the high school principal, the YMCA director, one Catholic (coach at the Catholic high school), a black woman, a junior high school teacher (the mayor's son in fact), a Protestant minister, a physician (interested in the welfare of youth), a university faculty member (in physical education), and a nurse, who said she was appointed because "they needed a housewife" (pp. 243–44).

Apparently, however, the mayor was not careful enough, for as we saw earlier, by virtue of personality factors the first two came to dominate the Commission, at least in its first year.

Sometimes, the representation on the board is designated formally. A 1971 bill of the Quebec legislature, for example, formally specifies the membership of the boards of directors of Quebec hospital centers as follows: two persons elected by the "users" of the center, two appointed by the provincial government, one elected by the clinical staff, one elected by the center's council of physicians and dentists, one elected by all nonclinical staff, one elected jointly by the affiliated community service centers where affiliated with a university, one appointed by the university and another elected by the center's interns and residents, and, where the center's immovable assets are owned by a nonprofit corporation (such as a religious order), four elected by that corporation.

In some cases, the board of an organization with a Divided EC will remain under the grip of a previously dominant external influencer. Unable to gain representation, the other external influencers are forced to rely on different means of influence. In the American universities of the late 1960s, the students perceived the governing boards to represent status quo interests, such as the business community and the political party in power. As the boards would not yield to their demands, the students resorted instead to pressure campaigns. That in fact brought changes in many boards, opening up places for students, blacks, faculty members, and representatives of different shades of political opinion.[3]

Similar trends can now be seen in the large business corporation. Traditionally it was the owners who dominated the External Coalition and controlled the Internal Coalition. With the dispersion of stock, as we saw earlier, the management gained much of the power at the expense of the shareholders in particular and of the External Coalition in general, and the board became a tool or a facade. But as the power vacuum in the External Coalitions of these important organizations has become increasingly apparent, special interest groups have stepped up pressure campaigns and governments and unions have imposed increasing numbers of formal constraints. More recently, signalled by the 1971 attack on General Motors by Ralph Nader and his associates (discussed at length in Part V), all kinds of influencers—representing women, blacks, consumers, the "public interest," and so on—have been seeking formal representation on boards of directors. They wish to bring the board in line with what they see as an External Coalition in the process of being realigned. In Germany, as noted earlier, the employees already control one-half of the directorships of the large corporations.

Of course, no matter how carefully designed the board, some external influencers will always resort to other means to make their power felt. For one

[3]In some cases, as in my own university, the Senate—a kind of internal formal coalition—broadened its representation instead, and gained considerable power at the expense of the board, which retained its traditional representation to a considerable extent.

thing, as we saw earlier, the power of the board over specific organizational decisions is highly limited; this is especially true when the board itself is divided actively avoid board representation in favor of other means of influence because they do not wish to legitimize their power in the External Coalition. No Mafia boss, for example, wishes to announce his influence in a racetrack by virtue of a seat on its board! And the United States government may now be an important influencer of the Chrysler Corporation, but American norms preclude the formalization of that relationship, too. (The head of the autoworkers' union was, however, less shy about breaking with precedent in this case. He did negotiate his way onto Chrysler's board.)

What effect does the division of power in the External Coalition have on the Internal Coalition? We shall take up this issue in more detail later, after we have discussed the functioning of the Internal Coalition. But we can note here that just as a Divided EC has the effect of politicizing the board, so too does it help to politicize the Internal Coalition. Competing external influencers pull the organization in different directions, forcing it to pursue conflicting goals. Later we shall discuss studies of prisons, unlike those mentioned above, in which conflicts in society between custodial and rehabilitation goals get carried inside the organization through the guards who favor the former and the professional staff who favor the latter. Power struggles in the External Coalition tend to get mirrored in the Internal Coalition.

Divided External Coalitions appear in a variety of forms. As in the case of these prisons, the presence of two conflicting missions tends to polarize the External Coalition: the external influencers coalesce into two camps, one behind each mission. Another form appears when the various owners of an organization make war on each other, perhaps over differences of strategy, personality, or simply control, and so pull the organization in different directions. One classic manifestation of this in the large corporation is the proxy fight, where two alliances of shareholders battle until one wins (dominates) or an agreement is reached.

A third form of the Divided EC occurs when there are a number of distinct external interest groups in close and regular contact with each other. As a result, they seek some formalized, permanent arrangement to divide up their power. We saw this in one of the McGill studies, of an egg marketing agency. Its External Coalition consisted of farmers, clearly delineated as to small, medium, and large-scale producers, the egg distributors, wholesalers, and retailers, and the provincial government (represented by its market regulatory agency), as well as the less clearly defined groups of consumers and producers outside the system (from other provinces or black market operators within the province). All were fervently concerned about the price of eggs, which the agency set. The agency's External Coalition consisted, in fact, of a complex hierarchy of committees—formal coalitions—wherein some of the battles were fought, overlaid on a more intricate system of informal power. Figure 7-3 shows the Divided EC. The agency's board of directors was made up of its chief executive plus the presidents

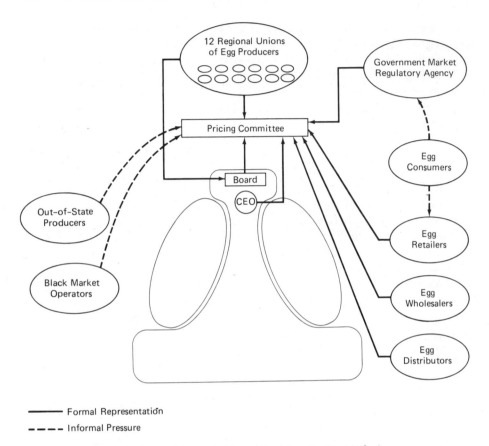

Figure 7–3.   *A Divided External Coalition: An Egg Marketing
Board.*

of each of twelve regional unions of producers (each a formal coalition in its
own right). But the price of eggs was determined not by this partisan body, but
by a separate seven-member pricing committee consisting of the same chief executive of the marketing agency, two other representatives of the agency's board
of directors (in effect, two representatives of the producers), one representative
each of the egg distributors, grocery wholesalers, and food retailers, and a
representative from the government market regulatory agency. Around this
committee were the informal groups whose presence was clearly felt despite
their lack of formal representation. The pricing committee met each Thursday
to determine the next week's price of eggs. That meeting was "extremely tense,"
with the sellers lined up on one side to keep the price up and the buyers on the
other to keep it down.[4]

[4]From a report submitted to the author in Management Policy 276-662, McGill University, 1971, by
Pierre Menard, Richard Brunet, Jean-Paul Masson, Chi Wu, and Mike Farkouh.

One last form of Divided EC occurs when the external influencers focus their attention on disparate issues and tend to pressure the organization only sporadically. Their natural inclination, therefore, is to rely on the pressure campaign and the imposition of formal constraints, rather than on the board of directors. The External Coalitions of some American corporations have begun to look more like this in recent years. Increasingly, governments and unions have imposed formal constraints, conservation groups have waged pressure campaigns, consumer groups have used the courts to impose product safety standards, and so on. Some groups, as noted, have attempted to broaden representation on the boards of these corporations, but their efforts have so far met with little direct success. Indirectly, however, as we saw in the last chapter, the corporations themselves have changed the composition of their boards, if not granting representation to any new groups at least eliminating the worst cases of facade and conflict of interest.

THE PASSIVE EC

As the number of external influencers continues to increase, the power of each becomes more and more diffuse until a point is reached where the External Coalition becomes passive and power passes into the Internal Coalition. This happens commonly when the shareholders of a corporation, the members of a union, or the clients or suppliers of a cooperative become very numerous. As we noted in Chapter 4, Jacobs argues that "fractionated and widely dispersed" clients are less able to exercise close control of the organization (1974; p. 55). Jacobs presents four arguments to support his point, three of which in fact apply to all highly dispersed external influencers, not just clients.[5] First, the more widely dispersed the influencers, the less likely they are to agree on what they want. The organization need only adapt itself to general, widely shared goals. Second, the individual influencer will not find it worth his or her own while to acquire the information needed to control the organization. And third, even assuming shared goals and the presence of the necessary information, there is the energy that must be expended to organize the dispersed influencers. Jacobs refers to the mathematical analysis of Olson (1965, 1968), which concluded "that large or latent groups have no tendency voluntarily to act to further their common interests" (1965; p. 165). Olson's point is that it pays no one member of such groups to invest the effort to organize it, or for that matter even to support it, when the benefits have to be shared among all the members, even those who remain passive, the "free riders." In other words, apathy is, to Olson, the "natural" strategy for the large, dispersed group. We shall soon discuss certain exceptions to this—influencers denied exit who are sufficiently aroused, those

[5]Jacobs' fourth point, which applies only to clients, is that fractionated consumers are generally interested only in the organization's products, not in its other areas of activity.

driven by normative beliefs, those already organized for related issues, and those led by "professional organizers." But in the absence of these conditions, we would expect the dispersed influencers to remain passive.

The analyses of both Mace (1971) and Zald (1969) suggest that the board of directors of the organization with a Passive EC does not concern itself with control. Rather it is the management that controls the board, presumably rendering it a tool of the organization if there is some need for service, otherwise a facade. In the widely held corporation, in principle the shareholders have the right to cast their votes for directors at the annual general meeting. In fact, however, before the meeting they each receive a proxy slip in the mail naming a block of individuals—typically existing directors, often managers—to whom they are requested to grant their voting rights. Like the voters of the communist state, they are offered an effective choice of one. In accordance with the points made by Jacobs and Olson, "The normal apathy of the small shareholder is such that he will either fail to return his proxy, or will sign on the dotted line. . . .The proxy votes are then used to rubber stamp the selections already made by those in control" (Berle and Means 1968; p. 76). The dissident stockholder "has only the expensive recourse of sending out a duplicate set of proxies and bidding for the stockholder's support in opposition to the management" (p. 76), almost always a wasted effort and therefore seldom attempted.

Thus, Mace concludes that the directors of large corporations are typically "selected by the president and not the stockholders. Accordingly the directors are on the board because the president wants them there. . . .in point of fact [they] represent the president" (1971; p. 188). Presidents tend to select directors "who are known as noncontroversial, friendly, sympathetic, congenial, and understanders of the system" (p. 196). These directors in turn act as if "This is somebody else's money" (p. 188). Even the choice of successor is typically dictated by the outgoing chief executive and rubber-stamped by the board (p. 190). There is no evidence that recent changes in corporate boards have been significant enough to render this picture outdated.

If the External Coalition has no power, then clearly—as Mace's comments show—the Internal Coalition moves quickly into the vacuum. And what happens there? Thompson (1967) hypothesizes that "When power is widely distributed, an *inner circle* emerges to conduct coalition business" (p. 140). Thompson notes further that "the central power figure is the individual who can best manage the coalition" (p. 142). And that person of course is the chief executive officer. Thus, as we shall see in more detail later in this book, when the External Coalition is passive, it is often the chief executive officer who seizes the lion's share of the power. The Passive EC then emerges as a special case of domination, except that here it is an insider who dominates.

But it is not always the CEO who comes out on top when external power is diffused. Later we shall see that other concentrations of power can emerge in the Internal Coalition as well, notably around ideologies or bodies of expertise or administrative systems in general.

There are a number of classic illustrations of Passive External Coalitions.

If the results of Berle and Means, Mace, and others we have discussed are to be believed, then clearly one is the widely held American corporation. The shareholders are so dispersed and unorganized, so ill-informed and uninterested, that management assumes full control of all actions, including the selection of directors. Perhaps the most pointed support for this conclusion comes from a brief analysis by Chandler (1975), who found that of the 502 individuals announced in the *Wall Street Journal* between January 1 and March 1, 1975, as having been elected to the boards of large corporations, only 7 of them—just over 1 percent—represented significant shareholder interests.[6]

Since the business corporation has been mentioned in our discussion of all three basic types of External Coalitions, it might be helpful to sort out these conclusions here. When corporations were entrepreneurial firms, they had Passive ECs, in the sense that their owner-managers had complete control, external influencers being few and generally distant. But as ownership was separated from management, the corporations moved toward the Dominated EC, since the owners were typically few and maintained tight control over the managers. Then as stock ownership became dispersed and as the corporations grew larger and gained power over their markets, the External Coalition shifted to the passive form. But nature abhors a vacuum, and society most of all abhors a power vacuum. And so, as the absence of external control of these giant organizations has become more obvious, and as their own impact on society has become more evident, all kinds of external influencers have been seeking new ways to control their actions. Today the giant American corporation, long used to a Passive External Coalition, is increasingly finding itself surrounded by a Divided one.

One interesting aspect of this last transition is that it seems to contradict the appealing argument of Olson. Why should consumers and others—with relatively little to gain as individuals—take on the giant corporation, in effect converting their apathy into concentrated, organized power? Zald and Berger (1978), among others, have addressed this important issue. They suggest, for one thing, that the incentive to organize—in Hirschman's terms, to use voice—goes up as the possibilities for exit are precluded. Sufficiently aroused, the latent group comes to life. The townspeople downriver have no choice but to fight the pollution; likewise important segments of the American population, apparently feeling more and more dominated by large corporations and less and less able to escape their actions, mobilize to influence them. Sometimes it is normative beliefs that mobilizes a group: acting for a cause they believe to be "right," its members do not care about personal gain. We saw this earlier in the case of the influencers of certain prisons who coalesced around the theme of custody. Their stand was, in their terms, ethical. So too is it to many of the groups that attack the giant corporation. To them the corporation is big, uncontrolled, polluting, dominating; their attacks render a service to society.

[6]Smith's (1978) more thorough data, on all 5,995 directors of the Fortune 500 of 1977, put that figure at 1.6 percent.

Second, voice is encouraged when related special interest groups already exist. That brings the price of organizing down drastically; indeed, existing groups look for new issues to sustain them. Once Nader's Raiders are established, each new pressure campaign becomes that much easier to mobilize. And what we have been seeing in America is a proliferation of such groups since the days of sit-ins and campus unrest, each group ready to take on the corporations in its own sphere of influence. Indeed, organizing means creating leaders— sometimes even paid ones, "professional organizers"—who do have more to gain from group action than the average member: Every successful pressure campaign solidifies their own reputation as organizers, and provides them with extra psychic if not material rewards, as well as helping to ensure the survival of their own organizations.

To return to our illutrations of the Passive EC, another is often that surrounding the large labor union. The members, ostensibly central to the functioning of the organization, often in fact act as outsiders who look on passively while those who hold office make all the decisions. Unions, too, may have democratic procedures but, as in the proxy elections of corporations, these often break down. The membership is simply too dispersed to resist the power of the incumbent leaders. The same thing frequently happens in other large volunteer organizations—in supplier cooperatives, such as farmer-owned distribution agencies, in client cooperatives, such as co–op retail chain stores, sometimes even in political parties. In a well-known study that we shall be reviewing later, Michels (1915) describes this phenomenon in European socialist political parties and labor unions at the turn of the century.

To this point, the emergence of a Passive EC has been described in terms of the dispersion of external influencers. But there are other causes too. Sometimes it is a source of power in the Internal Coalition that is able to pacify the External Coalition, one that might otherwise be divided or dominated. The leader of an organization can be so strong as to be able to beat all of the external influencers into submission. One is reminded of a de Gaulle in France, at least before 1968, or a Stalin in the Soviet Union. Likewise, a strong ideology can make an organization very aggressive, and so able to dominate its External Coalition. Sheer size alone can have the same effect. In Chapter 19 we shall see all kinds of techniques large organizations use to passify their external influencers—integrating themselves vertically to take control of their sources of supply and markets, merging or cooperating with their competitors, engaging in public relations exercises and lobbying government legislators, using their boards as coopting devices (as we saw in the last chapter), and so on.[7]

So too can critical expertise within the organization passify external influencers. Earlier we discussed how, as medical technology developed, the medical staff of hospitals came to draw power away from the trustees, in effect driving Dominated ECs to Passive ones. A similar phenomenon appears to have taken place in prisons. We noted that when influencers coalesced around the

[7]See Pfeffer and Salancik (1978) for a detailed treatment of these techniques.

mission of custody, the External Coalitions were dominated. Then, as rehabilitation was proposed as another mission, battles ensued between influencers favoring each, and the External Coalitions came to be divided. But Cressey notes how rehabilitation specialists in some prison staffs were able to use their expertise against the external influencers, and so to drive the External Coalitions toward the passive form. "The work of the prison's staff . . . was considered technical and 'professional.' The concomitant view was that it is to be judged by members of the technical or professional groups involved, not by 'the public' " (1958; p. 46).

Finally, we have some unexpectedly Passive External Coalitions. Earlier the case was mentioned of the corporate subsidiary or agency so inconsequential that the parent leaves it alone as long as it does nothing to draw attention to itself. An ostensibly Dominated EC becomes an effectively Passive one. An ostensibly Divided EC can also become effectively passive when the external influencers become so embroiled fighting with each other that they have no energy left to control the organization. We are reminded here of the power sometimes preempted by civil servants operating under highly politicized coalition governments. Frank (1958–59) describes a related curiosity in the Soviet factory. Here not lack of governmental attention, but, ironically, an excess of it enabled an External Coalition that should have been dominated to become in some sense passive. The Soviet hierarchy—the various agencies of the central government—imposed more rules and regulations than any factory could possibly have handled. The government bureaucrats knew this, and so did not expect the factory to meet all of them. The result, as we shall see when we return to this example later, was more freedom for the management than the casual observer would expect. In other words, as the dominant influencer became more and more demanding, some point was reached beyond which the organization could no longer respond; instead of greater domination by the External Coalition, the result was less, to the point where the whole system of controls broke down and the External Coalition seems to have emerged as passive.

To conclude, we have seen that **an External Coalition tends to emerge as dominated to the extent that the organization experiences some form of dependency in its environment as well as the concentration of its external power either in the hands of a single individual or group (often an owner) or else in an active concensus among its external influencers. The External Coalition emerges as divided when external power is significant but shared by a limited number of individuals or groups with conflicting goals. And an External Coalition tends to emerge as passive especially when the external influencers are numerous and dispersed (notably when they can easily exit, are not aroused or driven by normative beliefs, and are not already organized or inclined to be by a "professional organizer"), but also when the External Coalition is extremely politicized or overcontrolling, or when the organization is very inconsequential to it or else strong enough to pacify it by virtue of its leadership, ideology, expertise, or its**

sheer size. Our discussion has also made clear that the kind of External Coalition around an organization affects to a considerable extent the kind of Internal Coalition it develops. **A Dominated EC tends to weaken the Internal Coalition; a Divided EC tends to politicize it; and a Passive EC tends to strengthen it,** often at the level of top management.

But no matter what the External Coalition, it is through the efforts of the Internal Coalition that the organization functions and determines its goals. This is the heart of the organizational power system. We now turn our attention to it.

PART II

THE INTERNAL COALITION

Now we turn our attention from power around the organization to power inside of it. We focus on the internal influencers—those people identified earlier as the full-time employees—and their means of influence. In terms of power, being full-time employees distinguishes individuals in three fundamental ways:

1. They tend to have a serious commitment to the organization by virtue of their dependence on its well-being.
2. They come to know the organization intimately, by virtue of the amount of time they spend there.
3. They are the ones who make the decisions and take the actions; the initiative rests with them; the external influencers must influence their behavior.

We begin this section in Chapter 8 by discussing how power passes formally into the Internal Coalition, and then how it necessarily gets diffused once inside to the different groups of internal influencers. Chapter 9 then discusses the power and needs of each of our five basic groups of internal influencers. These influencers are described in this section as having, as their prime means of influence, four basic systems. The first, based on authority, is discussed in Chapter 10; the second, based on ideology, in Chapter 11; the third, based on expertise, in Chapter 12; and the fourth, based on politics, in Chapter 13. Finally, Chapter 14 seeks to reconcile our conclusions about these different internal systems of influence by discussing, first, how they work in concert, and second, how each of them can also exist in domination, in one way or another, giving rise to five basic types of Internal Coalitions.

8

Design of the Internal Coalition

THE PASSING OF POWER
INTO THE INTERNAL COALITION

In principle, the power of the External Coalition is supposed to be represented by the board of directors, the formal coalition. The board, in turn, is supposed to control the behavior of the organization. But we have seen that even the board that truly fulfills this mandate does not manage the organization. It must appoint a *chief executive officer* (CEO) as its trustee, to take formal charge of the running of the organization. As we saw in Chapter 6, that individual is given wide freedom of action, with the stipulation that the board may replace him or her at its discretion. The result is that formal power over organizational decision making passes almost completely from the board to the CEO. This reflects a kind of symmetry in the organizational power system, as shown in Figure 8–1: the board represents the formal power of the External Coalition, while the CEO, its trustee, represents the formal power of the Internal Coalition. Formal power passes from one to another as sand passes through the neck of an hourglass.

Not only the formal power but also a good deal of the informal power of the External Coalition passes into the Internal Coalition through the chief executive. The implication of Cyert and March's (1963) *A Behavioral Theory of the Firm* is that the influencers meet in some kind of direct bargaining to

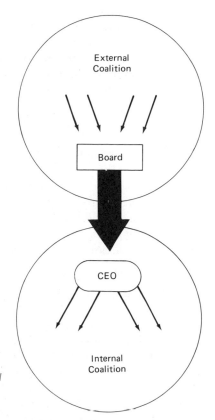

FIGURE 8-1. *Symmetry of Formal Power Between the External and Internal Coalitions*

rationalize their needs and thereby establish organizational behaviors in the form of standard operating procedures, budgets, and the like. But that theory overlooks one important element. The external influencers meet directly only on the board of directors, and we have just seen that the board is only one—and usually not the most important one—of the external means of influence. The others—social norms, formal constraints, pressure campaigns, and direct controls—are applied on the organization independently, sporadically, and often in contradictory manners. In other words, the external influencers do not talk to the organization in one clear voice. So there remains the important task of reconciling the demands of the different external influencers. And a good deal of responsibility for that reconciliation falls to that person with the highest formal position in the Internal Coalition, namely the chief executive officer. And in the capacity to effect this reconciliation lies a good deal of the CEO's informal power.

In Papandreou's term—to recall our discussion of Chapter 2—there exists a "peak coordinator," a single figure at the "apex" (what we call the *strategic apex*) of the organization who coordinates conflicting demands "with a sense of the whole. . . . At levels inferior to that of peak coordination, this complex totality is lost" (1952, p. 190). McDonald (1970*a*) captures this notion well with the word "melding," a blend of melting and welding. The chief executive sits at the crossroads where the demands of different influencers converge. "Seeking a satisfactory solution of the interest of all parties, the chief executive internalizes what would otherwise be bargaining among the parties" (p. 121).[1]

Thus, the CEO functions at a critical point in the process by which influence is converted to action. From one direction, he receives the demands of the external influencers, formally through the board and informally through the other external means of influence. And in the other direction, he stands formally responsible for the actions of the organization, for ensuring that it performs its mission effectively while satisfying its various influencers. In other words, the CEO is supposed to see to it that external influence is converted into internal action.

THE CREATION OF THE ORGANIZATION

But how can one person convert influence into action? The whole game of power in and around the organization is played over one thing: the actions that the organization takes—the products it markets, the clients it serves, the equipment it buys, the people it promotes, the surpluses it distributes, the air it pollutes, and the air pollution it reduces. But action is generally preceded by *decision*, that is, by commitment to action.[2] To elaborate the procedure, as shown in Figure 8–2, information is collected; analyses of it lead to advice; advice in turn helps to generate decisions, or choices; these choices may be subjected to authorization; and the authorized choices are executed—they become actions. "Organization" means that all of this is beyond the capacity

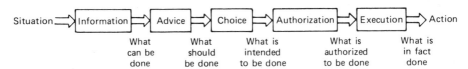

FIGURE 8–2.   *The Decision-Making/Action-Taking Process (from Mintzberg, 1979, p. 188)*

[1]See Mintzberg (1973, p. 73) for quotations from chief executives who depict themselves in this capacity.

[2]Of course, an action may be implicit, or subconscious, or inadvertent. Companies do not typically *decide* to pollute; it just happens as a byproduct of deciding to do something else, such as processing chemicals. But they do typically have to decide to reduce pollution.

of one person. So the CEO must engage other people to take care of different parts of the process; in other words, he must design an organization.

In the simplest case, the CEO need hire people only to execute his choices, maintaining personal control of all the other steps—including the making of all the important decisions. These executors—the ones who take the actions that produce the basic outputs of the organization—we have called *operators*, and the part of the organization where they take their actions we call the *operating core.* But most organizations have to make a great many decisions, far too many for a single person. So the chief executive officer must engage other *line managers* and must *delegate* to them formal responsibility for the decisions and actions of certain parts of the operating core. In other words, he names his own trustees, people who are given the formal power over certain kinds of decisions together with the responsibility for their consequences. In fact, most organizations are large enough to require a *hierarchy* of such managers. Those at its base (called "first-line supervisors") are responsible for specific parts of the operating core, while the others are responsible for ever more comprehensive clusters of these parts until all the managers come together in one total cluster under the chief executive officer. All these managers below the CEO form a part of the *chain of authority* that we call the *middle line.*

But looking back on Figure 8–2, we see that information must be collected and analyzed prior to the making of decisions. And that often requires an expertise that the CEO and line managers do not possess, as well as time free from operating responsibilities which they may not have. Moreover, the organization has need for a variety of services to support its activities. In other words, the organization needs a *staff* structure—a structure of people free of responsibility for managing the "line" operations (those concerned with producing the basic outputs). That staff, as noted earlier, falls into two groups. The *analysts* of the *technostructure* concern themselves with advising on, designing, and in part running the formal systems to achieve coordination, notably those of planning and of control. And the *support staff* provides advice on certain specialized decisions and also runs various support functions. In the typical manufacturing firm, analysts include planners, work study specialists, production schedulers, and accountants, while the support staff includes those people working in the cafeteria, mailroom, payroll office, public relations department, and legal counsel office.

In this way, therefore, the CEO designs the organization—with operators to execute the basic mission, line managers to take responsibility for parts of the operating core and the decisions these parts require, and analysts and support staffers to advise, help control, and support the rest of the organization. Figure 8–3 shows these five basic groups of full-time employees, with the CEO at the apex, the operators at the base, the line managers joining the two in an unbroken sequence, and the two staff groups on either side.

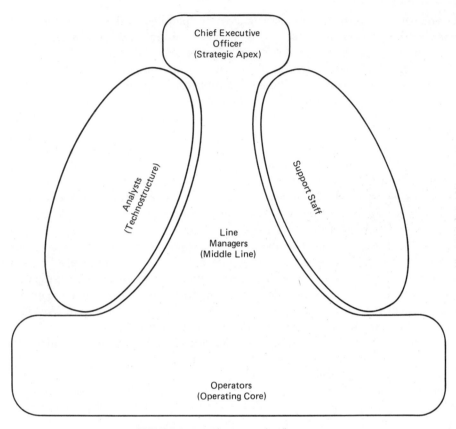

FIGURE 8-3. *The Internal Influencers*

THE SYSTEMS OF INFLUENCE
IN THE INTERNAL COALITION

As soon as the CEO delegates any of his formal powers—in essence, as soon as he hires a second individual—the problem of control arises. How can he ensure that the other participants—themselves all potential internal *influencers,* with their own needs to fulfill through their participation in the organization—suspend voice and instead function on behalf of the external influencers whom the CEO represents (or, indeed, on his own behalf, since he, too, is an influencer)? Specifically, how can he control the behavior of the managers to whom he has delegated formal power, and they in turn control their own "subordinate" managers, down to the first-line supervisors whose problem is to control the actions of the operators? In essence, the question becomes one of maintaining a *System of Authority*, of legitimate or formal power vested in office.

In our scheme of things, authority is considered to be maintained primarily by two distinct systems of control. The *personal control system* includes those means of influence by which the CEO and the managers of the middle line intervene directly in the work of their employees to control their behavior. They give work orders, set the premises of decisions, review decisions, and allocate resources. And the *bureaucratic control system* includes those means of influence by which the organization imposes standards on its employees. These standards may apply to the work itself, through job descriptions, rules and regulations, and the like; or else they may apply to the outputs of the work, through plans, schedules, formal objectives, and so on. It should be noted that the analysts of the technostructure play a key role in designing and operating the bureaucratic control system.

In the ideal world—at least from the narrowest perspective of the CEO— these two systems of control would serve to determine all the behavior of the insiders. But the world of organizations is far more complex than that. In effect, once the organization has been designed, it takes on a life of its own—it becomes more than just the positions and the controls that have been formally set in place. Other independent systems of influence arise in it, perhaps unintended ones from the CEO's initial point of view—systems that sometimes supplement the integrative effects of authority and other times counteract it.

First there is another system of influence that can serve to knit all of the insiders into a cohesive unit, although it does not derive from formal authority. That is the *System of Ideology*, based on traditions, beliefs, myths or stories of the organization that the different insiders share, as "members." Essentially this system draws on the *loyalty* of the insiders, causing them (as does the System of Authority), to suspend voice (except in support of the organization).

And then there are the systems of influence that can be used to resist cohesion or integration, fractionating the power of the Internal Coalition. To the extent that the employees of the organization are skilled and knowledgeable specialists, or "experts," in their own right, a *System of Expertise* arises in the Internal Coalition. This serves to distribute power unevenly, on the basis of talent, giving rise to voice wherever it is found. Here coordination of the work is achieved, not through personal or bureaucratic controls or the normative power of ideology, but by virtue of the mutual adjustment among different experts or else from another body of standards, based on skills and knowledge. In effect, to the extent that the employees have "internalized" their working standards through extensive training, typically received before they joined the organization, they can free themselves of the influences of authority and even ideology.

Finally, all of these systems—functioning separately or together—are often imperfect and incomplete. They leave a certain degree of discretion for the insiders to act independently of the influences of formal authority, accepted ideology, or certified expertise. A *System of Politics* arises in the Internal Coalition—one of illegitimate power, in the technical sense, typically coupled with conflict. The System of Politics is one of voice, but often of a clandestine nature. The internal influencers, as "players," use this system to circumvent, resist, or even disrupt the other systems of influence in order to accomplish ends they personally believe to be important. Indeed we shall see that the System of Politics is at times used by all the internal influencers, from operators who may have little other recourse to power to the chief executive who may have to rely on it to circumvent fundamental weaknesses in his systems of control.

Thus we have four basic systems of influence that can be used by the various participants in the Internal Coalition: the System of Authority, consisting of personal and bureaucratic controls, which views the internal influencers as "superiors" and "subordinates"; the System of Ideology, which views them as "members"; the System of Expertise, which views them as "experts"; and the System of Politics, which views them as "players." How each of these systems is used inside a particular organization, and what mix of the four results, determines what kind of Internal Coalition the organization will have. Once we discuss the power and the needs of each of our five groups of internal influencers in the next chapter, we turn our attention to each of these systems of influence in turn. Then we close this part with a discussion of how these systems can work in concert and then in domination to form different types of Internal Coalitions.

9

The Internal Influencers

In this chapter, each of the five basic groups of internal influencers are discussed in turn—the chief executive officer, the managers of the middle line, the operators, the analysts of the technostructure, and the support staff. We discuss, for each, their power in the Internal Coalition, their use of the different systems of influence, and their own needs as influencers in the play of organizational power. This provides the foundation for our discussion of the Internal Coalition. Once we have completed that discussion, we are able to summarize various characteristics of the internal influencers. This is done in Table 14–1, which can be found on pages 232–33.

THE CHIEF EXECUTIVE OFFICER

THE POWER OF THE CEO   Our discussion in Chapter 8—of the passing of formal power into the Internal Coalition through the chief executive officer and of his attainment of informal power through his responsibility to reconcile conflicting demands on the organization—leads us to the conclusion that **the CEO is inevitably the single most powerful individual in the whole system of power in and around the organization.** That is not to say that the CEO has the power to dominate *everyone* else, but rather that no *single* individual is typically more powerful. As Tannenbaum and Katz note, "The power of the membership is distributed among a large number of people; that of the president is in the possession of one person" (1957, p. 133). Of course, the CEO's actual power depends on a number of conditions, including how power is distributed in the External Coalition and how the insiders are able to use the other systems of influence to counter formal authority. But even in the case of the Dominated EC, where one external influencer is very powerful, that influencer must rely on the CEO to manage the organization. And in the case of professional organizations, such as universities, in which some theorists are prepared to argue that the operators hold authority over the managers (Etzioni 1959, p. 52), there is evidence to suggest that the CEO remains "The most powerful man of all":

> When we arrange the average scores that presidents receive [in a questionnaire distributed widely among people in American universities], the lowest score is 4.26 and the highest is 4.92. This means that the presidents, alone of all powerholders, occupy the unique position that *everywhere* they were perceived as having very high power, well over 4.00 on a five point scale. . . .even the least powerful are very powerful indeed. (Gross 1968, p. 542)

The power of chief executives seems to be most clearly indicated in the battles that ensue over their replacement. We saw this earlier in Zald's (1965) description of succession in a welfare agency.[1] A prime reason for their power seems to lie in the fact that major strategic change in an organization often accompanies and indeed often seems to require a change in the leadership (Miller and Friesen 1980). Thus Zald shows how the welfare agency reoriented itself under its new leader, changing a number of its major strategies. The CEO, it would appear, can set the whole tone of the organization.

THE CEO's MEANS OF INFLUENCE   What gives the CEO so much power? We have already discussed the CEO's *external* bases for power: he serves in a formal sense as the board's trustee to manage the organization and in an informal sense as the reconciler of pressures of various external influencers. In the terms introduced in Chapter 3, the CEO controls the legal prerogatives and he has the best access to the external influencers. But what about his bases of power vis-à-vis the internal influencers?

The most widely used categorization of power is probably that of French and Raven (1959). They distinguish five types: reward, coercive, legitimate, referent (based on identification), and expert. The power of the CEO is in the first instance clearly legitimate: it derives from the fact that, as the board's trustee, he is granted sweeping formal powers over the activities of the organization. These in turn enable him to demand a certain compliance from the other

---

[1]Zald's analysis suggests a curious irony. The intensity of the conflict over the choice of successor indicates the power of the position. Yet the very fact that there was conflict shows that the position is not *all*-powerful; that is, the chief executive could not simply name his own successor. Either extreme—no conflict, where the CEO simply names his own successor and no one cares, to extreme conflict, where he has no say—would suggest less CEO power than some middle ground. Zald's case seems to stand in that middle ground.

insiders. Typically, the CEO has the formal power to hire and fire many if not all of the other insiders and to impose decisions on them as well as to veto any they propose to him. Moreover, his formal power often extends to the mediation of their rewards—the setting of their salaries and other benefits (at least to the extent that unions do not preempt these prerogatives). In other words, three of French and Raven's basic forms of power—legitimate, reward, and to some extent coercive—serve the CEO first of all, and vest him with a great deal of power. When the chief executive speaks, others in the organization have a number of incentives to listen. Another way to put this is that the System of Authority is the chief executive's most important system of influence. And its two control systems—personal and bureaucratic—are in the first instance his own means of influence to ensure compliance with his wishes. So to the extent that the power of the Internal Coalition resides in office, it falls first and foremost into the hands of the CEO.

But the CEO is not restricted to this one system of influence. In other words, he has considerable informal power in the Internal Coalition as well. That power of course stems from office too—after all we are discussing the power of the incumbent of the office—but it takes a less official form.

First, the System of Ideology can serve the CEO. When an organization has a well-established ideology, it is typically the leader who "embodies" it— who is looked up to as representing and reflecting it. No one, as the saying goes, can be more Catholic than the Pope. And this enables the CEO to "lead" the organization in the sense that Selznick (1957) uses the term, to "infuse it with value," build "purpose" into its social structure, "transform a neutral body of men into a committed polity" (pp. 17, 90, 61).

Of course, leaders are not chosen at random. They emerge from the crowd because of their personal characteristics. They may have what is called "charisma," another way of saying that they attract followers, have intrinsic "referent" power. And that, of course, reinforces their leadership role in the System of Ideology. Moreover, leaders typically exhibit well-honed political skills, those of persuasion, negotiation, and so on. They could not have made it to the top without these skills. And so, ironically, the CEO is probably the most adept at using that system of influence on which those who wish to counter his power must often rely—the System of Politics. The cards of the game of organizational power are strongly stacked in his favor.

But why should a chief executive, with all those other powers, turn to politics? As we shall soon see, the control systems may be important, but they have their own deficiencies. And these drive the CEO toward the other systems of influence, including that of politics.

A key means of influence in the Internal Coalition is special knowledge. His position at the strategic apex puts the CEO in possession of a very powerful base of special knowledge. Research on managerial work suggests that the manager is the nerve center of his own organization, normally the single best informed member of it (see Mintzberg 1973). As its highest-ranking formal authority, he alone is formally linked to all of the insiders, and so he tends to establish the best internal channels of information. Furthermore, each of these insiders is a specialist relative to him, charged with some specialized activity. He alone can see the totality. Hence the CEO emerges as that individual most knowledgeable about the organization's internal activities. And his status as chief executive officer puts him into direct contact with other managers, themselves nerve centers of their own organizations. This provides him with the best sources of external information as well, especially the soft information that seldom gets documented (and therefore remains inaccessible to others). Moreover, as noted earlier, the CEO is that person best able to understand the needs of the different external influencers. So in total the CEO emerges as the most knowledgeable member of the Internal Coalition, the expert if not in any one function then about the organization itself. He may not know everything, but he typically knows more than anyone else. And in knowledge is power. In fact, as we noted earlier, the board of directors often proves impotent because it is unable to reinforce all of its formal power of law with the informal power of knowledge.

THE CEO AS INFLUENCER   Naturally, the chief executive officer can do more than just reconcile the wishes of everyone else. He too is an influencer with his own needs to fulfill in the organization. But the CEO is no ordinary influencer: he is an inside influencer, and the most powerful one of them all. This enables him, in the words of Chamberlain, to emerge as the "residual claimant" on the organization (1962, p. 74). Once all the other claimants—owners, suppliers, employees, and so on—are satisfied, "whatever discretion management has not bargained away remains its to follow as it chooses" (p. 74).

The goals that top managers try to impose on their organizations can, of course, vary widely, as can the goals of anyone else. But again what interests us here are only those goals related to their jobs as top managers. And in this regard, two points should be borne in mind. First, of all the influencers, the CEO is the one most committed to the organization. "Top management must personify, if not, as Maitland quipped of the British monarchy, parsonify the institution" (Long 1960, p. 211). As noted earlier, in the words of Selznick (1957), the CEO "embodies" organizational purpose. In some sense, it is *his* organization. England (1967) administered a questionnaire to 1,072 senior American managers and found that 91 percent ranked "my company" as being of high importance, whereas only 52 percent so ranked its owners.[2] And Brager (1969) found in his study of Mobilization for Youth that the degree of commitment to the organization's values varied by hierarchical level, with 48 percent of the executives falling into the upper third on the commitment scale, compared with

[2]Only customers were so ranked by more executives (92 percent); employees were so ranked by 78 percent of them, while of the seventeen groups ranked, unions received that ranking by the fewest executives (21 percent).

38 percent of the supervisory and consultant staff and only 26 percent of the operators. (For the board members the figure was 11 percent!) Thus, the CEO sees his interests as very much tied up with the organization. If it fails, he fails. And so the survival of the organization becomes a key goal for him.[3]

Second, it should be borne in mind that chief executives tend to be very achievement-oriented individuals. Not everyone makes it to the top of the hierarchy; the selection process tends to send up those more concerned with success. Thus, in the England questionnaire, 83 percent of the senior managers ranked achievement as of high importance as a personal goal, followed by success and creativity (at 70 percent). Only 28 percent so ranked money and 11 percent leisure.[4]

An achievement-oriented individual can expend his energies climbing up the hierarchy. But what happens when he finds himself at the top of it, with nowhere else to go (short of leaving the organization in which he has spent so much time and energy to succeed)? A CEO's status is associated with the size of the organization he runs; the natural conclusion, therefore, widely supported in the literature, is that the CEO typically manifests his achievement orientation in trying to expand the size of his organization. In other words, *growth* is a key goal that the CEO seeks to impose on the organization.

This leaves us with two principle goals of the CEO—survival and growth of the organization. The two may complement each other: in many circumstances growth is necessary for survival. But they may also contradict: growth can be risky, threatening survival. And so the behaviors of CEOs can range from the conservative, survival-obsessed to the entrepreneurial, growth-obsessed.

What about the profit goal in the case of the business firm? Some profit is obviously necessary for survival, so the question becomes: Is profit singled out as an especially important goal of the chief executive of the corporation? A number of writers have addressed this question, generally concluding that

[3]Another result of this commitment is that senior managers see the legitimate areas of organizational action as being far broader than other people do. Schein and Ott (1961–62) asked labor leaders, students (in MBA and management programs), and company executives to indicate on a questionnaire whether or not each of fifty-five behaviors were legitimate concerns of the corporation (e.g., tidiness of the employees' office, their working hours, the degree of formality of their clothing, how much they drink at home). The executives saw far more of these areas as legitimate corporate concerns than did the students and especially the labor leaders. The strongest differences between the executives and the labor leaders occurred on the items related to loyalty to the company, the subordinates' presentation of themselves during the working day, their degree of autonomy, personal morality, and some other specific items.

[4]Job satisfaction was the one item rated higher than achievement as a personal goal (at 88 percent), but curiously, the managers rated job satisfaction very low on the success scale. England believes achievement to be the highest "operative" value for managers. For the record, it should be noted that prestige was ranked as of high importance by 21 percent of the managers, influence by 18 percent, and power by 10 percent. The pejorative nature of these words may have had a significant effect here.

where ownership is separated from management and is diffused, some reasonable level of profit is treated as a constraint—a requirement for survival and for keeping the shareholders passive—but growth emerges as the real goal of the management.

This is the position taken by Alfred D. Chandler in his Pulitzer Prize–winning book, *The Visible Hand*: "in making administrative decisions, career managers preferred policies that favored the long-term stability and growth of their enterprises to those that maximized current profits" (1977, p. 10). Similarly, John Kenneth Galbraith argues in *The New Industrial State* that once the survival of the giant American corporation is assured by earnings large enough for an adequate level of reinvestment, the management has "a measure of choice as to goals" (1967, p. 171). Galbraith has "little doubt as to how, overwhelmingly, this choice is exercised: It is to achieve the greatest possible rate of corporate growth as measured in sales" (p. 171). Whereas

> . . . profit maximization as a goal requires that the individual. . . subordinate his personal pecuniary interest to that of the remote and unknown stockholder. . . growth, as a goal, is wholly consistent with the personal pecuniary interest of those who participate in decisions and direct the enterprise. (pp. 171–72)[5]

And Gordon Donaldson, a well-known professor of finance, argues that despite CEO claims that their primary duty is to "make money for the stockholder" (1963, p. 118), the interests of the two differ importantly, the CEO being committed to one particular corporation, the shareholder being in the market of many for capital gain. His is a "loyalty to superior financial performance. . . and to nothing else" (p. 125). Thus, when funds are to be invested, while the manager asks only "Now or later?", the shareholder adds "Here or elsewhere?" (p. 124). And so Donaldson ascribes to "professional" management "the absolute priority of the corporate interest—its continuity and growth—over the financial objectives of ownership" (p. 129).

One way to test these conclusions is to compare the performance of tightly held, owner-controlled corporations with widely held, so called "professionally" managed ones, in our terms those with Dominated as compared with Passive ECs. Monsen, Chiu, and Cooly (1968) found in a study of seventy-two firms, six manager-controlled and six owner-controlled in each of twelve industries, that the owner-controlled ones performed 75 percent better in terms of average profitability over the course of twelve years (12.8 percent versus 7.3 percent net income to net worth), and that the presence of management control "very strongly" affected performance in all twelve industries. Similarly, as we saw in Chapter 6, Smith (1978, p. 154) finds that the ten boards of the Fortune 500 in 1977 with the highest proportion of inside directors—presum-

---

[5]Galbraith discusses two other goals as well, technological virtuosity and a progressive rise in the dividend rate. But he calls these "secondary," arguing that they must not interfere with survival and growth.

ably an indication of being widely held—had lower average returns on stockholders' equity than the ten with the most outside directors.

In another paper, Monsen and Downs (1965) built a whole conceptual theory on the assumption that top managers of widely held corporations seek to maximize their own lifetime earnings. This would result in their striving to maintain a good public image, especially with shareholders, so as to avoid controversy and criticism; to ensure that dividend rates and stock prices rise regularly but smoothly; to avoid risky decisions, allowing the firm to grow carefully; to diversify, especially through merger; to finance internally or through borrowing; to spend expense account money freely and to contribute to community causes that enhance their prestige; and to concede more easily than managers of other firms to the demands of labor unions. As Monsen himself suggests in another paper, the sensitivity to outside criticism of top managers in widely held firms makes them, compared with those of closely held corporations, more like Papandreou's peak coordinators:

> The professional manager, unlike the owner-manager, is probably more responsive to pressures from the various constituent groups of the firm such as workers, consumers, suppliers, or stockholders, and the government. The professional manager is apt to respond to conflicting demands from these groups by balancing one off against the other or by utilizing compromise as an issue-settling device. The owner-manager, who views each dollar given to workers, suppliers, consumers, or the government as coming from his own pocket, is less likely to compromise. (1969, p. 48)

In a similar approach, Williamson (1963, 1964) built a mathematical model on the assumption that managers seek to maximize their self-interest. The model is developed in part around the notion of "expense preference," the propensity of managers to favor those expenses that help them to meet their personal goals—a polite way of saying that they like to build empires. Williamson argues that where favorable economic conditions prevail, managers will spend more on advertising, research and development, entertainment, travel, office improvements, and so on.

These conclusions are in fact supported in some research. Pondy (1969), for example, found that the ratio of administrative to operating personnel in forty-five manufacturing firms increased as ownership was separated from management. He believes this finding reflects the professional manager's "stronger preference for hierarchical expense *per se*" (p. 57). And Wolf studied ten firms with stated goals of improving profitability that had changed presidents, five promoted from within and five brought in from the outside. All of those with the outside CEOs subsequently reported significantly increased profitability, which correlated with decreases in selling, general and administrative expenses, while only one with a president promoted from within had a profit increase, and that was small and not related to decreased selling, general, and administrative expenses (reported in Lewin and Wolfe 1973, p. 12).

The obvious conclusion is that there was a good deal of slack in what Pondy calls "hierarchical expense."

To conclude, we have seen that **not only does the CEO tend to have distinct goals for the organization—notably survival and growth—but as the single most important player in the game of power, with the System of Authority at his command as well as his ability to use the Systems of Ideology and Politics and his own special knowledge, he also has the unique opportunity to orient the organization toward these goals.**

THE MANAGERS OF THE MIDDLE LINE

THE POWER AND MEANS OF INFLUENCE OF THE LINE MANAGERS   Everything that we have said about the chief executive applies to the managers of the middle line, but to a decreasing degree as we descend the hierarchy of authority. In other words, **those executives near the top, who report to the CEO directly, to some degree share his goals, his power, and the internal systems of influence he uses to fulfill them, while the first-line supervisors, at the bottom, are left with only vague echoes of these goals, power, and systems of influence.**

But while the managers who report directly to the CEO may often be the second most powerful influencers in the Internal Coalition, they are a distant second. For one thing, there are a number of them, but only one of him. Whatever formal powers he delegates down the chain of authority must be divided up among them, and, in turn, the people who report to them. Moreover they lack the same access that he has through the chain of authority to all of the insiders as well to the wide range of external influencers. So they cannot develop the same broad base of information to use as an informal means of power. And all of these factors become greater impediments to the development of a power base as we descend the hierarchy of line managers.

Yet, from another perspective, we see shades of all of the same bases of power in the middle line. Each manager is, by definition, in charge of an organizational unit—a division, department, factory, shop, or whatever. And within that unit he is like a mini-CEO, with many of the same types of power over it that the CEO has over the whole organization. For one thing, because he is a "line" manager to whom the CEO has delegated some formal power, he possesses the legitimate authority of his unit. As March and Romelaer (1976, p. 273) note in the case of deans and department chairmen in universities, they can exercise discretion and thwart initiative through their formal power to approve, delay, or deny certain decisions—the making of appointments and the granting of tenure, the spending of extra resources, the fixing of agendas, and so on. In addition, the control systems of the unit are at its manager's command. Moreover, the manager serves as the nerve center of his own unit, its only member with formal access to all of its other members and to the manager over it as well as informal access to the managers at his level who run sister units. So he can also develop informal power in his unit by virtue of his sources of information. Finally, like the CEO though again to a lesser degree, to the extent that the organization has traditions, beliefs, and values, the line manager is able to use the System of Ideology as a means of influence.

The analogy of the mini-CEO cannot, however, be carried too far. For a fundamental difference between the managers of the middle line and the CEO is that control over them is concentrated whereas control over him is often diffused. That is to say, whereas the CEO faces out to a somewhat ill-defined and ambiguous External Coalition which pressures him sporadically (especially in the case of a Passive or even Divided EC), the manager of the middle line looks up to a clearly defined hierarchy of authority supported by a system of continuous controls. In a sense, the "External Coalition" of the middle line manager is dominated—by a full-time "superior" with some potent means of formal control. And as we descend the hierarchy, these controls become more and more onerous: the weight of personal controls increases and the bureaucratic controls become more intense, more stringent. In many organizations, by the time we reach the level of first-line supervision, the individuals there cannot really be called managers at all, in the sense of really being in charge of their units. The personal controls of their own superiors and, more importantly, all of the bureaucratic controls imposed on the workers they ostensibly supervise leave them with hardly any more discretion than those workers. Thus, the irony of the job of managing in the middle line is that the control systems serve both as the means to power and the means to take it away. The middle manager is truly caught in the middle.

In a sense, the managers of the middle line are inclined to rely on the control systems for downward influence (with limitations to be discussed below) and the System of Politics and sometimes that of Expertise for upward influence, to check the controls on them. The lower in the hierarchy the manager, the greater his incentive to deflect orders and technocratic standards downwards, and to withhold information flowing upward or else to exploit it, as well as the expertise contained in his unit. But the irony is that while it may be the lower-level managers who have the greater incentive to rely especially on the System of Politics, it is the upper managers who are better able to exploit it. They have wider contacts and better information, and, by virtue of having made it to a higher place in the structure, they typically possess stronger political skills.

Figure 9–1 seeks to summarize this discussion of the managers of the middle line. It shows their overall power and reliance on the different systems of influence as a function of their level in the hierarchy. Obviously, the power of a particular line manager will vary markedly from one situation to another (as we shall see in Part IV). But on average, we see the following: In contrast to the CEO above who can rely first and foremost on the formal power of the control systems, and the operators below who are often forced to fall back on the informal power of politics (as well as expertise, where possible), the line managers came closest to striking a rough balance in their use of these (and

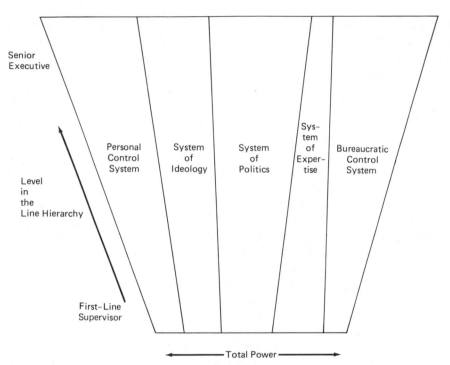

FIGURE 9–1. *Reliance on Systems of Influence by Level in the Line Hierarchy*

the other) systems of influence. In general, the *relative* reliance on politics is shown to increase at lower levels (although its actual influence decreases). The same is shown for the reliance on expertise—here actual as well as relative—since the technical knowledge and skills of most organizations tend to rest low in the hierarchy. But the use of the two components of the System of Authority—personal and bureaucratic controls—decreases markedly. This is especially true of the bureaucratic controls, which serve primarily the higher-level managers as well as the analysts, often at the expense of the lower-level managers. As for the System of Ideology, its use diminishes only slightly (in an actual sense, and increases in a relative sense), since it serves all of the members of the organization more equally than any of the other systems of influence. Finally, the overall figure is shown to narrow toward the base, to represent the fact that total power diminishes as we descend the middle line.

THE LINE MANAGERS AS INFLUENCERS   Again in discussing the goals of the line managers, we see a reflection of the goals pursued by the CEO, specifically survival and growth.

The higher the manager in the hierarchy, the stronger his commitment to the organization, and so the more important its survival to him. His rewards have come—and will continue to come—from climbing the hierarchy, so it stands to reason that the more he gets promoted, the more he has a vested interest in seeing the organization survive. Cummings and ElSalmi (1968), in their review of the research on managerial motivation, find good reason for managers to identify more strongly with the organization as they advance up its hierarchy: a number of studies show that high-level managers—in unions and the military as well as in business—express more satisfaction in their jobs and greater fulfillment of their needs for autonomy and self-actualization than do those at lower levels; the jobs of the latter tend to focus on the security and social needs. But even for lowest-level managers, there is often some satisfaction in having left operating work behind and attaining a new status. And this leads to some level of commitment beyond that of the operators. Thus, figures cited earlier in the chapter showed that, while the first-line supervisors of Brager's (1969) Mobilization for Youth organization exhibited less commitment to the organization's values than the managers at upper levels, theirs was still a good deal higher than that of the operators.

Organizational growth may be an even more important goal for the managers of the middle line than for the CEO. The hierarchy narrows as it rises, like a funnel, such that promotions become less and less available. But an expanding organization is always adding new units, thereby opening up new opportunities for promotion. So it is in the interest of the ambitious line manager to promote growth. Moreover, even for the manager who stays in his job, growth means a larger unit, a bigger budget, more room to maneuver, more "perks," also less conflict. There is plenty for everybody. It is in the static or declining organization that people tend to clash more often, since there is less slack to go around.

But more important to the line manager than the growth of the whole organization is growth of his own unit. Line managers, especially those at higher levels, have been found to exhibit strong needs for both autonomy and achievement (Rossel 1971; Cummings and ElSalmi 1968). "Empire building" is a natural practice for such managers, since their power and status, not to mention the salaries they earn, is a function of the size of the units they manage. And so there are strong pressures for the managers of middle-line units to add personnel, and to grab new functions for their units as well as take over old ones. As C. Northcote Parkinson puts it, "An official wants to multiply subordinates, not rivals" (1957, p. 33). And, of course, the resulting vector of all these forces points in one direction—toward the growth of the whole organization.

But another goal is implicit in the above findings too. The drive for autonomy encourages not only the expansion but also the balkanization of the organization—its division to allow the maximum discretion to each of the units of the middle line. One way to achieve this—and so often fought for by middle managers—is to have the units grouped on the basis of products or markets, so that all the necessary functions can be contained within each and its dependence on other units thereby minimized.

To summarize, **the needs of the line managers are reflected in two different forces: on one hand, an identification with the CEO and his goals of survival and growth, especially at higher levels in the hierarchy, and on the other hand, an attempt to satisfy their own drives for autonomy and achievement through the aggrandizement of their own units and the balkanization of the overall structure.** But both forces favor expansion of the organization at large, and so growth emerges—advertently and inadvertently—as the key goal promoted for the organization by the managers of its middle line.

THE OPERATORS

The operators, as noted earlier, are those people who do the basic work of the organization—the input, processing, and output functions, as well as the *direct* support activities, associated with producing the products and rendering the services offered by the organization. Operators include machinists and assemblers in factories, barbers in barbershops, doctors and nurses in hospitals, professors in universities, and so on. Their job is to execute the final decisions of the organization, that is, to take the actions—build the cars, cut the hair, transplant the hearts, teach the classes—as well as make any of the associated decisions that the managers of the middle line do not. One fact, therefore, stands out about the operators, as is evident in Figure 8-3. All the weight of the administrative structure—the middle-line hierarchy plus technostructure—rests upon them. Moreover, they are the farthest removed from the CEO, and from the pressures he feels from all the various groups of external influencers. The result is that the operators tend to have much weaker identification with the organization than the managers (as was shown, for example, in the Brager data cited earlier).

Yet operators too have needs which they seek to fulfill in the Internal Coalition. In other words, they too are influencers. In order to discuss their power and the systems of influence they favor, we must distinguish two fundamentally different kinds of operating work.

UNSKILLED OPERATORS   At one extreme are the operators who do simple and routine work—like that of the assemblers in the automobile factories. As a result, their work is easily standardized by the system of bureaucratic controls, and the operators end up with very little discretion in what they do. Essentially, they execute very specific decisions. This means that the control systems are not means of influence available to them (with certain exceptions that we shall come to shortly), but rather ones available to administrators to control them. Likewise, unskilled operators by definition have no complex knowledge or skills, and so neither is the System of Expertise available to them. Finally, in organizations with this kind of work, the System of Ideology is generally weak, especially among the operators. Tedious work does not often engender a strong identification with the organization. Among all the groups in the organization, the unskilled operators are the ones most predisposed to accept a strict inducements-contributions contract—to do as told in return for a set remuneration.

But unskilled operators have needs to fulfill as well. And so the question then becomes: How do these workers, at the bottom of the hierarchy of formal power and with no valued technical expertise, gain any power in the Internal Coalition? Each is easily replaced, since anyone can learn to do the job quickly. In other words, none has any of the prime bases of power discussed in Chapter 3, formal *or* informal—a critical resource, skill, or knowledge, a legal prerogative, or good access to the people with these. Each is close to powerless.

As Cartwright notes, research in a variety of settings has indicated "that when individuals find themselves powerless, they tend to form groups whose norms and leaders represent values contrary to those of the dominant social system" (1965, p. 36). In other words, **the one system of influence that remains open to use by the unskilled operators is the System of Politics, which can give them a good deal of power when they act in concert.** It should be remembered that, as a whole, the operators are critical to the organization—their work is its raison d'être. And so their disruption of the operations damages the organization at its core. In those organizations with simple and routine operating work, the operators typically constitute a majority of the internal influencers. And, as we shall see in Chapter 13, with the will to expend energy coupled with some degree of political skill, the unskilled operators acting in concert can become a significant force in the Internal Coalition, deflecting certain actions toward their own ends.

What goals do the unskilled operators seek to impose on the organization? Two points seem clear. First, the goals are those of the group, not the individual operator, because the group is the agent of their power. And second, the unskilled operators cannot take much satisfaction in their work, since it is simple and routine and tightly controlled by the administrators. In other words, they cannot hope to satisfy what Maslow (1954) calls the higher-order needs—status and self-actualization. At best they can only hope to alleviate some of their physiological and safety problems, and perhaps satisfy some of their social needs as well.

Physiological and safety needs are satisfied largely outside the Internal Coalition, by the operators' use of their unions to negotiate with management for wages and fringe benefits. But their social needs may be satisfied partly within the Internal Coalition. **One of the social needs of the unskilled operators is the conservation of established social relationships**—namely, protection of the group's own social structure—to impede managers and analysts from imposing changes that may interfere with it. When threatened, the group can act informally by resisting commands, or more formally, through its union, by striking, that is, withholding effort. The group can also use its power to force rules and procedures on the administrative structure in order to reduce the arbitrariness of personal supervision (Crozier 1964). Promotion by seniority—instead of by the preference of the first-line supervisor—is a prime example. Here, ironically, the unskilled operators working in concert are able to make use of the bureaucratic control system, indeed to turn it around on the administrators. In effect, they use it as a means of influence to counter the personal control system. Operators can also turn the bureaucratic control system to their advantage in a very different way, when they "work-to-rule," a form of strike in which they apply the standards so rigorously that the organization cannot function. What we have here, in effect, is a political (that is, technically illegitimate) use of the System of Authority.

In recent times, especially in Europe, unskilled operators have sometimes sought to challenge formal authority directly by establishing their own councils of elected workers to negotiate with managers about workplace issues, or else by seeking representation on the board of directors in order to influence major decisions. But as we shall see in Chapter 27, the evidence suggests that such efforts have not had a major effect on the lot of the unskilled operator; their only effect seems to have been a strengthening of the hand of the chief executive at the expense of the middle management.

PROFESSIONAL OPERATORS   So far we have discussed operators who do simple, routine work that has no attraction for them. At the other extreme, generally referred to as *professional*, are the operators who do work that requires a high degree of skill or knowledge. Not only does that work become interesting and attractive to the operators, but its complexity precludes close administrative control, giving rise to a whole new power relationship between operator and administrator.

Professional operators have an important basis of power—the possession of critical knowledge and skills. This means that alone or in small groups, they must be given considerable discretion in their work, and so come to amass a good deal of power. This is enhanced by the fact that the professional operators generally provide a skill which is in great demand, resulting in a good deal of job mobility. As a result, their dependence on the organization is reduced as is their commitment to it. In other words, ideology is typically not a strong force in the case of professionals, at least not organizational ideology. (Professional ideology—belief in the profession and its norms—certainly is.) All of this means that **the professional operator relies on the System of Expertise as the prime means of influence.**

Professional operators can also band together to exercise group power, either through the System of Politics in the Internal Coalition or else through the power of their professional societies in the External Coalition. These societies often control entry to the profession and also establish many of the standards of professional conduct and behavior. In fact, it is these professional standards, imposed on the organization from the External Coalition, that preclude the administrators from imposing their own bureaucratic standards on the operators.

Thus, the professional operators can emerge as relatively powerful influencers in the Internal Coalition (and, for that matter, in the External Coalition as well, through their societies). In fact, in organizations where the operating core is made up in large part of professional operators—as in hospitals and universities—individual and group operator goals play a major role.

The group goals—as in the case of unskilled operators—include protection of the group, in this case not only its social but also its work relationships. Professional groups and societies put a great deal of effect into maintaining their autonomy, from administrators within the organization as well as from other influencers outside of it. As we saw in Chapter 7, only the professionals were supposed to judge the work of rehabilitation in prisons, not "the public," even though it paid the expenses. Group goals also include trying to enhance the prestige, the strength in numbers, and the resources of the various kinds of professionals. In the hospitals, the surgeons lobby for more operating rooms, the radiologists for more and better equipment, the cardiologists for more beds, and all of them for more staff. The overall effect, again, is pressure on the organization for growth. Another effect of this vying for prestige and resources, which is inherent in the System of Expertise, is the establishment of pecking orders between and even within different professional specialties. As we shall see later, this typically pits the System of Expertise against that of Ideology, which as we shall see stands for equality among the members of the organization.

There are also professional goals of a more individual nature. One is often the pursuit of professional excellence, because the professional operator, unlike the unskilled one, tends to take pleasure in his work, and so becomes strongly committed to it. The professional's rewards are, in Etzioni's words, "normative": "high intrinsic satisfaction" (1961, p. 53). Of course, professional excellence can sometimes be pursued in spite of the needs of the organization or its clients, as in the case of the surgeon prone to cut in order to hone his own skills or the professor so obsessed with research that he has no time for his students. As Perrow notes: "...professionals have interests of their own which shape the organization. They may develop an identity and ethic which cuts them off from the needs of the community and favors specialized, narrow and—to critics—self-serving goals" (1961, p. 862).

But the self-serving tendency can be mitigated by another of the individual goals pursued by some professional operators. Because they often work closely with the client—as in the case of the doctor with his patient—the two develop a personal relationship. As a result, many professionals tend to treat the service they render—in other words, the actual mission of the organization—as another important goal of their own. Indeed, a curious switch can take place in the organization staffed with professionals: The operators uphold the needs of the clients, while the administrators, who may have little direct contact with the clients, support the more abstract, impersonal goals of efficiency and growth, sometimes in opposition to the mission.[6]

To conclude, **the goals professional operators tend to pursue in the Internal Coalition are first of all protection and especially autonomy of the group, then enhancement of the prestige and resources of the specialty and professional excellence (sometimes in spite of client need), and finally, when client-professional relationships are close and personal, support of the organization's mission.**

THE ANALYSTS OF THE TECHNOSTRUCTURE

As noted in Chapter 8, the analysts of the technostructure fill those staff positions concerned with the design and running of the formal systems of control and adaptation. Analysts tend to adopt the titles of the systems they work on—planner, accountant, budget analyst, operations researcher, MIS (or systems) analyst, and so on. To understand the analyst as influencer, four points need to be appreciated: (1) that the analysts are supposed to have no formal authority to make decisions; (2) that they are usually professionals; (3) that, by virtue of the work they do, they are committed to organizational change yet are obsessed with stability; and (4) that they require operational goals in order to apply their techniques.

THE POWER AND MEANS OF INFLUENCE OF THE ANALYSTS   The analysts serve in "staff" positions, technically impotent next to the "line" managers. Their role is to advise; they have no formal authority to decide. But they have needs for power too, as Cummings and ElSalmi found in their review: "Line and staff managers did not differ on the importance they attach to each type of need with the exception of autonomy needs. These were considered more important by staff managers" (p. 129). This results in frustration for the analysts: "Staff jobs produced greater deficiencies in fulfillment of most of the higher order needs than did the line jobs," and "Line managers tended to be more satisfied for almost all types of needs. This held at all four management levels from vice-president down to lower management" (p. 129). And this, in turn, has inevitably led—as so much of the literature bears witness—to all kinds of political conflicts between staff analysts and line managers.

[6]The same thing can, of course, happen with unskilled operators when their contact with the clients is close (as, say, in the case of waiters in a restaurant), although these operators have less power with which to uphold the goals of the clients. Alternately when contact between client and professional operator is less personal, the opposite result can occur, as Stymne (1972, pp. 255–88) shows in an interesting content analysis of the remarks made by professional employees and member representatives of an industry association.

In the power games that ensue (to be discussed in Chapter 13), the analyst is at an inherent disadvantage, since all of the formal means of influence as well as many of the informal ones favor the manager. The manager has the political skills, the nerve center information, and the formal authority to make decisions and allocate resources. But the analyst is not powerless. First of all, he is usually an expert, a professional. That is to say, he is hired by the organization to apply complex techniques that he has learned outside the organization. And so, it is in the System of Expertise that the analyst's basis for power in the Internal Coalition lies. Second, the analyst's techniques often serve to "institutionalize" the job of the manager, particularly at lower levels, that is, to remove responsibility for control and decision making from the manager's personal responsibility and put it instead into formal systems. In other words, analysts are employed to replace personal controls by bureaucratic ones. Thus, while both control systems are ostensibly under the formal authority of the line manager, in fact the analysts gain power over certain line managers by favoring one of those systems—the bureaucratic one that they help to design and run. A work study team that standardizes the job of a machine operator, at the same time reduces the power of a foreman to supervise that operator's work. And a budget planning system installed by analysts removes from the middle-level line manager the discretion to allocate resources within his unit as he wishes. In organizations that rely heavily on bureaucratic systems of control, the technostructure is typically very powerful (Mintzberg 1979a, chap. 18). So **the analyst must rely on the System of Expertise as his prime means of influence, yet gains power to the extent that he does so to build up the system of bureaucratic controls.**

As for the System of Ideology, later we shall see that it has its own built-in mechanisms of control—essentially the norms that are shared by members of the organization. Thus, to the extent that an organization has a strong ideology, it has no need for bureaucratic controls—or the analysts who design them. Thus, analysts often stand in direct opposition to the development or perpetuation of organizational ideologies. But, as we shall soon see, they too have their own ideology.

THE ANALYST AS INFLUENCER   What goals do the analysts pursue? One we have already seen is bureaucratization. Analysts encourage the organization to use as many of their technocratic systems as possible, as someone once commented, to worship at the altar of administrative science.

As professionals, the goals of the analysts in part also resemble those of the more skilled operators. In particular, professional excellence—what Galbraith calls "technological virtuosity" in *The New Industrial State* (1967)— also motivates them. Moreover, the analysts' techniques are general—applicable across a wide range of organizations—and are generally in demand, and so the analysts are typically mobile. That means that they, too, tend to have a weak identification with the organization itself, in fact, typically weaker than the professional operators since they do not even have direct contact with the clients.

Analysts also have a paradoxical relationship with organizational change. On one hand, the perfectly stable organization needs no analysts. Analysts are hired essentially to design systems for adaptation and control. But under conditions of perfect stability, adaptation is unnecessary and everything is under control. And so to augment their own indispensability and power, the analysts are encouraged to promote perpetual change in the organization. They have, as Mumford and Pettigrew note, "a vested interest in change" (1975, p. 205). Thus Pettigrew notes of the computer specialists he studied: "It was in their interests to push for change, even when, from the company's point of view, it was economically unjustifiable. The computer specialists' slogan became 'if it works it's obsolescent'" (1973, p. 77). Indeed, it is probably fair to conclude that the obsession with change in the large, contemporary organization—and in industrial society in general—originated in good part with the establishment of large corps of technocratic analysts. The first wave came in the 1920s, following Frederick Taylor's time study work; another began in the 1950s around computers and the field of Operations Research, and so on.

But at the same time that they promote change as a key goal of the organization, the analysts also represent a strong force for conservation and stability. These goals are inherent in the very nature of their techniques. The control analysts develop bureaucratic systems to standardize everyone else's work, while the adaptive analysts seek to bring the external environment under the organization's control, in effect to stabilize it (Katz and Kahn 1966, p. 109). And so, ironically, these proponents of organizational change often represent the forces for conservation and the status quo in the organization. Too much change disrupts the neat systems they work so hard to install. Thus, we can conclude that the change the analysts seek to impose on the organization is of a rather special kind, their kind—perpetual but moderate, careful and conservative, well regulated, under their control.

Finally, the analysts are motivated by the need to demonstrate the tangible worth of their technocratic systems. The way to make the top manager believe that the newfangled bureaucratic system they propose—which he may not even understand—is better than the old system of personal control is to "prove" it, in black and white. This means that the analyst is forced to favor the most operational goals of the organization—those that best lend themselves to actual measures of performance. Moreover, since keeping the organization efficient is his raison d'être, it is logical that the analyst should prefer as that operational goal an economic one. And this means profit in the business firm and some equivalent benefit-cost ratio in other organizations. Indeed (as we shall see later), efficiency has at times become such an important goal to certain analysts—an end in its own right—that a whole professional ideology has grown up around it, called "the cult of efficiency."

And so we are left with an interesting irony: those who identify least with the organization, those who have the least to gain personally from the profit which the organization earns, indeed those who by *personal* inclination care least about economic measures (since these are rather far from professional excellence), become in fact the most enthusiastic maximizers of profit (or efficiency). More so even than many a CEO, who, in the large, widely held corporation at least, has more to gain from growth than profit, as we have seen. In a curious way, the analysts of the Internal Coalition and the owners of the External Coalition form a kind of implicit alliance around the goal of profit. Strange bedfellows.

To conclude, **because of the nature of their professionalism, their work, their staff status, and their need for operational goals to prove the worth of their systems, the analysts of the technostructure favor as goals, professional excellence, perpetual but moderate and well-regulated change in the organization, ever increasing bureaucratization, and, as the criterion for choice, economic efficiency (as measured by profit or some other benefit-cost ratio).**

THE SUPPORT STAFF

As noted in Chapter 8, the support staff can include groups that provide a wide range of services, everything from the plant cafeteria and mailroom to the public relations department and legal counsel. As these examples suggest, the support services—like the work of the operators—can be split roughly into two types, those unskilled in nature and those with more of a professional orientation. But whereas one type or the other often dominates an operating core, we would expect to find both types in the support staff—typically the unskilled relating more closely to the operating activities and so reporting in at lower levels of the hierarchy, and the professional ones working more closely with the senior managers at higher levels.

UNSKILLED SUPPORT STAFFERS   Much of what was written about the unskilled operators applies equally well to the unskilled support staffers. We need only highlight the differences here, two of which appear evident. First, because the organization has a choice of whether or not to provide its own support services—it can just as easily "buy" as "make" in most cases—these services are not very critical to it. They are peripheral, almost incidental, and can easily be replaced. As a result, the unskilled support staffers emerge as even weaker than the unskilled operator. As we saw earlier, the operators as a whole are critical to the organization, and can seriously disrupt it when they so choose. But the unskilled support staffers have no such power to disrupt.

Second, while there are usually a great many unskilled operators doing similar work, the support staffers are typically more dispersed—a few employees in the mailroom, some in the cafeteria, and so on. As a result, their power to organize—to form unions or even to get together on common positions—is considerably less than that of the unskilled operators. The result of both these points is that **the unskilled support staffers emerge as rather impotent, the weakest members of the Internal Coalition.**

PROFESSIONAL SUPPORT STAFFERS   As for the professional support staffers, much of what was written about the professional operators and especially about the analysts applies equally to them. They are mobile, with strong professional affiliations. These factors together with their knowledge and skills mean that **the professional support staffers use the System of Expertise to gain power.**

But there are important differences. Compared with the analysts, the professional support staffers are not wedded to analysis per se, but rather to its application in some specialized branch of expertise. As a result, they have no particular obsession with operational goals or economic efficiency, nor do they have any special reason to favor bureaucratic controls. Also, as they work in small, fractionated groups offering rather vulnerable services to the organization (since these can usually be bought externally), it is in their interest not to pressure for autonomy but rather the reverse—to encourage their involvement in decision processes. **Collaboration is important to the professional support staff.**

With regard to change, they too are caught in a curious paradox of needing change yet being threatened by it, but in a way different from the analysts. The analysts deal with *organizational* change, whereas the professional support staffers often deal with a specialized kind of *environmental* change (or uncertainty). Like the analysts, therefore, they become committed to the perpetuation of that kind of change. But the more success the professional support staffer has in helping the organization cope with his specialized kind of change, the more routine that change becomes to the organization, and the less need it has for his particular expertise. In other words, the expert loses power when the change in which he specializes becomes rationalized. As Crozier notes:

> ...experts have power only on the front line of progress—which means they have a constantly shifting and fragile power... Of course, experts will fight to prevent the rationalization of their own tricks of the trade. But contrary to the common belief, the accelerated rate of change that characterizes our period makes it more difficult for them to resist rationalization. Their bargaining power as individuals is constantly diminishing. (1964, p. 165)

As a result, the support specialist learns to temper his actions—to push for change but to ensure that it remains under his control.

This completes our discussion of the five groups of internal influencers. We have seen that their striving for power evokes a complex and sometimes curious mixture of the systems of influence. The managers of the strategic apex and middle line rely on the System of Authority yet often need the System of

Politics to back it up (not to mention to resist the imposition of authority on themselves from above). Alternately, the unskilled operators need to rely on the System of Politics, yet can sometimes turn the System of Authority (namely bureaucratic controls) to their advantage. The analysts must rely on the System of Expertise, yet do so to favor the imposition of the bureaucratic controls of authority. And the System of Ideology serves to equalize power in the organization, somewhat favoring the CEO (though often less than do the Systems of Authority or Politics) and rendering the analysts redundant. But to this point, our discussion of those systems of influence has been superficial. To understand how power gets distributed in the Internal Coalition, we now turn to a more detailed description of each of them.

10

The System of Authority

Authority is power vested in office or position, what we have been referring to as *formal* power, also a form of legitimate power. And a person who has it can transfer it—"delegate" it—to another. To recapitulate our story thus far, authority originates in the External Coalition, with those influencers who have legitimate power, such as the owners of the organization or the government that granted its charter. Much of that authority is necessarily delegated to the chief executive office, typically through the board of directors—the organization's formal coalition—which names that individual as its trustee to manage the organization. The CEO in turn creates a hierarchy or chain of authority down which he delegates some of his own formal powers—to execute actions, and usually to decide on many of them as well.

But we have just seen that the "subordinates" who make up the rest of the organization are influencers too, with their own goals to fulfill. (In the spirit of the System of Authority, we shall sometimes refer to internal influencers in this chapter as "subordinates" and "superiors." In the spirit of the next chapter, on the System of Ideology, we shall call them "members"; in that of Expertise, "experts"; and in that of Politics, "players.") Moreover, these other employees lack the CEO's strong commitment to the organization. So the CEO requires some means of influence to back up his delegation, to ensure that the other insiders exert their efforts cooperatively, on behalf of the interests of the organization, at least as the CEO sees them. In the words of the behavioral scientist, the CEO must achieve an "integration" between the personal goals of the employees and the overall goals of the organization, as defined and imposed on the Internal

Coalition by the top management, what we shall hereafter refer to as the organization's *formal goals*. To exercise his authority, the CEO designs the superstructure, establishes the system of rewards, and utilizes the two formal systems to control behavior, one personal, the other bureaucratic.

DESIGN OF THE SUPERSTRUCTURE
AND REWARDS SYSTEM

To seek the integration of personal and formal goals, the CEO must first of all design the organization's superstructure. The work of accomplishing the organization's mission is divided into a series of tasks, which are grouped into positions that single individuals can fill. These positions are in turn grouped together into units, under managers, which are grouped again and again into ever larger units until the entire organization comes together in one final unit under the CEO. Underlying this design of the superstructure is the premise that if each individual pursues his or her own work diligently, the overall mission of the organization will be accomplished. Thus, organizational design represents a kind of "visible hand" whereby the CEO and others designated by him intervene consciously to create an integrated, smoothly functioning structure.

But even with the completion of the superstructure—that "rationally" designed instrument for accomplishing organizational purpose—the CEO's problem of ensuring the integration of personal and formal goals is not solved. For while the insiders may be grouped into appropriate positions and units, they will not necessarily carry out their tasks on behalf of the overall organization as expected. What is expected of them may still be unclear, it may be clear but problems of coordination between their tasks may remain, or they may simply resist performing as expected. Thus the skeleton of the superstructure must be fleshed out with other devices of organizational design. Some of these, such as standing committees and task forces, are not closely related to authority per se, and will not be discussed here.[1] Others, however, are of prime interest, and will be.

One of these is the system of rewards controlled by the CEO and the line managers to whom he delegates authority. They typically have considerable power over the setting of salaries, the distribution of fringe benefits, the determination of promotions, the firing of personnel, even the distribution of psychic rewards such as tokens of accomplishment or "praise from the boss." In other words, they have the power to reward those employees who comply with their wishes and penalize those who do not. To quote a Russian proverb, "Whose bread I eat his songs I sing" (Simon 1957, p. 216). Employee associations can, of

---

[1]The design of the superstructure, as well as that of the other parameters of structure, are discussed at length in the *Structuring* book (Mintzberg 1979a, chaps. 4–11).

course, limit these powers, by imposing formal constraints such as promotion by seniority, standard pay scales, and life tenure for certain positions. But a good deal of reward and coercive power inevitably remains in the System of Authority. To use the terms introduced in Chapter 2, it is primarily the managers who offer the inducements in return for the contributions. According to Simon, the employee "offers the organization not his specific service but his undifferentiated time and effort. He places this time and effort at the disposal of those directing the organization, to be used as they see fit" (Simon 1957, pp. 115-16).

But not all employees comply so passively, even when the inducements are generous. To repeat our findings of Chapter 9, any insider can be an influencer with his or her own goals to pursue, if necessary through the use of the System of Politics. The professional operator, for example, certainly places his services at the disposal of the organization—that, obviously, is what he is hired for. But those services come with all kinds of strings attached: that he perform only certain tasks and then only under the control of his professional society, that certain support services be provided to him, perhaps that the goal of professional excellence be paramount, sometimes even when it conflicts with the needs of the organization and its clients. And so it is, although perhaps to a lesser degree, with unskilled operators as well as all the other insiders.

Thus, authority in the form of the prerogatives of organizational design and the mediation of important rewards is not enough to ensure compliance with the organization's formal goals, as defined by its top management. And so that management must do more: in particular, try to express the goals in forms that make clear to others what is expected of them and that enable the management to assess whether or not they have complied with these expectations. And that brings us to the last and most potent of the means of influence related to authority, the control system, which we divide into two parts. One involves the more personal forms of control by the CEO and the managers to whom he delegates power down the middle line. And the other encompasses the more impersonal—bureaucratic—forms of control, in systems designed by the analysts of the technostructure on behalf of the System of Authority. Of course, as we have already seen, the fact that the bureaucratic control system is developed to secure formal authority does not preclude it from being in part captured by other internal influencers for their own purposes. But we shall come to that point in due course. Here our interest is in the control systems as the means to secure and complete the System of Authority.

THE PERSONAL CONTROL SYSTEM

At one extreme, the managers exercise control in a direct, personal, ad hoc, and, if they so choose, arbitrary manner. In other words, they manage by "direct supervision" (see Mintzberg 1979a, chap. 1). Operating through the chain of authority, the managers make certain decisions for their units and issue these as orders to be carried out by their subordinates; they establish the premises for some other decisions that are delegated to their subordinates; for still other decisions, they review the completed decisions made by their subordinates; and finally, in their absence of direct involvement in decision making, they allocate the resources that establish the overall limits to the decisions their subordinates can make. We refer to these four means of controlling behavior, listed in a rough order of diminishing potency, as constituting the *personal control system.*

1.   *The giving of direct orders:* At the limit, the manager can tell a subordinate exactly what to do. In effect, he makes the decisions, and the subordinate executes the actions. When this works, particularly for the most simple of tasks and with the most compliant of subordinates, the manager faces no difficulty in ensuring that his wishes are complied with.

2.   *The setting of decision premises:* Instead of giving direct orders, the manager can set the premises for the decisions made by his subordinates, in other words, established guidelines or specific constraints within which the subordinates must decide. The new piece of equipment is not to cost more than $3,000; the color of the part is to be pastel; only women are to be hired for the job. Here the manager delegates the power to make the decision, but controls its bounds. These limit the subordinate's freedom of action, while the manager remains free to change his premises at will. Of course, decision premises need not be communicated explicitly. Managers indicate their beliefs—in effect their implicit decision premises—every time they communicate informally with their subordinates, by the words they use and their manner of expressing them: "The language used in an organization is a powerful weapon: it colours the perceptions of organization members affecting the decisions they make. We came across many examples of leaders systematically using value-laden words (sometimes even slogans) to steer the ambitions of their organization in the 'right' direction" (Rhenman 1973, p. 63). It is here—in the subtle use of communication to set decision premises—that we find the most evident manifestation of Selznick's (1957) notion of leadership as "infusing the organization with value."[2]

3.   *The reviewing of decisions:* The manager can delegate to a subordinate the power to make a specific decision, but then exercise his formal right to review that decision before it is turned into an action. This can be looked upon as a mild form of direct supervision: instead of giving a subordinate specific guidelines or premises within which to make the decision, the manager instead gives him wide latitude but then supervises the result. If a decision displeases him, he cancels or modifies it.

[2]Note that we exclude here decision premises that are formally specified standards, ones that cut across whole ranges of decisions—to use one of the above examples, that parts always be pastel. The specification of formal standards takes us into the bureaucratic control system, as we shall soon see.

4.   *The allocating of resources:* Finally, the manager may delegate power to make decisions fully but retain one final means of personal control: the setting of the resource constraints within which the consequences of all the subordinate's decisions must fall. The CEO, who formally controls the organization's resources, allocates them (typically in the form of budgets) to his subordinate managers who in turn allocate them to their subordinates and so on down the line of authority. This is a powerful means of personal control, for it enables the manager to determine arbitrarily whether a subordinate will have wide or narrow latitude in his decision making. Subordinates who comply with the manager's wishes can find themselves resource-rich and so rather unconstrained; those who do not may find themselves having to make all of their decisions within very tight resource constraints. Thus, as Boulding notes, the budget is perhaps "the most important" of the control mechanisms, the one "by which the upper members of a hierarchy seek to impose their will and image on the lower members" (1962, p. 183).

These four personal means of controlling subordinate activities—the giving of direct orders, the setting of decision premises, the reviewing of decisions, and the allocating of resources—together provide the manager with a good deal of arbitrary power to orient the decisions and actions of his unit in the directions he thinks appropriate.

THE BUREAUCRATIC CONTROL SYSTEM

In addition to a system of personal controls, the System of Authority also contains a *bureaucratic control system*. Here the managers do not arbitrarily impose their will on subordinates on ad hoc bases, for example, through the imposition of specific decisions. Rather, impersonal standards are established that guide the behavior of employees in general, across whole ranges of decisions (much as external influencers impose formal constraints instead of direct controls).

In principle, three kinds of standards may be formally imposed on employees: (1) the content of the work of an individual may be standardized through its formalization by rules, procedures, job descriptions, and the like; (2) the output or performance of the individual's work may be standardized through what are known as planning and control systems; and (3) the skills and knowledge that the individual brings to bear on his or her work may be standardized through the establishment of procedures for training and selection. The first provides for very close control of the activities of the individual by the System of Authority, and the second allows for some intermediate level of control. (But both, it should be remembered, are typically developed not by the managers but by the analysts of the technostructure—the accountants, work study engineers, planners, and so on.) In contrast, as we shall see, skill and knowledge standards are generally developed by professional schools and societies in training programs outside of the organization. As such, the organization dependent on such standards is forced to surrender a good deal of control over its employees to these institutions. For that reason we do not include this third form of standardization under the bureaucratic control system; indeed, its effect is to weaken that system. All three forms of standardization have been discussed at length in the *Structuring* book[3]; in this chapter we discuss only how the first two support the System of Authority in the Internal Coalition (and, in Chapter 12, how the third supports the System of Expertise).

THE STANDARDIZATION OF WORK CONTENT THROUGH BEHAVIOR FORMALIZATION
Bureaucratic standards of work content may be used in place of specific direct orders or decision premises to formalize *in general* the content of an individual's work, specifically what he must do and when. A worker on an assembly line is given standing orders, or else instructions are attached to each part that goes by, telling him exactly what he must do next. Such standards are relied upon where work is simple and repetitive (unskilled). They generally remove most of the decision-making discretion from the worker, passing control over the work to the designer of the standards, as noted earlier, typically an analyst in the technostructure.

THE STANDARDIZATION OF OUTPUTS THROUGH SYSTEMS OF PLANNING AND CONTROL   Where the work content itself cannot be specified, the organization may settle for a looser means of formal control. It may seek to standardize the output (or performance) of the work—the result if not the process. Specifically, a planning and control system is designed which specifies what outputs are expected of given individuals or units in given periods of time. Two types of planning and control systems may be delineated. The *action planning system* seeks to predetermine the results of specific decisions or actions before the fact, for example that new products be painted pastel or be introduced in September, that holes be drilled with a diameter of 2.000 ± 0.001 centimeters. Critical path scheduling and strategic planning are examples of action planning systems. The *performance control system* seeks to measure output after the fact and thereby to control the overall results of whole sets of decisions and actions, for example that manufacturing costs not exceed $200,000 per week or that the growth of the pastel paint division reach at least 5 percent each quarter.

It is in the performance control system that the formal goals of the organization are most directly operationalized, that is, expressed in terms of

[3]See Mintzberg 1979*a*, especially Chapters 1, 5, 6, and 9.

specific objectives, or quantitative measures. If the management wishes the organization to grow, for example, it may set high performance targets for the salespeople; if it favors profit, it will demand high return on investment from its divisions.

To operationalize its formal goals as completely as possible, the organization sometimes attempts to develop a full blown *hierarchy of objectives,* which is superimposed on its superstructure to ensure that every unit and perhaps even every position has quantified goals to pursue for each period of time. (A variant of this, in which subordinates can negotiate with their managers in the setting of these performance standards, is called Management by Objectives, or MBO. And the system that in part reports the results back up the chain of authority is called a Management Information System, or MIS.) In effect, just as the superstructure partitions the tasks of the organization, so does the hierarchy of objectives partition the formal goals of the organization. These goals—let us say growth and profit—are first converted into overall organizational objectives—say 15 percent sales growth and 20 percent return on investment for a given year. Each is then elaborated down the hierarchy into an ever widening set of more specific objectives—more operational, more short-run, and more constraining. The sales department may be asked to achieve quarterly sales of 10 million units and a market share of 35 percent, while the manufacturing department may be asked to reduce costs by $600,000 in a quarter. Near the bottom of the hierarchy, these objectives end up as a monthly sales increase of 80 units requested of a particular salesperson and a reduction of $800 in costs for the month for a particular plant foreman. Another example of such a hierarchy of objectives, in this case together with action plans, is shown in Figure 10–1, taken from Khandwalla's work. Such systems of objectives have been referred to as means-ends chains because, looking upward, each objective is the *means* to achieve some higher-level objective, while, looking downward, it is the end (or goal) for the objective that follows it.

The intention of the hierarchy of objectives—and of planning and control systems in general—is fundamentally the same as that of behavior formalization: to elaborate a set of standards that will integrate the behavior of the individual with the formal goals of the organization. In theory, with the system properly designed, should all units achieve their respective standards, the formal goals of the organization will be achieved. In other words, the organization is conceived to be a perfectly regulated system in which rationally designed means combine to achieve given ends.

But all is not what appears on paper. In Chapter 13 we shall note a number of ways in which the theory breaks down. What is of interest at this point, in the case of performance control systems in particular, is that the link between objective and behavior is not a direct one. On January 1, the manager of a unit may be handed his list of objectives for the next twelve months—an 8 percent growth in sales, a 5 percent reduction in costs, and so on. During the next twelve months he makes various decisions subject to all kinds of pressures—the options

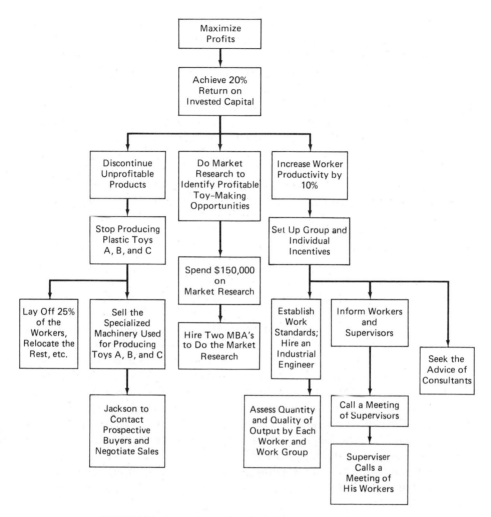

FIGURE 10-1. *A Hierarchy of Objectives and Actions (from Khandwalla, 1977, p. 376)*

available, the demands from customers and suppliers, not to mention the personal impositions of his superior, changes in technology and in personnel, the need to time his actions, and so on. When December 31 rolls around and his superior pulls out the objectives to see how he has done, the manager may have half forgotten about them. What decisions he made, and what performance he achieved, were in large part a function of what he was able to do on a day-to-day basis. In other words, the system of objectives notwithstanding, the line manager runs his unit on a day-to-day basis, in a stimulus-response environment. As noted in another book reprinted in this series, "The pressure of the managerial environment does not encourage the development of reflective planners, the classical literature notwithstanding. The job breeds adaptive information-manipulators who prefer the live, concrete situation" (Mintzberg 1973, p. 38).

Does this mean that the presence of objectives has no effect on a manager's behavior? Not at all. It means only that the effect is indirect, that the objectives sit in the back of the manager's mind during the year, as general standards against which he knows his performance will eventually be measured. Properly designed, these standards do help to orient his behavior, but implicitly, indirectly.

As such, systems of objectives are not only devices of measurement but also ones of *motivation*, establishing targets to direct behavior. There is in fact a considerable body of research, under the label "aspiration level theory," that seeks to explain the relationship between objectives and the effort expended to achieve them. Much of this research has been based on simplified decisions in the behavioral science laboratory, and is reviewed by a number of authors. It has been found, first of all, that just the presence of clear, specific targets (standards or objectives) influences the level of effort (Melcher 1976, p. 227). Second, the level at which the targets are set has been shown to influence behavior, effort declining when they are either too easy or too difficult to attain (Melcher, pp. 227 ff.; Stedry 1960). In effect, just as there is a perfect place to set the bar for each high jumper, so also would there seem to be some theoretically optimum profit target for each corporate division. Third, feedback is a factor, a necessary component to inform the individual of his performance vis-à-vis the standards (Melcher, pp. 229–32). Likewise, fourth, reinforcements or reward also influences effort. The more directly rewards are tied to performance, the more effective are the setting of standards in guiding behavior (Kast and Rosenzweig 1974, p. 183). And the longer the time lapse between behavior and reward or feedback, the less effective the setting of standards (Kast and Rosenzweig, p. 181). Khandwalla also notes, citing Skinner, that intermittent reinforcement tends to evoke the desired behavior more frequently than continuous reinforcement (1977, p. 99).

A fifth important factor is the previous level of attainment, success raising the level aspired to and failure decreasing it (Feldman and Kanter 1965, p. 633; Cyert and March 1963, p. 115). This leads to what has been referred to as the "crawling peg" (Eilon 1971) or "ratchet" phenomenon (Melcher 1976, p. 251), which management can use to exploit success: Each time an objective is approached, management raises it to be progressively more demanding. Sixth, targets set externally seem to lead to lower levels of performance than those set by the individual himself (Feldman and Kanter, p. 633). This presumably is what has attracted organizations to systems such as MBO, to involve the individual in the objective-setting process in order to secure commitment. And yet, seventh, it has also been found that the performance levels attained by referent individuals or organizations, such as competitors, influences the levels at which the targets are set. These typically lead to higher targets than would the simple application of past performance (Cyert and March, p. 115; Melcher, p. 252).

> One reason competition in athletics is so effective is that winning requires that one surpass the performance of the best existing competitor. This typically results in the standard of success becoming progressively more difficult with time. . . .The result is progressively better performance. (Locke, quoted in Melcher, p. 238)

A similar result would be expected in the case of competition between organizations, or, indeed, between units of the same organization. And note in terms of Khandwalla's point that the results of such competition are typically intermittent, not continuous, in all likelihood leading to a persistence of high aspiration behavior.

Thus the evidence from aspiration level research suggests what good performance targets, or objectives, are: ones that have clear, specific standards frequently but intermittently adjusted to optimum levels above current performance, developed in cooperation with those to whom they are to apply and in reference to related organizations, and with frequent feedback to these people and rewards tied to performance. For the management able to design such objectives, the performance control system is presumed to serve as an important tool to elicit effort by the internal influencers on behalf of the formal goals of the organization.

To conclude our discussion of the bureaucratic control system, we note that while the standards can sometimes be captured by nonmanagers, in essence they serve as prime means to secure and maintain the System of Authority of the organization, in particular to help operationalize the formal goals decided upon by the senior management.

THE FULL CHAIN OF AUTHORITY

This completes our discussion of the System of Authority. Figure 10–2 summarizes the full chain of authority we have been discussing, from those with formal power in the External Coalition—owners and perhaps the government which grants the organization's charter—through their representatives on the board of directors to the CEO as their trustee, and then on down the hierarchy of authority. The CEO sets in place a superstructure, this hierarchy of specialized units and positions to whose managers and workers he delegates formal power to make certain decisions and take certain actions. And then to try to ensure that delegated authority is used in the organization's interests—in other words, to effect an integration of individual needs with formal organizational goals, as defined by the senior management—the CEO and the other managers below him rely especially on the two control systems, one personal, the other bureaucratic, coupled with the system of rewards.

This whole System of Authority constitutes in the words of Allison (1971) the "rational actor" model of the organization. Concrete, tangible goals are fed in at the top and the whole organization is then consciously designed as a logically integrated chain of means and ends to accomplish them. All very neat

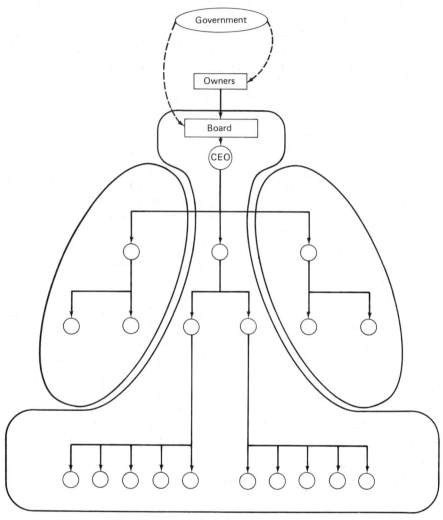

FIGURE 10-2. *The Full Chain of Authority*

and efficient. Unfortunately, however, less than half the picture. Glossed over are a number of tricky issues hidden in the assumptions, for example, that the external influencers manifest their power only through the CEO, that senior management is in fact able to express clear, unconflicting formal goals for the organization and then operationalize them through the control systems, that the CEO and managers of the middle line are able to maintain full command of the Internal Coalition, indeed even that they need to. In fact, other forces are alive in the Internal Coalition, some that knit it together in different ways, others that drive it apart, sometimes overriding and sometimes distorting the wishes expressed through the System of Authority. We now turn to these other kinds of systems in the Internal Coalition—informal ones.

11

The System of Ideology

As we have just seen, the System of Authority is the means by which the CEO and the managers to whom he or she delegates formal power seek to knit by conscious logical design the efforts of the various internal influencers into a unified, integrated effort. But there is another unifying force in the Internal Coalition—another means for control and coordination—although it is quite separate from the System of Authority. This is the *System of Ideology*. As a player in the Internal Coalition, ideology is distinguished by its ostensibly inanimate nature. Unlike the other players, it cannot be seen or touched. And so it is often forgotten in the literature, especially by those researchers and writers who insist on tangible measures for the phenomena they wish to consider. But to the observer who has come to know different organizations well, ideology clearly emerges as a potent force in many Internal Coalitions. The ideology "lives." And it infuses "life" into the organization.

Simple mathematics tells us that $2 + 2 = 4$. But general systems theory, under the concept *synergy,* suggests that it can also equal 5. A flashlight and batteries add up to so many pieces of hardware; together they form a working system. So also an organization is more than just the sum of its parts, more than a collection of people and machines. The behavior of the group cannot be predicted solely from an understanding of the personality of each of its members. Various social processes intervene. From some of these, the group develops a "mood," an "atmosphere"; it is said to have some kind of "chemistry." In the context of the organization, we talk of a "style," a "culture," a "character." One senses something unique when one walks into an office of IBM; the Canadian Broadcasting Corporation just does not feel like CBS or

NBC; the chemistry of the Harvard Business School is simply not the same as that of the MIT Sloan School, serving the same mission on the other side of the Charles River. It is all of these phenomena—intangible yet very real, over and above all of the concrete components of the organization—that we here refer to as *organizational ideology*. Specifically, organizational ideology is taken here to mean a system of beliefs about the organization, shared by its members, that distinguishes it from other organizations.[1]

The key feature of an ideology (the adjective "organizational" will be assumed from here on), for our purposes, is its unifying power. An ideology ties the individual to the organization; it generates an "esprit de corps," a "sense of mission," in effect, an integration of individual and organizational goals. Ideology gives rise to the third element in Hirschman's (1970) framework: It discourages exit and quells voice, instead encouraging "loyalty."

The development of an organizational ideology will be discussed here in three stages. The roots of the ideology are planted when a group of individuals band together around a leader and through a sense of mission to found an organization. The ideology then develops over time through the establishment of traditions. And finally, an existing ideology is reinforced through the identification of new members with the organization and its system of beliefs.

STAGE 1: THE ROOTING OF AN IDEOLOGY IN A SENSE OF MISSION

Typically an organization is founded when a single prime mover (an "entrepreneur") identifies a mission—some product to be produced or service to be rendered in a special way—and collects a group around him to accomplish it. Sometimes one organization is founded by another, as when a new agency is created by a government or a subsidiary by a corporation. But the basic ingredients remain the same—a founding leader, a unique mission to be accomplished, and the establishment of a group.

These individuals do not come together at random, but coalesce because they share some norms associated with the fledgling organization. At the very least they see something in it for themselves. But in some cases, in addition to the mission there is the "sense of mission," that is, a feeling that the group has banded together to create something new and exciting. This is common in new

[1]It is the focus of the beliefs on the organization, and its uniqueness, that is meant to distinguish *organization* ideology, by this definition, from ideology in general. The professionals of an organization may share an ideology—a strong system of beliefs—with their colleagues in other organizations; indeed, all the members of a given organization may share, say, a utilitarian ideology. But these are not organizational ideologies, that is, not ones focussed on the organization itself, that distinguish it from all other organizations. In the spirit of Kaplan (1964), that definitions are explained in the full text rather than in the sentence so labelled, this definition will be elaborated in this chapter and in Chapter 21.

organizations for a number of reasons. First, unbounded by procedure and tradition, new organizations offer wide latitude for maneuver. Second, they tend to be small, enabling the members to establish personal relationships. Third, the founding members often share some strong basic beliefs, perhaps a sense that they wish to work together. Fourth, a sense of "charisma" is often associated with the founder of a new organization. Charisma, as Weber used the term, means a sense of "personal devotion" to the leader for the sake of his personal qualities rather than his formal position (1969; p. 12). People join and remain with the organization because of a sense of dedication to the leader and what he seeks to accomplish. All of this contributes to the sense of mission, the esprit de corps established at the outset. Thus the roots of on organizational ideology are planted in the founding of the organization.

STAGE 2: THE DEVELOPMENT OF THE IDEOLOGY THROUGH TRADITIONS AND SAGAS

As the organization establishes itself, it makes decisions and takes actions which serve as commitments and establish precedents that reinforce themselves over time. Actions become infused with value. When these forces are strong enough, ideology begins to emerge. Furthermore, stories—sometimes called "myths"—develop around important events and the actions of great leaders in the organization's past. Gradually the organization develops a history of its own. All of this—the precedents, habits, myths, history—form a common data base of tradition which the members of the organization share. Over time, this tradition influences behavior, and that behavior in turn reinforces the tradition. Eventually, an ideology may become established.

As this happens, in Selznick's terms, the organization is converted from an expendible "instrument" for the accomplishment of externally imposed goals into an "institution," a system with a life of its own—". . . it acquires a self, a distinctive identity" (1957, p. 21). When organizations become institutions

> They take on a distinctive character; they become prized in and of themselves, not merely for the goods or services they grind out. People build their lives around them, identify with them, become dependent upon them. The process of institutionalization is the process of organic growth. . .(Perrow 1972a, p. 190, in reference to Selznick)

Perhaps the best illustration of this process in the research literature on organizations comes from Burton Clark's study of the "distinctive college" (1970, 1972). In discussing the strong ideologies of these institutions, Clark introduces the notion of an "organizational saga. . .a collective understanding of a unique accomplishment based on historical exploits. . . . Believers give loyalty to the organization and take pride and identity from it" (1972, p. 178).[2] The saga, "embellished through retelling and rewriting" links the organization's present with its past, and "turns a formal place into a beloved institution, to which participants may be passionately devoted" (p. 178).

Clark studied the organizational sagas of three "distinctive colleges"— highly regarded private, liberal arts colleges in the United States—Reed, Antioch, and Swarthmore. He distinguishes two stages in the development of the saga: initiation, which takes place during a short time, and fulfillment, which is more enduring. At Reed, initiation took the form of an autonomous new organization wherein its first president, "a high-minded reformer," could escape what he believed to be the "corrupt" Eastern universities; at Reed, he felt he could build "an academically pure college, Balliol for America" (p. 180). At Antioch, "a crisis of decay" caught "the attention of the reformer looking for opportunity" (p. 180), opportunity to change a system of beliefs. And in the case of Swarthmore, it was simply ready for evolutionary change by another new charismatic leader.

(It might be noted that while Clark finds the roots of the saga in the changes introduced by the charismatic leader, Rhenman [1973], who bases much of his study of organizations on the existence of ideologies, emphasizes the " one critical experience." For example, "The Development Company had what amounted to an internal calendar with two eras—'before' and 'after' The Conflict. This referred to a conflict with a large privately-owned company. The names of certain persons who had taken part in these events were still strongly emotive, although many of the present employees could never have known them personally," p. 63.)

While the conditions of initiation seemed to vary in these three institutions, those of the second stage, fulfillment, appeared to be more consistent. As Clark describes it, the leader initiates the changes, but these emerge in an organizational saga only if, once he is gone, the important members of the organization become committed to them, and conserve and perpetuate them. Three sets of members were involved in the distinctive colleges—the faculty, the students, and the external supporters (notably the alumni). The senior faculty, for example, "undertook the full working out of the experiment" (p. 181); the students supported the emergence of the saga when they defined "themselves as personally responsible for upholding the image of the college" (p. 182); and the alumni did the same when they sought "to conserve what they believe[d] to be a unique liberal institution and to protect it from the conservative forces of society that might change it—that is, to make it like other colleges" (p. 182).

The saga manifests itself in the form of various practices of the organization which stand out as unique, "that things had been done differently, and so

---

[2]Clark traces the word "saga" to medieval Iceland and Norseland, where it represented an account of achievement and events in the history of a person or group that deeply stirred the emotions of the participants and their descendents.

much against the mainstream, and often against imposing odds. . . ." Supporting such practices are various symbols and rituals, "invested with meaning." These are recorded in written histories and current catalogs, "even in an 'air about the place' " (all above quotes from Clark 172, p. 182). Finally, Clark notes that the organizational saga serves as a powerful force to integrate the goals of the individual with those of the institution:

> The most important characteristic and consequence of an organization saga is the capturing of allegiance, the committing of staff to the institution. Emotion is invested to the point where many participants significantly define themselves by the central theme of the organization. . . . Deep emotional investment binds participants as comrades in a cause. . . . An organizational saga turns an organization into a community, even a cult. (1970, p. 235)

STAGE 3: THE REINFORCEMENT OF THE IDEOLOGY THROUGH IDENTIFICATIONS

Our description to this point makes it clear that an individual entering an organization does not join a random collection of individuals but rather a living system with its own distinct history and tradition—its own ideology, whether weak or strong. He may come with his own preformulated goals, but there is little doubt that the ideology of the organization can weigh heavily on the behavior he will exhibit once inside of it. We say that the individual develops an *identification* with, or a *loyalty* to, the organization. This identification develops for a number of reasons—a natural attraction, the result of selection procedures, specific organizational attempts to evoke it, and the calculated cultivation of it by the individual.

NATURAL IDENTIFICATION   The simplest type of identification occurs when the new member gets attracted to the ideology of the organization he has joined —to use the vernacular, he gets "caught up" with it. As Daniel Webster pleaded the case before the U.S. Supreme Court in 1818 to recognize Dartmouth College —also "distinctive"—as a private corporation: "It is, sir, as I have said, a small college, and yet there are those who love it. . ." (quoted in Clark 1970, p. 3).

In his book, *Administrative Behavior*, Herbert Simon discusses a pointed example of two very different forms of identification: "Two soldiers sit in a trench opposite a machine-gun nest. One of them stays under cover. The other, at the cost of his life, destroys the machine-gun nest with a grenade. Which is rational?" (1957, p. 76). Obviously Simon's question is not meant to be answered. What can be said is that under the circumstances one individual opted for his personal goals while the other exhibited a strong identification with those of his organization. Simon goes on to develop the theme of identification. About natural identification, for which he uses the word "loyalty," Simon comments:

> ...almost all the members of an organization become imbued, to a greater or lesser degree, with the organization aim, and are influenced by it in their behavior. This has already been pointed out in the case of volunteer organizations; it is also true, although to a lesser extent, of governmental agencies and commercial organizations.... If the objective has any appearance of usefulness, the organization members, whose attention is continually directed to it by their everyday work, will acquire an appreciation of its importance and value (often an exaggerated appreciation), and the attainment of the value will come, to that extent, to have personal value for them. (p. 115)

Such behavior gets carried to the extreme in certain religious movements where, presumably because of the strength of their identification with the organization's mission, the members come to be known as "missionaries."

We have so far discussed natural identification as related to the organization's mission and goals. But as Simon notes (p. 205), a member of an organization may also identify with its leader, or even with the organization itself as an entity distinct from its purpose. Simon suggests that this last form of identification leads to very different behavior than does identification with mission or goals. In one case, the individual will support "opportunistic changes" in mission to enable the organization to survive and grow; in the other, he will resist them and may even leave to express his discontent:

> Some of the most striking manifestations of conflict between these two types of loyalty are to be found in religious and reform organizations, where there is often controversy as to the extent to which organization objectives shall be modified to insure survival. This was certainly one basis for the Stalinist-Trotskyist rivalry. (p. 118)

In one case the identification is ideological in nature—with the traditions, the system of beliefs; in the other the attachment appears to be more self serving—a belief in the organization as a system unto itself for what it can offer.

SELECTED IDENTIFICATION: RECRUITMENT AND PROMOTION   Many organizations cannot rely solely on identification that develops naturally. Their needs for loyalty are too great. And so they must take steps to influence the process of identification. This is most obviously done in the selection process: The organization chooses job candidates not only for their ability to do the work, but also for the match of their values with its ideology. As is so often heard, "Will he fit in here?" Recruiting becomes a device to reinforce identification with the organization's ideology.

But selection is a two-sided process, and just as the organization is careful to select the right candidates, so too are the candidates careful to select the right organization. They do not arrive at random, nor solely to negotiate material inducements for their contributions. "As Schallschneider has written, the members of the American League to Abolish Capital Punishment are not active in that group's work because they expect to be hanged" (Lindblom 1965, p. 224). People often seek to join organizations because they already identify with the ideologies they perceive to exist there. Thus at Antioch College, Clark reports that "Public image...grew strong and sharp, directing liberals and radicals to the college and conservatives to other places" (1972, p. 183).

The initial job interview often serves as the screening device for both parties; this is followed by an implicit or explicit trial period during which the graft of the new individual onto the existing organization is tested. Where it does not take, the individual is rejected (or leaves voluntarily), as is foreign tissue from the human body.

Those who stay may enter into a new phase of selection, that for positions in the hierarchy. When an organization's ideology is strong, it is those most committed to it who rise, because such organizations can afford to have only the most ideologically committed in positions of formal power. This applies increasingly as one climbs the hierarchy so that at the top, the chief executive tends to exhibit the strongest identification with the organization's ideology. The CEO is the person, as noted earlier, who "embodies" the ideology.

EVOKED IDENTIFICATION: SOCIALIZATION AND INDOCTRINATION   In many cases, natural and selected identification do not satisfy the organization's needs for loyalty. Also because the decisions to join and to leave an organization are, in Soelberg's words, "nonsymmetrical"—that is, people "will be predisposed toward staying with whatever organizations they have chosen to work for" (1967, p. 28)—they often stay despite an absence of natural or selected identification with the organization. The organization may, therefore, try to *evoke* the necessary identification, and at the same time to reduce outside identifications that might interfere with the employee's ability to serve it. In this regard, two processes can be relied upon, an explicit one called *indoctrination* and an implicit one called *socialization*.

The term *indoctrination* encompasses that set of formal techniques used by organization to develop identifications on the part of their members. Indoctrination can take extreme forms, as in the use of "brainwashing" by the Chinese forces during the Korean War to break the resistance of captured American pilots and get them to identify with Communist ideology. But most techniques of indoctrination are less extreme, if not always less subtle:

> Beatrice [Foods Corporation] tries to keep its managers fired up by what might be called "cheerleading." Each of the fourteen divisions holds a convention every year, and the company uses these occasions to pump enthusiasm and pride into its managers. At a recent dairy-division meeting in Nashville, 700 employees joined lustily in the chorus of a song led from the podium. "We're Number One," they

sang, thrusting their fingers into the air. The theme of the convention, registered in the placards, banners, and speeches, as well as the song, was "Number One," i.e., Beatrice now makes more money than any other food processor. (Martin 1976, p. 126)

Organizations in need of strong loyalty—for example, those whose members are sent off alone to distant, difficult assignments, as in certain religious orders, spy agencies, and police forces—put their new recruits through extensive courses where they learn not only skills and knowledge but also ideology. Many business firms also use programs of indoctrination: They, too, require loyalty, but their utilitarian nature often impedes its natural development. Few rely on "lusty" choruses of "We're Number One," but many publish internal magazines, stage retreats, distribute company ties, publicize their credos, hand out gold watches for long service. Large corporations make extensive use of job rotation, which some writers see as a means of uprooting local identifications in place of ones with the corporation. Long, for example, refers to "branch plants run by bureaucratic birds of passage with career lines stretching onward and upward to the magic haven of the head office" (1960, p. 203). And Bower notes the case of the Montgomery Ward store manager who moved twenty-six times in twenty-eight years, "only an extreme example of a common phenomenon" which "drastically weakens the ties of a man to his community" (1974, p. 203).

Socialization is an implicit, and therefore more subtle, means of evoking identification. As such, however, it may ultimately be more powerful. The individual is subjected to a host of informal pressures, all of which carry one message: "Conform to the ideology." Gradually the values of the organization "become 'internalized' and are incorporated into the psychology and attitudes of the individual participant. He acquires an attachment or loyalty to the organization that automatically—i.e., without the necessity for external stimuli—guarantees that his decisions will be consistent with the organization objectives"; in this way, he "acquires an 'organization personality' rather distinct from his personality as an individual" (Simon 1957, p. 198).

In the 1969 Douglas McGregor Memorial Lecture at MIT, Edgar Schein (1968) spoke on the topic of Organizational Socialization. He described it as focussing "clearly on the interaction between a stable social system and the new members who enter it" (p. 3). As the price of membership, the member learns the values, norms, and required behavior patterns of the group he is about to enter. During the process of socialization, the individual acquires this new learning from "the official literature of the organization; the example set by key models in the organization; the instructions given to him directly by his trainer, coach, or boss; the example of peers who have been in the organization longer and thus serve as big brothers; the rewards and punishments which result from his own efforts at problem solving and experimenting with new values and new behavior" (p. 6).

CALCULATED IDENTIFICATION   But what of the individual who runs the gauntlet of all these forms of identification and remains at the end firmly committed to his own goals? He has no natural identification with the organization, its mission, or its leadership; somehow he successfully passed all of the selection procedures; and he has been able to resist all of the pressures of indoctrination and socialization. He remains a private person, self-serving to the core. Must we assume that his personal interests put this person into opposition with the organization's established ideology? Not at all. This may be the very person who finds that his self-interest can best be served by an identification—albeit a calculated and therefore fragile one—with the organization's ideology. In other words, it may be in his very best interests to accept the organization's ideology.

Our explanation for this proceeds on the assumption that the individual acts purely on his own—that he enters the organization with no special outside identifications, no particular external influencers to whom he is committed, and no special goal system to champion, save that of serving of himself. We also assume him to be the rubber man, bending to any force that will serve his own needs. For a number of reasons, it is to this person's advantage to work with the system instead of against it, to cooperate with it and act in accordance with its ideology. For one thing, cooperation is much easier than rebellion. Rebellion takes effort, arouses anger, and leads to conflict, from which everyone can come out worse. In contrast, it often pays to cooperate.

Mary Parket Follett (1942) suggests that disagreements can be settled in three basic ways—by domination, where one party imposes its will on the others; by compromise, where each party gives up a little to reach agreement; and by integration, where the parties invent a solution that better accommodates all of them. She obviously favors the last approach, arguing in effect that few real-world games are zero-sum. Crozier mentions this theme of cooperation as well, outlining three general reasons why the members of the industrial monopoly he studied chose to cooperate with each other. First, they had to "live with each other...a minimum of harmony and good fellowship [had to] be maintained." Second, their privileges were "interdependent"—everyone knew, without saying it openly, that "their privileges depend[ed] to quite an extent on the privileges of the other groups and that an attack upon another group [could] endanger the whole system and indirectly, the special interest of the attacking group." And third, there had to be "general agreement of all groups about what constitute[d] a reasonable degree of efficiency" (1964, pp. 167–69).

Another reason for the self-serving employee to cooperate is that organizations, as noted earlier, have a propensity to promote to higher positions those who demonstrate strong commitment to their ideologies. Berlson and Steiner (1964, p. 376), to support this relationship, cite evidence linking American soldiers' scores on a "conformity scale" with their subsequent promotions during World War II. Of the Privates First Class (PFC), 27 percent scoring high were promoted to Non Commissioned Officer(NCO) within four months versus 13 percent of those scoring low; for the promotion from private to NCO, the respective figures were 31 percent and 17 percent, while for that from private to PFC, the figures (in this case after six months) were 87 percent and 62 percent. Even for the employee who does not get promoted, if his organization is on the move, he is likely to be as well:

> Many of [his] personal values are dependent not only on his connection with the organization, but also on the growth, the prestige, or the success of the organization itself....Growth of the organization offers to him...salary increases, advancement, and opportunity to exercise responsibility. (Simon 1957, p. 209)

The organization's success becomes its member's success. Thus the employee wishing to get ahead often finds it in his best interest to accept the organization's ideology.

Calculated identification need not, however, be as Machiavellian as all that. Every person interested in his own welfare has all kinds of obvious reasons to cooperate with the organization that employs him. He may simply get pleasure from his work and so wish to support the system that provides him with it; he may get psychological rewards from belonging to a social group; he may take pride in the success and reputation of the organization and the fact that his work contributes to those ends. In the distinctive college, participation meant "pride in one's identity," a reduction in the members' "sense of isolation" and an increase in their "pleasure in organizational life" (Clark 1972, p. 183).

Thus, for any employee, the organization can be a convenient place to satisfy his needs for belonging, status, and self-actualization. After all, the organization is not just another part of his life; it is the place where he spends one-third of his waking hours. Thus, he has an obvious propensity to cooperate with it, and to identify with its ideology.

To summarize this discussion, Figure 11–1 shows a continuum of various means of integrating individual and organizational goals. Natural identification is the strongest of these means, as it requires no organizational effort to achieve the desired integration. Selection is next strongest, since once the identification is discovered, it, too, requires no further effort. Evoked identification stands in the middle, requiring socialization and indoctrination. Calculated identification is clearly the weakest of the forms of loyalty, and differs from the others in that the identification is not really internalized by the individual. He identifies with the organization only because—and only so long as—it is in his best interests to do so. His identification, being calculated, is fragile. Whereas the truly indoctrinated or socialized member, or the one who identifies in a natural way with the organization, has a greater propensity to stay with the organization through hard times—to exhibit a strong loyalty—the member whose identification is calculated will be more fickle. But the individual who calculates his identification is also different from the one who contributes his efforts in return for inducements, subject to the authority of the control systems. And so this form of integrating individual and organizational goals is shown on the weak end of the

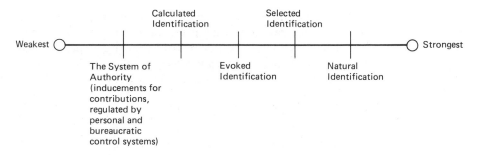

FIGURE 11-1. *A Continuum of the Means of Integrating Individual and Organizational Goals*

continuum. In both these last cases, the members calculate their involvement. But the one who remains only because of the inducements he receives is totally passive about the organization's ideology. He identifies with nothing organizational; the relationship is purely contractual—work for pay. Calculated identification, in contrast, is also psychological: It involves some emotional commitment to the organization beyond remuneration, small and fragile but present nevertheless.

In concluding this discussion of ideology as a player in the Internal Coalition, it should be noted that while some degree of ideology can be found in virtually every organization, that degree can vary considerably. At one extreme are those organizations, such as religious orders or radical political movements, whose ideologies are very strong and whose identifications are primarily natural and selected. Edwards (1977) refers to organizations with strong ideologies as "stylistically rich," Selznick (1957) as "institutions." It is the presence of such an ideology that enables an organization to have "a life of its own," to emerge as "a living social institution" (Selznick 1949, p. 10). At the other extreme are those organizations with relatively weak ideologies, "stylistically barren," in many cases business organizations with strongly utilitarian reward systems. History and tradition have no special value in these organizations. In the absence of natural forms of identification on the part of their members, these organizations sometimes try to rely on the process of indoctrination to integrate individual and organizational goals. But usually they have to fall back on calculated identifications and especially the formal controls contained in the System of Authority.

One final point. What is the influence of a strong ideology on the power distribution in the Internal Coalition? The answer has been implied in our discussion of this chapter, and will be dealt with at length in a later chapter. Here we need only note two effects, both of which stem from the fact that when an ideology is strong, the members identify naturally with the organization and the goals it has traditionally pursued, what we shall call its *ideological goals*. And in so doing, they subjugate their private interests to those of the organization as a system. The first consequence of this is that other means to control behavior are unnecessary, as are the various means to attain personal power. In other words, **when the System of Ideology is strong, the Systems of Authority, Expertise, and Politics tend to be weak.** And second, a strong ideology has a strong levelling effect on power in the Internal Coalition. Since everyone shares the same set of beliefs, everyone can be trusted equally to make decisions. At the limit there are no higher and lower status members, only those who accept the ideology (and stay) versus those who do not (and so leave). Under a strong ideology, **power in the Internal Coalition tends to become rather evenly distributed.**

We have now discussed, in the last two chapters, a number of means by which individual and organizational goals can be integrated. These include, primarily, two systems of control rooted in the System of Authority, and the System of Ideology, which exists quite apart from the System of Authority. One system leads to a set of formal goals for the organization, the other to a set of ideological goals for it. Both tie the individual to the organization, and so encourage the Internal Coalition to function as one integrated entity. But there are two other major forces in the Internal Coalition, which typically have very different effects on its members.

12

The System of Expertise

In the last two chapters, we have been discussing two systems of influence that serve to knit together, or integrate, the efforts of the insiders to accomplish the organization's goals and mission. Were these two systems complete in their capacity to determine behavior, our description of the Internal Coalition would be over. But they are not. In two important ways they are inadequate, giving rise to two other systems in the Internal Coalition, each of which allows the insiders considerable discretion in the execution of their tasks and so can result in tendencies toward *dis*integration in the Internal Coalition. First, needs for coordination over and above that supplied by the Systems of Authority and Ideology give rise to a system based on the expertise of the insider. And second, imperfections and inadequacies in all of the internal systems of influence—but especially that of Authority—leave considerable discretion in the hands of the internal influencers, opening up the way for the play of informal power of a more clandestine nature—"political" power. We take up the System of Expertise in this chapter and the System of Politics in the next.

THE POWER OF EXPERTISE

Work in an organization that is complex cannot be coordinated or controlled in any of the ways already discussed. Its content cannot be standardized directly by formalization nor its outputs standarized in formal planning and control systems. In other words, bureaucratic controls will not work. Nor will personal ones—coordination through forms of direct supervision by managers—because to be complex means that the work cannot easily be understood or controlled by those who do not actually do it. Moreover, the ideological forms of coordination and control—essentially the standardization of norms through socialization and indoctrination—are likewise inadequate, for they too are suited only to handling the more simple forms of coordination. So the organization must find some other means to coordinate the work.

Specifically, faced with having to accomplish complex work, the organization must engage people who have been highly trained to do it. In other words, it must hire "experts" or "professionals." In essence, a professional is someone in whom the capacity to carry out some complex, specialized work has been internalized through extensive training. His specific activities are not dictated by technocratic rules; rather, all of his tasks are guided by internalized procedures, or "programs," accompanied by a body of specialized knowledge, learned before he took his first job and subsequently applied in his professional work.

Now because the formal training of the professional is a long and arduous business, it is usually beyond the capacity of the organization. Therefore the responsibility for it falls on professional societies and training institutions, often universities. And so the organization gets the capabilities it needs by selecting individuals trained by these institutions, but at a high price: it surrenders to these professional institutions the power to train and even in large part to select its employees—ultimately the power to program their work. The hospital, for example, does not provide for or even design most of the formal training activities of its physicians. Even the less formal, practical training that takes place on its own premises is in significant part controlled by the professional societies and universities. And while the hospital has some say in the recruiting of its physicians, it is forced to choose from the small pool of candidates already selected by the universities which trained them.

Moreover, because their work is complex, professionals or experts themselves must be allowed considerable discretion in performing it. In other words, the work must come under the direct control of those with the knowledge and skill to do it. So the organization—and when we use that term in this context, we really mean the System of Authority controlled by the administrators—must surrender even more of its power to its professional employees themselves. In other words, an informal *System of Expertise* emerges to draw power away from that of formal authority.

Professionals can coordinate work among themselves in two ways. First, where the application of their work is rather standardized—in other words, where the professionals apply their internalized programs in rather routine fashion—coordination can be achieved simply by virtue of their knowledge of each others' skills. For example, the surgeon coordinates with the anesthesiologist largely through the fact that each knows what to expect of the other. The two have been seen to perform a five-hour open heart operation without exchanging hardly a single word (Gosselin, 1978). Their coordination is effected automatically, through what we have called the "standardization of skills." And that allows each professional to work rather autonomously, relatively free of the direct influences of his colleagues. We have referred to the structural configuration of organizations that rely on such coordination as Professional Bureaucracy, because of the standardized nature of the professional programs in their operating cores.

Second, where the professionals apply their knowledge and skills in nonstandard ways, in order to innovate, they must typically combine their expertise by working in small groups, and so must coordinate informally—by what we have called "mutual adjustment." The structure of organizations composed of such groups is looser, more organic, less bureaucratic, forming a configuration we have called Adhocracy.[1]

When an organization has to grant considerable discretion in the performance of its work to experts or professionals—whether they work autonomously or in small groups—and has to surrender power over their selection and training to professional institutions, its System of Authority is significantly weakened. In other words, power resides less in the formal systems of the administrators—less in the personal controls of the line managers or in the bureaucratic controls of the staff analysts—and more in the informal bases of influence of the specialists—in expertise based on specialized knowledge and skills. Specifically, it is the skilled operators and support staffers who typically stand to gain the most from the System of Expertise, at the expense of the managers of the middle line and the analysts of the technostructure who might otherwise control their work directly.

Likewise the System of Ideology is weakened, since power in expertise means power in the hands of individuals or small groups as distinct from power in some characteristics of the organization at large. Whereas the essence of ideology is the *equalization* of power throughout the organization—everyone shares the same belief system and acts in accordance with it—the essence of expertise is the *differentiation* of power—power distributed according to specialized capability. Central to the System of Expertise is the notion of the pecking order—not only between expert and nonexpert, but also among different kinds of experts according to the complexity of their particular specialities and even among different experts of the same specialty according to their personal skills in performing it. Thus, by its generation of all kinds of status differences in the Internal Coalition, the System of Expertise conflicts fundamentally with the System of Ideology.

As a result, the System of Expertise can emerge as a system unto itself, relatively free of the impingements of authority or ideology. So too, as we shall

---

[1]Those points about the two basic forms of coordinating professional work and the two resulting structural configurations are developed at length in the *Structuring* book (see Mintzberg 1979a, chaps. 19 and 21).

see more clearly in subsequent chapters, while it serves in one sense to coordinate work in the organization, the System of Expertise can also serve as a force for disintegration—for the pursuit of the goals of the individual or the small group in opposition to those of the organization at large.

THE NOTION OF CRITICAL FUNCTION

We have seen that expertise is one condition for power in the Internal Coalition. But it is not a sufficient one. The staff physician, to take a silly example, has no great power in the accounting firm, nor, for that matter, to take a more realistic example, does the staff accountant in the hospital. For an individual to acquire power, his expertise must also be *critical* to the successful functioning of the organization. The organization must be dependent on some body of knowledge or some core of skills that the individual possesses.

What makes a function critical in an organization? Gouldner (1959, p. 419-20) suggests that certain functions are inherently critical—for example, manufacturing as opposed to public relations in a business firm. The latter is dispensable in times of crises; the former is not. Such functions are critical because "their cessation would quickly and substantially impede a major work flow in the organization" (Hickson et al. 1971, pp. 221-22). Kanter associates the critical function with whatever "the organization finds currently problematic: sales and marketing people when markets are competitive; production experts when materials are scarce and demand is high; personnel or labor relations specialists when labor is scarce; lawyers, lobbyists, and external relations specialists when government regulations impinge; finance and accounting types when business is bad and money tight" (1977, pp. 170-71). As Kanter's examples suggest, sometimes a function is critical because it alone can access resources that are scarce. In a study of the University of Illinois, which at the time received 40 percent of its budget from government grants and research contracts, Salancik and Pfeffer (1974) found that the best predictor of the power of an academic department was its ability to raise such outside funds. Finally, Kanter notes that the ability to introduce major change can also be a critical function: "The rewards go to the innovators"—the first ones in new positions, those who make changes in the organization, those who take major risks and succeed. "Pulling off extraordinary risks was . . . power-enhancing . . . Very few people dared, but those who did became very powerful" (pp. 177, 179). Thus McCall asked a young manufacturing executive with a great deal of power in a large firm what was the key to his success: "'I love messes.' He had moved rapidly from one part of the organization to another, solving problems as he went. . . . he became an expert at fixing messes and gained more and more power" (1979, p. 192).

Of course, if a function such as manufacturing, or even fixing messes, is critical, but its tasks are so simple that anyone can understand and do them, then little power accrues to whomever performs them. In formal terms, that person is "substitutable." To be critical the function must require some rare and specialized expertise. Thus, while Crozier notes that by virtue of the division of labor, "every member of an organization is an expert in his own way" (1964, p. 163), only those who provide an expertise difficult to replace gain power. That is why Kanter found power flowing to the successful risk taker, the one who accomplished what few others were willing to do. She contrasts this person with those who did "the ordinary and the expected." Even if they did it very well, they got no "credit" for it and were rendered powerless (1977, p. 177).

Often it is the highly skilled operator who performs a function that is critical and cannot easily be substituted, because of skills that took years to develop. Combining such criticality and nonsubstitutability with the considerable discretion such specialists require results in the accrual of considerable power to them. Thus Crozier describes the maintenance men in the French tobacco factories, whom he saw as the guardians of the last remaining bit of discretion in a highly bureaucratic workplace:

> ...machine stoppages are the only major happenings that cannot be predicted and to which impersonal rulings cannot apply. ...the people who are in charge of maintenance and repair are the only ones who can cope with machine stoppage. They cannot be overseen by anyone in the shop. No one can understand what they are doing and check on them.
>
> With machine stoppages, a general uncertainty about what will happen next develops in a world totally dominated by the value of security. It is not surprising, therefore, that the behavior of the maintenance man—the man who alone can handle the situation, and who by preventing these unpleasant consequences gives workers the necessary security—has a tremendous importance for production workers, and that they try to please him and he to influence them. From this state of affairs, a power relationship develops....
>
> Supervisors cannot check on maintenance. They may be competent in the various aspects of their work, but their competence does not extend to the only problem about which the workers care, because only its outcome is uncertain. A supervisor cannot reprimand the mechanics who work in his shop. There is likely to be a perpetual fight for control, and the supervisors will usually be the losers. (1964, p. 109)

In a major study of power in the Internal Coalition, Hickson, Hinings, and their colleagues sought to operationalize a number of the concepts we have been discussing here, but in the context of functional units rather than individual experts. They studied three branch breweries in Western Canada and two breweries in the Midwest United States, as well as two semi-autonomous divisions of a Canadian container company (Hinings et al. 1974; see also Hickson et al. 1971). In each organization, the sample consisted of four units—engineering, marketing, production, and accounting.[2] The researchers began with "prolonged exploratory interviews" with the chief executives and department heads, and followed these up with "semi-structured but open-ended interviews" in all of the organizations, as well as a questionnaire on perceptions of facts completed by each of the unit managers (p. 24). Hinings et al. made some formative attempts to operationalize a number of the dimensions of power, as follows:

* *Substitutability* was measured by the perception of "how easy or difficult it was to obtain personnel"; data collected for "actual substitutability" included, among other measures, the level of formal education required for the job, the rank of expertise and training required, and the number of tasks contracted out; for "hypothetical substitutability," the measures included whether particular tasks could be done by other members of the same department, of other departments, or by groups outside the organization.

* *Workflow pervasiveness* reflected "the degree to which the workflows of a subunit are linked to the workflows of other subunits" (p. 26); the researchers collected data on where and how frequently inputs came from and outputs went to.

* *Workflow immediacy* reflected "the speed and severity with which the workflow of a subunit affects the final output of the organization" (p. 27); this was measured by classifying the effect of every output as immediate (within a few weeks), long run (within a few months), or nil.

* *Uncertainty* meant "a lack of information about future events" (p. 27); a scale was devised and applied to the inputs for each unit; the resulting range was "from an accounting department facing no uncertainty, to a marketing department facing frequent variations in various aspects of demand, such as market share, volume and order mix" (p. 28).

* *Coping* was "defined as effectively dealing with uncertainties," which the researchers believed a unit could do in three ways—by preventing it, forecasting it, or dealing with it when it occurred (which they called "absorption"); a measure was devised related to the number of coping items for each unit, and this was then related to the amount of uncertainty in the unit.

* *Routinization,* "the process of rationalization and proceduralization" (p. 30), was the only variable represented by questionnaire data alone, with questions covering the existence of stable, set procedures to do the work.

* *Power* itself was defined as "the determination of the behavior of one social unit by another" (p. 30); due to controversy over the measurement of power, a "multimethod, multimeasure strategy" was used, unit power being assessed: in interviews and through questionnaires; by chief executives and unit managers (of their own and other units' power: "the accounts tallied overwhelm-

---

[2]The two container divisions shared common engineering and accounting services. These were included twice in the research, once for each division, thus making a total of twenty-eight units.

ingly," p. 31); about formal or position power and participative power in decision making and action taking; and in more concrete terms (how much power
in each of seventeen of the most central and frequent problem areas encountered
in the organization) as well as in broader terms (on a five-point scale, "How
much influence do you think each of the following departments has on problems about [issue X]?").

The researchers were rather successful in their measures, only two of the
variables not correlating positively with power.[3] Coping scored the highest,
followed by immediacy, nonsubstitutability, and pervasiveness in that order.

The researchers then analyzed the interrelationships among the variables.
Their analysis was complicated, but essentially Hinings et al. found five recurring power profiles, which explained the power rankings of twenty-four of the
twenty-eight units studied. Units in the most powerful profile recorded top scores
on *all* of the variables. Those scoring in the second most powerful profile received a high score only on coping with uncertainty. Thus, all of the units falling into the first or second power profile scored high (first or second) on their
ability to cope with uncertainty; *none* of the other units did. The third profile
showed high nonsubstitutability alone, while the fifth showed high pervasiveness alone. Apparently a significant power position requires more than just being difficult to replace or tightly linked to other units. Above all it requires having
some kind of expertise to cope with uncertainty. (The fourth profile was a weak
pattern with lower coping than the most powerful unit, not compensated for
by the other variables.)

Although the specific context of their research must be borne in mind,
Hinings et al.'s comments about some of the units in question are of interest.
In general, the production units of these firms were powerful and the accounting units weak. Marketing units rivaled those of production in the container
firms, because production was dependent on them to write orders before they
could act and also because marketing influenced the design of each order. In
the breweries, where production was not to order and where the marketing staff
lacked the technical training required of the brewers, the marketing departments
had less power. Accounting generally ranked low in power because it took no
action on all the reports it developed and "hence influenced no one" (p. 39).
Hinings et al. conclude their analysis with advice on two routes for the power
seeker, as shown in Figure 12–1:

> For dominant power, take advantage of immediacy, reduce your substitutability,
> and then make a bid for a decisive area of uncertainty; or alternatively, first go

---

[3]These were perceived procedures (nonroutinization) and perceived uncertainty. The researchers
believed the questions they used were too broad for such complex phenomena. Note that the correlations for the different variables were rather consistent across all nine measures of power. Finally,
except for workflow pervasiveness, the correlations for the nonquestionnaire data were higher than
those for the data of the questionnaires.

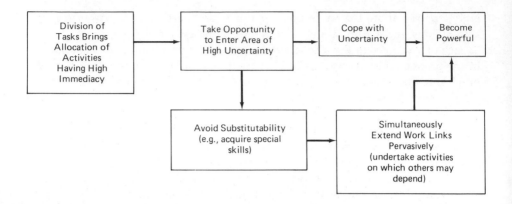

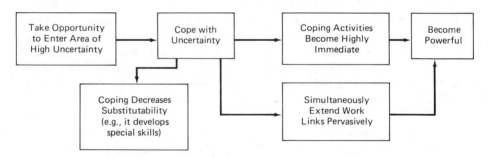

Figure 12-1. *Two Routes to Power in the Internal Coalition (from Hinings, et al, 1974)*

for the vital high coping with uncertainty, though this carries a risk of being left frustrated in second place unable to increase immediacy and decrease substitutability sufficiently to become first-rank, but don't get involved in a network of interaction links before you can dominate it. (pp. 40–41)[4]

More simply, to conclude in terms of the two central themes of this chapter, **power in the organization is bestowed on those who find a critical function in which to practice their irreplicable expertise.**

[4]Hinings et al.'s efforts to study power in this quantitative way were criticized by Crozier and Friedberg in their book *L'acteur et le système* (perhaps in response to their earlier criticisms of Crozier's work, in Hickson et. al. 1971, pp. 219–20, 224, and 225). Arguing that because a source of uncertainty exists and becomes important only when an actor, by virtue of his investment, exploits it to pursue his strategies, they add in a footnote: "That is why qualitative analysis will always take the lead over quantification in such a perspective. That is what also renders the approach of David Hickson and his colleagues very open to criticism" (1977, p. 72; this and subsequent passages from the Crozier and Friedberg book are my translations from the French).

13

The System of Politics

So far the insiders of the organization have been rather obedient, contributing diligently toward the needs of the organization at large. They have accepted the System of Authority and contributed to the formal goals defined for the organization by its senior management. Or else they have identified with the ideology of the organization and pursued its ideological goals vigorously. And even if they did neither, but instead worked as experts subject to the standards of their professional training, the effect was still to serve the organization, since that is the basic purpose of their expertise. In other words, insiders who work strictly within the confines of the Systems of Authority, Ideology, or Expertise are in effect contributing directly to the needs of the organization at large.

But the insiders are not always so obedient. They are influencers, too, with their own needs to fulfill, not just inert devices for accomplishing broader organizational needs. Moreover, being insiders, they are special influencers—the ones to whom is delegated the power to make the decisions and take the actions that create the outcomes. To the managers of the middle line is delegated formal power to make many of the decisions. To the analysts of the technostructure goes the power to design the systems of bureaucratic control which regulate everybody else's behavior, while to the support staffers goes the power to perform specialized services and to advise managers precisely where they are least informed. And to the operators is delegated, at the very least, the power to execute managerial decisions. In delegation is discretion. And discretion opens the way to the play of another, special kind of power, political power. A *System of Politics* arises in the Internal Coalition.

What exactly do we mean by "politics"? In our scheme of things, both authority and ideology serve to integrate the activities of the insiders, to achieve coordination and consensus. As such, these may be called "organizational" phenomena. They sanction behavior for the common good, though through two very different forms of consensus. The consensus of authority is formal and passive: The members accept the power of office as legitimate and respond to its demands. That of ideology is informal but active: The members positively identify with the norms and traditions of the organization and act in accordance with them, even though, strictly speaking, these are outside the System of Authority (and therefore informal). And the power of ideology is essentially legitimate as well: The sharing of a single set of beliefs by all the insiders makes it so. Expertise does not achieve a consensus per se, but, as noted above, it does serve as a device to coordinate and get the work of the organization done. In fact, the expertise is sanctioned by formal authority even though it operates outside of it. In that sense, power lodged in the System of Expertise is, though informal, also legitimate. Politics, in contrast to these, usually means three things:

1. Behavior outside of the legitimate systems of influence (or at least outside their legitimate uses), and often in opposition to them, in other words, behavior that is technically illegitimate, and often clandestine

2. Behavior designed to benefit the individual or group, ostensibly at the expense of the organization at large, (although, as we shall soon see, not always)

3. As a result of points 1 and 2, behavior typically divisive or conflictive in nature, pitting individuals or groups against the organization at large, or against each other

Distilled to its essence, therefore, **politics refers to individual or group behavior that is informal, ostensibly parochial, typically divisive, and above all, in the technical sense, illegitimate—sanctioned neither by formal authority, accepted ideology, nor certified expertise (though it may exploit any one of these).** The System of Politics arises either by default, in the weakness of the other three systems of influence, or by design, to resist (or in some cases to exploit) them. Thus, in contrast to "a highly co-ordinated organization," under politics we find "An alternative conception...that of the [organization] as a mass of competing power groups, each seeking to influence [organizational] policy in terms of its own interests, or, at least, in terms of its own distorted image of the [organization's] interest" (Strauss 1964, pp. 148, 137). As shown symbolically in Figure 13-1, formal power flowing down the chain of authority (or ideological or expert power flowing throughout the organization) gets blocked or sidetracked—in the formal terms of organization theory, it gets *displaced*. In its place is substituted political power, in the form of a set of what we shall call *political games* that the insiders play with each other—unofficial,

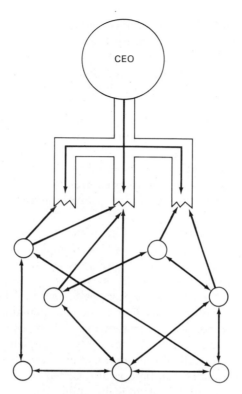

Figure 13-1. *The Displacement of Legitimate Power by Politics*

nonsanctioned processes by which inside influencers seek to satisfy ostensibly parochial needs.

We discuss the System of Politics in this chapter in three parts. First we find out why political games arise in the Internal Coalition—why formal, ideological, or expert power gets displaced. Then we take a look at the equipment these games are played with—the political means of influence. Finally, we look at a number of the games themselves, and then, to close, consider them in the context of legitimate power.

WHY PLAY POLITICS?
THE DISPLACEMENT
OF LEGITIMATE POWER

We have seen that a System of Politics arises in the Internal Coalition to "displace" legitimate power. This system would seem to arise in the presence of (a) problems or gaps in the other systems of influence, and (b) influencer needs not satisfied within these systems. The problems and gaps give rise to discretion in work, and unsatisfied needs stand ready to exploit that discretion. We shall discuss here six basic reasons for the displacement of legitimate power by politics, all of which were mentioned in passing in our Chapter 9 discussion of the internal influencers. The first two describe common problems in the System of Authority—distortions in the system of objectives and in the design of the superstructure. Ironically, we shall see that it is in the very design of these elements of the System of Authority—indeed, sometimes even in the complete absence of parochial insider needs—that the power of authority gets displaced. And the last four describe the sources of parochial insider needs, some of them exclusively personal, others abetted by the Systems of Authority or Expertise—job characteristics, group pressures, direct links to external influencers, and the intrinsic needs of the insiders themselves.

1. DISTORTIONS IN OBJECTIVES   One major purpose of the system of bureaucratic controls is to operationalize the formal goals of the organization down the hierarchy so that each unit knows exactly what is expected of it. And the most direct way to do this is through the system of objectives, which provides each unit with quantitative measures of its performance. The presence of such measures allows the use of "computational" methods in making choices, thereby precluding judgement, politics, or "inspiration" (Thompson and Truden 1964).

But the system of objectives is inevitably incomplete—unable to operationalize all the formal goals of the organization—and thereby misdirects effort toward those goals that can be operationalized. And even for those that can, the process of operationalization is inevitably imperfect, leading to other forms of distortion.

The members of the Internal Coalition have a strong propensity to favor the goals that get operationalized as objectives. With tangible measures of performance, they know exactly what is expected of them, and can demonstrate their accomplishments. Analysts can "prove" the payoffs from their technocratic systems; managers can be "objective" in rewarding their subordinates; and so on. So there is a strong incentive in most organizations to operationalize goals wherever possible, and to favor those goals.

To be operational, goals must be agreed upon, they must be stable, and they must be translatable into quantitative terms—and the top managers must be willing to do the translation. In these points lie the reasons why many goals do not find their way into the system of objectives. Even for a goal that can be quantified, the CEO may hesitate to operationalize it for fear that it is not shared by all of the major external influencers: so doing might bring it to their direct attention and evoke conflict. Thus, in the organization with a Divided External Coalition, there are good reasons not to operationalize goals. As for the organization with a Passive External Coalition, where a good deal of power can flow to the CEO, that individual may prefer to rule arbitrarily, through personal controls, and so not operationalize any goal—in other words, not release even a little of his power to the system of bureaucratic controls. (After all, the standards apply across the board, restricting even his flexibility.)

Sometimes, there is an incentive to operationalize goals, but this cannot be done simply because the goals are unstable. A dominant external influencer, for example, may simply be unsure which goals he or she wishes to favor for a given period of time. And then there are the goals which, however clearly stated and stable, simply cannot be expressed in operational terms. Everyone agrees that a major goal of the university is to advance knowledge. But no one knows how to measure this. Indeed, any conceivable activity can be argued to advance knowledge. Thus the university is reduced to having no objectives to guide faculty behavior, or to having silly ones, such as increasing the number of publications, as if one printed page is as good as another. The mission of a psychiatric hospital is to cure the mentally ill. But how is anyone to measure its performance when psychiatrists themselves cannot even define mental health, let alone illness. (There are psychiatrists who claim that the healthy individuals are the ones inside the asylums, since anyone able to cope with modern society must be mad.)

When an organization—such as a university or hospital—can operationalize virtually none of its goals, its System of Authority is weakened and expertise takes over, or else ideology or politics. But at least all the goals start on an equal footing. What is sometimes worse is the organization where some goals can be operationalized while others—equally important ones—cannot. In that case, even the most dedicated employee—the one who stands ready to support authority to the hilt—is driven to favor those goals that get operationalized, in effect to displace some formal goals in favor of others. Later in this book, we shall see how in the business corporation the goals of growth and profits—easily operationalized—tend to drive out those of employee welfare, safety, and environmental protection, for which measures are difficult to develop. Even when the top managers wish to achieve a balance between these different sets of goals, their systems of bureaucratic controls still preclude it (Ackerman 1975). This happens in nonbusiness organizations as well. Demerath and Thiessen (1966) point out how the goal of salvation in a religious group is difficult to operationalize, and so the goal of recruiting members— easily measured as to success—tends to displace it.

But even when all the relevant goals can be operationalized, problems remain. As noted in Chapter 2, it has never proved feasible to develop preference or utility functions to describe the desired tradeoffs among different goals. So employees have no way to know how to weigh different goals, even operational goals. Stressing growth may under certain circumstances, for example, reduce profit (Ridgway 1956).

But leaving this problem aside, even when the process of operationalizing a goal in the system of objectives appears to be simple, it is inevitably imperfect. That is, no goal can ever be completely translated into an objective; something

is always lost in the process of measurement. Every measure is an approxima-
tion, a *surrogate*. Take the case of the goal that seems most easily operationalized—profit. A time period must be chosen. How long? A long period
may make it impossible to detect downturns and correct them in time. But a
short one may enable the manager being measured to play games—for example, to cut costs that are really investments, let us say in maintenance or advertising, and thereby to trade off long-term profits for those in the short run.
Buckley tells the story of "a department head who got promoted to the presidency of his organization because he showed the most impressive departmental
profits over a three-year period. It was his successor who faced the deferred
maintenance that created the 'profits' in the first place. By that time, the person
who should have been axed had become the executioner" (1972, p. 21).

   If such problems can arise in the operationalization of profit, imagine what
can happen with other goals. The literature provides examples of the employment agency whose employees were appraised by the number of interviews they
conducted and so tried to complete as many as possible rather than trying to
place people in jobs; tax inspectors who processed tax forms toward the end
of the month more or less carefully than normal depending on whether or not
they had already filled their monthly quotas; and the Chicago policemen who
received points for the number of people they arrested and so were sometimes
inclined to pick up innocent bystanders (Ridgway 1956; Blau 1963; Terkel 1972,
p. 140). Ijiri, Jaedicke, and Knight provide us with an amusing example from
the Soviet Union:

> ...the project of the Novo Lipetsk steel mill...comprises 91 volumes totaling
> 70,000 pages. (One is not surprised to learn that the designers are paid by sheet...)
> Literally, everything is anticipated in these blueprints; the emplacement of each
> nail, lamp, or washstand. Only one aspect of the project is not considered at all:
> its economic effectiveness. (1970, p. 432)

   To conclude, every system of objectives is inadequate in two respects. First,
it is inevitably incomplete, often operationalizing only some goals and thereby
driving even dedicated employees to attend to those at the expense of others.
And second, whatever goals it does operationalize are done so imperfectly. So
one way or another, the formal goals of the organization get partially displaced.

   2. SUBOPTIMIZATION   Not only the design of the control systems but also
that of the superstructure drives insiders—even those with the best of
intentions—to displace legitimate power. By virtue of the division of labor and
departmentalization, the overall mission of the organization is divided into a
series of tasks. Each is then assigned to a specific position, and then to a unit.
Moreover, organizations with multiple goals and missions often use the
superstructure to assign responsibility for each of them. For example, a corporation with a number of distinct product lines will often set up a separate

division to manufacture and market each of them. And when it needs to pay attention to some particular social issue, it may set up a special unit to deal with it, for example an urban affairs department to consider urban problems. In effect, as we noted earlier, the organization is designed as a chain of means and ends in which the ultimate ends—basic missions and the formal goals—are partitioned into a series of means and then assigned to units as the ends or goals that they are to pursue. Each unit, and finally each position, is then expected to pursue its goals to the exclusion of all others. In other words, it is *expected* to *suboptimize*—to do the best it can on its goals and forget about the rest.

The assumption behind suboptimization is that if everyone does his or her bit, the overall mission will be accomplished and the organizational goals achieved. The interdependencies will take care of themselves, through the design of the superstructure. But a good deal of evidence suggests that this is a crude assumption. The design of the superstructure is imprecise, and because units naturally overemphasize their own goals, organizational performance deteriorates.

That units lose sight of the broader organizational perspective is well documented in the literature. As the saying goes, where you stand on an issue depends on where you sit.

> . . . a proposal to withdraw American troops from Europe is to the Army a threat to its budget and size, to the Budget Bureau a way to save money, to the Treasury a balance-of-payments gain, to the State Department Office of European Affairs a threat to good relations with NATO, to the President's congressional adviser an opportunity to remove a major irritant in the President's relations with the Hill. (Allison 1971, p. 168)

Dearborn and Simon (1958) asked twenty-three middle managers from various departments of a large corporation to read a business policy case and note the problem that they, as president, should deal with first. Most of the sales managers (83 percent vs. 29 percent of the production managers) mentioned sales as the key problem, while most of the production managers (80 percent vs. 22 percent of the sales managers) focussed on an organizational problem related to manufacturing. Even graduate students, when "asked to make estimates from identical figures, first as 'chief cost analyst' and then as 'chief market analyst,' tended to overestimate cost in the former job and underestimate sales in the latter" (Guetzkow 1965, p. 55).

With a perfectly designed superstructure, such biases would make no difference. But no superstructure can be perfectly designed. And so, when the balance of power tilts in favor of one unit, as it inevitably must, suboptimization can produce major distortions in the goals pursued by the organization.

3. MEANS-ENDS INVERSION The phenomenon known as the inversion of means and ends is close to suboptimization, except that the reason for it, as described here, is different and its effect is usually more pronounced. In means-ends inversion, the employees treat their own tasks as ends in themselves, for personal advantage. In other words, whereas we described suboptimization as an inadvertent distortion of goals, we describe means-ends inversion as an intentional one. And whereas suboptimization maintains the assumption of the dedication of the employee, means-ends inversion drops it. Organizational power is displaced because it suits the employee to do so. At this point, the employee enters our discussion as an independent influencer, one who has neither been successfully bought off by the inducements-contributions contract nor developed some overriding form of identification with the organization.

Nevertheless, that employee still remains rather innocent in this case. He or she is simply taken with their work—that which the organization pays them to do—to the point where it becomes an end in itself rather than a means to accomplish some broader organizational end. As such they displace the goals of the organization, even those of their own unit, in favor of those of their own work (Selznick 1966, p. 258). Examples of such behavior abound: the researcher who prizes elegant methodology over insightful result, the surgeon who boasts of a successful operation even though the patient died, the bureaucrat who is more interested in the form to be filled out than the client to be served. Crozier (1964) quotes one of the executives of the government-owned industrial monopoly he studied: "We are here to write reports and process paper . . . [the service given to the public] is only a by-product." In a related footnote, Crozier notes that despite this man's joking tone, "The rest of the interview, as a matter of fact, shows what exaggerated importance he himself gives to written documents and to formalism" (p. 200).

Means-ends inversion is common among unskilled operators, often, ironically, because they follow bureaucratic procedures to the letter. Such procedures must always be interpreted with some flexibility. But where means and ends get inverted so that the rules become ends in themselves, that flexibility disappears and the purpose which the organization is supposed to serve gets displaced. This phenomenon has been discussed in the literature in organizations under a number of different labels. Merton refers to it as "sanctification," commenting on the "emotional dependence upon bureaucratic symbols and status"; Davis uses the term "ceremonialism" in a study of the U.S. Navy Officers Corps, where ritual, designed to maintain morale, "may become an end in itself at the expense of the organization's capacity to perform efficiently its manifest functions"; Dimock has called it "traditionalism," and Selznick, "routinization"; but most of us simply call it "red tape" (all cited in Sills 1957, pp. 66–67).

The inversion of means and ends is perhaps even more common among skilled operators and staff specialists, because the System of Expertise within which they work frees them from the controls of authority and grants them so much discretion in their work. In other words, these people invert means and ends not because of powerlessness but because of power. The source of this power, the professional skills—operating on a patient or conducting an elegant experiment—become more important to the worker than what the skills are supposed to accomplish. The rule of the tool comes into play: "Give a little boy a hammer and it will just so happen that everything he sees needs hammering." Hire a planner and it just so happens that every managerial decision needs to be formally planned; hire a psychotherapist and suddenly everybody needs to be psychoanalyzed.

The inversion of means and ends can infuse not only a single individual but also a whole department and even an entire organization. Mission gets forgotten. Michels (1915) tells how the European socialist movements at the turn of the century lost sight of their mission of achieving governmental power as their leaders strove instead to maintain their own personal power. In discussing this study in the context of his own, of how right-wing factions infiltrated the Tennessee Valley Authority to divert its given goals, Selznick comments on how difficult it is "to avoid the tyranny of means and the impotence of ends" (1966, p.X). And Perrow discusses what is probably the most disheartening example in the literature:

> The vast majority of [New York City welfare] agencies for the blind are oriented to providing service for the "attractive blind," as one might call them—the children and young adults who might be employable. The child taps the sympathy of the generous public, and the young adult promises an adequate return on investment for those who respond to more calculated arguments. Consequently, about 80 percent of the blind—the old, those with other disabilities, and those in minority groups with high unemployment rates—are more or less neglected by the agencies. With only 20 percent left, the competition to tie an "attractive blind person" to a particular agency is fierce. Since in New York City the number of agencies for the blind is large, there are barely enough clients to ensure modest-sized programs for each agency. As a consequence, once a client has "signed up" with an agency, they are reluctant to make him independent, for then the size of their program dwindles. Agencies have been accused of keeping the blind in a dependent state to justify their appeal for funds. Yet there is little effort to serve the aged blind or the totally handicapped. (1970, pp. 128-29)

These organizations may perhaps satisfy the goals of their internal influencers, but those of their clients—and of the community which they are supposed to serve—get displaced.

4. GROUP PRESSURES   A fourth reason for the displacement of legitimate power is the emergence of social pressure within the organization to satisfy the needs of particular groups. Here we have a more direct and conscious subversion of organizational interests in favor of personal ones, especially the social and belonging needs of the individual—the ones often satisfied in groups. But we have not yet left the domain of imperfections in the System of Authority, for, as we shall soon see, much of this group behavior is evoked by the nature of the superstructure.

It is said that there is power in numbers. Even the best control system or ideology cannot counter a large group that chooses to resist it. This was the message of the first intensive study of the role of the group in factory work, the famous Hawthorne studies of a half-century ago:

> The workers constituted a cohesive group which had a well-developed normative system of its own. The norms specified, among other things, that a worker was not to work too hard, lest he become a "rate-buster"; nor was he to work too slowly, lest he become a "chiseler" who exploited the group (part of the wages were based on group performance). Under no condition was he to inform or "squeal". By means of informal social control, the group was able to direct the pace of work, the amount of daily and weekly production, the amount of work-stoppage, and allocation of work among members. (Etzioni 1961, p. 114)

Merton notes that when a white-collar social group is threatened, "the *esprit de corps* and informal social organization often leads the personnel to defend their entrenched interests." They withhold information, or else "have documents brought to [their superior] in such numbers that he cannot manage to sign them all, let alone read them" (1957, p. 201).

Group pressures develop, not independent of the superstructure, but very much as part of its design. Departmentalization creates groups based on function, location, line, staff, and level in the hierarchy. "We-they" relationships inevitably emerge. These often lead to stereotyping, as Tagiuri (1965) found in a study of nearly a thousand scientists, research managers, and executives. Each group tended to exaggerate the values of the others. For example, while the scientists rated themselves 51 on a scale of theoretical values and 34 on one of social values, the research managers rated them 60 and 28 respectively; similarly, while the executives rated themselves 45 on economic values and 44 on political ones, the research managers rated them 55 and 51. Balke et al. (1973) found even grosser misjudgements by managers and labor negotiators of each other's values in a simulation of a labor-management bargaining experience.[1]

Such stereotyping can lead to all kinds of conflicts in the Internal Coalition. Well known are those that arise between groups of staff specialists and line managers. Also common are the conflicts between groups at different levels of the hierarchy. Hierarchy introduces status differences among insiders that bind them together at given levels but separate them between levels. Crozier argues that "A bureaucratic organization...is composed of a series of superimposed strata that do not communicate very much with each other. Barriers between strata are such that there is very little room for the development of cliques cutting across several categories." The "pressure of the peer group" emerges within each strata (1964, p. 190).

---

[1] Using an intriguing methodology, these researchers replicated a real conflict with the actual participants, feeding back graphic representations of each other's perceptions, at different stages, to see how their behaviors would be affected.

5. DIRECT LINKS TO EXTERNAL INFLUENCERS   As noted earlier, inherent in the division of labor and in the factoring of the organization's mission and goals into a means-end hierarchy is the creation of units to look after specific functions, markets, and goals. In theory, each of these units is supposed to look up to one center of authority for guidance. But in practice, many of these units work directly with external influencers and come to represent their interests in the Internal Coalition. As shown in Figure 13-2, the chain of authority from the External Coalition through the board of directors to the CEO and then down the hierarchy is bypassed by direct links between insiders and outsiders. Instead of the CEO reconciling the demands of the external influencers, that reconciliation comes instead to be accomplished by various internal influencers, who negotiate with each other in political processes. And the result is often a displacement of formal goals, as the demands of certain external influencers get more weight than the senior management prefers to give them. The sales department sees its role as the protection of the customer, the research department as

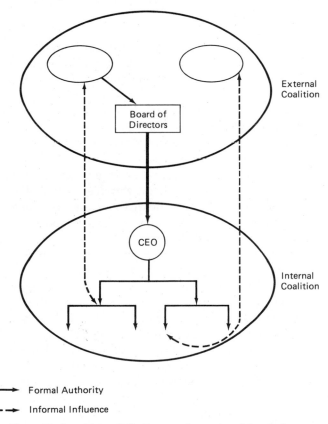

Figure 13-2.   *Direct Links Between Internal and External Influencers*

representing the interests of the scientific community, and the purchasing department as reflecting those of the suppliers. Whichever happens to be most influential in the System of Politics ensures that its "clients" in the External Coalition gets preferential treatment. Similar direct links are created by the System of Expertise. As we saw earlier, each group of experts may have a corresponding professional society outside the organization, whose interests it represents inside of it. The frequent result is politics and goal displacement.

The effect of these links between internal and external influencers can be akin to suboptimization: the employees displace broader organizational goals in their enthusiasm for carrying out the roles assigned to them. But direct links can also arise because of personal interests. The insider may consciously favor the goals of some outsider, or simply be paid to do so, and so seek to subvert those of the organization. Thus Boulding discusses the employee who accepts a formal role in the organization in order to carry out sabotage: "This is the boring from within of the Communists, the union activity of the labor spy or *agent provocateur,* and the undercover work of the cloak-and-dagger man" (1962, p. 180).

6. INTRINSIC NEEDS OF THE INSIDERS   In each of the five reasons for goal displacement so far discussed, something beyond the employees had contributed to the rupturing of legitimate organizational process in favor of politics. Distortions in the system of objectives or in the superstructure drove them to it; they got carried away with the importance of their own work; some internal group or external influencer got to them. In this final point we look at political power in its rawest form: the employees displace legitimate power simply because it serves their own personal interests to do so.

That all kinds of intrinsic personal needs exist for insiders is a foregone conclusion. In Chapter 9, we showed how the roles people play in the Internal Coalition create needs for them—growth for managers, moderate perpetual change for analysts, excellence for the skilled operators, and so on. Superimposed on these are all kinds of other personal needs. Some people rise to positions beyond their level of competence—a phenomenon known as the "Peter Principle" (Peter and Hull, 1969)—and then do whatever they can to hang on. Others struggle for personal autonomy by resisting authority per se, or else for power by trying to build personal empires within the organization. One individual may have a grudge against the organization, and so seek to displace its formal goals by holding back his efforts. Another may be caught up in a personal rivalry, and take the attitude that "I'm against it because he's for it" (Pettigrew 1973, p. 78). And finally there are the whole host of very private needs—the woman who works in a travel agency so that she can pursue her goal of building up a stamp collection and the man who works there so that he can pursue his goal of pursuing that woman.

In general, the organization represents to most insiders the most important place to satisfy their intrinsic needs. Unlike most external influencers, to whom the organization is an incidental place to pursue their goals—one place among many—to the insiders who spend their working lives there, it is *the* place. And so they bring to it a great many of their most important needs for fulfillment through the work they do. And in the process, they displace the more legitimate forms of power designed to serve the organization at large.

To conclude, six reasons have been discussed as to why legitimate power gets displaced in organizations. We have seen that any one of these can often suffice—for example, a distortion in the systems of objectives can force even the most well-meaning employee to distort formal goals, while a strong personal need can be sufficient for an ill-meaning employee to displace legitimate power, given the incompleteness of the control systems. But typically, of course, these six reasons work in concert. Organizations are complex places where all of these forces—distortions in objectives, tendencies to suboptimize and to invert means and ends, the direct pressures of the group as well as those of external influencers, and the intrinsic needs of the internal influencers—all blend together to give rise to a System of Politics, which often acts in contradiction to the Systems of Authority, Ideology, and Expertise.

PLAYING POLITICS WITH WHAT EQUIPMENT? SOME POLITICAL MEANS OF INFLUENCE

What equipment do the inside influencers use to play their political games? It should be emphasized at the outset—in light of the fact that the System of Politics represents, by definition, the illegitimate use of power—that the inside influencers turn to whatever means of influence they can get their hands on. At one extreme, those who can rely on nothing else make use of the personal will and political skill they have; at the other, those who have access to the more legitimate systems of influence try to exploit them politically, that is, illegitimately. And in between are those who can make use of privileged information and privileged contacts with the influential to enhance their political power.

POLITICAL WILL AND SKILL   Will and skill were discussed in Chapter 3 as bases for all forms of power in and around the organization. But they merit a special place in this discussion of the internal political means of influence, for two reasons.

First, players with no other means of influence (political or legitimate) can nevertheless turn to these—to their will to act, their capacity to expend energy, and to the skills they possess to win at politics. We shall see some pointed examples in our discussion of ostensibly powerless insiders who won political games simply because they were able to exert a good deal of effort in a politically astute manner.

And second, even for those who can use other political means of influence, will and skill are typically crucial ingredients to facilitate their use. The player who can rely on the power of authority, or ideology, or expertise—in other words on legitimate or widely accepted forms of power—is half way to getting his or her way. With authority, one sometimes need only give an order to get something done; with ideology, things tend to happen by themselves; and in many cases the player who has technical expertise can easily come to dominate those who do not. But forced to rely on one of the political means of influence, such as privileged information or access—means less sure and more likely to provoke resistance because they are not legitimate—the player must try that much harder and be that much smarter. In other words, he or she must show more will, and possess more skill of a political nature. The player must be adept at persuasion, manipulation, negotiation, and must have a special sense of how power flows in the Internal Coalition—where the formal and informal influence lies, which issues arouse attention, what friendships and rivalries exist, what the implicit and explicit rules of the organization are, and which of these can be broken and which evoked to win an issue.

It should be added that the players who control the more legitimate systems of influence are only "half" way there because they, too, must often possess skill and exert will of a *political* nature in order to make use of their nonpolitical powers. This is the clear message in Neustadt's book, *Presidential Power*, subtitled *The Politics of Leadership*. Even (Neustadt might say especially) the legitimate power of the President of the United States is worth little without the incumbent's energy and ability to back it up through political means. "Effective influence for the man in the White House stems from," among other sources, "the expectations of [other men he must persuade to act] regarding his ability and will to use the various advantages they think he has." Roosevelt succeeded, in Neustadt's opinion, because politics was "a vehicle for *him*"; Eisenhower failed because politics "defined the merely personal" (1964, p. 169).

And so, while will and skill are found wherever power is exercised in or around the organization, they assume an especially important role in the System of Politics of the Internal Coalition.

PRIVILEGED INFORMATION: GATEKEEPING AND CENTRALITY   As we have already noted a number of times, in information lies power. And so, just as technical knowledge generates expert power, so too does privileged nontechnical knowledge generate political power. This power arises in two ways: (1) from controlling an important flow of information into the organization, by playing a role known as "gatekeeper," and (2) from standing at the crossroads of important flows of information within the organization, by playing a role sometimes called "nerve center," or by being in a position of "centrality."

The gatekeeper serves as the channel through which some important type of external information flows into the organization (Allen and Cohen 1969). This information may of course be of a technical or expert nature, but it need not be. When it is not, what produces the power is the *access* to the information. And that of course means that the power is only as good as the channel: As soon as the source is lost, or as soon as others can establish parallel access to equivalent channels, the political power dissipates.

Akin to gatekeeping, but within the Internal Coalition, is centrality and the role of nerve center. Here an insider sits at the intersection, or "node," of important flows of internal communication and so gains political power. He or she can withhold important information from some people and filter what they send to others, transmitting only what benefits themselves. (Another trick available to the nerve center is the release of too much information in a channel, thereby hopelessly overloading the person at the end of it.) Pettigrew describes one nerve center, to whom we shall return, whose

> ...strategic placement as the communications link between the technical specialists and the [top executives], together with his degree of political access, constituted his greatest advantages. With control over the information flow in the decision process, he was able to focus attention successfully on his demands and, at the same time, to hinder others from generating support for theirs. (1973, p. 233)

Sometimes centrality is just a matter of physical location. The post of receptionist, for example, is typically valued for its access to information. But one can sit at crossroads symbolically as well as physically. As we noted in Chapter 9, senior executives by virtue of their links to so many insiders, tend to emerge as important nerve centers of organizational information. So too do certain staff people, the ones who move freely about the organization with wide-ranging contacts. Considerable attention has been paid in the recent literature of organizational design to the role of integrator or liaison person, that individual who links different departments, such as the project scientist who serves as the intermediary between the scientists in the laboratory and the engineers in the shop, or the sales liaison person who links the field sales force with the factory. The formal power of these people is often low, but their centrality in workflows usually ensures them considerable informal or political power.

PRIVILEGED ACCESS TO THE INFLUENTIAL   Direct and unique access—what Mumford and Pettigrew call "political access" (1975, p. 201)—to those with an important means of influence is a means of influence in its own right in the Internal Coalition. We have already seen this in the External Coalition, and also discussed it as a general basis of power in Chapter 3. But this too merits special mention here because of its importance in the exercise of political power within the organization. Although a player may lack his or her own means of influence, personal links to those who possess them—insiders or outsiders, with important external, formal, ideologic, expert, or political means of influence— may be enough to attain a position of power.

The best insider to have access to is, of course, the chief executive. And those people who have the best of it are the ones who serve that individual personally, every day. Hence the CEO's secretary and "assistant to" inevitably emerge as centers of power in their own right in the Internal Coalition. (Often, in addition, they have their own means of influence in their centrality, since important information flows around them continuously.) Of course, not everyone can work directly for the top manager, but any powerful manager can generate power for those around him. Being "sponsored" by someone with influence means sharing that influence.

> There are real as well as symbolic payoffs in working for someone who is power-ful in systems where resources are scarce and there is constant scrambling for ad-vantage. Powerful authorities can get more for their subordinates. They can more effectively back up both promises and threats, they can more easily make changes in the situation of subordinates. They offer the possibility of taking subordinates with them when they move...(Kanter 1977, p. 172)

An insider can also gain power by having privileged access to the places where the powerful sit, where important decisions are made. Thus Kanter talks about "visibility," the "chance to be noticed," as a source of power, which may be gained "through participation on task forces and committees" (p. 179).

Privileged access to influential outsiders—for example to a dominant ex-ternal influencer or one who controls a critical dependency for the organiza-tion—can also be a source of power in the Internal Coalition. Such access may grow out of a personal friendship, a family relationship, or simply a long associa-tion. Thus the salesman who has a unique "in" with a major customer—perhaps because its purchasing agent is his brother-in-law or his golfing partner or simply someone he has served well for years—can accumulate significant power in the Internal Coalition.

As the examples show, privileged access provides power not primarily for the information it brings—although this can be a factor too—but for the resources that can be made available, the decision that can be swung by a word dropped at an opportune moment, the favors that can open up, all the crumbs that fall around those with power. But this political means of influence, like the others, is a vulnerable one, worth nothing the day the connection is broken.

POTENTIAL TO EXPLOIT LEGITIMATE SYSTEMS OF INFLUENCE   Finally, among the *political* means of influence must be counted the *legitimate* means of in-fluence when they can be used in political ways. In other words, authority, ideology, and expertise become political means of influence when they are drawn upon in illegitimate ways—ways not sanctioned in the normal manner of behavior. They are *exploited,* for ostensibly parochial ends, not the ends intended.

We have already seen a number of examples of this, and shall see others in the discussion that follows. A group of analysts, for example, promotes a technocratic system not because it is good for the organization but because it extends their own power. Similarly, a CEO upholds the organization's ideology in order to enhance his own status as the true guardian of it. Experts—medical practitioners in hospitals, staff engineers in manufacturing—distort cost-benefit analyses in order to hoodwink managers into buying unnecessary equipment that gives them more influence. And managers, in turn, flaunt their authority in order to extend their control over the operators or staff personnel, just as the operators themselves flaunt the authority they have over the clients. In all these cases, legitimate power is used illegitimately, that is, politically.

To conclude, political power inevitably requires political will and political skill; in addition, it may draw on privileged information or privileged access to those with any kind of power, and it may exploit in illegitimate ways the legitimate systems of influence.

HOW PLAY POLITICS?
THE POLITICAL GAMES
OF THE INTERNAL COALITION

The best way to characterize the System of Politics of the organization seems to be as a collection of goings on, a set of "games" taking place throughout the Internal Coalition—"intricate and subtle, simultaneous, overlapping" (Allison 1971, p. 162), a kind of multiple-ring circus. But as Allison notes, these political games are neither as unstructured nor as independent of each other as they may seem. "Games proceed neither at random nor at leisure" (p. 162). They are guided by rules:

> Some rules are explicit, others implicit. Some rules are quite clear, others fuzzy. Some are very stable; others are ever changing. But the collection of rules, in effect, defines the game. First, rules establish the positions, the paths by which men gain access to positions, the power of each position, the action-channels. Second, rules constrict the range of . . . decisions and actions that are acceptable. . . . Third, rules sanction moves of some kinds—bargaining, coalitions, persuasion, deceit, bluff, and threat—while making other moves illegal, immoral, ungentlemanly, or inappropriate. (pp. 170–71)

Crozier and Friedberg also base their analysis on "the concept of the game," and describe it in similar terms:

> The game for us is much more than an image. It is a concrete mechanism thanks to which men structure their power relations and regulate them, at the same time allowing these relations—and the men as well—their freedom.
> The game is an instrument that men have developed to regulate their cooperation. It is an instrument essential to organized action. The game reconciles freedom and constraint. The player remains free, but must, if he wishes to win, adopt a rational strategy according to the nature of the game and respect its rules. (1977, p. 97)

In the literature on power in organizations can be found some studies that probe deeply into specific games commonly played there (though many more such studies are sorely needed). But no study was found that investigates the relationships among games, or seeks to develop a conceptual framework to help understand the system of games—in essence, the System of Politics of the organization. Thus, our discussion must deal more with the structure of individual games than with that of the system of games, although we conclude it with some comments on the latter. In discussing each game, we shall be interested in who plays it (chief executive, line managers, professional operators, unskilled operators, support staffers, analysts), which political means of influence they rely upon to play it (political will and skill, privileged information or access, potential to exploit the legitimate systems of influence), and what reason they have for playing the game. We shall, in fact, categorize our games at the outset according to the reason for playing, under the following headings: those played to resist authority, to counter its resistance, to build a power base, to defeat a rival, and to effect a change in the organization. In all, thirteen types of political games will be discussed, which fall into these categories as follows:

Games to resist authority:	The insurgency games
Games to counter the resistance to authority:	The counterinsurgency games
Games to build power bases:	The sponsorship game (with superiors)
	The alliance-building game (with peers)
	The empire-building game (with subordinates)
	The budgeting game (with resources)
	The expertise games (with knowledge and skills)
	The lording game (with authority)
Games to defeat rivals:	The line versus staff game
	The rival camps game
Games to effect organizational change:	The strategic candidates game
	The whistle-blowing game
	The young Turks games

THE INSURGENCY GAMES   The insurgency games are usually played in order to resist authority, and will be discussed as such, although they may also be played to resist expertise or ideology, and may also be used as a means to effect a change in the organization. These games range from mild resistance of legitimate power and distortion of its goals to outright mutiny, "from protest to rebellion" (Zald and Berger 1978, p. 841). They are often played in the execution phase of decision making, when someone down the hierarchy is instructed to carry out some action—to implement a decision taken higher up. Recall that we defined a decision as "a *commitment* to action." Between commitment and action inevitably lies some discretion: there is no guarantee that the action will be carried out to the letter. The executor can intervene to tilt or distort the action to suit his personal ends. For the decisions he favors, he can "go beyond the spirit if not the letter," for those he does not, he can "maneuver, to delay implementation, to limit implementation to the letter but not the spirit, and even to have the decision disobeyed" (Allison 1971, p. 173).

In the nature of the System of Authority, decisions are taken at higher levels in the hierarchy and executed lower down. The CEO decides the widgets should be green; the factory manager decides to apply the paint with brush instead of roller; the worker does the painting. Hence, those employees Mechanic (1962) calls the "lower participants," especially the operators at the bottom of the line, are the prime executors, and so they are the chief players of insurgency games. Especially the ones without skills and so most subject to the weight of the control systems. These are the internal influencers who have the most to gain from resisting authority. Indeed, that is all they can do to gain power in the Internal Coalition. "Lower participants do not usually achieve control by using the role structure of the organization, but rather by circumventing, sabotaging, and manipulating it" (Mechanic 1962, p. 356).

Of course, the insurgency games can be played by anyone subjected to the weight of any form of legitimate power: by professional operators against authority, in this case rather easily won because of their control of the operating work (Thoenig and Friedberg 1976); by unskilled operators against professionals (Scheff 1961); by whole sections of an organization against central authority, as when the long-tenured civil servants seek to impede the reforms of a new government or a union local holds out against the settlement negotiated by headquarters. Managers frequently play insurgency games against their own superiors, as illustrated by the evidence Guetzkow (1965) cites of the distortions in the information they send up the hierarchy. Even in a laboratory study:

> The average number of messages with critical content sent by lows to highs, when no power was involved, was three times the quantity sent when the highs had both desirable position and power over the advancement of the lows...Critical comments were simply omitted by those whose fortunes depended upon those with higher hierarchical rank. (p. 555)

And the most senior of line managers have been known to resist the authority of chief executives. Zald and Berger (1978) mention the famous "admirals' revolt" of 1949 against changes in the U.S. Defense Department that were to diminish the role of the Navy. And Allison quotes an aide to U.S. President Franklin D. Roosevelt who claimed that "Half a President's suggestions, which theoretically carry the weight of orders, can safely be forgotten by a Cabinet member" (1971, p. 172).

The insurgency games can be played in two very different ways: subtly by individuals or small groups, which Zald and Berger (1978) believe is the preferred approach of line managers and professionals, or aggressively by large groups—in the form of what Zald and Berger call the "mass movement"—which they believe is the approach usually taken by the less skilled operators.[2] As noted earlier, while these operators have little power as individuals, they are still the ones who perform the organization's most critical function—producing its basic products and services. Moreover it is they who are in most intimate touch with the organization's daily functioning. And so, when they are willing to act in concert—a whole work force cannot easily be replaced—and to expend the effort required to resist authority, they can develop a good deal of political power.

These mass movement insurgency games can, of course, only be played occasionally, since no organization can tolerate perpetual disruption of its operations. They tend to occur when senior management seeks to impose some change on the operators that threatens their established social relationships, or perhaps threatens an ideology dear to them. Sometimes the operators are aggravated by some other issue—by something as small as the quality of food in the cafeteria (Zald and Berger 1978, p. 846), or as significant as the weight of the bureaucratic controls imposed on them—and they take out their frustration in any change management cares about. Often these games are fought shortly after a transition in senior management, because the new chief executive does not understand, or accept, the compromises made by his predecessor for the sake of peace in the organization. The operators test out his political power.

Insurgency by unskilled operators can take a variety of forms. Sometimes the operators exploit the System of Authority by turning the bureaucratic rules back on their superiors, for example in working-to-rule. "If [the rules] restrain the freedom of the subordinates, they do likewise for the zone of discretion of the superior. He can no longer exercise his power of sanction, for example, except in specific circumstances" (Crozier and Friedberg 1977, p. 76). More common forms are the restriction of output, the disruption of operations, and the outright refusal to work. Workers stage slowdowns or seize plants, prisoners riot, soldiers desert, and sailors mutiny.

Such tactics are not new. Udy, for example, discusses slavery in the second century B.C. Roman estates, where "discontent was rampant . . . with constant revolts and frequent collusion between slave supervisors and workers in 'stalling' on the job" (1959, p. 83). And Sterba (1978) describes how over the course of thirteen centuries in imperial China, clerical subordinates and lesser functionaries were able to manipulate and corrupt the orders of their superiors, the first known civil servants. The setting was not unlike that of contemporary insurgency games. The civil servants were carefully selected and highly educated, then sent out to the regions to run the Chinese government. But they were out of touch with the day-to-day realities of the operations—even with the dialects and customs of the people there—and so their authority was easily thwarted by the clerks they had to recruit locally to do the operating work:

[2]Zald and Berger describe the former as played "to change some aspect of organizational function" in the face of resistance by the organization's formal authority, which makes it akin to what we call the young Turks game. But small groups of line managers and/or professionals can also play to resist authority per se.

Partly resulting from their resort to deceit, obfuscation, chicanery, collusion and the selective performance of assigned tasks, and partly due to their mastery over administrative detail and operating procedure, these low ranking subordinates were able to confound, frustrate, inveigle and even intimidate their more prestigious superiors. (p. 70)

The clerks exercised "a kind of veto power not only over decisions made by officials directly above them, but, in the extreme, over policies promulgated at the ministerial levels as well" (p. 75). They procrastinated, feigned misunderstanding, preoccupied themselves with minutiae. By their control of information, they omitted, exaggerated, and even falsified data. In what must have been the ultimate game of insurgency, such tactics were believed to have undermined every measure of state trade and land reform introduced by the government of the Sung dynasty over a period of fifty years! And throughout all this, the civil servants were reluctant to antagonize the clerks, on whom they depended to administer their regions. The result, in Sterba's view, was a reversal of implicit authority, a "clandestine management" (p. 76).

None of this seems to have been lost on players of present-day insurgency games. In fact, the description by Scheff (1961) of "Control Over Policy by Attendants in a Mental Hospital" bears striking resemblance to Sterba's description of the imperial Chinese bureaucracy. Scheff studied the successful resistance by six hundred attendants, the largest group of workers by far in a large state mental hospital, to an attempt by management to replace custodial practices by "social treatment," a program of reform the attendants found "impractical, fraudulent, and immoral" (p. 94).

The weak link in the chain of authority between administrator and attendant was the physician. In theory, the physician was the "focal point" for administrative control of the ward, "responsible for the treatment of the ward patients, and for insuring [attendant] obedience to hospital regulations" (p. 95). In fact, the physician was dependent on the attendants to get his work done. While his tenure tended to be short and his visits transitory—physicians had many duties outside their wards and some physicians were assigned to as many as four wards—the attendants were "all but rooted to the ward" (p. 95), spending all day on the same ward, sometimes for as long as five years. In other words, theirs was a more serious commitment to the specific workplace, and so they were more predisposed to exert effort to gain informal power over it. Not only was their presence permanent, but the attendants were also well organized, in cohesive groups that did not break rank (even though a sizeable minority was apparently in sympathy with the administration's program of change).

All of these conditions constituted a "typical setting for 'bureaucratic sabotage,'" enabling the attendants to "capture" the physicians (p. 96). Physicians who did not cooperate with them—who took the side of patients or favored the administration—were subjected to a whole array of sanctioning techniques. In their absence from the ward—especially overnight and on weekends—the physicians depended on the attendants for reports on the behavior of their patients. These were withheld. The attendants also controlled the flow of patients to the physicians, normally allowing only those with appointments to see them. But when the attendants were dissatisfied with the attitude of a physician, they sometimes "encouraged" patients "to accost him with their requests," sometimes almost to the point of "mob scenes" (p. 96). Sanctions also took the form of outright disobedience and the withholding of cooperation. Physicians were responsible for more than they could possibly handle, to take one example, for ordering all adjustments in tranquilizer dosages, ideally several times each week for each of 150 patients. So an arrangement usually had to be worked out with the ward attendants to make most of the decisions and consult only on specific problems. If that cooperation was withheld, "the physician had absolutely no recourse but to do all the work himself" (p. 97).

The choices open to the physicians were to quit or "reach a tacit under-standing" with the attendants. Those "new to the ward soon got the point, and arrived at a working arrangement which involved the continuation of much of the old ward system in return for cooperation" (p. 97). Thus, the attendants were able to "stalemate a vigorous program of reform" (p. 104). The admin-istration "relied largely on formal control, without the informal system of con-trols which usually supports changes in organizations" (p. 105). In other words, legitimate power was not sufficient to effect the desired change. Because the administrators were unwilling to use political means of influence, they lost the game.

THE COUNTERINSURGENCY GAMES   Commonly, those in authority fight back when faced with insurgency. In imperial China, three solutions were tried: "(a) increasing the severity of punishment for proven misconduct; (b) expand-ing the likelihood of detection and exposure of wrongdoers; and (c) improving methods of supervision and control to prevent or discourage clerical knavery" (Sterba 1978, p. 76). In other words, the attempted solution to resistance to authority was more authority—a tightening of the controls. But the problems were "due to faulty organizational design rather than to human frailty and fallibility" (p. 77), and so these solutions did not work. One that did in part— until rescinded by political opponents—was to involve the civil servants more deeply in the intimate details of the operations while bringing the clerks "within the pale of Confucian ethical and social norms, and to inspire in them a sense of loyalty and dedication" (p. 77). In other words, an ideological basis was established to encourage the cooperation of the clerks.

So too in this day and age, the natural inclination is to fight resistance to authority with more authority, to increase the controls, tighten the rules, and levy the penalties. The Church excommunicates; the union puts its recalci-trant local under trusteeship. It sounds like a game we call "lording," which we shall get to in due course. Such tactics can sometimes work in extreme cases of insubordination. But we have just seen that the roots of the problem often go beyond insubordination, and that authority often proves inadequate to counter political resistence, even by unskilled operators.[3]

Thus, when the managers are unwilling to give in to the operators, they must typically resort to political means of influence to counter the insurgency. In other words, the managers are forced to fight fire with fire. They have to expend a good deal of effort, make use of their political skills together with their nerve center information, and persuade, cajole, and bargain with the operators to get what they want. Of course, the managers also use the resources and legal prerogatives provided by their positions to the fullest, and sometimes beyond, in illegitimate, or political, ways. As Neustadt notes in his study of the U.S. presidency, "effective power has to be extracted out of other men's self-interest" (p. 156). Neustadt emphasizes how chief executives must immerse themselves in operating details so as not to be manipulated by better-informed subordinates, and how they can foster competition among their subordinates to serve themselves. Thus a favorite technique of Roosevelt, to whom politics was a vehicle,

> was to keep grants of authority incomplete, jurisdictions uncertain, charters over-lapping. The result of this competitive theory of administration was often con-fusion and exasperation on the operating level; but no other method could so reliably insure that in a large bureaucracy filled with ambitious men eager for power the decisions, and the power to make them, would remain with the President. (Schlesinger, quoted in Neustadt 1964, p. 150)

THE SPONSORSHIP GAME   Next we come to a series of political games played to build power bases. The first three that we discuss use people in dif-ferent places to do so—in the first, superiors; in the second, peers; and in the third, subordinates. Kanter in fact argues that those who wish to have any real power in the organization had better play one of these three games: "People without sponsors, without peer connections, or without promising subordinates remained in the situation of bureaucratic dependency . . ." (1977, p. 188).

The sponsorship game is a simple one, about which little need be said. The individual attaches himself or herself to a rising star—or one already in place—and professes loyalty in return for "a piece of the action." In other words, sponsorship involves an implicit contract—service in return for a share of the power. The sponsor is typically one's official boss, but need not be, although subordination is always implied for the player. (Kanter describes a salesman who had a sponsor four steps removed from him in the hierarchy. In professional organizations, such as hospitals or universities, a high-status, senior professional

---

[3]In the case of professional operators, formal authority is even less likely to prevail. Direct orders are likely to be ignored, technocratic standards do not apply, staffing is often beyond the managers' control, rewards may be subject to the standards of the professional societies, and even budgets may be partly out of the managers' hands.

will often sponsor a junior one.) Thus sponsorship is not a contract among equals, but of a more powerful influencer with a less powerful one. The former gets the lion's share of the power, the latter the crumbs (which can, nevertheless, be substantial).

Martin and Simms suggest that "the executive system in a firm is composed of complexes of sponsor-protégé relationships" (1959, p. 517). Kanter elaborates on these, noting that sponsors—who in the company she studied were known as "rabbis" or "godfathers"—"are often thought of as teachers or coaches whose functions are primarily to make introductions or to train a young person to move effectively through the system" (p. 181). But she finds that sponsors in fact provide three other important services. First, they fight for their protégés, stand up for them in mettings and promote them when opportunities arise. Second, they enable them "to bypass the hierarchy: to get inside information, to short-circuit cumbersome procedures, or to cut red tape" (p. 182). And third, "sponsors also provide an important signal to other people, a form of 'reflected power.' Sponsorship indicates to others that the person in question has the backing of an influential person, that the sponsor's resources are somewhere behind the individual" (p. 182).

Of course, all of this lasts only so long as the relationship is maintained, which makes sponsorship a very vulnerable means of power. The "fast trackers can. . . fall when sponsors fall if they have not developed their own power base in the interim" (Kanter, p. 183). And the protégés, in their discussions with Kanter, referred to sponsorship as "embryonic," "tenuous," "a father/son issue." "There is great danger if you go against a godfather. . . . God help you if you are not grateful for the favors given" (p. 183).

Anyone can play the sponsorship game, although it is probably most common in the middle line, where managers attach themselves to others on the move. It is also commonly played by professionals at different places in the pecking order, as noted, and, of course, by personal staff, such as secretaries and assistants-to who attach themselves to managers.

THE ALLIANCE-BUILDING GAME   This game to build a power base is played among peers—often managers of the middle line, sometimes professionals in the staff or operating functions—who negotiate implicit contracts of support for each other.

> The middle manager attempts to develop a network of social relations with others in strategic positions and to surround himself with allies in a position to supply him with resources such as information. . . With the help of allies, the middle manager is able to expand his influence and thus overcome the structural limitations of his role. (Izraeli 1975, p. 60)

Kanter concludes that in the company she studied "high 'peer acceptance'. . .was necessary to any power base or career success" (p. 184). She notes that "Strong alliances among peers could advance the group as a whole," and that "certain cohorts sometimes seem to produce all of the leaders in an organization" (p. 185).

The process of building an alliance, which requires a good deal of political skill and the expenditure of much effort, as well as the exploitation of legitimate means of influence, would seem to proceed as follows: an individual develops a concern for an issue, and seeks supporters. Alternately, a group of individuals concerned about an issue seek out an informal leader around whom they can coalesce, someone who can adequately represent their interests. In this way, the nucleus of an *interest group* is formed. Many interest groups are only temporary. They form over specific issues and disband when the issue is resolved. But others endure, because the players have a number of issues in common. These groups are sometimes referred to as *factions*. (When the faction forms around a leader—because of his charisma or his political ability—rather than around an issue, with the followers willing to be taken wherever he sees fit, then he may be said to have a *constituency*, a loyal group whose support is more or less guaranteed, and we are back to the sponsorship game.)

Often the interest group—whether it focusses on one issue or emerges as a more permanent faction—lacks the power to win an issue by itself. And so it must enlist other adherents to its cause—other individuals, but more importantly, other interest groups or factions—in order to enlarge its power base. As it grows, it becomes an *alliance*. Some groups are easily persuaded to join, others must be enticed, through the threat of reprisal if they do not join, or, more likely, the promise of reward if they do—a share in the winnings or perhaps a modification in the stand of the alliance. "Peer alliances often worked through direct exchange of favors. On lower levels information was traded; on higher levels bargaining and trade often took place around good performers and job openings" (Kanter 1977, p. 185).

The alliance may continue to grow until it runs out of players willing to join; until it becomes large enough to dominate, or at least to win the issues of importance to it; or until it meets head on with another alliance (in which case it finds itself in a "rival camps" game, which is discussed below). Over time, as issues are won and lost, new members join the alliance and old ones leave it. But the concept of alliance implies some stability in membership. A core of individuals and interest groups hold together over time to provide mutual support across a number of issues.

THE EMPIRE-BUILDING GAME   Whereas alliance building is a mutual game played in cooperation with peers, empire building is an individual one played by single individuals, typically managers in the middle line, who set out to enhance their power bases by collecting subordinates and subunits.

The empire-building game—the attempt to create "independent sovereignties with spheres of influence," to use Dahl's phrase (1961, p. 189)—makes use of all the political means of influence. Especially favored is privileged access to the influential, notably those who design the superstructure. But also important are privileged information through gatekeeping and centrality, exploitation of the legitimate systems of influence, as well as the political skills of the player and especially the effort the player is willing to expend to build the empire.

As in the worlds of animals and nations, so too in the world of organizations is the empire-building game fought over territory. Territory in the organization consists of positions and the units that contain them. Not only are salaries based on the number of subordinates a manager has, but resources are allocated and decisions delegated on the basis of the positions he or she controls. Moreover, positions and units provide managers with built-in constituencies of political supporters. Political battles require armies; position and units supply them. And so the empire-building game is played under departmental barriers, in the course of the design of the superstructure.

Managers can be gentlemanly when fighting over a new function or position. But, especially in organizations with slow growth, empire building also requires the takeover of existing ones. And it is difficult to remain polite when the object of the game is control of one another's sphere of influence, or, more to the point, of one another. So empire building can become among the riskiest and most highly politicized of the games we are discussing. Strauss describes how aggressive purchasing agents, hungry for power and status in their firms, sought "to win control over allied functions such as receiving, inventory control, stores, and production control" (1964, p. 139), hoping to build what is grandly known in their trade as "materials management." These expansion desires—especially to gain control over what to buy—brought them into head-on clashes with the engineers, resulting in "a running battle" between the two (p. 140).

Pettigrew (1973) describes in vivid detail a similar battle, in which the manager of a systems analysis department set out to capture the programmers. He was quite explicit about his intentions:

> They were like a bunch of sixth-formers, sixth-form mathematicians. They were slick, witty in a sarcastic sort of way. They hid behind their technology. Trying to get to grips with them was extremely difficult....
> They were a little "in" group. They larked around at Wolverhampton like a bunch of school kids. I thought, I must get control of them. (pp. 98–99)

From 1957 to 1961, the programmers had significant expert power in the organization due to uncertainty in the implementation of the necessary new computer systems. The programmers used that expert power to gain status, high salaries, and the right to flaunt bureaucratic rules and to exhibit a general arrogance. They were resented but, because they were needed, they could survive as an isolated social system in the organization. But between 1962 and 1967, the function of systems analysis emerged to challenge that of programming. Territorial wars ensued, in this firm and many others, essentially over the issue of "How near the computer are the analysts going to get?" (p. 82) As the programmers' position in the firm deteriorated, their department became a prime takeover candidate by that of system analysis.

Hanging on as best they could, the programmers resorted to four tactics to protect their power base: norms of secrecy and ones that denied outsider's competence, protective myths, and protection of their knowledge base through control over training and recruitment. In other words, they played expertise games (described below). The head of the systems analysis department in turn worked to reduce the myths of their expertise, by getting their programs written, and to make that expertise substitutable, by bringing in alternate programmers. He also had them moved physically, to isolate them from their source of power. Eventually he won out. The programming department was, so to speak, acquired by systems analysis.

THE BUDGETING GAME   This game is very similar to empire building—in some sense a subset of it—except that here the method of building the power base is not to acquire new positions and units but simply to expand those the manager already has. In other words, the object of this game is to get more—more positions, more space, more equipment, more resources of any kind, and especially more money. And because such resources are usually allocated through financial devices called budgets, those budgets—whether capital or operating—become the central focus of the game.

The budgeting game is perhaps the best-known of the political games, and the one most extensively studied, probably because it must be played more overtly and with more clearly defined rules than any of the others. Managers must make their cases explicitly and formally, in accordance with set procedures at set times of the year. This results in open bargaining—horse-trading as it can be seen in no other political game. Thus budgeting is the most formalized kind of empire building. As one well-known student of these games writes, budgets may be conceived of "as attempts to allocate financial resources through political processes. If politics is regarded as conflict over whose preferences are to prevail in the determination of policy, then the budget records the outcome of this struggle" (Wildavsky 1968, p. 192).

The tactics of the budgeting game are simple. In the case of operating budgets, use every trick available to gain the largest possible allocation for the unit; always ask for too much in the knowledge that a given percentage will be cut; evoke all the "rational" arguments that support a large budget and suppress those that do not, if need be distorting the truth about the real needs of the unit; and finally, when the budget is determined, make sure that every last penny is used up at year end, even if some of it must be wasted, for whatever gets turned back will be subtracted from next year's request. In fact, it is wise to hide some of the excess as slack in the unit, so that it can be drawn on when there is a financial squeeze. Schiff and Lewin, in a study of a two-year budget sequence in three divisions of large corporations, "detailed the process whereby managers satisfied personal aspirations through the use of slack in 'good years' and reconverted slack into profits in bad years" (1970, p. 262). These researchers estimate that the slack in these budgets may have accounted for as much as 20–25 percent of the total expenses.

Capital budgets are manipulated in similar ways. In particular, the costs of the capital project are biased on the downside and the benefits on the upside. Thus Cyert and March cite the "classic statements" of the staff analyst who said of a pet project: "In the final analysis, if anyone brings up an item of cost we haven't thought of, we can balance it by making another source of savings tangible" (1963, p. 81). Even that archtechnocrat, Robert McNamara, as Secretary of Defense deliberately distorted the figures he gave to Congress on the Vietnam War during the 1965–67 period. He commented later: "Do you really think that if I had estimated the cost of the war correctly, Congress would have given any more for schools and housing?" (quoted in Halberstam 1972, p. 610).

Such distortion often works, since many projects involve technical information known only to the unit doing the proposing, not to the management higher up doing the approving. Moreover, that management is busy, and so usually cannot take the time to review the cost-benefit figures carefully.

But the tactics of this game do not stop here. Bower tells the story of one division that avoided review altogether by chopping a capital project into small enough increments so that each could be passed through the operating budget. The assistant comptroller explains:

> Our top management likes to make all the major decisions. They think they do, but I've just seen one case where a division beat them.
>
> I received for editing a request from the division for a large chimney. I couldn't see what anyone could do with just a chimney, so I flew out for a visit. They've built and equipped a whole plant on plant expense orders. The chimney is the only indivisible item that exceeded the $50,000 limit we put on the expense orders.
>
> Apparently they learned informally that a new plant wouldn't be favorably received, so they built the damn thing. I don't know exactly what I'm going to say. (quoted in Bower 1970, p. 189)

THE EXPERTISE GAMES   If a political base of power cannot be built with superiors, subordinates, or peers, then one can always try to fall back on expertise, exploiting it as a political means of influence. This can take two forms: the *flaunting* of expertise by the professional and the *feigning* of expertise by the nonprofessional.

Professionals—those who really have highly developed skills and knowledge—play these games offensively by exploiting their assets to the limit, emphasizing the uniqueness of their skills and knowledge, the importance of these to the organization, and its inability to replace them. At the same time, they play defensively by seeking to ensure that all of this is in fact true, specifically, as we saw in Pettigrew's description of the programmers, by keeping their skills and knowledge to themselves and above all by discouraging any attempts to rationalize it. In other words, experts—and the professional societies that support them—do what they can to build mythologies around their skills, to render them inaccessible to ordinary mortals. In Crozier's tobacco factories, the maintenance workers

> ...prevent both production workers and supervisors from dealing in any way with machine maintenance...The one unforgivable sin of a machine operator is to "fool around" with her machine. Maintenance and repair problems must be kept secret. No explanation is ever given. Production workers must not understand. Maintenance workers keep their skill itself as a rule-of-thumb skill. They completely disregard all blueprints and maintenance directions, and have been able to make them disappear from the plants. They believe in individual settings exclusively, and they are the only ones to know these settings...These practices are necessary for preserving the group's absolute control over machine stoppages. (Crozier 1964, p. 153)

Nonexperts have two choices when faced with these games. Those with some other kind of legitimate power who feel threatened by the experts—notably the managers who sense a challenge to their authority—seek to rationalize the expertise. Again, as we saw in the Pettigrew study, they try to reduce it to easily learned steps so that anyone can do it. This would make it easily substitutable, and no longer a basis for power. "As soon as a field is well covered, as soon as the first intuitions and innovations can be translated into rules and programs, the expert's power disappears" (Crozier 1964, p. 165).

Nonexperts with no legitimate basis of power sometimes try to do the opposite. They seek to join the experts rather than fight them, in other words to have their own work declared professional so that it will be put under their control and removed from the influence of the managers, analysts, and even the real experts in the operating core. After all, if they too are certified experts, then no one can tell them what to do. Strauss, who notes that "as one group dons the cloak of professionalism, other groups seek to do likewise in self-defense" (1964, p. 148), documents this case for the purchasing agent. When faced with resistance from groups such as engineering, and in the absence of support from management, the purchasing agent "turns to professionalism, which helps bolster his self-image and which, hopefully, strengthens his position in interdepartmental conflict" (p. 137). In the "extreme case" of the hospital, according to Strauss, where the authority of management is relatively weak but the tyranny of one professional group—the physicians—legendary:

> ...We see a vast proliferation of professional and semiprofessional occupational associations, covering groups ranging from housekeepers through medical librarians

and lab technicians. Each [association] fights for the economic and social welfare of its members, and many seek the full accouterments of professionalism, such as certification, professional training, a code of ethics, and the right to exclude nonprofessionals from their special work. (p. 148)

Such use of pseudoprofessionalism—professional-type power in the absence of professional-type expertise—has been a powerful means of influence in such trades as plumbing and carpentry, used especially to restrict entry. But, to conclude, it should be stressed that this means of influence is political—based not on the technical knowledge or skills of the workers but on the political will they exert and the political skill they possess to have it declared expert.

THE LORDING GAME   Here we come to the last of our games to build power bases, the one in which insiders "lord it over" those subject to their influence. This is a game in which legitimate power is exploited in illegitimate ways. A boss may lord his authority over a subordinate to force him to do something, or an operator, at the bottom of the hierarchy of authority, may lord whatever formal power he has over the clients by evoking bureaucratic rules or by threatening to take disputed issues to his boss, who has more authority. Experts, too, play a form of this game, by lording their expertise over their clients, as do members of organizations with strong ideologies, who lord their norms and beliefs over outsiders.

But lording is really the game favored by those who feel the full weight of the bureaucratic controls, namely the unskilled operators and the line managers close to them in the hierarchy. In part, lording is encouraged by these controls. As Merton (1957) describes it, the demand for "strict devotion" to the rules sees them transformed into "absolutes" so that the need to interpret them flexibly, according to the needs of the client, is lost (p. 200). The rules, designed as means, emerge as ends unto themselves. But there is more to lording than just a direct reaction to the controls. As Kanter points out, lording is the favored game of the powerless, the game by which players with the least influence in the organization consciously try to enhance their own positions:

> When a person's exercise of power is thwarted or blocked, when people are rendered powerless in the larger arena, they may tend to concentrate their power needs on those over whom they have even a modicum of authority. There is a displacement of control downward... People will "boss" those they can, as in the image of the nagging housewife or old-maid schoolteacher or authoritarian boss, if they cannot flex their power muscles more constructively and if, moreover, they are afraid they really are powerless. (1977, p. 189)

Thus lording, as the simplistic tactic of falling back on authority in the face of resistance, while giving the player a sense of control over someone, is no way to build a substantial power base. As Strauss found in his study of the purchasing agents, recourse to the System of Authority was a tactic avoided by the effective agents. Appealing to the boss was considered a drastic step, one favored only by the low-status agents, "an admission that the agent could not handle his own problems" (1962–63, p. 169). Similarly, those agents who relied on rules tended to be the weaker ones, with lower education, who worked for the larger, more static companies. The more successful agents tended to rely on the rules to bolster their positions only when there was conflict.

THE LINE VERSUS STAFF GAME   From the games to build power bases, we now move to two games of sibling-type rivalry, played not so much to enhance personal power—although this is always a factor—as to defeat rivals. In effect, we move into the realm of what are known formally as "zero-sum games," in which, by definition, one player wins because another loses.[4] The first of these games pits line managers against staff specialists, while the second describes the clashing of two rival camps.

Line versus staff is a classic power conflict, pitting managerial decision makers in the middle line with formal authority against staff advisors in the technostructure with specialized expertise.[5] (Note that the managers' authority is here by definition not *direct*. That is, the staff specialists do not report to them directly but rather into the line hierarchy at levels above them. Hence the two are in some sense peers.) Ostensibly, the object of the game is to control choices—the line managers by trying to retain their discretion to make choices, the staff analysts by trying to preempt it. This the analysts can do in two ways: as advisors they can try to control the information that guides choices, or as designers they can try to enact bureaucratic rules that limit choices. But the nature of the confrontation, and the opposing interests of the players, soon reduce it to a game of rivalry between peers.

In a basic sense, the line versus staff game is a clash of formal and informal power. The managers seek to invoke their authority as members of the line hierarchy, while the analysts try to counter by exploiting their expertise. In other words, one tries to play the game of lording, the other the various games of expertise. But line versus staff is much more than that. It is a clash of personalities as well. The two sets of rivals tend to differ in age, background, and orientation. The line managers are typically older, more experienced, more pragmatic, and more intuitive, while the staff analysts tend to be younger, better educated, and more analytical (e.g., Huysmans 1970; Hammond 1974; Doktor and Bloom 1977). Moreover, as we saw in Chapter 9, the managers tend to identify more strongly with the organization (and are more subject to

---

[4]The insurgency and counterinsurgency games together reflect some of these characteristics as well, although games between superiors and subordinates can hardly be called ones between rivals.

[5]The more skilled advisors in the support staff can also engage the line managers in this game, although the classic play is between the analysts and the managers.

suboptimization tendencies), while the staffers tend to identify with their professions (and so are more apt to invert means and ends). In Gouldner's (1957–58) terms, this game pits the "locals" against the "cosmopolitans." All of these differences strengthen cohesion within each group and aggravate the conflict between them, as indicated in studies by Dalton (1959) and many others. The result is that the game heats up, and draws on all the political means of influence, not just the potential to exploit the legitimate means of authority and expertise.

As noted earlier, the line manager has behind him not only the weight of the organization's System of Authority—which gives him the right to make certain choices—but also some potent political means of influence. Being the nerve center of his own unit and being directly linked to the operating functions through the formal hierarchy, he develops a certain centrality in the flow of information. Moreover, of the two, the manager probably has the greater will to fight the political battles—not to mention the greater skill at doing so—for power is part and parcel of his job. Staff analysts are often lost in the world of organizational politics.

But, in the other corner, the staff analyst should not be underestimated. His expertise is a potent force, especially to the extent that he can use it to pull the wool over the manager's eyes. He, too, has a kind of centrality in information flows, since as advisor he often moves freely about the hierarchy. Mumford and Pettigrew (1975), for example, refer to a "dirty linen strategy," whereby "as part of their investigations into other departments, specialists may uncover the inefficiencies and incompetencies of others" and then use this knowledge against "recalcitrant clients" (p. 200). Also many staffers act as "technical gatekeepers" (p. 200), linking the organization to important sources of external information.

But, as Mumford and Pettigrew also note, while expertise and privileged information may be necessary means of influence to the staff analyst, they are not sufficient to win this political game. "To the specialist interested in the acceptance and implementation of his ideas, political access [to insiders of high authority] is likely to be critical," as is "assessed stature with the appropriate figures in his political network" as well as support from other staff groups (pp. 201, 206). Ironically, it is sometimes the staff analysts who can, in a sense, lord authority over the line managers, at least indirectly. The analysts, being outside the line hierarchy, can "often go to management to seek support for the proper execution of their plans" (Litterer 1973, p. 618), whereas the line managers often cannot even make direct contact with managers above their own bosses. Indeed, as we saw earlier, top managers sometimes plant staff analysts into line units in order to provide them with alternate channels of information. And these channels, as Dalton (1959) and others have so clearly shown, not only bring information up to the top managers, but also bring political power down to the staff analysts.

Where is the line versus staff game played? One major field of play is in the adoption of systems of bureaucratic control. In establishing such systems to control the operating work, the analyst not only formalizes the work of the operator but also "institutionalizes" the job of that worker's manager. In other words, impersonal bureaucratic controls replace the personal controls of the managers, and so reduce their discretion, and their influence over their subordinates. Thus, although the analysts have no formal authority themselves, ironically they are the ones who mediate between the two major systems of formal authority. Each time they put in a system of bureaucratic control, they weaken the system of personal controls, thereby reducing the power of managers lower down in favor of those higher up (not to mention the analysts themselves, who design the formal systems on behalf of the senior managers). As a result, the establishment of each new system of bureaucratic control becomes a zero-sum game between analysts and managers, with one pushing hard for its adoption and the other doing what they can to block it.

More generally, the line versus staff game is played on fields of change. As noted in Chapter 9, the staff analysts find their raison d'être in continuous although moderate change—they have, to repeat the words of Mumford and Pettigrew, a "vested interest in change" (1975, p. 205). So they are always looking for something to change. But many of the line managers find their raison d'être in smooth operations, which means a minimum of disruption. Managers "have quotas to reach, deadlines to meet and empires to protect"; they have "a vested interest in relative stability" (p. 205). And so they resist change. As Litterer notes, "Change can be a disquieting thing" (1973, p. 610). Thus line versus staff battles often arise over issues of change.[6]

Much of the actual conflict of the line versus staff game revolves around the issue of "rationality." As noted earlier, analysts have no special personal affinity for the profit an organization earns or whatever other measure of economic efficiency it uses. But that is the goal that serves them. It provides the operational criterion by which they can support their proposals for change, enabling them to "prove" their advice is right. And so economic efficiency becomes the analysts "rationality," and in the line versus staff game, they use it as a club to support their proposals. The analysts flaunt their brand of rationality, accusing the line managers of being empire builders and suboptimizers whose parochial departmental interests harm the organization at large. The managers who reject their advice are accused of being "political," "self-serving," or—the ultimate insult—"irrational." After all, the analysts have "hard data"—the facts—to back up their arguments.

[6]On the other hand, major, high-risk change—which must often be assessed on an intuitive rather than an analytic basis—may reverse the roles, with the entrepreneurial-type manager in favor and the conservative analyst against. But in organizations with rigid hierarchies of authority—where, as we shall see, the line-staff game tends to be played most commonly—such change, when it occurs at all, is usually the prerogative of the *top* management.

Line managers of course become defensive under such attacks, partly at least for good reason. For one thing, if line managers tend to suboptimize, then staff analysts tend to invert means and ends. Whereas the managers may pursue narrow ends, the analysts may pursue broad ends with narrow means. Many see the solution to all problems in their technocratic tools. But in another sense, the ends pursued by the analysts are not so broad as all that. Efficiency, as we shall see more clearly in Chapter 16, can be a narrow goal, such that the analyst's rationality can turn out to be not very rational at all. That rationality tends to be based only on what is quantifiable, often only what is economic. Whatever can't be measured doesn't count, so to speak. In this respect, the line manager works with a broader rationality, one beyond formal analysis, in Pfiffner's terms, an "administrative rationality" that "takes into account an additional spectrum of facts. These are the facts relative to emotions, politics, power, group dynamics, personality and mental health" (1960, p. 126). In contrast, the economic or classical model of rationality "takes a mechanical attitude toward human motivation and regards human behavior as conditioned by considerations of self-interest, mainly financial" (p. 130). So the line manager threatened by a technocratic analysis has a simple recourse: He dismisses it as narrow, invoking his broader "experience," his intuitive "feel," his greater "wisdom."[7]

Of course, both players use their respective rationalities to cheat a little in the bargain. The staff analysts exploit their command of the facts to state them in ways favorable to themselves, as noted in examples earlier of understating the costs of the proposals they favor. And the managers can attribute any conclusion they like to their intuition. Who beside they can distinguish the true messages of their subconscious from the results of conscious political analysis? And so, for the disinterested observer—if there are any—line versus staff can be the most intriguing game of all.

THE RIVAL CAMPS GAME   The building of alliances or empires cannot continue forever. Either one alliance or empire takes over the organization and dominates it, or else it is stopped by others. When those others are reduced to one—in other words, when the settling of the dust after alliance and empire building leaves only two major power blocks facing each other—then we enter the realm of the rival camps game. N-person games become two-person, zero-sum games, in which there must be losers whenever there are winners.[8]

In the rival camps game, because two opponents are clearly pitted against each other, all the stops are generally pulled out, and some of the most divisive political infighting takes place. The game itself can take a variety of forms—between units, between personalities, between those for or against a major change. Sometimes suboptimization tendencies in the superstructure pit units

[7]All of these points about the manager's and analyst's rationality are developed at greater length in Mintzberg 1979b.

[8]A CEO may sometimes encourage a rival camps game in order to try to maintain a balance of power—under him—in the Internal Coalition.

against each other. Marketing and production are old rivals in many manufacturing firms, each a center of power, one favoring the goals of growth and
customer service, the other of efficiency and stability. The game also frequently
develops around rival personalities. Zaleznik and Kets de Vries cite an example:

> "The palace revolt," in the words of the *Wall Street Journal*, that led to Semon
> Knudsen's departure from Ford Motor Company illustrates a failure in the forma-
> tion of coalition. It is true that Henry Ford named Knudsen president of the com-
> pany, but his actual position of power as a newcomer to an established power
> structure depended on the formation of an alliance. The individual with whom
> an alliance seemed crucial was Lee Iacocca. For some reason, Knudsen and Iacocca
> became competitors instead of using cooperatively a power base to which both
> contributed. . . . In the absence of a coalition, the opposing postures of rivalry
> were assumed and the battle for control was waged. (1975, p. 129).

Proposed changes of a significant nature can also lead to the rival camps game
as the organization splits into two factions—an "old guard" against the change
and the "young Turks" for it. (The one-sided view of this is discussed below
as the "young Turks" game.) Such rivalry is common when the change involves
a shift in mission. As we saw in the case of custody and rehabilitation in prisons,
the organization splits into two, with each mission becoming the primary goal
of one of the camps.

How do these rival camps games work out? In the case of a personality
clash, as between Knudson and Iacocca, typically one individual wins and the
other leaves. Organizations that must be hierarchical cannot long afford to be
split in two by warring camps. Similarly, in the battles between young Turks
and old guards, normally the issue will then be settled in favor of one or the
other, and the organization will get on with its work. But in some cases, no
side can win decisively. Manufacturing firms need to pursue both the service
goals of the marketers and the efficiency goals of the producers. Modern correctional institutions can ignore neither the custodial nor the rehabilitation missions. So while the balance may sometimes tilt to one side or the other, the
war goes on, although on a more subdued scale, and small battles continue to
be won and lost.

THE STRATEGIC CANDIDATES GAME   Finally we come to three types of games
played primarily to effect some change in the organization. In the first, an individual or group seeks a strategic change by promoting through the system
of legitimate power its own proposal or project—its "strategic candidate." In
the second, called "whistle blowing," the change is usually of a nonstrategic
nature, but legitimate power is questioned, to the point where internal influencers
go to the External Coalition for support. And in the third, legitimate power
is also questioned, but here the change is fundamental. A group of "young Turks"
seeks to change the basis of the organization's strategy or structure or even to
overthrow its central authority or ideology.

The central playing field of the System of Politics is the decision-making process itself, for here is where the organization commits itself to taking specific actions. And so here are where the great political battles take place, especially when decisions are "strategic," that is, important—committing large amounts of resources or setting important precedents. If a decision is a commitment to action, then a strategic decision is typically a commitment to a great many actions. Thus, a player is far wiser to try to influence a strategic decision in the making than to try to resist the many actions that result from it. In other words, those who can save the game of insurgency as a last resort. Moreover, power in the Internal Coalition is significantly redistributed during periods of strategic change, and that power tends to flow to those who proposed the change in the first place. As noted earlier in citing Kanter, those who succeed—even once—in effecting risky change gain great amounts of power in the Internal Coalition. Finally, the processes by which strategic decisions get made are fundamentally unstructured ones—that is, they follow no formal or set procedures—and so are filled with ambiguity and inevitably involve considerable discretion (Mintzberg, Raisinghani, and Théorêt 1976). Hence they invite political gamesmanship, as different groups or alliances promote or "champion" their own pet projects—their candidates for strategic change.

The strategic candidates game is perhaps the most interesting of the political games played in the Internal Coalition, because it combines elements of all the others. Strategic candidates are often promoted in order to build empires, and they often require alliances; rivalries frequently erupt between line and staff or between rival camps during the game; expertise is exploited in this game and authority lorded over those without it; insurgencies sometimes occur as byproducts and are countered; capital budgets often become the vehicles by which strategic candidates are promoted; and sponsorship is often a key to success in this game. In other words, a good deal of the action of the System of Politics focusses on the promotion of strategic candidates.

One would expect the CEO to control all strategic decision making, and in some organizations indeed that person does. But as Allison notes, Chiefs are busy people, and in most organizations—certainly in complex ones, even those with strong Systems of Authority—the Indians must get involved too. And that inevitably means political struggle. "Most problems are framed, alternatives specified, and proposals pushed. . .by Indians. Indians fight with Indians of other departments. . . . But the Indians' major problem is how to get the attention of Chiefs, how to get an issue on an action-channel, how to get the [organization] 'to do what is right'" (1971, p. 177).

Anyone can play the strategic candidates game, that is, can assume the role of "sponsor" or "champion." All it takes is a candidate to propose and a significant means of influence, although clever players have been known to succeed with no more than an immense amount of effort and a good deal of patience. They just keep pushing until someone finally listens. In this game, staff analysts have been known to form temporary alliances with line managers to push a candidate both favored. Even chief executives get involved in these games.

In professional organizations, for example, where they know they cannot execute their wishes without the support of others, they promote their own strategic candidates politically before they do so formally.

How does a strategic candidates game develop in the System of Politics? Stymne (1975) describes the process in three basic steps, as shown in Figure 13-3. The first step is the "generation of the strategic candidate," which may originate inside or outside the organization. The second step involves "the attachment of values to candidates." Different power groups in the organization have a "go" at the candidate, deciding to support it, oppose it, or modify it to support their own ends. Gradually, the candidate may develop support, while being modified: "In an organization there are always persons and groups with different interests, beliefs and values. The presence of a strategic candidate may be a major occasion for the different groups to present their ideas and to try to make the candidate 'theirs' or in some way become associated with it" (p. 13).

What is known as the "bandwagon effect" occurs when it becomes evident that a candidate will be successful, and all the as yet uncommitted influencers rush forward to support it: ". . . the slightest sign of plurality [converts itself] into an overwhelming majority" (Schelling 1957, p. 32). Of course, sometimes an alliance proposing a candidate may wish to avoid consensus, because that may require too much compromise or dilute each member's share of the winnings. It prefers what Riker calls a "minimum winning coalition": "Excess members of a winning coalition both cost something to acquire and lessen its gains" (1962, p. 107). The sponsors want just enough support to be sure of winning.

Gore (1956), in his study of decision making in federal field offices, also discusses this second stage of the strategic candidates games. He found that sponsors who did not actively seek out political support for their candidates were notably unsuccessful in promoting them. Successful sponsors followed one of two approaches—"selling" their given candidate to enough people willing to support it as such, or, more commonly, "accommodating" to the interests of others by modifying the candidate in order to win their support. Of course, modification does not necessarily mean weakening the candidate. To return to the ideas of Mary Parker Follett, instead of compromise, where each side gives up a little to reach agreement, both sides with a little bit of good will and imagination may be able to improve the candidate for their common good. "Integration involves invention, and the clever thing is to recognize this, and not to let one's thinking stay within the boundaries of two alternatives which are mutually exclusive" (1942, p. 33). In other words, this game need not be zero-sum.

Stymne's third and final step is the selection of a candidate. As he notes, "In organizations the selecting body is often a single person or a small group of decision makers" (p. 15). They accept the candidate if they believe the values embodied in it are sufficiently consistent with their own. But when selection is not by a central authority, as, say, in a university senate, where certain specialists may have considerable power, or in a highly ideological organization, where everyone must agree with the proposal, then the processes discussed

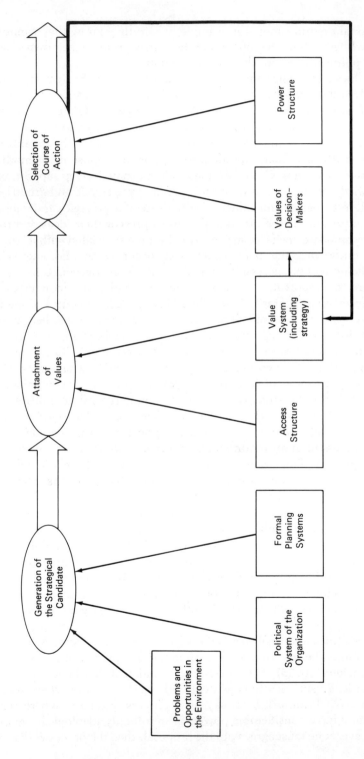

Figure 13-3. *Steps in the Strategic Candidates Game (from Stymne, 1975)*

above—of gaining consensus or negotiating sufficient support—become the direct means to selection.

A number of strategic candidate games are described vividly in the literature. We encountered one in Chapter 6 in Zald's (1965) description of how various insiders (as well as outsiders) lined up behind different candidates—in this case people—for the position of chief executive officer of a welfare agency. Pettigrew (1973, also 1972) describes another game in considerable detail, this one played over the choice of a computer system. He notes in his introduction:

> Political behaviour is likely to be a special feature of large-scale innovative decisions. These decisions are likely to threaten existing patterns of resource-sharing . . . New resources may be created and appear to fall within the jurisdiction of a department or individual who has not previously been a claimant in a particular area. Those who see their interests threatened by the change may invoke resistance in the joint decision process. (p. 169)

In this decision process, three rival factions developed at middle levels, each supporting its favored manufacturer of computer systems. But as the member of one faction noted about another: "Their choice of manufacturer in the decision process wasn't just a matter of their technical orientation. Bill was actively concerned with putting forward a different installation, one that was his alone" (p. 216). Since the selection rested with the senior management, each faction tried to manipulate the information and advice going to it in order to influence the outcome. But one of the three factions had an inside track: its leader controlled the flow of technical information from the other two to the senior management. To use Pettigrew's term, control of information was his power resource. Pettigrew's depiction of this is shown in Figure 13–4. Thus it was inevitable that he would eventually win.

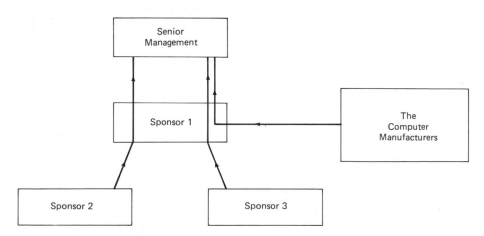

Figure 13–4. *Control of Information to Senior Management in a Strategic Candidates Game (adapted from Pettigrew, 1973, p. 235)*

THE WHISTLE-BLOWING GAME   This is a very specific game, typically brief, designed to use privileged information to effect a particular kind of change in the behavior of an organization. In essence, the player—usually an insider low in the hierarchy of authority, often an operator, sometimes a staff specialist—perceives a behavior taking place in the organization that he or she believes violates some social norm and, usually, a formal constraint as well, such as a law. And so the player "blows the whistle" on the culprits, that is, informs an external influencer who can remedy the situation. Since the informer is bypassing legitimate power—the chain of authority, certified expertise, or accepted ideology—and is questioning its legitimacy with respect to this behavior, his or her action can bring retribution. Hence the player usually attempts to make the contact secretly, sometimes even anonymously, for example, through an unsigned letter.

In one well-known case of whistle-blowing in the United States, an inspector at the Fisher Body plant provided Ralph Nader with critical data about the dangers of driving General Motor's Corvair. Nader went on to write *Unsafe at Any Speed* and to a career of organizational pressure campaigns, while General Motors suffered a series of embarrassments and, among other things, eventually had to withdraw its Corvair from the market. Another well-known case involved A. Ernest Fitzgerald, a systems analyst for the U.S. Defense Department who testified before a Senate committee on the massive cost overruns in building the Lockheed C-5A cargo plane.

THE YOUNG TURKS GAMES   Now we come to the last of our political games, and also the one played for the highest stakes. For here the intention is not to effect one simple change, as in our last two games, nor to counter authority, as in the very first game we discussed, but to effect a change so fundamental that it throws the legitimate power itself into question. The "young Turks," as the proponents of such changes are sometimes called, may wish to reorient the organization's basic strategy, to displace a major body of expertise, to replace its ideology, or even to overthrow its leadership directly. Thus, while these are games played to effect change in the organization, they also resemble insurgency, although in many cases the term is too mild: rebellion or even revolution would be a better one.

In their paper, "Social Movements in Organizations: Coup d'Etat, Insurgency, and Mass Movements," Zald and Berger (1978) touch on a number of the games we have been discussing. But their real focus is on what we here call the young Turk's games. To cite two examples:

> ...in the fall of 1975 Robert Sarnoff, president of RCA and son of the founder of the company, took a trip around the world to visit RCA's foreign plants. He had recently announced the reassignments of some of the senior executives; also, the company had suffered alarming financial reverses from the 1973–75 recession

and Sarnoff's strategic decision to enter the computer industry. In his absence, senior executives convinced RCA's board that Sarnoff's reorganization was inappropriate and that he should be replaced. It is reported that when he returned he was handed a letter of resignation for his signature...

In a similar vein, in the late 1950s Brigadier General Hutton (faced with official opposition based on written agreements among the Department of Defense, the army, and the air force) developed the armed helicopter. Starting with baling wire and lashing machine guns to the frame, a group of midrank officers evolved the quick-strike, mobile air cavalry. The army's air force is now the third largest in the world, behind the United States Air Force and that of the Soviet Union... (p. 824)

As these examples show, young Turks are often rather highly placed in their organizations, sometimes right up to, but of course never including, the chief executive officer, at least so long as that person is perceived to be the problem. Also they tend to constitute a small group, at least at first, since the game must be played very secretly. In fact, we might expect that the greater the power of the young Turks, the fewer they need be to accomplish their aims. A few vice-presidents may be able to convince a board of directors of the failings of the president, but it will take more people than that to convince it of the failings of the whole team of senior executives. Indeed, a last resort of unsuccessful young Turks—short of exiting the organization altogether—is to try to turn their conspiracy into an outright rebellion. In Zald and Berger's terms, they try to provoke a "mass movement," involving a large number of "lower participants"—the ultimate insurgency game.

Zald and Berger describe social movements in organizations as "unconventional opposition," "unconventional politics" (pp. 825, 830). And so, whereas the organization "defines legitimate mechanisms for attempts to reach decisions and allocate resources," social movements must operate in the zone of "proscribed" behavior or at least behavior not specified by organizational authority (p. 830). In other words, the young Turks must rely on the political means of influence.

Leeds (1964) elaborates on the characteristics of these groups of young Turks, which she calls "enclaves." They tend to be led by charismatic leaders— who "have tendencies toward nonconformity and unorthodoxy" and "a flair for originality" (pp. 119, 121). These leaders in turn are strengthened by the support of able lieutenants. The atmosphere of the enclave is unorthodox, in some sense ideologic. But "it maintains a high commitment to the basic goals of the organization" (p. 122), if not to its authority, strategy, or ideology.

> The enclave itself is endowed with a militant spirit; its members are eager to undertake large-scale tasks and to execute them with novel strategies. The organization, grown weak internally in one or several respects, either cannot or prefers not to initiate change. (p. 119)

The authority under challenge may try to condemn the enclave, avoid its challenge, or expel its members, and will succeed if the enclave is weak. But it may instead choose to "absorb" the protest of the nonconforming enclave— accept its challenge and integrate it "into the organization by converting it into a new legitimate subunit" (p. 116). In other words, an accommodation can be reached whereby the enclave "is given some autonomy to pursue a specific activity...but, at the same time, it is expected to abide by the regulations and restrictions to which all legitimate subunits adhere" (p. 116). Leeds argues that this pattern of protest absorption is most frequent in "normative" organizations, that is, ones with strong ideologies.

Zald and Berger discuss a number of other forms of these games. One is "organizational coup d'état"—"the infiltration of a small but critical group from within the organization's structure to effect an unexpected succession" (p. 833). As in nation-states, the purpose is not to overthrow the *System* of Authority but rather the *holders* of authority, keeping that system intact for the new leaders. Here the young Turks need direct access to board members who have the power to replace the CEO, or else to dominant external influencers who control the board. (Otherwise they need to be able to bring so much pressure on the CEO that he will resign voluntarily. This point in fact applies to all forms of the young Turks games: either the young Turks are able to create alliances with powerful external influencers to impose their change on the Internal Coalition, or else they must get the central authority to acquiesce through the intense pressures they are able to bring to bear.) Another form of this game Zald and Berger discuss is designed to change some aspect of the organization's functioning, as in the helicopter example cited earlier.[9] Whereas coup d'état usually involves higher level executives, Zald and Berger believe that this form "usually range[s] deeply into the organization, throughout middle management" and even down to the operating core when it is staffed with professionals (p. 838).

The young Turks games are perhaps the ultimate ones of zero-sum, because the intensity of the challenge is such that the organization can never be the same again. Should the existing center of legitimate power yield to the wishes of the young Turks, it will have difficulty retaining its previous status. Only with great skill at reversing its stand—making accommodation after resistance seem perfectly natural—might it maintain its position. Otherwise it is quite possible that one of the young Turks will eventually take over the leadership. On the other hand, should the challenge be completely squashed, it is the young Turks who are permanently weakened. In these circumstances, they frequently exit, sometimes effecting a schism by taking a piece of the organization with them. This last of our political games is frequently all or nothing.

[9]Zald and Berger call this game "bureaucratic insurgency." But in their description of it—"an attempt by members to implant goals, programs, or policy choices which have been explicitly denied (or considered but not acted upon) by the legitimate authority" (p. 838)—it is closer to what we call the young Turks game.

THE POLITICAL GAMES IN THE CONTEXT
OF LEGITIMATE POWER

We have seen that the System of Politics of the organization can be described in terms of a set of political games played by the various internal influencers. We have described thirteen of these games in all. Some of their characteristics—including one to be introduced below—are summarized in Table 13-1.

To this point, our discussion has perhaps captured the flavor of the political games, but not their interaction. In part, as noted earlier, this reflects a lack of research on the subject. We have no evidence on these interactions. But it also reflects the fact that in contrast to the Systems of Authority, Ideology, and even to some extent Expertise, there is less order in the System of Politics. It is a system of everyone for himself or herself, with no sense of unity or integration, of pulling together for the common good. The games, in other words, do not interact very systematically; they come and go, in various relationships with the legitimate system of influence. To conclude this chapter and lead into the next, which draws together our findings about power in the Internal Coalition, we can express these relationships in three broad forms:

- Games that *coexist with* the legitimate systems of influence
- Games that are *antagonistic to* the legitimate systems of influence
- Games that *substitute for* the legitimate systems of influence in their weakness

A number of political games depend on one or other of the legitimate systems of influence. These games are relatively mild and pose no real threat to legitimate power. Indeed, they could not exist unless one of the legitimate systems was strong. These games are equivalent to the parasites that live off—but in coexistence with—other living organisms, like the sea squirt that attaches itself to the scallop shell and shares its food.

Lording comes immediately to mind as one of these *coexistent* games—it most often takes place only when authority is the paramount system in the Internal Coalition. And by exploiting authority, in some sense this game reinforces it. In other words, ironically, when the political game of lording is present, the implication is that the System of Politics is weak, that of Authority strong. The same could be said—perhaps to a slightly lesser extent—of the games of sponsorship, budgeting, and from the line perspective, of line versus staff (since the System of Authority defines a sharp distinction between line and staff). Empire building, the strategic candidates game, and to a lesser extent alliance building, often emerge within a strong, stable System of Authority as well, although these can also arise under very different conditions, as we shall soon see.

The expertise games similarly arise commonly when the System of Exper-

TABLE 13–1. Some Characteristics of the Political Games of the Internal Coalition

Game	Main Players	Common Political Means of Influence	Reason Played	Relationship to Other Systems of Influence
Insurgency	Unskilled operators (in large groups), lower-level managers and sometimes professionals (singly or in small groups)	Political will and skill, privileged information	To resist authority (or other legitimate power)	Antagonistic to legitimate systems
Counterinsurgency	Senior managers	Privileged information, exploitation of authority, political skill	To counter resistance to authority	Coexistent with legitimate systems
Sponsorship	Any subordinate or junior, usually managers, personal staff, or younger professionals	Privileged access	To build power base (with superiors or seniors)	Coexistent with authority or expertise
Alliance Building	Line managers	Political will and skill, exploitation of legitimate systems of influence	To build power base (with peers)	Substitutable for legitimate systems, or else coexistent with authority or expertise
Empire Building	Line managers	All, but especially privileged access and political will	To build power base (with subordinates)	Coexistent with authority or expertise; sometimes substitutable for legitimate systems
Budgeting	Line managers	Privileged access and information, and political skill	To build power base (with resources)	Coexistent with authority or expertise
Expertise	Operators and staff specialists	Exploitation of expertise or else political will and skill to feign it	To build power base (with real or feigned knowledge and skills)	Coexistent with expertise, or substitutable for it

Lording	Unskilled operators and their managers (sometimes professionals)	Exploitation of authority (or expertise or ideology)	To build power base (usually with authority, especially bureaucratic rules)	Coexistent with authority (or expertise or ideology)
Line versus Staff	Line managers and staff analysts (sometimes support staff)	Exploitation of authority and expertise, privileged information and access	To defeat rivals	Coexistent with authority for line, antagonistic to it for staff
Rival Camps	Any alliances or empires, usually in middle line	Privileged information and access, exploitation of legitimate power, political will and skill	To defeat rivals	Substitutable for legitimate systems
Strategic Candidates	Line managers, CEO, professional staffers and operators	Political will, privileged access, also political skill and privileged information	To effect organizational change	Coexistent with legitimate systems, sometimes substitutable for them
Whistle-Blowing	Usually lower-level operators or analysts	Privileged information	To effect organizational change	Antagonistic to legitimate systems
Young Turks	Usually higher-level line managers and/or staffers, sometimes professional operators	Privileged access, privileged information, also political will and skill	To effect organizational change	Antagonistic to legitimate systems

tise is strong. In fact, by exploiting expertise, just as lording exploits authority, their effect is to reinforce the importance of expertise in the Internal Coalition (sometimes at the expense of authority or ideology). The true professionals play to enhance their power as experts; the other play to create new (if pseudo) areas of expertise. A number of the games mentioned above as being played under strong Systems of Authority and posing little threat to them, are similarly played under strong Systems of Expertise. Included are sponsorship (of junior by senior professionals), lording (of expertise over clients or co-workers), budgeting, alliance and empire building, and strategic candidates, all favorite games of groups of experts seeking to build power bases or to effect change in the professional organization. None does great damage to the System of Expertise; in other words, all can comfortably coexist with it.

In the case of a strong system of Ideology, the equality it dictates tends to preclude almost entirely games such as sponsorship and empire building in the Internal Coalition. Perhaps the only political games that can coexist with a strong ideology are that of strategic candidates, as insiders promote favored changes within the context of the ideology, and a form of lording, where the members lord the ideology of the organization—its strong norms—over outsiders.

Another group of political games also depends on the existence of one of the legitimate systems of influence, but is played to weaken or even to destroy it. In other words, while these games could not be played without that system, the relationship is not one of coexistence but *antagonism*. This kind of parasite requires its host in order to destroy it, like the lamprey eel that attaches itself to a trout, bores into its flesh, and consumes it. Insurgency, young Turks, and to a lesser extent whistle-blowing games, as well as line versus staff (at least from the perspective of the staff), usually arise to challenge authority itself, or those in authority, or in some cases to confront established ideology or expertise. As such, these antagonistic games are usually far more intense, and more divisive, than the coexistent ones.[10]

Finally there are the political games that arise in lieu of the presence of a strong System of Authority, Ideology, or Expertise (and perhaps help to weaken it as well, although that is not their intention per se). Once the lions leave, the scavengers move in. In other words, here it is the System of Politics itself that dominates the Internal Coalition. Political games pervade it and—unconstrained by legitimate power—can become extremely intense and divisive. Rival camps would seem to be the best example of these *substitute* games—since it splits the entire Internal Coalition into two warring groups, precluding a strong role for authority, ideology, or even expertise. Alliance building would seem to be another, although it can also coexist with a moderately strong System of Authority or Expertise as well. And to a lesser extent, we might also include

[10]Counterinsurgency of course arises because of insurgency. In that sense, it is associated with antagonism to legitimate power, although it itself is of course coexistent with it.

empire building and the strategic candidates games here. While they are common under strong Systems of Authority or Expertise, they can also be played aggressively when legitimate power is weak. The same is true of the expertise games, which, although often played under a strong System of Expertise, can also arise in the absence of any strong legitimate system of influence, as different groups try to gain power by having their work declared professional.

The presence of these three possible relationships of political with legitimate power—coexistent with it, antagonistic to it, or substitutable for it— imply two basic levels of the System of Politics. On one hand, it can exist as a kind of fifth column of power in the Internal Coalition—present but not dominant. It becomes just another force, one system of influence that coexists with the others. Here the System of Politics seems to consist of a number of mild political games, some of which exploit the more legitimate systems of influence, and in the process actually strengthen them, others which weaken them, but only to a point, so that politics remains a secondary force in the Internal Coalition. **On the other hand, the System of Politics can emerge as the dominant force in the Internal Coalition, weakening the other, legitimate systems of influence or simply arising to replace them after they have weakened themselves (or each other).** Here we might expect to find fewer kinds of political games, but played far more intensively and pervasively.

In fact, thinking back to the last three chapters, the same conclusion was present there as well. Ideology was described as sometimes just another system in the Internal Coalition, sometimes the dominant one, driving out authority, expertise, and politics. So too was expertise described as just another system of the Internal Coalition or one that prevails over the others, weakening especially authority and ideology. And we have seen that authority, while often showing a tendency to dominate the others through its formal power, must also coexist with them in many circumstances. This, then, is how we shall reconcile our descriptions of these four very different systems of influence. We shall show first how they coexist, indeed can even work in concert with each other, and then how each can emerge as the preeminent force in the Internal Coalition, dominating the others.

14

Reconciling the Systems of Influence in the Internal Coalition

We have now invested a good deal of space in discussing the various systems of influence in the Internal Coalition—authority, ideology, expertise, and politics. But our discussion has not, on the whole, been an integrative one. We have implied that each of these systems acts very differently on the organization, but we have made little attempt to reconcile these differences.

We described the System of Authority as tending to draw power into the middle line of the organization, and there up to its apex (with some filtered off to the technostructure). The System of Ideology, in contrast, was described as tending to diffuse power widely, to all who share its norms. And although both these systems were characterized as serving to integrate the efforts of the insiders, our discussion also implied that they might do this in mutually exclusive ways. The System of Expertise, while also described as serving to get the work of the organization done, was shown to distribute power unevenly in the Internal Coalition—in effect, to act as a force of disintegration. And the System of Politics was described as having both disintegrative and parochial tendencies—ostensibly serving individual needs at the expense of the broader need to get the work of the organization done.

Yet we have also mentioned contradictions to most of these tendencies. We have seen examples of centers of authority—including the CEO—using the System of Politics or that of Ideology to consolidate their own individual power. Likewise, we have seen examples of people farthest from the center of authority—operators at the bottom of the hierarchy—exploiting authority as a means to gain individual power to the detriment of the functioning of the organization. And then there were the young Turks who sometimes use the System of Politics to fight authority or ideology for the good of an organization in need of change. In other words, in the complex world of organizations, everything seems to get stood on its head once in a while.

How do we reconcile all of this?

One way is to take up the point introduced at the end of the last chapter— to consider first how the different internal systems of influence can coexist, indeed work to support each other, and then how each might come to dominate the Internal Coalition, driving some of the others out and relegating the rest to places of secondary importance. We pursue these two themes in this chapter, in order to try to reconcile the disparate elements introduced in our discussion of the Internal Coalition and also to show that there is an underlying logic to the play of power in the Internal Coalition. We present a first set of propositions to describe how the systems of influence work in concert. We then present a second set of propositions to describe how each can come to dominate the others (pointing out that dominance by one does not necessarily exclude the others from working in concert). These latter propositions lead us into a description of five basic types of Internal Coalitions.

THE INTERNAL SYSTEMS OF INFLUENCE
IN CONCERT

Throughout our discussion of the Internal Coalition, we have seen hints of a certain logic in the functioning of the internal systems of influence, whereby they seem to work in concert to complement one another. Our first two propositions describe how these systems sometimes move in unison, for the good of the organization, while the subsequent propositions describe how each of the systems of influence can serve to support the others or correct their deficiencies.

1. The internal systems of influence can at times act in concert to concentrate power in the Internal Coalition, while 2. at other times, they can act in concert to diffuse power, in both cases to serve broad needs of the organization. Power in the organization seems to be a *pulsating* phenomenon, at times imploding or concentrating toward a center, at other times exploding or diffusing to the peripheries.

We have seen how a number of the systems of influence can favor the chief executive officer at the strategic apex. To reiterate, formal power is ultimately his—he sits at the pinnacle of the hierarchy of authority—and so the personal and bureaucratic control systems ultimately serve him. Ideology too can favor him, since he embodies the beliefs and represents them in his role as the organization's figurehead. Many CEOs even have a potent form of expertise, retaining personal control of functions critical to the organization—selling in the consulting firm, finance in the conglomerate, government relations in the utility. Finally, even the political means of influence can favor the chief executive. As the organization's nerve center, the CEO develops a privileged position with respect to both internal and external information; his position at the apex of the hierarchy enables him to exploit the legitimate systems of influence and also provides him with the best access to powerful influencers in the External Coalition; as the one who made it to the top of the hierarchy, his political skills are often the most highly developed in the organization; and no one is better placed or has more will to expend effort in the political games than the CEO, since power is his business. Kanter supports this notion of the concentration of power, arguing that "power is likely to bring more power, in ascending cycles, and powerlessness to generate powerlessness, in a descending cycle," those without power being "caught in a downward spiral" (1977, p. 196).

Yet we have seen evidence of the opposite effect too, that some law of diffusion also seems to be at work in the organization. How else can we explain the power that Scheff's attendants were able to amass in the mental hospital?

The fact is that a number of forces work to diffuse power in the Internal Coalition. Earlier we quoted Crozier that in some sense each employee is an expert. That is, each carries out a specialized function that he or she knows best. And every function is critical to some extent, or it would not exist in the organization. Therefore, every insider can make use of the System of Expertise to gain some power in the Internal Coalition. Patchen supports this with his finding that insiders tend "to defer to [the] preferences" of that decision maker in whose realm a particular decision falls: "The most frequently mentioned characteristics [of people most influential in a decision process] are ones which have to do with the extent to which a person *will be affected* by the decision" (1974, pp. 217, 209). Next most frequently mentioned were characteristics associated with an individual's particular "expertise," followed in third place by those associated with formal responsibility. The implication of these findings is not only that power tends to be diffused in the Internal Coalition more widely than implied by the System of Authority, but also that the System of Politics may be less pervasive than many people believe, while that of Expertise may be more so, even in the absence of complex technical skills and sophisticated technical knowledge. Insiders often defer to each others' areas of specialization—expert or not—rather than challenge each other.[1]

Of course, it is not only the System of Expertise that serves to diffuse power in the External Coalition. Indeed, in Patchen's results we can see some of the same tendencies even in the System of Authority, for that is what places the responsibility for specific functions in the hands of individuals in the first place. Ideology, too, serves as a force to diffuse power among the insiders. It may favor the CEO as that person who embodies it, but it also puts a good measure of power in the hands of its adherents.

[1]The context of Patchen's findings—purchasing decisions—must, however, be borne in mind. His findings would seem to hold best for decisions that fall clearly into the realm of single decision makers. Strategic decisions, which have broader implications, as we have seen tend to evoke all kinds of political activity.

Likewise, while the CEO has certain advantages in the use of the System of Politics, in other, perhaps more important ways, that system also works to diffuse power widely in the Internal Coalition. We can see this, for example, in the use of privileged information and access, since many insiders serve as gatekeepers, occupy positions of centrality in information flows, and maintain direct contacts with influential outsiders. Moreover, a variety of insiders can exploit the legitimate systems of influence, as when analysts use their power as the designers of the bureaucratic controls to weaken the line managers or when operators lord their formal power over the clients.

But the diffusing effects of political power come out most clearly in the expenditure of effort as a means of influence. While it is true that power is the chief executive's business, it is equally true that this one person's time and effort is severely limited. "Time for decision activity is a scarce resource," March and Olsen (1976, p. 45) tell us: "A person who has many interests has less energy to attend to any one of them; a person of many talents has less time to use any one of them; a person with many responsibilities devotes less attention to any one of them" (p. 46). And, in general, no insider has more interests and more responsibilities, sometimes also more talents, than the CEO. As a result, the CEO cannot fight every political battle that matters to him; he must select only the most important, and leave the rest to others. And so it is, to a decreasing extent, with each of his subordinates down the line. The result, ultimately, is that something is left in the Internal Coalition for everyone—a few crumbs at least. For everyone, that is, willing to expend the effort to collect them.

> . . .secretarial staffs in universities often have power to make decisions about the purchase and allocation of supplies, the allocation of their services, the scheduling of classes, and, at times, the disposition of student complaints. Such control may in some instances lead to sanctions against a professor by polite reluctance to furnish supplies, ignoring his preferences for the scheduling of classes, and giving others preference in the allocation of services. (Mechanic 1962, p. 359)

Mechanic agrees that such power "may easily be removed from the jurisdiction of the lower participant," especially when it is abused, but only "at a cost—the willingness to allocate time and effort to the decisions dealing with these matters" (p. 359). Thus we saw how the ostensibly powerless attendants of the mental hospital were able to manipulate the doctors—the experts, and with formal authority to boot—because collectively they had more time and effort to invest.

Thus we find both the concentration and the diffusion of power in the Internal Coalition. And by the pulsating phenomenon mentioned above, power can flow one way or the other depending on where it is needed. Sometimes the organization must act as a highly integrated entity, adapting quickly and decisively in totally focussed fashion. At these times, the concentration of the various forms of power at one center is critical. But at other times, there is the need for local adaptation—for being in touch, for nuance. Then diffusion is required to put power where it is most needed, where the specialist, who best understands the particular situation, can act. By alternate impulses of concentration and diffusion of its power, the organization adjusts to its different needs.

But while the different systems of influence may sometimes pull together, more commonly they pull in different directions, each serving its own special purpose. Acting alone, any one of them can throw the organization out of balance. But acting together, as a *set* of forces, they can provide for the different needs of the organization and also serve to correct each other's deficiencies. In this way, they help to maintain a basic balance in the organization. Below we review what each of the systems of influence contributes to achieve this balance.

3. Personal control, in the System of Authority, provides necessary focussed responsibility and overcomes the sluggishness of the other systems of the Internal Coalition. When organizational change must be effected quickly and decisively—as when a sudden shift in the environment threatens the survival of the organization—there is the need for pinpointed responsibility (Hamblin 1958). The organization requires one center where all the necessary information can be gathered and where tightly integrated decisions can be made for the good of the organization as a whole.

The System of Ideology provides no such focussed center; instead it distributes power widely. It also tends to be the most sluggish of the systems of influence, resisting change for the sake of maintaining tradition. Even within the System of Authority, bureaucratic controls pose problems for such change, because they are oriented to standards—to accepted, repetitive ways of doing things. They actually impede significant change. (They also encourage an analytic approach to decision making, which means analyzing any proposed change laboriously before accepting it.) As for the Systems of Expertise and Politics, they so diffuse power that no change can ever be effected through them quickly. Too many people must be involved, and convinced. The process of change bogs down in debate or negotiation. It is only personal control in the System of Authority—free of tradition and standards, able to focus responsibility and rely on intuition—that can allow for quick, decisive change. This it does by enabling one person—the chief executive officer—to make all the necessary decisions and then impose them on everyone else.

Even under normal operating conditions, organizations still require some degree of personal authority to maintain a certain order and credibility. Centuries ago, the political philosopher Thomas Hobbes argued that without personal authority, there is a "war of each against all" with the result that "the life of man is poor, nasty, brutish, and short." Hobbes was talking about government, but the same argument can be used in today's organizations. In the absence of personal authority, the war occurs in the form of uncontrollable political games, which result in "poor, nasty, brutish, and short" lives for organizations. The Hobbes quote is taken from a book by Kenneth Arrow (1974), who sees authority as providing "the focus of convergent expectations": "An individual obeys authority because he expects that others will obey it" (p. 72). In that sense, authority serves to pull the disparate elements of the organization together. Indeed, authority serves to achieve the very concept of "organization."

4. Bureaucratic control, in the System of Authority, provides for stability and regularity, and serves to overcome the inefficiencies in the other systems of influence. While authority in the personal sense serves one set of needs, that in the bureaucratic sense serve another. Every organization requires some level of stability, rationalization, and standardization if it is to perform its mission efficiently. And the only system that can assure all of this is the one of bureaucratic control.

Personal control is arbitrary and often irregular, varying according to the whim of the individual manager. The System of Expertise, because it diffuses power among so many individuals, can lead to irregularities in the exercise of that power, especially when the experts work in teams on ad hoc projects. Political power, based on the principle of everyone-for-oneself, naturally elicits behavior that is unstable and inefficient. Politics is no way to achieve regularity in the organization. Even ideology, which imposes stability on the organization through standardizing its norms, can fail to achieve a logical rationalization among the different tasks. It, too, is not designed for efficiency. The bureaucratic control system is. That is its central purpose in the Internal Coalition.

5. The System of Ideology is required to infuse life into the shell of the organization created by authority and expertise, and to overcome parochial tendencies in the other systems of influence so that the insiders are drawn to consider the needs of the whole organization. Authority alone cannot be relied upon to integrate the efforts of the insiders with the needs of the organization. The organization that tries to do so emerges as a lifeless shell, devoid of human feeling and identification. (Or else, those feelings and identifications are deflected into the System of Politics, where the insiders are driven to displace formal goals in favor of parochial ones.) Likewise, the organization that tries to rely exclusively on expertise emerges as another kind of shell, devoid of a life of its own, whose members direct their identifications to external professional societies.

These shells come to life when the organization is infused with some form of its own ideology. Ideology, because it elicits the deepest, most sincere form of identification of the individual with the goals of the organization, achieves the strongest integration of individual effort with organizational need. Rather than buying the individual off materially, as under authority, or offering the chance to control his or her own work, as under expertise, or allowing free reign to pursue parochial interests, as under politics, ideology attracts the individual directly to the mission of the organization as an end worthwhile in itself. Operators, no matter what their skills, find their work more meaningful—its end comes into view, comes to have a broad purpose. Likewise, staff specialists come to see their methods as means to broader ends rather than as ends in themselves. And the managers of the middle line come to consider not only the narrow goals of their own units but also the broader goals of the whole organization. All the reasons for goal displacement—some due to authority, others to expertise or politics—tend to disappear under a strong ideology.

This point is developed by Selznick in his book *Leadership in Administration* (1957): ". . . policy attains depth," he argues, when "a neutral body of men [is transformed] into a committed polity" (p. 90). More specifically, "A well-formulated doctrine is remarkably handy for boosting internal morale, communicating the bases for decisions, and rebuffing outside claims and criticisms" (p. 14). Moreover, it "ensures that in the performance of assigned tasks the spirit as well as the letter will be observed. Similarly, emotional identification with the organization creates resources of energy that may increase day-to-day effort and, especially, be summoned in times of crisis or threat" (p. 18).

6. **The System of Expertise is required to ensure that power is put where the critical technical skills and knowledge of the organization are located, rather than being allocated arbitrarily according to office or rules, given to any believer in the ideology, or allowed to flow to those most adapt at the political games.** Authority is hardly a finely tuned distributor of power. It puts power in offices not people, and, through bureaucratic controls, allocates it according to rules and standards of performance. In other words, its distribution of power is formal and inflexible, and therefore often well behind the situation at hand. As Hickson et al. note, "Perhaps today's authority hierarchy is partly a fossilized impression of yesterday's power ranking" (1971, p. 218). For its part, ideology is not tuned at all. It distributes power indiscriminately, to any believer. And politics puts power into the hands of those insiders most adept at playing the political games—those with the time, the will to play, the right contacts, the political skills—not those who can necessarily best serve the needs of the organization.

To the extent that the organization requires expertise in its functioning, all of these systems of influence tend to misallocate power. When the experts must work under the System of Authority, they become subservient to line managers, or to technocratic rules, and so lack the discretion to make proper use of their skills and knowledge. When they are subject to the System of Ideology, their skills and knowledge are restrained—by themselves as well as other people—for fear of creating pockets of status and power. And, of course, under the System of Politics, political skills count for more than technical ones. When they lack the former, even though the organization may badly need the latter, the experts are submerged in the play of politics.

Given the need for technical skills and knowledge, only the System of Expertise can ensure that power flows to those who can best serve the organization. In terms of our conclusion of Chapter 12, power flows to those who perform the critical functions with irreplaceable bodies of expertise. In other words, the System of Expertise imposes a kind of law of natural selection on the organization, whereby those who have the necessary skills and knowledge get the power they require to use them.

7. **The System of Politics is necessary to correct certain deficiencies and dysfunctions in the legitimate Systems of Authority, Ideology, and Expertise—to provide for certain forms of flexibility that the other systems of in-**

fluence deny. Our initial description of the Internal Coalition, as noted, rested on the assumption that a so-called "rational" System of Authority is used by the CEO to impose formal goals on the organization, and that this is opposed by an illegitimate System of Politics in which insiders seeks to displace the formal goals in favor of their own personal ones. (We also enlarged our description of legitimate power to include the Systems of Ideology and Expertise, but that of Politics remained illegitimate.) This dichotomy is, in fact, common in the literature. Pfeffer and Salancik (1974, citing Baldridge) contrast the "bureaucratic model" with the "power model." In one, "subunit interests are presumed to be subordinated to overall [universalistic] organizational objectives"; in the other, "there is conflict among participants and the answer to what decisions will be made is to be found in examining who has power to apply in a particular decision context. Thus power, rather than what is optimal for achieving some organizational objective, becomes an important decision variable" (p. 136).

At this point in our discussion, it is time to ask whether the goals that the CEO seeks to impose on the organization through authority—or those imposed by that person and others through ideology or expertise—are always legitimate, while those imposed through politics are not.[2] We have seen that the CEO is an influencer too, with his own personal goals to pursue. So too is this the case with all the other internal influencers, including the line managers and the experts. In other words, those who have power by virtue of authority or expertise can abuse that power for private ends. Moreover, we have seen that authority, ideology, or expertise can be used to impede change necessary for the organization, whereas politics can bring about that change. This was most apparent in our discussions of the whistle-blowing and young Turks games. We have also seen, in our discussions of suboptimization and distortions in objectives, that employees truly dedicated to serving the organization must ignore ill-conceived demands of the System of Authority and play politics instead. In other words, each of the legitimate systems of influence can be abusive...and abused. Repeatedly, our discussion has shown that these systems can be dysfunctional and, in terms of the needs of the organization, irrational.

There is no doubt that the System of Politics has its dysfunctional and irrational side too. It tends to be divisive and destructive; it wastes energies, requiring far more time and effort than the other systems of influence to get things done; and it often ends up putting power in the hands of the most mercenary elements in the organization. Yet the functional side of the System of Politics must be recognized too, for it is an important side. To quote McCall, "power [illegitimate as well as legitimate] is a two-edged sword. It can be used to solve im-

---

[2]We are here referring only to the ends achieved. As we described politics earlier (*"behavior* outside of the legitimate systems of influence," or outside their legitimate uses), the means are always illegitimate, although the ends need not be (to continue our description, "behavior designed to benefit the individual or group, *ostensibly* at the expense of the organization at large").

portant organizational problems... On the other hand, use of power can be misdirected to problems of power preservation... (1979, p. 203). As Stymne argues, based on his study of three trade organizations, while political processes consume a great deal of energy in the organization, energy that might otherwise go into work processes, "the structure would break down rather quickly if political processes could not take place" (1972, p. 59). And so, while in Chapter 13 we talked of political games at best coexisting with the legitimate systems of influence—like the sea squirt on the scallop shell—now we can talk of them as being in a *symbiotic* relationship with the legitimate systems—like the pilot fish that by picking at the food scraps in the teeth of a shark helps keep them clean and healthy. Let us now, therefore, consider in terms of four subpropositions the ways in which the System of Politics can be functional, can work on behalf of the organization, when the Systems of Authority, Ideology, or Expertise are deficient or dysfunctional.

7(a). **The System of Politics acts in a Darwinian way to ensure that the strongest members of the organization are brought into positions of leadership.** Situations frequently occur in organizations where the System of Politics allows natural leaders to rise in the face of their suppression by the System of Authority. Authority is based on the principle of a single, "scalar" chain of command. A weak link can create problems further down. Weak leaders can, for example, suppress the most capable of their subordinates, encouraging only the "yes men." The best people are held back. But the System of Politics provides for alternate channels: It allows these people to develop contacts elsewhere in the hierarchy, sometimes enabling them to bypass their superiors. (Moreover, it is often only through the System of Politics that the weakness of a link in the chain can become evident. Managers, as we have seen, are able to filter the information that goes up the hierarchy. Information on poor performance can be held back or distorted. Senior managers may have no idea what is really going on until a subordinate bypasses his superior to tell them.)

Even when the promotion system works as it should in the System of Authority, the System of Politics can supplement it. We saw this most clearly in the sponsorship game, where a manager supports a promotable junior, thereby helping that person to climb the hierarchy faster than authority alone would allow. We can see this also in the political games played between peer managers. Games such as strategic candidates and alliance and empire building can serve as testing grounds to reveal those managers with the most highly developed political skills. Need for power and the ability to use it subtly in the interests of the organization—in neither mercenary nor timid ways—have been shown to be important characteristics of leaders (McClelland 1970; McClelland and Burnham 1976). This is especially true at the top of the hierarchy, where the games are not between units but between whole organizations. The second-string players may suffice for the scrimmages, but only the stars can be allowed to meet the competition. Senior managers, therefore, who have to make choices about future leadership, need information on the candidates' political wills and skills. And it is the political games that provide such information. Indeed, these games sometimes serve to make the choices. When the dust settles, only the best players are left standing. They go forward to play again, while the losers fade quietly into the background.

In all of these ways, therefore, the System of Politics, by serving to ensure the survival of the fittest, serves to strengthen the leadership of the organization.

7(b). The System of Politics can ensure that all sides of an issue are fully debated, whereas the Systems of Authority, Ideology, and sometimes even Expertise tend to promote only one. The System of Ideology assesses every issue in terms of the "word." If the prevailing ideology is Marxist, or capitalist, or whatever, then only that interpretation of events is acceptable. And the System of Authority likewise promotes but a single point of view, although for a different reason. It aggregates its information up the hierarchy into successively narrower channels. The manager who represents ten subordinates, perhaps with ten different opinions, in turn serves as the sole channel of information to his superior. The tendency is to pass up the hierarchy only one point of view, often in fact the one already known to be favored above. The literature is replete with stories of decisions gone astray because the appropriate information was blocked in the hierarchy. As for the System of Expertise, ostensibly it is more eclectic than the other two, supporting all kinds of different bodies of expertise. But as we saw earlier, in Patchen's findings, under this system there is a tendency to defer to the expert on each issue. Thus, unless an issue cuts across more than one body of expertise, the System of Expertise too can promote only one point of view.

The System of Politics, on the other hand, contains a number of devices to encourage a fuller airing of issues. In politics, "responsible men are obliged to fight for what they are convinced is right" (Allison 1971, p. 145). In authority, right is vested in office; in expertise, it is vested in the specialist; in ideology, there is only one right. Employing political means of influence, employees who feel strongly enough about nonprevailing viewpoints can make themselves heard. They can, for example, bypass their managers and access those higher up. Or if that doesn't work, they can use the whistle-blowing game to take their point of view right out of the organization, to external influencers. The rival camp's game also provides for a full exploring of the issues, since each side marshalls arguments to support its own case and weaken that of its opponents. Points come out that would never emerge through the legitimate systems of influence:

> Interdepartmental conflicts encourage the free competition of new ideas (as well as giving top management a chance to evaluate subordinates' behavior). Since each department has only a partial picture of the entire organization, competition improves the quality of each department's thinking and forces it to take the other department's point of view into consideration. In large organizations such internal competition tends to substitute for the external competition of the marketplace. (Strauss 1964, p. 148)

The line versus staff game is another device of the System of Politics to ensure the full airing of issues. Here it is not just two sides that are heard, but two very different orientations. One prefers "soft" data, processed in an intuitive way, the other "hard" data subjected to formal analysis. An organization often requires both approaches, and this political confrontation may be the best way to ensure that it gets them.

What really forces the System of Politics—ostensibly so parochial and distorted—to actually broaden the organization's approach to decision making is the requirement that it operate within the sphere of organizational "rationality." In other words, no matter how self-serving one's position, it must be presented in "objective" terms—in terms of what is best for the organization.

> Normally, either side in any conflict called political by observers claims to speak in the interests of the corporation as a whole. In fact, the only recognized, indeed feasible, way of advancing political interests is to present them in terms of improved welfare or efficiency, as contributing to the corporation's capacity to meet its task and to prosper. . . . this is the only permissible mode of expression. (Burns 1961–62, p. 260)

Burns elaborates in an amusing footnote:

> It is impossible to avoid some reference from the observations made here to F. M. Cornford's well-known "Guide for the Young Academic Politician." Jobs "fall into two classes, My Jobs and Your Jobs. My Jobs are public-spirited proposals, which happen (much to my regret) to involve the advancement of a personal friend, or (still more to my regret) of myself. Your Jobs are insidious intrigues for the advancement of yourself and your friends, spuriously disguised as public-spirited proposals." (p. 260)[3]

Thus, no matter how heavy the infighting, the System of Politics is often highly effective at bringing out all the issues. The proponents of an idea present the "pros," and their opponents retort with the "cons." Wildavsky notes that research on Canadian, British, Dutch, and Soviet government practice indicates that when disagreement between the budgeting agency and a department arise, both sides "come to a meeting armed to the teeth to define their respective positions" (1968, p. 194). The same thing, of course, happens in business and other organizations. In such an atmosphere, only the valid arguments tend to survive. Ultimately, therefore, victory in political games is often decided on "rational" grounds—organizational rather than parochial.

And this fact is not lost on the players, which further encourages objectivity. For if the debate is likely to be heavy, then it is in the interests of each

---

[3]Burns with his colleague Stalker elaborates in another publication that "We do not mean to represent the conduct of management in firms as a continuous melodrama of hypocrisy and intrigue. These do, of course, exist, but the real problem, here or elsewhere, is most often that to the parties themselves, their opinions and policies seem utterly sincere and disinterested and their maneuvres aimed at serving what they see as the best interests of the firm" (1966, p. 145).

player to present only the arguments that are likely to stand up, and to propose only the most defensible strategic candidates. It is dangerous to be caught with the best arguments on your opponent's side. After all, one has only so much energy to expend on strategic candidates. It is best to support likely winners, those for which strong arguments can be marshalled, which means arguments that cater to organizational, not parochial, interests. And so political power often goes to those who support what is best for the organization. The System of Politics becomes an agent of organizational need, in spite of itself.

7(c). **The System of Politics is often needed to promote necessary organizational change blocked by the Systems of Authority, Ideology, and / or Expertise.** No one in the organization has a monopoly on foresight. Needed change can come from the powers that be, but it must sometimes also come in spite of them, or even against their opposition. "I beseech you, in the bowels of Christ, think it possible you may be mistaken," Cromwell told the Scottish authority (in Arrow 1974, p. 75).

McCall points out that the locus of power has to shift when the demands on an organization change, otherwise "the organization's ability to survive becomes threatened" (1979, p. 189). In other words, whatever system of influence is strong, or whoever is strong within that system, usually has to give way when major change becomes necessary. A new legitimate form of power must eventually emerge. But to create that change, it would appear that the "illegitimate" System of Politics must often take over the Internal Coalition for a time, displacing the preeminent authority, ideology, or expertise.

The very fact that authority concentrates so much power into the line hierarchy of the organization and then up to the chief executive at its apex, creates the danger that when authority cannot adapt, the organization will become threatened. Authority is often unable to adapt, or refuses to, for a number of reasons. For one thing, the senior managers often exhibit a strong psychological commitment to the organization's existing strategies, because they have long lived with them and perhaps even introduced them in the first place, and so they resist changing them (Mintzberg 1978). In other cases, the senior managers simply grow old and tired. They become unprepared to make needed changes, yet hang on to their power nonetheless. Change may have brought them to power, but now it is change that threatens them. Another reason why authority impedes change, as Salancik and Pfeffer note, is that the "institutionalized forms of power," such as centralized control and MIS, "tend to buffer the organization from reality and obscure the demands of its environment" (1977, p. 3). In other words, managers who rely on the system of bureaucratic control for information may be the last ones to realize the need for major change. And finally, bureaucratic controls are based on standards—whether of work in the form of rules and the like, or of outputs in the form of action plans and performance controls—and that means they put greater emphasis on maintaining stability than on promoting change.

The case for ideology is even more clear-cut. Important components of the strategy are often embedded in the ideology. So to propose change in the strategy is to put into question the ideology itself. And that is a taboo when the ideology is strong. The System of Ideology is rooted in the past—in traditions—not in the present or the future. So it is especially resistant to change. The organization is committed, in Selznick's words, "to specific aims and procedures, often greatly limiting freedom of the leadership to deploy its resources, and reducing the capacity of the organization to survive under new conditions" (1957, p. 18).

As for expertise, the commitment is to sets of skills and bodies of knowledge, not to the organization per se. Moreover, the standardization of these skills and knowledge can make them as resistant to change as the standards contained in the system of bureaucratic controls. Professional organizations that apply standardized skills—universities, accounting firms, and the like—are not noted for their adaptability (Mintzberg 1979a, pp. 374–76). Thus the System of Expertise, by concentrating power in the hands of those who are often more interested in maintaining their professional standards or in serving their professions rather than in serving the organization where they practice them, can also act as a force to impede change in the organization.

Here then is where the System of Politics often comes in. For it, ironically, can be the most flexible of the internal systems of influence, the one that often forces the organization to make necessary changes. In other words, the System of Politics seems to work as a kind of "invisible hand" in the organization—"invisible underhand" would be a better term—to set things straight. When change must be made without questioning the basic legitimacy of existing power, it is the strategic candidates games that can be used. When legitimate power must be bypassed, say for the sake of correcting an unethical practice, then it is the whistle-blowing game that can be called upon. And when the necessary change is so fundamental that it must challenge the legitimate power directly—as in the replacement of a whole strategy, ideology, or even the central authority itself—then politics in the form of the young Turks game is usually necessary. "There is a certain naive tendency to assume that all conflicts are bad," Stagner has stated (1967, p. 142). But as Burns argues in a paper called "Micropolitics: Mechanisms of Institutional Change" (1961–62), what appears as self-serving political activity can often be in the best interests of the organization.

All of this is to say that the System of Politics seems to be an almost inevitable component in major organizational change, even when that change is from one legitimate power to another. Indeed, as we shall see in our next and last point, recourse to politics is often necessary even when the CEO himself wishes to effect strategic change. Political action is the instrument of social change.

7(d). The System of Politics can ease the path for the execution of decisions. In point 7(b), we saw the role of the System of Politics in ensuring the completeness of the information that goes into decision making. And in the last point, we saw its role in promoting the decision process itself. Now we see its role in the execution of the completed decision.

We saw very clearly in our discussion of the insurgency games—especially in the stories of the Chinese clerks and the hospital attendants—how easy it is for operators who are well organized to block the execution of decisions imposed on them from above. As a result, the senior manager who wishes to ensure the successful execution of his decisions must play political games too. If he does not smooth the way for his own strategic candidates—by persuading, negotiating, and so on, as well as by building alliances, before he announces his choices—he may well find himself embroiled in a counterinsurgency game after he does so. And then it may be too late to save his candidate. As Saunders has noted, in a political situation, management must ensure that its strategies have "the necessary support through the organization to gain effective implementation. If the political process is not open and vigorous, then the product of the process is less likely to meet the needs of the organization and will certainly not have the widest possible support" (1973, p. 18).

To conclude this discussion, we note that while the System of Politics is not always functional—"rational" in terms of organizational needs—neither are the Systems of Ideology, Expertise, or Authority. Both a functional and dysfunctional side of each of these systems must be recognized. In that way, we can better appreciate how these systems of influence are able to work in concert.

THE INTERNAL SYSTEMS OF INFLUENCE IN DOMINATION: FIVE TYPES OF INTERNAL COALITIONS

To work in concert, even to achieve a balance in the Internal Coalition, does not necessarily mean that one of the Systems of Influence cannot take precedence over the others, indeed come to dominate them. A certain balance can be maintained so long as the other systems stand ready to correct difficiencies or distortions in the dominant one. For example, a small degree of politics may be sufficient to correct the maladaptive tendencies in a dominant System of Authority. Or else, should that correction require intense politics, the organization may become dominated by the System of Politics for a brief time to effect the necessary change before returning again to a state of stable, dominant authority. Thus, the two themes of this chapter—the systems of influence acting together in concert and singly in domination—are not necessarily contradictory. Later in this book we shall take up the question of how this occurs; at this point we need only make the point that it does and get on with our description of how each of the systems of influence can come to dominate the Internal Coalition.

In each part of the organization, one of the systems of influence may emerge as most important. For example, personal authority may be key at the strategic apex, bureaucratic authority for the technostructure, expertise in the operating core when it is staffed with professionals, politics under certain circumstances in the middle line, and so on. Table 14-1 summarizes for each of our

TABLE 14–1. The Internal Influencers and Their Play of Power

	Chief Executive Officer	Line Managers	Staff Analysts	Support Staffers	Professional Operators	Unskilled Operators
Their *role* in the Internal Coalition	Overall management of it	Management of its individual units	Design and operation of its systems of bureaucratic control and adaptation	Indirect support of its operating functions	Provision of its operating functions	Provision of its operating functions
The goals they favor	Survival and growth	Growth above all (of units and organization), survival, balkanization	Bureaucratization, economic efficiency, perpetual but moderate and well-regulated change, professional excellence	For professional staff: collaboration, perpetual but moderate change, professional excellence; for unskilled staff: protection of social group	Autonomy, enhancement of specialty, professional excellence, mission	Protection of social group
Their prime *means* of influence	Authority (personal and bureaucratic), privileged knowledge, privileged access to the influential, political skills, sometimes ideology as well	Authority (decreasing as descend hierarchy), privileged information, political skills, sometimes expertise	Bureaucratic controls, expertise	Expertise (for professional staff), political will (for unskilled staff, when act in concert)	Expertise	Political will (when act in concert)

Their *reasons for displacement* of legitimate power	Maintain personal power	Distortions in objectives, suboptimization, direct links to external influencers	Means-ends inversion, direct links to external influencers	Suboptimization, means-ends inversion, direct links to external influencers	Means-ends inversion, direct links to external influencers	Group means-ends inversion
Their *fields of play* of internal power	Decision making	Decision making, advice giving, and execution (with respect to upper levels)	Advice giving	Advice giving	Decision making, execution	Execution
Their favorite *political games*	Strategic candidate, counterinsurgency	Sponsorship, alliance and empire building, budgeting, line vs. staff, strategic candidate, rival camps, sometimes lording, insurgency, and young Turks	Expertise, line vs. staff, strategic candidate, sometimes whistle blowing and young Turks	Expertise, strategic candidate (for professional staff)	Expertise, strategic candidate, sometimes young Turks	Insurgency, lording, whistle blowing

main groups of internal influencers, their role in the Internal Coalition, the goals they favor, their prime internal means of influence, why they tend to displace legitimate power, where they do so, and the political games they use to do so. But these groups seldom share power equally in the Internal Coalition. As described in the *Structuring* book, depending on the circumstances, one group often assumes the position of greatest importance. And when this happens, the system of influence favored by that group emerges as the strongest.

We saw in Chapters 10 to 13 how, when strong, each of the internal Systems of Influence tends to overwhelm the others, driving them out of the Internal Coalition or at least relegating them to positions of secondary importance. Strong ideology, for example, being based on normative control, largely precludes the need for the personal or bureaucratic controls of the System of Authority; its egalitarian norms can also be incompatible with a strong System of Expertise, which creates all kinds of status distinctions in the Internal Coalition; and the strong identification with the organization that it develops in its members precludes almost all political activity. In other words, when the System of Ideology is strong, the Systems of Authority, Expertise, and Politics tend to be weak. And so it is with each of the other systems of influence. Situations can arise where two or more of these systems attain equal importance in the Internal Coalition—we call these *hybrids*. But here we hypothesize that **the natural tendency in the Internal Coalition is for one of the systems of influence (and, in the case of authority, one of the forms of control) to emerge as paramount, at least temporarily, and to dominate the others.** In this part of the chapter, we describe five ways in which this can happen, giving rise to five types of Internal Coalitions (much as in Chapter 7, we saw the emergence of three types of External Coalitions). We introduce these below in terms of a series of propositions which describe what happens to each of the other systems of influence when one dominates.

8. When personal control in the System of Authority dominates the Internal Coalition, the System of Politics tends to be precluded and those of Expertise and bureaucratic control are discouraged, although a mild form of the System of Ideology may reinforce the personal authority. What we call the *Personalized IC* emerges.

9. When bureaucratic control in the System of Authority dominates, the System of Ideology tends to be precluded, and the System of Expertise is discouraged, although personal controls may reinforce bureaucratic ones at higher levels and the System of Politics coexists in mild form to resist or exploit certain aspects of authority and to correct its deficiencies. What we call the *Bureaucratic IC* emerges.

10. When the System of Ideology dominates, the Systems of Authority (in personal and bureaucratic forms) and of Politics are largely precluded, and the System of Expertise is usually discouraged. What we call the *Ideologic IC* emerges.

11. When the System of Expertise dominates, the Systems of Ideology and

Authority (in personal and bureaucratic forms) are usually discouraged, but the System of Politics coexists as a secondary force in the Internal Coalition. What we call the *Professional IC* emerges.

12. And when the System of Politics dominates, it tends to discourage all the other, legitimate systems of influence (or else it arises in their weakness). What we call the *Politicized IC* emerges.

THE PERSONALIZED IC   In the first of two types of Internal Coalitions dominated by the System of Authority, it is the personal control system that rules. And since personal control focusses power in the hierarchy of authority, and specifically at its top, the chief executive officer emerges as the absolute ruler of this Internal Coalition. In other words, here power pulses to one center.

Personal control means that the CEO makes the strategic decisions, and monitors their execution closely by maintaining an intimate contact with the operating core of the organization. In other words, not only does that one person possess the formal authority, but he or she also controls the critical functions and maintains centrality in all of the information flows. When one individual so controls everything, the other insiders have little chance to play political games. As a result, the Personalized IC emerges as one of the least politicized of the types of Internal Coalitions.

The System of Expertise also tends to be weak in this type of Internal Coalition, discouraged by a CEO who prefers not to have to delegate power to experts whom he cannot control personally. In other words, expertise and personal control tend to be incompatible—either a chief executive dominates, or he does not and another kind of Internal Coalition emerges. Bureaucratic control tends to be weak here for the same reason. The chief executive who controls personally will not tolerate bureaucratic standards. They diminish his flexibility, his power to maneuver. Thus we conclude that of all the Internal Coalitions, the Personalized one concentrates power to the greatest extent, making it the closest equivalent to the Dominated External Coalition.

One other system of influence can, however, coexist with personal control so long as it is clearly subordinate to it. That is the System of Ideology. When the ideology revolves around the leader and his own ideas—as it tends to do in its first stages (discussed in Chapter 11), as it forms under so-called "charismatic" leadership—then rather than challenging his personal power, it enhances it. And so at this stage ideology is compatible with personal control. But in later stages, when the ideology becomes rooted in tradition, and acts to diffuse power in the Internal Coalition, it becomes a threat to personal control and is discouraged.

In the *Structuring* book (Chapter 11), the concept of *decentralization*—the extent to which decision-making power is dispersed among the members of the Internal Coalition—was broken down into two dimensions, each composed of two types. The first dimension concerned where the power is decentralized. *Vertical* decentralization referred to the delegation of formal power down the chain of authority, from the CEO to the line managers at different levels. *Horizontal* decentralization referred to the extent to which informal power flows out of the System of Authority, in other words, to nonmanagers—the operators, analysts, and support staffers. The second dimension concerned the extent to which the decentralized power is focussed. In *selective* decentralization, the power over different kinds of decisions is dispersed to different places in the organization, while in *parallel* decentralization, the power for many different kinds of decisions concentrates in the same place.

In these terms, the Personalized IC can be seen to be vertically and horizontally centralized, in parallel. In other words, power over all important decisions is concentrated at the top of the hierarchy of line managers, in the strategic apex. This form of centralization was seen to give rise to what we called *Simple Structure*. We noted that this is commonly found where a single individual can maintain close personal control in the absence of bureaucratic standards and expertise. Organizations that are small and young lend themselves to such control, since one individual can easily comprehend everything. Indeed, they often require such control to get themselves going. Similarly, an environment that is simple enables one individual to comprehend everything in the absence of experts and one that is also dynamic precludes bureaucratic standards. Sometimes, nothing more than the strong will of a leader may ensure the primacy of personal controls. The existence of a great deal of hostility in an organization's environment can have the same effect, since power may have to be wielded arbitrarily by one individual for a time to ensure a fast, integrated response. The classic example of the Personalized Internal Coalition is the entrepreneurial firm, where the owner-manager controls everything.[4]

THE BUREAUCRATIC IC   In the second type of Internal Coalition, power is again concentrated in the System of Authority, but this time in its bureaucratic controls. In other words, authority is maintained primarily by the standardization of work processes and of outputs.

Under the system of bureaucratic controls, authority retains its primacy. In other words, these controls ultimately serve the insiders with formal power. But because the bureaucratic standards, as noted earlier, tend to "institutionalize" the job of the lower line manager—reducing his capacity to use personal control—they tend to concentrate formal power near the top of the hierarchy. It is on behalf of the senior managers that the bureaucratic controls are designed. So we can call this type of Internal Coalition vertically centralized. But it must also be remembered who does the designing of the bureaucratic controls: the

[4]The evidence for any of the findings cited here or subsequently in this chapter which refer to the structural configurations can be found in Mintzberg 1979a. We review the conditions of each of these Internal Coalitions—as related to its corresponding structural configuration—only briefly here because these conditions are discussed at greater length in the section on the power configurations.

analysts of the technostructure. As the designers, they gain influence whenever their systems do. It is, after all, their standards that control everyone else's work. So the Bureaucratic IC also involves a limited form of horizontal decentralization, selective in nature. In other words, informal power over some decisions flows out of the hierachy of line authority, to the staff analysts.

The personal control system is not fully impotent in this Internal Coalition, although it is clearly subordinate to the bureaucratic one. With that much power concentrated near the top of the hierarchy, personal controls can be used there as well. But only there, because institutionalization of the jobs of lower-level managers precludes them from making extensive use of personal control. On the other hand, ideology does tend to be impotent in this type of Internal Coalition, because the emphasis on standardization usually breeds an impersonality that discourages strong traditions and beliefs. Most insiders contribute their efforts in a purely utilitarian fashion, in return for material inducements. They develop no special identification with the organization. This is the type of Internal Coalition closest to the lifeless shell we talked of earlier. Likewise, the System of Expertise is weak in this Internal Coalition. When internal rules control everything, expertise—necessarily subject to the self-control of the expert as well as the external control of his profession—cannot establish itself on a firm footing. To put this another way, the Bureaucratic IC cannot tolerate strong pockets of expertise; these are discouraged as incompatible with its form of control.

In the Personalized IC, close personal control by one individual precludes politics. But not here. The dominance of bureaucratic controls does serve to keep the System of Politics under control. But some political games nevertheless arise. Some are encouraged by distortions in objectives and suboptimization tendencies inherent in the bureaucratic controls themselves. Others arise because of the general rigidities of the Internal Coalition and because of its various inherent status differences, for example between line and staff or operator and manager. Unskilled operators, feeling crushed by the weight of the bureaucratic controls, lord the rules over the clients or else engage their managers in insurgency games, as do these managers their own superiors higher up in the hierarchy. Managers of the middle line try to build empires and enlarge their budgets and to be sponsored by the more senior managers with greater authority. It is in the Bureaucratic IC too that the line versus staff game is most often played, since this type of Internal Coalition gives staff analysts the responsibility but not the authority for the design of the bureaucratic controls. That authority remains with the line managers whose very jobs these systems institutionalize. And so conflict ensues between the two. Thus, while the Bureaucratic IC cannot be called highly politicized, neither can it be described as devoid of politics.

In *The Structuring of Organizations*, this type of structure was referred to as *Machine Bureaucracy*, and, when the organization was divided into a number of machine bureaucratic divisions, the *Divisionalized Form*.[5] It was found to be associated with operating work that is simple and routine, in other words, unskilled, so that it could be easily standardized. The conditions that typically give rise to this kind of work are technical systems of mass production, environments that are simple and stable, organizations that are mature and large or that are controlled externally. Classic examples are mass production manufacturing firms as well as service organizations with large numbers of unskilled operators, as in the cases of large banks and post offices.

THE IDEOLOGIC IC   In the third type of Internal Coalition, it is the System of Ideology that dominates. The result is a tight integration around central organizational goals, perhaps tighter than in any of the other Internal Coalitions. Here the insiders do not merely accept the central goals; through identifications, they share or "internalize" them as their very own.

The chief executive of the Ideologic IC would seem to have a great deal of power, because as leader he or she embodies the ideology. But the fact is that in sharing the beliefs, everyone also shares the power. In other words, this tends to be the most egalitarian of the Internal Coalitions. All who have been duly socialized or indoctrinated, or who simply identify naturally, are able to take part in the decision making. They can all be trusted to decide in accordance with the prevailing set of beliefs. Thus, this Internal Coalition can be described simply as "decentralized," with power to make decisions diffused rather evenly throughout—not horizontal in the sense that nonmanagers have more or less power than managers, not vertical in the sense that to lower managers are or are not delegated formal powers from above.[6]

Its tight integration means that the Ideologic IC has little need for either of the control systems. Its own means to control behavior, by the standardization of norms, is far more effective. Likewise, politics is excluded here because of the sharing of beliefs. Since all the insiders subscribe to the prevailing ideology, they have little basis for conflict. And no one is inclined to pursue parochial goals. At most they lord their beliefs over outsiders, and occasionally promote strategic candidates within. Hence the Systems of Authority and Politics are the least developed in this Internal Coalition. The System of Expertise also tends to be weak here. Because it creates status differences among the members, it is discouraged as incompatible with a strong ideology.

Loyalty is the ingredient needed to bring about an Ideologic IC, and that comes typically from a mission whose uniqueness or inspiring character attracts adherents, as in many religious or radical political movements. Sometimes an

---

[5]The Bureaucratic IC is not, however, to be confused with *Professional* Bureaucracy as discussed in that book, which we shall come to shortly.

[6]A structure corresponding to the Ideologic IC is not discussed in the *Structuring* book (although its existence is suggested on the very last page of that book).

ordinary mission attracts adherents because of a unique way of accomplishing it. Charismatic leadership at some point in the organization's past is another characteristic often associated with the Ideologic IC.

THE PROFESSIONAL IC   In our fourth type of Internal Coalition, it is the System of Expertise that dominates, power flowing to those with the technical skills and knowledge critical to the success of the organization.

As noted earlier, its need for sophisticated skills and knowledge forces an organization to engage highly trained experts—professionals—and to surrender a good deal of its power to them and the institutions that train and certify them. In other words, a strong System of Authority is incompatible with a strong System of Expertise. The work, being complex, cannot be controlled personally by managers or bureaucratically by the simple standards that can be developed within the organization. This means that the chief executive, the managers of the middle line, and especially the analysts of the technostructure are relatively weak in the Professional IC. Ideology is usually weak here too, for the same reason that expertise tends to be weak in the Ideologic IC—the two are in some ways incompatible. In this case, strong ideology is discouraged because it interferes with the need to allocate power unevenly—to create pecking orders on the basis of ability.

Politics, on the other hand, is not a weak force in this Internal Coalition, although it does take a second place to expertise. Power allocated on the basis of internal expertise tends to be fluid power because what is critical to the organization changes from time to time. Moreover, the abilities of the different professionals vary, and as new ones enter and old ones age, the pecking orders among them have to change. Also, bodies of expertise inevitably overlap, creating zones of conflict. At the margins, conflicts occur, as the experts vie with each other for control of activities. Were the System of Authority strong, managers could resolve these conflicts, and politics could be precluded. But since it is weak, the Professional IC becomes the playing field for all kinds of political games—alliance and empire building, budgeting, rival camps, and strategic candidates, not to mention the sponsorship game as junior professionals seek the support of senior ones, and the expert games, as the more skilled members of the organization seek to protect their expertise while the less skilled ones struggle to attain professional status. But while the dominant System of Expertise encourages some of theses games directly, it also keeps the System of Politics in check because ultimately it ensures that power flows to those most skilled at the functions critical to the organization.

As described in the *Structuring* book, two types of decentralization correspond to the Professional IC. In one, called horizontal and vertical decentralization, decision making power flows all the way down the chain of authority and at its bottom out to the professionals who man the operating core. Here the operators work individually with their clients, applying repertoires of standard programs to predetermined contingencies, as in universities or accounting firms. Because of this standardization—based on the operators' skills, not on technocratic systems, it should be noted—the organization takes on the characteristics of bureaucracy. Hence this was called *Professional Bureaucracy.* Because the professionals work rather independently, this emerges, as we shall see more clearly later, as the most fragmented of the Internal Coalitions—as much a *federation* as an integrated organization.

The second type of decentralization corresponding to the Professional IC was referred to as selective horizontal and vertical, because in this case the experts are found in various places in the structure—notably in the operating core, support staff, and various levels of the middle line. These experts join together in small project teams to innovate on ad hoc bases. Hence this structure was called *Adhocracy* and was found commonly in industries such as film making, electronics, and aerospace. Again power—both within and between the project teams—tends to be distributed primarily on the basis of expertise, although because this structure is more fluid than Professional Bureaucracy, politics plays a bigger role. Both structures tend to occur whenever an organization finds itself in a complex environment, since this forces it to rely on highly developed expertise to function. When that environment is also stable, Professional Bureaucracy results; when it is dynamic, we find Adhocracy.

THE POLITICIZED IC   In our last type of Internal Coalition, power rests not in office, not in bureaucratic controls, not in ideology or expertise—in other words, not in any of what we have called the legitimate systems of influence—but in politics. Here it is the political games that dominate the Internal Coalition, not so much those described as coexisting with the legitimate systems of influence, but the antagonistic games, those that drive legitimate power out, or that substitute for it in its weakness—games such as young Turks, rival camps, alliance and also empire building in their most divisive forms.

There is some focus of power in each of the other Internal Coalitions—a leader, bureaucratic rules, a shared set of beliefs, or expertise. The Politicized IC can be defined as that Internal Coalition with no focus of power. Politics is pervasive, and it weakens authority, ideology, and expertise, or, emerging when they are already weak, it maintains them in that state. Conflict dominates, allocating power to whomever happens to win at any of the political games running concurrently in the Internal Coalition. Thus, there is no stability in the distribution of power, as there is in the other Internal Coalitions, more or less. Rather we find complete fluidity. And this means that we cannot describe a form of decentralization. Sometimes power flows to one or a few major alliances, other times it diffuses to all kinds of individuals and groups.[7]

---

[7]Adhocracy was described as having a fluid power structure as well, but at least there expertise guided the flow of power. (In fact, later in the book we shall see that the Adhocracy form of the Professional IC most closely resembles the Politicized IC, although we argue that it falls short of meriting that label.)

All the characteristics of the System of Politics are prominent here. The insiders tend to be guided by their personal needs and the pressures of their own groups; direct links to external influencers abound; all the political means of influence are used to the fullest, especially privileged information and access and political will and skill. Effect expended is especially important since under the rule of politics, unlike that of authority, ideology, or expertise, no one person's word is sacrosanct. Victory often goes to that person willing to expend the energy in some political game, assuming that person has some political skill.

Any major unexpected ambiguity or uncertainty, which destabilizes existing power relationships in the organization, tends, in the resulting confusion, to give rise to the Politicized IC for a time. Sometimes a major change in the environment weakens the existing center of power, sometimes that center falters of its own accord (as when a dominant leader dies), sometimes politics itself weakens the established order in the first place. In all these cases, strong politics is likely to emerge and perhaps to take over the Internal Coalition until a new stability emerges. Later we shall see that many transitions from one legitimate power system to another require a period in the Politicized IC to make them happen. Even when, for example, formal authority seeks to replace prevailing ideology, or one leader in authority has to be replaced by another, the existing ideology or leader must often be pushed aside. And it is typically political power—illegitimate power—that does the pushing. In other words, power must pulse out to the periphery before it can once again be concentrated at a center.

The Politicized IC can also dominate on a more permanent basis, for example, when authority, ideology, and expertise are naturally weak and the internal influencers are tightly interdependent (because they depend on each other in their work, or because resources are scarce and must be shared). In the absence of any stable mechanism to distribute power, conflict arises, just as it does when too many rats are confined in a small cage. With no leader to exercise authority, no standards or norms to reconcile the interdependencies, and no expertise as the basis of allocating power, the interdependencies must be negotiated among the players by political means. Some government regulatory agencies seem to be examples of this. The Politicized IC can also arise when two or more systems of influence find themselves in equal balance—say the bureaucratic form of authority on one hand and expertise on the other. Unable to resolve essentially inconciliable differences, the two legitimate systems clash, and politics takes over. The hybrid becomes a Politicized IC. Later, when we return to the case of the System of Politics as the dominant force in the organization, we shall see how varied and interesting the forms of the Politicized IC can be.

This completes our description of the five types of Internal Coalitions. Each description has been brief and rather stylized, stated in simple and absolute terms. This is because we wish at this point only to introduce the five. Later, in Part IV, when we combine them with the three types of External Coalitions to describe our basic configurations of power, we shall investigate each in more detail, paying closer attention to the nuances.

This also completes Part II of the book, on the elements of organizational power in the Internal Coalition. One set of elements remains to be discussed before we can synthesize our findings in terms of the power configurations. These express the results of the decisions made and the actions taken by the Internal Coalition. We turn next to our discussion of these elements, the goals of the organization.

PART III

ORGANIZATIONAL GOALS

Four sets of questions were posed when we began our discussion of the elements of power in and around organizations. Let us see where we stand on each.

  * First the overriding questions: How do all of the personal goals, values, intentions, needs, and expectations of the individual actors get translated into organizational decisions and actions? In other words, how is power operationalized? What takes us from individual need to organizational action? These questions have, of course, served as the basis for our discussion up to this point. We have traced the flow of power from the External Coalition with its means of influence to the Internal Coalition where authority, ideology, expertise, and politics interact in the making of decisions and the taking of actions.

  * Second, how does the organization deal with multiple goals, or conflicting pressures? Does one dominate, leading it to maximization behavior? If so, how does the concept of maximization become operational? Or if multiple goals must coexist, how are the conflicts reconciled? A number of answers have been hinted at in our discussion to this point, but these questions have yet to be addressed directly. That is one of the purposes of this section of the book.

  * Third, are goals dependent or independent variables? In other words, is the organization the instrument of some group which imposes goals on it, or is the organization a political arena in which individuals vie for power? Or is it perhaps a system unto itself with its own intrinsic goals? Our discussion has, I believe, made clear that all three answers are possible. The organization can be

conceived of as an instrument operated on behalf of specific influencers, as a political arena in which various games of power determine outcomes, or as a system unto itself. Which it is would appear to depend on the organization's own particular circumstances. To the question, For whom does the organization exist? our evidence indicates that the answer must be, For anyone who can gain the power to determine its actions. We shall elaborate on this answer in this section and in the next, on the different power configurations.

   *   And fourth, can organizations be said to have goals at all, or only their participants? Bearing in mind our definition of goals—the intentions behind decisions or actions—can the organization as an entity be said to have a "collective intent"? Or can we say no more than that the individual actors have intentions which get translated into organizational actions? Is there, in other words, a common intent as distinguished from the sum of individual intentions? Is the organization endowed with a character or personality separate from those of its actors, a consistent system of goals separate from theirs? I believe the answer to this set of questions has been implied repeatedly in our discussion to this point. But it remains here to draw these implications into a cohesive statement.

   This section of the book comprises two chapters. The first, entitled "The Determination of Organizational Goals," opens on this last point, seeking to make the case that organizations can indeed be said to have goals, as inferred from their actions. We then describe various ways in which goals can be conceived to emerge and to be reconciled in organizations. The second chapter then describes a number of specific goals that many organizations pursue in common.

15

Determination of
Organizational Goals

Our intention in this chapter is to describe various goal systems that emerge in organizations. First, however, we must make two points: that organizations do indeed have goals, sometimes distinct from those of their participants, and that these goals are inferred from their actions. Then we go on to describe the various ways in which organizations try to reconcile conflicts among their different goals.

THE ORGANIZATION HAS GOALS

In their book *A Behavioral Theory of the Firm*, which contains one of the major contributions to the theory of goal formation, Cyert and March begin their discussion of this topic by specifying that "the problem is to specify organizational goals without postulating an 'organizational mind'" (1963, p. 26). They also claim that "To define a theory of organizational decision making, we seem to need something analogous—at the organization level—to individual goals at the individual levels" (p. 26). Herbert Simon, in his important paper, "On the Concept of Organizational Goal," seeks to deal with the concept "without reifying the organization—treating it as something more than a system of interacting individuals" (1964, p. 1).

But why not? What need is there for such assumptions? Why cannot different people sometimes share goals and so act as a single "organizational mind"? If a theory of organizational decision making needs something at the organizational level analogous to goals at the individual level, why cannot that "something" be the goals of the organization itself. Indeed, does the concept "organization" really have any meaning if it involves nothing more than "a system of interacting individuals"? Hill notes that "if there were only individual goals, there would be no point in organizing" (1972, p. 82).

In Chapter 1, we defined a goal as the intention behind a decision or action. It seems reasonable, therefore, to conclude that an organization can be said to have a goal to the extent that there is some consistency in the intentions behind the decisions and actions taken by its participants, in other words, that the organization as a system can be said to pursue a certain outcome consistently. Thus we have two prime characteristics of organizational goals: *consistency in* and *intendedness of* organizational behavior, that is, certain preferences realized consistently. And what emerges from our discussion of the flow of power in and around organizations is that a whole range of such intended consistency is possible:

1.   Most clear is the case of a strong ideology (in what we called the Ideologic IC), where all of the members of the organization share a set of beliefs, in effect a set of preferences about organizational outcomes. Such an organization can be said to have goals—clear goals—because there is consistency across decision makers and across time. Indeed, the goals of such an organization can be distinct from those of its individual participants in the sense that sometimes it is only through the existence of the organization that the individuals are able to pursue these goals. Had there been no religious orders, there would certainly have been far fewer missionaries. These people accepted the goals of the orders when they joined them; in other words, these goals became their personal goals only because the organizations existed and they joined them. Organizations with strong ideologies seem almost to come alive—to have an existence of their own distinct from that of their individual participants; why, therefore, should they not be considered to have goals of their own? We have called these *ideologic* goals, and as our example implies, they usually focus on the mission itself of the organization, or some aspect of it (such as the quality with which that mission is pursued).

2.   Next most clear is the case of a dominant influencer able to impose his or her *formal goals* on the organization through the use of authority. Here again, we have a strong intended consistency in organizational behavior. So long as the controls of authority are effective, the insiders pursue a given set of goals. Of course, they do not necessarily share these goals intrinsically. Rather they accept them to benefit themselves—whether in return for material inducements or through calculated identification in order to advance their own interests. In either case, the goals of the organization emerge as distinct from the intrinsic personal goals of the participants. The organization's ends are simply the means to their private ends. Except, of course, for the dominant influencer—usually either the key external influencer in a Dominated EC or else the CEO in a Personalized IC—whose private goals *are* the formal goals of the organization.

3.   Organizational goals can also emerge in the absence of strong ideology and authority. When various individuals rally around a particular organization as a convenient place to pursue goals which they all have in common, the *shared personal goals* become organizational goals. In other words, the individuals reach a tacit consensus, as sometimes happens in a Professional IC. Professors may join a particular university or doctors a particular hospital because they find it a tolerant place to pursue their interests in research. So research becomes a prime goal of the organization. No ideology or control system is required to weld together individual and oganizational need. Indeed, the individuals may have joined the organization, or perhaps even established it in the first place, in order to escape the ideologies or controls of other organizations, ones that interfered with their abilities to pursue their own interests. Note that this case of personal goals becoming organizational goals is not precluded by politics in the Internal Coalition. For example, if every insider vigorously pursues a personal goal of power attainment through the empire-building game, the result can be that the organization pursues a consistent goal of growth. Thus, even the Politicized IC can conceivably exhibit identifiable goals.

4.   Individuals may also find it in their interests to share voluntarily common goals which are not intrinsically their own. The most obvious case of this is where the individuals benefit from the very existence of an organization—as a system independent of what mission it happens to pursue—and so rally around any goals that help to maintain it. We call these the *systems goals*, noting that they typically include first, survival; second, a certain level of efficiency to ensure survival; third, control of the organization's environment to ensure an adequate degree of independence (especially from external influencers); and fourth, above all, growth. Growth ensures security and control, and also increases the booty to be shared by the insiders. Note that none of these goals are inherently those of the influencers: what matters to them is not the survival of the organization, its efficiency, control, or growth per se; these are merely the means by which each of them can pursue their own personal goals (of security, power, belonging, or whatever). Once again, even in a highly politicized organization, certain of these systems goals can emerge in this way. For example, no matter how severe the political games, the one goal all the players may share is the need for a common playing field. So survival of the organization may be one goal all have in common, which enables it to emerge as an organizational goal. Without it, all the players would have to find somewhere else to play.

These four cases—of ideologic, formal, shared personal, and system goals—all describe strong forms of intended consistency, consistency across whole ranges of behaviors over time in particular types of organization. Of course, weaker forms of consistency can also occur, encompassing the behavior of parts of organizations, perhaps for shorter periods of time. What this means is that we can always find a great many goals in every organization, pursued with varying consistency.

Thus we conclude that the organization has goals. Out of all the ferment of decision making and action taking in the organization emerges identifiable, intended consistencies in behavior over time—due primarily to strong ideologies which create shared beliefs, to a dominant influencer able to impose his or her goals on everyone else, or to many influencers who share personal goals or who rally around a set of systems goals. This is not to say that the organization's influencers do not have goals of their own, which they seek to impose on the organization at the expense of those pursued more consistently. One clearly does not preclude the other. Indeed, the two sets of goals—shared and non-shared, organizational and personal—coexist in all imaginable organizations. But it is to say that organizations can be conceived of as living systems that exhibit consistencies of their own, consistencies that cannot always be expressed as the sum total of the personal goals of their individual participants.

THE INFERENCE OF GOALS FROM ACTIONS

Given that organizations have goals, how do we recognize them? A point made at the outset of this book merits reiteration at this point: goals exist only in terms of the behaviors of organizations, specifically as the intentions that can be imputed to their decisions and, better, their actions. It is unacceptable simply to ask the members of an organization, including its chief executive, what its goals are, or to read the pronouncements of what we have called the *official* goals. The manager "must put his resources where his mouth is if something is to be considered a goal" (Buck 1966, p. 109).

Official goals are often developed as public relations pronouncements for external consumption only. As such, they are often stated in motherhood terms, and are not intended to influence actual behavior. How many corporations put "service to the public" or to their clients first on their list of official goals, well ahead of earning a profit, with growth not even mentioned? Some organizations cannot even mention in their official pronouncements what they are driven to achieve. "Suppose a minister is asked why he wants his church to grow. The probability that he would say 'large churches pay more than small ones' is practically zero, whatever his personal feelings" (Starbuck 1965, p. 465). Zald (1963) found in his study of four institutions for delinquent boys that because "rehabilitation is considered in the society as a more noble aim than containment" (p. 214), the official goal statements of these organizations all emphasized the former and denied the latter, in some cases in direct contradiction to their behavior.[1] In other cases, what the members wish to achieve is mentionable, but unattainable, and so not pursued. Thus it never becomes a goal as we are defining it—that is, it never influences actual behavior.

The assumption behind much of the traditional thinking in economics and

[1] Interestingly, in prisons for adults, the concerns of the public are such that the containment or custodial goals must be kept close to the top of the official pronouncements, even when rehabilitation is strongly emphasized.

decision theory is that we first establish what it is we want and then we act to achieve it. But what we want is a function of what we can get, and that is not always clear at the outset. As a result, what we thought we wanted is often not the same as what we end up setting out to get. And that can mean a divergence between official goals and real goals, as we have defined them. An individual or organization cannot be said to have a goal in our terms if no action is ever taken to realize it. Note that this can apply to formal goals too. If senior management cannot operationalize the goals it wishes the organization to pursue—if it cannot use the control systems to get the other insiders to pursue them—then these cannot be considered as goals of the organization. This divergence between official or formal goals and real ones becomes sharpest in the Politicized IC, where power is so fluid that the pronouncements of those in authority cannot be relied upon at all. Indeed, even a knowledge of the intentions of all of the players is not sufficient to infer goals, because it is only in the bargaining process that power gets manifested.

For all of these reasons, we conclude that goals cannot be ascertained reliably simply by asking the members of an organization what they are or by reading what these people write about goals. True we must understand intentions, but only in the context of studying actual outcomes—the actions taken by organizations:

> Two kinds of evidence are necessary before one can confidently assert that a goal is present: *intentions* and *activities*. By "intentions" we understand what, in the *participants' view*, the organization is trying to do. . . . By "activities" we understand what persons in the organization are in fact *observed to be doing*, how they are spending their time, how resources are being allotted. (Gross 1969, p. 284)[2]

Given that we must study both actions and intentions, how do we make the link between the two? One way to proceed is to consider actions in terms of their benefits to specific influencers. In this regard, we can describe three kinds of actions organizations take, three ways in which they "pay off" the influencers for their power or support—in the orientation of their basic strategies, the granting of side payments, and the distribution of their surpluses. Our description of these forms of payoffs connects the final link in the continuous chain of organizational power we have been describing, for it shows the feedback loop

[2]The Scandinavian Institutes for Administrative Research (SIAR) have devoted a good deal of attention to the study of organization goals. In their 1973 annual report, they outline the steps involved in such study, concluding that "in practice the interview method combined with an exhaustive study of critical events in the company's history have provided, from many points of view, the best insight into the values and ideas dominating the organization concerned" (SIAR 1973, p. 15; see also Rhenman 1973, for an elaboration of this approach as well as a number of illustrations, and Stymne 1972, for an example of one detailed study). Other researchers have developed more systematic techniques for imputing goals to choices, but these are really only suited to laboratory or experimental work where similar decisions can be made repeatedly under controlled circumstances (see for example, Balke, Hammond, and Meyer 1973; and Pfeffer and Salancik 1974, p. 137).

from organizational action back to the influencers of the Internal and External Coalitions.

1. THE ORIENTATION OF BASIC STRATEGIES   Strategy, as enacted, can be defined as consistency in behavior—a pattern in a stream of decisions (Mintzberg 1978). The greatest reward for influence is the right to dictate, or at least to affect, the most important of these decision patterns, or strategies, the ones concerned with the basic directions that the organization takes—what it produces, in what quantities, for whom, with what equipment, and so on. Thus, the orientation of basic strategies to suit personal interests is the ultimate payoff, reserved for the most powerful of influencers. A prison shifts from a custodial to a rehabilitation orientation as a reflection of the growing power of its professional operators; a parts producer introduces certain new product lines in response to the influence of its one client, an automobile company.

2. THE GRANTING OF SIDE PAYMENTS   Few influencers can dictate basic strategies. Many must instead content themselves with payoffs incidental to the basic directions of the organization. Payoffs to specific influencers in the forms of actions peripheral to the basic strategies may be referred to as *side payments*. Some side payments are byproducts of major decisions. For example, in deciding to build a new factory, a corporation may put it in an economically depressed area as a side payment to an influential government, install pollution abatement equipment as a side payment to a powerful conservation group, give the construction contract to a certain company as a side payment to one of its directors who owns that company. Other side payments are not byproducts of anything, but decisions in their own right, although still incidental to the organization's basic strategies. Earlier we saw the example of the McGill student study of the racetrack, where, in order to maintain the support of the horsemen, the track executives intervened on their behalf to negotiate the settlement of a tax dispute with the government. The organization acted, but to serve an influencer, not to serve any of its own needs directly. As Maniha and Perrow note, in the natural course of their operations, organizations generate power which can be put to uses quite independent of their basic purpose:

> The potential power of a business firm is being utilized when it is a source of testimonials, sponsorship, or support for political, social, or economic activities that are unrelated to its basic task of providing goods or services. When the American Medical Association supports the farm organizations in their relentless war on daylight-saving time, or takes a stand on the treaty-making powers of the presidency, its power as a medical group is being used by other groups. (1965–66, pp. 255–56)

Sometimes side payments are given as "consolation prizes." In a battle over some basic strategy, the loser may be given a side payment instead of a say in the strategy. Thus, a government seeking to roll back a corporate price increase may settle instead for the corporation's support in the implementation of some of its new legislation.[3]

Cyert and March (1963), who introduced the term side payment to the management literature,[4] note that these types of payments are becoming increasingly popular at the expense of direct monetary payments, not only in political parties where they have long been used, but also in business corporations.

3. THE DISTRIBUTION OF SURPLUSES   The classic means of satisfying an influencer, at least in the context of business, is to pay him off with money or the like. Organizations often generate surpluses from their operations—in fact, business firms must do so in order to remain viable. These surpluses then become a booty to be divided up by the influencers. In the corporation, owners ask for them in the form of dividends; managers in the form of bonuses, or longer vacations or thicker carpets on their floors; powerful clients in the form of prices lower than economic conditions would dictate or else special delivery arrangements or tickets to hockey games; unions in the form of higher than normal wages or special fringe benefits; special interest groups in the form of charitable donations; governments in the form of taxes. In the hospital, "profit," Perrow notes, "can be paid out to doctors in the form of rent-free office space; to administrators in the form of high salaries and lush perquisites; to trustees in the form of special services and rates for friends and relatives" (1970, pp. 129–30). "Patronage" is a form of the distribution of surpluses usually associated with governments, but as Pettigrew (1973, p. 19) notes, it can apply elsewhere as well. He uses the term in his study of a business corporation to describe certain rewards of promotions, new appointments, and the distribution of goods and privileges. Similarly, we have Perrow's example of the company that "was obliged to hire, during summer vacations, the incompetent and disruptive college-going son of a purchasing agent in a large firm" (1970, p. 123).

Influencers demand a share of the surpluses in accordance with the power they have. Occasionally, when conditions are stable and all the influencers are fully informed, they may work out a precise formula for the distribution of the surpluses. The McGill group that studied the racetrack came across such a formula, shown in Figure 15–1, where the exact percentage allocation of every dollar bet was predetermined. But more commonly, both the supply of surpluses

[3]Note that in the case of a consolation prize, the payment is *aside* from that which the influencer really wants. In our previous examples, the side payment was of central interest to the influencer, as in the conservation group insisting on the installation of pollution abatement equipment; the payment was *aside* only from the central functioning of the organization. In Game Theory, side payment is defined in the former sense, that is, with respect to the recipient. We define it in the latter sense, with respect to the organization making the payment.

[4]Although they include our third payoff, the distribution of surpluses, in their use of the term.

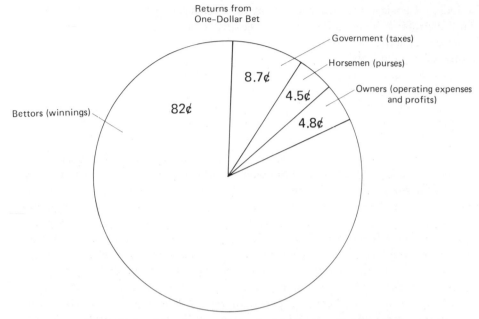

Returns from
One-Dollar Bet

Government (taxes)

Horsemen (purses)

Owners (operating expenses
and profits)

8.7¢

4.5¢

4.8¢

82¢

Bettors (winnings)

Figure 15-1. *A Precise Formula for the Distribution of Surpluses in a Racetrack (adapted from a report submitted to the author by C. Rinfret and C. Sabourin, Management Policy 701, McGill University, 1969)*

and the demands for them are unstable and vague, and influencers make ad hoc demands on the management. As a result, supply and demand are not always balanced. When the demand exceeds the supply, management can try to tighten up and explain that the organization is being squeezed. But when supply exceeds demand, management is inclined not to explain anything. Here another claimant typically comes into the picture, the organization itself. It becomes, in effect, the "residual claimant" on its own surpluses. In effect, these excess surpluses are stored as *slack*—excess cash, more employees than absolutely necessary, and so on. This slack provides the margin of safety which protects the organization when demands rise again to exceed supply.[5]

Of course, excessive slack is an invitation to influencers in the know to increase their demands. And those most in the know are the senior managers of the organization, the ones who oversee the distribution of the surpluses in the first place. Being "full-time, in a position to perceive potential slack early, or [having] some flexibility in unilateral allocation of resources" (Cyert and March 1963, p. 37), the senior managers tend to get first crack at the excess surpluses.

[5]The term slack was popularized in the literature of management by Cyert and March (1963), but again our sense of it differs slightly from theirs. They define slack as the "difference between total resources and total necessary payments" to keep the influencers happy, and then state that "slack consists in payments to members of the coalition in excess of what is required to maintain the organization" (p. 36). In our case, slack is taken as that surplus which is kept in the organization itself, not paid to influencers.

But they must siphon them off prudently, taking care not to bring their disproportionate rewards to the attention of other more distant influencers. Thus, business corporations that find themselves with large profits seek all kinds of ways to announce only moderate ones, so as not to whet the appetites of unions and tax collectors, not to mention shareholders. They invest in research and in advertising, buy a new corporate jet, redo the executive dining room.

To review our conclusions of this chapter so far, we concluded that organizations do indeed have goals and that these must be inferred from the intentions that can be imputed to the specific actions they take. The way to make these inferences is to consider the organization's actions in terms of how they benefit different influencers—whether it orients basic organizational strategies toward their needs, grants them side payments peripheral to the functioning of the organization, or distributes the surpluses of the organization to them. Our discussion to this point also suggests that we might look for four particular kinds of organizational goals. First are the *formal* goals, which can in fact be the formal manifestations of the other three kinds of goals. The formal goals are the easiest to uncover because these are the ones operationalized in the control systems. However, as noted, care must be taken to ensure that these are actually pursued and so stand as true goals of the organization. Second are the *ideologic* goals, usually tied to mission. While these are not formalized, when strong they may be clearly indicated in the established traditions of the organization. Third are the *systems* goals—survival, efficiency, control, and growth—which are typically present, more or less, in all organizations. These tend to be easy to uncover, because they are typically reflected in a wide range of organizational actions. Finally, there are the *shared personal* goals of the influencers. These may be the most difficult to uncover because they tend to vary considerably between organizations and may not be articulated.

One last point seems to be clear. All or at least many of these kinds of goals coexist in most organizations, and so must often conflict with each other. Thus, the overriding question in the study of organizational goals remains to be answered: How are conflicts among competing goals reconciled?

THE RECONCILIATION
OF CONFLICTING GOALS

No organization—indeed, no human being—can attend to only a single goal. At the limit, such behavior becomes pathological, as Kenneth Boulding (1966) has noted, pointing out that the logical behavior for a production manager intent on minimizing costs is to produce nothing. Perrow (1970, pp. 147–50), in fact, recounts the story of Eastern Airlines under Eddie Rickenbacker who eventually became so obsessed with cost reduction that, in times of increasing demand for service and comfort, he nearly drove the line into bankruptcy. Starr (1971) recounts the theme of the play "The Monkey's Paw" in which a family is given a paw which allows its possessor three wishes. But the family is informed that the third wish of the first possessor was for death. The father wishes for enough money to clear the mortgage on the house, and is granted it as compensation for the death of his son in an industrial accident. The mother then requests that the son be brought back to life, but the father, realizing the possible side effects of this, used the third wish to cancel out the second. Starr presents the story to point out that multiple goals are present in all decisions, even though some are taken for granted. And so it is with every organization, which is subject to a great number of goals, many of which its members never think about. How then does the organization deal with and reconcile all of these goals? How does it signal out some for specific attention, and what happens to the rest?

There are no simple or agreed-upon answers to these important questions, which have in fact been the focus of intensive debate in the management literature for decades. Many answers have been proposed, and while some seem to have conceptual validity, few has been derived from, or tested by, systematic empirical research. The following four theories are perhaps the best known:

1. That different goals are combined into a single utility or preference function

2. That goals are treated as constraints, minimum levels to be attained

3. That one goal is singled out for maximization, and the others are treated as constraints

4. That different goals are attended to sequentially over time, perhaps in some orderly fashion such as in cycles or in a hierarchy

The first theory—the notion that goals are weighted and combined in some mathematical-type function—has held up in none of the empirical research on organizations (e.g., Carter 1971; Cyert, Simon, and Trow 1956). Indeed, even in a study of decision making by individuals (Master of Science students at the MIT Sloan School of Management, heavily trained in such concepts), it was found that "the goal weights which the subjects provided during decision making could not be trusted" (Soelberg 1967, p. 218). This researcher was led to conclude that:

> ...scalar utility theory is a poor way of representing the structure of human values. Decision Value attributes are usually multidimensional: they are not compared or substituted for each other during choice. No stable utility weighted function can be elicited from a decision maker prior to his selection of a preferred alternative, nor do such weights appear to enter into each person's decision processing. (p. 224)

Utility theory, as we noted in Chapter 2, does not stand up in a world of multiple and changing preferences. Hence it is of no help in explaining how organizations reconcile conflicting goals.

But there seems to be at least a measure of truth in each of the other three theories. Let us discuss each in turn and then see if we can combine them into a common theory.

ALL GOALS AS CONSTRAINTS   Herbert Simon, in his important paper "On the Concept of Organizational Goal" (1964), provides a convenient conceptual trick as well as a highly plausible notion to explain how organizations are capable of dealing with the great multitude of goals they face. They simply treat all of them as *constraints*, as minimum levels to be attained in the making of choices.

> What is the meaning of the phrase "organizational goal"?... it is doubtful whether decisions are generally directed toward achieving *a* goal. It is easier, and clearer, to view decisions as being concerned with discovering courses of action that satisfy a whole set of constraints. It is this set, and not any one of its members, that is most accurately viewed as the goal of the action. (p. 20)

Thus, every proposed course of action is simply assumed to be acceptable or unacceptable in terms of each of the relevant goals. The new machine is safe or it is unsafe; the project's return on investment is sufficient or it is insufficient; the quality of the product is up to the organization's usual standards or it is not. Of the great number of constraints an organization faces, Simon believes that only a few are singled out in any given decision process. The rest remain dormant. The active ones represent, as in a linear programming problem, an n-dimensional space within which a solution must be found—in Hill's terms, "a feasibility polygon" (1969, p. 207).

Of course, there are constraints that are not goals, in the sense of not representing the intention of any influencer. A machine, for example, is constrained as to the number of operations it can perform per hour. But a great many constraints are goals, imposed by specific influencers. The government demands that food products be of a certain minimum quality, the shareholders expect a certain minimum dividend rate, the unions insist on promotion by seniority, a special interest group anticipates a donation of $1,000 each year.

Some constraints are defined clearly for the organization, as in the ones we called "formal" that are imposed by the External Coalition. A government regulation requires that supermarkets remove tomatoes from shelves after five days. But many are vague, and it is only by testing them out that the decision makers can get an idea of where they lie. (That can sometimes be a painful experience, as shown in the story of "The Monkey's Paw.") Of course, most constraints can be violated at a price, that being confrontation with the influencer behind them. Occasionally, to relieve the pressures of other constraints, the decision makers prepare themselves for this. Earlier we recounted Frank's (1958–59) description of the managers of the Soviet factories, caught in a complex web of constraints. Many of these came from the government bureaucracy and were contradictory. They included plans and "countless" directives on the "type, quantity, quality, and assortment of production; amount of materials and labor to be used; wages to be paid; and production norms" for the workers to achieve (p. 8). Other constraints came from the Communist Party, and concerned priorities, campaigns, and socialist competition. And then there were the usual pressures from workers and unions, the press and the local community, contracts with suppliers and customers. How could the factory managers function? Frank suggests that they simply cheated, by feigning the meeting of constraints, lying about performance, or meeting the letter but not the spirit of certain constraints. They also peddled their influence to negotiate their way out of certain constraints and strove to have others set generously so that they could easily be met.

In effect, we can characterize the goal system of the organization as a room with a great many walls—an n-dimensional space—within which sits a single person, symbolizing all the decision makers. The walls are made of foam rubber and are movable; behind each sits an influencer who pushes occasionally to change the location of his wall. The game our decision maker is playing forces him to float around that room perpetually. For the most part, he tries to remain in open space. But sometimes he bumps into a wall, perhaps because he never noticed it before (it may, in fact, be brand new), perhaps because it moved since the last time he noticed it. Also, because our decision maker is near-sighted, the location of even the walls he knows is not always clear to him. There are times when he deliberately collides with a wall in order to determine where exactly it is, how deeply into its foam he can penetrate without damage, how much effort it would take to move that wall, and whether anyone is ready to push back on the other side. Sometimes, as his luck would have it, one wall moves against another, and our decision maker begins to get squeezed. If both walls turn out to be hard rubber, and he can push neither back, the game may be over for him.

ONE GOAL MAXIMIZED   One issue is missing in our story of the room, as it is in Simon's description of all goals as constraints. When there is open space to float in that room—when the constraints allow the decision maker some measure of discretion—what determines which way he moves? There must be some other force at play—something other than passive walls in the room, simple constraints in the organization. There must be some force that elicits or evokes action, that guides rather than merely limits decision making.

Some decision makers are of course so delighted to find themselves with free space that they do nothing. They pull up a nice soft chair and relax. But others have more energy; they too have goals to pursue. Likewise, the influencers behind some of those walls have extra energy, energy to exploit the discretion they see on the other side of the walls. The goals that underlie that energy—those of energetic influencers who are not satisfied with mere levels of acceptability—emerge as more than simply constraints. To distinguish these goals—the ones that come into play whenever discretion is available—we call them *primary* goals (after Soelberg 1967). They differ from constraints in that there are no predetermined levels at which they become satisfied. They are insatiable. More is always better.[6]

When one such primary goal dominates, we can talk of *maximization* behavior. Thus, **maximization is here taken to mean that one single goal tends to absorb the discretion of the organization, as soon as all of the constraints have been met.** In this sense, we treat maximization as being synonomous with single-mindedness, with obsession. One goal is treated as primary, and can never be satisfied; all the others are treated as constraints, satisfied at given levels of attainment. Maximization occurs when the decision maker in that room always uses his free space to move in one direction, sometimes even trying to knock over the walls that get in his way. Or else it occurs when a powerful influencer behind one of those walls keeps pushing so that the decision maker inside must keep moving in one direction.

Note that our definition of maximization discards many of the usual trappings associated with the word. Maximization is not taken to mean, for example, the generation of all the alternatives in decision making or the selection of

---

[6]A new constraint can have the effect of initiating action too, but only once. Only when change in a constraint occurs repeatedly would we call it a primary goal. Simon (1964) in fact acknowledges a distinction between primary goals and constraints:

> A river valley development plan that aims at the generation of electric power, subject to appropriate provision for irrigation, flood control, and recreation will generally look quite different from a plan that aims at flood control, subject to appropriate provision for the other goals mentioned. Even though the plans generated in both cases will be examined for their suitability along all the dimensions mentioned, it is almost certain that quite different plans will be devised and proposed for consideration in the two cases, and that the plans finally selected will represent quite distinct points in the feasible set. (p. 9)

But later in his paper, in a discussion of cause and effect, Simon denies the distinction. He argues that cause—motivation—is often difficult to ascertain in an action, a conclusion that seems warranted. But that conclusion leads Simon to draw another which can be questioned:

> If we select any of the constraints for special attention, it is (a) because of its relation to the motivations of the decision maker, or (b) because of its relation to the search process that is generating or designing particular courses of action. Those constraints that motivate the decision maker and those that guide his search for actions are sometimes regarded as more "goal-like" than those that limit the actions he may consider or those that are used to test whether a potential course of action he has designed is satisfactory. Whether we treat all the constraints symmetrically or refer to some asymmetrically as goals is largely a matter of linguistic or analytic convenience. (p. 20)

As Simon's own example of the river valley development plan illustrates, which goals are treated as constraints and which as what we have called primary goals is more than a matter of "linguistic or analytical convenience": it makes a difference in terms of the outcome of the decision-making process. Only where the set of constraints is so tight as to dictate the choice, in other words, where there is no discretion, does it make no difference. Eilon (1971) develops the same argument as Simon, although in somewhat more rigorous language, concluding that "the distinction between goals and constraints is an artificial one" (p. 295). Again, it is artificial, as Eilon's own analysis indicates, only when the constraints are so tight as to prevent decisional discretion.

the best alternative. In other words, maximization here does not mean "best"; it means "perpetually more."

How can we take this concept and operationalize it in the context of the organization? Clearly, maximization must mean that the discretion of all the decision makers and action takers tends to be absorbed in the pursuit of one primary goal. They may have to spend certain periods of time satisfying constraints, as for example during crises, when the survival of the organization is threatened. And even in other periods they must always respond to a multitude of constraints. But if, whenever the pressures are off, they immediately turn their attention to one primary goal, then their organization can be said to maximize. Polaroid under Edwin Land, obsessed with perfecting that self-developing automatic camera, seems to be one such example, as was the early American labor movement under Samuel Gompers, who when asked what it was labor wanted, replied simply "more."

But what is it that gets a collection of people to direct their discretion toward the pursuit of one goal? We can see this best in terms of our different types of coalitions. In the cases of the Personalized and Ideologic ICs, the explanation is simple. The organization with the Personalized IC can maximize whenever its chief executive exhibits a single-mindedness about one goal. Since he controls everything—including everyone else's discretion—he simply imposes his goal on all the decisions and actions. As for the Ideologic IC, while no one person directs others to pursue a single goal, all do so naturally because of their identification with the organization and its mission. In other words, every member tends to exhibit a single-mindedness about some aspect of the organization's mission, and so the organization tends to maximize with respect to it. Note that in both these cases, the primary goal need not be an operational one, that is, one that lends itself to quantitative measure of performance.

What of the other cases, when a chief executive cannot rely on personal controls and the ideology is weak? Is maximization still possible? How, for example, can it be achieved in a Bureaucratic IC, or a Dominated EC, where the dominant influencer promotes a primary goal but neither controls the organization personally nor can fall back on ideological forms of control? In both cases, maximization is possible, but only if the primary goal is operational, that is, can be expressed within the system of objectives. As this system works, all of the objectives are expressed as constraints—targets, or levels of performance, to be reached by units in the organization over given periods of time. The plastics division is directed by top management (or top management itself is directed by a dominant external influencer) to attain 10 percent growth in sales in the next quarter and to earn a return on investment of 15 percent. How then does, say, growth get singled out for maximization?

It would appear that while all the other objectives retain their levels, *even when they are reached,* the level of the one singled out for maximization keeps getting increased *as soon as it is reached.* The principle is that of the ratchet, which, when it advances, can never go back (Berliner 1965, p. 91–92). Actual performance of 11 percent growth and 16 percent ROI means targets for the next quarter of 12 percent growth (an increase of 2 percent) and 15 percent ROI (unchanged). The message to the unit (or organization) is to redirect its excess efforts into growth; the return on investment is sufficient, perhaps even too high if it is interfering with the rate of growth. In other words, maximization means that one carrot is always kept out in front, to guide movement; the others can be consumed when reached. That one objective keeps getting increased, to keep it clearly fixed before the decision makers.

Thus can the concept of maximization be operationalized in the system of objectives. On all dimensions but one, the organization can be said to "satisfice" in Simon's (1957, p. xxiv) terminology—to accept performance that is good enough. On only one does it maximize—always seek more. The job of the CEO—or of the dominant external influencer seeking to control the organization through the CEO—is to keep the level of that objective high enough and to move it fast enough so that all the discretion in decision making is used up in its pursuit. To return to our decision maker in the room, if the walls stay in place but the floor keeps moving up, he will have to forget everything else and race up the stairs to higher and higher levels just to avoid being crushed against a ceiling.[7]

What about maximization in the other coalitions? Clearly the Passive EC cannot be considered to try to maximize anything—indeed, it hardly tries to impose any goals at all on the organization. As for the Divided EC, by definition it tries to impose conflicting goals on the organization and so cannot be said to promote maximization. The Professional IC can conceivably maximize when the various experts share one primary goal in common, such as professional excellence, and pursue it obsessively. Normally, however, we would expect to find a range of competing goals in this form of Internal Coalition. The same is certainly true of the Politicized IC, although as noted earlier, if growth of the organization benefits all of the players, a crude form of maximization can conceivably appear here as well.

MULTIPLE GOALS ATTENDED TO SEQUENTIALLY   So much for a predominant primary goal. But what happens when the organizational power system is dominated neither by one external influencer, the CEO, nor ideology, and no one goal is shared by the various influencers, in other words, when different influencers promote conflicting primary goals (or a dominant influencer himself does so)?

Cyert and March (1963) propose an ingenious solution, as we saw in Chapter 2. The organization attends to these goals sequentially, ignoring the resulting inconsistencies:

---

[7]Such maximization behavior may be self-reinforcing. Researchers have found that when aspirations do not get realized, their levels tend to fall (Feldman and Kanter 1965, pp. 632–33). The system of objectives that we have described here, by frustrating the decision maker's ability to attend to his own goals, may cause them to diminish in importance for him. He is kept firmly focussed on someone else's goal.

> Organizations resolve conflict among goals, in part, by attending to different goals at different times. Just as the political organization is likely to resolve conflicting pressures to "go left" and "go right" by first doing one and then the other, the business firm is likely to resolve conflicting pressures to "smooth production" and "satisfy customers" by first doing one and then the other. The resulting time buffer between goals permits the organization to solve one problem at a time, attending to one goal at a time. (p. 118)

Over time, if not for each particular decision, the goals of the different influencers get attended to, and, in the bargain, direct confrontations between them are largely avoided. Thus the school board can point to one set of decisions to convince the taxpayers that it is keeping costs down, and to a second set of decisions to convince the parents that it is keeping the standards up. (No matter that taxpayers and parents may be the same people; they too attend to their various goals sequentially.) If an influencer squawks loudly enough about the last decision, the next one can serve him.

We can return to Frank's story of the Soviet factory manager to show an interesting, if special, case of sequential attention to goals. It will be recalled that this manager was in the tightest room of all; indeed, the walls frequently pushed past each other such that no human being should have been able to survive there at all. But the walls turned out to be very soft indeed. Everyone knew that the factory could not possibly function if all of the standards were applied simultaneously. So a great deal of discretion was allowed in their interpretation, and the situation essentially became one of sequential attention to goals. Factory managers were expected to ignore most of the goals so long as they did not flaunt this fact, acted within reason (in effect, within implicit, less stringent constraints), and attended to the formal goals periodically:

> Each subordinate appeals to those standards which are most in accord with his incentives and the circumstances of the moment and to those which are most likely to be invoked by superiors in evaluating his performance. Superiors, in turn, make their assessment of priority to guide their necessarily selective evaluation of subordinates' performance and enforcement of standards. The entire process is continuous: superiors modify the set of standards to comply with their changing objectives; subordinates adapt their decisions to changing standards and to changing circumstances; superiors enforce standards in accordance with changing priority. (1958–59, p. 11)

The behavior that results from sequential attention to goals suggests that the organization does not maximize anything, at least not in the long run. Over a short period of time, however, the organization may maximize: it may attend to one primary goal before turning to another. Faced with censure by a professional association, the school board may forget about cost reduction and seek instead to maximize the improvement in the quality of its programs.[8]

---

[8]Although one can doubt whether sporadic attention to such a goal can really make a serious difference.

This notion of maximizing for a time raises the possibility of extending Cyert and March's notion in at least two ways. First, conflicting goals can be attended to alternately, in cycles; and second, different and possibly complementary goals can be attended to in a hierarchy associated with the stage of development of the organization.

ATTENDING TO MULTIPLE GOALS ALTERNATELY, IN CYCLES   When two (or more) conflicting goals vie for primacy, organizations often appear to attend to them alternately, favoring one for a time and then the other. The result is a pattern of cycles in the attention to the different goals. There is a certain logic in this. Instead of continuously trying to balance conflicting demands, it is often far easier to favor one for a time, until the situation gets out of balance, and then to correct it by favoring the other. The pendulum swings back and forth, enabling the organization to concentrate its efforts on one thing at a time—to maximize temporarily. Many corporations reconcile the pressures for growth and efficiency by alternating strategies of expansion and consolidation (e.g., Mintzberg and Waters 1982). Jönsson and Lundin (1975) find a similar phenomenon in the municipal government of the city of Gothenburg with respect to the conflict between the spending inclinations of the politicians oriented to social need and the economizing inclinations of those oriented to fiscal responsibility. Figure 15–2, drawn from their work, shows that instead of working out a balance between these two, the politicians (and the city population that elected and defeated them) instead attended to them alternately, giving rise to clear cycles.

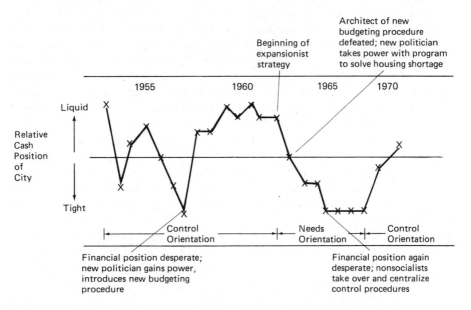

Figure 15–2.   *Cyclical Attention to Goals in a Municipal Government (adapted from Jonsson and Lunden, 1975).*

Such alternating behavior is of course compatible with divided power in the External Coalition and politicized (and perhaps also expert) power in the Internal Coalition, as was the case in Gothenburg with socialist and nonsocialist political parties. Each group of influencers has its day in court, so to speak, eventually overdoing things, and so needing to be displaced by the proponents of the opposing point of view who redress the balance. Eventually they, too, overstep their bounds, and the first group remerges to take power.

ATTENDING TO MULTIPLE GOALS IN A HIERARCHY   An organization will sometimes concentrate its efforts on one primary goal for a time, and then move on to others, never giving the first a place of prominence again. The implication is that this goal was appropriate at one stage in the organization's development, necessary to get it to other stages. This goal was not in conflict with those that displaced it; rather, they all seem to exist in some kind of complementary hierarchy. The earlier goals are the lower-order ones, in effect, the means to attain some higher-order, ultimate ones.

What we are describing here is, in fact, an equivalent on the organizational level to Maslow's (1954) needs hierarchy theory on the individual level. Just as, according to Maslow, the individual must satisfy his physiological needs before he can worry about safety, and must feel secure before he devotes much attention to love and belonging, and so on up through status to self-actualization, so too we have repeatedly found in our studies at McGill that entrepreneurial firms are first obsessed with survival and then with profit in order to build secure financial bases; after that their attention turns to growth as the primary goal. A comparable phenomena has also appeared on a much larger scale (Mintzberg 1974). In looking at public spending, we concluded that governments could be described as pursuing five primary goals, arranged in hierarchical order according to the stage of development of their society. These goals, which in fact correspond to Maslow's five human needs, are citizen protection (which corresponds to the physiological needs), economic development (safety), social freedom (love and belonging), national identity (status), and human development (self-actualization). Thus, the governments of the poorest and least developed nations seem to stress citizen protection, with few resources left over for economic development or the protection of social freedoms. Only the economically developed nations seem to be able to devote considerable resources to the protection of social freedoms, while only the most democratic nations and those secure in their sense of national identity seem to invest significantly in human development.

This notion of organizations (or governments) attending to multiple goals in some kind of hierarchy would appear to have a certain plausibility, as would a conclusion that all kinds of other patterns among goals exist but have yet to be uncovered. Clearly we need a great deal more empirical research on how organizations reconcile their multiple goals.

To draw our conclusions together, we have seen that **organizations can indeed be said to have goals, in fact a great many goals.** Most of these goals seem to enter into decision making merely as constraints—acceptable levels to be attained—and probably remain rather stable over time. But others do not, for at least two reasons. First, discretion typically remains in decision making after all the constraints have been satisfied. And second, the more powerful influencers stand ready to exploit discretion in terms of their own goals. These emerge as what we have called primary goals, ones that are insatiable. When one primary goal predominates—is pursued singlemindedly, all the other goals being treated as constraints—we can talk of an organization that maximizes. This appears to be possible when a chief executive rules the Internal Coalition through personal controls, when a strong ideology or some other force ensures that all the internal influencers pursue a common goal, or when a dominant external influencer or the management is able to control the Internal Coalition by operationalizing one favored goal in the system of objectives. That goal is expressed as a performance target that keeps getting increased as it is attained. But when a number of primary goals vie for preeminence—as is usually the case in a Divided EC or a Professional or Politicized IC—some mechanism for reconciliating them must be found. The most logical appears to be the sequential attention to these goals with each goal attended to periodically. The pattern of attention to the different goals may be random, but some evidence suggests it can also be orderly. Sometimes two or more goals are attended to alternately, in cycles; sometimes a number of them are attended to in a hierarchy of lower- and higher-order goals related to the organization's stage of development. In either case, the organization can be said to maximize its attainment of each goal for some limited period of time.

To conclude, we can place the different goal systems we have discussed in this chapter along a continuum, from the most consistent to the least.

1. *Maximization*—of one goal perpetually—clearly belongs at one end, as the most consistent of goal systems.

2. Next would be the *hierarchy of goals,* where certain goals exist in some predetermined order, such that each is maximized for a time before the organization moves up to the next one.

3. Then would follow the *alternating cycles of goals,* where each of two or more goals is alternately maximized in turn.

4. Less consistent would be *sequential attention to goals* but in *no special order.* Various primary goals are attended to, but not in any clear pattern.

5. Finally, we have the least consistent goal system, where no primary goals are pursued at all; the organization does no more than seek to satisfy a whole *set of constraints.*

16

Specific Goals in Organizations

In the last chapter, we discussed four common types of goals that tend to be pursued by entire organizations—ideological goals, formal goals, systems goals, and shared personal goals. Of these, we can generalize least about the shared personal goals, because they can take so many forms—virtually anything that the influencers believe in, from perfecting a favorite product to keeping the factory spotlessly clean. The same is true for the formal goals, except that when they are imposed through bureaucratic instead of personal controls, they must be operational in nature.

We can more easily generalize about the systems and the ideological goals because they tend to be more specific. Four systems goals were identified in the last chapter—survival, efficiency, control, and growth. And the ideological goals were associated with the organization's mission, specifically with the preservation, extention, or perfection of it. Because we can generalize about these goals, and, more importantly, because they are common to a great many organizations, we focus on them in this chapter.

We begin with a discussion of each of the four systems goals in turn—those goals that organizations as systems unto themselves pursue—seeking to show in conclusion that these goals are most logically thought of as existing in a Maslow-type hierarchy. Then we look at mission as a goal of certain organizations, and follow this with a note on the relationship between the systems goals and mission, arguing that mission as a goal of the business firm has gradually been displaced over the course of the last two centuries by the systems goals. Finally, to close this section of the book—and our discussion of the elements of power in and around organizations in general—we describe the power and goal systems of the organization as a dynamic equilibrium.

SURVIVAL AS A SYSTEMS GOAL

Survival—what some writers have referred to as "conservation" or "systems maintenance"—is the ultimate constraint for every system. Failure to satisfy it results in the incapacity to pursue any other goal. Thus survival stands at the base of the systems goals. (The temporary organization, set up to do a particular job and then disbanded [Becker and Neuhauser 1975]—such as an Olympic Organizing Committee—would seem to be an exception to this. As we shall soon see, however, survival sometimes becomes a base goal even in these organizations.)

But survival is a tenuous concept, difficult to get a grip on. As long as an organization is functioning, it has survived. As a result, the members of the organization tend to think in terms, not of survival, but of means of safety. One such means, introduced in the last chapter, is the slack that the organization accumulates. During times of plenty, excess resources are stashed away, which can be drawn upon when conditions deteriorate, much as bears accumulate fat in the summer to nourish them through the winter. These surpluses, which could have been paid out to influencers, are stored as excess working capital, a conservative debt-equity ratio, extra inventory, employees with free time, and so on.

Another means to ensure safety is to diversify the products and services. By increasing its range of markets and missions, the organization can reduce its vulnerability in the event of a crisis in any one of them. For the same reason, organizations also engage in a variety of what are sometimes called "maintenance" activities, ones peripheral to the accomplishment of their basic missions (Gross 1969, pp. 282–83, Selznick 1948, pp. 29–30). For example, they seek to legitimize themselves, as we saw in Chapter 6, by appointing prestigious individuals to their boards of directors.

Survival would normally be thought of as a constraint. So long as the organization can ensure a reasonable degree of safety, then it should be expected to get on with the accomplishment of other goals. But survival can also become a primary goal, even an obsession (*the* primary goal). In other words, some organizations behave as if to maximize their survival. Examples are the business firms run by aging, risk-averse chief executives, or by the children of their founding leaders who, lacking their parents' courage and abilities, spend their lifetime trying to conserve their inheritances. (Of course, such behavior may be self-defeating; risks must usually be taken in order to survive.)

More naturally, during severe crises—when the organization's survival is threatened—protection of the system itself becomes the overriding goal, at the expense of all others. "The system in jeopardy sheds first the relations least essential to its survival," as in the case of "an organism in danger of death from cold [that] restricts its surface blood vessels," thereby risking peripheral frostbite in order to protect its more vital organs (Vickers 1965, pp. 30–31). But organizations often go well beyond their peripheries in order to protect themselves as systems. Some exhibit a willingness to shed everything but the shell of their actual existence—their beliefs and strategies, even their ideologies and missions. It is as if an animal were willing to give up its heart and brain in order to protect its skeleton. To return to Brager's story of the political attack on the Mobilization for Youth (MFY), introduced in Chapter 5:

> ...the day following the attack, MFY's executive directors assured the staff that no one would be fired for suspected communist affiliation. "What matters," they said, "is not really whether we survive, and that indeed is an open question—what matters is the issues on which we stand and fight. ..."Three days later, however, in response to pressure from federal officials who believed that MFY could not otherwise be saved, the executive directors agreed that current members of "subversive" organizations would be dismissed. (1969, p. 167)

Similarly, Perrow cites the study of the Townsend organization, which "managed to stay alive by transforming its political goal of increased support for the aged through a radical economic plan into social goals of fellowship and card playing and fiscal goals of selling vitamins and patent medicines to its members" (1972a, p. 182).

Earlier, in Chapter 13 on the System of Politics, we talked of the *displacement* of the formal goals *in* the organization—the deflection of the intentions of the senior managers by other insiders. What we have here is goal displacement on an organizational level, *by* the senior management—the deflection of what have been the basic goals *of* the organization in order to save it as a system. A related phenomenon, called *goal succession* (Blau 1963, pp. 241–46), occurs not when failure threatens the survival of the organization but when success does. The organization that has achieved what it set out to do, instead of closing its doors, finds a new purpose in order to keep going.

Well known in the literature of sociology, thanks to Sill's excellent book *The Volunteers* (1957), is the story of the Foundation for Infantile Paralysis, which ran the effective "March of Dimes" campaign to raise funds to eradicate that disease. With the development of the Salk and Sabine vaccines, the Foundation's tangible goal was realized and it lost its raison d'etre. Success created a crisis of survival. As Etzioni (1964) puts it, the Foundation was "so to speak 'unemployed' ":

> Here was a vast network of volunteers who experienced a variety of social and normative gratifications from working for the Foundation, and national leadership and staff, all coordinated in an efficient and obviously effective organizational machine—but the machine was without a purpose. (p. 13)

And so the Foundation "had to find a new goal [and a new mission[1]] or cease its

[1]Perrow (1970, pp. 136–37), one of the few theorists to distinguish clearly between goal and mission (he refers to the latter as "product goal"), believes that the failure to make this distinction has led to considerable confusion in interpreting Sills's study. He argues that the primary goal of the Foundation did not need to be changed, only its mission. But it could be argued that in this case—later in this chapter we shall argue in the Ideologic IC in general—goal and mission were closely associated. The collection of funds to aid research on infantile paralysis was certainly the mission (or product goal) of the Foundation, but the eradication of *this particular* disease was clearly the primary goal. In that sense, both goal and mission needed to be changed. Only another goal—that of survival—remained.

activity" (p. 13). It should come as no surprise that it did the former. With its powerful ideology and great momentum, the Foundation was not about to let so minor a detail as the loss of its fundamental goal and mission end its life. It found a new mission—the combating of birth defects—and changed its name to the National Foundation. The organization survived even if its primary goal did not.[2]

Sills reviews in his book the cases of other organizations faced with similar crises of survival. A few dissolved, such as the "Sons of Liberty" after the success of the American Revolution. But most carried on, suggesting that even temporary organizations have a habit of becoming permanent. Some organizations, such as the Women's Christian Temperance Union, failed to adapt to changing environments, and "exist today as fossil remains of their previous life" (p. 258). Others, however, rebounded effectively. The American Legion, "established in order to preserve the spirit which characterized the American Expeditionary Force in World War I" (p. 257), came to protect the rights of veterans and to carry out community projects; Dartmouth, founded to educate and Christianize the Indians of New England, became a liberal arts college; and the YMCA and the Red Cross were able to change a number of times as the societies in which they were embedded changed.

What is so important about the survival of an organization anyway? Classical economic theory tells us that it is healthy to have companies go bankrupt once in a while; the same is presumably true for nonprofit institutions that become ineffective or irrelevant. Moreover, if the argument that organizations are mere collections of individuals is true, why don't those individuals readily disperse to other organizations and let their own die when it has outlived its usefulness? The fact of the matter is that the demise of an organization means more than just the dispersal of its personnel and the loss of power by a few managers. It means the dissolution of a whole system of investments, psychic as well as material, often the evaporation of an ideology as well. An organization is brought into being, usually with a great deal of effort, by a group of founders; thereafter its members invest much time and energy to consolidate its operations, develop an impetus for it, and establish its niche in the community. Traditions develop, commitments are made, identifications are established. All of this is lost when an organization dies. Thus when a 100-year-old daily newspaper collapsed in Montreal a few days before this was written, the com-

---

[2]The transition was not immediate, as is evident in the confusion in the literature. (Sill's study, published in 1957, ended before the organization adopted its new goal and mission.) Hall refers to the Foundation as dealing with " 'other crippling diseases,' with particular emphasis on birth defects" (1972, p. 92), Perrow as dealing with "all childhood diseases" (1970, p. 136), and Etzioni as dealing with "arthritis and birth defects" (1964, p. 13); Thompson plays it safest in commenting that the Foundation "entered several new disease domains" (1967, p. 47). In fact, the *New York Times Index* of 1958 reports the same change and the expansion of the program "to include arthritis and congenital defects," while the *Encyclopedia of Associations* of 1964 lists the program as concerned with "certain birth defects, crippling arthritis, polio melitis, and all types of virus diseases." By 1968, that listing was down to "the area of birth defects," and the 1980 edition shows another name change to "March of Dimes Birth Defects Foundation" whose "purpose is prevention of birth defects."

munity mourned it like the death of an elder statesman, as if a cherished living organism had suddenly stopped functioning. It is reactions such as these—and the lengths people go to to save threatened organizations—that perhaps most decisively counter the claim that an organization is merely a collection of individuals. Time and time again, organizations show clear signs of having lives of their own.

EFFICIENCY AS A SYSTEMS GOAL

A second goal intrinsic to the system called organization is *efficiency*. "The commandment, 'Be efficient!' is a major organizational influence over the decisions of the members of any administrative agency..." (Simon 1957, p. 14). Simon devotes a whole chapter of his major work, *Administrative Behavior*, to "The Criterion of Efficiency," which he defines as dictating "that choice of alternative which produces the largest result for the given application of resources" (p. 179). In other words, to be efficient means to get the most of whatever goal an organization wishes to pursue—the most growth, the happiest employees, the most prizes, the highest quality. Efficiency means the greatest *benefit* for the *cost*, or in the words of MacNamara's whiz kids at the Pentagon back in the 1960s, the biggest bang for the buck. And since resources—not only money and material but also human time and energy—are always limited in a competitive world, efficiency must be a goal of every organization, business and non-business, and so is one of the systems goals.

Indeed, efficiency can be a rallying point for many of the influencers. For the insiders, especially the senior managers to whom the survival of the organization is most important, efficiency is a means to that survival. Inefficient organizations run out of resources, and cease to function. To the analysts of the technostructure, efficiency is especially important. As we saw in Chapter 9, efficiency is their raison d'etre: they exist to develop systems to improve the efficiency of the organization. Without it as a goal, they would be out of a job. To the public at large and the government in particular, efficiency means productivity: the prudent expenditure of society's resources. No matter what the goal, better that it be pursued efficiently. For the clients, efficiency can mean that the products and services are being produced as cheaply as possible,[3] and for the owners, that the surpluses—in the business firm, the profits—are as large as possible, thereby maximizing their return on investment.

Of course, one can ask; Efficient for what? If the goal of a firm is to fleece its clients, then efficiency works against these clients: the more efficient the firm, the worse off the clients. Similarly, if the goal is to have happy employees no matter what the cost, efficiency can mean a reduced return on investment for the owners. In the popular literature of management, whereas efficiency is the con-

---

[3]Which benefits them as long as markets are competitive, so that the savings are passed along to them.

cept associated with "doing things right," effectiveness is the one associated with "doing the right things" (Drucker 1973, p. 45). In other words, an organization can be efficient without being effective—doing the wrong things well, as in the expression "arranging the deck chairs on the Titanic"—or it can be effective without being efficient—doing the right things badly, as when a great film runs 200 percent over budget. There are, of course, no absolutes in determining "right" things—things are right only in the eyes of particular influencers. What is right for the owners or the clients can be wrong for the workers or for conservation groups. Thus, effectiveness is a concept laden with values, with preferences, whereas efficiency is ostensibly value-free, in Simon's words, "completely neutral" (1957, p. 14). How well or badly one does something should be quite independent of whether or not it is a good thing to do. All of this suggests that efficiency is the motherhood goal, the one rightfully pursued by every well-meaning management, in conjunction with other goals. How could anyone possibly be against efficiency?

The irony is that many people are indeed against it, that efficiency is a dirty word in many quarters. Even at the Harvard Business School, one teaching note refers to the label "efficiency expert" given a manager in one of its cases as "most uncomplementary in connotation."[4] How can this be?

Some attribute the reaction to an obsession with efficiency, what is sometimes called the "cult of efficiency," its pursuit as an end in itself. "Years of Taylorism, scientific management, and now operations research and management science have led to the maximization of efficiency as a value" (Pfeffer and Salancik 1978, p. 35). But as Simon has defined the term, an obsession with efficiency simply means an obsession with whatever goal efficiency helps the organization to pursue. So something more than this must be involved with people's reaction to the word.

Others in search of an explanation look to the goals pursued efficiently, and suggest that the problem lies with the uses to which the techniques of efficiency are put. It is the so-called "professional" manager who sees his function as the efficient attainment of whatever goals the organization happens to have. He is the hired gun, so to speak, in the business of efficiency, not effectiveness: "...they say given your ends, whatever they may be, the study of administration will help you to achieve them. We offer you tools. Into the foundations of your choices we shall not inquire, for that would make us moralists rather than scientists" (Selznick 1957, p. 80). But when that goal is considered to be antisocial, efficiency gets a bad name. Singer and Wooton (1976) document from a management perspective the case of Albert Speer, the super efficient manager of the Third Reich's armaments production, a man who "stressed functional effectiveness and amoral judgment" (p. 88). They argue that managers may be "so caught up in the procedural demands of their work that they easily lose sight of the important end results of their activities" (pp. 98–99). As Tom Lehrer parodied one of Speer's colleagues in song:

---

[4]Teaching note for "The Rose Company," Case 9-453-002, Intercollegiate Case Cleaning House, Graduate School of Business Administration, Harvard University.

"Once the rockets are up, who cares where they come down.
That's not my department," says Wernher von Braun.
(©1965 Tom Lehrer. Used by permission.)

Yet even this cannot fully explain the negative attitudes toward efficiency, because surely for every Speer there are many other managers concerned with the efficiency of organizations that pursue perfectly acceptable goals—hospitals and post offices, for example. Again, as Simon has defined the term, efficiency should be a force for good or evil. Yet even in hospitals and post offices, let alone the Harvard Business School, the efficiency experts are often the bad guys. So what is the real problem?

In my opinion, the root of the problem lies not in the definition of the term efficiency, but in how that definition is applied. For efficiency in practice does not really mean just the greatest benefit for the cost; it means the greatest *measurable* benefit for the *measurable* cost. In other words, efficiency means *demonstrated* efficiency, *proven* efficiency, above all, *calculated* efficiency. A management obsessed with efficiency is a management obsessed with measurement. The cult of efficiency is the cult of calculation.

Consider these examples. If I call a restaurant efficient, what is your immediate thought? (Think about it before you read on.) That its food tasted good for the price? Not likely, because we cannot measure that. I polled fifty-nine MBA students on the question (cold, at the start of a class, before we had ever discussed efficiency), asking them to write down the first thing that popped into their heads when I said that a restaurant was efficient. Most of them—forty-three in all—mentioned a most quantifiable goal, speed of service, in one way or another (e.g., "fast service," "no delays"). Thirteen did comment positively on the food, typically something like "serves good meals" or "tasty food," but five others commented negatively, for example, "terrible food," "serves what should be thrown out," "bland, boring, and dehumanizing."[5] Another individual to whom I posed the question answered: "I don't see what efficiency has to do with food," but then, on further reflection, added "If I heard that a restaurant was efficient, I would wonder about the food!" Similarly, when I say that my house is efficient, hardly anyone thinks of its comfort or the beauty of its design; the most common first thoughts relate to quantitative items, for example, that it takes only nineteen minutes to vacuum, or that we can get from the kitchen to the bedroom in thirteen steps, or that it takes only 3,000 liters of oil to heat it in the winter.[6] In practice, therefore, efficiency ends up being associated with factors that are measurable. And this has three major consequences.

[5]A few students commented on price, cleanliness, or profitability. Note that some students noted more than one point, hence the number of answers exceeds fifty-nine.

[6]I polled the fifty-nine students on this one too. Forty of them referred to the house being well planned or organized to get chores done, to tidiness or neatness, to things being in their place, and seven referred to low energy comsumption ("well insulated," "low fuel bills," etc.). One student mentioned comfort, another, a "good family relationship"; none mentioned aesthetics. A year later I polled twenty-two students on the two questions. This time all but two mentioned speed of service (fourteen exclusively), and ten each mentioned something related to fuel consumption and to some aspects of tidiness and organization.

1. Because costs are typically more easily measured than benefits, efficiency all too often reduces to economy. Costs are typically more easily expressed than benefits in quantitative terms—dollars, man-hours, materials, or whatever. University administrators know with some precision how much it costs to train an MBA student; but no one really has a clue how much is learned in such programs, or what effect that learning has on the practice of management. So the all too frequent result of an obsession with efficiency is the cutting of tangible costs at the expense of intangible benefits. What university administrator cannot cut 10 percent of the cost of training an MBA with no *noticeable* effect on the benefits. Even in the business firm, it is a simple matter for a chief executive to cut the budget—he simply reduces expenditures on activities with intangible results, such as research or advertising. The effect on profits may not show up for years, long after he has left. In other words, all too often efficiency comes to mean economy, with benefits suffering at the expense of costs, so to speak.[7] And efficiency gets a bad name.

2. Because economic costs are typically more easily measured than social costs, efficiency all too often results in the escalation of social costs, treated as "externalities." The business firm in particular likes to operate where things can be measured. Peter Drucker makes this quite clear: "[The] task can be identified. It can be defined. Goals can be set. And performance can be measured. And then business can perform" (1973, p. 347). The problem is that some things are more easily measured than others. The dollars required, the number of man-hours involved, the materials necessary—all these are easily quantified. The air polluted, the minds dulled, the scenery destroyed—these are costs, too, but they are not so easily measured. In general, the economic costs—the tangible resources deployed—are usually more easily measured than the social ones—the consequences on modes of living. In business especially, but not exclusively, an emphasis on measurement means a tendency to attribute only the tangible costs to the organization, while the intangible social costs get dismissed as "externalities," the responsibility of the society at large. (We shall elaborate on this notion in Part V of the book.) The implicit assumption is that if a cost cannot be measured, then it has not been incurred. And so it is not the concern of a management responsible for "efficiency." As a result, the economic costs tend to be closely controlled by that kind of management, while the social costs escalate. And efficiency gets a bad name.

[7]Among the "criticisms of the efficiency criterion," Simon dismisses the one about economy as follows:

> One group of criticisms need not concern us here, for they refer to definitions of the term different from the one proposed here. In this category must be placed attacks on efficiency which equate the term with "economy" or "expenditure reduction." As we have used "efficiency," there is no implication whatsoever that a small expenditure—or, for that matter, a large expenditure—is *per se* desirable. (1957, pp. 182–83)

But our point is that while there may be no implication in Simon's definition per se, there is one in how his definition gets operationalized in practice. The issue is not one of definitions but of the consequences of them.

3. Because economic benefits are typically more easily measured than social benefits, efficiency all too often drives the organization toward an economic morality which can sometimes amount to a social immorality. All human activities create multitudes of benefits, ranging from the very tangible to the highly ambiguous. But the efficiency conscious manager will naturally favor the former, those that he can measure. The dean who must base his promotion decisions on "hard facts" will naturally be driven to count the publications of his professors rather than to make a subjective assessment of their quality. In other words, an obsession with efficiency means that tangible, demonstratable, measurable benefits are allowed to drive out vague, obscure, ill-defined ones, often when the former even miss the point. The criterion of efficiency comes to mean the largest *measurable* result for the given application of resources. It is not the quality of the food that counts so much as the speed with which it is served, not the comfort of the house that comes to mind so much as its facility to keep the heat in. Again, it is those things economic—speed, heat retention, the goals associated with tangible resources—that best lend themselves to measurement. The social goals—quality, comfort—often get left behind.

Pirsig, in his popular book *Zen and the Art of Motorcycle Maintenance* (1974), takes this conclusion one step farther, suggesting that social values such as these may be beyond our skills of logic and analysis: "I think there is such a thing as Quality, but as soon as you try to define it, something goes haywire. You can't do it. . . . Because definitions are a product of rigid, formal thinking, Quality cannot be defined" (p. 200). And yet, "even though Quality cannot be defined, you know what Quality is" (p. 201). But do the efficiency experts? Or at least, do they allow themselves to "know" that which is beyond the power of their tools?

And so efficiency emerges, in practice if not in theory, not as a neutral concept at all, but as one associated with a particular system of values—economic values. In fact, an obsession with efficiency can mean a dominance of economic goals over social ones that drives the organization beyond an economic morality to a social immorality. Ackerman (1975) shows how the systems of objectives used in large corporations "may actually inhibit social responsiveness" (p. 56) by driving out the less operational social goals.[8] Bower (1970) notes that it was the turning of the financial screws in one such system, at General Electric, that contributed to the famous price fixing scandal of 1961. In the giant corporation,

> Men are rewarded for performance, but performance is almost always defined as short-run economic or technical results. The more objective the system, the more an attempt is made to quantify results, the harder it is to broaden the rules of the game to take into account the social role of the executive. (Bower 1974, pp. 202–3)

Thus does proeconomic behavior become antisocial behavior.

[8]We shall return to a more detailed discussion of the Ackerman study, and the interplay between the large corporation's economic and social goals, in Chapter 30.

In practice, therefore, efficiency has come to represent economic values. The call to "be efficient" is the call to calculate, where calculation means economizing, treating social costs as externalities, and allowing economic benefits to push out social ones. At the limit, efficiency emerges as the pillar of an ideology that worships economic goals, sometimes with immoral consequences. Thus does efficiency, that "completely neutral" concept, get a bad name.

This ideology tends to be most highly developed in certain quarters of the business community, for the obvious reason that the costs and benefits most important to businessmen are easily measured, both in the same units. As a result, the costs can be subtracted from the benefits, to calculate the surplus, called profit. And profit thereby becomes the prime measure of efficiency in the firm, indeed the central notion of an entire economic system. To make profit means to be efficient which means to serve society. Any behavior that produces the right numbers on that all-important bottom line becomes acceptable, so long as does not break a law. Food may be thrown into the sea to raise prices, rivers polluted to process minerals, prices set to bring in whatever markets will bear, assembly lines speeded up to reduce costs, all this because the social consequences of these acts cannot easily be measured and attributed to specific organizations. In other words, in the particular case of business, efficiency has all too often interfered with effectiveness from the perspective of many groups in society. It is some businessmen's obsession with this kind of efficiency that has led business's sharpest critics to comment in terms such as the following:

> . . .it would be perfectly easy to show how the extrapolation of business criteria into family life destroys families and how the insistence that schools operate according to canons of efficiency, measured in terms of dollars and cents, is guaranteed to ruin any school, no matter how good the school may have been before these business criteria were imposed. Businessmen tend to be blinded by the holy light emanating from the word "efficiency," as though somehow the invocation of this word dispelled any foolish notions about the importance of other criteria. One rarely hears anyone asking "Efficient for what?"—and whether the "what" that is stated has anything to do with the values sought in family life or schooling or religion. (Tumin 1964, p. 125)

But not all businessmen, or other kinds of managers, are so obsessed with efficiency. Efficiency, like survival, while *a* goal of virtually every organization, usually takes its place along side others. In fact, as we have described it, efficiency seems to be more often a constraint then a primary goal. Attention must be paid to keeping the economic benefits up and the economic costs down, but only to a point. Even in the widely held business corporation, as we saw earlier, profit tends to be treated as a constraint. Once the needs for efficiency or profit are satisfied, attention then turns to other goals, often to our two remaining systems goals.

CONTROL AS A SYSTEMS GOAL

The third goal pursued by virtually all organizations as systems is the attempt to exercise some control over their own environments. We have seen that every organization experiences a host of external forces designed to constrain and control its actions. But by the same token, the organization as a system seeks to control these forces too, to take the initiative in mastering them. "In adapting to their environment, systems will attempt to cope with external forces by ingesting them or acquiring control over them" (Katz and Kahn 1966, p. 24). Here again we see the phenomenon of reciprocity in power relationships, with control flowing in both directions.

The control goal may be pursued in two ways. On one hand, the organization may simply try to retain its autonomy, to relieve the pressures on itself. In this case, control is a constraint: the organization pursues it to the point where it feels it has enough room to maneuver, in order to pursue other goals. On the other hand, control can also be an end in itself, just like survival or efficiency, even an obsession. The organization may become so obsessed with dominating the forces in its environment that the quest for autonomy comes to look more and more like the lust for power. As in the parallel case for individuals, to distinguish these two—stopping others from interfering with the pursuit of one's own goals versus controlling the goals others pursue—can be very difficult in practice. Indeed, some of the most blatantly power-hungry individuals or organizations often claim to be, and sometimes really believe themselves to be, simply searching for autonomy. How much power given inidividuals or organizations really need to control their own affairs is a matter of opinion.

The most thorough description in the literature of the methods organizations use to control their environments is, ironically, contained in a book entitled *The External Control of Organizations*. The authors, Pfeffer and Salancik (1978), in fact devote roughly half their book to discussion of external control *by* organizations. Their point is that organizations, which are subjected to all kinds of external influencer pressures, do not always comply passively with the pressures. At the very least, they try to avoid some of the pressures—for example, by restricting information on available surpluses and payoffs that have been made to other influencers, or by playing conflicting influencer groups off against each other. Taking a more active stance, many organizations try to manage some of the pressures for their own advantage—for example, by seeking to select who it is that will exert the pressure, as in the selection of members of their boards of directors. Finally, some organizations try to turn the game of power around, and seek to control their environments directly.[9]

Pfeffer and Salancik devote three chapters to their discussion of the means

[9]Richards (1978, pp. 78–82) argues, in similar fashion, that possible organizational reactions to external demands include compliance, direct resistance, rhetorical support (without action), tactical diversion, attempted cooptation, and proaction and advocacy.

organizations use to pursue their goal of control. The first, subtitled "Controlling the Context of Control," discusses expansion and diversification:

> We argue that *vertical* integration represents a method of extending organizational control over exchanges vital to [the organization's] operation; that *horizontal* expansion represents a method for attaining dominance to increase the organization's power in exchange relationships and to reduce uncertainty generated from competition; and that *diversification* represents a method for decreasing the organization's dependence on other, dominant organizations. (p. 114)

Citing a good deal of evidence from the empirical research, Pfeffer and Salancik make the point that the merger—a prime means to expand and diversify—is undertaken not to increase profitability or efficiency, but to reduce external dependency and to achieve stability in the organization's environment. "One organizational response to interdependence is to absorb it" (p. 139).

When the organization cannot or does not wish to control the source of the pressure through outright absorption, a second choice is to negotiate with it, thereby "establishing collective structures of interorganizational action," the subtitle of Pfeffer and Salancik's second chapter. Here, they discuss a number of arrangements organizations use to "coordinate" or cooperate with each other, including the establishment of trade associations, cartels, joint ventures, and reciprocal trading agreements, as well as the use of interlocking boards of directors as a means of cooptation. These arrangements are "more flexible than managing dependence through ownership," but at the expense of "less than absolute control" (p. 144). In fact, there are costs to these arrangements, in the form of "restricted discretion," which organizations are "willing to bear. . .for the benefits of predictable and certain exchanges" (p. 183). Thus, reciprocity appears again: cooperation means giving up one kind of power to gain another.

When absorption and cooperation do not work, then the organization may turn to a third alternative, "controlling interdependence through law and social sanction," the subtitle of their final chapter on control by the organization. ". . .organizations will attempt to use the larger social power of the state to benefit its operating environment" (p. 222). They may request from the government direct financial support (in the form of subsidies, defense contracts, or whatever), market protection (in the form of tariffs, quotas, the establishment of regulatory agencies, and so on), or some other helpful piece of legislation or action (as in the building of new roads to aid trucking companies). Otherwise, the organization may try to enlist existing legislation or governemnt agencies in its cause, as when a business firm charges a competitor with antitrust violations. Because "the courts and the government are increasingly replacing the market in determining which organizations will survive and prosper" (p. 189), organizations in turn try to use these agencies to control their environments. The result is that "laws, social norms, values, and political outcomes reflect, in part, actions taken by organizations" in their own private interests (p. 190).

Pfeffer and Salancik conclude that "organizations, in addition to being coalitions of interests, are markets in which influence and control are transacted" (p. 259). And just as they are subject to external controls, so too do "organizations seek to avoid being controlled" (p. 261). But, "ironically, to gain some control over the activities of another organization, the focal organization must surrender some of its own autonomy" (p. 261).

GROWTH AS A SYSTEMS GOAL

All organizations experience strong natural pressures to grow, for a number of reasons. Earlier we noted that all the internal influencers, but especially the middle-line managers and the chief executive, are rewarded directly by the growth of the organization, in terms of larger salaries, greater opportunities for advancement, and more power and prestige: ". . .as the pond grows bigger, so does the size of the frog" (Perrow 1970, pp. 152–53). Growth is also a particularly effective way to deal with internal strain, when ambitious managers come into conflict:

> If one department brings pressure against a second department because the second unit seems overstaffed and overprivileged with respect to status and frequency of promotions, the tendency of management is not to cut back the one department but to upgrade the other. . . .it is easier for management to meet internal problems by adding rather than subtracting. (Katz and Kahn 1966, p. 101).

Thus, just as the system of competitive markets makes economic efficiency the natural goal of the owner, so too does the system of organization make growth the natural goal of the manager.

Growth can also help the organization to meet the other systems goals, namely to survive, be efficient, and control its environment. In many spheres of activity, the small organization is vulnerable; the larger one more secure. The latter has more slack to fall back on in hard times, and more external influencers concerned that it not disappear. The United States government will intervene to save a Chrysler or a Penn Central, while it allows thousands of small firms to go bankrupt every year. Efficiency relates to size through economies of scale. In many industries, especially ones reliant on elaborate or complex technical systems, organizations must grow large to become efficient. As for the goal of control, Pfeffer and Salancik point out that "Organizations that are large have more power and leverage over their environments. They are more able to resist immediate pressures for change and, moreover, have more time in which to recognize external threats and adapt to meet them" (1978, p. 139). Moreover, as John Kenneth Galbraith (1952) notes in his theory of "countervailing power," bigness begets bigness: so as not to lose control, organizations must grow large when other organizations that can influence them grow large. Big unions are needed to stand up to big business, big suppliers encourage the development of big clients and vice versa, big government emerges as a reaction to big business and big labor, and in turn forces them as well as other organizations to grow even bigger to deal with its influence. It is the big university that can best confront the big government that finances it.

But while growth may be a subordinate goal and a constraint to some organizations—a means to survival, to an acceptable level of efficiency, and to control—it turns out to be a primary goal, indeed *the* primary goal, to a great many. That is to say, ours is a society of organizations obsessed with growth:

> No other social goal is more strongly avowed than economic growth. No other test of social success has such nearly unanimous acceptance as the annual increase in the Gross National Product. And this is true of all countries developed or underdeveloped; communist, socialist or capitalist....
>
> Given a secure level of earnings the esteemed firms are those that are large—that have a record of achieved growth—or which are growing with particular speed. (Galbraith 1967, pp. 173, 177)

But this phenomenon is hardly restricted to the private sector. Today all kinds of organizations prize growth, even in those service sectors where *dis*economies of scale render large organizations inefficient in carrying out their basic missions. We have multiversities, mammoth hospital complexes, comprehensive high schools, giant old age homes, and various other organizational dinosaurs, which often seem more adept at conducting political battles among themselves than rendering services to their human clients. In other words, the dictates of power are too often allowed to override human and even economic criteria.[10] Indeed, Pfeffer and Salancik (1978, pp. 133–35) cite a good deal of evidence that even in business corporations, growth often comes at the *expense* of profit. Thus, growth can and does emerge as an end in itself, bigness the ultimate measure of the success of a system in a world of big systems.

To conclude our discussion of the systems goals, we have seen that they can interrelate in a variety of ways. Growth may be necessary for survival, just as survival is obviously necessary for growth. A certain degree of control may

---

[10]This point was driven home to me some years ago when I was once asked to respond to a proposal at our university to merge what was at that time our small management library into the large central one. On any performance criterion for which there was data, (e.g., number of people served per day), the small library proved two to three times as efficient as the much larger one. The explanation seemed to lie in those notions behavioral scientists use to try to patch up the human problems of large organizations: in our small library, jobs were naturally varied and "enlarged," and the structure was organic; everyone, including the chief librarian, did everything. Because this library could not "afford" a rigid division of labor, it's three or four employees enjoyed their work, and worked hard. They also knew their clients personally and served them well (the critical performance criterion, for which, as our discussion of efficiency would lead us to expect, no measures were available). In cases such as these, where the human factors of motivation and service replace the technical ones of machine economies of scale, small size would seem to be most efficient, even if we cannot always measure that efficiency and even if that size is not always the most politically astute in this world of countervailing powers.

also be necessary for survival (at least survival as an independent entity), and may also enable growth to take place. Alternately, growth may be a prerequisite for control. Growth brings efficiency under certain conditions, and efficiency can generate the surpluses needed to support growth. But then again, an obsession with any of the systems goals can also conflict with pursuit of the others. For example, too much growth may interfere with efficiency, and ultimately even with survival, while too great an obsession with control may hamper efficiency or growth. And, finally, we saw that an obsession with survival can in fact backfire and lead to violation of itself, that most fundamental of constraints—with the result that efficiency, control, and growth can no longer be pursued.

But if one major relationship stands out among these four goals, it would appear to be the hierarchical one, a close parallel to Maslow's hierarchy of human needs. Organizations must survive in order to pursue other goals. But once survival is ensured, efficiency is pursued. But only to a point. Certainly organizations strive for more than the bare minimum of efficiency needed for survival, but they are typically satisfied at some point sufficient to generate the resources necessary to pursue other goals. One of those other goals is control. But that, too, seems to be a means to another final end, that being growth. In other words, **most often, survival, efficiency, and control seem to be treated as constraints, goals subordinate to growth, the most common primary goal of the system called organization.**

MISSION AS A GOAL OF THE ORGANIZATION

The systems goals appear to be common to all organizations, no matter what other goals are pursued or even dominate. Survival, efficiency, control, and growth are inevitably the intentions behind at least some of the actions of every organization, and frequently emerge as primary goals.

At the outset of this book, the term *mission* was introduced, as describing the organization's basic function in society, the reason for its existence in the eyes of the world at large: to produce specific products or services. And the point was made then, and is repeated now, that mission may or may not be a goal of an organization, that what it does for a living may be central or only incidental to its controlling influencers.

Thus, to draw on the example cited in Chapter 1, the mission of the hamburger franchise is to feed its clients, its goal perhaps to make money (or friends, or whatever). If the owner could make more money selling fanbelts, he probably would. In contrast, the gourmet chef who runs his own restaurant prepares the meals to satisfy himself as well as his clients; he would no sooner sell fanbelts than hamburgers. In other words, both organizations pursue the same mission, but only in the second one is that mission also a goal—an end as well as a means. The primary goal of this gourmet restaurant is to perform its mission well.

Under what conditions does mission become a primary goal of an organization? One condition, obvious in the above example, is when an important influencer believes in the mission as an end in itself. That person can be an owner and, even better, the chief executive officer. (In fact, as we shall soon see, this is more likely to happen when the owner *is* the chief executive officer.) That influencer can also be an associate, for mission is intrinsically important both to the organization's clients, who look to it for specific goals and services, and to its suppliers, whose sales to it depend on the vigor with which it pursues its mission. Thus, associates in positions of power—for example, monopsonists or monopolists—naturally encourage the organization to treat mission as a primary goal. So too do owners who create organizations to serve themselves—parent firms that establish subsidiaries to supply certain of their needs, suppliers or clients who establish cooperatives. When farmers set up agencies to market their produce or brokers create stock markets to trade their securities, they care only that these organizations perform their missions well. Unfortunately—as we shall see later—owners of cooperatives often become passive influencers, and so lose control to the full-time managers. And the latter tend to pursue other goals, sometimes even ones that conflict with the initial mission, as when the managers of a farmer cooperative promote substitute products to increase sales.

Mission tends to enter the goal system in organizations that pursue different and competing missions. We saw this earlier in the example of custody versus rehabilitation in prisons. In these cases, alliances form around each mission, which then comes to be treated as an end in itself. Pfeffer and Sherwood cite a doctoral thesis by a former prison warden who concluded that "a fundamental conflict in goal philosophy in modern correctional administration between social treatment of offenders as the paramount value (Goal 1) and custody as the important consideration (Goal 2) ramified through every administrative tendon of the prison" (1960, pp. 406–7).

Mission also tends to emerge as one, if not the, primary goal in the particular case of the Professional IC. This occurs because some of the professional operators, who have a good deal of the power, are inclined to favor the goal of professional excellence—essentially the quality with which the mission is pursued—sometimes at the expense of efficiency and occasionally even of survival.

Finally, and perhaps most commonly, mission and goal become synonomous in the Ideologic IC—the organization with a strong ideology. Here the preservation, extension, and/or perfection of the mission becomes an end in itself, forming the basis for the ideology. Perrow describes the Daimler-Benz Company (circa 1961), manufacturer of the Mercedes automobile, where "quality is a goal in itself." He contrasts this with the Ford Motor Company, were "quality becomes a problem. . . only when it appears to drop below the standards of its competitors" (p. 167). Referring to a 1961 *Fortune* article entitled "Daimler-Benz: Quality uber Alles," Perrow describes the firm's behavior:

The firm built the world's first practical automobile and has been building quality cars in small numbers for over 75 years. The chief engineer of the company described the 75-year-old tradition as "constant experimentation, concentration on new developments, and continuous improvement." This has meant that the Mercedes has incorporated, as standard equipment, all significant innovations as soon as they appear, whether the public demands them or not and without regard to the increase in the cost of the car . . . The company is dominated by engineers and has an adequate pool of skilled labor. Its workers have lived and worked for generations in the German towns where the cars are produced, and they take a fierce pride in their skilled craftsmanship. (1970, p. 168)

Organizations obsessed with their missions are sometimes called, appropriately enough, "missionary." Common examples are religious movements and radical political parties. Save perhaps survival in times of crisis, no goal takes precedence over the preservation, extention, and/or perfection of the mission. At the other extreme are organizations sometimes referred to as "utilitarian" (Etzioni 1961), whose ends are quite independent of their means. Mission has no special meaning for them, no place in their system of goals.

Perrow (1970) describes different firms in the textile industry which exhibit a range of attitudes toward mission as a goal. At one extreme were those with strong product identifications:

Their [executives'] attachment to fibers such as wool, cotton, or silk and their resistance to new synthetic fibers, was so strong in the early 1960s that, at a meeting of the Fashion Institute of Technology, an executive of one large textile company was hissed by "silk men" in the audience when they felt that their true love had been slurred. (p. 161)

In between was the J. P. Stevens Company, an old firm with a commitment to textiles, but not to any special kind. As the chairman claimed in 1963: "If the public wants straw, we'll weave straw. We're not wedded to any particular product or fiber" (p. 161). And at the other extreme was Indian Head, bought in a period of difficulty by a "professional manager," a Harvard Business School graduate with no experience in textiles. He retained the profitable parts of the company and sold off many that were losing money, taking tax losses where he could. Unlike the J. P. Stevens executive, he invested nothing to improve the parts that were left over. He prepared a policy manual which stated that the company was *not* in business

to grow bigger for the sake of size, nor to become more diversified, nor to make the most or best of anything, nor to provide jobs, have the most modern plants, the happiest customers, lead in new product development, or to achieve any other status which has no relationship to the economic use of capital.

Any or all of these may be, from time to time, a means to our objective, but means and ends must never be confused. Indian Head Mills is in business solely to improve the inherent value of the common stockholders' equity in the company. (p. 164)

The top official of one old, established textile company asked ("bitterly" in the words of *Fortune*): "Is he trying to build up a textile business or just to make money?" On this, the chief executive of Indian Head had no doubts. "We have no emotional involvement in the textile industry. We're in it through happenstance" (p. 164; quotations from *Fortune* magazine article [Rieser 1962]).

To conclude, we have seen that mission can take a variety of forms in the organization's goal system:

* The preservation and extention of the mission per se can be one of the organization's primary goals (as in the example of custody or rehabilitation in prisons).

* The perfection of the mission can be a primary goal (as in Daimler-Benz).

* The mission can be incidental, a dispensible means to another goal (as in Indian Head).

* The mission can conflict with the goal (as in the farmer cooperative whose managers promote substitutes).

These are various forms mission *can* take in the goal system. But which are most common? What are the long-term trends? I should like to argue that the two groups of goals we have been discussing in this chapter stand in one major relationship to each other. **While mission remains the primary goal of some organizations—notably those with strong ideologies—the trend over the course of the last two centuries, particularly in business firms but also in other types of organizations, has been its displacement by the systems goals.** In effect, a major consequence of the introduction of more and more sophisticated systems of control—that is, of the rise of machine bureaucratic and divisionalized forms of structure—since the advent of the Industrial Revolution has been the weakening of mission as a goal and the strengthening of the emphasis on survival, efficiency, control, and especially growth.

A NOTE ON THE DISPLACEMENT OF MISSION BY THE SYSTEMS GOALS

In a crude, stylized way, we can trace in Western societies over the course of the past two hundred years a number of steps in the gradual displacement of mission as a goal by the systems goals. Prior to the Industrial Revolution, a good deal of work was craft in nature, which "meant that all the workers—masters as well as servants, apprentices and journeymen—had to be skilled in every aspect of the craft" (Olton 1975, p. 9). The craft worker, whether artisan in the city or farmer in the country, was personally responsible for the final product, and so had a propensity to identify strongly with it. The cobbler made shoes to earn a living, but the quality of the shoes he made and how well shod were his customers likely mattered to him.

The Industrial Revolution brought mechanization and mass production to certain trades. As a result, many workers were brought together in single factories, and their labor was divided and specialized so that each contributed a small task to the final product. Products became standardized and their cost decreased, the the workers lost responsibility for the final products and also lost personal contact with the clients, so that their identification with both diminished. How was the man who sat tacking heels onto shoes all day to care about those shoes or the people who wore them? So mission tended to become incidental to the factory workers, a means to an income.

However, the workers had a boss, typically an entrepreneur who both owned and managed the factory. And that entrepreneur was generally committed to a single product in a single industry for a lifetime. As Chandler noted, "in the single-product enterprise, the question of what to produce is solved once and for all with the establishment of the works and reappears only in cases of critical reorganization" (1962, p. 14). The entrepreneur was certainly motivated by the systems goals—especially profit—but he retained personal responsibility for the mission and therefore tended to identify with it. The shoe company was devoted to the shoe business; its owner was perhaps active in the trade association and his friends wore *his* shoes. He took pride in what his factory produced.

But industrialization proceeded. Frederick Taylor's experiments with "Scientific Management" at the turn of the century led to the rise of the technocratic component of organizations. And this was accompanied by an elaboration of functional structure, at first in railroading and telegraph communication, then more generally into mass production and mass distribution, in order to effect "administrative coordination" (Chandler 1977). In effect there came about a strong division of *administrative* work, which resulted in what we have called the machine bureaucratization of the manufacturing organization. Managers proliferated in the middle line and experts in staff units. Both, specialized by function, naturally developed strong identifications with their functions. In other words, what had happened to the operating workers earlier was now happening to the middle-level administrators: the fragmentation of their work was driving the wedge further between mission and goal. The administrators were being increasingly encouraged to suboptimize and to invert means and ends, to pursue narrow goals and to treat their tasks and functions as ends in themselves. In this way, many of them, too, lost touch with the ultimate products and customers of the organization, with mission as an end in itself.

The systems goals emerged as the primary ones for the new administrators. The line managers typically favored growth as an organizational goal, for all the reasons previously outlined—growth opened up promotion possibilities for ambitious managers, it lessened the strain when many were trying to build empires, and so on. As for the analysts, as noted earlier they were mobile professionals concerned with their techniques, not the organizations where they happened to apply them. If the shoe factory no longer wanted the services of the time study analysts or, later, the operations researchers or long-range planners, then they could always go to the wheelchair factory, or the hospital. Mission had no special significance for them. The one organizational goal the analysts were likely to pursue was efficiency, for as noted earlier, efficiency provided the operational criterion by which they could demonstrate the worth of their proposals. Indeed, with the proliferation of the technostructure in the middle years of this century, as a result of Taylor's earlier work, efficiency became a virtual obsession—as some said, a "cult"—in the large manufacturing organization, and later elsewhere. But as already noted in this chapter, this was not efficiency broadly defined as the pursuit of any goal of the organization's choosing in light of the resources available; it was *measurable* efficiency, which meant the favoring of operational goals. And since the systems goals were so much more operational than those associated with mission, the rise of the technostructure meant the further fall of mission as an organizational goal. And so bureaucratization of the administrative components of the organization drove a further wedge between mission and the organizational goal system, which came increasingly to be based on the systems goals.

So long as the organization concentrated its efforts in one industry, some identification with mission inevitably remained. This was at least true at the strategic apex, and especially where entrepreneurs survived in the office of chief executive. But increasingly they did not. As discussed in Chapter 4, ownership became increasingly separated from management. As Chandler (1977) so carefully describes, over the course of this century, as firms grew in size and diversity, control fell to the "salaried manager." In other words, the owners moved into the External Coalition, although by dominating it they retained control over the firm. But that detached them from a direct involvement with mission, even though they could retain some identification with it so long as their ownership remained concentrated in one firm. In a sense, the firm was theirs, if not the shoes.

But that control, and its related identification with mission, was not to last. As we also saw in Chapter 4, ownership began to disperse, to the point where in most large corporations the owners came to look more and more like investors, detached from any personal relationship with the corporation:

> . . . the domineering founders of family fortunes were dying off, leaving their stockholdings to numerous heirs, foundations, charities, trust funds, and the like, so that the ownership unit which once exercised absolute control over many enterprises became increasingly amorphous and leaderless. Thus the larger corporations gradually won more and more independence from both bankers and dominant stockholders, and their policies accordingly were geared to an ever greater extent each to its own interests rather than being subordinated to the interests of a group. (Baron and Sweezy 1966, p. 18)

And that new independence was of course largely the prerogative of the salaried managers, who came increasingly to be called "professional," because management was both their occupation and their means of livelihood.

Sometimes these managers rose from the bottoms of the hierarchies they controlled, so that they retained a personal identification with the mission. As Perrow noted, there remained textile men, even cotton men and wool men. But more commonly, as the notion of professional management came to mean skill or training in the practice of management itself—at the limit the capacity in theory to manage anything—people entered the firm, and the industry, at middle levels of the administrative hierarchy or higher. Inexperienced MBAs were hired into technocratic staff positions, managers experienced in other industries were hired directly into line positions. Indeed, a firm sometimes even filled its top slot with an outsider, an individual experienced in the practice of management but not in the industry where he was to practice it. (Thus, for example, an advertisement in the *Financial Times* of Canada, on November 3, 1980, placed by an executive recruiting firm, invited applications for a post of president and CEO: "One of the largest and most widespread Canadian organizations is on the brink of change. It requires an operations-minded C.E.O. with sound management systems knowledge and good practical sense." Neither the company nor the industry were ever mentioned.)

The result of this, increasingly, was that those who reached the top, as well as most of the managers who reported to them, had no direct experience in the operating core—the place where the mission was carried out. They never experienced its problems firsthand, they never handled a product in production, they may never even have spoken to a customer. Indeed, some corporations appointed chief executives who never had line experience at any level—which would at least have constituted second-hand involvement with the mission—as in the electric or telephone utilities which felt it more important to have lawyers who could deal with the government than engineers or marketers could deal with the operating core. The inevitable result of all this was a further loosening of the identification of the managers with the mission of the organization, so that its importance as a goal further diminished.

Of course, so long as the organization remained concentrated in one industry, with close ties to one identifiable set of customers, mission could retain some place in the organizational goal system. In other words, despite the separation of ownership from management and the professionalization of the management itself, at least the managers still knew what business their firms were in. But further changes incurred by the professionalization of management reduced that place, in some cases to virtually nothing. As we saw earlier, the professional managers favored growth as the prime goal of the organization. Efficiency, an obsession with profit, was reserved for the owner-managers. As a result, the firms run by the professional managers experienced greater pressures to grow. They were also in a better position to grow, because there was no entrepreneur fearful of losing personal control and because, in Chandler's (1977) opinion, their systems of administrative coordination were highly effective. And so they grew, and as they did, their managers were further and further separated from the operations—from products and customers, from mission. As a small western Canadian cattle rancher being forced out of business noted,

"The big operators don't feel for cattle; they feel for cash."[11]

But the firm operating in only one industry could grow only so large. At some point it had to run out of room for expansion, and so begin to look elsewhere. In other words, the largest corporations were tempted to "diversify," and then to "divisionalize" to bring their structures in line with their new strategies. What we have in fact seen in this century are a series of waves of consolidation and then acquisition—first with competitors to attain large size, then of suppliers and customers to integrate vertically, finally of anyone in sight to diversify into new businesses (Nelson 1959, Reid 1968). In other words, the larger organizations have grabbed up many of the smaller ones, with the overall result that in America, and increasingly in Europe, the private sector has become dominated by enormous divisionalized corporations (Wrigley 1970, Rumelt 1974, Scott 1973). Companies that concentrated their efforts—despite some evidence of their greater profitability (Rumelt 1974)—began to go out of style sometime in the middle of this century.

Pure, or conglomerate, divisionalization—where the divisions pursue totally unrelated missions—represents the final blow to the notion of mission as a goal. For here, mission—particular products and services for specific markets and customers—is wholly irrelevant to the top management that sets the formal goals. They oversee a multitude of missions, and shift into and out of them at will, according to where profits and more importantly potential for growth in sales seem to lie. Today shoes, tomorrow steam shovels. It almost became old-fashioned to care about what was produced. Thus *Fortune* magazine commented on the chief executive officer of one conglomerate:

> Mason often refuses to listen to his top officers when they talk about operating problems, and his lack of interest is reflected even in his hunt for acquisitions. When he tried to buy a steel company last spring he never bothered to learn what kind of blast furnaces it had, how old or inefficient they were, or how much smoke they spewed into the atmosphere. Practically all he was concerned about was the company's projected earnings. . . . "He refuses to have his mind cluttered with it." (Loving 1975, pp. 121, 177).

So if any sense of identification is left for the employees of the divisionalized corporation—the kind of firm that is the natural culmination of a long series of steps since craftsmen began leaving their shops to find work in factories two hundred years ago—it is not with the mission but with the organization itself, and that means with the systems goals of survival, efficiency, control, and especially growth. At the top level—the headquarters—there are often too many missions to care about any one. The commitment is to growth. At the level of division management, single missions are certainly pursued, but various administrative procedures used by the headquarters discourage a real commit-

[11]Quoted in a *Weekend Magazine* article entitled "No Room for the Little Man," by Don D. LaRoque (*The Montreal Star,* December 13, 1975).

ment to them. First, the professional managers are sometimes moved around in ways that do not allow them to become very attached to any one mission. "Young Flexo over there, who runs the baby bottles division. He's capable and logical, and besides he's already been there for three years. Let's let him try to sort out the problems in the coffins division." Second, the divisionalized corporation expressly designs its control system to keep the attention of its division managers clearly riveted on the tangible systems goals—notably growth and efficiency, measured in financial terms—not the fuzzier social goals or missions (Ackerman 1975). As for those below the level of division management, we have seen that the division of labor, first at the operating and later at the administrative levels, the introduction of functional structure, the proliferation of the technostructure, all have driven a firm wedge between the mission performed by the organization and the goals that its operators, staff specialists, or other line managers are encouraged to pursue.

And so we have seen that virtually every development associated with industrialization and the establishment of the corporate form of organization—mechanization, mass production and the creation of factories, the growth and bureaucratization of them, the evolution of the administrative component, the separation of ownership from management, the dispersal of ownership and the rise of "professional" management, the increase in market diversity and the accompanying introduction of the divisionalized form of structure—all have caused mission to be displaced as an organizational goal in favor of the systems goals, notably profit and especially growth. What we have been really seeing is various stages in the death of organizational ideology. It began in those organizations that produce society's consumer goods. But more recently in a parallel way and for many of the same reasons, it has been taking place in those organizations that provide society's public services as well. Or perhaps it would be more accurate to say that we have been seeing the destruction of one ideology, organizational and missionary in nature—service to clients and attention to products and services as ends in themselves,—by another ideology, utilitarian and transorganizational in nature—the obsession with economic efficiency and growth as ends in themselves.

With this note, we have completed our discussion of organizational goals and indeed of the elements of power in and around organizations. To draw this part of the book to a close, and create the link to the next, we conclude with a brief discussion of the system of power and goals as a "dynamic equilibrium."

THE SYSTEM OF POWER AND GOALS AS A DYNAMIC EQUILIBRIUM

As we have described the system of power and goals of the organization in these last thirteen chapters, it may be characterized as existing in a state of dynamic equilibrium. In other words, it displays characteristics of both stability and dynamism. We have seen that the organization does indeed have goals, some of which remain stable over time. But we have also seen that the organization constitutes a complex game of power among the influencers, in which the distribution of that power shifts continuously, causing shifts in the mix of goals pursued as well.

The main forces for stability in the systems of power and goals are the organization's ideology and its systems of control. Other forces include organizational slack and the presence of the chief executive officer. Finally, there is the natural propensity of the power system to seek a state of equilibrium and remain there. Let us look at each of these five forces for stability in turn.

1.   The role of ideology as a force for stability need not be dwelled upon. Clearly the presence of a body of traditions serves as a major factor to dampen change in the goals pursued by the organization. Organizations with strong ideologies seek to preserve their "characters," to use Selznick's (1957) term. But even in those with weaker ideologies, past precedents create a momentum difficult to arrest. Thus, Cyert and March (1963) admit that organizational goals are far more stable than is suggested by their model of a bargaining process that "goes on more or less continuously, turning out a large series of commitments" (p. 32). They explain this stability by the establishment of precedents:

> In most organizations most of the time...the elaboration of objectives occurs within [tight] constraints. Much of the structure is taken as given. This is true primarily because organizations have memories in the form of precedents, and individuals in the coalition are strongly motivated to accept the precedents as binding... Past bargains become precedents for present situations; a budget becomes a precedent for future budgets; an allocation of functions becomes a precedent for future allocations. Through all the well-known mechanisms, the coalition agreements of today are institutionalized into semipermanent arrangements. (pp. 33–34)

2.   As the above quotation suggests, the control systems also act as a stabilizing force, in effect as a set of techniques to enforce precedents. A budget, for example, "is an explicit elaboration of previous commitments" (Cyert and March, p. 33). Litterer (1965) argues that budgets and other formal controls fix organizational goals for given periods of time, usually at least a year (p. 430). They also create a host of arrangements that discourage changes in goals:

> ...to make any basic agreement work, there has to be an enormous number of sub- and sub-subagreements worked out.... The cost of changing such sub-agreements, accommodations, and arrangements may be so great that basic objectives are not changed even when most people recognize the necessity. (p. 429)

3.   By storing slack resources, organizations are able to resist some

pressures to change their goals. A new influencer can be "bought off" with payment from slack instead of with a more fundamental change in the goal system. Moreover, as Cyert and March note, slack serves to stabilize the levels of aspiration in an organization, in two ways: "(1) by absorbing excess resources, it retards upward adjustment of aspirations during relatively good time; (2) by providing a pool of emergency resources, it permits aspirations to be maintained (and achieved) during relatively bad times" (p. 38).

4.   In his role as peak coordinator, the chief executive is charged with achieving a balance—an equilibrium—among the influencers in the organization's power system. As such, he serves as a force for stability, seeking to ensure that pressures for change are viewed in the context of the existing power balance. Typically, the CEO will try to resist a new influencing force. Should it persist, and require recognition, he will try to incorporate it into the existing power coalitions so as not to cause undue disruption. This applies even to changes he himself would like to make. Thus, to complete Zald's story of succession in the welfare agency, even though the reformer was the one finally chosen as the new chief executive, this person had to act prudently:

> ...the movement into the executive position has required Leaf to take on a new role, one in which he has to create the conditions of organizational maintenance. Only a radical and immediate attempt to reshape the character of the organization would be seen as a violation of his mandate. He selects from his mandate those elements which are most useful at the moment. Some of the pressing issues which would create great conflict are shoved aside in favor of other, more attainable and more consensual goals. Other issues are handled so as not to appear divisive. (1965, p. 59)

5.   The final force for stability is the fact that the members of the coalitions themselves prefer a kind of equilibrium in which the relative positions of all of the influencers are more or less fixed. It takes considerable effort to change an existing coalition; it is far easier to establish some kind of agreement—albeit an imperfect one—and remain with it:

> ...people have limited time and energy, and bargaining over goals consumes great amounts of both. Hence, in order to accomplish goals, people seem willing, once a basic agreement has been reached, to let it stand. It may not be perfect from their point of view, but it is perhaps not so bad as to justify the effort of seeking a better arrangement, which might never come about anyway. (Litterer 1965, p. 429).

What all of this suggests is that the power coalitions of the organization, both internal and external, stabilize around established influencer forces. As a result, the goal system of the organization can be described as *homeostatic*: that is to say, it achieves a steady state, in which "any internal or external factor making for disruption of the system is countered by forces which restore the system as closely as possible to its previous state" (Katz and Kahn 1966, p. 23).

Thus, just as the human body acts to bring its internal temperature back to normal when the temperature of the environment changes, and just as a cherry in a bowl of jello will, when disturbed, vibrate for a while and eventually settle back to its initial spot, so too does the organization return as closely as possible to its previous goal system following the shock of a change in one of its power coalitions.

But the other side of the coin is that power and goals do change—they are dynamic, at two levels, surrounding their states of equilibrium. At the micro level, the same power and goal system that from a distance looks rather stable from close up seems to be in a perpetual state of movement. That, of course, is what the microscope would also reveal about the cherry in the jello. In the organization, new constraints are constantly being encountered, and shifts in the preferences of individual influencers and in the relationships among different influencers are always taking place. "As circumstances change, or as the facts come in, our one-time intermediate preferences are amended or abandoned in favor of others. . . . Every new fact or experience remolds our policy preferences" (Lindblom 1968, p. 102). Most of these changes are in fact minor, indeed imperceptible. But they are happening all the time, just as that stable cherry is a bustle of activity under the microscope, or as a generator vibrates as it produces its steady stream of energy.

At the other extreme are the macro changes which, although infrequent, alter the system of power and goals significantly and permanently. A new pressure campaign signals the entry to the External Coalition of a significant new special interest group; an unexpected reorientation of social norms requires a whole new attitude toward the society; an expanded technostructure introduces new bureaucratic procedures that weaken the old system of personal controls; a group of young Turks succeed in taking over the executive suite and change the course of the organization. In other words, power systems do change, requiring goal systems to achieve new states of equilibrium. Shake the jello vigorously enough, and the cherry will have to find a new resting place.

To conclude, the system of power and goals of the organization can be characterized as in a state of dynamic equilibrium. Viewed from an intermediate perspective—at some distance but across a short time frame—it seems to be rather stable. But viewed more narrowly or broadly, its dynamic characteristics dominate. Close up, it can be seen to be in a perpetual state of minor movement, while from a distance, across a longer time frame, periodic but important shifts can be perceived. And if the observer waits long enough, he or she may get to see one of those sudden and profound transitions that leads to a whole new state of equilibrium.

Once we recognize this notion of states of equilibrium and dynamism, our next step in describing power in and around the organization becomes evident: to describe them. Specifically, we must now draw together all of the elements of power we have introduced in these many pages—the external influencers, their means of influence, and the types of External Coalitions they form, the internal influencers, their systems of influence, the types of Internal Coalitions they form, and the types of goals and goal systems that emerge. We draw these elements together in terms of various possible states of equilibrium that they can assume, which we call *power configurations*. Then we look briefly at some of the dynamic characteristics of the system of power and goals, specifically at common transitions between these power configurations.

PART IV

THE POWER CONFIGURATIONS

It remains now to draw together—to synthesize—the elements of power in and around organizations that have been introduced in this book. This will be done by showing how these elements—the influencers in the Internal and External Coalitions, the means and systems of influence they use, the types of Internal and External Coalitions they form, and the goal systems that result—combine in various ways. These combinations, which represent the steady states discussed at the end of the last section, will be referred to as *configurations* of power. Six are introduced here, as pure types that seem to best caricature the most common states of power equilibrium encountered in organizations. The first chapter of this section introduces the six, presenting reasons for their primacy. Each of these configurations is then described in a subsequent chapter of its own. The final chapter of this section considers transitions among these six configurations of power, and presents a general model of stages of organizational development.

17

Deriving Configurations from Coalitions

In theory, a great many configurations of our elements of organizational power are possible, specifically e^n if we have e elements that can each take on n different forms. But there are a variety of reasons to believe that the world of organizations—like the world of ants and of stars—tends to order itself in certain natural clusters. As we have argued elsewhere (Miller and Mintzberg 1980), organizations are driven to these clusters in order to achieve consistency in their characteristics, synergy in their processes, and harmony with their situations. Moreover, forces of natural selection would seem to favor those organizations best able to achieve mutual complementarity among their elements. Thus, of the thousands of combinations of the elements of power conceivable in theory, we should expect to find a far smaller number occurring in practice, with only a subset of these—perhaps just a handful—able to explain a good deal of the power behavior in and around organizations. Such a small set of combinations, or "types," is sometimes referred to as a typology or taxonomy, depending on how formally it is derived. And the members of the typology are sometimes called "ideal types"—what we prefer to call "pure types"—because they do not precisely describe commonly occurring reality so much as reflect common tendencies in reality.

Accepting the premise that a handful of pure types can explain a good deal of organizational power behavior, our job then becomes to isolate that handful. Statisticians have developed various techniques for clustering elements in the computer to produce taxonomies. But none shall be used here. The "hard" data required by such techniques has been lacking in the study of power. Moreover, the recognition of pure types is an exercise in pattern recognition, and human brains seem better suited to it than electric ones. Our approach, therefore, will be less rigorous, although still systematic. But before we describe how we derived our typology, let us consider other ones in the literature.

TYPOLOGIES OF ORGANIZATIONAL POWER IN THE LITERATURE

A few typologies of organizational power have been proposed in the literature. Among the best known are those of Blau and Scott (1962), Etzioni (1961), and Rhenman (1973).[1]

Blau and Scott (1962) categorize organizations according to their "prime beneficiaries"—in effect, those influencers for whose benefit the organization was ostensibly created. They propose four types of organizations, whose prime beneficiaries in fact correspond closely to our four types of external influencers:

- *Business concerns*, whose prime beneficiaries are the owners, examples being manufacturers, retailers, and banks
- *Service organizations*, whose prime beneficiaries are the clients, examples being hospitals, schools, and social work agencies
- *Mutual benefit associations*, whose prime beneficiary is the membership, examples being political parties, unions, and religious sects
- *Commonweal organizations*, whose prime beneficiary is the public at large, examples being police and fire departments, armies, and government revenue collection agencies

This is an interesting classification scheme, but one based more on intent than result. In other words, it is based on who is supposed to benefit, not on who really does—on who actually seizes power in the External Coalition. As we have seen, and as Blau and Scott acknowledge, the fact that an organization has been set up to benefit one group has never stopped other groups from displacing its interests.

While Blau and Scott base their typology on an external characteristic— on who in the External Coalition the organization is supposed to serve—Etzioni (1961) bases his on an internal characteristic, namely, control. He classifies organizations according to (a) the means of control (or influence) used by the upper management to elicit the desired behavior from the "lower participants," and (b) the corresponding involvement (or identification) these participants develop with the organization. This leads Etzioni to propose three basic types of organizations:

---

[1]Rhenman's typology is well known among management researchers in Europe, particularly Scandinavia and Britain, if not the United States.

- *Coercive organizations*, where the means of control is "coercive" and the employee involvement is "alienative," examples being traditional prisons, custodial mental hospitals, and prisoner-of-war camps

- *Utilitarian organizations*, where the means of control is "remunerative" and the employee involvement is "calculative" (corresponding to the inducements-contributions formula), examples being factories, mines, banks, and many government agencies

- *Normative organizations*, where the means of control is "normative" and the employee involvement is "moral" (corresponding to our ideological forms of identification), examples being churches, general hospitals, universities, and voluntary associations

As far as it goes, Etzioni's typology is perhaps the more useful one since it is based on actual behavior. But it does not go very far—essentially not beyond the Internal Coalition, and even there not beyond two dimensions.

The Rhenman (1973) typology links the Internal and External Coalitions in a two-by-two matrix. On one dimension is the presence or absence of "internal or strategic goals," by which Rhenman means strategic focus, or the direction in which the internal influencers wish to take the organization. On the other is the presence or absence of "external or institutional goals (sometimes also called the *mission* of the organization)" (p. 55), which describes whether or not the external influencers wish to impose a mission on the organization. Four pure types emerge in the Rhenman typology:

- *Marginal organizations*, with neither internal strategic focus nor externally imposed mission; strategic changes are opportunistic, following no prescribed plan (Rhenman notes that marginal organizations usually shift to the second type after reaching a certain size)

- *Corporations*, with internal strategic focus but no externally imposed mission (in our terms, a strong Internal Coalition and a weak External Coalition), which therefore exist for their own purposes

- *Appendix organizations*, the opposite of corporations, operating solely on behalf of outside interests; these organizations are often created by parent organizations to pursue one particular mission, and may even be dissolved when that mission is accomplished

- *Institutions*, with both internal strategic focus and externally imposed mission, which may or may not correspond to each other; whereas internal power is more or less centralized in the other three types, here it is divided in the Internal as well as the External Coalitions[2]

At first glance, Rhenman's typology seems less intelligible than the other

[2]Rhenmann selected the term "institution" to correspond with Selznick's (1957) use of it.

two, since his two dimensions are unclear and perhaps not even distinct from each other. (Can strategies be considered independently of missions?) Yet the types that result—with the exception of the marginal organization, which appears to be an uncommon aberration[3]—seem to be more useful than those of Etzioni or Blau and Scott.

Two other typologies are worth mentioning in passing here. One, although its author does not name the resulting types, is that of Hirschman (1970, p. 121), whose two-by-two matrix is based on whether or not the members of the organization use exit and voice to express their discontent. Strong use of both is found in voluntary associations, competitive political parties, and certain business enterprises; weak use of both in totalitarian one-party states, terrorist groups, and the like; strong use only of voice in tribes and single parties in nontotalitarian states, and so on; and strong use only of exit in competitive business concerns (in relation to customers). The second typology is that of Allison (1971), which, although ostensibly one of models of decision making, also distinguishes types of organizational power. Allison describes a Rational Actor Model, in which the organization is viewed as acting in a purposive way as a single unified entity; the Organizational Process Model, in which the organization's actions are ascribed to the interplay of loosely coupled repertoires of standardized programs; and a Governmental Politics Model, in which the organization's actions are seen as the resultant of various bargaining games among different players.

RELATIONSHIPS BETWEEN THE COALITIONS

The typology of power configurations introduced in this book differs from the others (except that of Allison) in that it attempts to synthesize a large number of dimensions of organizational power instead of combining just one or two. Thus it cannot be described in any single matrix or along any one continuum; indeed we shall suggest various ones along the way (and shall also relate our types to those of these other typologies where possible). But in one respect our typology is similar to that of Rhenman: it derives in the first instance from a consideration of the relationships between external and internal power. Specifically, we introduce it by considering the likely combinations of the three types of External Coalitions discussed in Chapter 7 with the five types of Internal Coalitions discussed in Chapter 14, themselves each, of course, pure types made up of the dimensions of their respective coalitions.

---

[3]Can it really be said that the small Swedish printing firms Rhenman cites as examples of marginal organizational lacked any strategic focus? They were, after all, in the printing business (and being opportunistic is a strategic focus of sorts). Perhaps this category should be reserved for those few organizations that really exhibit nebulous behavior, such as Maniha and Perrow's (1965–66) "reluctant organization" before it was found and enlisted for political action (and thereby presumably became an "appendix").

A pure type, as implied earlier, is a caricature of reality, an overstatement, if you like, of the real world in order to highlight certain of its pronounced characteristics. To derive a typology of pure types, therefore, it is necessary to make certain assumptions to simplify the reality. Our prime assumption is that certain of the various External and Internal Coalitions fit naturally together, like the proverbial horse and carriage. While examples of each of the fifteen possible combinations (the three ECs times the five ICs) can always be found, only a subset is assumed represent "natural"—if you like, consistent or harmonious and therefore somewhat stable—relationships. A related assumption is that the Internal Coalition is in its most natural, consistent, and therefore stable state when dominated by *one* of its systems of influence—by personal or bureaucratic control, ideology, expertise, or politics. We have not forgotten our conclusion of Chapter 14 that these five systems act in concert. But, as we saw there, to act in concert does not mean that one cannot play a leading role at any one time. We state these two points as assumptions at the outset, although in fact we shall present a series of arguments along the way to support specific instances of them.

We have used the word "natural" in the paragraph above, and will repeat it frequently throughout this part of the book. In using it, we mean to imply that there are certain forces inherent in organizations that drive them to behave in certain ways. Barring the intervention of random or external forces, these behaviors can commonly be expected. These are the ones we call the "natural" behaviors.

Below we present three hypotheses which describe what we believe to be the natural combinations of the two coalitions, assuming the dominance of one of the systems in the Internal Coalition. A fourth hypothesis then describes what we believe happens when other combinations of the two coalitions or of two or more of the internal systems of influence are attempted. It is the results of these hypotheses that led to our basic configurations of organizational power. Because of the sparsity of research on these issues, we have little empirical evidence to support three of our four hypotheses. Nevertheless there is a certain logic behind each of them, as we shall soon see.

1. A Dominated External Coalition fits most naturally with a Bureaucratic Internal Coalition, and so tries to give rise to it. Domination in the External Coalition means that, typically through control of some kind of organizational dependency, a single external influencer, or a group of them acting in concert, has significantly more power over the organization than all of the others. This concentration of external power forces the insiders to be responsive to the demands of the dominant external influencer. But, being external, this influencer does not manage the organization. And so he or she must find ways to control its behavior indirectly. And the most effective ones are the following two, used concurrently. First, the external influencer holds the chief executive responsible for all of the organization's actions as well as its performance. This has the effect of strengthening the System of Authority and centralizing whatever power remains in the Internal Coalition. And second, the external influencer imposes on the chief executive clear—that is, operational—goals, ones that the CEO can, in turn, formalize in the system of objectives. This has the effect of strengthening the bureaucratic side of the System of Authority. With such goals, no one can mistake what the wishes of the external influencer are, or whether the Internal Coalition has actually pursued them. Moreover, with external control concentrated, the organization must be especially careful about its actions, and so it also tends to formalize its own procedures voluntarily, in order to be able to justify them. And since the combination of centralization with formalization means a Bureaucratic IC, we conclude that this is the type of Internal Coalition that fits most naturally with a Dominated External Coalition.

Indeed, to reverse this relationship, we contend that in the absence of operational goals and centralized internal authority, a single external influencer would have great difficulty controlling the Internal Coalition, and a change in form of both of the coalitions would likely take place. Without centralized authority and operational goals, power would flow to many insiders who could use it with a good deal of discretion. The only way for the external influencer to stop this and reassert his control would be to develop strong personal links with each of these insiders. But in order to do so, in all but the simplest organizations, the external influencer would have to become the chief executive officer, in effect if not in fact. And that would convert the Internal Coalition to the Personalized form. Should he not do this, the power of the external influencer would be diluted, and the External Coalition would revert to the Passive form, or, if other external influencers moved into the void, the Divided form, while the Internal Coalition would take on another form, perhaps Politicized or Professional.

This particular relationship between a Dominated EC and Bureaucratic IC was discussed in the *Structuring* book, in the following terms: "The greater the external control of the organization, the more centralized and formalized its structure" (Mintzberg 1979a, pp. 288–91). Among the researchers cited there as providing support for this hypothesis were Samuel and Mannheim (1970), Hydebrand (1973), Holdaway et al. (1975), Pugh et al. (1969), Reimann (1973), and Pondy (1969). Pugh et al., for example, concluded in their study that "Dependent organizations have a more centralized authority structure and less autonomy in decision making; independent organizations have more autonomy and decentralize decisions down the hierarchy" (1969, p. 108).

Can other types of Internal Coalitions combine with a Dominated EC? Yes, but... In a way, our discussion suggests both that a Personalized IC is possible and that it is less desirable for the external influencer, and therefore less likely to be encouraged and to occur. It is possible when only one of the two conditions discussed above is present, namely that the external influencer holds the chief executive responsible for the organization's actions and performance—thereby centralizing its structure—but does not impose operational goals on the CEO. In other words, the external influencer allows the CEO personal, and therefore full, control of the Internal Coalition, but denies the CEO's use of that control in his own personal interests. His personal control is to be exercised on behalf of the external influencer's interests.

Such an arrangement is certainly conceivable, at least when a close rapport exists between the two individuals. But it is also likely to be unstable. It establishes two centers of individual power—one outside the organization, the other inside—with a high probability of an eventual clash between them. To maintain personalized control of the Internal Coalition requires a strong, independent leader, one unlikely to accept someone else's goals for long. The leader's natural temptation would be to undercut the external influencer, in order to render the Dominated EC passive. As for the external influencer, such a person does not usually take kindly to an all-powerful chief executive, one who can challenge his influence. Moreover, he is likely to worry about transition, and the losses he can incur from it when so much power is concentrated in one person. And so his natural inclination is to diffuse the CEO's power while maintaining central authority in the Internal Coalition. And the one way to do this is to encourage the depersonalization, or institutionalization, of the CEO's influence, in other words to encourage bureaucratic control of the Internal Coalition. And to go along with this, he is likely to replace a strong personal CEO with a weaker, more "professional" one, who is willing to accept a bureaucratic form of internal control (Kipnis 1974, p. 92).

The combination of a Dominated EC with an Ideologic, Professional, or Politicized IC would seem to be even less stable. Ideology is not usually imposed from without; typically it establishes itself within the organization, intrinsically, and is there internalized by the members. When the ideology is strong—as it is in the Ideologic IC—deep-rooted loyalties are established among the members, which provide them with a clear sense of direction. These people will hardly be predisposed to taking orders from an outsider. As a result, they will strive to pacify his influence, and he, in turn, will try to weaken their ideology, by replacing normative controls with bureaucratic ones.

A similar thing happens with the experts of the Professional IC. Their work is complex. As a result, they must be highly skilled and knowledgeable, and they themselves must control the work, and, as a consequence, the Internal Coalition. For an external influencer to control the Internal Coalition instead, he must wrest that power from the professionals. But how can he do this while maintaining a Professional IC? He cannot; his natural inclination is not to maintain it at all, but to try to convert it into Bureaucratic IC. This he does by attempting to have the complex work broken down into simple component parts that can be regulated by work standards and executed by unskilled workers. Barring that, he will try to have the outputs of the work controlled by measurable standards. These efforts are, of course, resisted vigorously by the experts, with the result that political games ensue, notably lording by the administrators and the various expertise games by the professionals. We see this, for example, when governments try to take control of school systems, hospitals, or universities.

As for a Politicized IC facing a Dominated EC, the natural inclination of the different insiders is to draw other external influencers into their political games, to enlist their support and to reduce their own dependence on one individual. For his part, the dominant external influencer knows that the benefits of a Politicized IC are few, while the long-run risks to his power base are great. So his natural inclination is to rely on authority to depoliticize the Internal Coalition, as soon as possible, thereby bringing it under his control to pursue his goals. In other words, both sides resist the combination of a Dominated EC with a Politicized IC.

2. A Divided External Coalition fits most naturally with a Politicized Internal Coalition, and vice versa, and so each tries to give rise to the other. Conflict in one of the coalitions has a habit of spilling over to the other. In other words, the natural combination is of a Divided EC with a Politicized IC. Earlier we referred to our natural combinations as ones of consistency or harmony and stability. While we can hardly call the presence of conflict in both of the coalitions a state of harmony, what we can say is that there is greater consistency between the coalitions when both, rather than just one, experiences conflict. Likewise, while conflict throughout both coalitions hardly seems like a state of stability, as we shall soon see, it is more stable than when conflict exists in only one of the coalitions. Let us consider both these points in terms of what happens when only one of the coalitions is in a state of conflict.

When political battles rage in the Internal Coalition, the inside influencers naturally seek to enlist the support of different outsiders, as we have already noted. In the case of a Passive EC, it is often only a matter of time until the insiders succeed in engaging external influencers in their politics, thereby dividing the External Coalition. (Sometimes, of course, no outsider cares very much, and politics can remain an internal phenomenon.) So too will a Dominated EC tend to become divided as other external influencers get drawn into the conflict, unless the dominant external influencer is able to impose his will and thereby restore the primacy of authority over politics. As we noted earlier, it is not in the long-term interests of the dominant external influencer to allow a Politicized IC to endure. (Sometimes, however, there can be short-run benefits. When intense political games, such as young Turks or rival camps, arise to change an organization, a truly dominant external influencer may let them continue for a time to hear both sides before declaring a winner in his own interests. Here the insiders would vie for the ear of the external influencer, and a Dominated EC would combine with a Politicized IC. But the external influencer cannot let such a situation endure for long, for fear of losing control of the Internal Coalition.)

In the same manner, when the External Coalition is divided it will tend to pull the Internal Coalition in different directions and thereby encourage the breakdown of any form of concentrated power there. The insiders will, in other words, be attracted to different camps or alliances, and the Internal Coalition driven toward the Politicized form.

For a Divided EC to coexist with a Personalized or Bureaucratic IC would be to assume the willingness of different external influencers to channel their conflicting demands through one central authority—namely the chief executive officer—rather than bypassing that one individual to access other insiders directly. In other words, all would have to be willing to keep the System of Authority—the unity of command—intact. In the case of the Bureaucratic IC, the additional assumption would be required that most of their demands are willingly channelled to the CEO in terms of operational goals. To make such assumptions in the case of a Divided EC—where different centers of power actively vie for influence—seems unrealistic in general. Conditions such as these do occur, but they would seem to be less stable than those in which some external influencers seek to bypass the CEO and to impose nonoperational as well as operational goals on the organization.

The assumption that has to be made in the case of an Ideologic IC combining with a Divided EC would seem to be even less realistic, namely that the external influencers are somehow willing, and able, to state their conflicting demands in terms of the existing ideology. More realistically, the tight integration of the Internal Coalition around the ideology would preclude the pursuit of conflicting external demands. Or else, in the Personalized and Bureaucratic ICs no less than in the Ideologic one, enduring division of the External Coalition would tend eventually to break down the unifying focus of power in the Internal Coalition, and to politicize it. In other words, when conflict in the External Coalition confronts unity in the Internal Coalition, or vice versa, something usually has to give. Either unity gives way to conflict, or else it suppresses it.

The case of a Professional IC combined with a Divided EC is less clearcut. As we shall see, organizations staffed with many professionals often experience conflicting forces in their External Coalitions, in part, perhaps, as we noted in Chapter 14, because their internal Systems of Politics are fairly active. Thus, their External Coalitions naturally appear to be divided. But as we shall argue in the next hypothesis, and in more detail in Chapter 22, in other, more important ways, these are better described as passive. In other words, in the Professional IC, the natural effect of expertise is to dominate the entire power system, not only to contain politics and the other systems of the Internal Coalition, but also to pacify most of the external influencers, even those intent on control. And this leads to our general conclusion, namely that dominant legitimate power of any form in the Internal Coalition—of expertise, personal or bureaucratic authority, or ideology—is incompatible with divided power in the External Coalition.

3. A Personalized, Ideologic, or Professional Internal Coalition fits most naturally with a Passive External Coalition, while a Bureaucratic Internal Coali-

tion can fit with it, and all four try to give rise to it. Our first hypothesis connects a Bureaucratic IC with a given Dominated EC, while our second one connects a Divided EC with a Politicized IC, no matter which comes first. Our third hypothesis is really a combination of the first two, since it describes the set of natural relationships that remain possible between the Internal and External Coalitions. Specifically, a Passive EC can fit with a given Personalized, Ideologic, Professional, or Bureaucratic IC, indeed *should* fit with the first three (the fourth, the Bureaucratic IC, fitting also with a given Dominated EC).

The point is that passiveness in the External Coalition allows considerable leeway in the establishment of power relationships in the Internal Coalition, with one qualification. The power vacuum should naturally be filled by some focussed system of power in the Internal Coalition. (Or, perhaps more exactly, the only way to ensure that power in the External Coalition remains passive is to have power clearly focussed in the Internal Coalition.) All but one of our types of Internal Coalitions do in fact focus power in one way or another. Two focus it clearly in the System of Authority, a third in ideology, and the fourth in expertise. In other words, power defined in terms of a single leader, bureaucratic standards, shared beliefs, or expert skills would seem to be compatible with weak external control of an organization.

But more to the point, it is the natural inclination of each of these systems of influence, when dominant internally, to try to give rise to a passive coalition externally. And in three of the four cases, the natural solution is for it to succeed. The Personalized IC tends to be led by a strong-willed chief executive, one not inclined to accept any imposing form of outside control—whether from one external influencer or many. Either he will try to take his organization away from such control—as when an entrepreneur seeks out markets free of dependency on any one client or supplier—or else he will try to diffuse such control when he cannot escape it. As we have already noted, such a leader will tend to clash with a dominant external influencer and try to weaken him, while the latter will try to bureaucratize the Internal Coalition to weaken the personal control of its leader. Faced instead with a Divided EC, the leader will try to pacify the external influencers, while they will try to bypass his authority which will tend to politicize the Internal Coalition. Ultimately, then, the only form of External Coalition fully compatible with a chief executive's need for complete personal control is the passive one. That is the most harmonious, and therefore most stable, combination.

Likewise, only perhaps more so, an Ideologic IC will strive to ensure that it faces a Passive EC, clashing with any strong forces in its External Coalition until it overwhelms or escapes them. Its need for tight integration and strict adherence to its own internal norms and beliefs precludes it from being dominated by one external influencer or being pulled in different directions by several. In other words, an Internal Coalition functions naturally and harmoniously in the ideologic state only when its External Coalition is passive.

The same can be said for the Professional IC. Earlier we saw why this kind of Internal Coalition avoids a Dominated External Coalition, why expert control of the work is incompatible with focussed external control of the organization. To control the organization, the dominant external influencer must break down the expertise and impose bureaucratic standards on the workers. But this, as we noted, is resisted by the experts. Likewise, a fully Divided EC is also discouraged by the experts, because that allows the external influencers to usurp some of the power the experts have to control their own work. It also raises the level of politics internally, displaying expertise as the prime system of influence. And so the experts encourage passiveness in the External Coalition. To do so, they try to use against the external influencers the same means with which they so successfully overwhelm the unskilled insiders—their control of critical functions with their irreplaceable skills and knowledge. Specifically, they rebuff external attempts at influence with their claim that outsiders lack the technical knowledge needed to decide on the important issues. If the experts succeed in these attempts, then the relatively stable combination of a Professional IC with a largely Passive EC emerges. If they do not, then the Internal Coalition tends to revert to another form—typically bureaucratic if the experts give in or politicized if they do not.

As for the Bureaucratic IC, combination with a Passive EC is *one* natural occurrence, but not the only one. As we saw in our first hypothesis, a Bureaucratic IC can also coexist with a Dominated EC, indeed arises naturally in the presence of the latter. But the natural inclination of the Bureaucratic IC itself is to try to give rise to a Passive EC. In other words, in the absence of a dominant external influencer, and sometimes in spite of one, the Bureaucratic IC tries to diffuse power in its environment. Being pervaded by standards, and as a result developing an obsession with control (Mintzberg 1979a, pp. 319–21), the Bureaucratic IC tries to regulate everything—even its environment. That is to say, it vigorously pursues the systems goal of control of its own environment, in order to protect its internal procedures—to buffer itself from environmental uncertainty so that it can function without disruption. Since external influence, particularly when it comes from more than one source, means uncertainty, disruption, and loss of control, it is resisted.

Thus, faced with a Divided EC, the Bureaucratic IC tends to pacify it (just as the External Coalition tries in turn to politicize the Internal Coalition). And while the Bureaucratic IC can obviously function smoothly when faced with a Dominated EC, and is typically forced to, it also shows an inclination to nip away at that source of external influence. Eventually, perhaps without even being aware of it, that source can become pacified. Earlier, we discussed the gradual diffusion of stockholding in the large American corporation, until closely held organizations dominated by their owners become widely held ones controlled by their managers. What we are suggesting here, based on the evidence presented by Pfeffer and Salancik (1978) discussed in Chapter 16, is that the corporations themselves likely played an important role in pacifying their owners, through their efforts to grow, merge with and acquire other firms, and so on.

To summarize to this point, we have hypothesized that six of the fifteen possible combinations of the Internal and External Coalitions are most natural. Now let us consider the remaining combinations.

4. Other combinations of the coalitions, or of the internal systems of influence, frequently generate moderate or intense levels of conflict. This hypothesis, our most ambitious, claims that violation of one of the first three hypotheses frequently creates some significant level of conflict. Specifically, trying to function with what we have argued is a less natural combination of power can have the effect of politicizing the Internal Coalition and/or dividing the External Coalition.

One point has permeated our discussion to this point: what we have called a "natural" combination of the coalitions arises when there is one central focus of power; otherwise conflict is natural. In one case, that focus is in the External Coalition, in the form of a dominant external influencer (or a consensus among many), and the Internal Coalition falls into line in its Bureaucratic form. In the other cases, that focus is in the Internal Coalition, in one of its systems of influence—in authority, either through the personal controls of an all-powerful leader or the bureaucratic controls of the administrators, in ideology, through powerful norms and beliefs, or in expertise, through the skills and knowledge of the experts. As a result of the internal focus, the External Coalition is weak, that is, passive.

But what happens when a focus of power is absent in both of the coalitions? We saw part of the answer in our second hypothesis. When power in the External Coalition remains divided, or power in the Internal Coalition remains politicized—either way lacking one central focus—the tendency is for the other coalition to follow suit, to become conflictive as well. In other words, a prolonged absence of focussed power in either of the coalitions tends to lead naturally to a pervasive state of conflict as all kinds of influencers jump into the void.

Of course, the absence of *a* focus of power does not preclude the presence of several. Power may, in other words, be concentrated in more than one place. There may be one focus of power in each of the coalitions, or there may be two or more foci of power in the Internal Coalition. What happens in either of these cases?

Our discussion to this point has rested on the assumption, stated at the outset, that the Internal Coalition is in its most natural, and consistent or harmonious state when one of its systems of influence dominates, at least for a time. The others act in concert either by reinforcing it where it is weak, or else by standing ready to displace it when it falters. When two or more systems of influence try to coexist as focussed centers of power in the Internal Coalition, one of two things is likely to happen.

The first possibility is that the supporters of each system of influence battle outright—intensively—for the supremacy of their favored system. For example, when the believers in a strong traditional ideology face administrators intent on imposing bureaucratic controls to replace the normative ones, severe political battles are likely to errupt. The same thing can happen when a strong personal leader tries to stave off a challenge to his authority from a new group of experts. In these cases, the Internal Coalition can become fully politicized, all the insiders getting drawn into the battles. And so, too, can the outsiders, as we saw in the second hypothesis, with the result that the External Coalition becomes divided. Note that the period of battling must be brief, for no organization can tolerate intense conflict for long and survive.

The second possibility is that proponents of the two internal systems of influence reach a kind of accord, and so moderate their conflict, enabling the combination to endure. They reach a kind of *shaky alliance*, creating a *hybrid* form of Internal Coalition. For example, the personalized power of the leader may come to coexist with the expert power of the operators, as in a symphony orchestra. In this situation, following from our fourth hypothesis, we conclude that the requirement that different focussed systems of influence coexist within the same organization often leads to higher levels of conflict than when one system dominates. What we are saying is that the different internal systems of influence tend to be incompatible in some ways, and combining them often generates a certain degree of conflict, moderate if not intense. The musicians, for example, by accepting the personal control of the conductor, allow the symphony orchestra to survive and endure, but not without a certain tension between authority and expertise. Similarly, when strong personal control exists side by side with significant bureaucratic control, there will invariably be recurring friction between the CEO and the analysts of the technostructure.

What of the case where power in the Internal Coalition is focussed in only one of its systems of influence, but then confronts incompatible focussed power in the External Coalition? In other words, what happens when a Personalized, Ideologic, or Professional IC, confronts a Dominated EC? As we saw earlier in each of these cases, the result tends to be a state of conflict. That conflict, too, can take one of two forms. Initially, it may emerge as a war between the coalitions, each united around its center of power (that is, each acting as a "coalition" in the usual sense of the term). Thus, the CEO of the Personalized IC, or the experts of the Professional IC, or all the members of the Ideologic IC, challenge the dominant external influencer. Such a war tends to be intense, a brief but all-out confrontation between two sides until one wins. But again the conflict can also be moderate, and prolonged. The result can be another form of shaky alliance between unlikely partners, although eventually there may be a gradual politicization of the Internal Coalition and division of the External Coalition as each side seeks supporters in the opposing ranks.

Finally, to close a last loop, what happens when conflict in one of the coalitions meets focussed power in the other? As we saw in the earlier hypotheses, especially the second, if the focussed power fails to suppress the conflict, then the conflict is likely to engulf it. In other words, when faced with an intractably Divided EC, the level of conflict within the Bureaucratic, Personalized, Ideologic, or Professional IC will likely rise, often to the point where it comes to be more accurately described as a Politicized IC. So too is the level of friction between the two coalitions likely to rise. We believe it unlikely that any of these focussed types of Internal Coalitions can confront divided power in the External Coalition and still maintain their normal degrees of harmony and stability. We expect a similar result when an intractably Politicized IC faces a Dominated or Passive EC, namely, first, increased conflict within the External Coalition, as new outsiders are drawn into the power system, and second, increased tension between the two coalitions.

What we are saying in this fourth hypothesis is that the first three hypotheses define natural, consistent or harmonious combinations of the two coalitions, combinations that are therefore more likely to occur and more likely to be stable when they do. The nine other possible combinations are more likely to generate significant levels of conflict within each of the coalitions and/or between the two of them. That conflict can be either intense, in which case it is likely to be brief, or else moderate, in which case it may be able to endure for some time. Of course, this conclusion is not new here, for we have already described the conflicts that arise in each of these nine other combinations. We have shown why internal power concentrated in personal control, ideology, or expertise naturally conflicts with an External Coalition that is not passive, why a Dominated External Coalition naturally conflicts with an Internal Coalition that is not bureaucratic, and why a Divided External Coalition is incompatible with any Internal Coalition but a politicized one, and vice versa.

We should point out in closing this discussion that while we have described these nine combinations as less natural—less consistent and harmonious, probably less stable and common than the others—they should not necessarily be viewed as dysfunctional aberrations. Sometimes of course, they are just that, as we shall see in examples later—combinations that impede the organization from accomplishing its basic mission. But these "unnatural" combinations can be functional too. How, after all, is an organization to effect a necessary but contentious transition from one of the natural combinations to another except by passing through a period of unnatural combination? How, for example, is a critical new expertise to gain recognition in the face of a worn-out ideology, or needed bureaucratic controls to displace ineffective personalized ones, except through the organization experiencing a less harmonious combination of the two competing centers of power for a time? In other words, an "unnatural" combination, with its resulting conflict, must often serve as the necessary way station in the transition from one natural combination to another. Likewise, how can an organization that faces various needs for power avoid the use of an enduring hybrid? To return to our earlier example, how can the symphony orchestra avoid an equilibrium between the Systems of Expertise and Authority (in its personalized form)? To tilt the balance in favor of the leader at the expense of expertise, or in favor of the players at the expense of central coordination, would be less functional for the orchestra. In other words, to operate with one of the less natural combinations, involving higher levels of conflict, is in fact *more* natural for organizations that face conflicting needs for power or that require a transition from one natural combination to another.

THE SIX POWER CONFIGURATIONS

Our first three hypotheses propose a specific set of relationships between the Internal and External Coalitions as being the most natural. These are shown in Figure 17-1 and listed below:

- A Dominated EC fits most naturally with, and so tries to give rise to, a Bureaucratic IC.
- A Divided EC fits most naturally with, and so tries to give rise to, a Politicized IC.
- A Politicized IC fits most naturally with, and so tries to give rise to, a Divided EC.
- A Personalized IC fits most naturally with, and so tries to give rise to, a Passive IC.
- An Ideologic IC fits most naturally with, and so tries to give rise to, a Passive IC.
- A Professional IC fits most naturally with, and so tries to give rise to, a Passive IC.
- A Bureaucratic IC can fit naturally with, and tries to give rise to, a Passive IC.

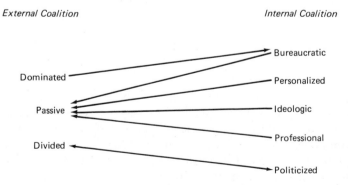

Figure 17-1. *Natural Relationships Between the Types of External and Internal Coalitions*

What these relationships define are six natural combinations of the two coalitions. And these form our six configurations of organizational power—a slightly oversized handful.[4] As for the nine other possible combinations, according to our fourth hypothesis:

a. Each, being less natural, is probably less likely to occur than the others, but

b. when it does, it is likely to be less stable and to involve some degree of conflict, between the coalitions and/or within them, taking the form of either

b₁: intense conflict for a brief period, perhaps a necessary way station in the functional transition between two natural combinations, or

b₂. more moderate conflict that can endure, sometimes the consequence of achieving a necessary hybrid, or shaky alliance, between different concentrations of power.

Below we list the six natural combinations of the Internal and External Coalitions, together with the label given to each configuration, followed by the nine other combinations, showing the forms they can take:

External Coalition	Internal Coalition	Power Configuration
Dominated	Bureaucratic	The Instrument
Passive	Bureaucratic	The Closed System
Passive	Personalized	The Autocracy
Passive	Ideologic	The Missionary
Passive	Professional	The Meritocracy
Divided	Politicized	The Political Arena
Dominated	Personalized	
Dominated	Ideologic	
Dominated	Professional	Probably less common and
Dominated	Politicized	less stable, likely to be Poli-
Passive	Politicized	tical Arena (sometimes in
Divided	Bureaucratic	form of functional hybrid
Divided	Personalized	or way station in transition)
Divided	Ideologic	
Divided	Professional	

[4] In the *Structuring* book (Mintzberg 1979a, p. 300), in which I presented five configurations, I quoted from the *Dictionnaire des Symboles* on the symbolism of the number five. That source offers less on the number six, but it does say: "In the Apocalypse, the number 6 would have a clearly pejorative meaning; it would be the number of sin. It is also the number of Nero, the sixth emperor. One could say here that things ended up badly (l'épreuvé a mal tourné)." How fitting, then, is six configurations for a book on power! (Quotes from the *Dictionnaire des Symboles*, sous la direction de Jean Chevalier avec la collaboration de Alain Gheerbrant, Editions Robert Laffont, 1969, p. 709; my translation from the French).

TABLE 17-1. Characteristics of the Power Configurations

Characteristic	Instrument	Closed System	Autocracy
External Coalition	Dominated	Passive	Passive
Internal Coalition	Bureaucratic	Bureaucratic	Personalized
Key Influencer(s)	Dominant outsider (or group in concert)	Administrators (senior managers and analysts)	CEO
Flow of Power between Coalitions	EC → IC (IC controlled)	Nil or EC → IC (IC autonomous or controlling)	Nil (IC autonomous)
Freedom of Action	Some and little: choice of means to pursue given ends	Much (due to size); but constrained by bureaucratic standards and conservative administrators	Much (due to independence of CEO); but constrained by size and precariousness
Type of Board	Control device, otherwise facade	Tool or facade	Facade
Integration of Insiders (identification)	Inducements (minimal)	Inducements (calculated)	Inducements (calculated, some natural)
Favored Use of Exit/Voice/Loyalty:			
by Insiders	Exit	Mild voice or exit	Loyalty or exit
by Outsiders	Voice (dominant influencer only, exit for others)	Exit	Exit
Favored Political Games in IC	Lording, line vs. staff, some empire building and budgeting	Insurgency and counterinsurgency, sponsorship, empire building, budgeting, line vs. staff, strategic candidate, whistle blowing, some young Turks	Sponsorship
Favored Goals	Any clear, operational ones	Systems goals, notably growth	Any personal goals (often including mission and survival)
Goal System	Can be maximization	Maximization in goal hierarchy	Can be maximization

Principal Conditions Favoring (n = necessary; s = sufficient; f = facilitating; o = overriding)[a]	External power focussed (n) and organized (n), operational goals (n), critical external dependence (f), focussed legal prerogative (f), external concensus (f), simple and stable environment (f), simple and regulating technical system (f), unskilled work force (f), precarious organization (f)	Maturation of organization (i.e., growth and aging) (f), simple and stable environment (f), simple and regulating technical system (f), unskilled work force (f)	Formation of organization (s), young organizations (f), small organizations (f), founding leadership (f), simple and dynamic environment (s), strong leadership (o), crisis (o)
Principal Conditions Weakening (ex. = external to config.; in. = can be intrinsic to config.)[a]	Success and growth of organization (in.), diffusion of external influence (in.), breakdown of consensus or of ability of external influencers to organize (in.), lapses in external surveillance (in.), emergence of nonoperational goals (ex.)	Exploitation of insider power (in.), illegitimacy of power distribution (in.), inability to adapt to changing environment (in.)	Precariousness of organization (in.), stabilization of environment (in.), growth and aging of organization (in.), solution of crisis (in.), departure of founding leader (ex.)
Stage in Organizational Development[a]	Development to maturity	Maturity	Formation (also renewal)
Purpose of Configuration[a]	To ensure organization serves relevant (or at least dominant) constituencies, to institutionalize procedures for efficiency, to establish new organizations in absence of entrepreneurial initiative	To accelerate institutionalization of procedures and facilitate large-scale systematic pursuit of mission	To create new organizations, to see established organizations through crises, to enable small organizations (especially in simple, dynamic environments) to function effectively and to innovate
Vis-a-vis Other Typologies	Machine Bureaucracy (Mintzberg 1979a), Coercive or Utilitarian org. (Etzioni 1961), Appendix (Rhenman 1973), Paralytic organization (Butler et al. 1977–78)	Machine Bureaucracy, especially Divisionalized Form (Mintzberg 1979a), Utilitarian organization (Etzioni 1961), Corporation (Rhenman 1973)	Simple Structure (Mintzberg 1979a), Corporation (Rhenman 1973)
Government Equivalent	Colony, also government elected by clear consensus (welfare state as well?)	Communism (plus all large contemporary governments to some degree)	Dictatorship (or dictatorial leadership in democracy)

aDiscussed at length in Chapter 24.

TABLE 17-1. Characteristics of the Power Configurations (cont.)

Characteristic	Missionary	Meritocracy	Political Arena (primarily pervasive forms)
External Coalition	Passive	Passive	Divided
Internal Coalition	Ideologic	Professional	Politicized
Key Influencer(s)	All insiders	Experts	Varies
Flow of Power between Coalitions	Nil or EC ← IC (IC autonomous or imposing)	EC ⇄ IC (IC quasi-autonomous)	EC ⇄ IC (IC controlled and controlling; reciprocal flow; can be war between the two)
Freedom of Action	Much in principal (due to independence of organization), but little in practice due to constraints of norms and traditions	Considerable (due to power of expertise, but constrained by professional standards and norms (especially Professional Bureaucracy)	Little; organization and influencers constrained by conflict
Type of Board	Facade (or tool)	Intended control device, but actually tool	Intended control device and tool
Integration of Insiders (identification)	Shared goals, socialization and indoctrination (natural, selected, evoked)	Shared goals (selected and evoked, with profession)	Bargaining (none with organization)
Favored Use of Exit/Voice/Loyalty:			
by Insiders	Loyalty (or else exit)	Voice and exit (loyalty to profession)	Voice, then exit
by Outsiders	Exit (sometimes loyalty)	Exit (attempted voice)	Voice, then exit
Favored Political Games in IC	Lording, some strategic candidates	Alliance and empire building, budgeting, rival camps, strategic candidates, lording, expertise	All, but especially alliance building, rival camps, young Turks
Favored Goals	Ideologic (preservation, extention or perfection of mission)	Mission, profession autonomy and excellence	Any personal goals
Goal System	Maximization	Sequential attention to few primary goals; many constraints	At best sequential attention; possibly set of constraints; at worst paralysis (no goals pursued)

Principal Conditions Favoring (n = necessary; s = sufficient; f = facilitating; o = overriding)[a]	Clear, focussed, distinctive, inspiring mission (n, s, o), distinguished history (n), charismatic leadership in past (n), small size (f), middle age (f), simple environment (f), simple technical system (f), volunteer membership (f)	Complex technology or technical system (n, s, o)	Challenge to existing order or between existing influencers (n, s, o), fundamental change in important condition (f), breakdown in established order or none to begin with (f), maladaptation to a previous change or breakdown (f), balanced and irreconcilable forces on organization (f), visible, controversial mission (f), death throes of organization (f)
Principal Conditions Weakening (ex. = external to config.; in. = can be intrinsic to config.)[a]	Time (atrophy of ideology) (in.), need for administrative apparatus (in.), need to interact with outsiders (in.), vulnerability of organization (in.)	Rationalization of expertise (ex.), shift to new mission (ex.), callousness of experts (in.), challenges by external influencers (in.)	Demise of organization (in.), overpoliticization (in.), resolution of challenge (in.), tilting of power balance in shaky alliance (ex.)
Stage in Organizational Development[a]	Development to maturity	Development to maturity and maturity	Decline, and transitions between other stages
Purpose of Configuration[a]	To change certain societal norms, to add inspiration to work and enthusiasm to pursuit of mission	To provide necessary complex skills and knowledge	To induce necessary but resisted change in organizational power, to enable necessary hybrids to function, to speed up recycling of resources of spent organizations
Vis-a-vis Other Typologies	Normative organization (Etzioni 1961), Institution (Selznick 1957)	Professional Bureaucracy and Adhocracy (Mintzberg 1979a), Institution (Rhenman 1973), Organized Anarchy or Garbage Can (March and Olsen 1976)	Governmental Politics Model (Allison 1971)
Government Equivalent	Cultural Revolution	Meritocracy (see Young 1959)	Revolution, Anarchy, Pluralistic Government (and all contemporary governments to some degree)

[a]Discussed at length in Chapter 24.

Our six power configurations are also listed in Table 17-1 together with various of their characteristics. These characteristics include the elements of power introduced in the first three sections of this book as well as other factors of interest, to be discussed later. By describing the configurations as combinations of all of these elements, this fourth section of the book serves not only to synthesize the material we have presented on power in and around organizations, but also to summarize it. The six configurations are reviewed briefly below, in a rough order of declining concentration of power and clarity in its use.[5]

* The *Instrument* is a power configuration in which the organization serves a dominant external influencer (or a group of them acting in concert). Because external control of an organization is most effectively achieved through the use of bureaucratic controls, the Internal Coalition emerges as Bureaucratic, pursuing and if necessary maximizing whatever operational goals the dominant influencer chooses to impose on it. Insiders are induced by utilitarian means to contribute their efforts, with little opportunity to play the power games. Such a configuration tends to emerge when an organization experiences external power that is focussed and organized, typically around a critical dependency or key legal prerogative, wielded by an external influencer (or a group of them acting in concert) with clear and operational goals.

* The *Closed System* also has a utilitarian, Bureaucratic IC, internal control being based on bureaucratic standards of work and output. In other words, its Internal Coalition closely resembles that of the Instrument. The fundamental difference is that the Closed System faces no focussed power in its environment, but rather a dispersed and unorganized set of external influencers. In other words, its External Coalition is Passive. This enables the Internal Coalition—notably the administrators, particularly the senior managers and the analysts who design the bureaucratic standards—to seize the lion's share of the power, and to direct the organization toward the systems goals. Specifically, survival, efficiency, control, and growth are pursued in that hierarchical order, with growth the goal that is ultimately maximized. This means that the Internal Coalition, being autonomous or even in control of its own environment, ultimately serves itself. The Closed System, while controlled by its administrators, has more room for political activity than the Instrument, particularly games of the empire-building sort. The Closed System tends to appear in more established organizations, typically large ones in simple, stable environments with unskilled operators and dispersed external influencers.

* The *Autocracy* also faces a Passive External Coalition, but develops a quite different Internal Coalition. All the power focusses on the chief executive officer, who controls by personal means. This tight form of control means a

[5]Except for the Autocracy, which follows the Instrument and Closed System for convenience of discussion, although its power is somewhat more clearly defined and concentrated.

virtual absence of political games—insiders express loyalty to the chief or leave. The Autocracy can pursue and if need be maximize any goals to the CEO's liking. Autocracies tend to be small and nonvisible organizations—so that single individuals can maintain personal control—also new organizations or older ones still led by their founders, ones operating in simple, dynamic environments, sometimes ones with strong leaders or ones facing severe crises.

* The *Missionary* is dominated by ideology, so much so that its External Coalition is rendered Passive. Indeed, rather than experiencing influence from its environment, the Missionary often seeks to send influence the other way, imposing its mission on the environment. The strong ideology serves to integrate the Internal Coalition tightly around the ideologic goals. It also allows the members to be trusted to make decisions, since each shares the traditions and beliefs—indeed embraces them through natural or selected identifications, or by virtue of being socialized and indoctrinated. Hence, political games are hardly played at all in this configuration. All efforts are devoted to pursuing to the maximum the goal of preserving, extending, and/or perfecting the mission of the organization. The Missionary tends to emerge when an organization has experienced charismatic leadership in its past and perhaps a distinguished history, and develops strong traditions around a clear, distinctive mission attractive to its members.

* The *Meritocracy* focusses its power on its expertise, of which it has a good deal in its operating core and/or support staff. Hence its Internal Coalition is Professional. But the presence of different types of experts typically means a fair amount of political activity too, especially in the administrative structure where the experts squabble over resources, territorial boundaries, and each other's strategic candidates. Pressures frequently develop in the External Coalition, but internal expertise is able to deal with most of them. Hence the External Coalition is best described as Passive, although it appears to be divided. The integration of the efforts of the experts is achieved through their standardized skills and knowledge, developed in training program that preceeded the job, or else through extensive mutual adjustment on the job among the experts trained in different specialties. The training programs make the experts highly mobile, so that loyalty to the organization is a weak factor, although the experts tend to be loyal to their professional societies, since socialization and indoctrination is a part of their professional training. The Meritocracy can maximize no single primary goal, but rather tends to pursue a few sequentially, including that of professional excellence, while responding to a host of constraints. But whatever the primary goals, in keeping with the complexity of work in the Meritocracy, they are typically nonoperational. The key condition that gives rise to the Meritocracy is the need for an organization to perform complex work, which requires a high level of expertise in its Internal Coalition.

* Finally, the *Political Arena* is characterized by conflict, often both in an External Coalition that is divided and an Internal Coalition that is politicized.

In other words, conflicting pressures are imposed on the organization from the outside, and political games abound inside, particularly those that pit alliances against each other. Voices are loud, exits frequent, loyalty absent. As a result, at best the organization attends to a large number of constraints or to personal goals in sequence, at worst it expends all its energies in political bargaining and achieves nothing. Sometimes the Political Arena has no concentration of power, neither a single key influencer nor any one focused system of influence. Instead conflict and politics are pervasive. In other words, with no natural focus of power, conflict emerges as natural. Other times the Political Arena has two or more concentrations of power that prove incompatible with each other in some ways, which results in conflict between them—either between one concentration of power in each of the coalitions or between different concentrations in one of the coalitions. Also, some Political Arenas are characterized by intense conflict, which must be of brief duration if the organization is to survive, while others are characterized by more moderate conflict. The latter can endure, sometimes in the form of a shaky alliance between a few centers of power, sometimes as a system of general bargaining among many. While the Political Arena seems to be dysfunctional— harmony better enabling most organizations to achieve their missions than conflict—it need not be an aberration. It can serve as a functional, indeed a necessary, way station in the transition from one of the other configurations to another (or from one set of actors to another in a given configuration). It can also serve as a functional hybrid, the only way that an organization experiencing conflicting power needs can function. The Political Arena emerges when an organization experiences a challenge to its existing order of power or between its existing influencers (to realign a coalition or change the configuration), perhaps because of a fundamental change in one of its important conditions or the breakdown of its established order of power. It also emerges when there are balanced and irreconcilable forces in the organization. The Political Arena endures when the conflicting demands placed on it cannot be resolved and none will abate.

We can highlight the key distinctions between these six configurations of power by reviewing them in terms of some of the characteristics listed in Table 17–1:[6]

* In terms of *key influencers* and *concentration of power,* as noted earlier, five of the six configurations can be considered to concentrate their power, though to different degrees, while the sixth is characterized by an absence of any such concentration. In the Instrument, power is firmly concentrated in the hands of one or a group of dominant external influencers, and in the Autocracy, in the hands of the CEO. In the three remaining cases, power is concentrated not so much in the hands of single individuals as in internal systems of influence, which nevertheless has the effect of defining which of the insiders get the power.

[6]Other characteristics included in the table are not discussed in this chapter but will be covered either in each of the chapters on the configurations or else in Chapter 24.

In the Closed System, power resides in the bureaucratic controls of the System of Authority, which concentrates it in the hands of the administrators, especially the senior managers and, to a lesser extent, the analysts of the technostructure. In the Missionary, power resides in the System of Ideology, which diffuses it to the believers, typically all the members. And in the Meritocracy, it resides in the System of Expertise, which concentrates it in the hands of the experts. It is the Political Arena that is distinguished by an absence of power concentrated in the hands of any one identifiable individual or group. Power in this case resides in the hands of many influencers, or in a few which challenge each other, but who these are can vary widely from one Political Arena to another.

* Turning to the *flow of power* between the External and Internal Coalitions, and the residual *freedom of action of the organization itself,* we see sharp differences among the configurations. At one extreme is the Instrument, with a clear flow of power from the External to the Internal Coalition, with the result that the organization is tightly controlled, and weak. Yet, ironically, it can act fairly freely, at least in its choice of means, so long as these serve the ends of the external influencer. At the other extreme are the Closed System and the Missionary, with organizations so independent that if power flows at all, it is from the Internal Coalition to the External, as the organization seeks to impose its will on its environment. The Closed System organization is typically the most powerful of all, and so is often able to dominate its would-be influencers by sheer force. The Missionary, in contrast, is not so much powerful as aggressive, often with a mission designed to change certain norms in its environment. Rather than respond to outsiders, it seeks to have outsiders respond to it. Close behind these two is the Autocracy, in which there is the least flow of power between the coalitions. The organization is rather independent of external infuence, yet lacks the power, and the intent, to control its environment. Ostensibly, all three of these organizations can act freely, but in fact all are constrained in important ways. The first two are constrained internally by themselves—in one case by bureaucratic standards and conservative administrators,[7] in the other by established norms and traditions. And the Autocracy, which can be the most flexible of all internally—because it is fully responsive to the wishes of one individual in complete personal control, with no standards of any kind—is usually constrained externally by its own small size and by its inherent precariousness. Power flows two ways in the Meritocracy, which cannot escape external influence. But its ability to use expertise to pacify much of that influence means that the Internal Coalition emerges as the more powerful. In other words, the organization retains a good deal of freedom to set its own direction, although

[7]The Instrument is ostensibly constrained by bureaucratic standards and conservative administrators too, but in fact these are less significant, for two reasons. First the standards are designed to pursue, not given systems goals, but any operational goals of interest to the dominant external influencer(s). And second, the conservative administrators must respond to the wishes of that external influencer.

professional norms and standards constrain it somewhat (especially in the case of Professional Bureaucracy). It is in the Political Arena that we find the most reciprocal flow of power, the organization in some ways being both controlled and controlling (especially when there is war between the two coalitions). However the intensity of conflict can also render the organization impotent, utterly unable to act. And even when action is possible, the question arises as to whether this is organizational in nature, as opposed to individual.

     *   Considering *the means of integration of insider efforts with organizational needs* and their corresponding *form of identification* with the organization, in three cases—the Instrument, Closed System, and Autocracy—integration is achieved by material inducements in return for contributions. Identification is minimal in the case of the Instrument, calculated at best in the case of the Closed System, and in large part calculated in the case of the Autocracy, with perhaps some natural identification with the values of the chief executive as well. The insiders of the Meritocracy and Political Arena also share little inclination to identify naturally with their organizations, although the experts of the Meritocracy do exhibit strong identifications (selected or evoked) with their professions. Bargaining is the means of integration, if it can be called that, in the Political Arena, while shared goals among the experts integrates their efforts with organizational need in the Meritocracy. Finally, we come to the Missionary, where the strong forms of identification with the organization can be found (natural, selected, and evoked). Integration is achieved through shared goals which are encouraged by socialization and indoctrination.

     *   As Hirschman (1970) notes, the participants in and around an organization can use *exit, voice, or loyalty* to express themselves. At one extreme is the Instrument, whose insiders can use only exit to express their grievances, voice being reserved for the dominant external influencer. At another extreme is the Political Arena, in which voice is relied upon by everyone—insiders and outsiders—with exit as an alternative. Loyalty is weakest in the Political Arena, but weak too in the Instrument. In contrast, loyalty is emphasized almost to the exclusion of voice within the Missionary. Members socialized into the organization stay and conform, or leave. So the Instrument, Political Arena, and Missionary sit at the three nodes of Hirschman's triad. In between are the Closed System, whose insiders can use mild voice or can exit, the Autocracy in which the insiders express loyalty to the chief executive or else exit, and the Meritocracy in which voice and exit are both common due to the mobility of the professionals, loyalty being reserved for the professional societies, not the organization. Outsiders in the Closed System are denied voice and are encouraged to exit if they do not wish to express loyalty to the organization. The same is true of the Autocracy (although few bother to express loyalty to the chief), and even more so of the Missionary (where, in some cases, loyalty can be expressed only by entering the organization). As for the ousiders of the Meritocracy, they attempt to use voice, but typically end up exiting if unhappy with the behavior of the organization.

* As for the *favored goals* and *goal systems* of the configurations, our contention that the organization has goals of its own is most strongly supported in the Missionary, with its strong ideological goals, and the Closed System, which vigorously pursues the systems goals, notably growth. Both these configurations can be called maximizers. The Instrument and Autocracy also have clear goals—those of their dominant influencers—and both can maximize should their dominant influencers so will it. Least describable as having goals of its own is the Political Arena, which pursues any and all of the personal goals of its influencers, and sometimes succeeds in pursuing none at all as the players tie themselves up in knots (although sometimes it can attend to some primary goals sequentially, or at least satisfy a whole set of constraints). The Meritocracy falls in between. Because the goals associated with professional work tend to be nonoperational, and because power is divided among various professional groups, the Meritocracy attends to a number of goals sequentially with no chance to maximize any one of them. But some goals—for example, those associated with professional autonomy and excellence—can emerge as more significant.

* Next, we look at how this typology of six power configurations maps unto *other typologies* we have discussed. In terms of our five structural configurations (Mintzberg 1979a), Simple Structure clearly corresponds to Autocracy while Machine Bureaucracy can be found here in two forms, the Instrument and the Closed System, depending on whether it is externally controlled or autonomous. For reasons we shall discuss later, the Divisionalized Form is most closely associated with the Closed System. Professional Bureaucracy and Adhocracy are two forms of Meritocracy, in one case where the professionals work alone, in the other, in groups. That leaves two of the power configurations, which are in fact additions to the other typology. The Missionary is the sixth structural configuration alluded to on the last page of the *Structuring* book, while the Political Arena can be viewed either as another addition (alluded to in that book in the discussion of the hybrids), or else as a less stable combination of the elements and therefore not one of the configurations. Our preference is to include it in its functional form, giving rise to a combined typology of seven configurations:[8]

— Simple Structure (Autocracy)
— Machine Bureaucracy as Instrument
— Machine Bureaucracy as Closed System (including Divisionalized Form)

---

[8]To return to symbolism, the "Dictionnaire des Symboles" devotes five pages to the number seven. Interestingly, what repeats in culture after culture is seven as the number of "perfection" and, correspondingly, completion (for example, to the Egyptians, seven symbolizes "a complete cycle, a dynamic perfection"; to the Chinese, "the *Yang* numbers. . .achieve their perfection at 7"; in Africa, "seven is the symbol of perfection and unity"; pp. 687, 688, 690). As Miller (1956) notes in a famous article, seven is the "magic number." Presumably it is the place for us to stop in the development of configurations!

— Professional Bureaucracy (Meritocracy)
— Adhocracy (Meritocracy)
— Missionary
— Political Arena (when a functional hybrid or a way station in a functional transition)

Turning to other typologies, Rhenman's Appendix Organization is our Instrument, his Corporation, our Closed System (and perhaps Autocracy as well), while his Institution seems closest to our Meritocracy. (As noted earlier, his Marginal Organization seems to be an uncommon aberration.) Etzioni's Utilitarian type can be either our Instrument or Closed System (sometimes Autocracy as well), while his Coercive type is probably closer to our Instrument than our Closed System, because it seems typically to be dominated by a concensus of its external influencers, as we shall see later. And his Normative type is clearly our Missionary. Blau and Scott's typology does not easily map unto ours, in our opinion because it represents intended rather than actual control. We shall see Business Concerns that are Autocracies, Instruments, Closed Systems, and even Political Arenas (not to mention Meritocracies and Missionaries on occasion), and Mutual Benefit Associations which are designed to be Missionaries but often end up as Closed Systems. His Service Organizations are perhaps most often Meritocracies, while his Commonweal Organizations, designed as Instruments, again often end up being Closed Systems. Allison's typology works somewhat better. His Government Politics Model clearly fits our Political Arena, his Organizational Process Model reflects in some limited ways our Closed System, while his Rational Actor model may fit most closely with our Autocracy or Instrument (probably the latter).[9]

    *   Finally, in terms of *government equivalent*, our Instrument has its closest equivalent in the colony, ruled by a mother country (and, as we shall see, seems to have another close equivalent in the government elected by a clear consensus of the population). The characteristics of our Closed System seem to be mirrored to some degree in all large contemporary governments, but it is really the communist state that seems to reflect them in virtually every detail. Our Autocracy is clearly equivalent to dictatorship (or dictatorial leadership even in democracy), while our Missionary is most closely reflected in cultural revolution as in the experience of China a few years ago (as we shall see). Our Meritocracy seems not to have appeared yet in government per se, although Young (1959) argues that it is about to, under that title. And our Political Arena finds its parallel in both of what are labelled anarchy and revolution, as well

[9]These last speculations are not shown in Table 17–1. But some other pure types, of whose relationships with ours we are more sure, are shown, namely Butler et al.'s Paralytic Organization as Instrument, Selznick's Institution as Missionary, and March and Olsen's "organized anarchy" or "garbage can" as Meritocracy (although it exhibits signs of the Political Arena as well). These relationships are discussed in the relevant chapters.

as in pluralistic forms of government (although, again, all contemporary govern-ments reflect the characteristics of the Political Arena to at least some degree).

In the next six chapters, we shall discuss these power configurations in turn, each characterized as a particular "play" of power. But first a word of caution. As noted earlier, we are here describing pure types, caricatures or simplifications of reality. No real power situation will exactly match any of these types, although if the typology proves to be any good, many will seem to resemble one or another. We are describing tendencies in and pressures on organizations as much as types in this section, although our points are best made in terms of the latter.

18

The Instrument

A COMMAND PERFORMANCE IN TWO ACTS

Starring: One or a group of dominant external influencers, often an owner, with the CEO and the analysts in supporting roles.

Synopsis of Act I: One external influencer (or many who reach a consensus), with clear, operational goals—ideally the maximization of a single one—dominates the External Coalition and so is able to impose his will on the Internal Coalition through formal constraints supplemented by direct controls (sometimes using the board of directors as well), and thereby to render it his Instrument.

Synopsis of Act II: By virtue of this external control, the Internal Coalition emerges as Bureaucratic; rigidities in this form give rise to some political games, but these do not seriously displace the formal goals; the cycle of power is completed when the Internal Coalition orients its strategies toward and/or puts its surpluses at the disposal of the dominant external influencer(s).

Now Playing: Where external power is focussed and organized, normally around a critical dependency or legal prerogative, and the goals imposed from the outside are clear and operational, typically involving organizations in stable environments with simple, mass output technical systems and unskilled work forces; notably in closely held business corporations, subsidiaries of other organizations, public service

bureaucracies such as fire departments and post offices, coercive
organizations such as custodial prisons, and certain cooperatives with
organized owners, such as stock exchanges.

> In the rational model, the organization is conceived as an "instrument"—that is, as
> a rationally conceived means to the realization of expressly announced group
> goals. Its structures are understood as tools deliberately established for the effi-
> cient realization of these group purposes. Organizational behavior is thus viewed
> as consciously and rationally administered. . . .
>   Fundamentally, the rational model implies a "mechanical" model, in that it
> views the organization as a structure of manipulable parts. . . The long-range
> development of the organization as a whole is also regarded as subject to planned
> control and as capable of being brought into increasing conformity with explicitly
> held plans and goals. (Gouldner 1959, pp. 404–5)

In our first configuration, as described in this Gouldner quotation, the
organization acts as an Instrument to execute the wishes of some power beyond
itself. In our terms, a Bureaucratic Internal Coalition responds to a Dominated
External Coalition; in those of Rhenman (1973), the organization is the "appendix" of some outside agency. Butler et al. see this organization as "paralytic,"
meaning, in the terms of the Oxford English Dictionary, "an inability to move or
use free will; a reliance on external means of support, a state of utter powerlessness," in their own terms, "a focal organization dominated by and influenced by
external interest units which effectively immobilize it" (1977–78, p.48). From
our perspective, however, the Instrument is not immobilized at all. Rather it is
mobilized to pursue the goals of its dominant external influencer(s). Within this
major imposition, it can move rather easily. (We shall, in fact, use the term
paralytic for a form of the Political Arena, one so immobilized by politics that it
can accomplish nothing for anybody.)

We begin this chapter with a description of the External Coalition of the
Instrument, where its power originates, and then we describe its Internal Coalition. Following some comments on its goal system, we conclude by describing
some forms that this power configuration can take.

THE EXTERNAL COALITION:
DOMINATED (AND DOMINATING)

One prime conditon is prerequisite to the emergence of the Instrument:
Power in the External Coalition focussed in the hands of a single influencer or a
group of them acting in concert, typically in control of a critical dependency or a
prime legal prerogative.

Given a single dominant external influencer, access to the Internal Coalition can be personal, with the result that this individual is able to impose direct

controls on it. He can select the CEO as his own trustee, plant other represen-tatives inside to serve as his watchdogs, authorize key decisions and even im-pose some on the organization. Yet, even though the external influencer has a strong incentive to keep close personal control—for the organization is in effect if not in fact his private property—he cannot get too involved. For after all, he is an *external* influencer, which means that his time for the organization is limited. (Were it not—in other words, were he to control the organization personally, on a full-time basis—he would become in effect its chief executive officer and the configuration would revert to Autocracy.) With limited time, therefore, the ex-ternal influencer must fall back on another external means of influence, one that is less personal in nature yet enables him to maintain his control of the organization. That is what we have called the formal constraint. Specifically the external in-fluencer imposes tangible objectives on the organization—goals that he has operationalized. This way, he can let the management run the organization, while he need only monitor its performance periodically.

Indeed, for all but the smallest and simplest of organizations, operational goals are virtually the only means by which an influencer can maintain tight control of an organization yet remain outside of it. With such goals, manage-ment knows what is expected of it, and knows that its results can and will be evaluated in terms of these expectations. So its pursuit of the interests of the ex-ternal influencer is ensured. In other words, the Instrument emerges when an organization must respond to focussed external power that speaks with a clear voice. Without such a clear voice, the organization cannot, or need not, respond with consistent behavior, and so does not act as an Instrument. With it, the organ-ization has no choice but to respond consistently, since control of it is unchallenged.

Thus, formal constraints emerge as the prime external means of influence in the Instrument, supplemented by direct controls. What of the other means? Social norms are obviously unimportant here, and pressure campaigns un-necessary, since these are far less direct and effective than formal constraints and direct controls. The board of directors may be used as a means of influence, as the vehicle by which the external influencer can access the CEO formally on a regular basis, in order to impose his operational goals and direct controls. But it need not be, since that influencer can easily bypass the board and access the CEO informally. This is what the external influencer is likely to do, in which case the board will probably become a facade. Given the weakness of the other external influencers, the organization has little need to use the board as its tool—to coopt influencers, legitimize itself, and so on.

Who tends to emerge as a dominant external influencer? The most obvious candidate is the owner of the organization—at least where ownership is concen-trated—since that person legally controls it. Another candidate is an associate in control of a critical dependency—a monopsonist or monopolist who controls a key market or source of supply. Sometimes dominance is established by a group of external influencers. In these cases—we referred to them in Chapter 7 as *con-census-dominated* External Coalitions—different external influencers coalesce around a central theme, expressed in terms of operational goals. By acting in unison, these influencers emerge as a single force able to control the Internal Coalition, much as does a single dominant external influencer.[1] In Chapter 7, we cited Cressey's (1958) study of the prison with a custodial orientation, whose significant external influencers—police, judges, prosecuting attorneys, and others—all favored the goal of protecting society from criminals, rather than rehabilitating them. As a result, the prison emerged as Instrument: "...the prison operated according to a conception of public service expressed in a proposed code of ethics for employees and officials of Arlington County, Virginia: 'Those holding public office, *as servants of the public*, are not owners of authority but agents of public purposes' " (p. 46, italics in original).

THE INTERNAL COALITION: BUREAUCRATIC AND RESPONSIVE

We have already seen in the last chapter how external control of an organization generates both centralization and formalization within its structure, in other words, drives it to what we have called as Machine Bureaucracy, or the Bureaucratic IC. This is the fundamental hypothesis that underlies the Instrument: a Dominated EC naturally gives rise to a Bureaucratic IC. In essence, the external influencer renders an organization his Instrument by centralizing its power in the hands of a single individual—the CEO at the strategic apex—whom he holds responsible and accountable for its actions, and then by imposing on that individual goals which the CEO can in turn translate into bureaucratic standards—into objectives, rules, regulations and the like—through the hierarchy of authority. These standards in fact serve to protect the insiders, by enabling them to "prove" that they have performed in the interests of the external influencer. Thus we see the Instrument in Figure 18–1 as a fully developed chain of formal authority, from the external influencer into the organization through the CEO (perhaps via the board) and then down through the complete hierarchy of authority to its base in the operating core.

The CEO of the Instrument is weak compared with the dominant external influencer, since the former holds office at the latter's discretion. But compared with the other insiders, the CEO has a great deal of power. He is the main channel to and from the true center of power. Influence flows into the Internal Coalition, and information back out to the dominant external influencer, primarily through the CEO. Thus the other insiders are dependent on the CEO for information and delegated authority. Moreover, the strategic apex is the one place where all the different functions of the Machine Bureaucracy come together for coordination. Hence power flows not only down to it from above but also up to

---

[1]When the group of influencers names one of their number to act on their behalf, consensus and individual domination become synonymous.

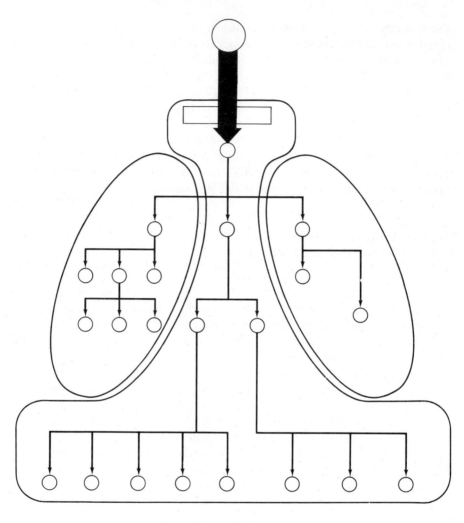

Figure 18-1. *The Instrument*

it from below. "The bureaucratic machinery of modern organizations means that there are rather few people who are really powerful," Kanter tells us (1979, p. 197). As a consequence of his authority and centrality, the CEO emerges as the center of formal as well as informal power in the organization as Instrument.

But little of that power can be exercised through personal controls, at least relative to the CEOs of most other configurations. (Some CEO powers must, of course, always be exercised personally, because of the unprogrammed nature of his job.) As we discussed in the last chapter, the external influencer prefers bureaucratic controls; a center of personal control is a threat to his own power. As Kipnis notes:

...in several studies...it has been found that appointed leaders who...perceived themselves as externally controlled were reluctant to invoke personal resources as a means of inducing behavior in others.... [They] either did nothing or else relied exclusively on institutional resources. (1974, p. 92)

The insiders of the Instrument do not generally develop a sense of identity with their organization's goals, for these are imposed on them from outside. Hence, Instruments do not typically develop strong ideologies. They emerge, in fact, as the closest of the configurations to the lifeless shells we described in Chapter 14. The Instrument is a tool—an expendable one at that—designed to achieve outside ends, with no acceptable life of its own.

What then induces the insiders to exert their efforts on the organization's behalf? The answer of course is implied in the wording of the question: the inducements-contributions formula. They contribute their efforts passively in return for tangible inducements, notably pay. For the most part, they leave the determination of organizational goals to the dominant influencer and the CEO acting as his agent. Thus, this configuration corresponds to what Etzioni calls "utilitarian," where the members' involvement is "calculative." And this, of course, greatly reduces the influence of the System of Politics (although, as we shall soon see, it does not eliminate it). As Butler et al. note, "the paralytic organization would be associated with a calm interior. After all, it is almost a non-decision making situation, and people will be quietly getting on with their routine jobs" (1977–78, p. 49). Should political games get out of hand, the inclination of the dominant influencer is to step in quickly and squelch them. The System of Expertise is also weak in the Instrument, discouraged as a threat to the existing centers of power. Expert work does not lend itself to bureaucratic work standards, measurable outputs, or external controls. Hence the Instrument cannot tolerate a great deal of it.

With this in mind, we can consider the power of each of the insiders of the Instrument. The managers of the middle line typically represent specific functions or subfunctions, such as manufacturing or maintenance. Because of the bureaucratic nature of the organization, they tend to be weak relative to the CEO, in fact increasingly weak at successively lower levels in the hierarchy. As layer upon layer of authority is heaped upon them, and as bureaucratic standards increasingly institutionalize their jobs, their ability to use personal controls, never strong at any level, reduces to almost nothing near the bottom of the hierarchy. Like everyone else, the line managers are motivated by the inducements-contributions formula, although a few at higher levels may develop some calculative identification as well, in the realization that one day, one of them will probably become CEO.

The rigidity of the structure does, however, lead to mild forms of goal displacement and political activity in the middle line. In particular, the machine bureaucratic structure sometimes encourages the line managers to distort objectives, to suboptimize, and to invert means and ends, although the highly operational nature of the goals keeps this to a minimum. And, in a structure in which status is associated with level in the hierarchy and size of unit managed, the line managers are somewhat encouraged to play the political games of empire building and budgeting. If they cannot influence the goals of the organization significantly, then at least they can seek a larger share of its material rewards. Perhaps more popular as a political game, especially at lower levels in the hierarchy, is lording, as managers take out their powerlessness on subordinates and others.

> In the bureaucratic mode, the middle manager adopts a style that consists of applying rules and procedures inflexibly and treating compliance as an end in itself. . . .
> Since he lacks the power to change the rules and lacks resources to motivate subordinates, he protects himself from upward criticism by narrowing his responsibility to a strict interpretation of the letter of the law. (Izraeli 1975, p. 59)

The analysts of the technostructure have little *formal* power here, since Machine Bureaucracy keeps it all in the line hierarchy. But *in*formal power they do have, at least in small amounts, because they are the designers of the bureaucratic standards that regulate everyone else's work. The design of these standards is a critical function in the Instrument—one important island of discretion in a sea of regulation—and the analysts are the ones who control it. That of course brings them into conflict with the managers at lower levels of the middle line, whose little personal discretion is further threatened by each new bureaucratic standard. Hence, line versus staff emerges as another political game in the Instrument, pitting line managers with the status (if not the substance) of power against staff analysts with its substance (if not its status).

The support specialists of the Instrument, being in staff positions, also lack formal power. But unlike the analysts, most of them control no critical function, and so they generally lack informal power as well.

Finally, at the bottom of the pecking order are the operators. Because their work is generally routine and unskilled, they feel the full weight of the System of Authority in the form of bureaucratic controls. Their discretion is minimal, their inducements almost purely utilitarian. About the only political games they can play are lording, at least when they serve clients directly, and, occasionally, insurgency, when they are able to act in concert against the management. But the presence of a strong and unified System of Authority, legitimated by external control, makes insurgency a risky game.

The operators' relationships with the central authority are typically conducted by their unions, negotiating outside of the Internal Coalition. Indeed, these negotiations can usually be viewed as outside of the External Coalition as well. Because the organization's goals are so clearly those of the external influencer, the unions concentrate not on influencing the organization's behavior but on getting the best material inducements possible for their members. As a result, they act more as economic associates—suppliers of labor—than as full-fledged influencers. Even the strike comes to look less like a campaign of political pressure than a tool of economic negotiation, resembling the behavior of any other supplier who refuses to sell until the price is right (Zald and Berger 1978, p.842).

To conclude, while political games are not absent from the Internal Coalition of the Instrument, neither are they a central element in its power system. Too much power is concentrated in one place—in the hands of the dominant external influencer and, in turn, the chief executive as his trustee. Politics just doesn't offer many benefits. Political games become, at best, grabs for status or personal advancement, at worst, mere expressions of frustration. The energies of the organization as Instrument remain focussed on the goals imposed from without. As noted earlier, the Instrument can act—and act decisively—but only in the interests of its external influencer(s), never its own as a system or those of its insiders.

THE GOAL SYSTEM: OPERATIONAL

Earlier we noted that to act as an Instrument, the organization must have a clear idea of what is expected of it. As Allison (1971) points out, the organization cannot function as a "rational actor" unless its goals are specified a priori—before actions are taken. Hence the goals of the Instrument must be clear, specifically, operational. Vague and nonoperational goals discourage control by an *external* influencer, forcing him either to enter the Internal Coalition or to relinquish control of it. Clear, operational goals, on the other hand, enable the CEO to operationalize the external influencer's wishes and so to ensure that all the other insiders act in accordance with them.

The susceptability of vague goals to displacement is easily explained. Every organization experiences a tension between "rationality" and politics— between the formal goals imposed through the System of Authority and the personal ones with which insiders seek to displace them. As we saw earlier, political games must typically be played on the terrain of rationality. Even the most blatant grab for power must somehow be justified in terms of the formal goals. Where these are vague, virtually any action can be justified in their terms. (As noted earlier, what doesn't serve the cause of the "advancement of knowledge" in a university?) And so it stands to reason that the clearer and more operational the formal goals at the top, the less easily they can be displaced lower down, and so the less room there is for politics in the Internal Coalition (Warner and Havens 1968).

A corollary of this is that the fewer the goals, the less each can be displaced, and so the less politicized is the organization. The existence of multiple goals—even operational ones—opens the door to interpretation and debate about weighting them. This creates discretion, a breeding ground for politics. A single primary goal, on the other hand, focusses all discussion over choices on a single dimension, encouraging the use of calculation in place of judgment or bargaining. Thus, we can conclude that the purest form of the Instrument is the one whose dominant influencer imposes but a single goal on the Internal Coalition, and thereby forces it to maximize. We see this, for example, in the case of the owner of the closely held business corporation who demands the highest possible profit.

The goal system of the Instrument is complete, and the loop in its continuous chain of power closed, when the major payoffs from its activities are made to its dominant external influencer: its basic strategies are oriented to his needs and its surpluses are put at his disposal.

The systems goals—survival, efficiency, control, and growth—are not major factors in this power configuration, at least not as systems goals. That is to say, the Instrument has no worth as a system unto itself; it exists to serve outside needs, not its own. Thus, survival is not a goal per se, the organization being dispensable as far as the external influencer is concerned. (Of course, should he lose interest in it, rather than consciously try to liquidate it, the insiders may seize control to perpetuate it as a Closed System.) Control by the organization of its environment is certainly not a goal; quite the contrary, it is a threat to the external influencer. And growth may or may not be a goal, depending on the external influencer's needs and preferences. Efficiency usually is a goal, however, because it tends to serve the external influencer. Since his goals are operational, efficiency becomes the measure of their attainment. Mission has no special role in the goal system of the Instrument per se, unless of course it serves the external influencer's interests. (In fact, we shall soon see examples where it does, in cases where clients dominate the External Coalition.)

FORMS OF THE INSTRUMENT

Aside from an external concentration of power, the Instrument tends to be found under the same conditions as the Closed System, and the Machine Bureaucracy in general, namely those that drive the operating work of an organization to be routine and unskilled and so amenable to tight standardization. This happens when an organization's environment is simple and stable, allowing its operations to be rationalized, and when its technical system tends to regulate (but not automate) the work of its operators, as in mass production and mass services. It is under these conditions that an external influencer can most easily control the organization through operational goals.

Machine Bureaucracies are typically mature and large organizations, so that their operating tasks have had the time and the volume to become repetitive and hence to lend themselves to standardization. But external control, because it encourages bureaucratization, can speed up these processes somewhat, so that relatively small and young organizations can sometimes appear as Instruments as well. Indeed, as we shall see in the next chapter, time and especially growth of the organization can rob the external influencer of his power over it, so that the Instrument becomes a Closed System.

According to these conditions, one classic example of the Instrument has to be the *closely held business corporation* operating in a mass output industry. Here power is concentrated in the hands of the owners. As Dill has noted:

> Business firms traditionally have been more unabashedly authoritarian than many other kinds of organizations. Both in ideology and practice, the main locus of formal power starts with the owners... Strong central control is assumed necessary in order to achieve the focussing of action, the coordination of effort, the means of conflict resolution, and the control of results that are required to deal effectively with the organization's external environment. (1965, p. 1097)

The other external influencers of the closely held business corporation, especially one that is not large, tend to be relatively passive. The associates are inclined to remain in straight economic relationships, as are the unions, and governments typically content themselves with imposing certain formal constraints. As for the dominant owners, as we saw earlier they tend to favor the goal of profit— one of the most easily operationalized of goals. Growth for them, unlike for the managers, tends to be viewed as a means to the end of profit. Etzioni (1961) presents as his prime example of the utilitarian organization the blue-collar business corporation, as well as such white-collar ones as banks and insurance companies. He attributes their emphasis on remunerative forms of reward to their economic goals and their bureaucratic structures. Such forms of reward "can be readily measured and allocated in close relation to performance," a necessity in these highly rationalized structures (p. 80).

Subsidiaries operating in mass output industries also tend to be Instruments, even when their controlling parent firms are themselves widely held (that is, Closed Systems). One of the studies carried out by a team of McGill University MBA students involved a metallurgy firm, recently acquired by a conglomerate. Before the acquisition, as shown in Figure 18–2(a), the firm was a near-perfect Autocracy: small, dominated by its president who had "his finger in every pie," with a highly organic structure (no job descriptions, no personnel function, etc.) Its main goals were described as survival and stability. The conglomerate, on the other hand, as shown in Figure 18–2(b), was a Closed System— widely held, divisionalized, with a goal system best described as the maximization of growth. The sudden parachuting of a dominant influencer into the External Coalition of the acquired firm, as shown in Figure 18–2(c), produced the expected result, which proved traumatic for it. Although the president was retained (at least up to the time of the study), the parent clearly exercised its power. First, it took over the board and used it as a control service. Second, it imposed bureaucratic controls on the firm, such as requiring it to develop a five-year plan and an organigram with clearly delineated lines of authority, and to submit for

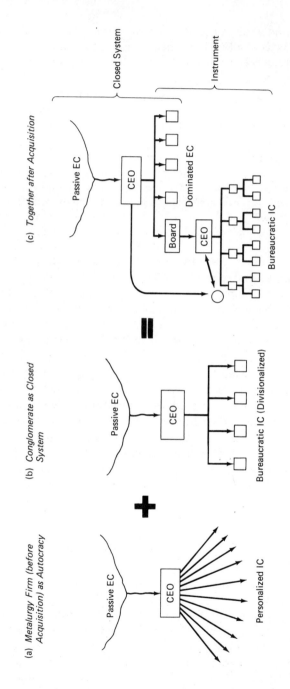

(a) *Metalurgy Firm (before Acquisition) as Autocracy*

Passive EC

CEO

Personalized IC

(b) *Conglomerate as Closed System*

Passive EC

CEO

Bureaucratic IC (Divisionalized)

(c) *Together after Acquisition*

Closed System

Instrument

Passive EC

CEO

Dominated EC

Board

CEO

Bureaucratic IC

Figure 18–2. *The Shift to an Instrument*

approval all decisions involving expenditures of more than $50,000. And third—worst of all for the old president—it planted one of its own people in a highly sensitive technocratic position, that of secretary-treasurer, to keep watch over the president and his actions. Note the position in the technostructure—a key one concerned with performance control in this firm. Thus, the acquisition resulted in a sudden shift from Autocracy to Instrument, with the External Coalition becoming dominated and the Internal Coalition bureaucratized. Likewise the goals of the firm changed, with growth emerging ahead of the rest after many years of stagnation.[2]

Butler et al.'s (1977–78) "paralytic" organization—a local electricity board dominated by the Electricity Council of the British Government—is a more extreme example of the subsidiary as Instrument, in this case in the public sector. Its prices were dictated by the Council; it was restricted to the supplying of electricity and could not diversify; it did not even have marketing decisions to make, since it had to serve every customer in its own area and could not expand elsewhere. In total, its "strategic alternatives [were] negligible" (p. 51). As for the Internal Coalition, there was "anything but a jostling for power. . . .no suggestion of politicking, competing for resources or pushing new activities" (p. 52). The electricity board was the perfect Instrument, in the view of Butler et al. for many of the reasons discussed earlier: it was linked "to the externality of power"; it used "an energy form that is understood and controlled" and a technology that is "highly developed and stable"; its operating work was "routine" and its performance "readily counted and evaluated" (pp. 56, 57).

What Etzioni (1961) calls the *coercive organization* also seems to be a form of the Instrument. Custodial prisons and mental hospitals, prisoner-of-war camps and the like, all have simple, stable missions and "highly routinized" operations; their goals are clear and easily operationalized, for example, in terms of "runaway rates"; as a result, "little conflict" is expected among their employees (Zald 1962–63, p. 29). Earlier we saw that these organizations tend to be dominated by a consensus among their external influencers around the theme of custody. The employees of the custodial prison, for example, are perceived as "agents" or "servants of the public" (Cressey 1958, p. 46).

In McCleery's (1957) description of "The Authoritarian Prison," we see that the internal structures of these organizations can take the form of Machine Bureaucracy in the extreme, in terms of regulations, hierarchy of authority, and centralization. To quote from his report, this institution "was totalitarian in the sense that all the processes necessary to sustain life within its walls were subject to regulation in detail." For example, "perfect control involved a knowledge of where every man was at any moment." The structure of the custodial force "was borrowed directly from military organization," with employees advancing in a hierarchy "from guard through Sergeant, Watch Officer, and Senior Captain." "All communication flowed upward, leaving each superior better informed

[2]Based on a report submitted to the author by D. J. Kalman in Management Policy 701, McGill University, 1971.

than his subordinates and limiting the information on lower levels on which discretion could be based." As a result, "a monopoly of discretion [was placed] in the hands of the executive," with the "warden and his deputy the only policy-making officials of the institution." Even liaison with outsiders was carefully restricted to the chief executive, making him the center of power. "All communication to and from the prison crossed [the warden's] desk, giving him the broadest prespective and, hence, widest discretion in external affairs. The respect accorded to the Warden by the prison community was far above that given to his Deputy." All others—subordinate officers as well as inmates—"were forbidden to mention institutional affairs to outsiders." In general, "violation of the chain of command" was prohibited as a threat to "the stability of the authoritarian social system" (quotes from pp. 10–15, 39). Here, then, we have the ultimate case of the Instrument.

Another form of the Instrument is found in the *public service bureaucracy* with a stable, well-defined mission, which becomes the goal around which the various external influencers coalesce. For example, whether or not the fire department has a dominant external influencer, virtually all those who surround it promote the goal of extinguishing fires quickly and efficiently so as to minimize the loss of life and property. And so it is with the post office in delivering the mail, the airport in serving the flying public, and so on. Governmental activities do not always elicit agreement among different external influencers. But these organizations elict that kind of agreement. That is because they provide well-defined, routine services to the mass of the population, services minimally subject to misinterpretation and conflict and with easily operationalized criteria of performance. These organizations fit into the category of Blau and Scott's commonweal organizations, in which everyone is effectively a client. Hence the consensus.

Consensus-dominated Instruments can also be found outside of the public sector. One McGill MBA group studied a recording studio set up by four artists with a very clear (if not exactly operational) goal—to produce the perfect sound. Another group, that studied the racetrack we discussed earlier, found it to be controlled externally by its owners, the government, and the horsemen. Each wanted the largest share of the pie—the money left over once the bettors had received their average 82¢ return on each $1.00 bet. The government wanted more taxes, the horsemen higher purses, the owners larger surpluses after operating expenses were paid. In this sense, they formed a Divided External Coalition. But once they agreed on a distribution—a precise formula, shown back in Figure 15-1, on page 252, they were able to act in concert, functioning as a consensus-dominated External Coalition to promote the goal of maximizing the amount of money bet. The organization became their Instrument to generate revenues.[3]

---

[3]Possibly the best indication of this is that the racetrack paid dividends to its owners that amounted to 70–80 percent of its net earnings. Indeed the figure was no higher because the owners made a promise when issuing a debenture to limit dividends to 80 percent!

Another form of private Instrument dominated by an external consensus occurs when a consortium of private organizations forms an "appendix" organization to serve some common need. For eample, brokerage firms create a stock exchange to trade their stocks efficiently. Since the owners and dominant influencers are also the customers of the exchange, it stands to reason that its mission should emerge as its prime goal.

The stock exchange is, in fact, just one example of the class of organizations called "cooperatives," mutual benefit associations in Blau and Scott's terms. Farmers also create cooperatives to market their produce, consumers form retail cooperatives to supply themselves, and manufacturing firms establish trade associations as cooperatives to represent their interests. All are designed as Instruments of their owners, although, as we shall soon see, many revert to Closed Systems because their owners, who are dispersed, lose control to the managers, who are centrally organized. *Owner-controlled cooperatives* as Instruments, may in fact be rarer than manager-controlled ones as Closed Systems. Indeed, democratic government itself, the ultimate cooperative, or mutual benefit association, intended as the Instrument of the people, these days often looks more like a Closed System designed to serve the politicians and civil servants (as we shall discuss in the next chapter). But when a government is elected by a clear concensus of the population, to carry out a particular mandate, then it is more likely to act unequivocally as the Instrument it is supposed to be. Of course, one might also view the welfare state, carried to its logical extreme, as a form of Instrument of the people as well.

In conclusion, while we see in these last examples that the Instrument can shift to another power configuration when its managers, or others, wrest control from its dominant external influencer(s), nevertheless many organizations do remain as the Instruments they were intended to be. They spend at least part of their lives serving, not themselves, not their employees nor their leaders, but specific members of their External Coalitions who speak in clear voices.

19

The Closed System

> **Now Playing:** Primarily in large, mature organizations operating in simple, stable environments, that would otherwise be Instruments except that their potential external influencers, particularly their owners, are dispersed and unorganized (perhaps as a result of actions taken by the administrators); notably in widely held corporations, especially of the divisionalized type, certain large volunteer organizations including some revolutionary political parties and unions; also in some organizations ignored by their dominant external influencers (such as "little fish" subsidiaries), some public service bureaucracies, and, more and more, large government itself.

Society is adaptive to organizations, to the large, powerful organizations controlled by a few, often overlapping, leaders. To see these organizations as adaptive to a "turbulent," dynamic, ever changing environment is to indulge in fantasy. The environment of most powerful organizations is well controlled by them, quite stable, and made up of other organizations with similar interests, or ones they control. (Perrow 1972a, p. 199)

In the Instrument, we saw a continuous chain of power, from the dominant external influencer(s) to the CEO and then down the hierarchy of authority to the operators. In this second configuration, we see the beginning of the collapse of this chain, notable the lopping off of the links between the External and the Internal Coalition, as indicated in Figure 19-1. There is a chain associated with this second configuration, as we can see, but it runs exclusively within the Internal Coalition, from the CEO on down. In other words, the difference between these two power configurations is that in this second one, the External Coalition is Passive. The owners are typically diffused and unorganized, and the other outsiders are generally unaggressive, indeed often dependent on the organization rather than vice versa. And this makes all the difference to the distribution of power. The organization exploits this situation, in fact, as we shall see often creates it in the first place, to emerge as a system unto itself, for all intents and purposes closed to external control. The organization can do as it pleases. Indeed, if any control does take place, it is the organization that controls its environment.

Each of the next four configurations of power that we shall be discussing is in fact a system to some extent closed to influence from its environment. Yet as we shall soon see, three of these base their impermeability on some more or less legitimate form of power within the organization, while one does not. That one is closed not because it must be, but because its administrators have been able to exploit one of its characteristics—frequently its size—to make it so. They have suceeded in blocking out or even dominating legitimate forms of external in-

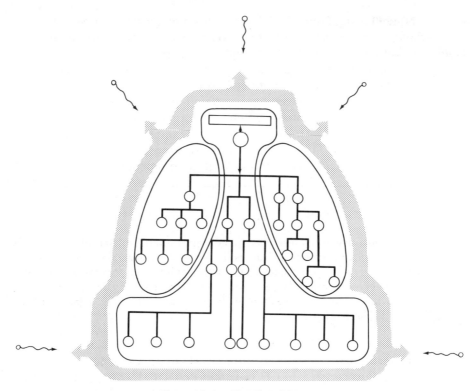

Figure 19-1. *The Closed System*

fluence. In their place, they promote the organization as a system—as an end in itself. Hence we reserve the label *Closed System* for this configuration.

Leaving external influence aside, in most other ways the conditions of the Closed System resemble those of the Instrument: its goals are well defined and operational, its environment simple and stable, its technical system frequently mass output, and its operating tasks routine and unskilled. As a result, the Internal Coalition of the Closed System is also Bureaucratic, its prime system of influence being bureaucratic control within the System of Authority.

Earlier we described authority as one, in fact the prime, *legitimate* system of influence in the Internal Coalition. Why then do we describe the Closed System, which emphasizes authority, as an illegitimate configuration of power? Simply because that authority has no roots, no source—it does not exist to serve any power or purpose beyond the organization. Unlike the Instrument, and even, though to a lesser degree, the Autocracy, Missionary, and Meritocracy, the Closed System, as noted above, serves itself above all.

The Closed System corresponds most closely to what Rhenman calls the "corporation," and encompasses many of Etzioni's utilitarian organizations. Some of Blau and Scott's business concerns, commonweal organizations, and mutual benefit associations also fit in here. Ironically, the Closed System is the true mutual benefit association, but not as Blau and Scott envisaged it. They use the term for the organization whose members are supposed to be the prime beneficiaries. That is the result in the Closed System, but not the intention! In other words, erected to benefit others, the Closed System instead benefits its own inside members, notably its administrators. (Indeed, we shall soon see that many of Blau and Scott's mutual benefit associations do turn out to be Closed Systems, because the result is exactly the opposite of what these writers suggest: the administrators, as insiders, shut out the true members, as outsiders.)

THE GOAL SYSTEM:
PURSUIT OF THE SYSTEMS GOALS

The key to understanding the Closed System lies in its goal system, hence we begin our discussion here. To understand this system, three points must be borne in mind. First, with a Passive External Coalition, no important goals are imposed on the organization from the outside. This organization is the instrument of no outsider. Second, the insiders, to whom the power naturally flows, are there primarily for the inducements they can get, not for any ideological considerations. So mission counts for little as a goal, in fact probably less here than in any of the other configurations. What the organization happens to produce and who it happens to serve are simply means to other ends. Those ends are the direct payoffs to the insiders, in the form of salaries, fringe benefits, positions, social satisfactions, and so on. Their involvement is, to use Etzioni's term, calculative. So the insiders are prepared to coalesce around whatever goals will produce the largest pie to be shared. Third is the fact that the machine bureaucratic nature of the organization's structure requires it to have a clear, operational system of goals.

And so the question becomes, Around what set of operational goals, providing the largest pie to be shared, can the inside influencers coalesce? And the obvious answer is, Those goals that can best protect and nourish the organization itself, as an independent system, the font of their rewards. In other words, the systems goals emerge as paramount in the Closed System—survival, efficiency, control, and growth, in that hierarchical order, as we described them in Chapter 16.

Growth is the primary goal of the Closed System, because as we saw in Chapter 9, it is the one goal around which the insiders most naturally coalesce. Growth enlarges the pie form which they can be rewarded. For the managers especially, it leads to larger salaries, better opportunities for promotion, lusher fringe benefits, and more playthings such as jet airplanes. Growth, as we noted in Chapter 16, also enables the line managers to build empires with a minimum of internal stress and conflict. In the growing organization, there is plenty for everybody. That is why the Closed System tends to be a growth maximizer.

Efficiency, in contrast, tends to be a constraint in the Closed System, not a primary goal. The insiders know that the organization needs a certain level of efficiency to survive and grow, but they also know that an obsession with efficiency can be costly to them. A lean, efficient organization has to be less generous than a fat, growing one: "...managerial salary, prestige, options, and the like tend to be far more closely correlated with the size of a firm than with its profitability" (Findlay and Williams 1972; p. 73). Thus, we saw evidence in Chapter 9 that the owner-controlled firms—the Instruments, or sometimes Autocracies—average substantially higher profits than the management-controlled firms—the Closed Systems—and that the managers of the latter may even show a preference for administrative expense per se, the result, presumably, of building empires as a part of the growth process.

Closely behind growth is the goal of survival, or conservation of the system. Closed Systems tend to be rather conservative in their behavior, even in their pursuit of growth, for two reasons. First, the survival of any organization is an important matter to its full-time employees; when they have been able to seize control if it—to make it serve them—its survival becomes especially crucial. Not only their daily livelihood is at stake; all those cozy deals they have managed to develop over the years will be lost if the organization dies. So whereas the death of some other kind of organization may be incidental to its key influencers—a necessary eventuality, as in the case of a spent Instrument—it is not to the insiders of the Closed System. They will hang on for dear life and, more importantly, will run the organization in the first place to avoid such an eventuality.

The second reason for conservative behavior is that the Closed System is very sensitive to attack. The insiders know that the power arrangements they have managed to establish are vulnerable, difficult to justify to outsiders. The Instrument, in contrast, has nothing to hide—its power, both in theory and in practice, is legitimate, rooted in a force beyond itself. Ultimately, it serves someone else. The Missionary is legitimate because it serves some*thing* else. Its members can point to its mission or purpose, rooted in its ideology, as supreme. Even the Autocracy can often justify the absolute power of its leader: as we shall see in Chapter 20, that person may be the organization's legitimate owner, or may have been necessary to establish the organization in the first place or to have seen it through a major crisis later. And even in the absence of these factors, the Autocracy is typically so small and insignificant that no one worries much about its legitimacy. As for the Meritocracy, while it may seem as closed and as self-serving as the Closed System—its inside experts getting the lion's share of its benefits—the fact is that it can function in no other way. Because of the complexity of its work, its power must be rooted in its expertise.

But the Closed System *can* function in another way: it can be an Instrument. The obvious question is, Why isn't it? In other words, the inability of outsiders, even ones with legal prerogatives, to penetrate its Internal Coalition, the self-serving nature of its goals, the incidental nature of its mission—all these are difficult to support in public debate, especially when the organization is large and visible, as the Closed System tends to be. Better to aviod debate by not disrupting anyone. Hence the conservative behavior.

Thus, Monsen and Downs note of the widely held corporation:

> ...stockholders have so few contacts with management that any widely circulated criticism of top management is likely to convince many stockholders that "where there's smoke, there's fire." Therefore, top management is often highly sensitive to criticism from major groups outside the firm. (1965; p. 231)

These authors suggest, as we discussed in Chapter 9, that this drives the managers to engage in a variety of behaviors: to screen carefully all information forwarded to stockholders and the public at large; to pay satisfactory, steadily increasing dividends (instead of more lucrative but erratic ones); to settle more easily with unions; to avoid risky decisions; and in general to maintain a public image of competence by the avoidance of criticism and controversy. Thus it is not only survival and maintenance of the organization that matters here, but survival and maintenance of the power configuration—of the Closed System.

The final systems goal is that of control of the environment. And the striving for such control amounts to a virtual obsession in many Closed Systems, almost on a par with the goal of growth: "...instead of efforts at efficiency, there are efforts at 'efficiency of control' " (McNeil 1978; p. 69). Why should an organization with a Passive External Coalition, in essence with an environment that does not seek to control it, in turn seek to control its environment? The reasons are obvious. The line between controlling and being controlled can be fine, at least in the minds of those who administer so vulnerable a power configuration. Actions to control the environment may have been how they created the Closed System in the first place. Such actions become habit forming. More importantly, no matter how it came to be, the whole power arrangement is predicated on the External Coalition remaining passive. That is absolutely crucial.

The organization need not confront its external influencers directly to pacify them. It can take defensive actions, to avoid them. For example, it can diversify, since this reduces its dependence on any one market or set of trading associates. And it can try to finance internally, from slack, to reduce its dependence on lenders and investors. Even by growing, the organization reduces external influence, since the larger the organization, the more diffuse its ownership is likely to be, the greater its market power, and the more difficult it is to penetrate and control.

But these defensive actions are apparently insufficient for many Closed Systems, since they commonly take offensive ones as well. To ensure a Passive EC—as well to guarantee the environmental stability their machine bureaucratic procedures require—many Closed Systems act aggressively to bring parts of their environment under their own control. The actions they can take, as we saw in Chapter 16 in our review of the Pfeffer and Salancik (1978) text, are numerous. Closed Systems often integrate vertically to absorb their suppliers and customers, and they provide many of their own services in their support staffs, rather than buying them on the open market. Some establish cartels, others form trade associations, to collude in one way or another with their competitors, while some develop reciprocal trading arrangements with associates. Many manage demand for their products through mass media advertising, and lobby with politicians to ensure favorable legislation. At the limit—we shall see examples of this later—Closed System have been known to buy themselves from their owners, so that they need never again bother with the legal prerogatives of ownership. Of course, the more of these things that they do, the more the Closed Systems' ostensible quest for autonomy comes to look like a lust for power.

Thus the goal system of this configuration shows how closed a system it really is. It is obsessed with its own growth and with controlling others; it is sensitive to attack but will fight with great vigor any attempt to open it up to serious external influence; it treats efficiency—likely to be a primary goal of its owners, clients, and the public alike—as a secondary constraint. Ultimately the Closed System exists not to provide some product or service, but to serve itself. The mission is the means; the conservation and strength of the system is the end. From the perspective of society, this is the configuration that most profoundly inverts means and ends.

THE EXTERNAL COALITION: PASSIVE (AND PACIFIED)

As noted repeatedly, the key feature of the External Coalition of this configuration is its passiveness. Typically, the organization is widely held, that is, owned by many individuals who, because they are widely dispersed, do not, and often cannot, communicate with each other independently of the management. The stockholders of the widely held corporation, for example, typically act not as influencers—as owners entitled to the surpluses—but as suppliers of capital who expect no more than an acceptable return on their investment.

Other external influencers remain passive, too, sometimes because the organization does not much matter to them, but often because the large size and the attitude of the organization impede any efforts to control it. It just isn't worth trying. Even big government can hesitate: "The Federal Communications Commission confesses it is not big enough to investigate the telephone company's long-distance rate structure. Who is big enough?" asks Bruckner. "There are now hundreds of businesses, and banks, which have simply extended themselves beyond the sovereignties of nations and thus, in effective ways, beyond the reach of national laws and controls" (1972; p. 11). Like any organization, the Closed System must respond to social norms and some formal

constraints, and perhaps to the occasional pressure campaign as well. But otherwise it is independent, a "sovereign state" to borrow the title of a book about one
commercial giant (Sampson 1973).

The board of the Closed System does not exercise a control function. Indeed, as we saw in Chapter 6, the flow of informal power in the widely held corporation is the exact reverse of what is specified by law: The directors are
selected by the CEO; it is *they* who sit at *his* discretion. But if the board does not
control, it can still be used as a tool *of* the organization, particularly to create a
legitimate front for it. This can help avoid certain embarrasing questions. "After
all, if General Goldbuttons is on their board, he must be keeping an eye on
them." In fact he probably is not; he was likely chosen, and is remunerated,
because he is not only well known but also cooperative—good window dressing
to hide the fact that the system is closed to external influence. Sometimes even
this is unnecessary. The organization names a so-called "inside board," one that
precludes representatives of the External Coalition altogether, and, as we saw in
Chapter 6, renders the board the ultimate facade. The pure inside board is no
longer possible in most large American business corporations, due to stock
market requirements for outside directors, but it lives on in spirit:

> Last year one of the largest petroleum companies solicited my proxy for the annual
> meeting for which this slate had been nominated: the CEO, seven senior officers,
> the ex-CEO, two lawyers whose firms together had received more than $800,000 in
> fees from the company in 1973, and a single truly outside director. (Chandler 1975;
> p. 75)[1]

Boards such as these serve only one purpose: to demonstrate precisely the
nature of the configuration of power.

THE INTERNAL COALITION:
BUREAUCRATIC AND AUTONOMOUS

The Internal Coalitions of the Instrument and Closed System are rather
similar, since both are Machine Bureaucracies. In both, a good deal of the power
remains within the System of Authority, expecially with the senior management, which relies on bureaucratic standards of work and output as the prime
means of influence. Both tend to discourage expertise as a threat to authority.
Also in both, material inducements are used to evoke the involvement of the
employees, so that organizational ideology has difficulty establishing itself.

But the differences between the two, though subtle, should not be ignored.
Our discussion will highlight those differences, assuming that otherwise the

---

[1]Dooley (1969) finds that as the proportion of insiders increases, the frequency of board interlocks
decreases, a further indication of the closed nature of the system.

description of the Internal Coalition of the Instrument applies to the Closed System as well.

Earlier we argued that the presence of external control serves to increase the degrees of centralization and bureaucratization of an organization. The most important difference between these two configurations is that the *absence* of external control in the Closed System renders it somewhat less centralized and less bureaucratic than the Instrument. In some sense, the CEO here picks up a form of power he lacks in the Instrument, namely personalized power. With no external influencer overseeing his activities and worrying about his power, the CEO is able to exercise a certain degree of personal control over his subordinates. But in a broader sense, the CEO looses more power than he gains, for the centralizing effect of external influence is gone. No one outside the organization is acting to draw its internal power up to its apex. So, paradoxically, while the CEO of the Closed System has more *personal* power than his counterpart in the Instrument, and more *absolute* power—because the organization he leads itself has considerable power to do as it wishes—he has less *relative* power in the Internal Coalition. In effect, the absence of a dominant external influencer gives him more room to maneuver, but also forces him to share a greater proportion of that room with other insiders. Remember that in this power configuration the CEO acts not as the trustee of some external influencer, but as the leader of the internal influencers in pursuit of their own self interests. The result, compared with the Instrument, is a slightly weaker System of Authority (and of bureaucratic control in particular)—though dominant nonetheless—and a stronger System of Politics. With a substantial pool of rewards up for grabs in the Internal Coalition, there is more incentive to play political games to gain a share of it.

Who gains power at the expense of the CEO? Above all the administrators do, notably the staff analysts and the line managers. First, as in the Instrument, come the analysts of the technostructure. Here they operationalize the goal system around which all the insiders coalesce. Because they carry out this critical function, the analysts gain a good deal of informal power in the Internal Coalition, somewhat more than their colleagues in the Instrument.

Second are the managers of the middle line. The absence of external control, with its centralizing effect, causes more power to filter down the entire length of the managerial hierarchy. Part of this power is formal, as delegated authority, and part is informal, appearing in the form of the political games the line managers are able to play. Empire building is an especially popular game in the middle line of the Closed System, because it represents one of the most natural ways to grab a share of the available rewards. Indeed, this game is fully compatible with the emphasis on growth as the primary goal, since the pressure for unit growth encourages organizational growth and vice versa. Whereas in the Instrument the external influencer waits at the gates to siphon off the surpluses, in the Closed System the line managers are busy inside absorbing the surpluses by building empires. We can say that the line managers here need not so much distort objectives as suboptimize in their pursuit of them.

Thus Pondy (1969) found in his research that as the management of corporations became increasingly separated from its ownership, the ratio of administrative to operating personnel increased. This he took to signify that the line managers were increasingly able to build empires: "The central idea of the theory is that the number of administrative personnel employed in an organization is *chosen* so as to maximize the achievement of goals of the dominant management coalition" (p. 47).

But while there can be a greater diffusion of power through the middle line of this configuration, it remains far from evenly distributed. The system of bureaucratic controls still predominates in the Internal Coalition, which means that the jobs of the managers at lower levels in the line hierarchy get somewhat institutionalized, and therefore weakened. Moreover, with the propensity to grow large and diversify into different markets to protect their autonomy, many Closed Systems are consequently encouraged to divisionalize their structures—that is, to divide themselves into quasi-independent units, each charged with performing all the functions necessary to serve one distinct market.[2] This requires the delegation of considerable power to the manager of each division, subject only to the control of its overall performance. Each of these managers, then, emerges as a kind of mini-CEO. As we saw in the case of the subsidiary in the last chapter, the divisions become the effective Instruments of the headquarters, which means that each tends to emerge as a centralized Machine Bureaucracy ruled by its manager who operationalizes the goals imposed upon him from above. Thus, in the Closed System that is divisionalized, as many are, one set of managers high in the middle line gains a good deal of power at the expense of all those below.

For the manager of a division of a Closed System, empire building is manifested primarily in the form of the budgeting game. In a structure where the relationship between the strategic apex and the senior line management is governed largely in impersonal terms, power is gained by receiving as large an allotment of the financial resources as possible, and then making sure that all of it is spent or at least hidden within the division as slack. Where the line managers are instead organized on a functional basis—in the absence of divisionalization or below the level of division manager—budgeting games are typically supplemented by ones of strategic candidates. In other words, empires are built first by promoting projects that enhance the importance of the function; only then can claims be made for increases in staff, facilities, and equipment.

The ultimate prize of the empire builder in the Closed System is, of course, the position of the CEO itself. And this position is inevitably reserved for an insider, since that is the surest way to keep the system closed:

---

[2]This relationship between diversification and divisionalization—well supported in the research— was discussed at length in the *Structuring* book (Mintzberg 1979a, pp.278-81, 393-97). Later in the chapter we shall see why the Divisionalized Form is more likely to be a Closed System than an Instrument.

> Management is a self-perpetuating group. Responsibility to the body of stockholders is for all practical purposes a dead letter. Each generation of managers recruits its own successors and trains, grooms, and promotes them according to its own standards and values. (Baron and Sweezy 1966; p. 16)

And with that prize dangling before everyone's eyes, two other political games gain popularity. One is sponsorship, a way up to the top or at least to bigger and better things. And for those passed over, there is always the possibility of the young Turks game, in the form of coup d'etat. It makes little sense to try to overthrow the CEO of the Instrument, who is named by the dominant external influencer. But in the Closed System, much like in the communist state (which, we shall soon argue, acts like a giant Closed System), there is no power higher than the top management, and no provision made for succession other than one CEO naming the next. But being highly bureaucratic and closed to external influence, Closed Systems tend to lose touch with their environments and resist change. And the CEO who has led the resistance will hardly appoint a radical to succeed him. And so young Turks who believe the organization must change are predisposed to trying to overthrow the holders of authority while, of course, keeping the System of Authority intact for their own use. In other words, it is change in strategy or in players they promote, not change in power configuration. What political game could be more natural for the change agents or the power hungry of the Closed System than coup d'etat?

Line versus staff is another popular political game in the Closed System, more so than in the Instrument. Here again, because the structure is machine bureaucratic, the line-staff distinction is maintained. But since both line managers and staff analysts have more power and discretion in the Closed System, they are inclined to battle more often and more openly.

The operators of the Closed System, as of the Instrument, find themselves at the bottom of the structure, with little expertise and the full weight of the bureaucratic controls upon them. But they too, are better off here. After all, they must also be accommodated in the distribution of rewards, that is to say, receive greater benefits than economic factors alone would dictate. The operators work within the system, and many well know what the other insiders are getting. Denied their share, they can make trouble. As individuals they may be powerless. But collectively, as we noted in Chapter 9, they are the action takers of the organization. Working in concert, they control the organization's most critical function—its workflow. When they are willing to make the effort, through various forms of insurgency, they can bring the organization to a halt. Far worse from the perspective of the management, they can engage in the whistle-blowing game, thereby calling into question the legitimacy of the whole power configuration.

Thus the operators too must be paid off, collectively—in generous wages and fringe benefits as well as special deals, such as rules of promotion by seniority. As Galbraith notes in his theory of countervailing power, "there are strong unions in the United States only where markets are served by strong corporations. . . . [such unions] share in the fruits of the corporation's market power" (1952; p. 122). And Monsen and Downs (1965; p. 223) conclude, as we saw earlier, that it is the top managers of the widely held business firms who most readily make concessions to the labor unions. After all, it is the system's money that they are giving away, not their own or that of some dominant external influencer.[3]

In general, then, the Internal Coalition of the Closed System experiences somewhat more political activity than that of the Instrument. but the System of Authority remains predominant, so that the most popular political games are those that coexist with or occasionally perhaps challenge authority, not those that substitute for it. Thus, while most of the political games discussed in Chapter 13 are played in this configuration, a few—such as rival camps and perhaps alliance building—are less common.

FORMS OF THE CLOSED SYSTEM

As another form of Machine Bureaucracy, the Closed System is found under many of the same conditions as the Instrument—namely, a simple, stable environment, a simple and regulating technical system, typically mass output in nature, and an unskilled work force. The main difference is that in the Closed System, external power is dispersed and unorganized. Moreover, there is evidence that Instruments tend to convert to Closed Systems as they grow large, integrate their operations vertically, and diversify their markets.

The general growth of the organization is discussed by Pfeffer and Salancik (1978) as a means to bring the environment under control. In their terms, growth "alters organizational interdependence"; in ours, it pacifies the External Coalition. It stands to reason that the larger an organization, the greater the number of owners and associates it is likely to have and the less likely any one of them will be able to dominate its External Coalition or come to grips with its internal workings. As Zald (1969; p. 104) notes, in the small organization, directors are able to comprehend the market situation and to maintain personal contact with the employees at different levels; in the large ones, they become dependent on the top management for their information, and so become subject to manipulation.

Growth may take a variety of forms—expansion in existing markets, vertical integration to take control of the markets of associates, and horizontal

[3]Collective payoff means that the workers gain most of their power in the External Coalition through their unions. But by no stretch of the imagination can the unions be called dominant in that coalition. Their efforts are generally restricted to getting greater financial remuneration and perhaps imposing certain changes in work processes for the benefit of the workers. Attempts to involve the workers more deeply in decision making—through what is known as industrial democracy—as well as the reasons why we believe such attempts usually fail to increase the workers' power significantly, will be discussed in Chapter 27.

diversification into new markets. All three forms can be shown to help pacify the External Coalition. When it expands, the organization becomes more dominant in its own markets—at the limit it becomes a monopolist or monopsonist—and so gains power at the expense of its associates. This point is presented forcefully by John Kenneth Galbraith (1967) in *The New Industrial State*. He describes the giant corporation as an independent state that controls its environment through planning systems which are made self-confirming by the corporation's ability to manage demand through mass advertising and the like. Such organizations are, in Galbraith's view, controlled by their "technostructures," a term he uses to designate not only their analysts (as we do), but their line managers and other staff specialists as well.

In the case of vertical integration, the organization literally takes control of its direct suppliers or clients, converting potential external influencers into subordinates. As for horizontal diversification, Pfeffer and Salancik provide evidence that conglomerate acquisitions are made for growth not profit—indeed sometimes at the expense of profit. This suggests that such diversification serves the managers, not the owners. Moyer (1970) in fact makes this point directly, arguing that conglomerate acquisitions, by bringing different firms under one umbrella, restrict the shareholders' choices in the stock market and impede their ability to inform themselves about the different businesses they hold (since the conglomerate can report a consolidated statement). Such acquisitions often also force the shareholders to pay a premium which they would not incur if they diversified their own portfolios instead. But most significantly, Moyer concludes that the conglomerate acquisition or merger serves to pacify the owners as influencers in the External Coalition.

> In general, the impact of a merger is to increase the diffusion of ownership in the surviving firm. Quasi-ownership capital instruments have been shown to be of great importance in large mergers. The near term effect of the use of these instruments is the surrender of voting power by the acquired firm's stockholders to the stockholders of the acquiring firm. As these instruments are converted, voting power becomes increasingly diffused among a larger and larger group of stockholders. (P. 29)

All of this suggests that the *large, widely held corporation,* especially the *diversified firm,* is the classic example of the Closed System, as we have already seen in the examples used repeatedly in this chapter. That the vast majority of the large American corporations—the Fortune 500—are vertically integrated and especially diversified has been well established (Wrigley 1970; Rumelt 1974). That their External Coalitions have become passive has been a more hotly debated point, but one whose opponents have lost a lot of ground over the years.

As far back as 1918, observers were noting that "the entreprise assumes an independent life, as if it belonged to no one" (Walter Rathenau, quoted in Berle and Means 1968; p. 309). But it was in 1932, when Berle and Means published the first edition of their famous *The Modern Corporation and Private Property* to show that managers have wrested control from the owners in many of America's largest corporations, that the debate really heated up.

> Men are less likely to own the physical instruments of production. They are more likely to own pieces of paper, loosely known as stocks, bonds, and other securities, which have become mobile through the machinery of the public markets. Beneath this, however, lies a more fundamental shift. Physical control over the instruments of production has been surrendered in ever growing degree to centralized groups who manage property in bulk, supposedly, but by no means necessarily, for the benefit of the security holders. Power over industrial property has been cut off from the beneficial ownership of this property. (1968; p. 8)

The debate about who is in control has raged furiously since 1932. But it has largely been one of degree—not whether management control exists but how encompassing it is. And time has favored Berle and Means. When they published the revised edition of their book, they found by the measures they used that management control had increased from 44 percent of the two hundred largest U.S. corporations in 1929 to 85 percent of them in 1963. Only five of the firms were found to have majority ownership and only eighteen to have minority owner control.[4]

All kinds of other evidence has accumulated about the closed nature of the widely held corporation. For example, one study of all 5,995 directors of the Fortune 500 in 1977 found that only 1.6 percent of them represented major shareholder interests (Smith 1978). Indeed a survey of 855 corporations (Bacon 1973; p. 40) found that 84 percent of them did not even formally require their directors to hold any stock at all![5] In Chapter 6 we saw examples of the inside board—the ultimate facade—and now we read of outside boards that seem no better. Consider that of Coca Cola, as reported by Smith (1978; p. 153). There were fourteen "outsiders" on the sixteen-person board, including three retired officers as well as one's brother, a retired partner from one of the company's investment banks, two commercial bankers who do business with the company as well as the retired chairman of one of these banks, and a vice-president of a univeristy that has received substantial contributions from the company over the years.

Elsewhere we read comments from directors that

> When I go to the board meetings of the three companies I serve, that is not my property. I don't own more than 100 shares, and when I go along with the management's request for approval of new leases on executive space on upper

---

[4]The later study defined minority owner control as 10 percent of the stock in single hands; the earlier study had used a cutoff figure of 20 percent. Note that another eight firms in the 1963 study were defined as controlled by a "legal device."

[5]Although four hundred of them did have "an informal expectation" (p. 40). But these expectations, like the formal requirements, were almost always for the ownership of one hundred shares or less.

Third Avenue, or for approval of a larger jet airplane, I am not behaving as a trustee or an owner. (quoted in Mace 1971; p. 64)

We hear of the generally accepted "taboo" that "outside directors must not deal directly with management personnel except with the chief executive's knowledge and consent" (Bacon and Brown 1975; p. 26). More blatantly, we read the finding that "If a director feels that he has any basis for doubts and disapproval [of the management], most of the presidents interviewed believe that he should resign" (Mace 1971; p. 188).

The American corporation has certainly come a long way from the days when the very word "corporation" referred to that organizational form in which a board of directors controlled the management! But this is not an exclusively American phenomena. In Canada, we find that the Sun Life Assurance Company has bought back all of its shares, making its policyholders its ostensible owners and thereby achieving the widest conceivable diffusion of ownership. And then there were those executives of another firm who sought to stop a takeover bid by voting in their own interests company stock held by a subsidiary, until an Ontario court quashed that idea. In effect, the managers were trying to keep their Closed System from becoming an Instrument by using ownership to fight the owners!

While the giant, widely held corporation may be the most evident form of the Closed System power configuration in Western society, it is certainly not the only one. In fact, virtually any organization whose conditions call for it to be an Instrument but whose external influencers fail to organize to control it tends to revert to a Closed System. We have, for example, the fund-raising agency free of external control that becomes increasingly charitable to itself—giving its administrators lush salaries, plush offices, generous expense accounts, and so on. We also have the closely held corporation that acts as if it were widely held because its owners, having inherited their shares through two or three generations, do not care to control it (Mace 1971). Likewise, though on a more temporary basis, we have the subsidiary controlled by a parent too busy with its own difficulties to care about its Instruments. Then there is the "little fish," discussed in Chapter 7, the subsidiary or agency so inconsequential to its parent that it is free to act as a Closed System so long as it brings no attention to itself. Only the big fish merit close surveillance, as Instruments.

In these cases, we have a dominant external influencer who for one reason or another fails to exercise control of the organization. A Closed System can also emerge when a number of conflicting external influencers, who ostensibly form a Divided EC, become so embroiled in their own politics that none is able to exercise any significant influence over the Internal Coalition. The External Coalition becomes effectively passive, the administrators seize the power, and the configuration becomes a Closed System.

A very different, but nonetheless important form of the Closed System frequently occurs in *large volunteer organizations*, whose members elect their leaders. Designed to be Missionaries—mutual benefit associations to serve some mission important to the members—they end up serving themselves as systems instead. This is the situation Michels (1915) describes in European revolutionary political parties and trade unions at the turn of the century. Observing how the leaders of these organizations, which were ostensibly committed to social reform and democratic principles, came to be more concerned with maintaining their own power inside the organizations than with achieving social power for the organizations, Michels proposed his "universally appliable" "iron law of oligarchy": "oligarchy is, as it were, a preordained form of the common life of great social aggregates" (p. 390). Michels concluded that "We find everywhere electors and elected. And we find everwhere that the power of the elected leaders over the electing masses is almost unlimited" (p. 401). Only in the small organization can everyone be kept involved and the leaders responsive to the members. As the organization grows large, the members become indifferent; those with leadership skills gain power and hold it; as new members with such skills emerge, the established leaders either coopt them or else purge them.

Michels' description may seem to resemble our Autocracy, but it is in fact much closer to our Closed System, because by leaders he seems to mean the administrators as a group, not just the chief executive officer. And he describes bureaucratic rule by these administrators, not personal rule. (Autocracy means personal rule by the CEO; Closed System means bureaucratic rule by an implicit alliance of all the administrators.) Thus we see in Michels' description of his "oligarchy" many of the features of our Closed System: organization as "an end" in itself, a smoothly functioning "machine" (p. 373), "a state within a state" (p. 394); the propensity to build up the size of the machine for its own sake; and the "need of a vast organization whose central strength is found in a trusted and stable bureaucracy, the members of which are well paid" (p. 394). So when Michels writes, "Who says organization, says oligarchy," he means that when the external members elect the leaders of the organization, they lose control to these leaders and the administrative bureaucracies they build. In the words of Jenkins: "an increase in the number of members is argued to lead inevitably to an increase in the number of administrators. Ultimately the effect is to transfer effective control over policy from members to officers and professional staff" (1976, p. 569). And "the principle cause," in Michel's view, "is to be found in the technical indispensibility of leadership" (1915, p. 400). At first leadership arises "spontaneously," and is provided gratuitously. But soon it becomes "professional" and "irremovable" (pp. 400–401).[6]

It is not only the administrators who can take an intended Missionary and convert it to a Closed System. When the members of a small volunteer organization, which they manage themselves, displace its ideology in favor of their own parochial needs, a form of Closed System can be considered to have emerged. For example, when holding office or gathering to socialize becomes more impor-

---

[6]In the next chapter, we shall discuss other kinds of unions and volunteer organizations that do in fact give rise to Autocracy. And in the chapter after that, we shall see some that manage to be Missionaries, as intended.

tant in a charity organization or a church than serving the poor or finding salvation, then we have an organization functioning to serve its own insiders—the essential characteristics of the Closed System.

These organizations are designed to be something else but emerge as Closed Systems. What seems like a Closed System but in fact emerges as something else is what Goffman (1961) calls the "total institution." As we saw earlier, by this he means the organization whose members live and work within its boundaries, such as orphanages, prisons, mental hospitals, ships, and monasteries. Such institutions are certainly closed in the physical sense. But in terms of power, some are very open—as we saw in Chapter 17, the Instruments of a society that wishes to put people away. And others, as we shall see in Chapter 21, are more accurately described as Missionaries—united by ideologic norms rather than bureaucratic rules.

But another kind of organization that is supposed to be an Instrument often emerges as a Closed System, much as does the corporation that grows large. This is the *large, powerful government department* around whose mission strong social consensus does not tend to form. When Dwight David Eisenhower, a president who himself came out of the military, complained at the end of eight years in the White House about the "military-industrial complex," he was suggesting that the Pentagon he knew so well had become, in concert with its giant suppliers, a system largely closed to external, political control. And we see a repeat of such occurrences in a great many other government departments.

The final and ultimate example of the Closed System might be *large government* itself. The communist state in particular seems to fit all of the characteristics of this power configuration. It has no dominant external influencer (at least the Soviet Union does not; its European "satellites" are so called because they seem to be its Instruments). And the population to which it is ostensibly responsible remains largely passive. Its election procedures, in offering an effective choice of one, resemble those of the directors of the widely held American corporation. The structure of the government is heavily bureaucratic, with a single hierarchy of authority and a very elaborate technostructure.[7] Indeed the economy is essentially set up as one giant, all-encompassing Divisionalized Form, with the industries and plants, as divisions, subject to extensive systems of performance control. All significant resources are the property of the state—the collective system—not the individual. And as in other Closed Systems, the administrators take the lion's share of the benefits:

> . . .far from increased productivity benefiting the majority, increases in productive capacity primarily benefit the bureaucracy itself. In the case of the Soviet Union, the standard of living of the bureaucracy has risen far more than that of any other group, and its tendency is to go higher still. . . .the gap in standard of living and

---

[7]As Worthy notes, Frederick Taylor's "Scientific Management has had its fullest flowering" not in America but in Soviet Russia (1959, p. 77).

status between the top and the bottom of the Russian social structure is far greater than in the United States and, even more significant, it is growing...(Constas 1961–62, p. 294).[8]

But the Western reader should not get too smug, because Western "democracy" shows similar tendencies. In France, for example, democracy means in part the right to elect the Président de la République every seven years, and the deputees of the National Assembly. Assuming the voter is not excessivley manipulated by the media campaigns, he or she has a real choice. But that may not make much difference, just as the right to elect directors of the corporate board makes little difference to the factory worker (as we shall see in Chapter 27). For the French citizen's life too is regulated importantly by a heavy bureaucracy over which he or she has little direct control. In the words of France's best-known organization theorist, who looks at his country as an organization in an article entitled "Why is France Blocked?":

> As a nation, we have gone to the end point of centralization, to a point where we are now completely jammed in a system where we all crush each other. Our present administrative system is characterized by a whole set of hierarchical dependence chains, through which national, regional, and local power is exercised. (Crozier 1974, p. 49)

It is not the nationally elected deputy who affects the French citizen's daily life so much as the local civil servant who serves in a straight chain of authority many levels below the president. The bureaucracy can be so thick that even the president's most powerful ministers are sometimes unable to penetrate it (Theonig and Fredberg 1976). For example, the education system employs about 1 million individuals all reporting up to one central ministry in Paris. Likewise the telephone, postal, and electricity systems are single massive bureaucracies for the entire nation, whose employees are not always civil nor servants. In other words, not only the whole government, but important parts of it emerge as Closed Systems. In addition, the president appoints directly the ninety-six department prefects, that office closest to state governor in the United States or provincial premier in Canada, except that in France it is charged with implementing the laws and rules set by Paris. The prefect, too, heads an extensive bu-

---

[8]On the day that Alexei Kosygin, Chairman of the USSR Council of Ministers, died, a Canadian diplomat who knew him was interviewed on the CBC radio network. Kosygin reminded him of an American businessman more than the head of a totalitarian state, he said, obviously having been surprised at the revelation. He need not have been. The Soviet Union is organized much like a large American business, and, conversely, as we have seen in this chapter, in many fundamental respects the large American business is managed internally much like a totalitarian state (which is defined in the Random House Dictionary as "absolute control by the state or a governing branch of a highly centralized institution").

reaucracy. Thus, "there is no intermediate power with sufficient authority to take risks and demonstrate initiative" (Crozier, p. 49).[9]

Thus, as shown in Figure 19–2, the individual French citizen—the "sovereign" of the "democratic" society—shoulders the weight of an immense and incredibly complex bureaucracy. How is he to reconcile its closed nature with the

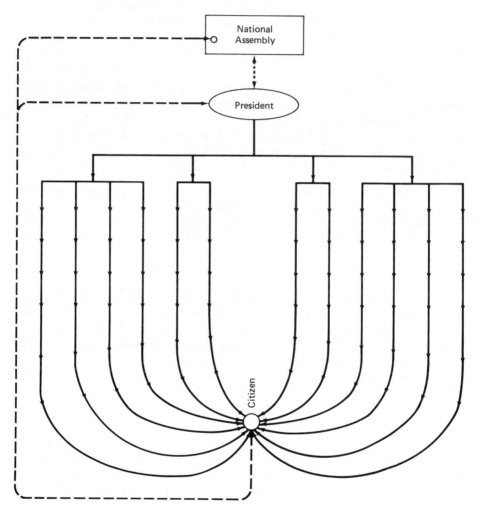

Figure 19–2. *Closed System "Democracy"*
Note: See footnote 9, below for a change introduced in 1981

[9]Mayors are elected, but with so much power remaining in the central hierarchy, their discretion is highly circumscribed: ". . . all technical experts to whom local authorities have to appeal are tied either directly or indirectly to the hierarchy of the civil service" (Crozier, p. 49). Charges promised by the Mitterand government and passed by the National Assembly, however, just as this book was going to press (mid-1981), introduce regional councils indirectly elected by the population. Whether this will seriously reverse almost two hundred years of steadily increasing concentration of power in the central government remains to be seen.

fact that somehow, somewhere, perched on top of it all sits the man he elected to control it?

The English-speaking democracies are not there yet. They tend to have smaller, more dispersed public services (with parts of them, like some telephone systems, in private hands). And they elect more types of officials, such as state governors or provincial premiers and school boards. As shown in Figure 19–3,

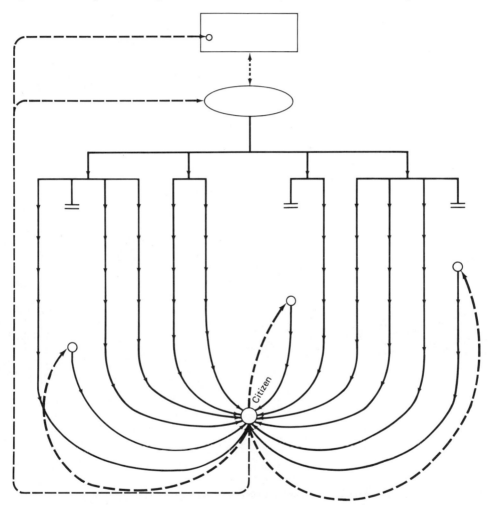

Figure 19–3. *Breaking the Chain of Authority to Open the System*

these have the effect of breaking the chain of authority at intermediate levels, opening the hierarchy up to public influence. But similar trends exist in these democracies, too. Indeed, there are those who see government in these societies not as the Instrument of the people, but as a coalition of politicians, civil servants, and related interest groups intent on enlarging the size of the public sector.

They see them doing so to build their own empires, much as the administrators of the Closed System promote its growth to increase the pie they share. When government as a Closed System combines with private organizations as Closed Systems—as in the military-industrial complex Eisenhower talked about—then it is the citizens outside these systems, like the members outside Michels' oligarchies, who ultimately suffer.[10]

---

[10]Another form of government as Closed System emerges—more direct, but less pervasive—when the elected representatives, perhaps intent on serving the public, get so caught up in their own politics that they lose control of the civil service which can then do what it likes. (This is a special case of a situation discussed earlier.) In our terms, the legislature as External Coalition (comparable to a board of directors) transcends a state of division to become effectively passive, and civil servants, the administrators of the Internal Coalition, seize the power. We see this, for example, in minority governments in the parliamentary system, not designed for this eventuality, or in the disarray of the Fourth Republic in France or in today's Italy, unfortunately designed, it would seem, to maximize political conflict.

20

The Autocracy

A SOLO PERFORMANCE

Starring: The Chief Executive Officer.

Synopsis of Solo: The CEO emerges as the only center of power, controlling the Internal Coalition personally, to the exclusion of all other forms of power; bureaucratic procedures and politics can be virtually eliminated from the Internal Coalition, while expertise is discouraged and ideology allowed to develop only to the extent that it revolves around the CEO and reflects his or her beliefs; the External Coalition is Passive, and if it shows signs of becoming active, the inclination of the CEO is to take the organization to another part of the environment, where external influencers can be avoided; hence this configuration experiences the least flow of power between the two coalitions; the goals of the organization are whichever the CEO chooses to impose on it, operational or not, mission and survival often being prominent ones.

Now Playing: Most commonly in small organizations operating in simple but dynamic niches, typically organizations with little visibility (and for all these reasons precarious), the classic case being the entrepreneurial firm; also in almost all young organizations as well as many older ones still led by their founders; finally in almost any kind of organization facing a severe crisis or led by a very strong-willed individual, as in many of the American "bread and butter" unions during their growing years as well as in dictatorial regimes.

In moving from the Instrument to the Closed System, we saw a partial truncation of the power system, specifically the virtual elimination of that component above the CEO. Here, we see a further truncation, the effective elimination of that component below the CEO. Our third power configuration is characterized by a Passive EC and a Personalized IC: The one individual who is left—the chief executive officer—rules the entire power system absolutely, as an Autocracy, as implied in Figure 20-1.[1]

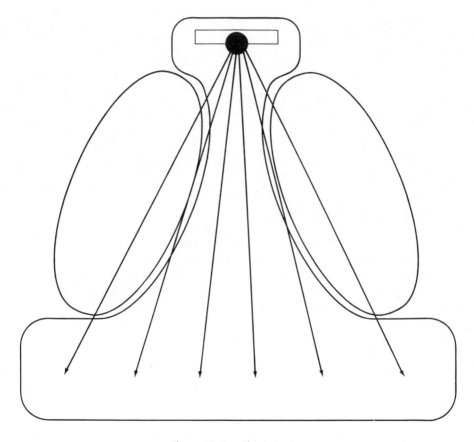

Figure 20-1.   *The Autocracy*

[1]The word *Autocracy* was chosen because it best describes this configuration of power—"uncontrolled or unlimited authority over others, vested in a single person," according to the Random House Dictionary. The more pejorative meaning of the word is not intended, nor is the CEO necessarily implied to be an "autocrat," as that word is often used. An alternative, more neutral term for this configuration was "Monocracy," but was not used because, being little known, it would have introduced an additional measure of jargon to the book.

CONDITIONS THAT FAVOR PERSONALIZED
LEADERSHIP

To be able to discuss the power distribution in the Autocracy, we must first understand how such a power system arises. Sometimes the presence of a powerful leader is sufficient—someone who can pacify the External Coalition and rule the Internal Coalition with an iron hand. Other times it is a severe crisis that drive an organization this way, at least temporarily. When an organization is threatened with survival, no matter what its natural configuration of power, its influencers tend to defer to its leader so that he can set things right. The external influencers suspend their demands—what is the use of pressuring a system that may collapse and deny them anything in the future—while the internal influencers set aside their bureaucratic procedures, political games, and so on. Thus Hamblin (1958) shows that under laboratory conditions of crisis, the group will centralize its power in the hands of its leader, at least long enough to give him a chance to try to deal with it.

But under normal conditions—no crises, ordinary leaders—one prime condition that gives rise to Autocracy is an environment that is dynamic yet simple to comprehend. A dynamic environment calls for an organization that is flexible and responsive. Bureaucratic controls must be avoided for their rigidity, as must an excessive reliance on ideology, steeped as it is in tradition. And when that environment is also simple, one individual can easily comprehend it. So the most effective way to ensure flexibility and responsiveness is to centralize power in the hands of a single individual, most obviously the CEO, and then allow that individual to control the Internal Coalition personally. The Autocracy is, therefore, the Simple Structure introduced in our *Structuring* book.

Two other conditions associated with Autocracy are youth and small size. Almost all organizations have to rely on strong leaders to get them started, hence new organizations are almost inevitable founded as Autocracies, and remain so at least until they become established. In fact, as we shall see later, many retain this configuration so long as their founding leaders remain in office. As for small size, it is in the small organization that personalized authority is most effective, since one individual is able to maintain direct contact with everyone else. Only when the organization grows large must the organization turn to more impersonal forms of communication and control. Of course, youth and small size fit naturally with simple, dynamic environments. That is to say, organizations tend to begin their lives with small operations in those kinds of environments—specifically in dynamic but easily understood niches in the market. Here is where their strong leaders can retain personal control yet avoid confronting the larger, more established bureaucracies. As we saw in our discussion of the Instrument and Closed System, the latter tend to seek out more stable environments.

All of this suggests another characteristic often associated with

Autocracy: precariousness. Small size and location in a market niche make an organization precarious in the economic sense. Combining this with power centralized in the hands of the chief executive makes the organization precarious in another, more important sense. There is no one around to protect it when it falters. All the characteristics of Autocracy serve to discourage external influence. That has the positive effect of bringing a certain independence to the organization. But it has a corresponding negative effect. Just as the external influencers do not bother the organization, so too do they not bother about it. If the organization is one of little visibility, and, at that, the instrument of its chief executive, then it just isn't worth worrying about when it is in trouble. Thus, while the U.S. government cannot possibly let a Penn Central go under, it does not even notice when a Lionel, the maker of toy trains, almost does.

Hence autocracy—among the most autonomous of our power configurations, certainly the one in which there is the least flow of power between the two coalitions—pays a price for its independence. When the organization has problems no one is there to jump to its aid. Even the insiders, who should have some commitment to it by virtue of their full-time status, may hesitate because they have never been given any real responsibility. Morever they are few in number and weak in power. Years of personalized rule can render them unorganized and unmotivated. The CEO is the only one who really cares—he has made his bed and in it he must lie.

This makes the Autocracy precarious for a third reason. Power is so concentrated that when the CEO falters, for whatever reason, there is no natural means of succession. In the Instrument, the dominant influencer stands ready to replace the CEO. In the Closed System, a corps of ambitious line managers stand ready to take over his job themselves. Sometimes they even give him a little nudge. And as we shall see in our discussions of the other configurations, each has equivalent people ready and willing to take over. But none is there in the Autocracy, with the result that when the CEO becomes incapacitated or, worse, becomes so wedded to his strategy that he cannot perceive the need to change it, the very survival of the organization becomes threatened.

We referred to precariousness, or more exactly vulnerability, in our discussion of the Closed System, too. But note the fundamental difference. The Closed System appears to be vulnerable as a *power configuration*, on grounds of legitimacy. But as we described its conditions—large, bureaucratic, powerful—the organization itself is far from precarious. In Autocracy, it is the *organization* that is precarious. Indeed, compared with the Closed System, the Autocracy power configuration should be rather secure. (That it is not, and that the Closed System, ironically, emerges as rather secure despite its illegitimacy, will be discussed in Chapter 24.) Most people accept Autocracy as a legitimate power configuration (even if in principle they reject the autocratic form of governing as incompatible with democracy), for a number of reasons. First, many Autocracies are owned by the people who control them, and so are considered their legitimate instruments. Second, strong personalized authority can be seen as the only way to establish an organization and to see it through severe crises. And third, it is often this kind of leadership that establishes new and exciting directions in society. Hence, this kind of leadership comes to be highly valued under certain conditions, despite its inconsistency with democratic principles. As Larçon and Reitter note, "legitimacy...is much easier to achieve under a charismatic system," where clearly defined, innovative purpose is embodied not only in the leader, but even in those who willingly follow (1978; p. 6; see also 1979).

With these points in mind, let us now consider the power distribution in this configuration before looking at its goal system and various forms that it can take.

THE POWER DISTRIBUTION: NO DISTRIBUTION

As noted in Chapter 17, external influencers do not take kindly to personalized control of the Internal Coalition. Such control is too tight, too impenetrable, leaving them too little influence. Besides such control makes the organization too precarious. So they tend to look elsewhere when confronted with such an organization, especially if the organization is not a very significant one. If they do not—if they show signs of trying to exert influence in order to render the organization their Instrument—the chief executive will be inclined to try to move the organization away from them, to find another niche that provides greater autonomy. The CEO will certainly fight back when cornered, but his natural inclination is to avoid a confrontation because he knows how small and precarious his organization is.

These characteristics reflect themselves in various forms of passiveness in the External Coalition of the Autocracy. The associates in the organization's chosen markets tend to restrict themselves to straight economic relationships, as do the employee associations, at least when they exist at all. (While few face unions, many of those that do either have "house" unions under the control of their chief executives or else deal with locals that get lumped together in industry-wide negotiations.) Likewise outside owners may not exist—many CEO's owning their own Autocracies—or else may be inactive. And governments and special interest groups tend to pay little attention to the organization.

As a result, the organization experiences few formal constraints, pressure campaigns, or direct controls. And because of its insignificance to outsiders, it is typically far less affected by social norms than other organizations. Its environment is what Rhenman calls "value free"—containing "a minimum number of norms...all of which are of a very general nature, applying to all organizations" (1973; p. 46). And with the minimal flow of power between the two coalitions, in either direction, the board, which is supposed to stand between them, tends often to be no more than a facade, existing only because of legal requirements.

With an External Coalition that passive, all of the power resides in the Internal Coalition. And here it sits in one place, with no significant delegation of formal authority and little chance for centers of informal power—expert or political, even bureaucratic—to arise. One person possesses all the formal authority, controls all the critical functions, and maintains centrality in all of the information flows. That person—the chief executive officer—makes all of the strategic decisions, and ensures their execution through his own personal orders, often given directly to the operators. That person also designs his own information gathering system—based on personal contacts with clients and operators—thereby denying informers and advisors control over the inputs to his decision making.

Thus, through the system of personal control, the CEO maintains absolute power—both formal and informal—in the Internal Coalition. And that, of course, helps keep the structure simple: With the absence of bureaucratic controls and the presence of personal contacts between the CEO and the operators, there is little need for either a technostructure or a middle line. Indeed, personal control becomes self-reinforcing in this structure, driving out other forms of control. Autocracies tend to be run by leaders who abhor the rigidities of bureaucratic control, not to mention the thought of surrendering power to the technocratic analysts who design them. Hence such controls have difficulty establishing themselves, even when they become needed. Likewise, while personal control may arise in the absence of significant expertise in the Internal Coalition, subsequently its presence tends to discourage such expertise when the need for it does arise. Expertise calls for decentralization, which is incompatible with Autocracy. Thus, the operators of Autocracies tend to be unskilled, as do the support staffers, who tend to be few in number in any event since every attempt is made to keep the organization as lean as possible.

As the most power concentrated of all the configurations, Autocracy (together with the Missionary) is the least politicized. With individual control so close, personal, and aboslute, little is to be gained from trying to displace the goals of the leader and to play political games. The choice open to the insiders is essentially one of loyalty or exit, not voice.[2] There are no formal objectives to distort, few external influencers with whom to establish direct links, little opportunity to create informal groups, and, with a simple administrative structure, not much pressure to suboptimize, to invert means and ends, or to engage in the games so popular in the bureaucratic structures, such as line versus staff or empire building. There is room for the building of only one empire in this configuration, that of the chief executive. Insurgency games are risky—challenges to the CEO's power are quickly snuffed out—and young Turks and whistle-blowing games are futile since there is no one but the CEO to listen. Even the strategic candidates game is discouraged by the CEO's tight control of the information needed to make strategic decisions. Sponsorship is perhaps the one game to be expected—to get on the good side of the CEO.

[2]And in line with Hirschman's arguments (1970; p. 84), the possibilities for exit are usually numerous.

Ideology can be a factor in this power configuration, so long as it backs up the power of the CEO. Strong leaders often have charismatic qualities as well as strong beliefs, that is, ideologies of their own. These can attract followers who identify with the leaders' style or sense of mission. The organization, therefore, adopts the ideology of its leader. But there are limits to·the influence of the System of Ideology. Too much ideology can become a threat to personalized power, since it may require a sharing of power. Thus, while the CEO may encourage ideology forming around himself, he discourages it forming around the organization—as an end in itself. And this means that ideology alone cannot induce the necessary contributions from the insiders. They necessarily view this as the CEO's organization, not theirs. They are there to carry out his orders, to serve him. Hence their identification can be weak, so that material forms of inducements are required to secure their efforts.

THE GOALS:
THOSE OF THE LEADER

Obviously, the goals of the Autocracy are those that the CEO chooses to impose on it. He has complete discretion to pursue his own personal goals, whether they be to maximize profit or find excuses to travel. The organization becomes, in effect, an extension of the CEO's own personality.

Despite the wide range of goals possible in the Autocracy, some general comments can nevertheless be made about some that are probable. First, because the organization is an extension of the CEO's personality, its mission often takes the form of a goal. What the organization produces, as well as how it produces it—with what quality, reliability, or innovativeness—can become ends in themselves, viewed by the leader as reflecting directly on himself. As a result, many Autocracies become wedded to particular industries, even single products or services. The CEO in this configuration is not typically a professional manager flitting from one industry to another; he is an individual dedicated to one particular sphere of human endeavor.

Second, because these configurations tend to have strong leaders—people with something to say or do—they often have strong goal systems as well, that is, ones in which a single goal is maximized. Sometimes that goal is unique to the particular organization, such as the perfection of a particular technology or the changing of some aspect of society. Later we shall discuss the example of Hans Isbrandtsen who used his shipping company to fight the U.S. government's support of the international shipping cartel (Perrow, 1970, pp. 157–58).

It should be noted that the goals of the Autocracy, even when strong, need not be operational. That is, the CEO need not express his goals quantitatively in a system of objectives so as to guide other decision makers. Here, after all, there are no other important decision makers. The CEO decides on all of the important issues. The goals need only be clear in his own mind. Thus, nonoperational goals, including social ones, do not get displaced by economic ones in this configuration. Quite the contrary, the fact that the behavior of the organization reflects directly on its leader sometimes sensitizes that person to social issues. And his actions can be decisive in this regard, since only he need be convinced of the value of an issue. Of course, the same forces can work in the opposite direction: the CEO can take a public-be-damned attitude, and it may be well nigh impossible to make him change his mind.

Finally, there is one goal that often emerges as paramount in these organizations—survival. As noted, these tend to be precarious organizations, and so often become obsessed with just keeping themselves afloat (a concern that can, of course, work against the pursuit of social goals). Many of the McGill studies involved small business firms set up as Autocracies. Overwhelmingly, the MBA student groups described their goals as above all else survival, followed by other goals, such as product quality, when possible. Growth was also mentioned. But that goal is limited in this configuration by one major factor: the CEO knows that large size creates the need for bureaucratic procedures which reduce his internal power and external flexibility, eventually making inevitable the shift to another power configuration, probably the Instrument or Closed System. So he may hesitate to pursue the goal of growth wholeheartedly. And, of course, without growth, the goal of control of the environment cannot be pursued very vigorously either. That is why, while the Closed Systems tend to confront directly attempts to influence them, the Autocracies tend to avoid such attempts by trying to go elsewhere.

FORMS OF THE AUTOCRACY

From what we saw earlier, the classic Autocracy would be small, so as to be susceptible to the personal control of the CEO and insignificant to most external influencers, and young, so as not to be ready for bureaucratic procedures; it would be led by its founder and owner; and it would operate in a simple, dynamic niche in its environment. All of these characteristics suggest that the *entrepreneurial firm* is the classic Autocracy. It is typically small and young—many do not survive to ripe old ages, at least not without becoming large professionally managed bureaucracies; it typically operates aggressively in a market niche; and it is usually closely controlled by its owner-founder.

But not all of these conditions need be satisfied in order to have Autocracy. In fact, Autocracies exist that satisfy only one or two of these conditions, indeed some that satisfy none of them, but other, overriding conditions instead.

Consider the *mature owner-managed firm*, the entrepreneurial company that has grown older, perhaps even larger, yet remains tightly and personally controlled by its chief executive. It may have lost some of its entrepreneurial drive, but not its power configuration. The last years of Henry Ford, whose reliance on inappropriate personal controls nearly destroyed the giant automobile company he created, represent this in the extreme. Probably more common—and more appropriate because of its small size—is the case of an auto dealership studied by one of the McGill MBA groups. Its External Coalition was passive except for some constraints imposed by its major supplier, an automobile manufacturer. The CEO consciously kept the internal structure organic, in his words, operating under "planned confusion" and keeping the employees off guard so as to prevent a "strong man" from emerging on whom he would have to depend. To this chief executive, motivation meant the carrot and the stick, nothing more. As a result, in the opinion of the students, he had very docile employees who did as they were told but were prepared to take no initiatives. The students believed that the goals of the firm reflected its chief's "definite need for achievement, his very real need for being independent, and his need for success." Above all, he "had little trust in anyone but himself."[3]

In this last example, the organization maintained all of the characteristics of the entrepreneurial firm, except that it was not young. Our next form of Autocracy is the opposite: the organization need maintain none of the characteristics except youth. The *young organization*—no matter what its size, market, or ownership—tends to resemble Autocracy simply because organizations usually need to rely on their leaders to get them going. At the outset their structures are inherently organic: Everything they experience is new and untested, standardized procedures have yet to be worked out, social relations are fluid. Only centralized leadership based on personal control can knit all this together. Thus, even though the organization—say a government department—may more appropriately emerge in the form of another power configuration when it reaches steady state, in its formative years, or maybe just months, it functions as an Autocracy. The wolves at the door—the various internal or external influencers who will eventually move into positions of power—give the CEO time to establish the organization. After all, if the lambs were all eaten at birth, who would ever get a chance to wear wool?

Many organizations maintain Autocracy configurations so long as their founding chief executives remain at the helm. It is the founder who selects the people and establishes the procedures. As a result, the people tend to be loyal to him—they are *his* people, as the saying goes—while the procedures tend to cater to his style and strengths. So long as he remains, power tends to concentrate around him. Moreover, these *founder-led organizations* tend to be Autocracies because founding chief executives tend to be strong and independent individuals. Such individuals tend to be selected to found organizations and they tend also to select themselves. They are selected in the realization of how critical the formative years of an organization can be. This is the time when patterns of behavior are established that persist throughout the life of the organization. It usually takes time to destroy an organization that was built on firm founda-

---

[3]From a report submitted to the author in Management Policy 276–661, McGill University, 1971, by F. Pitre, E. Cahady, R. Gee, A. Kane, and B. Rickhaus.

tions, while it is typically very difficult to correct an organization that was badly constructed in the first place. And strong, independent individuals select themselves in the sense that they seek out new organizations because of the discretion such organizations allow them. Here, at least for a time, they can build their own thing, with a minimum of interference.

Then there are the forms of Autocracy that satisfy none of the conditions listed above. Some Autocracies in fact arise simply because a leader is so strong that he is able to dominate all the influencers in and around the organization. Perrow recounts the story of Eastern Airlines under Eddie Rickenbacker, the famous fighter pilot of World War I, who despite his small holdings (3 percent of the stock, the rest dispersed) and the large size of his company, "from 1935 to 1959. . .ran it as if he owned it all":

> No one was disposed to quarrel with his leadership, for the company was the most consistent money-maker in the volatile airline business. . . .Rickenbacker ran a one-man show, and the main act was economy. . . His frugality became an industry legend. He actually lectured his employees on the importance of saving not just pennies, but mills (a mill is one-tenth of a cent). His main goal for the company appeared to be cost reduction, and it worked for a good many years. (1970; p. 147)

But Rickenbacker's obsession turned sour when the company faced competition from more service-oriented airlines, and, like the Ford Motor Company twenty years earlier, it nearly went bankrupt shortly after its chief executive retired. Both examples show how precarious the Autocracy can be despite even large size.

Strong leadership, of course, tends to arise in a power vacuum, which is what helps to explain the presence of Autocracy in many of the large American unions (the so-call "internationals") during their years of great growth. These unions were taken over by extremely strong-willed individuals who ran them as their private empires, sometimes for decades. In the last chapter, we saw that the ideological unions of Europe, whose members were dispersed, became Closed Systems. Here we see that the American unions, whose members were dispersed but whose concerns were ones of "bread and butter," not ideology, became Autocracies. Tannenbaum (1965) cites evidence that such "business unions," concerned with wages, working conditions and the like, were inclined "to develop strong leadership and autocratic government" (p. 752). Their national headquarters came to exercise "important control over locals" (p. 744); their constitutions prohibited the publication of criticism "not approved by the officers" (p. 745); and "alleged breaches of union law [were] often judged by those who administer[ed] the law, usually the president" (p. 745).

Tannenbaum attributes the rise of what we might call *leader-imposed Autocracy* in these unions to a number of factors. Above all perhaps was the need for strong leadership to negotiate with management across the table. Indeed, "there is some indication that control by strong leaders may be precisely what many members want—especially if this proves effective in 'bringing home the bacon' " (p. 744). Moreover, because the leaders often had nowhere else to go except back to rank-and-file jobs—with a significant loss of status, income, and stimulating work—they tended to "devise means to protect their positions, and this often means the restriction of opposition in the union" (p.752). And these tendencies were reinforced by the unions' own large size, which distanced the leaders from the membership, as well as by the size of the organizations with which they had to negotiate, and not incidentally by the preference of the managements of these organizations to deal with autocrats: "...most would rather deal with a union leader who can control his membership" (p. 753). Hence, a set of other factors combined here to overcome the usual requirement that Autocracies remain small to ensure the viability of personal control.

Thus, ironically, whereas the ideological unions of Europe moved toward the Closed System configuration, the bread and butter unions of America appear to have favored Autocracy. At least they did so until their strong leaders passed on, at which point many shifted toward the Closed System configuration as weaker, more "professional" leaders succeeded the strong ones and other administrators consolidated their power under bureaucratic procedures.[4]

Another form of Autocracy tends to arise when an organization faces a severe crisis, for example a threat to its survival. A crisis is no time for debate or politics, or, for that matter, standard procedures. The organization must act quickly, decisively, and in tightly integrated fashion. And so the tendency is to suspend whatever distribution of power is normal in the organization and instead grant unusual power to the chief executive. In such cases—we can call them *state-of-seige organizations*—the CEO can get away with behaviors, such as squashing dissidents, that might be unacceptable in calmer times. There is nothing like trauma to fuse all the disparate influencers into one cohesive easily led body, as Kenneth Boulding has noted:

> A conflict usually simplifies the purposes of an organization, simply because the objective of winning or surviving the conflict comes to dominate over all others. Thus, a nation in peacetime has a diversity of purposes and objectives....factions and diverse interests within the nation tend to pull it apart. A strong enemy, however, is a great unifying force...(1962; p. 162)

Of course, if the leader is strong enough he may be able to retain his power after the crisis has subsided, much as the founder retains power after the formative years of the organization, and for many of the same reasons. Periods of crisis can be ones of intense internal chaos, allowing the leader to shift people and procedures around to suit his own needs and generally to consolidate

---

[4]Thus, a number of years ago, Tannenbaum (1965) and especially Wilensky (1961) saw some "embryonic" tendencies toward the growth of bureaucracy in unions and the increasing power of the full-time employees in general. These tendencies have clearly strengthened since then. Also, Tannenbaum found evidence that American unions concerned with "larger social goals" tended to maintain democratic structures (p. 753), which presumably meant that they formed and retained Missionary configurations (as we shall see in Chapter 21).

around himself a good deal of power, which he can hold for many years. The leader in other words, can exploit the confusion of crisis for his own advantage.

Crises are sometimes related to the political state of the organization itself, giving rise to a form of Autocracy we call the *postpoliticized organization*. Here the organization transcends a state of severe politics to emerge as an Autocracy. Conflict in the coalitions becomes so intense, and the atmosphere of confusion so great, that a strong CEO is able to exploit the situation to seize power for himself. Just as room for maneuver can be found even in the most highly bureaucratized structure, for example by playing one rule off against another, so too can room for maneuver be found even in the most highly politicized situation, by playing one influencer off against another. This is a dangerous game, played effectively only by the most clever and ambitious chief executive. But it is played nevertheless. The influencers expend so much of their energy battling among themselves that somehow the object of the exercise—to control what the organization does—becomes lost. The CEO steals the prize behind their back, and when they come to their senses it is too late.[5]

We have the same phenomenon, on a far grander scale, in the emergence of the *dictatorship* in government, the ultimate Autocracy. Here, usually after a period of intense political or economic turbulence, a leader manages to pacify the population (the equivalent of the External Coalition) through charisma or terror, and then rules the structures of government (the Internal Coalition) in a tight, personalized way. We saw this in the Soviet Union under Stalin and in France under Napoleon, in both cases after revolutions. (Interestingly, both eventually gave rise to highly bureaucratic administrations—essentially Closed Systems—after their leaders passed on.) Even de Gaulle, elected to lead the Fifth French Republic, was in many ways an autocratic who emerged to deal with the confusion of the Fourth Republic and the crisis in Algeria.

To conclude, the opportunities for Autocracies to establish themselves in the societies we call democratic are numerous. Indeed, such societies cannot function without this power configuration in certain places. Leadership—firm leadership, free of external control or internal procedure—remains a major factor in the world we know.

---

[5]When the conflict is restricted to the External Coalition, its intensity rendering it more Passive than Divided, as we noted in the last chapter, the administrators in general and not just the CEO may seize the power, in which case the organization emerges as a Closed System.

21

The Missionary

Alcoholics Anonymous and the Israeli kibbutzim as originally conceived, designed to change society by attracting members and then changing them; and "cloisters," such as remote monasteries and certain religious orders that turn in upon themselves to avoid any external contamination of their strong ideologies; also in some organizations that should fall under different power configurations but in fact emerge as what we call quasi-missionaries because of their strong ideologies, typically derived from distinguished histories and/or past charismatic leaders (but not in organizations that, while seeming to satisfy many or all of the characteristics of the Missionary, in fact behave so as to serve the personal needs of their insiders instead of the lofty ideals of their missions, and so emerge as Closed Systems instead, what we call pseudo-Missionaries).

When the mission of an organization is (a) clear and focussed, so that people are able to identify easily with it, (b) distinctive in purpose or execution, thereby depositing the organization in a niche, and (c) attractive or inspiring, to some people at least, so that they are drawn to that niche to identify with the mission, then a power configuration called the Missionary is likely to emerge. Of course, the range of missions that can fit these criteria is infinite, everything from the building of excellent automobiles to the clothing of animals. Ideologies tend to build up around missions with these characteristics, which commit followers to their pursuit, loyalty being the chief element in this power configuration. Thus Clark writes of the organizational saga: "...the most telling symptom is an intense sense of the unique. Men behave as if they knew a beautiful secret that no one outside the lucky few could ever share" (1970; p. 235). Other characteristics usually associated with this power configuration are a highly charismatic leader in the organization's past and a long, distinguished history in some field of endeavor. Commonly, these two characteristics work in concert. The charismatic leader expounds the ideology in the first place, clearly and eloquently so as to attract the initial followers, and this in turn leaves the organization with a rich set of traditions, sagas, and beliefs—a distinguished history.

Our Missionary is Etzioni's normative organization (except for the professional organizations he includes here, which we consider Meritocracies), and Selznick's institution. "As an organization acquires a self, a distinctive identity, it becomes an institution" (Selznick 1957; p. 21).

We begin our discussion with the goal system, the key to understanding this power configuration, and then we look at its distribution of power before considering various forms it can take.

THE GOAL SYSTEM:
MISSION AS THE PRIMARY GOAL

This is the power configuration in which mission and goal coincide. Decisions and actions are motivated above all by a desire to further the organization's mission—to preserve it, extend it, or perfect it. The mission, as noted above, must be distinctive, it must be attractive, and it must be clear and easily understood, although it need not be operational in the formal sense of the term. The members typically join the organization not primarily for material inducements, not to build a power base, not to satisfy a social need, but because of an identification with the organization's basic purpose, its ideologic goals. They see the organization as a means to serve and perhaps to improve society, not themselves. Thus, to adapt an old story, when asked what he is doing, the bricklayer of the Instrument, Closed System, or Autocracy answers that he is laying bricks, and the one in the Meritocracy is likely to say that he is constructing a church; but in the Missionary, he replies that he is participating in the creation of a great monument.[1]

As a result of their attachment to its mission, the members of the organization resist strongly any attempt to change it, to interfere with tradition. The mission and the rest of the ideology must be preserved at all costs.

> [Emotional identification binds] the organization to specific aims and procedures, often greatly limiting the freedom of the leadership to deploy its resources, and reducing the capacity of the organization to survive under new conditions. . . .
> . . . there is a resistance to change. People feel a sense of personal loss; the "identity" of the group or community seems somehow to be violated; they bow to economic or technological considerations only reluctantly, with regret. (Selznick 1957; pp. 18, 19)[2]

This is in sharp contrast to the Closed System, whose members will dispense with the mission—which they view as an arbitrary means to generate their material rewards—without hesitation. There it is the system, not what it does, that must be protected at all costs. In Simon's words:

> The individual who is loyal to the *objectives* of the organization will resist modification of those objectives, and may even refuse to continue his participation if they are changed too radically. The individual who is loyal to the *organization* will support opportunistic changes in its objectives that are calculated to promote its survival and growth. (1957; p. 118)

[1]In the Political Arena, he is likely to say that he is constructing a personal power base.

[2]This raises the interesting point that while the Missionary may be radical in trying to change the world, it is conservative with regard to changing itself: ". . . thus in the Marxist parties, factors in conservative ideology such as dependence on tradition, depreciation of youth, and rigidity in *organizational* procedure may go hand in hand with a thoroughly revolutionary program with respect to *outside* political events" (Selznick 1943, p. 54).

Thus, the systems goals have no special importance in this configuration. They are subordinated to the ideologic goal of mission. Survival is important only to sustain the mission, not the organization. The same is true of efficiency, which helps to further the mission. Control of the environment is not a goal per se, only (in some cases as we shall see) the imposition of the mission on the environment. And growth matters to the extent that the mission must be extended, although, as we shall see, growth is often limited to preserve the ideological nature of the organization.

As a result of the members' attachment to the organization's mission, their prime rewards are collective and psychic in nature. These derive from a sense of participation in what the organization itself accomplishes. Thus, many Missionaries are volunteer organizations, whose members—sometimes even full-time ones—donate their efforts for no material gain. We see this in the extreme in religious orders where the new recruits, upon joining, take vows of poverty, in effect turning over to the order all remuneration that will accrue from their work. These are organizations that really do "plow back all of their earnings," to use a phrase normally associated with the Closed System: every resource—material as well as emotional—is invested in furthering the mission. In this sense, the Missionary is the truest maximizer of all.

THE DISTRIBUTION OF POWER: INTERNAL PARTICIPATION

The power of this configuration resides essentially in its ideology, which all the members share. And the key to the configuration is loyalty, strict devotion to the ideology. As Niv notes in the case of communes:

> The survival of the commune depends on its members' commitment. Individuals are to completely surrender and conform with basic norms and rules as developed over time. Surrender and compliance are central terms in all communes' vocabulary. (1978; p. 13)

The members typically join the Missionary or are selected by it because of their natural propensity to identify with the ideology. Thereafter this identification is solidified by socialization, coupled with indoctrination where necessary. And once this process—which can be a lengthy one—is completed, loyalty is secured, and different forms of control are unnecessary. The members are firmly wedded to the organization's ideology; left alone, each will make decisions and take actions in accordance with its goals:

> St. Augustine once gave as the only rule for Christian conduct, "Love God and do what you like." The implication is, of course, that if you truly love God, then you will only ever want to do things which are acceptable to Him. Equally, Jesuit priests are not constantly being rung up, or sent memos, by the head office of the

Society. The long, intensive training over many years in Rome is a guarantee that wherever they go afterwards, and however long it may be before they even see another Jesuit, they will be able to do their work in accordance with the standards of the Society. (Jay 1970; p. 70)

In effect, the Missionary achieves its coordination through the standardization of its beliefs, or norms (not to mention the standardization of its members, through selection). This makes it a form of bureaucracy—which we defined in the *Structuring* book as a structure whose "behavior is predetermined or predictable, in effect standardized" (Mintzberg 1979a, p. 86). And this, of course, is consistent with the Missionary's unwillingness to change or adapt. But the Missionary is a very different form of bureaucracy, not machine or professional but *normative bureaucracy*. Unlike the bureaucracies we have so far discussed in this section, and Simple Structure as well (in other words, unlike the Instrument, Closed System, and Autocracy), the Missionary's whole System of Authority—encompassing personal as well as bureaucratic controls—is weak. Power rests in ideology, not authority, in beliefs, not offices. But in another way, the Missionary more closely resembles Simple Structure (and Autocracy) than the other forms of bureaucracy: It requires very little structural elaboration. With most of its coordination effected by the standardization of norms, it needs few bureaucratic controls, or the staff analysts who design them. As Sills notes of the Foundation for Infantile Paralysis, an excellent example of the Missionary: ". . .comparatively few bureaucratic procedures involving purely internal matters have been established. Chapters do not have regular meeting places. . .and most Chapter business is conducted over the telephone or at committee meetings" (1957, p. 204). Likewise, there is little need for managers of the middle line, or the elaborate hierarchies required to contain them. In effect, a mission clearly understood by everyone need not be factored into a means-ends chain with an extensive division of labor. As a result, the Missionary experiences little specialization or departmentalization. Even its support services tend to blend in with its basic operating activities. The Missionary consists, essentially, of a group of people who know what they have to do and do it, with a minimum of supervision, work standards, action plans, performance controls, and all the other formal paraphernalia of structure. Its bureaucracy is inherent in its norms (although in that sense can be far more deep-rooted than when it must be imposed by formal procedures).

All of these characteristics enable the Missionary to achieve the purist form of decentralization. In other words, it emerges as the most participative—egalitarian or democratic, if you like—of the six power configurations, as indicated in Figure 21-1. As the founder of the Benedictine order instructed:

Let him make no distinction of persons in the monastery. Let not one be loved more than another, unless he be found to excel in good works or in obedience. Let not one of noble birth be raised above him who was formerly a slave, unless some other reasonable cause intervene. (St. Benedict, *Holy Rule*, chap. 2, quoted in Goffman 1961, p. 339)

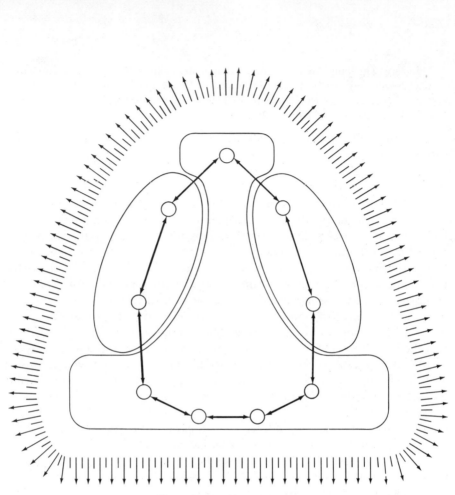

Figure 21-1. *The Missionary*

As we saw in the case of the Jesuits, once accepted as ready—as having internalized the ideology to the existing members' satisfaction—each new member can be trusted to act in the best interests of the organization, and so can be given a good deal of autonomy. Whatever coordination cannot be effected by the standardization of norms can be left to mutual adjustment among the members themselves, free of hierarchical authority. The members have every incentive to cooperate with each other, since they share common goals and seek no personal rewards. As Khandwalla notes, when an organization exists as "a tightly knit community in which members...share a sense of destiny," then "the job of coordination is not left to a few charged with the responsibility, but assumed by most individuals in the organization, much in the way members of a well-knit hockey or cricket team all work spontaneously to keep its activities focussed on the goal of winning" (1976, pp. 5, 10).

But to maintain such equality, it is important that any potential source of status differences among the members be eliminated. And that means discouraging not only authority and office, but also expertise. The System of Expertise promotes individual achievement and personal power, not to mention the fact that it requires a surrendering of control over norms to outside professional societies which proves incompatible with the ideology of the Missionary.

In the largest of Missionaries, China during its Cultural Revolution, in order to reduce the influence of office and expertise, the managers had to work in the factories and the city officials on the farms for a certain number of days each year. In the Foundation, Sills (1957) describes the "deep-rooted antagonism toward hierarchical and bureaucratic organizations in general" (p. 207), and to the paid, full-time "organizers" of other charities in particular, especially those of the Red Cross. "People resent someone coming in here with a Packard station wagon on a salary to supervise fund raising," said one Foundation volunteer (p. 208). The Foundation even went so far as to forbid medical doctors from holding office in local chapters in order to avoid the development of a specialized elite. We see the same phenomenon in the Israeli kibbutz, in its purest form a classic example of the Missionary. Consider Rosner's (1969, p. 38) comparison of the principles of pure bureaucratic organization, as defined by Max Weber (found in Instruments and Closed Systems), with those of the kibbutz organization:

Principles of Bureaucratic Organization	*Principles of Kibbutz Organization*
1. Permanency of office.	Impermanency of office.
2. The office carries with it impersonal, fixed privileges and duties.	The definition of office is flexible—privileges and duties are not formally fixed and often depend on the personality of the official.
3. A hierarchy of functional authorities expressed in the authority of the officials.	A basic assumption of the equal value of all functions without a formal hierarchy of authority.
4. Nomination of officials is based on formal objective qualifications.	Officials are elected, not nominated. Objective qualifications are not decisive, personal qualities are more important in election.
5. The office is a full-time occupation.	The office is usually supplementary to the full-time occupation of the official.

From Rosner, 1969, p. 38

The participative nature of the Internal Coalition should not, however, cloud the fact that the leaders still have special influence in this configuration. But this is an influence that derives from their relationship with the ideology, not with authority. To understand this, let us back up a bit. Charisma, as we noted earlier, figures prominently in the emergence of this configuration. It was typically a charismatic leader who created the organization or at least established the ideology in the first place. So long as he was in command, the configuration was one of Autocracy, that is, hardly egalitarian. But once he passed on, his ideology was institutionalized—consolidated through traditions, in the form of precedents, myths, sagas, and so on—and the configuration changed to a

Missionary. Then a different kind of leader was required, charismatic still, but less an independent person to create new beliefs than a devoted one to reinforce and represent the beliefs already created. In other words, the leader of the Missionary *embodies* the ideology, and thereby gains his influence. In the Foundation:

> Identification with National Headquarters personnel sometimes verges on adulation. "I think the heads of the organization are so uplifting," reported the Chairman of Women's Activities in Steel City. "They are wonderful speakers.... I enjoy every meeting when they are there. You know, when we come home, that we're going to give everything we've got." (Sills 1957, pp. 216–17)

To put this conclusion another way, the members of the Missionary quite naturally and *voluntarily* put their faith in their leaders, literally so in a study Etzioni cites of 245 churches, almost all of whose lay leaders "were willing to accept the pastor's advice, direction, decisions, or even complete control. Only 6.1 percent insisted on sharing power equally with the pastor" (1961, p. 104).

The leaders, of course, maintain their influence only so long as they support the ideology. The one thing they cannot do is change the basic traditions, unless of course they wish to rule by authority or personality alone and in the process convert the Missionary back into an Autocracy. And this suggests the fundamental difference in leadership between the Missionary and the Autocracy, consistent with a distinction in managerial styles that McClelland (1970) makes in his paper "The Two Faces of Power." In the Missionary, the leader "does not force [his followers] to submit and follow him by the sheer overwhelming magic of his personality and persuasive powers" (or, we might add, of his formal authority), for that is associated with a "kind of personalized power syndrome" (p. 37), which we identified with Autocracy. Instead, in keeping with the members' needs for active participation, the leader inspires them, strengthens and uplifts them, makes them feel "more powerful, rather than less powerful and submissive.... The leader arouses confidence in his followers. The followers feel better able to accomplish whatever goals he and they share" (pp. 37–38). In the absence of ideology, the leader says, "Do as I say because I am strong and know best" (p. 38), or else "because I am in charge." With ideology established, the leader says instead, "Here are the goals which are true and right and which we share. Here is how we can reach them. You are strong and capable. You can accomplish these goals" (p. 38).

In the Missionary configuration, as Etzioni points out, the formal and informal structures tend to coincide. There is no need for informal or clandestine leadership because, through a process he calls "absorption," "potential informal leaders are recruited into full-time organizational positions" (1961, p. 103). This occurs because of "the high degree of concensus...concerning the ultimate values, mores, and norms" shared by the members and the leaders, because of the "strong positive commitment" to serving the organization and cooperating with its leaders, and because the "most active members...tend to be highly committed to the organization" and highly supportive of its actions; "those most alienated from the organization—including those who have leadership potential—tend to be inactive or to drop out" (p. 105).

This correspondence of formal and informal power, together with the other characteristics discussed earlier, suggest another key feature of the Internal Coalition of the Missionary: an absence of politicization. ". . .doctrine defines a straight line that rules out the zigs and zags of opportunism" (Clark 1970, p. 9). As implied in the Etzioni quotes above, voice is muted in the Missionary, or at least it is channelled by loyalty; those unwilling to conform are expected to exit.[3] In this configuration, there are no informal centers of power to play the political games; no bureaucratic controls to resist or distort; with personal ambition subjugated to common mission, no private empires to build; with clear, widely-shared goals, no means to invert with ends, no reasons to suboptimize, no incentives to create alliances; with weak departmentalization and the discouragement of status, no rival camps to battle or expertise to flaunt; with authority weak, no insurgency, line versus staff, or young Turks games to play. Strategic candidates may be promoted, to improve the organization's effectiveness. But with no empires to build, and with the inherent resistance to change, even this game tends to be mild, played in the context of the given ideology. Perhaps the only political game played with any enthusiasm is lording, as the members sometimes lord their beliefs over outsiders. In effect, the only real conflict within the Missionary power configuration occurs over interpretation of "the word"—the inherited ideology—as when Talmudic scholars debate endlessly the real meaning of some minute passage in their ancient books. The fact is that all of the members of the Missionary unite to build one empire, that which will best achieve the organization's mission.

Little need be said about the External Coalition of the Missionary, because in this configuration, the Internal Coalition is the active force; the External Coalition is passive by comparison. For one thing, the organization's distinct mission typically positions it in a niche that is relatively free of external influence. For another, even when there is potential influence, the organization's ideology tends to act as a protective shield. That is what the aura of Figure 21–1 is supposed to signify.

Organizational autonomy can be achieved in a number of ways, as Niv notes in the case of the commune:

> Autonomy means that the commune maintains clear boundaries. A unique ideology . . . is one way for defining such a boundary. Other ways are by setting criteria for membership, by locating the commune in a separate geographical setting, by controlling members' movement into and outside the commune and by developing the commune as an independent system [containing all the functions needed to satisfy members' physical and emotional needs] . . . . In short, the commune, regardless of its size, is a mini-universe. (1978, pp. 1–2)

[3] As Hirschman (1970) notes, "In organizations entry into which is expensive or requires severe initiation, recognition by members of any deterioration will . . . be delayed and so will be the onset of voice" (p. 93). Even then, voice will be colored by loyalty (p. 84).

Some Missionaries, such as secluded monasteries, take the notion of autonomy to the extreme, selecting their missions and their sites to seal themselves off as completely as possible from the rest of the world. But others do quite the opposite. They pursue missions that, while not allowing a great deal of power to flow *into* the organization, encourage the organization to exercise its own power *over* its environment (hence the arrows emanating from the aura in Figure 21-1). Here the Missionary becomes the aggressor, seeking to impose its mission directly on its environment—to convert the heathens, wipe out infantile paralysis, or whatever.

Sometimes an aggressive mission requires the cooptation of outsiders—the attraction of passive (and not-so-passive) external influencers to a position of loyalty, so that they will provide external support for the mission. As Clark notes of the "distinctive" colleges, where strong ideologies made Missionaries out of what would otherwise have been Meritocracies:

> . . .a college seeking distinctiveness must make believers out of thousands of people on the outside whose lives are not directly bound up in the fate of the college. To the extent that outsiders believe in it, the college achieves a differentiated, protected position in the markets and organizational complexes that allocate money, personnel, and students. (1970, p. 250)

Such efforts have sometimes been so successful that the external influencers have emerged as the chief guardians of the ideology. Indeed, many a distinctive college in need of adaptation has found it vigorously resisted by the alumni. The old alma mater can do no wrong. . .so long as it never changes.[4]

Unlike the Closed System, however, the Missionary seeks not to control its environment per se, but, in certain cases at least, to change it. Of course, the result is similar: power, when it flows at all in this configuration, flows from the Internal Coalition to the External Coalition, not vice versa. Thus, formal constraints imposed on the organization are few, social norms (as opposed to internal ones) are relatively insignificant, pressure campaigns are infrequent, and direct controls are virtually absent. Indeed, often the reverse flow of power means that it is the organization that seeks to change some accepted social norm of society, by mounting its own pressure campaigns against other organizations. This is one of the real purposes of the Missionary configuration—to change some aspect of society. A final indication of the relationship between internal and external power is that when the Missionary has a board of directors, this tends to be either an inside board (a facade in terms of external control) or

---

[4]And it remains a Missionary configuration if it never does. But an interesting situation can arise when the insiders try to effect changes in the face of alumni resistance. The former may be seeking to convert it to another configuration, perhaps Meritocracy or a Closed System, or even a Missionary with a different ideology, while the latter, by virtue of resisting such changes, end up working not so much to retain it as a Missionary as to render it their Instrument. And until one side wins, the conflict is likely to convert the Missionary into a Political Arena.

else one that serves as a tool to coopt external influencers, and so, like everything else, to help in the pursuit of the mission.

FORMS OF THE MISSIONARY

We find it convenient in discussing forms of the Missionary configuration to distinguish *classic Missionary*, *quasi-Missionary*, and *pseudo-Missionary* organizations. Essentially, the first is expected by its conditions to be a Missionary and is, the second is *not* expected to be but is nevertheless, and the third *is* expected to be but in fact is *not*.

What conditions would cause us to expect a Missionary power configuration? As mentioned, loyalty is the chief ingredient of this configuration, and this is encouraged above all by a sense of mission—an intention to better some aspect of society, for its own sake rather than for private advantage. That is why a distinct, inspiring mission commonly gives rise to this power configuration. In contrast, we would not expect the typical business concern—created for the material benefit of its owners—to emerge as a Missionary. More generally, we would not expect to be Missionary any organization that naturally fits the conditions of one of the other configurations—in other words, one that is constituted to benefit primarily an external influencer or the CEO (and so to be an Instrument or Autocracy), one that caters to the material, status, or social needs of its administrators (a Closed System), or one that serves the various personal needs of all its influencers (a Political Arena). As for the Meritocracy, its mission may also be inspiring—for example, to cure the ill. But its need for expertise typically creates status differences and introduces external norms that prove incompatible with strong internal ideology. Ultimately its prime beneficiaries are its experts.

Other conditions we might expect in the Missionary are volunteer membership, or at least membership that joins for other than material gain, and a simple environment. The Missionary must have a mission that is clear and easily understood, and that can be achieved without too great a reliance on expertise. This means that, no matter how bold it is, the mission must in principle be simple to execute, and so must be designed for an environment that is likewise simple to understand.

Finally, what can we say about the age and size of the Missionary? Interestingly, both of these characteristics cut two ways. On the one hand, we should not commonly expect the organization to be very old, since it is difficult to retain a sense of missionary fervor for long periods. Time should dull the enthusiasm, driving the organization to another configuration. On the other hand, ideology is by its very nature rooted in history and tradition, and so time should strengthen it. Hence, we would expect the typical Missionary to be neither very young nor terribly old, although we can easily find exceptions. There are the flash fire Missionaries—the sudden movements that quickly burn themselves out—and the smoldering Missionaries—the ones that develop slowly and glow more brightly with age. (Of course, a flash fire can also leave smouldering embers behind.)

As for size, on one hand we should expect the Missionary to be small, because personal contact among the members is crucial in retaining a sense of cohesiveness and identification with the ideology. The impersonality of large organizations has to be avoided at all costs. On the other hand, small organizations cannot easily change the world. Of course, not all Missionaries have such ambitious goals. For those with missions of limited scope, small size is perfectly acceptable. But how do the ambitious ones reconcile this dilemma? As we shall see in a number of examples, they achieve large and small size simultaneously by federating themselves—forming into small, intimate, and rather autonomous *enclaves*, linked to each other by the common ideology (with one perhaps serving as the archives, the depository of the relics). If each enclave succeeds in changing its immediate environment, together they can change the world.

Thus, as Niv notes (in personal correspondence), Missionaries may "grow" but they do not "develop" in the ways of conventional organizations—by the division of labor and differentiation into ever more complex forms. Rather, they retain their simple structures, splitting like amoebae into similar smaller units when they have grown too large. Niv points out that "Deganya, the first kibbutz, split into Deganya A and Deganya B when it reached a membership of 30. The reason at that time: it is impossible to maintain the special quality and spirit of the community with a larger number of members."

We can describe at least three forms of Missionary that meet all or most of these expected characteristics, in other words, three *classic* Missionaries. We call them the *reformers*, the *converters*, and the *cloisters*.

THE REFORMERS   An important form of Missionary is what Selznick (1952) calls the "organizational weapon," which we shall call the *reformer*. As Selznick describes it, the organization is designed as a weapon to foment revolutionary change in society. Selznick studied the Russian Bolsheviks, but other similar groups spring to mind—the IRA of Northern Ireland, the Mau Maus of Kenya, the Red Guard of Italy.

Here, clearly, the organization is viewed as an instrument of ends beyond itself—an instrument of an ideology. Some organizational weapons can be classified as flash fire Missionaries, in that they start out like houses on fire but burn out just as quickly. The Bolshevik party of course did not. As Selznick describes it, the core of the party was its skeleton of trained members, who became "leaders of wider groups." "Total conformance" was demanded of adherents, and "through activity and indoctrination, [the party] absorb[ed] and insulate[d] the member, severing his ties to the outside world and maximizing his commitment to the movement. . . .political contention within the party [was] minimized. Power centers which challenge[d] the official leadership [were] prohibited. . .The full potentialities of Marxist ideology for morale-building" were exploited (pp. 72–73).

Selznick points out that these organizations face some tricky problems of balancing, ones in fact common to all forms of the Missionary. First is the need to maintain discipline without reverting to authority. The danger is that an inner circle will seize power, in our terms converting the Missionary into a Closed System, or perhaps an Autocracy. We saw clear examples of this in the last two chapters, particularly in Michels's description of what happened to the revolutionary political parties in Europe. And second, perhaps more serious, are the "twin inherent dangers of liquidation and isolation" (p. 73). On one hand, the Missionary is drawn into the larger society where it tends to dissipate its energy and lose its ideology. *It* gets coopted, and ceases to be Missionary. On the other hand, the Missionary that closes in on itself becomes incapable of rendering its desired change. Its own isolation kills it. How to keep its members loyal, unadulterated by external forces, yet out there working among those forces, is the reformer Missionary's prime dilemma, one that it can resolve only partially through the use of socialization and indoctrination.

Of course, a Missionary need not foment revolution or use violence to serve as an organizational weapon, a reformer. It need only seek to change some aspect of the external society. Social activist groups such as Nader's Raiders or the Society to Clothe Animals are reformers, as are small local unions whose members unite to change a management or larger unions that strive for broader social change (so long, at least, as they do not succumb to oligarchy).[5] So too is the organization formally known as "missionary"—the religious order whose members take vows of poverty and then set out to convert the heathens.

Sills' Foundation for Infantile Paralysis, which, as we have already seen, illustrates a great many of the characteristics of the Missionary, is another good example of the reformer. Over the course of two decades, the Foundation kept its attention firmly riveted on the one central change it sought in society:

> If we examine the record of achievement of the Foundation it is quite apparent that the organization has not been deflected from achieving its major goals. In fact, in the nearly two decades since its establishment it has sponsored research which has vastly increased medical knowledge of infantile paralysis; it has brought about revolutionary changes in the methods of treating victims of infantile paralysis; it has introduced a completely new concept of how payment for medical and hospital bills may be shared by all the members of a community; it has sponsored the development of the Salk polio vaccine; and it is now on the threshold of achieving its major purpose—the elimination of epidemic infantile paralysis. (1957, p.69)

Among the factors Sills discusses as contributing to this singleness of purpose

[5]Thus Tannenbaum finds that local unions tend to be more democratic than national ones due to "close personal contact" in the plant (1965, p. 744). He also finds that "A union's commitment to larger social goals...is sometimes considered to be associated with democratic procedures"; ideology leads it to sacrifice immediate, materialistic goals for longer-range ideals (p. 753).

were the Foundation's volunteer nature and its absence of vestiges of bureaucracy: "...the ratio of employees to volunteer members is very low"; there existed no elaborate organization hierarchy, for example, "no state societies...occupy an intermediate position between National Headquarters and local Chapters"; there was a "relative absence of status rewards associated with holding office" (p. 70); and there existed "few opportunities for Volunteers to advance upward in the Foundation hierarchy" (p. 71).

THE CONVERTERS   Our second form of classic Missionary is the one that tries to change society simply by trying to change its own members. In other words, it seeks to attract members and then to convert them to a new way of life. Those *converters*, as we shall call them, that attract enough members—and some attract millions—change society. The difference between our first two classic forms of the Missionary, between reformers and converters, is the difference between the Women's Christian Temperence Union and Alcoholics Anonymous—between organizations which try to force or convince outsiders to change their ways and those that try to change the ways of their own members. One attacks the external environment, the other concentrates on its internal membership. Many of the religious movements that promise salvation in return for commitment are converters, as are some of those movements that spring up in California every few months to promise some new secret to the inner life (although many more seem to be Autocracies, entrepreneurial ventures parading under the Missionary banner to make a quick profit).

The Israeli kibbutz may be seen as a converter or a reformer. Niv (in personal correspondence) describes it as a reformer, a leader in the Jewish state in the implementation of basic Zionist goals and in the promotion of socialist ideology and practice. The kibbutzim helped settle remote areas, developed the country's agriculture, contributed by their locations to the defense of frontiers, and played a major role in the Labor governments and in the establishment of the cooperative sectors of the economy in general. But the kibbutzim were also converters. As originally conceived, they encouraged settlers to Israel to live and work according to the purest of socialist principles. In the ideal kibbutz, jobs are rotated, all forms of wealth are shared equally, overt differences in status are discouraged, and important decisions are made in open meetings of all the membership. The country took on a socialist character in good part because of the conversion activities of its kibbutzim.

Conversion often requires the full commitment of the individual, with the result that in this form of Missionary, the members often work and live physically inside the organization. In other words, here we find some of Goffman's (1961) "total institutions." Even when it is not total in this sense, the converter Missionary nevertheless extends its influence well into the private lives of its members. For example, to belong to Alcoholics Anonymous means to consider one's identification every time liquor is poured.

The twin dangers of liquidation and isolation weigh more heavily on the converter Missionaries than on the reformers. The reformers know what their choice must be: they cannot achieve their kind of change without getting out in society, even if that threatens liquidation. But the converters stand right on the knife edge. On one hand, they must be as closed as possible to avoid contamination of their conversion processes. After all, they seek to imbue in their members values that will differentiate them from the rest of society. This process requires the full commitment of the members, free of external influence. On the other hand, in order to survive and do their job, the converter Missionaries also need to sustain a certain level of membership as well as of physical resources. And this demands certain linkages—a certain openness—to the larger society.

Few manage to survive the dilemma in the long run. Niv (1978) studied the American commune as a "social experiment," and found in both the literature and his own research "a sad story of failure and disappointment" (p. 1). Despite the ease with which communes could be set up,

> the vast majority of communal experiments failed during their first few months of existence. Out of more than a hundred communal beginnings in nineteenth century America, only a dozen managed their way to maturity.... Comtemporary efforts do not enjoy higher rates of success. (p. 3)

But even maturity provided no safety. Those that "successfully overcame hardship associated with the take-off phase" and "developed the needed ingredients for long range success and maturity," "sooner or later...vanished into the graveyard of communal experimentation" (p. 4). They fell on one side of the knife edge or the other, disappearing either through "assimilation" or "stagnation," Niv's equivalents to liquidation and isolation. Thus, either the commune—and, presumably, the converter Missionary in general—opens up to the larger society, and is eventually absorbed by it, or else turns inward to protect its ideology (in effect becoming a cloister) and instead runs out of energy, disappearing typically from an inability to replenish the members who die and desert. It can hardly escape one form of "disintegration" or the other:

> Stagnation is a problem all kinds of social organization have to cope with. Not so assimilation. The latter is a unique issue that only deviant systems have to be aware of. In fact, successful avoidance of stagnation usually results in assimilation. (Niv, p. 12)

THE CLOISTERS   A few of the Missionaries that turn inward manage to survive, however, sometimes to perpetuate themselves for many years as large total institutions. The form what we call the *cloisters*, our third classic form of Missionary. If the converters sit on the knife edge, and the reformers take their place on one side of it, then the cloisters take theirs on the other, the side closed to the environment. The Hutterites, for example, described by Margaret Mead as "a fortress against the introduction of any new ideas" (1964, p. 209), have survived by maintaining a tremendously high birth rate and being careful to create new independent enclaves whenever established ones reached 130 members (Melcher 1976, p. 192). Religious orders, such as the Benedictines, have also managed to perpetuate themselves, in this case across millennia, in their various monasteries, convents, and other enclaves, despite their dependence on new members from the outside. Another impressive example is the Greek Orthodox Monastery called Santa Katherina, at the foot of Mount Sinai, where Christians believe Moses was given the Ten Commandments. The Monastery has stood in that one spot for fourteen centuries, despite its total isolation (until recently). Its membership has varied from six to three hundred, and now, with direct air and road access, stands at about fourteen.

These cloisters are truly closed systems, the most total of Goffman's total institutions, in terms of exchanges with their environments far more closed than the organizations for which we used that term earlier. But they are closed in a fundamentally different sense. What we called the Closed System seeks to take in as much as it can from its environment and to give back as little as possible so that its members can live off the surpluses. It is closed to influence, not inputs. (In fact, it might be better described as a valve, encouraging resources to flow in and influence to flow out.) The cloister Missionary, in contrast, is closed on all counts—to resources as well as influence on both the input and output sides. Its members join to escape society—not to grow fat by exploiting it. Indeed, the cloister can survive only as a Missionary: ideology is the one means by which it can attract and retain its membership.[6]

The recent experiences of the Israeli kibbutzim are indicative of many of the problems of Missionaries. As an experiment in pure socialism, the kibbutz was rather successful. So long as it remained small and restricted itself to simple agricultural pursuits, the single kibbutz seemed able to preserve its socialist ideals. In other words, as a cloister, it was a success. As a reformer, the kibbutz movement also had notable successes, as discussed earlier, especially in its impact on the social values of the state. A rather small number of "kibbutzniks" have been largely responsible for an extensive degree of socialism in the society. But as a converter, to encourage widespread communal life, the movement has not been very successful. For years it has been unable to raise its membership above 3 percent of the Israeli population. Many of its young members have left for city life or private farming,[7] and these have not been replaced at increasing rates.

As for those who remained, three forces have threatened the socialist

---

[6]Unless, of course, it reverts to coercion, as did the sect under Jim Jones, 779 of whose members committed mass suicide in Jonestown, Guyana in 1978. Coercion, of course, shifts the power configuration to the Autocracy, or perhaps the Instrument.

[7]Often in what are called "moshavs," farms owned privately but run in limited cooperative ways. The moshav proportion of the population has risen to match approximately that of the kibbutz.

ideology. One is materialism, typically as a direct result of financial success. Wealthier and less threatened directly by hostility in the environment, many kibbutzim have slackened in their ideological commitment. In our terms, they have come to look more like Closed Systems intent on benefiting their members than Missionaries intent on achieving some higher purpose. Second has been the growth of the individual kibbutz. Whereas the first kibbutz may have split in two when it reached thirty members, others were subsequently allowed to grow beyond the figure of one thousand. Large size, by impersonalizing relationships, weakens ideological fervor. But kibbutzim can be kept small, and increasingly are. (Today the figure of six to seven hundred members, meaning adults, is frequently cited as the largest desirable size, and few kibbutzim now exceed that number.)

The third force, perhaps the most threatening of all, has been the diversification out of agriculture, into industry (as well as the mechanization of agriculture itself). As the kibbutzim sought to maintain pace with the growing Israeli economy, and to accommodate their members' needs for more stimulating work, they established numerous small factories. The problem in the factories, unlike agriculture in its traditional form, is that the egalitarian norms are less easily maintained. Jobs in the orchards, including those of leadership, are so simple that they can be rotated frequently. An eyeglass factory, in contrast, requires a sharper and more permanent division of labor. It also introduces new needs for expertise. As soon as someone shows a talent for managing the operations or for establishing marketing contacts, the kibbutz is inclined to keep him there, and let him make the important decisions on his own. In other words, industry as well as advanced forms of agriculture require specialization and expertise, and these put the kibbutz on the road to other power configurations. Today, with increasing industrialization, the 3 percent who remain in kibbutzim are threatened with the dilution of their traditional ideology. Perhaps that ideology will be able to survive only in kibbutzim like Ein Gedi, a small community devoted to agriculture and tourism (and, on the shores of the Dead Sea at 400 meters below sea level, the lowest point on earth, more a cloister than a converter).[8]

All three of our classic Missionaries seem to come together in the most impressive example of them all—the Chinese Cultural Revolution that began in the 1960s. Was this a reformer, in which the Red Guard tried to change the larger society? Or a converter, in which all the citizens of the society (or, at least, those who survived the experience) were members to be changed? Or a cloister, in which the Chinese society sought to seal itself off from the rest of the world? Obviously, depending on your point of view, it was any or all of these three. In

---

[8]These conclusions are drawn from a personal visit to Israel in the summer of 1978, partly to spend a short time on a kibbutz, partly to attend a conference at the movement's Ruppin Institute with organization theorists who study kibbutzim.

Eoyang's opinion, "The Cultural Revolution of 1968 was a violent reaction to bureaucraticism and concomitant elitest values," designed to purge the leaders of the technocracy and reestablish the preeminance of socialist ideology (1972, p. 15). He sees it, in other words, as an attempt to reinstate a Missionary that had been displaced by a Closed System. In the Chinese enterprises during the Revolution, according to a study by Laaksonen (1977), top managers spent thirteen hours a week on ideological training in addition to the day a week they had to spend together with other office personnel working alongside the operators; every "human side of life" was "regarded as affecting the organizational behavior of the individual," including leisure time with workmates and family (p. 80); attempts were made "to avoid emphasizing the importance of expertise" since it "would destroy the initiative of the ordinary workers" (p. 81); and while norms prevailed, rules and methods were shaken up from time to time.

QUASI-MISSIONARIES   From this exteme we go to another, what we earlier called the *quasi-Missionary*, the organization that for all intents and purposes should not be Missionary but in fact turns out to be. Here we have an organization whose mission may, on the surface, seem ordinary, whose members may even have joined at the outset for material gain, whose general conditions seem to call for another power configuration. But just as a strong leader can override other conditions to create Autocracy, so can a strong ideology alone create a Missionary. Such an ideology can emerge slowly, by virtue of a long, distinguished history in some field of endeavor—perhaps just performing an ordinary mission in a distinctive way. Or else it may appear more quickly through the efforts of a charismatic leader.

In Chapter 16 we read Perrow's (1970) account of how a tradition of quality, experimentation, and perfection in the mission of producing automobiles became the basis of a strong ideology at Diamler-Benz. And in Chapter 11 we read of Clark's (1970) description of the "distinctive college." The factors Clark discusses as driving what would otherwise have been Meritocracies toward the Missionary configuration include a number already mentioned in this chapter: the organization's seizing of its "role in a purposive way that we call a mission"; "the innovating effort . . . conceived, enunciated, and put in motion by a strong-willed man in the president's chair"; "the development of belief and power in a personnel core . . . commonly the senior faculty"; a "program of work . . . as an embodiment and expression of distinctiveness"; and "the force of organizational ideology." "These major elements interconnect and seemingly are inescapably the fundamental tools of the making of a college saga" (pp. 8–9).

Ouchi and Jaeger (1978) show how the influence of culture can drive business firms toward the Missionary configuration. In the table reproduced below, they contrast the typical large American corporation (which we have already characterized as a Closed System) with its Japanese counterpart:

Type A (American)	Type J (Japanese)
Short-term employment	Lifetime employment
Individual decision-making	Consensual decision-making
Individual responsibility	Collective responsibility
Rapid evaluation and promotion	Slow evaluation and promotion
Explicit, formalized control	Implicit, informal control
Specialized career path	Nonspecialized career path
Segmented concern	Holistic concern

From Ouchi and Jaeger 1978, p. 308.

Every characteristic of what these authors call the Type J firm is consistent with our description of the Missionary. The personal relationship between the individual and the organization, the collective nature of responsibility and choice, the holistic concern instead of specialization, the discouragement of formal controls in favor of implicit (presumably normative) ones, all of these point to loyalty and a strong ideology as the central elements in the power configuration.[9] Ouchi and Jaeger present one example in which the Missionary and the Closed System configuration meet head on, which highlights a fundamental difference between them:

> ...during one of the author's visits to a Japanese bank in California, both the Japanese president and the American vice-presidents of the bank accused the other of being unable to formulate objectives. The Americans meant that the Japanese president could not or would not give them explicit, quantified targets to attain over the next three or six months, while the Japanese meant that the Americans could not see that once they understood the company's philosophy, they would be able to deduce for themselves the proper objective for any conceivable situation. (p. 309)

In a related empirical study, Ouchi and Johnson (1978) contrast a typical American corporation with one that resembles in certain of its characteristics the Japanese form (although it was American owned).[10] In the latter, they found many of the characteristics of the Missionary—greater loyalty, a strong collective orientation, less specialization, and a greater reliance on informal controls. Here, for example, "a new manager will be useless for at least four or five years. It takes that long for most people to decide whether the new person really fits in, whether they can really trust him." This was in sharp contrast to the "auction

[9]Further evidence comes from the tendency of Japanese firms to house their workers and even arrange their vacations, so that the organizations begin to look like "total institutions," as Goffman uses the term.

[10]They describe it as "an American version of the prototypical Japanese organization" (p. 293) and label it "Type Z." Ouchi (1981) subsequently wrote a widely marketed book called *Theory Z: How American Business Can Meet the Japanese Challenge.*

market" atmosphere of the other firm: ". . .it is almost as if you could open up the doors each day with 100 executives and engineers who had been randomly selected from the county, and the organization would work just as well as it does now" (p. 302).

PSEUDO-MISSIONARIES   Finally we come to what we earlier called the *pseudo-Missionary* organization. By virtue of its characteristics, this should be a Missionary. But it is not, emerging instead most often as a Closed System (and mentioned as such in Chapter 19). The organization may be staffed by volunteers, but these people are drawn to it not to pursue the external mission (the organization's ostensible purpose), but rather to satisfy some personal need they have—to socialize, gain power and prestige, or whatever.

> Considerable attention is given to the formulation of [official] goals for they are important in attracting contributors: goals must be socially acceptable, indeed socially applauded, for organizational prestige is of the essence. Nevertheless, [these] goals are essentially secondary. (Georgiou 1973, p. 302)

We find this form in many veteran associations, social clubs, and religious congregations. For their members, it is the group interaction that counts, not any real sense of mission—bingo instead of salvation. Or, as Etzioni notes, in some religious organizations "prayers are cut short. . .to leave more time for square dances" (1964, p. 13). Sometimes the Missionary orientation is hampered by the fact that the official, ideologic goals are neither clear nor attainable: ". . .salvation is neither clear cut nor easily achieved" (Demerath and Thiessen 1966, p. 684). And so the official goals get displaced. Typically it is the systems goals that emerge in their place, notably to conserve the organization as a social system and perhaps also to make it grow, even if that means sacrificing the mission. Thus the organization emerges as a Closed System.

Etzioni describes certain American Protestant and Jewish congregations where the lay elite is more powerful than the religious leaders, causing an "overemphasis on the congregation's instrumental activities; for example, facilities such as buildings are expanded, while salvation and other religious goals are relatively neglected" (1961, p. 108). Earlier we saw a similar phenomenon in the Israeli kibbutzim, where the goal of bringing collective living to Israeli society, having proven unattainable on a large scale, is in the process of being displaced in some of these organizations by more materialistic goals. And back in Chapter 13 we saw our most pronounced example of goal displacement, in the description of how certain rehabilitation agencies kept the "attractive blind" in states of dependence, in order to use them to raise funds, while older or needier blind people were ignored. By serving themselves instead of their clients—allowing parochial systems goals to displace broader ideologic ones—these organizations too emerge as pseudo-Missionaries, as Closed Systems.

In outward appearances, pseudo-Missionary organizations seem identical with classic Missionary ones. It is only when their specific actions and the intentions behind them are studied that the real differences show up. Sills' Foundation could have been a pseudo-Missionary organization; indeed, many charity foundations seem to be. But Sills is careful to stress the distinction at a number of points in his discussion. For example, in noting that the volunteers had little opportunity to advance in the hierarchy, he comments: "This situation contrasts sharply with that which prevails in organizations such as trade unions or the American Legion, where there is generally active competition for the position of local President or Post commander, and active competition among these offices for state or national position" (1957, p. 71). He also describes a number of "organization-related activities" that were discouraged because they might have interfered with the Foundation's single-minded pursuit of its mission: initiation rites, investitive ceremonies, uniforms and badges, and meeting places which could be "invested with ceremonial sentiments" (p. 74). In all of these ways, the Foundation ensured that its mission remained its central goal. That is what maintained it as a Missionary.

To conclude, we have seen that the Missionary configuration, while subject to all kinds of displacement pressures toward other configurations, remains an important one in our societies. Indeed, an increasing disillusionment with conventional and prevalent forms of bureaucracy, and fears of the instability of the alternatives, notably the currently popular Adhocracy, may make increasing attraction to the Missionary inevitable. The rash of mass movements in America of late suggests this. And as our discussion indicates, this would be for better *and* for worse.

22

The Meritocracy

A TALENT SHOW IN MANY ACTS

Starring: The experts of the operating core and support staff, sometimes with the CEO and other administrators in nonsupporting roles.

Synopsis of the Show: Experts who gain power on the basis of skill and knowledge dominate the Internal Coalition; their work cannot be regulated by analysts of the technostructure nor supervised by managers of the middle line, who often represent the experts in any event; as a result authority—in its personal as well as bureaucratic forms—tends to be weak, and the CEO emerges as the weakest in all of the power configurations (although far from impotent); likewise organization ideology is weak, in part because professional ideology is strong; weak authority and weak ideology, coupled with a wide but not sharply defined distribution of power, give rise to a good deal of politics, the most popular political games being alliance and empire building, budgeting, strategic candidates, rival camps, and those of expertise; the formal goals of the organization, being nonoperational (such as to advance knowledge or improve health) are easily displaced by the means and personal goals of the experts (notably professional autonomy and excellence) which, together with mission, are among the few primary goals attended to sequentially, subject to a multitude of constraints;

meanwhile in the External Coalition, although various influencers try to exercise power, most are pacified by internal expertise; only the professional societies may be able to gain considerable power, but rather than using it to dominate the External Coalition, and thereby control the organization, they instead use it in conjunction with the professionals to pacify everyone else; and so an External Coalition that appears Divided turns out to be better described as Passive.

Now Playing: In organizations whose environments or technical systems are complex, forcing them to rely on expertise; in a federated-type structure called Professional Bureaucracy, where each expert works autonomously in the operating core to apply standardized skills, as in general hospitals, universities and accounting firms; and in a collaborative-type structure, called Adhocracy, where experts from all parts of the organization work in project teams, sometimes on behalf of the clients directly, as in think tank consulting firms or film agencies (a form called Operating Adhocracy), sometimes on behalf of the organization itself, as in electronics firms or aerospace agencies (a form called Administrative Adhocracy).

Today we have an elite selected according to brains and educated according to deserts, with a grounding in philosophy and administration as well as in the two S's of science and sociology.... Today we frankly recognize that democracy can be no more than aspiration, and have rule not so much by the people as by the cleverest people; not an aristocracy of birth, not a plutocracy of wealth but a true meritocracy of talent. (Young 2034, pp. 18–19)[1]

Our first four configurations each have a clear focus of power. In two, that focus is on an individual—a dominant external influencer or the CEO. And in the other two, it is on an internal system of influence which the insiders as a group accept—the organization's ideology or the organization itself as a system, represented by bureaucratic authority. In each of these cases, the focus, by concentrating power, serves to preclude a good deal of conflict in the Internal Coalition and even, to a considerable extent, in the External Coalition. Now we come to a configuration in which, while the power is again focussed on an internal system of influence, that system serves not so much to concentrate power as to diffuse it. The system is that of expertise, and the result is that various insiders with different kinds and degrees of expertise attain different amounts of power.

[1]According to the author, his book *The Rise of the Meritocracy: 1870–2033*, was written in 2034 (although the publisher claims it was issued in 1959). Young adds in a footnote:

The origin of this unpleasant term [Meritocracy], like that of "equality of opportunity," is still obscure. It seems to have been first generally used in the 60s of the last century in small-circulation journals attached to the [British] Labour Party, and gained wide currency much later on. (p. 153)

The result is a more fluid configuration of power, with a greater degree of politics in the Internal Coalition and more disparate pressures from the External Coalition than we have seen in the four other configurations. Because power here flows to those with the skills and knowledge critical to operate the organization—to those who in some sense merit it—we call this configuration, after Young, the *Meritocracy.*

One prime condition gives rise to the Meritocracy. Because its environment, or perhaps its technical system, is complex, the organization must rely to accomplish its mission on highly trained employees—experts, usually professionals—in its operating core and perhaps support staff, and then give them considerable power. This is the case in hospitals with their doctors, universities with their professors, space agencies with their scientists, electronics manufacturers or automated process firms with their engineers.[2] But before we can describe the consequences of this—the distribution of power in the Internal Coalition and in the External Coalition, the flow of power between the two, and the resulting goals—we must first introduce two basic forms of Meritocracy.

TWO BASIC FORMS OF MERITOCRACY: FEDERATED AND COLLABORATIVE

Meritocracies can be divided into two fundamental types. Where their environments are stable, and therefore predictable, the experts are able to apply standardized skills directly to client needs, and so can work relatively autonomously in the operating core. Each time a client presents himself, the organization categorizes, or pigeonholes, his needs in terms of the repertoire of standard professional skills it has available, and sends him to the appropriate professional (or set of professionals in sequence). The result is a *federated-type* structure, which we referred to in Chapter 14 as Professional Bureaucracy. Where the environment is instead dynamic, client needs cannot be predetermined or responses standardized, and so the experts must pool their different skills to innovate, working in project teams. The result is a *collaborative-type* structure, earlier referred to as Adhocracy.

The *Federation,* which could have been treated as another type of power configuration, is that form of organization in which autonomous individuals or units band together to pursue a common mission. Brokerage firms create an ex-

---

[2]Power based on expertise in the operating core and support staff should not be confused with the power that flows to the analytic specialists of the technostructure. The two often are confused in the literature, primarily as a result of lumping all "staff" experts together. The power of the analysts of the technostructure is derived not from their expertise per se but from authority, specifically from their role in developing the bureaucratic controls in the System of Authority. And that power gives rise, not to Meritocracy, but to the Closed System configuration of power. Thus, when the literature refers to "staff" or "staff experts" taking control of an organization, the chances are good that it means technocratic staff and that it is describing the Closed System configuration.

change to trade their stocks, unions federate to consolidate their power, businessmen establish chambers of commerce to promote their city, the American Indian Nations years ago banded together for purposes of defense (Zald and Berger 1978; Swanson 1971;[3] Rice and Bishoprick 1971). In its simplest form, shown in Figure 22-1, the federation consists of no more than a governing council of the members or their representatives who meet periodically to make common decisions. Each unit retains its own autonomy, except in the area of common concern where they make decisions jointly. As a result, conflict is minimized, restricted to these areas of common concern, and there the politics are open, in the form of explicit bargaining (Zald and Berger 1978, p.833).

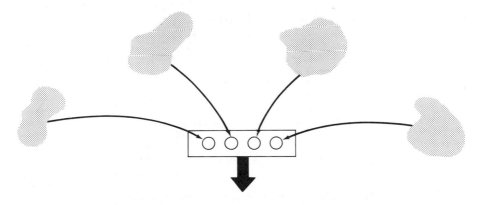

Figure 22-1. *The Simple Federation*

But the federation often requires an administrative structure to execute the council's decisions. And so the council becomes a board of directors that names a chief executive who in turn establishes an organization of full-time employees, as shown in Figure 22-2. In the true federation, that organization is designed to serve the members, not vice versa. In other words, it is their Instrument. As Zald and Berger (1978, p. 832) express it, the federation is an "upside down" organization, the administrators being dependent on the members; " . . . the leader does not dictate policy. Instead, he must gain support from the members" (Rice and Bishoprick 1971, p. 60).

In our discussion to this point, we have seen a number of organizations that looked like federations. First were those dominated by a consensus of their members, and described as Instruments in Chapter 18, as in the way stock markets were originally set up. Later we saw the case of the Missionary set up as a series of autonomous enclaves coupled together by a common ideology. This seems to be a federation of sorts, except that the organization is not created to serve its member units. Rather, the units are created—more exactly, spun off from existing units—to serve some mission. Nevertheless, when all is said and

---

[3]Swanson calls the federation a "heterarchy."

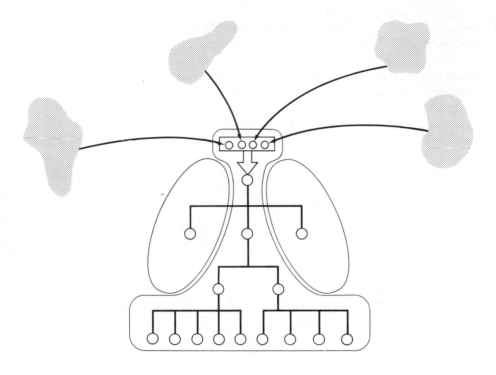

Figure 22–2. *Federation with Administrative Structure (as Instrument)*

done, the Missionary with multiple enclaves looks and acts much like a true federation.

Elsewhere we saw how the "upside down" power of the federation can get turned right side up (or, at least, conventional side up) when the full-time administrators seize control and convert it to a Closed System. As the administrators use the organization to serve themselves, instead of its constituent members, power begins to flow the other way. Many organizations that begin as true federations in fact suffer this fate. Sometimes they grow large and their members become passive, leaving control to the administrators, as Michels describes in the European socialist parties and labor unions. Other times, because the members are particularly dependent on their central administrative structure—as in the cases of farmers vis-à-vis their marketing agency—they become subordinate to the administrators. These become pseudo or false federations.

The Divisionalized Form is another version of the false federation, because while it consists of semi-autonomous units (divisions) around a central administrative core (the headquarters), the flow of power is from the headquarters to the divisions, not vice versa. In other words, "legitimate authority resides in the center"; the units are "owned" by it; they do not have "clear property rights and discretion. . .established in [a] constitution" (Zald and Berger 1978, p. 832). The divisions have power only because it is delegated to them from the head-quarters; as described in Chapter 18, they are its Instruments, not vice versa.

PROFESSIONAL BUREAUCRACY AS FEDERATED-TYPE MERITOCRACY   True federation, as we have discussed it, is not so much an integrated organization as a collection of individuals or units banded together for convenience. That is why we have chosen not to discuss it as another power configuration, but rather to treat its central administration (when one exists) as an Instrument.

But there is a configuration of power close in its characteristics to federation and that is our first type of Meritocracy—the Professional Bureaucracy. Professional Bureaucracy is in fact set up as an organization, but its component parts act as if they were the units of a federation. In that sense, this form of Meritocracy is the opposite of a false federation—it is federation de facto but not de jure, what we could call quasi-federation. In other words, it is not legally a federation—not "defined constitutionally by the rights reserved to the units" (Zald and Berger 1978, p. 853)—but it nevertheless exhibits many of the characteristics of a true federation. The experts are hired by the organization, but they consider it a structure of convenience where they can practice their professions as individuals, with common administrative support. Doctors, lawyers, accountants, and scholars who need that support come together in Professional Bureaucracies. Once inside, because they apply standardized procedures, they are able to serve their clients with a good deal of autonomy and personal responsibility. (Sometimes different groups of them form autonomous units—as in the case of university departments that do their own hiring, accept their own students, and provide their own degrees—thus leading to a kind of two-tier federation.) But together they share physical facilities and support staff. And because the members of this type of federation function within the organization—they are internal influencers, not external members—they are able to retain control of the administrative structure. That structure, often largely composed of representatives of the experts themselves, serves their own needs, for example by supervising the common support staff, reconciling the conflicts among the experts, and dealing with the external influencers. This *federated-type Meritocracy* is shown in Figure 22–3.

ADHOCRACY AS COLLABORATIVE-TYPE MERITOCRACY   Our second form of Meritocracy, called Adhocracy in the *Structuring* book, is quite unlike a federation. Here, because the environment of the organization is dynamic, the work arrangements must be far more flexible, and so the experts cannot apply standardized procedures per se. Rather they must use their talents to innovate, and that requires them to collaborate with each other—to work in temporary project teams, or shifting work constellations, in order to combine their different knowledge and skills. As a result, no expert can view him or herself as autonomous; all depend on the organization to bring them together. Moreover,

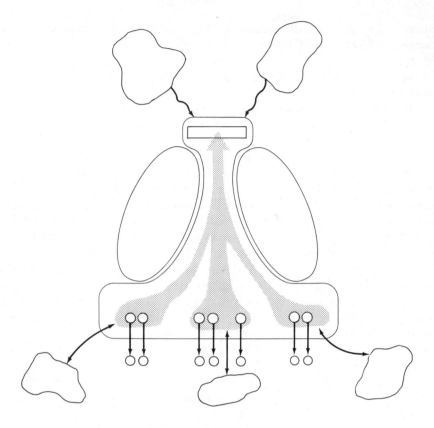

Figure 22-3. *Federated-Type Meritocracy: The Professional Bureaucracy*

whereas the administrators of the Professional Bureaucracy concern themselves minimally with the work of the experts—because it is so highly standardized and controlled by each of them in any event—the administrators of the Adhocracy must be intimately involved with that work. Because of the need for collaboration, and because of the fluidity of the work, coordination of it becomes a critical function. While a good deal of that coordination is achieved by mutual adjustment among the experts themselves, much is still left to be effected by the administrators—not so much by direct supervision but by serving in various liaison and integrating roles between the different teams or work constellations. Also, unlike Professional Bureaucracy, where the experts are concentrated in the operating core with unskilled workers in the support staff, in Adhocracy the various parts of the organization cannot be so easily distinguished. The experts can be found in the administration, the support staff, and the operating core. Thus, the whole organization can emerge as one amorphous mass of experts, hardly a suggestion of federation.

The administration of the Adhocracy tends to be controlled by experts too, but in a different and less representative way. In Professional Bureaucracy, certain professionals of the operating core occasionally volunteer their services as administrators. They do this on behalf of their operating colleagues, and often return to their jobs in the operating core at some later date. The Adhocracy needs experts in its administration too. But once an expert moves into the administration, he is more likely to remain there and perhaps climb the hierarchy, and is less likely to view himself as acting on behalf of his colleagues. In effect, the stronger need for coordination in Adhocracy creates a somewhat stronger administrative structure, less directly controlled by the expert workers.

What we can find then in Adhocracy are experts everywhere—in the support staff, operating core, and the administrative positions of the line hierarchy and the technostructure. The collaborative teams in fact draw their experts from all parts of the structure. As a result, whereas the federated-type Meritocracy is decentralized rather fully in the horizontal dimension—in other words a good deal of the power lies in the operating core, beyond the reach of administrators in the hands of individual professionals—the collaborative-type is decentralized selectively: power over the various decisions lies in all kinds of different places in the structure, at every level of the hierarchy and among line managers, staff specialists, and operators. In other words, there is no predictable distribution of power in Adhocracy; decisions are made wherever the required expertise happens to coalesce. This is shown symbolically in Figure 22-4.

One kind of collaborative-type Meritocracy, called *Operating Adhocracy*, carries out its projects directly on behalf of its clients. In fact, it often functions in the same sphere as Professional Bureaucracy but with a different orientation. For example, a consulting firm set up as an Operating Adhocracy treats each client problem in a unique way, setting up an interdisciplinary team of experts to deal with it. A consulting firm set up as a Professional Bureaucracy, in contrast, will pigeonhole the problem into a given category, and assign an individual expert (or a number in sequence) to apply to it a standard procedure. In effect, one selects the dynamic, the other the stable part of the industry in which it functions.

A second kind of collaborative-type Meritocracy is the *Administrative Adhocracy*, which innovates on its own behalf. For example, an electronics firm establishes project teams to develop new products to market or a chemical firm establishes such teams to bring a new automated facility on line. In this type, the operations are sharply separated from the rest of the organization, but in a way almost opposite to that of the Professional Bureaucracy. The operating core is truncated: set up as a separate structure (as in the case of an automated facility) or else simply done away with altogether (for example, by having the operating work contracted out to the other organizations). The expertise resides in what remains—in the administration and especially the support staff—the main role of which is to carry out projects to design, create, and modify the activities of the operating core.[4]

[4]Professional Bureaucracy as well as both types of Adhocracy are discussed at length in the *Structuring* book (Mintzberg 1979a, chaps. 19 and 21). An attempt has been made to repeat here only what is absolutely necessary to discuss the corresponding power configuration.

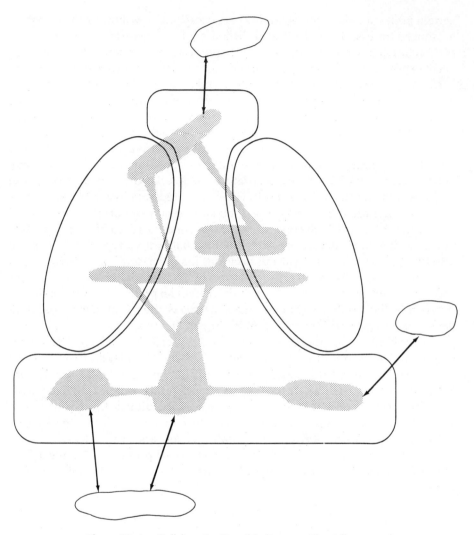

Figure 22–4. *Collaborative-Type Meritocracy: The Adhocracy*

POWER DISTRIBUTION IN THE INTERNAL COALITION: UNEVEN POWER, BASED ON EXPERTISE

Experts demand and receive considerable control over their own work. The work is too complex to be controlled personally by managers or bureaucratically by the simple standards of the analysts. It takes years to learn. Even the outputs cannot be regulated, because the goals of complex work are typically nonoperational. How is anyone to measure progress toward the "advancement of knowledge" in a university or toward "cure" in a psychiatric hospital?

As Zald notes for the goal of rehabilitation, associated with professional work in the correctional institution, "criteria of effectiveness are difficult to establish...since the success of rehabilitation can be established only over a long period of time" (1962–63, p. 30). Often, control over remuneration is also denied to the administrators, because the salaries of the experts are set by their professional associations and standardized across organizations. Moreover, expert power is enforced by the fact that those who possess it are typically in demand and so are mobile, which makes them minimally dependent on the organization.

For all of these reasons, the System of Authority tends to be relatively weak in Meritocracy. In fact, as noted earlier, in Professional Bureaucracy it often comes under the direct control of the professionals themselves, who staff the important administrative positions with people who act on their behalf. Even in Adhocracy, as noted above, most of the key administrative positions are typically filled by experts, although they do not see themselves acting directly on behalf of their colleagues. The result is that, one way or another, not only the operating but also the strategic decisions tend to come under expert control. Many are actually made by operating or staff experts—by the individual professionals in one form of Meritocracy, who decide what kind of work they wish to do and how, and by teams of experts in the context of their projects in the other. And those decisions that do fall to the administrators tend to be highly influenced by operating or staff experts before final choices are made.

Power distributed on the basis of expertise may suggest a kind of democracy, but in fact meritocracy is the more accurate term. It was chosen because what matters in this configuration is the kind of expertise one possesses and its importance to the organization. Power is distributed, not equally, on the basis of membership, but unequally, on the basis of critical knowledge and skill. And this introduces all kinds of status differences. Thus, the Meritocracy stands in sharp contrast to the Missionary which, by discouraging expertise and the associated distinctions in status, achieves a more even distribution of power—a purer form of democracy, if you like. Of course, the opposite conclusion holds as well. Meritocracies, because they must distribute power unevenly, discourage the development of strong organizational ideologies, which call for greater equality.

Unequal distribution of power can be found on a variety of levels in Meritocracy. For one thing, different kinds of experts possess different levels of skill, with the result that pecking orders develop among them, as between doctors and nurses in hospitals, or even between surgeons and other physicians. And of course the nonexperts of these organizations—the orderlies and other unskilled support staffers in the hospitals, for example—are the low people on the totem poles, and feel no sense of participation. Their units are treated as the private instruments of the experts. For another thing, even within given professions or fields of expertise, different levels of experience as well as of skill can be found, so that pecking orders establish themselves here as well. Thus we have distinctions between interns and residents in hospitals, between assistant, associate, and full professors in universities (the latter typically controlling the tenure decisions, for example), and between the more and less well known researchers in both these institutions.

Not only is power distributed unevenly in Meritocracy, but that distribution also tends to be fluid in at least part of the structure. Adhocracy, faced with continually changing conditions (what we called a dynamic environment), is required to shift its power distribution frequently, almost everywhere. As new bodies of expertise become critical, they must displace others in importance. Thus, teams are continually being formed and disbanded, and within each, power is redistributed frequently, according to which expert can best deal with the problem at hand. Hence, wherever the project teams are found—throughout Operating Adhocracy and in the administration and support staff of Administrative Adhocracy—highly fluid power relationships can be expected.

In Professional Bureaucracy, in the operating core the pecking orders are relatively stable, and so, therefore, is the distribution of power. But, as we shall see, ambiguities do arise at the margins—especially as a result of the pigeon-holing process and the vagueness of the goals. These create conflicts, pressures to redefine the distribution of power. But because these pressures tend to be highly disruptive, undermining the stability the professionals require to get on with applying their standardized skills, the conflicts tend to get pushed up to the administrative levels, where the professionals' representatives are expected to handle them. Thus it is at this level where the fluid power relationships of the Professional Bureaucracy tend to be found.

James March and his colleagues (see March and Olsen 1976), whose research has focussed largely on administrative decision processes in Professional Bureaucracies, describe them as "organized anarchies" or "garbage cans." By the latter term, these researchers mean that problems, solutions, choices, and people are all dumped into the decision processes at random, with no clearly defined relationships among them. Instead of stability in the administrative division of labor—in preferences, in participation, and in power—they argue (1) that "preferences are often problematic," that "the organization operates on the basis of a variety of inconsistent and ill-defined preferences. It can be described better as a loose collection of ideas than as a coherent structure"; (2) that "technology is often unclear. . . . its own processes are not understood by its members"; and (3) that "participation is often fluid. . . . involvement varies from one time to another" (Cohen, March, and Olsen 1976, p. 25). The result is that

> choices are fundamentally ambiguous. An organization is a set of procedures for argumentation and interpretation as well as for solving problems and making decisions. A choice situation is a meeting place for issues and feelings looking for decision situations in which they may be aired, solutions looking for issues to which they may be an answer, and participants looking for problems or pleasure. (p. 25)

THE MANAGERS OF MERITOCRACY: WEAKER BUT NOT IMPOTENT   Weak authority and power based on expertise combine to reduce the influence of the chief executive as well as other managers of this power configuration. Etzioni goes so far as to argue—in accordance with the upside-down notion of federation—that "if there is a staff-line relationship at all, experts constitute the line (major authority) structure and managers the staff" (1959, p. 52). But while there are indications of this—especially in Professional Bureaucracy—Etzioni's case would appear to be overstated. The CEO, and to a lesser extent the other line managers of the Meritocracy, while far from dominant, are certainly not impotent. As Cohen and March note about the U.S. college president: "He is resented because he is more powerful than he should be. He is scorned and frustrated because he is weaker than he is believed capable of being" (1976, p. 197).

Ironically, it is the very fluidity of the structures they administer, as well as their centrality within it, that provide the managers of Meritocracy—at least the astute ones—with room to maneuver, especially in Adhocracy. Their power is largely informal, and its main sources are two. First, as noted, differences in professional affiliation and in status give rise to considerable conflict in these structures. And it is the managers who are ideally suited to resolve much of it: ". . .the leader is a mediator, a negotiator, a person who jockeys between power blocks trying to establish viable courses of action" (Baldridge et al. 1978, p. 45). In other words, conflict resolution is a critical function in these organizations, and so the managers capable of dealing with it gain considerable power. "Without the 'superb politician,' metropolitan school systems, urban governments, universities, mental hospitals, social work systems, and similar complex organization would be immobilized" (Thompson 1967, p. 143).

The second source of managerial power in the case of the chief executive, at least, is that this person serves as the main liaison with a most important group of outsiders—the suppliers of the funds. It is typically the president of the university who negotiates with the government department of education, the executive director of the hospital who deals with the rich trustees, the partner in the consulting firm who brings in the new contracts.

These two sources of informal managerial power are reinforced by two others—namely political will and skill. First, it is the managers who have the time and the energy to devote to political activities; dealing with conflict, as we saw, is a main component of their jobs. The full-time experts are too involved in their own work. Second, the managers of these organizations are typically skilled politicians, for that is likely what carried them to administrative responsibility in the first place. The apolitical prefer to remain behind, practicing their expertise in the operating core or support staff.

But one major limitation to managerial power must be stressed. In this configuration, the manager serves at the discretion of the experts. So long as he maintains their confidence, he retains considerable power. Indeed, the experts are dependent on the effective administrator, for he is the one who frees them from political and economic concerns to get on with their chosen work. But his power—because it is based more on informal means than formal authority—diminishes quickly without their support. As Thompson notes, "an individual can be powerful, can symbolize the power of the organization, and can exercise significant leadership; but...only with the consent and the approval of the dominant coalition. Thus the highly complex organization is not the place for the dictator or commander to emerge" (1967, p. 142). This shows up clearly in Gross's massive study of the perceptions of goals and power in American universities. High-level administrators were consistently rated by the faculty as having considerable power. Yet among both administrators and faculty there was a "striking concensus" about what the goals were and should have been (1968, p. 538). In other words, the administrators apparently held power because they reflected the beliefs of the faculty.

This being said, it should be noted that the managers of Adhocracy, especially Administrative Adhocracy, tend to have more power than those of Professional Bureaucracy, as we have already seen in our discussion and will see again further along. Of course, the more powerful the administrators at the expense of the experts, the more the configuration comes to resemble a Closed System. Thus, while Professional Bureaucracy can perhaps be considered the purest form of Meritocracy, followed by Operating Adhocracy, Administrative Adhocracy can be considered the least pure, sometimes close to a hybrid structure in which expertise must coexist with authority. And that, of course, can drive it toward the Political Arena when the two systems of influence conflict with each other.

The managers of Adhocracy have more power in a different sense too. For no matter how much relative power a manager can or cannot muster within his organization, in a broader sense what really matters is what he can do with it on behalf of his organization. Professional Bureaucracies, as bureaucracies committed to standardized procedures, are difficult organizations to change. "The college president has more potential for moving the college than most people, probably more potential than any one other person. Nevertheless, presidents discover that they have less power than is believed..." (Cohen and March 1974, pp. 197-98). Presidents of Adhocracies, in contrast, may have more power than is believed, because they lead what is one of the most innovative and flexible forms of organization.

CONSIDERABLE POLITICAL ACTIVITY When power is concentrated in the hands of a single individual, as in the Autocracy or Instrument, there is little power left over for the taking. The dominant individual stands ready to rap the knuckles of anyone who tries. And when the insiders coalesce around a well-defined goal system, as in the Missionary or Closed System, the room for political maneuvering is circumscribed. But where there exists neither one center of power nor clear goals—the case of the Meritocracy—political games inevitably arise. The System of Expertise—the means by which power flows naturally to

those with the necessary skills—obviously precludes a good deal of political activity. But far from all. For one thing, the System of Expertise distributes power
widely, and rather than encouraging consensus, it introduces all kinds of opportunities to pursue parochial goals. For another, as a means of distributing
power, the System of Expertise is often vague, leaving considerable ambiguity,
within which politics thrives.

In general, all the characteristics discussed in Chapter 13 as causing displacement of formal goals and the rise of the System of Politics are present in
Meritocracy, in spades. First, because the output or performance of expert work
is not easily measured, goals imposed from above are easily deflected. Second,
because the experts are committed to their own skills, they have a notable
tendency to invert means and ends, to focus on the skills they provide rather
than the mission for which these skills are intended. Third, because professionals identify strongly with their own professional societies, and because the
Meritocracy tends to house professionals from a variety of such societies—psychiatry, surgery, and other specialties in the general hospital, various branches
of science in the research laboratory—groups form as factions and conflicts
arise between them. Fourth, in the federated-type Meritocracy, the fact that
professionals deal with their own clients directly leads both to suboptimization
tendencies and to the creation of direct links with external influencers. For the
experts of Professional Bureaucracy, there is no one central organizational purpose, only a host of special ones.

And so there is ample opportunity to play the political games in Meritocracy. Given the fluidity of its structure and the fact that most of the experts typically wish to get on with their specialized work, all it takes is a little effort, as
March and his colleagues point out in their description of the organization as
garbage can: "...influence over the flow of events appeared to depend [in part]
on...presence. Since few people were involved and those who were involved
wandered in and out, someone who was willing to spend time being present
could often become influential" (March and Romelaer 1976, p. 272).

The games that count in Meritocracy are not so much those to counter
authority—not insurgency, line versus staff, whistle blowing or young Turks—
simply because authority is weak in this configuration. In the case of line versus
staff in particular, a weak technostructure in Professional Bureaucracy and a
blurring of the line-staff distinction in Adhocracy renders this a minor game. Of
course, games such as insurgency and young Turks will be played when the
managers try to lord authority over the experts. But in this configuration, the
advantage does not lie with the managers, at least so long as various experts are
are able to cooperate with each other.[5] Moreover, since it is the senior professionals who have much of the power in this configuration, it is sometimes they

---

[5]Thus Zald and Berger (1978) could find no case of coup d'état in universities, although they did find
open calls for the resignation of CEOs. They believe that for coup d'état, "the subalterns must be
quite dependent on the executives for their positions" (p. 835), which is not the case where there is
professional mobility, especially when it is coupled with tenure for many of those who stay.

who find themselves challenged in these kinds of games, particularly by young Turks.

The games that really matter in Meritocracy are those to build power bases and those that pit peers against each other—notably alliance and empire building, budgeting, rival camps, and strategic candidates. The games of expertise are, of course, played as well, by the skilled seeking to protect their expertise as well as by the unskilled—the forgotten ones, numerous in the support staff of Professional Bureaucracy—seeking not only to resist authority like the experts but also to protect themselves from the power of those experts. (The sponsorship game is played, too, but not with managers so much as among experts, trying to further their careers by affiliating with colleagues of high status.) Lording (of expertise) is also used to pacify external influencers, as we shall see.

In the Professional Bureaucracy, political activity revolves first and foremost around the processes of resource allocation and pigeonholing, and second around the selection of strategic candidates.

Resource allocation is a natural focus of conflict in the Professional Bureaucracy, for a number of related reasons. First, the federated nature of the structure means that the professionals, and often their units as well, work rather independently of each other. All they need do is share common resources—funds, facilities, and support staff. (This is what Thompson [1967] calls "pooled" interdependence, as opposed to sequential or reciprocal interdependence, where the work different people do is directly linked.) So the allocation of resources emerges as a central source of conflict, especially when resources are scarce. If the outputs or performance of the professionals could easily be measured, an objective basis for resource allocation could be found—one tied to organizational needs. But they cannot, and so the basis of allocation can easily become political, allowing considerable opportunity for empire building. When the chief of psychiatry insists that the cure rate in his ward would increase dramatically if only he had three more beds, who can tell whether he is making a valid claim or trying to expand his empire.

Thus budgets tend to get allocated on the basis of power, in the first instance according to status associated with expertise, and then according to political clout. As Pfeffer and Salancik (1974) found in their research in a university, the size of the budgets received by departments was significantly correlated with their power, as perceived by department heads and reflected in their representation on major university committees, even after correcting for departmental workloads and number of faculty members. "The more powerful the department, the less the allocated resources are a function of departmental workload and student demands for course offerings" (p. 135).

Another major source of conflict in the Professional Bureaucracy is the procedure we have referred to as "pigeonholing" (Mintzberg 1979a, pp. 352–54). While the skills the professionals seek to apply may be well defined, the situations to which they should apply often are not. In other words, there is considerable overlap in the different professional skills, which leads to numerous jurisdictional disputes. Pigeonholing requires that each client be channelled to one professional or another, despite possible ambiguities in the client's needs. The university student interested in educational administration must choose between the schools of education and business administration; the hospital treats the patient for either physical or emotional symptoms—psychosomatic diseases are not recognized. Pigeonholing in the hospital assumes that the body is a collection of organs, not an integrated system. So too in the university, the Renaissance man does not exist; man's knowledge is partitioned into a series of often arbitrary boxes. In the absence of performance measures of professional work, the overlaps between these artificial distinctions cannot be rationalized analytically. And so they are fought out as political games. When the surgeons and the gynecologists argue over who should do mastectomies—the former specialists in surgical intervention, the latter in women's diseases—despite the appeals to patient welfare, it is clear to everyone that the dispute is one of power, of which empire will be expanded.

Interestingly, the processes of both resource allocation and pigeonholing, though messy and divisive, in fact also serve to reduce conflict and politics in the Professional Bureaucracy. That is because once the decisions about them are made, no matter how arbitrary, they serve to buffer or insulate the professionals and their units from one another. In effect, the political games are played at the administrative level; that is where the budgets are allocated and the pigeonholes established. Once this is done, these processes allow the professionals at the operating level to get on with their standardized work, free of political interference. The professionals are more than happy to leave these games to the managers who represent their interests, so that they can expend their energies on what they prefer to do—their professional work.

The strategic candidates game is sometimes played in the Professional Bureaucracy, but in unusual ways, because these organizations are not designed for major reorientation. For one thing, each professional operator is an independent strategy formulator: each develops his own strategy to deal with his own clients. For another, responsibility for strategic change is not clearly placed inside these organizations. Anyone—administrator or expert—may take on the role of prime mover, but it is the professional operators who must accept the change. Many candidates are in fact promoted by operators, although no one operator will do so very often. Typically an operator promotes an activity that he will perform for years, as when a professor works to create a research center or a physician promotes a new form of treatment.

Some of the strategic change comes not from the organization itself but from the professional societies which represent its experts. These societies decree regulations for all of their members and so, in effect, impose strategies on the Professional Bureaucracies. But the professional societies are notoriously conservative bodies, slow to accept innovative ideas. Thus the promotor of a strategic candidate—at least one involving a new professional procedure—must often confront resistance in his professional society as well as in his own organization. Indeed, some of the most important strategic candidates games are fought out in the professional societies.

Frequently it is the CEO who does the promoting, and the operators (perhaps in conjunction with their professional societies) who do the resisting. Thoenig and Friedberg (1976) describe the attempt by a minister of the French government to introduce structural reform in the Ministry of Public Works. The minister believed he could retain control over the formulation, leaving implementation to the professional operators in the field. He was wrong.

> Lacking relevant information, the reformers were forced to decide according to impersonal, abstract and universal criteria. Thus, to reform the local agencies they could only define a very general organizational chart which then had to be adapted to the prevailing local conditions. (p. 333)

And there the professionals with the power and knowledge that mattered subverted the proposed changes. In other words, it was the insurgency game that blocked the minister's strategic candidate, a game the operators could play rather easily. Thoenig and Friedberg conclude that "those at the top are just as much prisoners as managers of the organizations they are to run. . . . Organizational change . . . becomes a permanent bargaining process between the different groups in the organization" (pp. 314–15).

Thus, in the Professional Bureaucracy only the politically astute chief executive is able to effect strategic change. He pushes it along slowly, using persuasion, negotiation, and occasionally some interpersonal manipulation, exploiting whatever informal and formal power he has. Above all, he knows how far and how fast he can push each issue. The autocratic CEO drives the Meritocracy toward Political Arena as the professionals resist him; the weak one becomes the errand boy of the professionals, securing their funds and maintaining their external relations, while avoiding internal issues. Only the one with political finesse leaves his mark on the organization.

In Adhocracy—the collaborative-type Meritocracy—the mixture of political games is somewhat different, for two reasons. First, because the work processes are so much more fluid, there is a good deal more political activity. Politics in the federated-type Meritocracy is at least mitigated by the fact that the operators spend most of their time alone with their clients executing standardized procedures. But in Adhocracy, where almost all of the work is carried out in temporary project teams and shifting constellations of experts, the propensity to take advantage of the ambiguities to play political games is very high. When the energies of the experts can be directed into pursuits of a collaborative and constructive nature, the organization is able to perform its mission effectively. But when the politics gets out of hand, this form of Meritocracy, always on the verge of being a Political Arena, becomes one.

The second reason for a different mixture of political games in Adhocracy is that its process of strategy formation is far more complicated. Organizations using this structure do not so much have set strategies a priori—deliberate strategies—as they have fluid strategies that emerge from the consistencies in the streams of decisions coming out of their projects.[6] This means that anyone who has influence in a project has influence in strategy making. And in Adhocracy that can mean virtually everyone in the organization. It also means that the strategic candidates game emerges as paramount in Adhocracy. Indeed, given the project nature of the structure, the promotion of strategic candidates can almost be considered the very essence of the work of Adhocracy.

By no means do we wish to deny the importance of other political games in Adhocracy. Alliance and empire building, budgeting, expertise games, and especially rival camps are common too, as individuals and units vie for power in these fluid structures. Moreover, for the reasons cited earlier, the high level of fluidity gives the managers and especially the CEO more power than in the Professional Bureaucracy—someone must try to bring some order to the whole thing—and that increases somewhat the incidence of games such as sponsorship and young Turks.

THE EXTERNAL INFLUENCERS:
DETERMINED TO INFLUENCE

A number of groups of influencers tend or at least try to be active in the External Coalition of the Meritocracy. Not the least of these are a variety of professional societies, and often the government at various levels, in addition to client groups, and, when they exist, the owners of the organization. There are two reasons for the interest of these groups. First, the services provided by many Meritocracies—for example, hospitals and universities—are perceived as vital ones to society, and so attract the attention of external influencers. And second, numerous direct links exist between the internal experts and the outside influencers, with the result that the former sometimes seek to draw the latter into their conflicts.

The professional societies are perhaps the single most important group of external influencers, because they have certain powers over their members, who typically constitute the most important influencers in the Meritocracy. Through their members, these societies are able to impose certain constraints and even strategies on the organization. Much of this is accomplished indirectly, by virtue of the control these societies, together with the universities, maintain over the selection of candidates for the profession, the training of them, as well as their accreditation to practice. In other words, these societies are often able to dictate who can join the organization and with what knowledge and skills. Many also

---

[6]See Mintzberg (1978) for a discussion of deliberate strategies compared to ones that emerge from decision streams. Strategy formation in Adhocracy is described in some detail in the *Structuring* book (Mintzberg 1979*a*, pp. 442–47).

limit the supply of professionals, so as to increase the demand—and the salaries—of those already accredited. As noted earlier, protection of their members is a prime concern of these societies, sometimes at the expense of service to the clients. Once the professionals have been trained and have joined an organization, control of them can be less intense, since they have "internalized" the norms of the profession. But it can also be more direct, as the societies occasionally dictate specific regulations to their members, for example, that a specific procedure is mandatory or unacceptable for a given problem.

These forms of control impact more profoundly on the Professional Bureaucracy, which typically depends on the formal accreditation of its experts. Adhocracy is less sensitive to them, because it has less use for standardized procedures. But professional control can be present nevertheless, in the form of peer or social pressures over behaviors that are acceptable to the members of a given profession. In other words, professional norms, if not professional standards of behavior, are imposed on the organization. As we pointed out in an earlier chapter, experts identify with their own professions—that is the basis of their ideology. This results in a weak organizational ideology—since the loyalty of the Meritocracy's members lies elsewhere—but strong professional ideologies across different Meritocracies.

Finally, we should point out that the typical Meritocracy houses a whole range of experts, and so is subject to the influence of various professional societies. And these do not always see eye to eye. Sometimes they conflict, and so pull the Meritocracy in different directions. But they can also work at cross purposes and cancel out each others' influence.

Professional unions, in sharp contrast, which have emerged more recently in some Professional Bureaucracies, get around this problem by representing all of the professionals of a given organization. Given the importance of the System of Expertise in the Meritocracy, this should give the unions an enormous amount of power. Indeed, since, as we noted earlier, the union works in the *External* Coalition, this should really enable it to dominate that coalition. But the effect of unionization is quite different. We shall return to this issue later in this chapter; suffice it at this point to suggest that unionization works in contradiction to the System of Expertise, weakening rather than exploiting it, and in the process drives the organization away from the Meritocracy configuration (or further away if such tendencies encouraged unionization in the first place).

Government can be another important external influencer, particularly in the case of the Professional Bureaucracy. In part, government can get drawn into this role by the behavior of particular professional societies. Where a society is slow to protect the clients from abuse by callous professionals, the government is typically called upon to act in its place. The government can, of course, legislate directly against the professional society, in effect regulating the regulators. But professional work is difficult to regulate even by the professionals themselves, let alone by a distant government. So governments have instead been inclined to try to regulate the Professional Bureaucracies, through the imposition of controls of one sort or another. Many of these organizations, such as public universities and hospitals, in fact receive their funding from the government; indeed, many are effectively owned by the government. Thus, while a government concerned with overspending in the health sector can battle with the corporation of physicians and surgeons to change its fee schedule, it is usually far easier to cut the budgets of the hospitals under its control.

The power of government—at least as perceived by the participants—to influence the goals of certain Professional Bureaucracies shows up in the study by Gross, who found significant differences between private and public American universities on twenty-four of the forty-seven goal dimensions he studied:

> In private universities the goals emphasized revolve about student-expressive matters such as the student intellect, affecting the student permanently with the great ideas, and helping the student to develop objectivity about himself (no expressive goals distinguish the state universities at all), training the student in methods of scholarship and creative research, serving as a center for the dissemination of ideas for the surrounding area, and encouraging graduate work. In contrast, state universities emphasize to a distinctly greater extent than the private universities preparing the students for useful careers, assisting citizens through extension and doing applied research. Academic freedom, although it is high everywhere, turns out to be particularly high in the private universities reflecting their ability to maintain a greater degree of autonomy. (1968, pp. 533–34)

Evidently he who pays the piper can call some of the tunes, no matter how skilled the piper. But too much of this, as we shall soon see, and the Meritocracy becomes an Instrument. When the piper is forced to press the pedals of a player piano, the music just doesn't sound the same.

As we have seen, government can be the owner of a Professional Bureaucracy. So too can it be of an Adhocracy—as in the case of a NASA—although this is less common. Many other Meritocracies of both types are owned by their own experts, sometimes by all of them, sometimes by only the most senior ones, as in the law, accounting, and consulting firms owned by their "partners." In Blau and Scott's terms, these are mutual benefit associations (although Blau and Scott categorize what we call Professional Bureaucracies and Operating Adhocracies as "service organizations").

Some Professional Bureaucracies—private universities and hospitals, independent social work agencies, and the like—are constituted formerly as "corporations." They have no owners per se, formal authority ultimately resting in their boards of directors. The membership of these boards may be formally designated, but more commonly it is self-perpetuating, with existing directors naming the replacements. Wealthy donors have often come to dominate such boards, particularly where the organizations have been dependent on them for support, as in many private hospitals and universities in the United States. At one time, that may have enabled the donors to exercise considerable power over the organizations. But today, with the internal expertise of these organizations far more highly developed, the donors appear to be more coopted than controlling (Perrow 1961). In return for their donations, they happily accept the status and the trappings of power—the seat itself, the buildings in their name, and so on. An occasional side payment or reorientation of strategy may be requested, as when a businessman director of a university asks to have his son slipped past the admissions committee or encourages the establishment of a business school. But most often, formal cooptation seems to be effective.

Then there are the professional organizations that are privately owned, as in the case of the consulting firm started as an entrepreneurial venture. Many Administrative Adhocracies—especially ones operating in the business sector—are privately owned, although their stock may be widely held. When closely held, say in the case of an electronics firm, the owner of course has considerable power, but because of the importance of expertise, nowhere near that of the owner of a Machine Bureaucracy or Simple Structure. The organization may perhaps emerge as a hybrid of Meritocracy and Autocracy, if the owner serves as chief executive, or of Meritocracy and the Instrument, if he does not. When an Administrative Adhocracy is widely held and large—as in the case of, say, a petrochemical company—as implied earlier we might expect a hybrid of Meritocracy with the Closed System, as the experts are forced to share a fair amount of power with the administrators.

A final group of external influencers, particularly in the Professional Bureaucracy (and to a lesser extent the Operating Adhocracy), are the clients. They should have considerable power, for here more than in any other power configuration, the relationship between operator and client can be direct and personal. The doctor, lawyer, and accountant meet their clients on a face-to-face, one-to-one basis. This constitutes direct access by members of the External Coalition to the influential operators of the Internal Coalition, bypassing the board, the CEO, and the whole administrative structure. Thus the clients should be able to influence significantly the organization's behavior. Unfortunately, however, they lack an understanding of the critical skills of their "suppliers," and so typically remain passive, even subservient to them, although they may resent it. Only when the professional operators take it upon themselves to represent the interests of their clients—as professional ideals so encourage them—do the clients get a voice in the Internal Coalition. As Blau and Scott note:

> In the typical case...the client does not know what will best serve his own interest. For example, the patient is not qualified to judge whether or not it would be best for his health to undergo an operation. Hence, the client is vulnerable, subject to exploitation and dependent on the integrity of the professional to whom he has to come for help. The customer in a store, on the other hand, presumably can look after his own interests. Consequently, while the businessman's decisions are expected to be governed by his self-interest—as epitomized in the phrase *"caveat emptor"*—the professional's decisions are expected to be governed not by his own self-interest but by his judgment of what will serve the client's interest best. (1962, p. 51)

THE EXTERNAL COALITION:
APPARENTLY DIVIDED, ACTUALLY PASSIVE

(We have noted that Professional Bureaucracy appears to be the purest form of Meritocracy, followed by Operating Adhocracy, while Administrative Adhocracy, because of the power of the administrators and sometimes the owners as well, appears to be the least pure of the three, often tending toward a hybrid form. Consequently, the following discussion will, except where otherwise noted, relate primarily to Professional Bureaucracy and secondarily to Operating Adhocracy, although it will not be completely irrelevant for Administrative Adhocracy.)

From what we have said above, the External Coalition of the Meritocracy should be active and divided, a force to be reckoned with by the Internal Coalition. The clients may be subservient and the donors coopted, but governments, owners, and others seem intent on exerting influence. And then, of course, there are the professional societies. But from what we also said above, expert power in the Internal Coalition also acts to pacify the external influencers. Hence the flow of power between the External and Internal Coalitions—unlike that of our first four configurations, where it clearly flowed one way or the other (if at all)—seems to be rather complex, and able to go either way depending on the circumstances.

The setting for the confrontation is simple: the Internal Coalition seeks autonomy while the External Coalition seeks control. Bidwell (1965), in discussing school systems, puts "this problem...generic to professionally staffed organizations" (p. 1012) this way: "to maintain professional latitude without diminishing too greatly public responsiveness" (p. 1016). Professional latitude is required for "judgments regarding, first, what kinds of specific...outcomes best serve the...constituency and, second, what procedures are best adapted to these ends." Public responsiveness means "to remain responsive to the controlling constituency" (p. 1012).

Between the External and Internal Coalitions, each vying for power, sits the CEO. Due to the profusion of direct links between the experts and various external influencers, the CEO can look like a kind of spectator. Unfortunately for him, however, his seat is not in the grandstands but down on the ground, in the no man's land between the two coalitions. Sometimes shots are fired directly at the CEO in the expectation that he will deflect them to the other side. Governments, for example, as well as economic-minded directors, look to the chief executives of public hospitals, universities, and the like to keep the costs down, while the experts look to them to keep the budgets up. The CEO is viewed concurrently as the trustee of the powerful external influencers and the leader of the internal influencers. The problem discussed by Bidwell becomes the CEO's problem: how to maintain professional latitude so that those with the requisite knowledge make the important decisions yet still respond to the wishes of the public for the efficient pursuit of the goals it considers important.

But the battle for control is fought less in the middle ground than on either side. Looking at the External Coalition, as noted earlier, what especially activates the external influencers—particularly in welfare agencies, schools, hospitals, and the like—is the importance of the mission to society. And what gives them a basis of power is, above all, the dependence of the organization on external funding. The external influencers try to use all of the means of influence available to them. Social norms are invoked, and can weigh heavily on the conscience of the professional, since part of his training involved an indoctrination in the importance of service to society. Pressure campaigns are attempted, as in the case of the student uprisings against the universities in the late 1960s. The board of directors is another available means of influence, with its places sometimes formally designated to different groups of external influencers. In Chapter 7, we noted the example of the Quebec hospitals, with certain seats alloted to "users," government, clinical and nonclinical staff, affiliated universities, and so on. And then there are the formal constraints imposed on the professionals by their societies, as we have already seen, and the direct controls that can also be imposed by governments, as when they dictate university or hospital budgets.

Sometimes the insiders themselves activate the external influencers with whom they have direct links, to enlist their support in inside political games. Radical factions on university faculties, for example, seek the support of activist students, while conservative ones turn to the alumni for support of the status quo. In Professional Bureaucracy, the operators will often draw their respective professional societies into battle, while in Administrative Adhocracy, the different functional specialists will do the same with the external influencers they represent—marketing people will turn to the customers, researchers to members of the scientific community, and so on.

But while the experts sometimes seek to activate external influencers to help them win political games, more often they work to pacify them, in order to protect their own power and prerogatives. And here the insiders can rely on two things. First and foremost is their expertise, which they can lord over the "lay" members of the External Coalition. And that is often sufficient to tip the power balance in favor of the Internal Coalition. The professionals pacify the external influencers by claiming that only they possess the knowledge required to determine what the organization should do. We see this clearly in Cressey's discussion of the treatment or rehabilitation-oriented prison, compared with the one oriented to custody, the former requiring professional work in its operating core, the latter largely unskilled work. While we described the latter in Chapter 18 as a consensus-dominated Instrument, here we see the former as a Meritocracy with a pacified External Coalition. As Cressey notes, the treatment-oriented prisons tend to "maintain alliances" with external influencers that support the efforts of the inside experts, that allow them to "have their own views of their purpose, of policy and of appropriate means for achieving goals." Because the work is "technical and 'professional'. . .it is to be judged by members of the technical and professional groups involved, not by the 'public'":

Accordingly, professional groups such as psychiatrists and social workers, and technical groups such as visiting wardens and foremen of prison industries, made up the significant public of the treatment-oriented prison. This left evaluation of professional or technical competence in the hands of professional workers or technicians, not in the hands of the uninformed taxpayer. (1958, p. 46)

A second thing the insiders can rely on to help pacify the External Coalition is the difficulty of bringing expert work under bureaucratic controls. As noted in Chapter 18, bureaucratic controls are generally required to render an organization the Instrument of its external influencers. But expert work does not allow such control. The analysts of the technostructure cannot really formalize procedures, simply because these are too complex, requiring years of training. Hence they must be controlled by the workers themselves, backed up by their professional societies. Nor can the analysts easily measure the organization's outputs and performance, thereby specifying objectives for it. The university's mission, for example, is to develop and disseminate knowledge. But what conceivable activity, from reading comic books to swimming in the nude, cannot be argued to pursue that mission? That is why governments have been stifled again and again in their attempts to gain tight control of universities, as well as hospitals and the like. They have simply been unable to tie their funding to reasonable measures of performance. So they fall back on crude, artificial ones, like counting heads, or publications. Thus in the university studied by Butler et al.:

> Greater internal power...appears to be associated with greater "ambiguity" and with "lack of clarity"... Criteria for evaluating teaching and research are primarily in the hands of internal interest-units which relate them to an international cosmopolitan system of knowledge.... External organizational interests such as the [University Grants Committee], Government departments, or industry find it much more difficult to evaluate [the university] and so to impose their interests on it than they do with [the electricity board studied] (1977-78, pp. 56-57).

As the Butler et al. analysis indicates, the Internal Coalition is able to establish all kinds of devices to protect itself from external influence and thereby to render its External Coalition passive. This public university, for example, was in many ways legally autonomous from the government that funded it. Its chief executive was appointed by the University Council rather than the government, and its budget allocations were determined by a national committee of academics rather than civil servants. Internal power was further enhanced by career tenure for its faculty, by freedom to determine its own new programs and control its own admissions, and by its receipt of budgets on a global basis, enabling it to decide on the internal allocation.

All of this leads us to the conclusion that while *organizations of professionals* may face a wide variety of External Coalitions, *Meritocracies* face ones that, while apparently divided, are in fact best described as passive. Our point is that organizations of professionals can indeed face truly Divided or Dominated External Coalitions, but that the effect of this is to weaken the internal System of

Expertise, to the point where the power configuration cannot be described as Meritocracy, at least in its pure form. At best a hybrid results, which, in terms of our analysis of Chapter 17, may very well drive the organization toward a form of the Political Arena. We can expect this result whether the external pressures come from the government, the owners, even unions of the professionals themselves, or from all of them together, as they divide power in the External Coalition.

In the pure form of Meritocracy, of which Butler et al.'s university seems to be an example, the clients are overwhelmed by expertise and the donors are coopted, while government and the owners are somehow pacified. Perhaps they have given up after years of fruitless attempts to exercise direct influence. Only the professional societies retain some power in the External Coalition, but as was clear in the Cressey description, rather that trying to dominate, they in effect join hands with the professionals to help pacify everyone else. Thus, expertise inside the organization, supported by corresponding expertise outside of it, dominates the power system.

Of course, not all universities or other professional organizations achieve the autonomy of the one studied by Butler et al., which is another way of saying that not all can be described as pure Meritocracies. When external influencers, notably governments, do succeed in exercising considerable control over them, a hybrid form tends to emerge. This seems to be the case, for example, in the public American universities that Gross studied, according to the findings we cited earlier. Governments, whether in England, America, or elsewhere, control the budgets of the public universities. So long as they do no more than allocate these on a global basis, their control is loose, and professional autonomy to set direction can be maintained, at least within the resource constraints. But all kinds of pressures arise on governments to exercise more influence. Cases come to light of wastage and inefficiency, of the callousness of certain professionals, of the pursuit of goals that some segments of the population consider subversive. As a result, government sometimes attempts to control behavior more directly, to render the university society's Instrument. And as we saw in Chapter 18, that means trying to impose on it bureaucratic controls—work or output standards. Either government sends in its own analysts, to prescribe rules, regulations, performance measures and the like, or else it expects the analysts of the university's own technostructure to do these things for it. (Of course, in the absence of external influence, the internal administrators may try to do the same thing.)

Either way, since bureaucratic controls challenge the experts' control of their own work, they tend to fight it. And so long as they do, the experts are expending their energies on politics in place of practicing their expertise, and so the Political Arena configuration tends to displace that of Meritocracy. At best, a shaky alliance is reached between the experts and the administrators, with conflict just below the surface, ever ready to erupt. Should the experts stop resisting the bureaucratic controls completely, the System of Authority will displace that of Expertise as the predominant force in the Internal Coalition, and the organization will begin to look like an Instrument (or a Closed System if the internal administrators are behind the controls).

Such forces are, of course, dysfunctional to the extent that the organization requires expertise. Some external control is always necessary, to keep the lid on expenditures and limit exploitation of their power by the professionals. But too much can seriously effect the quality of the professional services. Thus Gross (1968) finds in his study of the perceived goals of American universities that "when the faculty have power the goal of student intellect receives strong emphasis. When legislatures have power, it is positively de-emphasized... Such is also the case for training scholarship and research, student careers, disseminating ideas, preserving the heritage, accepting good students only," and so on (p. 541).

Of course, the case for bureaucratic controls can become a self-fulfilling one. Control in the Meritocracy—self-control by the experts—presupposes professional excellence. In other words, the experts merit power when they are highly trained, highly skilled, *and* responsible. But bureaucratic controls reduce the organization's ability to attract competent experts, and rob the competent ones already there of their initiative. Skills atrophy, autonomy gets abused, and irresposibility becomes prevalent. In other words, the basis for expert control weakens, which leads to calls for its further curtailment through greater tightening of the technocratic screws. If the professors teach poorly, show no concern for their students, are unable to keep up in their fields, and avoid doing research, why then should their work not be more tightly regulated by the analysts or more closely supervised by the administrators? On what basis can incompetent professionals justify autonomy? A vicious circle therefore results, rendering the organization more and more machine bureaucratic and probably politicized as well, less and less able to perform its intended mission.

A NOTE ON THE UNIONIZATION OF THE PROFESSIONAL BUREAUCRACY　Lately, professionals faced with such pressures have tried a new form of resistance: they have unionized. In other words, they have chosen to vent their frustration collectively. Because expertise and conventional forms of collegiality have been insufficient to meet the pressures, the professionals have instead formally combined forces within the organization, across their different areas of specialization (or professions), much as unskilled workers do when they form industrial unions. Of course, unionization need not result only from dysfunctional forces already at play in the professional organization. It can also result from weak expertise to begin with, incompetent experts needing unionization to protect themselves and to conceal the fact that they will never be able to justify professional autonomy or achieve true professional collegiality. In fact, according to the vicious circle discussed above, we should expect to find these two sets of forces—dysfunctional administrative pressures and weak expertise—combining in many professional organizations that unionize. The strong Meritocracies, purer in form, have not generally been the ones to unionize.

In any event, unionization does not solve the basic problem; it aggravates it. It takes a weakened System of Expertise and further weakens it, driving the organization further from Meritocracy, closer to a form of Machine Bureaucracy (or Political Arena). The clients are worse off and so too are the competent professionals. The reasons for this are as follows.

The key to the effective functioning of the Professional Bureaucracy is *individual responsibility*—dedication of the professional to his client, based on a close, personal relationship between the two. (In Operating Adhocracy, the equivalent is project team responsibility.) A subtle point has to be stressed here. These are highly decentralized structures, with much power flowing right to the operating core. But this power is not dispersed to the collectivity of professionals, for them to make major decisions together. It is dispersed to individuals and small departmental groups to make the specific decisions that concern their own work and to lobby within the administrative structure on broader issues. That is to say, while it is true that the experts hold the reins of power in the Professional Bureaucracy, they do not do so as an homogeneous collectivity. These organizations house all kinds of experts, each with its own needs and interests. On the operating level, individuals are largely left alone to carry out their basic work; on the administrative level, they must vie with each other, often in departmental groups, to determine outcomes. Thus, decision making at the administrative level of the Professional Bureaucracy is a complex maze of negotiation, influence peddling, persuasion—in other words, of political activity.

Unionization, by paving over professional and departmental differences and, more importantly, challenging individual control of the work, seriously damages professional autonomy and individual responsibility. And collective responsibility can never replace individual responsibility in these kinds of organizations.

Unionization also damages a second characteristic key to the effective functioning of these organizations—collegiality, which means in part professional control of administrative decision making, either directly by the operating professionals or through their representatives in the administrative positions. Collegiality assumes that operating professionals and administrators work together, in common interest. Unionization, in contrast, assumes a conflict of interest between the two. By taking a we-they attitude, viewing the managers as "bosses" instead of colleagues, unionization drives a wedge between operator and administrator (or drives the existing wedge deeper when such dysfunctional forces preceeded unionization). This damages the notion of collegiality.

More significantly, unionization takes professional influence not only outside the administrative structure but outside the Internal Coalition altogether, as we noted in Chapter 4. By acting collectively through their representatives, who negotiate with the top managers directly, the professionals bypass the entire administrative structure. The effect of this, ironically, is to cede control of the Internal Coalition to the senior managers, thereby *centralizing* power in the organization. The managers at middle and lower levels, as well as *individual* professionals—key players when collegiality exists—are bypassed in the play of power between union representative and senior manager, and so come out seriously weakened.

Acting from the External Coalition, the union seeks to impose formal constraints on the organization on behalf of its membership. But what needs do the members have in common? The prime one is to control decision making individually and in particular groups, for the fact of the matter is that on most of the issues that matter to them, the professionals have different requirements. But that is the one need the union cannot serve. Having to present a united front in central negotiations with the administration, the union is forced to deny these differences and to focus on the commonalities. And these tend to be on the grossest, most self-serving issues, notably remuneration for professional services. So while the professionals may gain on this one issue, they lose on all others. All this is to say that the assumption of the collective interest of the professionals vis-à-vis the administration, the very basis for unionization, is a fallacy in the true Professional Bureaucracy.

Where the union does succeed in imposing formal constraints on the administration, what this amounts to is the imposition of standards, in the form of rules and regulations, across the entire organization. In other words, even though imposed on behalf of the professionals, the constraints by their very nature serve to formalize the structure, which serves to weaken the power of expertise in favor of authority. Formalization coupled with centralization, it will be recalled from Chapter 14, means Machine Bureaucracy. In other words, the direct effect of unionization is to drive Professional Bureaucracy toward Machine Bureaucracy, in the form of the Instrument or Closed System. Exactly the tendency that likely caused the professionals to unionize in the first place!

To summarize, while we can understand what makes external influencers—notably government—want to exercise close control over certain professional organizations, we must also recognize the consequences: the evoking of dysfunctional processes in the structure which can lead to responses by the professionals that are themselves more dysfunctional. The illustrations of this are everywhere around us—in overregulated and ineffective school systems, universities, hospitals, and welfare agencies. To correct the original problems—misuse of professional autonomy, weak expertise, and so on—society will instead have to improve professional training in the first place, encourage retraining where necessary, and above all play on the responsibility of the professional and the ideology of his profession (its "code of ethics") to render effective service to society. And the professional faced with excessive administrative pressure will have to counter it through the forces of collegiality—for example, by working bit by bit to reinstate expert control over decision making—rather than by unionizing. In other words, society and professionals themselves will have to reinforce individual responsibility, with competence. And that means reverting to a purer form of Meritocracy, away from Machine Bureaucracy.

THE GOAL SYSTEM:
NONOPERATIONAL, ORIENTED
TO PROFESSIONAL GOALS

To close this discussion, we review briefly the goals of the Meritocracy, and in the process draw together a number of our conclusions.

We have already seen that Meritocracies tend to have official goals, tied to their missions, that are vague and nonoperational, what are often called "motherhood" goals—to advance knowledge, to improve the lot of the under-privileged, to cure the mentally ill, and so on. Thus Bidwell comments that:

> The goals of schools tend to be stated in ambiguous, diffuse terms, presumably because educational outcomes are highly indeterminate, that is, variable above a minimum standard. This quality of goal statement no doubt causes internal dif-ficulties for school systems in specifying desired results of instruction and artic-ulating professional judgments and community demands. But it also provides them with fairly wide latitude to exercise such judgments while maintaining the legitimacy of their operations in the eyes of their public constituents. (1965, pp. 1016–17)

These comments apply particularly to Professional Bureaucracies; Adhocracies, especially of the administrative type, sometimes have clearer official goals—for example, to put a man in the moon before 1970 in the case of NASA, perhaps to grow and make a certain profit in the case of an electronics firm.

But what interests us here are the organization's real goals, those inten-tions that underlie the actions they really do take. Because the lion's share of the power rests with the experts, we would expect to see some consistency in the goals pursued. But because the organization houses all kinds of experts, and because external influencers have some power—to impose constraints if not dic-tate primary goals—we expect to see diversity as well. Thus the goal system is probably best described as a complex web of constraints coupled with a few pri-mary goals that are, in Cyert and March's (1963) terms, attended to sequentially. In this sense, Meritocracy looks more like the Political Arena than the Instrument of any influencer or the Closed System that pursues its own goals, although it does exhibit some characteristics of the latter two configurations as well.

The clients of the Meritocracy are obviously concerned with the mission itself as a goal. That should not make much difference, since as we already noted, they usually lack power in this configuration. But as it happens they are joined in their interests, to a certain extent at least, by the experts, especially in the Professional Bureaucracy. Even though the professionals have a good deal of discretion to displace mission as a goal by their own personal goals, the personal relationships they often have with the clients, as well as their professional ideologies, helps to place service and mission high up on their list of goals. And the professionals of course do have the power. In fact, given the weakness of the clients it is often the professionals who end up representing their interests, sometimes, ironically, in face of resistance from the administrators, who can be distant from the clients and more concerned with economic efficiency. (Not so, however, in those organizations such as consulting firms, where the top managers are the salesmen and so close to the clients and their needs.) Thus Brager found in his study of the Mobilization for Youth that the professional operators manifested "dramatically more commitment" to the organization's mission than the administrators or support staff (1969, p. 173).

Hence mission emerges as one important goal of the Meritocracy, as pointed out by writers such as Etzioni (1961) and Dent (1959). The latter found in his study that "whereas only two fifths of the business managers express a concern for public service, all of the hospital administrators give this as a goal" (p. 370). In fact, we shall see in the next chapter that when a professional organization pursues more than one mission, for example teaching and research in the university, a great deal of the political energy is expended battling over which is to get more attention.

For the experts of the organization, right alongside the mission—and frequently above it—is the pursuit of their own professional interests. Two goals are especially important for the experts, as we have seen throughout this discussion as well as that of Chapter 9 on the professional as influencer. One is the maintenance of their autonomy—individual or group—from interference by administrators or external influencers. And the other is professional excellence. What encourages the expert to produce is neither the carrot nor the whip—at least not those of the organization itself—but the fact that he has a strong commitment to his skills and to his profession. But this can also generate an obsession with perfecting skills, so that the expert forgets what he is perfecting them for—as in the case of the surgeon who claims that his operation was a success even though the patient died. This can sometimes result in the inversion of means and ends by entire Meritocracies. A third goal of importance to the experts, and especially to the administrators who represent specific groups of them, is the enhancement of the prestige of their particular specialty. This, of course, manifests itself in the empire-building game, as various factions of experts vie for wider latitude in the practice of their specialties and for greater resources with which to practice them. And such efforts create natural pressures for organizational growth.

In pursuing these two sets of goals—the mission of the organization and the personal interests of the experts—the Meritocracy may seem to have a goal system that resembles those of the Missionary combined with the Closed System. But neither resemblance is quite correct. The Meritocracy, for example, does not pursue the systems goals very vigorously, because the experts, who hold the lion's share of the power, typically believe they have relatively little to gain from the strengthening of the organization as an independent system. Their commitment is to their professions, not to the organization. They are skilled and mobile; many have no interest in administrative office; their remuneration is often tied to profession-wide standards, indeed, as Beyer and Lodahl note in the case of university professors, "many . . . receive an important part of their re-wards—recognition—from their scientific or scholarly communities" (1976, p. 124). Thus the survival and efficiency of the organization are not strong goals per se, although control by it of its environment tends to be, indirectly, since that is the means to ensure professional autonomy. And growth also tends to be, as noted above, because of the pervasiveness of the efforts at building empires.

The same factors also mitigate against the development of strong goals of organization ideology. Expert work can certainly be surrounded by a good deal of ideology and sometimes even a missionary orientation as well. But that is typically centered on the professions themselves—their own histories, tradi-tions, and sagas—rather than on the organization where the professions are practiced. An organizational ideology can, of course, grow up separately from the professional ideologies, as we saw in the case of Clark's "distinctive colleges." Indeed, the wide diffusion of power in both the Meritocracy and the Missionary would seem to make them compatible configurations. But, as noted in this chapter and the last, the status differences inherent in expertise conflict with the egalitarian norms of organizational ideology, and so create a certain in-compatibility between these two configurations. Hence, although many excep-tions can be found, in the general case we would not expect a strong ideology within the organization that assumes the characteristics of Meritocracy, especially in the federated-type where the experts' identification with the organization tends to be the weakest.

One systems goal—economic efficiency—is the subject of certain atten-tion in the Meritocracy. As we saw, it is the goal favored by the influencers who supply funds, notably the government and the donors. They are particularly concerned that the organization not squander its resources, a tendency they find particularly strong whenever experts are allowed to perfect their skills at some-one else's expense.

But it is not the experts they hold responsible for attending to the goal of economic efficiency, for two reasons. First, they deal with the organization for-mally, that is, through those of its members in positions of authority. Second, they themselves usually work in more authoritarian structures—the donors in business firms, the government administrators in public bureaucracies—typically either Autocracies, Instruments, or Closed Systems. None of these configura-tions reflects a particular appreciation for the wide distribution of power based on expertise. And so these external influencers tend to hold the CEO, and in turn the other administrators, accountable for the behavior of the experts, presum-ably through the imposition of bureaucratic controls, just as they themselves are held accountable for the behavior of their own subordinates.

But of course the Meritocracy does not work like this. Bureaucratic con-trols are anathema to the professionals, and they hardly accept the CEO as being accountable to someone else for what they do. And so, it is the goal of efficiency above all that traps the CEO in the no man's land between the External and

Internal Coalitions. On one side, the external influencers cannot understand why the "manager," supposedly in charge of the organization, cannot keep the costs down; on the other side, the professionals cannot understand why the "administrator," their representative, seems so obsessed with economic goals. The former fail to appreciate the power distribution in the Internal Coalition, the latter fail to realize that if the CEO did not attend to the economic goals, no one else would.

23

The Political Arena

endure, it must typically moderate itself, giving rise to what we call a "shaky alliance" if it remains confined, or to the "politicized organization" if it pervades all power relationships; while any form of the Political Arena appears to be dysfunctional because of the resources it wastes, those that cause or speed up functional realignments in coalition or functional changes of configuration, those that correct earlier dysfunctional changes in coalition or configuration, those shaky alliances that reflect natural, balanced, and irreconcilable forces on an organization, and even those complete Political Arenas that speed up the death of spent organizations, can be considered functional.

...each individual in [the] group is, in his own right, a player in a central, competitive game. The name of the game is politics... [The Politics Model] sees no unitary actor but rather many actors as players—players who focus not on a single strategic issue but on many diverse...problems as well; players who act in terms of no consistent set of strategic objectives but rather according to various conceptions of national, organizational, and personal goals; players who make...decisions not by a single, rational choice but by the pulling and hauling that is politics. (Allison 1971, p. 144)

As our discussion has proceeded from one configuration to another, we have seen a gradual reduction of the forces of integration, from the full chain of authority of the Instrument, to the truncated one of the Closed System, to the weak authority of the Meritocracy. And with this has come a gradual rise in political activity. But even the Meritocracy housed forces that mitigated political activity, keeping it under control. Now we come to a power configuration that is essentially political, one in which conflict predominates. It is the opposite of the Missionary, in which everyone voluntarily pulls together toward a common end. Here everyone can pull apart, toward what seem to be his or her own private ends. The organization emerges as a *Political Arena*, a system captured by conflict. The French have a graphic term for it—un panier de crabes, a bucket of crabs, each clawing at the others to come out on top.

Just as a strong leader can override other conditions to drive an organization toward Autocracy, and a strong ideology can do the same in favor of the Missionary, so too can strong politics override all other conditions to drive an organization to the Political Arena, at least until other conditions reassert themselves. In fact, we shall find that the Political Arena is often a temporary configuration, sometimes a necessary way station in the transition from one stable power configuration to another, sometimes an aberration of more natural power relationships or just an arbitrary attempt to realign power.

No matter where conflict arises, as it endures it has a habit of spreading in and around an organization. Sometimes it originates in the External Coalition, but because the members of that coalition cannot make the decisions, they impose their diverse and conflicting pressures on the insiders, and this tends to politicize the Internal Coalition. More often perhaps, the conflict originates in the Internal Coalition, but because it is to the advantage of internal influencers to seek the support of outsiders, there is an inclination to divide and politicize the External Coalition as well. The conflict can also arise not in either coalition but between the two of them, each united at the outset in its struggle against the other (as when insiders who share a strong organizational ideology battle with a dominant external influencer). But again, each side will try to gain supporters in the other, which tends to divide and politicize both of the coalitions.

When the conflict does in fact pervade both coalitions as well as the relationships between the two of them, and, in addition, is *intense* in nature, a form we call the *complete Political Arena* emerges.

Few Political Arenas can be complete in this way, at least for long. In other words, few organizations can sustain intense, pervasive politics without destroying themselves. Thus most of the Political Arenas we expect to find in practice, aside from some of brief duration, should be partial—confining their conflict to one of the coalitions or the relationships between the two of them or else moderating the intensity of the conflict that pervades them.

We open this chapter with a brief description of the complete form of the Political Arena, to show, if you will, the fullest flowering of this configuration, what it looks like in its purest, most absolute form. Then, we introduce three other, partial forms that appear to be common, and use them to explain various life cycles of Political Arenas—how they tend to emerge and resolve themselves. This discussion leads us to some conclusions about whether the Political Arena can be described as a functional or dysfunctional configuration. Finally, we look at some illustrations of the three partial forms of the Political Arena, in order to flesh out our discussion of this most fluid and complicated of the power configurations.

THE COMPLETE POLITICAL ARENA

This description, which will be brief and somewhat stylized, discusses conflict first in the External Coalition, then in the Internal Coalition, and finally between the two. It is the presence of conflict of an intense nature in all three of these places—essentially the complete breakdown of any focus of power, for the whole organization and even for either of its coalitions—that makes a Political Arena "complete." We end our discussion of this form of the Political Arena with a look at some of the goal systems it can adopt.

THE EXTERNAL COALITION: DIVIDED   As already noted, in its complete form, the External Coalition of the Political Arena is divided and politically particular situation, and in some situations virtually all of them do. Owners, government at every level and in all of its manifestations, suppliers, clients, competitors, all kinds of employee associations, and particularly special interest groups of every conceivable stripe seek to benefit from the organization's actions. The complete Political Arena experiences all kinds of external dependencies, and so must respond to external influencers. It comes under perpetual fire.

In some organizations, when the conflict originates in the Internal Coalition, the external influencers wish to remain passive. Sometimes they succeed, as we shall see later. But forces arise, as noted earlier, to draw them into the internal battles. And once drawn in, their very presence further intensify these battles. Consider Mumford and Pettigrew's example of the purchase of major equipment:

> With large-scale technical decisions involving the purchase of expensive hardware, the outside manufacturers of this hardware will have a major incentive to influence the internal decision process... It can be argued that one of the objectives of the sales staff of an equipment manufacturer is to generate uncertainty, particularly in relation to the proposals of their rivals.... A good salesman needs to understand the political factors within a firm which are influencing its technical decisions and to intervene in these in such a way that his firm's interests are favored.... These attempts to interfere with and influence internal political processes will, in turn, add to the uncertainty of the internal decision-making environment and may increase political activity within those groups responsible for taking the final decision. (1975, pp. 111–12)

Given the open-ended and divisive nature of politics, every one of the external means of influence tends to get used in the complete Political Arena. The external influencers try to impose all kinds of formal constraints on the organization, many of them contradictory; they watch over it carefully for violation of social norms—at least *their* social norms; they constantly seek direct access to insiders, and try to include themselves in decision processes and to plant their representatives inside the Internal Coalition whenever possible. But their most important means of influence is the pressure campaign. What characterizes the External Coalition of the complete Political Arena above all is the frequency and the intensity of the campaigns of pressure it brings against the organization.

Of course, as an available external means of influence, the board of directors also gets used. It is seldom a facade, for although it is easily bypassed, it remains a center of legitimate power. For the outsiders, it is a potential control device; for the insiders, a potential tool to ward off external control. "Boards may be most implicated in decisions when the unified chain of command is broken up. For instance, as hospitals have come to look more like pluralistic polities, boards may reenter the power arena either at the invitation of the contending parties...or on their own accord" (Zald 1969, p. 110). And so the influencers of the complete Political Arena fight for seats on the board, and then try to use these seats to gain personal benefits. Sometimes, because of historical factors, the board of a highly politicized organization remains the private domain of one set of influencers, forcing the others to find alternate means of influence. But in this environment of conflict, the old directors can hold on only so long before other influencers succeed in broadening the representation, thereby rendering the board itself an arena for face-to-face bargaining.[1]

THE INTERNAL COALITION: POLITICIZED   The Internal Coalition of the complete Political Arena features all the characteristics described in Chapter 13 on the System of Politics. Group pressures and direct links to external influencers abound; the personal needs of the insiders dominate their behaviors; formal goals and objectives, should they exist at all, get distorted; suboptimization is common; and means are commonly inverted with ends. Privileged information and access to the influential are used to their limits, games are won and lost on the basis of effort expended and the political skills of the players, and the legitimate systems of influence—to the extent that they exist at all—are exploited in illegitimate ways without hesitation.

The fact is, however, that these legitimate systems—especially Authority and Ideology, the keys to integrating the efforts of the insiders—tend to be weak in this configuration. Unity of command has no special importance, and tradition and sense of mission count for little. Everything is subordinated to the System of Politics. The Systems of Authority and Ideology might have been weak in the first place, creating a vacuum in which politics was able to arise. Or else, the intensity of the political activity might have weakened them, insiders having pursued conflicting or parochial goals, perhaps encouraged by outsiders who bypassed the chain of authority. In any event, what we see in the complete Political Arena is a breakdown of authority and ideology—in other words, of the forces of integration.

Likewise, conventional forms of expertise are overridden by political forces in the Political Arena. Here it is not technical skills that count so much as skills at politics—at persuading, bargaining, and coercing—and not technical knowledge so much as privileged knowledge, knowledge of the organization and its players—their interests and their vulnerabilities. In summary, in this configuration it is politics—the play of informal, essentially illegitimate power—that determines outcomes:

> . . . what happens is not chosen as a solution to a problem but rather results from compromise, conflict, and confusion of officials with diverse interests and unequal influence; *political* in the sense that the activity from which decisions and actions emerge is best characterized as bargaining. . . (Allison 1971, p. 162)

Political games abound in the complete Political Arena, especially the most

[1]See the discussion of the Divided External Coalition in Chapter 7 for more detail on the nature of the complete Political Arena's External Coalition and the possible forms it can take.

intense ones, those that are antagonistic to or substitute for (rather than coexist with) the legitimate systems of influence: alliance building, rival camps, young Turks. Alliances are especially important because, under conditions of conflict, there is strength in numbers. And alliances are encouraged because all of the insiders can get involved in the political games. Indeed, in this kind of configuration—where "if you're not for us, you're against us"—it is difficult to remain neutral or passive. Unlike the games played in, say, the Instrument, those played in the Political Arena lack referees. In that sense, they are more like wars. Operators, line managers of every kind, analysts, even support staffers, all get drawn in.

The position of chief executive is a difficult one in the complete Political Arena. For one thing, the CEO stands between the Internal and External Coalitions, each conflictive in its own right and the two in conflict with each other. Moreover, the CEO's prime means of influence—the personal and bureaucratic systems of control—are of little help here. Even ideology is of no avail. At least in the Meritocracy, the CEO knew with whom he had to deal. Power was distributed on the basis of expertise, and it was clear who had that. In the complete Political Arena, the distribution of power is so fluid and the politics so intense that no one can ever be sure where the real power lies. External influencers take a good deal of the CEO's time—he must listen to them, negotiate with them, and try to pacify them. Likewise, as the occupant of a position that at least seems important, the CEO is constantly harassed by internal influencers. Of course, here again, as in Meritocracy and especially Adhocracy (which in some ways resembles the Political Arena), the fluidity of the power situation can also favor the CEO. The politically astute occupant of that office can exploit the ambiguity. He becomes a lion in the Political Arena. But without political skills, his role reverts to that of Christian, and he gets chewed to pieces by other lions.

THE FLOW OF POWER BETWEEN THE TWO COALITIONS: COMPLEX AND RECIPROCAL   The flow of power between the Internal and External Coalitions of the complete Political Arena is typically very complex, flowing in both directions through a wide variety of channels. To some extent, conflict in the complete Political Arena takes the form of war between the two coalitions, as the external influencers seek control over the organization's actions while the internal influencers seek to resist such control and to coopt the outsiders, hoping to keep the spoils for themselves. Favoring the power of the insiders is their intimate knowledge of the organization's functioning, as well as any technical expertise they happen to have. Moreover, as full-time participants, they have the energy to expend on the political battles. But the outsiders often control, not only critical resources on which the organization depends, but also its legal prerogatives. So the war can be somewhat balanced.

But much more than war takes place between the two coalitions. With conflict rampant in both of them, defections and clandestine alliances across them are common. This results in a jumble of complex relationships between the two, in many cases seeming to result less in war than in anarchy. The outsiders' means of influence are so direct, personal, and focussed, and the contacts between the two groups so pervasive, that is sometimes difficult to distinguish insider from outsider without looking at a list of salaried employees.

Here, in contrast to all the other power configurations, does the distinction between External and the Internal Coalition tend to break down. As suggested in Figure 23-1, the two blend into one continuous network of political activity. In the Instrument, Closed System, Autocracy, and Missionary, the boundaries between the two coalitions—between organization and environment—are sharply defined. Even in the Meritocracy, the distinctions are clear (especially in Professional Bureaucracy, although somewhat less so in Adhocracy[2]). In the Political Arena, however, with influencers coming and going, these distinctions blur. Certainly, as noted, some external power passes conventionally through the board and the CEO into the Internal Coalition—in the Political Arena no channel of influence is left ignored. But a great deal more bypasses the conventional channels and flows from external influencers directly to internal influencers, and vice versa. Nothing is simple or ordered about the flow of power in the complete Political Arena.

THE GOAL SYSTEM: FLUID AND UNSTABLE

Consider a round, sloped, multi-goal soccer field on which individuals play soccer. Many different people (but not everyone) can join the game (or leave it) at different times. Some people can throw balls into the game or remove them. Individuals while they are in the game try to kick whatever ball comes near them in the direction of goals they like and away from goals that they wish to avoid. The slope of the field produces a bias in how the balls fall and what goals are reached, but the course of a specific decision and the actual outcomes are not easily anticipated. (March and Romelaer 1976, p. 276)

As implied in the quotation, the complete Political Arena tends to have as many goals as it does influencers, since it is the convenient terrain on which all gather to pursue what seems to be their own personal or parochial goals. Even for the insider who wishes to express loyalty to the organization and pursue its goals, there is no easy way for him to know what these are.

Like the goals of the Autocracy, those of the Political Arena cannot be specified in general, since virtually any personal goals are possible. But at least in Autocracy, if one understands the CEO, one can predict what goals the organization is likely to pursue. And in the other configurations, one knows from the nature of the power system what goals will likely be pursued—systems goals in the Closed System, professional excellence in the Meritocracy, and so

---

[2]This is indicated by the similarities between Figure 22-4, an Adhocracy, shown on page 396, and Figure 23-1.

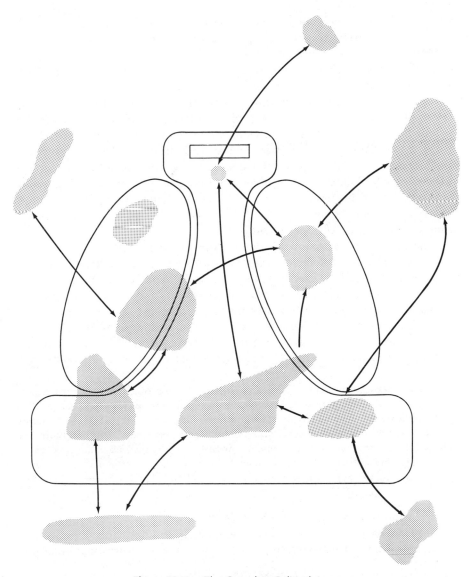

Figure 23–1. *The Complete Political Arena*

on. But in the complete Political Arena, with so many influencers pursuing personal goals in such a fluid situation, it is usually impossible to make any predictions—to know in advance what the results of any particular bargaining processes might be. Anyone can end up getting some piece of the action—in the form of surpluses, side payments, or the orientation of basic strategies. Again Allison says it best: "...action does not presuppose...intention." The outcome is "rarely intended by any individual or group. Rather, in the typical case separate individuals with different intentions contribute pieces to a resultant. . . . Actions. . . rarely reflect a coordinated. . . strategy and thus are difficult to read as conscious 'signals'" (1971, p. 175).[3]

What goal systems can emerge from all the conflict of the complete Political Arena? We suspect that four are possible, although one of these is probably less likely. First, in theory, the organization should be able to attend to certain primary goals sequentially, perhaps alternately in cycles. That is, the various influencers should be able to reach agreements to accommodate each others' needs. "You scratch my back today, and I'll scratch yours tomorrow." But this presupposes a certain level of cooperation, which is difficult to achieve in the complete Political Arena, given the intensity of its politics. We might, therefore, expect this first, and strongest, goal system to be more common in the less than complete forms of the Political Arena, notably in what we shall discuss as the shaky alliance.

Second, and perhaps more likely in the complete form of the Political Arena, is simply the satisfaction of a whole set of constraints. Given the pressures on the organization, little energy is likely to remain to pursue any primary goals. Or, as the third possible goal system, the constraints may become so tight that the organization cannot even satisfy many of them. At the limit, it becomes completely immobilized, unable to fulfill even important ones. In Pfeffer and Salancik's description of how New York City went virtually bankrupt, we see the case of one attempt to attend to goals sequentially that led to immobilization:

> New York City presents a good illustration of the problems of administering a system that is too tightly constrained. In the past, various interests that together provided the support for the city administration were enlisted in the coalition through the provision of special favors: large pensions (and salaries) for municipal workers, rent-controlled apartments for the middle class, public housing for the poor, and so forth. When the cost of these various concessions became overwhelming, the city administration had no discretion left and no room within which to maneuver. (1977, p. 22)[4]

The fourth goal system likewise reflects immobilization, but for a different reason. Here each influencer, not satisfied merely to impose his own goals on the organization, actively seek to block the organization from attending to the

---

[3]The possible exceptions to this, as implied in Chapter 15, are the systems goals of growth and survival. Politics encourages or reflects the building of empires. When everyone tries to do this, growth can emerge as a common goal. However, as we shall soon see, when politics causes each influencer, in addition to trying to build his own empire, to seek to destroy those of his rivals, the behavior that results may not reflect a common goal of growth at all. Likewise, all the influencers require the organization as a common arena in which to play their political games, and so all tend to share its survival as a goal. But, lacking loyalty to it, none will invest heavily in this. Other arenas can always be found.

[4]In the next chapter, however, we shall see the case of the organization that becomes so constrained that the constraints lose their meaning. Like the Phoenix that arises fresh from its own ashes, the organization reemerges as a Closed System.

goals of the others. Each takes the view that another's gain is his loss. Everyone is his rival. In effect, the influencers define themselves into, not even a zero-sum game, but a negative-sum game. Instead of agreeing implicitly to split the payoffs, as in the first goal system, they instead ensure that no one gets anything. And, of course, the only way to ensure this is to preclude the organization from taking any action at all, since action must inevitably benefit someone. So if we carry the complete Political Arena to its logical conclusion, the useful functioning of the organization is brought to a complete halt. The truly complete Political Arena becomes a system effectively closed to any influence—internal or external. All of the organization's energies are burned up in the spinning of its own wheels. To return to New York City, in this case its Board of Education:

> [Rogers] describes a policy decision system in which a multitude of factions—teachers, school administrators, neighborhood parent groups, ethnic and religious organizations, labor unions, and city officials—working exclusively for their self-interest, blocked each other and stalemated progress. The Board of Education dared not support any innovation consistently lest it be accused of being aligned with one or another faction. Instead it adhered to policies that satisfied no one. (op. perd., 1972, pp. 2–3)

These last two cases both describe a "paralytic" organization, one whose politics precludes it from accomplishing anything.[5] In effect, beyond some limit, the greater the level of conflict in an organization, the less its power as a system to get things done. Within that limit, certain influencers gain from conflict while the organization continues to function. We saw this in the Meritocracy, particularly in its Adhocracy form, which thrives on constructive conflict. Indeed it would atrophy without it. But beyond the limit, paralysis sets in and everyone seems to lose.[6] "Seems to" because, as we shall see shortly, even paralysis can serve a useful function in organizations.

To conclude, the main characteristics of the complete Political Arena are an active and Divided External Coalition, an intensely Politicized Internal Coalition, war as well as a complex network of relationships between the two, and a goal system that seems to reflect a host of personal needs rather than any specific organizational ones. While that goal system may sometimes enable certain primary goals to be attended to sequentially, more likely at best it allows for the satisfaction of a host of constraints, or, carrying the complete Political Arena to its logical conclusion, precludes the pursuit of any goals at all. The organization emerges as paralytic.

But few Political Arenas are complete. No organization can survive intense pervasive conflict for long. Thus we must introduce some partial forms

---

[5]Butler et al. (1977–78) also use the term "paralytic," but, as we noted in Chapter 18, to describe the Instrument, the organization that cannot accomplish anything *for itself*. The Political Arena we are describing here is more thoroughly paralytic—it cannot accomplish anything *for anyone*.

[6]Unless of course, there is an influencer who benefits from paralysis, a point we shall return to later.

that the Political Arena can take. But before we do this, we must first develop various propositions about conflict in organizations that we captured by conflict.

PROPOSITIONS ABOUT CONFLICT
IN CONFLICT-RIDDEN ORGANIZATIONS

The conflict of the Political Arena has to arise somewhere. Thus, we can conclude that **1. at the outset, the conflict tends to be confined**, arising within the Internal Coalition, the External Coalition, or between the two of them. This conflict may arise in an intense way, that is, flare up suddenly. Or it may build up gradually, or perhaps remain in moderate form. Let us begin with the case of intense conflict.

The assumption behind the complete Political Arena is that intense conflict, no matter where it begins, spills over its original boundaries, spreading to both of the coalitions as well as the relationships between them. Thus, we conclude that **2. when it is intense, the conflict tends over time to pervade the entire power system.**

But, **3. few organizations can sustain a state of intense conflict.** In other words, the complete Political Arena cannot last: It represents a valid tendency but an unlikely stable state. The complete Political Arena simply demands too much energy for what it offers in return. Eventually it must consume all of the organization's resources, and kill it.

Some organizations, of course, have benefactors that keep them alive artificially. But over time intense conflict will drive these benefactors away, not to mention the other influencers. It is not the conflict that provides their benefits, but its resolution. With no resolution or even moderation in sight, the influencers hesitate to continue investing their political energies. As they begin to leave, either the organization dies or else those who remain reach some kind of agreement. In other words, something has to give in the intense Political Arena.

Most simply, the conflict resolves itself, and the Political Arena disappears in favor of another power configuration. But not all conflicts are quickly resolved; in other words, not all Political Arenas are temporary. Some endure. But only if their conflict is moderated. In other words, **4. in order to sustain itself, the state of conflict must be moderated in its intensity.** The influencers must tone down their demands, perhaps even come to accommodate each other somewhat. They engage in cold war instead of hot. For example, the influencers may try to avoid direct confrontation with each other, enabling the organization to attend to various goals sequentially. This moderation allows the organization to put more of its energy into the pursuit of its mission, and so may enable it to survive. It cannot, of course, pursue its mission as effectively as an equivalent organization that is relatively free of conflict, but at least it comes out ahead of the organization that faces intense conflict.

Our second proposition argued for the tendency of intense politics to pervade the entire power system. But when politics is moderated, it can more easily be contained to one part of it. In other words, **5. moderate conflict can endure confined to one of the coalitions or the relationships between them**. Typically, two centers of power face each other—perhaps two alliances or camps, perhaps just two powerful influencers—but they do not seek to destroy each other. Rather, they reach some kind of loose and implicit accord, or alliance, muting their disagreements in order to keep the organization alive and their benefits flowing. These benefits are likely to continue to flow because conflict that is both moderate and confined is not especially taxing on the organization.

Of course, moderate conflict can spread too, so that rather than focussing on two mildly opposing parties, it encompasses many. But moderate conflict that pervades the organization is far more taxing than moderate conflict that is contained to one part of it. This leads us to the conclusion that **6. for a state of pervasive although moderate conflict to endure, the organization needs some artificial means of support**. With so much energy consumed by the pervasive conflict, the organization is not viable without some way to make up for its losses. It can, for example, be sustained by a benefactor, who may find some benefit to keeping it alive. Or the organization itself may find some political (that is, illegitimate) means to sustain itself, such as belonging to a cartel or coopting relevant politicians. Later in this chapter, we shall discuss organizations pervaded by moderate conflict that do in fact get such support, and in the next chapter we shall see why many do, essentially because of the residual powers they retain from the time when they were Closed Systems.

FOUR FORMS OF THE POLITICAL ARENA

Emerging from this discussion are three dimensions we have used to describe the Political Arena:

Intense	← →	Moderate
Pervasive	← →	Confined
Brief (or transient)	← →	Enduring (or stable)

The *intensity* dimension refers to the divisiveness of the conflict, whether the disagreements lead to all out fighting (hot war) in order to break the opposition, or the antagonists are somehow able to moderate their disagreements (cold war), perhaps even reaching implicit accords with each other. The *pervasiveness* dimension refers simply to whether the conflict is contained in some way, within one of the coalitions or between the two of them, or is to be found everywhere in and around the organization. And the *duration* dimension refers to whether the conflict lasts or not, ultimately to whether the state of conflict is brief and transient or can instead reach some kind of relatively stable state and endure.

Combining these dimensions in various ways yields four basic forms of the Political Arena:

*   What we shall call the *confrontation* is a Political Arena characterized by conflict that is *intense, confined,* and *brief* (transient). In other words, conflict of an intense nature flares up in one of the coalitions or between the two of them, but cannot sustain itself in this form. The confrontation seems to be the form in which Political Arenas most commonly arise, typically because of a sharp challenge to an existing order of power.

*   What we shall call the *shaky alliance,* characterized by conflict that is *moderate, confined,* and *enduring* (relatively stable), typically involves the reaching of some kind of implicit and loose accord between two or a few centers of power, in order to mute their conflict so that the organization can perform and sustain itself. The shaky alliance most commonly arises after a confrontation (but sometimes from a gradual buildup of conflict to a moderate level), when no side in the conflict is able to dominate the others, nor wishes to retreat, yet all depend on the survival of the organization.

*   What we shall call the *politicized organization* experiences conflict that is *moderate, pervasive,* and *enduring* (relatively stable). In other words, conflict is everywhere but in muted form, so that the influencers can tolerate the situation for some time. However, the pervasiveness of the conflict requires this form of the Political Arena to have a benefactor or to find some other artificial means of support in order to endure. Indeed, this form of Political Arena often emerges when the organization is no longer viable. The politicized organization most commonly arises from a gradual buildup and pervasion of moderate conflict, although it can also emerge from a confrontation that pervades the organization but moderates itself.

*   What we have already called the *complete Political Arena* experiences *intense, pervasive,* and *brief* (transient) conflict. It typically arises when a confrontation spreads, out of control, to pervade both coalitions and the relationships between them, or else when the conflict in the politicized organization intensifies, again, out of control. But this kind of Political Arena cannot easily last, and in fact often signals the imminent death of an organization.

One of our four forms of Political Arena is complete, according to our earlier description, and is so named. The other three are partial, one by moderating conflict, another by containing it, and the third by doing both. The two that moderate conflict are described as relatively stable, and somewhat enduring, although we have concluded that one of these—the politicized organization—is so only because of artificial support. In other words, left on its own, it could not survive. In that sense, it is less stable than the other—the shaky alliance—although certainly far more so than the two forms of the Political Arena whose conflicts are intense.[7]

LIFE CYCLES OF POLITICAL ARENAS

With these propositions and four forms of Political Arenas in mind, we can now describe how Political Arenas arise, sustain themselves (when they do), and eventually disappear. We do this in terms of a three-stage model of the "life cycles" of Political Arenas, comprising impetus, development, and resolution. Figure 23-2 shows our model in terms of these stages, and it positions our four forms of Political Arena within them. It also illustrates many of our propositions.

IMPETUS: CONFLICTING DEMANDS   We begin our discussion with the assumption that, unless it is new, the organization has achieved a steady state of power, a given order. In other words, it has one established focus of power (and thus a conventional configuration), or else two or more centers of power have achieved some kind of accommodation with each other to stabilize relationships.

Under one of these conditions, the Political Arena arises from a serious challenge to the existing order of power. In the absence of such an order to begin with (in the new organization), it arises from challenges among different influencers seeking to place themselves at the center of power. Either way the Political Arena reflects a state of conflicting demands placed on the organization. These demands may arise in one of three ways—of their own accord, due to changes in a fundamental condition of the organization, or due to a breakdown in the established order of power (or none to begin with).

First, the challenge simply arises of its own accord. A new influencer seeks to enter one of the coalitions in an important way, or an existing influencer

[7]Note that our three dimensions gave rise to eight possible combinations, in other words eight conceivable forms of the Political Arena. We have left out four of these. Two of them (intense, pervasive, and enduring; intense, confined, and enduring) were left out because they violate proposition 4, that a Political Arena cannot be intense and endure. The other two are forms that are both moderate and brief (one pervasive, the other confined). One of these at least is probably common—the confined one. (If conflict is moderate and brief, and, according to proposition 1, begins in confined form, then it would not likely have the time nor experience the pressure to spread.) But neither, we believe, merits the label Political Arena. Moderate conflict of short duration, especially when contained, does not really signal a change in power configuration. Rather, it implies a temporary increase in political activity within the confines of another power configuration, what we described in Chapter 13 as a fifth column of political activity, comprising the milder political games (ones able to coexist with the legitimate systems of influence). Only when conflict is intense, even if brief, or enduring, even if moderate, do we feel comfortable in describing it as having captured in some sense the power system of the organization.

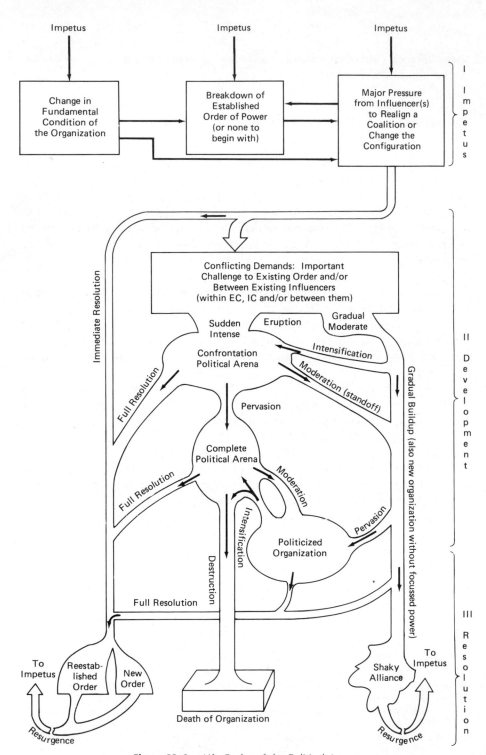

Figure 23–2. *Life Cycles of the Political Arena*

seeks a major new deal. The challenge may amount to an attempt to realign a coalition or even shift the whole power system to a new configuration. A group of young Turks challenges the existing management for control of a Closed System, seeking to retain the configuration but change its principal actors; or a group of shareholders organizes to challenge management control, seeking to convert a Closed System into an Instrument; alternately, the managers challenge the controlling owners of an Instrument, seeking to convert it into a Closed System; or the government decides to try to bring the public hospitals and universities under the control of its own technocrats, trying to convert Meritocracies into Instruments; and so on.

More commonly, perhaps, these demands for fundamental change in the distribution of power do not arise out of the blue. Rather they are provoked by a change in some fundamental condition of the organization. Perhaps a new technology requires the introduction of new expertise into the operating core, perhaps the organization has grown large and needs more formalized systems of control or is forced to draw on a new resource base, perhaps an environment long dynamic in nature has suddenly stabilized.[8]

Changes such as these are disruptive. Coping with them requires shifts in the distribution of power in and often around the organization—among influencers as well as among systems of influence in many cases. The influencers who believe themselves best able to cope with the new conditions, or at least able to exploit them for their own benefit, exert pressure to change one of the coalitions or perhaps the entire power configuration. As Mumford and Pettigrew note, "During periods of major change, it is probable that latent conflict will become overt"; "the very fact of change introduces an element of instability as long established methods and procedures are abandoned and new ones introduced"; overt political behavior arises because "individuals use the fluidity of the change situation to promote or protect their own interest" (1975, pp. 219, 208, 207).

Among the changed conditions most likely to bring on the Political Arena are major innovations and serious reductions in the resources available to the organization (Hills and Mahoney 1978; Mumford and Pettigrew 1975). In the case of a serious resource reduction, influencers who have hitherto been able to reach a stable equilibrium—for example, those of a Closed System who were more or less satisfied with the distribution of payoffs—suddenly find themselves in conflict with each other as each strives to maintain his or her share of a

[8]This last example is used to emphasize the point that it is not a *state* of environmental change that drives the organization to the Political Arena, but a specific discontinuity to the organization itself—a shift in its established patterns. When external change is continuous and therefore expected—in other words, when an organization faces an environment that is permanently dynamic—then that becomes its established pattern, its regular state of affairs, and we would expect it to fall under one of the stable configurations. As we argued in the *Structuring* book, that would likely be the Simple Structure (Autocracy) or Adhocracy (collaborative-type Meritocracy), depending on whether the dynamic environment was simple or complex. Sudden cessation of these dynamic conditions—in other words, a discontinuity—is what can bring on the Political Arena configuration.

diminished pie. As for major innovation, it opens up all kinds of opportunities to seize new power, and so tends to encourage conflict.

> Innovation usually implies some reallocation of scarce resources. It provides an opportunity for groups and departments to gain control of assets they did not possess before. This in turn implies some control over social pressures and makes it an intensely political activity. (Mumford and Pettigrew 1975, p. 22)

Much innovation requires a shift in the established order of power, and so in the power configuration itself, as when a new technology requires a Closed System to hire and depend on new experts in the operating core, thus pushing it toward Meritocracy. But innovation can also call simply for a change of actors, within the existing power configuration. For example, the development of a new product may require a change in strategy but not of systems of influence. When the top managers are wedded to the existing strategy, a group of young Turks may have to stage a coup d'état in order to replace them and their ideas.

The third impetus for the Political Arena is a breakdown in the established order of power (or none to begin with). New influencers jump into the power vacuum, and until one comes to dominate or some kind of accord is reached, conflict reigns. The CEO of an Autocracy dies, an ideology weakens, the dominant external influencer of an Instrument loses interest. Various insiders and perhaps outsiders as well vie for enhanced power, and the organization becomes a Political Arena until a new focus of power emerges. In some cases, as the death of an organization becomes imminent, there is a general breakdown in all legitimate forms of power. Everyone jumps into the fray to get some final benefits before everything is lost.

Of course, the absence of any focus or center of power to begin with has the same effect on the power system. Different influencers are attracted to the organization, like piranhas to a wounded animal, they challenge each other for control, and until one emerges as dominant, the organization functions as a Political Arena. As we noted in Chapter 20, in the new organization the CEO typically steps in at the outset to become the initial focus of power and that precludes politics. The organization is born as an Autocracy. In some cases, however, the CEO must share center stage with other influencers soon after birth, and so a form of the Political Arena develops to replace Autocracy.

These three forms of impetus for the Political Arena—a change in fundamental condition, breakdown in the established order, new influencer pressure for realignment—relate to each other in a number of ways, as shown in Figure 23–2. First, we should repeat that it is only one of those—major influence pressure for realignment of power—that is the necessary condition for the Political Arena. This alone is also a sufficient condition. In other words, influencer pressures, arising of their own accord, can create a Political Arena.

But we believe that influencer pressures are more often brought on by one of the other two factors. Breakdown in the established order of power or a change in a fundamental condition of the organization encourages influencers to seek more power, and so to challenge the existing order (or each other). These three factors can also work in sequence, as shown in Figure 23–2, a change in condition first breaking down the established order, which then provokes the challenge. Probably the most common form of impetus for the Political Arena begins with a change in condition, which provokes both breakdown and challenge concurrently, and these two reinforce each other, in Ping-Pong fashion, as shown in Figure 23–2. Growth may render an Autocracy too large for the personal control of one individual. Or a new technical system may render existing expertise in the operating core redundant, so that the experts of a Meritocracy lose their basis of influence. The line managers may try to usurp the power of the weakened chief executive or experts, or else staff analysts may challenge them through the imposition of technocratic standards. The CEO or experts resist, political means of influence come into play on both sides, and the conflict intensifies.

To summarize in the form of propositions, **7. a prerequisite to the emergence of the Political Arena is new major pressures from influencers to realign a coalition or change the power configuration. 8. These pressures can arise of their own accord or be evoked either by a breakdown in the established order of power or by a change in a fundamental condition of the organization (which itself may break down the established order, leading to such pressures). And 9. the pressures for realignment and the breakdown in established order tend to reinforce each other (whether provoked by a change in condition or not).**

DEVELOPMENT: SUDDEN OR GRADUAL BUILDUP OF CONFLICT　　No matter what the impetus, the result of the pressures tends to be an important challenge to the existing order of power, if there is one, otherwise challenges among influencers seeking to put themselves at the center of power. In other words, as shown in Figure 23–2, the one essential condition for the emergence of the Political Arena is a set of conflicting and irreconciled influencer demands on the organization. These cause it to have no focus of power for a time, or, what amounts to the same thing, more than one focus of power. Clashes occur between influencers—between established ones at the center and challengers at the periphery, or between different challengers—each seeking control of the center. Hence, an organization tends to be drawn toward the Political Arena configuration when it must make a transition from one configuration of focussed power to another or when it must achieve a major redistribution of power among the actors of a given configuration.

Of course, pressures for realignment need not always result in conflicting demands. In other words, the Political Arena configuration can be bypassed altogether, as shown by the line on the left side of Figure 23–2. Sometimes a challenge is nipped in the bud; sometimes it succeeds immediately because its opposition crumbles. Similarly, after the sudden breakdown of the established order, the pressures among competing influencers can sometimes be resolved immediately. The CEO of an Autocracy dies, his natural successor quickly seizes the power, and that is that. Or the young Turks of a Closed System stage their coup d'etat quickly and cleanly, so that there is a new management when everyone appears for work the next morning.

These examples describe changes of actors within a given configuration, because change is more likely to be free of conflict when the power configuration remains intact. When the means and systems of influence do not have to be changed, shifts in power can sometimes be effected quickly and decisively. Of course, even change from one power configuration to another can sometimes be effected with little conflict, that is, without having to revert to a transitional stage of Political Arena. This tends to happen when the transition is long overdue, recognized by everyone as necessary, and so is widely supported. Much as a liquid that is supersaturated freezes suddenly when disturbed, so an organization held back from making a natural transition may do so quickly and peacefully when it can. For example, the death of the founder of an Autocracy, who was able to maintain personal control to his last days despite the need for standardization and formalization, may bring on a quick and painless transition to Machine Bureaucracy in the form of a Closed System or Instrument.

But few transitions—of actors or whole systems of influence—prove that smooth, even ones that are obviously needed. Most involve resistance, and it is usually politics that must serve as the lubricant to get them moving. Thus we often find the Political Arena during transitions of power. And, of course, when power is changing but with no clear result—in other words, there is no obvious successor or succeeding system of influence—then the occurrence of the Political Arena must be viewed as almost inevitable. The organization is, so to speak, up for grabs: Everyone is encouraged to try to get a piece of it, and politics plays a major role in determining who does.

As noted earlier, conflict can arise in one of three places: (1) in the External Coalition, as when two shareholder groups engage in a proxy fight to control a corporation; (2) in the Internal Coalition, as when two rival camps fight for dominance or expert power confronts an established ideology; and (3) between the Internal and External Coalition in the form of a war, as when a dominant external influencer is challenged by the chief executive or by the experts of the operating core. In other words, as we noted earlier, the Political Arena tends to emerge first in one of its partial forms, confined in some way.

Commonly, the initial conflict involves two groups, usually an established set of influencers and a group of challengers, as we have said repeatedly, an old guard and young Turks. Even when there is no established order, the conflict will often quickly reduce to a battle for supremacy between two rival camps. In effect, while many different influencers may wish to vie for personal power in an ambiguous situation, the need for supporters will drive most of them into factions and alliances, which will tend to combine with each other until only two remain to confront each other (unless, of course, the balance of power tips strongly toward one, which may create a bandwagon effect, and consensus).

Whether or not the conflict spreads, and whether or not the resulting Political Arena is stable and can endure—in other words, what form of Political Arena results—depends on the speed and intensity with which the conflict develops. A change in fundamental condition can be sudden and harsh, as many firms found out when the OPEC nations raised their oil prices in 1973. Or it can be slow and gradual, as is typical in the case of economic pressures or changes in consumer tastes. Similarly, a breakdown in the established order of power can be sudden or gradual, the difference between a CEO suffering a stroke and growing old. Hence, the influencer pressures that result, and even those that arise on their own, can be sudden and intense—can erupt, or flare up—leading to a sharp challenge, or else they themselves can build up slowly, producing a more moderate challenge. (Our suspicion, however, is that the former is more common, with gradual changes or breakdowns being long ignored until they come to a head in the form of a sharp challenge.)

10. **Influencer pressures that errupt with suddenness and intensity lead to what we have called the confrontation form of Political Arena, which we believe to be unstable and therefore temporary or transient.** Being intense, 11. **the conflict can spread quickly, pervading the entire power system, so that the confrontation form turns into a complete Political Arena**, as shown in Figure 23-2. But this form tends to be even more unstable, and so cannot last. It risks destroying the organization, and even the actors involved. And so the intense conflict—whether confrontation or complete Political Arena—must quickly be resolved, or at least moderated so that a more stable form of the Political Arena can be reached.

Alternately, influencer pressures that develop gradually tend to lead straight to a more moderate and potentially more stable form of Political Arena (and so will be discussed under the resolution stage which follows). Of course, at any time, the gradually developing moderate conflict can itself flare up, leading to confrontation and perhaps subsequently to the complete form of Political Arena for a short time, as indicated in Figure 23-2.

RESOLUTION: VICTORY, MODERATION, OR DEMISE   What can ultimately result from all of this? In other words, what relatively permanent or stable distribution of power—steady states—are possible? As shown in Figure 23-2, four and perhaps a fifth steady state solutions are likely. In the first two, the conflict is fully resolved and the organization reverts to a stable, focussed configuration of power. In the third, the conflict destroys the organization. And in the last two, more enduring forms of the Political Arena emerge, one of them stable only if artificially supported.

First, and most obviously, the conflict is fully resolved. Some system of power, and the influencer(s) behind it, come out the winners. In other words, the organization reverts to some stable configuration of power, with a clear focus. Two steady state solutions are possible here—the old and the new. Sometimes the established order manages to fight off the challenge to its supremacy, and the old configuration and coalitions survive intact, with the previous actors. The government, for example, gives up trying to control a public hospital or university directly, though technocratic standards, and contents itself with setting its overall budget, as before, leaving control in the hands of its professionals. Other times, of course, the challenge is successful. A new configuration emerges, typically with new actors, as when a CEO replaces an external influencer as dominant, converting an Instrument into an Autocracy. Or else a new alignment emerges in the old configuration, as when the young Turks achieve their coup d'etat within a Closed System, changing the leadership, and maybe even the strategy, but not the systems of influence. One set of players merely displaces another. Even when no established order existed to begin with, one can obviously emerge from the conflict, so that the Political Arena gets converted into one of the other, more stable power configurations. A new focus of power forms around one set of actors and one system of influence.

12. Full resolution would seem to be the most likely result of the confrontation Political Arena, as is indicated in Figure 23–2, with a flare-up followed by victory for one side or another. The complete Political Arena may also resolve itself in this way, although with more points of conflict and more actors involved, one system of influence and set of actors has greater difficulty emerging as supreme.

Next, the conflict simply kills the organization. Politics takes so much out of the organization, and perhaps its participants as well, that the system can no longer function, and dies. The confrontation form of Political Arena can conceivably result in the demise of an organization directly, but our suspicion is that its contained conflict is more likely to be resolved fully or partially, or else to pervade the entire power system before it kills the organization. Thus, as shown in Figure 23–2, **13. the complete Political Arena most commonly precedes the death of an organization, either killing it or signalling its inevitable death from other causes.** On one hand, the complete Political Arena can easily kill an organization. The intensity and pervasiveness of this form of Political Arena simply takes too much out of the organization. On the other hand, in what ultimately amounts to the same thing, as it becomes clear than an organization is about to die from other causes, all the influencers jump in to get what they can at the last moment. The organization becomes a complete Political Arena, a free-for-all—a dying animal beset by scavengers—which, of course, speeds up its demise.

Finally, the conflict can abate, enabling the organization to survive with a moderate form of the Political Arena, one that is more stable and enduring. In effect, the conflict is partially resolved. Two of our four forms of Political Arena were described as moderate—the shaky alliance and the politicized organization—and here is where we would expect to find them.

The shaky alliance—moderate conflict that is contained in some way—is probably the more likely of the two to arise. **14. The shaky alliance emerges when the result of a confrontation Political Arena is standoff**: neither side can win, yet neither wishes to give up. So they moderate their conflict and reach some kind of accord to enable the organization to survive. The different centers of power—typically two, but in any event just a few—learn to live with each other.

Of course, an organization need not pass through a period of intense conflict—of the confrontation form of Political Arena—in order to find itself with a shaky alliance. **15. The shaky alliance can also emerge directly, from a gradual buildup of conflict.** In fact, this is probably the form of Political Arena most likely to occur when conflict builds up gradually in an organization, and is shown as such in Figure 23-2. **16. The shaky alliance can also appear near the outset of an organization's life, when there is no one obvious and natural focus of power, but two or more that must accommodate to each other.** Here, the conflict neither appears from an abatement of sudden, intense politics, nor builds up gradually in moderate form. It is there in moderate form almost to begin with (typically following, as we noted in Chapter 20, a short period of Autocracy to get the organization started). In other words, the organization grew up as a shaky alliance; from infancy, it never knew anything else.

The shaky alliance is, as noted earlier, the equivalent of cold war, in which influencers with fundamentally different goals—essentially opponents—reach accommodation so as not to destroy the organization. Somehow they agree—usually implicitly—to attend to each others' goals sequentially. One is reminded of the entrenched guerrilla group in the mountains that, after spending so many fruitless years trying to overthrow a government, reaches an implicit accord with it. Each side realizes that it cannot destroy the other, yet might very well destroy itself trying. So in order to survive and save face, the two maintain only the pretext of battle, carrying out an occasional raid, in an almost ritualistic manner. In a sense the two sides almost need each other, much as do grouchy older people their mates—they would be lost with no one to nag.

Of course, the fact that the two sides have reached some kind of implicit alliance should not obscure the fact that it is inevitably shaky. Outright conflict—hot war—is never far from the surface. Should one side falter, the other will quickly move in to usurp its prerogatives. In other words, what makes the shaky alliance relatively stable—no form of Political Arena can be described as fully stable—is a rough but delicate balance between the centers of power. They must be of more or less equal strength. Any change in that delicate balance—due to a changed coalition or a breakdown in power on one side—is likely to bring new pressures to redistribute power. In effect, we loop back through the model, to a new impetus (as shown by the arrow coming out of the shaky alliance in Figure 23-2). A confrontation type Political Arena will likely result until a new balance is attained or a fuller resolution achieved.

Many of the hybrids of our focussed configurations are really shaky alliances of this sort. We have already mentioned the example of the symphony

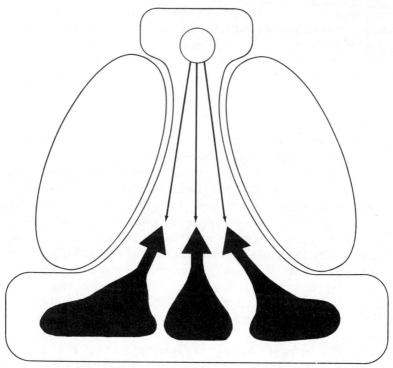

Figure 23-3. *A Shaky Alliance: Hybrid of Autocracy and Meritocracy*

orchestra—a hybrid of Autocracy and Meritocracy, which we illustrate in Figure 23-3. We might also find a shaky alliance of a dominant external influencer with a chief executive in personal control of the Internal Coalition (the Autocracy as Instrument), a strong ideology with established expertise (the Meritocratic Missionary), or extensive bureaucratic controls with established expertise (the dominated or Closed System Meritocracy).

Of course, not all hybrids (defined in terms of our six configurations of power) need be shaky alliances. In the fourth hypothesis of Chapter 17, we argued that these hybrid combinations *"frequently* generate moderate or intense levels of conflict." But not necessarily. Clark's "distinctive colleges" appear to be harmonious combinations of expertise with ideology, in other words, non-conflictive hybrids of Meritocracy and Missionary.

Nor must all shaky alliances be hybrids of the more focussed configurations. All kinds of other combinations are possible too, for example, of different actors rather than different systems of influence. Thus, Agersnap describes an organization divided in two, each half under the personal of its own manager—a kind of dual Autocracy:

The firm is privately owned by an old man who seldomly interferes with the business. He has two sons, the one in charge of production and the other in charge of sales. To minimize frictions, the two sons have agreed not to interfere in the operations of the division of the other. To secure this independence the production division maintains a large stock of the finished products listed in the catalogue. Most orders can be delivered with a short time of delivery, and the sales division [infrequently] accepts orders on products not listed in the catalogue. (1970, p. 98)

By the same token, we can imagine an organization divided into two ideological camps, or one with two dominant bodies of expertise, in each case the two forming shaky alliances with each other.

And not all shaky alliances—hybrids or not—need be stable. The most stable are presumably those whose different centers of power are supported by real needs of the organization—in other words, whose means of influence are based on natural forces. Such natural bases of influences means that neither side in the alliance is likely to falter, or be easily pushed aside by a political challenge. As a result, the power is likely to remain balanced and the alliance therefore stable (so long, at least, as the underlying conditions do not change). Thus the symphony orchestra is a stable hybrid because it can do without neither the top-flight expertise of the players nor the personal coordination of the conductor. (The Russians apparently tried a conductorless orchestra, called Persimfans, shortly after their revolution, but countless arguments among the musicians caused them to reintroduce the leader.) Conversely, an attempt by an external influencer to take control of a Missionary—to render it his Instrument—should prove unstable when there is no basis for the external control in the face of the strong internal ideology. Intense conflict should flare up until either the external influencer withdraws or the ideology is destroyed (unless, of course, the organization is destroyed first).

The second possible result of moderate conflict is what we called the politicized organization, where the moderate conflict pervades the organization. As we shall discuss later, certain regulatory agencies and large corporations appear to be examples of this.

In no form of Political Arena is one center of power dominant, whether a single external influencer or one set of internal influencers behind one of the legitimate systems of influence. But in the shaky alliance, at least a few, normally two, are relatively strong. In contrast, all are weak in the politicized organization. It is the System of Politics that dominates, even though it exists in moderate form. And because conflict pervades it, this form of Political Arena cannot sustain itself. As we argued earlier, without a benefactor or some other artificial means of support, the organization is likely to run out of energy and die. Hence we describe the politicized organization as only marginally stable, at best, and thus Figure 23–2 shows it as only half way into the stage of resolution, since it can be considered as much an intermediate stage of development as a form of final resolution.

The politicized organization can arise in a number of ways. **17. Most likely,**

the politicized organization arises directly, from the gradual buildup and pervasion of conflict, such that no other form of Political Arena preceeds it. Later we shall see that this form of Political Arena is, in fact, often preceded by the Closed System configuration. As various external influencers jump into the void in its External Coalition and as the different internal influencers find themselves in increasing conflict with one another, the Closed System gradually gets undermined by politics and emerges as a politicized organization. **18. But the politicized organization can also follow a more intense form of the Political Arena, notably when conflict is moderated (but remains pervasive) in a complete Political Arena, or, perhaps, is moderated but becomes pervasive in the confrontation form of Political Arena.**

Also the figure shows **19. the principal way out of the politicized organization is the eventual death of the organization, via the complete Political Arena.** Full resolution is, however, shown as a remote possibility in Figure 23–2 (as it is for the complete Political Arena as well). Fearing the death of the organization, the influencers might back off and allow a more focussed configuration of power to emerge. But our belief is that most organizations captured by pervasive conflict are unlikely to shake themselves free of it.

To summarize our conclusions on the resolution stage of the life cycle of the Political Arena, we have suggested that four or five relatively stable states are possible after an organization has been partially or fully captured by conflict. First, the conflict can be fully resolved, the organization returning to its established order of power or moving on to a new one. Second, the organization can die, perhaps killed by the conflict or the conflict simply arising when its death was imminent. And third, the conflict can be only partially resolved, so that a more moderate form of Political Arena arises—the shaky alliance which, potentially at least, is somewhat stable of its own accord, or the politicized organization, which appear to be stable only when it is artificially supported.

FEEDBACK LOOPS: NEW IMPETUS   Before completing our discussion of the life cycles of the Political Arena, we must emphasize that no system of power is ever completely stable. We made this point in Chapter 16 in our discussion of the power system as a *dynamic* equilibrium. Hence all the states of resolution shown in Figure 23–2 (except one) have feedback loops which are meant to return to impetus.

The shaky alliance, as we noted earlier, can easily flare up, looping back through the model to the confrontation form of Political Arena. But so long as the different bases of influence that have underlain the alliance are natural ones and remain in balance, we believe the confrontation will quickly moderate itself and the shaky alliance will reappear. Thus, power in the natural shaky alliance can be thought of as oscillating around some central mean, or balance point, in effect achieving a state of homeostasis. Other shaky alliances will however, have difficulty maintaining such a steady state. This includes the unnatural ones, where one or more of the centers of power is not rooted in a fundamental condition of the organization. The same is true of the shaky alliance, once natural, where a change in fundamental condition has undermined the basis of influence of one of the centers of power and thereby tipped the delicate balance in favor of another. In these cases, flare-ups will prove more frequent and more intense, as the influencers seek a new, more natural, and more stable distribution of power.

Even what we have called full resolution can prove unstable if the victor's basis of influence proves untenable, reflecting no natural condition of the organization. What this means is that false resolution is temporary resolution, whether it is the old guard that hangs on to power artificially or the young Turks who attain it on a spurious basis. **20. When power rests on an artificial base, pressure for realignment remains just below the surface, waiting to take the organization through a new cycle of the Political Arena to seek a more permanent correction.** Those at the center of baseless power can hang on for only so long before they must collapse or give way. Their challengers may have to retreat and lick their wounds a few times, but eventually they must win out (unless the organization dies first). The musicians may get their conductorless orchestra, but the stability that may follow is deceiving, conflict flaring up at the first opportunity. The experts who practice a new technology required by the organization, being few in numbers at the outset, may be destined to lose their first challenges to the established order of power. The old guard—guardians of the old technology—control most of the established means of influence. But time must be on the side of the experts, even if the organization may have to be severely weakened before they succeed with a subsequent challenge. Conversely, pseudoexperts who do manage to take power with no real basis of expertise form false Meritocracies which, as we described earlier, must eventually succumb to politics. Mismatch of power and situation can be sustained for only so long. It must eventually be corrected, or else the organization itself succumbs.

Of course, few cases are so cut and dried as these. A change in fundamental condition, or breakdown in the established order of power, is often gradual, so that early challenges are in fact premature, and thus are appropriately repulsed. Only when the change or breakdown more fully manifests itself is a successful challenge appropriate.

But even appropriate resolution of conflict must be viewed, ultimately, as unstable. No established order of power is ever safe from challenge. At any time, it may be challenged artificially or arbitrarily, or it may become vulnerable by breaking down of its own accord or by facing a changed condition that undermines its basis of influence. Only one place in all of Figure 23-2 is truly and permanently stable: the death of the organization!

VARIOUS COMMON LIFE CYCLES OF THE POLITICAL ARENA   This section has been titled life cycles of the Political Arena. To summarize and conclude it, we list what appear to be some of the more common of these cycles suggested in our discussion.

Life Cycle 1. Flare-up: Challenge to the established order gives rise to a confrontation Political Arena which resolves itself in favor of challengers or the established order (and can flare up again if not naturally resolved).

Life Cycle 2. Standoff: Challenge gives rise to a confrontation Political Arena, which results in standoff; neither side wishing to withdraw and both dependent on the survival of the organization, they moderate the conflict and form a shaky alliance which sustains itself so long as power remains naturally balanced and the organization remains viable; (in a perhaps less common variant, conflict in the confrontation form pervades, leading to a complete Political Arena, whose conflict then moderates but does not confine itself, resulting in a politicized organization, which remains stable so long as it is artificially supported; should the influencers refuse to moderate the conflict, in either case, but continue to fight intensively for dominance, the organization is destroyed).

Life Cycle 3. Gradual Politicization: Multiple challenges in and between both coalitions coupled with slow breakdown in legitimate power gradually lead to the politicized organization, which eventually dies if it can find or retain no artificial means of support (through cycle 5, as described below).

Life Cycle 4. Lifetime Shaky Alliance: Need for different bases of influence gives rise to a shaky alliance shortly after the birth of the organization, which remains intact (despite occasional flare-ups) so long as the bases of influence remain naturally balanced.

Life Cycle 5. Death Throes: Fundamental weakness of the organization (due to inherent ineffectiveness, loss of markets or basis of support, etc.) results in a total breakdown of legitimate systems of influence and the rise of the complete Political Arena, as the influencers engage in a free-for-all, which speeds up the inevitable death of the organization.[9]

THE POLITICAL ARENA AS A FUNCTIONAL CONFIGURATION

Political Arenas clearly appear to be dysfunctinonal—aberrations of power. They burn up energy that could instead go into performing the organization's mission. The purpose of an organization is, after all, to produce

---

[9]Other life cycles are of course possible, such as the gradual buildup of conflict that suddenly flares up, or the confrontation Political Arena whose conflict moderates but pervades, resulting in the politicized organization. But we believe these to be less common than the five described.

goods and services, not to provide an arena in which the participants can fight with each other. The other configurations, by limiting conflict, are able to accomplish more as systems and also to provide more benefits to their main influencers. Thus, organizational effectiveness appears to depend either on harmony, or in some cases (such as Adhocracy), on moderate degrees of conflict channelled to constructive ends.

But this conclusion assumes a short-run perspective. The Political Arena must not only be evaluated according to the energy it wastes; it must also be judged by its long-term effects, by what would have happened if it had never occurred. In this regard, the Political Arena can be clearly functional if it enables the organization to better pursue its mission in the long run. So the question is not whether the Political Arena wastes resources while it lasts, but whether its existence has a net benefit on the long-term effectiveness of the organization. And the answer to this question—as should be evident from our discussion to this point—is "sometimes." Specifically **21. the Political Arena is functional when (a) it causes or speeds up a realignment in a coalition or a shift in configuration necessitated by a change in a fundamental condition of the organization or a breakdown in its established focus of power; (b) it corrects an earlier change in coalition or configuration that was itself dysfunctional; (c) it exists as a shaky alliance that reflects natural, balanced, and irreconcilable forces on the organization; or (d) it speeds up the death of a spent organization.**

The first point of our proposition—labelled (a)—argues that when the established order has outlived its usefulness, typically because of a change in a fundamental condition of the organization or perhaps because it breaks down of its own accord, then a Political Arena which flares up to confront and change it can be functional. In effect, when politics is the only way to displace legitimate power that itself has become dysfunctional, then the Political Arena, based on technically illegitimate power, must be viewed as functional. The Political Arena becomes the means to achieve necessary change in the organization; it serves as the way station on the road from one focussed power configuration, or from one set of actors or beliefs within such a configuration, to another. That way station may be dysfunctional and unstable while it lasts, but it serves the functional purpose of enabling the organization to attain a new stability.

Each of the legitimate systems of influence—authority of a personalized or bureaucratic nature, ideology, expertise—can block necessary change. In contrast, politics, as noted in Chapter 14, can promote it, by allowing influencers to challenge those at the established center of power who support accepted but outmoded ways of doing things. To oust the chief executive whose age has robbed him of the faculties necessary to control his organization personally, or whose eyes have been sealed by years of dealing with the same conditions, to bring in technocratic controls which must replace a body of expertise no longer valid, or vice versa, to replace a worn-out ideology which serves as a force for tradition and continuity rather than change, intense political activity is usually called for.

Remember that four of our six configurations of power are virtually sealed off from serious external influence. As a result, when the need for change arises, they tend first to ignore it and then to resist it. Politics is the vehicle that society depends upon to change its organizations that have gone astray. A Passive External Coalition becomes active for a time, perhaps forming a consensus to challenge the insiders, perhaps dividing to impose diverse pressures on the Internal Coalition and thereby to politicize it. Or else certain insiders themselves challenge those at the center of power, politicizing the Internal Coalition as a result. Even when the necessary change is not one of configuration, but of strategy, ideology, or of the actors themselves within a given configuration, a challenge may still be necessary, as when a coup d'état by a group of young Turks is the only way to save an organization threatened by stagnant management. A Closed System becomes a Political Arena long enough to change its leadership, before reverting back to a Closed System.

Of course, such challenges do not always correct the situation. Some aggravate it, the solution proving worse than the problem. Likewise, politics can also serve as a means of influence for those near the center of power to block necessary change. Just as a dam can be used to block water from finding its natural level, so can politics be used to sustain or create an unnatural configuration of power, one that wastes resources and impedes the organization from pursuing its mission. A change in technology may necessitate a shift in power from one set of experts to another. But the administrators may use political means during the disruption to capture the organization instead, rendering it a dysfunctional Closed System instead of a necessary form of Meritocracy. In such cases, of course, the Political Arena proves dysfunctional.

But, as we argued earlier, such dysfunctional situations are not likely to remain stable for long. Renewed confrontation can be expected. An excess of water artificially contained by a dam will burst its confines and find its own level. So too will the System of Politics gravitate to where it is needed, and there build up pressure until it bursts its confines to effect necessary change. Lurking beneath every unnatural configuration of power is a latent Political Arena, waiting for the first opportunity to carry the organization to a more natural stability.

Politics is, then, an intrinsic component of every unnatural configuration of power, used by the established order as well as the challengers. Because their ostensibly legitimate bases of influence have become artificial, those at the established center of power must fall back on illegitimate means of influence, namely those of a political nature. They must, for example, lord or exploit their legitimate power in illegitimate ways in order to hang on to their positions. To flesh out an example introduced earlier, when specialists who are not very skilled or knowledgeable try to retain power through the System of Expertise—the situation we referred to as the false Meritocracy—intense politics must inevitably result. Because the expert basis for distributing power is essentially artificial, the specialists will have to revert to political means to retain their power. They will restrict information, form alliances, lord their status over others, and above all exploit insignificant forms of expertise, investing more energy in playing these games than in doing their normal work. We see a similar result in the opposite case, when an organization requiring high expertise is captured by the administrators, who run it like a Machine Bureaucracy, exploiting their authority in any way they can to keep the experts down. In any situation of this nature, because the established order uses politics to sustain itself, the challengers must also use politics to confront them. Conflict inevitably erupts, and this is what is likely to resolve the problem eventually.

Thus, aberrations of power certainly exist—misplaced focussed configurations as well as the dysfunctional Political Arenas that create them—but these carry their own built-in tensions that tend to correct things. Politics, as we stressed in Chapter 14, while it can be terribly dysfunctional, also has a way of sorting things out. Just as anarchists, who lurk everywhere, tend to succeed in fomenting revolution only when large segments of the population feel frustrated and sense the need for change, so too does politics, lurking in every organization, tend to capture it when what it promotes is ultimately necessary for it. Thus we argue in point (b) of our proposition that politics can serve the functional role of correcting an earlier dysfunctional change in power.

What about the political challenge that arises of its own accord, in other words, in the absence of any fundamental change in condition, breakdown in established order of power, or earlier dysfunctional change in power. Some influencer simply wants a new deal. Clearly such a challenge can be viewed as dysfunctional if it weakens the organization's ability to pursue a given mission, as when a government technostructure imposes controls on a school system that, besides not eliciting the desired behaviors, also manages to reduce the quality of the teaching. But such a challenge can also be viewed as neutral—neither functional nor dysfunctional—if the change it renders leaves the organization with the same ability to perform its given mission, or else replaces that mission with another, equally appropriate one.

Who can call the result functional or dysfunctional when one shareholder wrests control of a corporation from another (unless, of course, the challenger has the capacity to strengthen the organization)? Likewise, when two equally qualified individuals fight for the leadership of an Autocracy, or an external influencer tries to seize control of a Closed System to render it his Instrument, or experts try to convert a Missionary into a Meritocracy to concentrate on perfecting certain skills instead of expounding an ideology, then there may be no question of better or worse, no natural winners, just an arbitrary fight for power. The Political Arena will certainly be dysfunctional while it lasts—impeding the organization from pursuing its mission, whatever that is and might become—but the change it brings about can be termed neither functional nor dysfunctional.

We must, however, qualify this conclusion in one way. When a challenge is neutral, as we have just described it, we suspect that the resulting Political

Arena will tend to last longer than the one that arises from a clearly functional or dysfunctional challenge. The reason is that no natural forces exist to draw the organization back to its old system of power or on to some new one. So the conflict tends to get drawn out, which means that the period of Political Arena—of dysfunction—endures. And this, of course, can weaken the organization. Thus, while the challenge may be neutral from a political perspective, its effect may be dysfunctional from an organizational perspective. The organization would be better off with quick resolution, whether a return to the established system of power or a transition to a new one. Either way, the organization would perform more efficiently, with less wastage of energy. It is the absence of resolution that renders it worse off, even if the two sides form a shaky alliance.

This conclusion leads us into a discussion of point (c) of our proposition. As just implied, arbitrary shaky alliances—ones that reflect no natural forces on the organization—are dysfunctional because they use up in conflict resources that could otherwise go into the pursuit of mission. Because they must typically compete with organizations that are able to establish more harmonious configurations of power, they are not viable, and, like the politicized organization which tends to be not viable for the same reason, they are unlikely to survive unless supported artificially. Thus one McGill MBA group studied a university whose chief executive tried to organize it as an Adhocracy, with a fluid matrix structure of programs and departments, instead of the more stable Professional Bureaucracy, with strong departments, that its professors wanted it to be. The organization—being fully government supported—obviously survived, but experienced considerable conflict. Only when the power tilted toward the departments did conflict diminish to a more tolerable level.

As we have seen, however, many shaky alliances are not arbitrary at all. They reflect different forces on the organization that are natural, roughly equal, and irreconcilable. In other words, the organization could not function if it did not accommodate each of them. Hence it had no choice but to form into a shaky alliance, often a combination of our systems of influence which amounts to a hybrid of our configurations. This, for it, is functional, although not necessarily efficient. The conflict can be moderated to get the work done, even though some conflict is an inevitable consequence of getting that work done. (While the same case might be argued for the politicized organization, the pervasiveness of the conflict makes paralysis—an inability to get the work of the mission done—more likely.) Sometimes, in other words, it is *more* natural to function with a less than natural combination of the systems of influence.

To return to our favorite examples, the symphony orchestra is functional as a hybrid of Meritocracy and Autocracy because we can imagine no other way to coordinate the efforts of many talented musicians. So long as the musicians and conductor reach an alliance of sorts, moderating the natural conflict between them without necessarily removing all of the tension, the result sounds good. But tilting the balance one way or the other damages the system. Weakening the expertise of the operators replaces harmony with clatter, while weakening the leadership can produce anarchy. A recent film by Fellini, entitled *"Provo della orchestra" (Orchestra Rehearsal)* makes this point decisively. It shows that, as individualists who reject leadership, the musicians, however competent, can achieve nothing. Only when they accept the role of the conductor, however grudgingly, can they perform works of great beauty.[10] The school system, on the other hand, that must operate as a hybrid of the Instrument and the Merito-cracy (Machine and Professional Bureaucracy) in order to satisfy the needs of government administrators for control and order, can be considered dysfunc-tional. The purer configuration of Meritocracy (in the form of Professional Bureaucracy) seems to be more effective, by which we mean better at educating children. (We shall return to this example shortly.)

The fourth and final point of our proposition, labelled (d), considers the organization that is about to die anyway, because it can no longer perform its mission effectively. Perhaps it is so moribund that there is little hope of reviv-ing it (or, more to the point, it would be more efficient to create a new, more vibrant organization in its place). Or perhaps its mission is no longer required and the organization cannot easily be adapted to a new one. In any event, when death is inevitable, then the sooner it comes the better. This ensures that the wastage of resources during the death throes is minimized. And since, as we argued earlier, the Political Arena sometimes emerges in this period, in its com-plete form, with the effect of speeding up the demise, then it must be considered to serve a functional purpose. Much as the scavangers that swarm over car-casses are known to serve a positive function in nature, so too can the political conflicts that engulf a dying organization serve a positive function in society. Both help to speed up the recycling of necessary resources.

This, of course assumes that the conflict is allowed to take its natural course. When artificial forces sustain the organization in a state of pervasive politics—as governments sometimes do with giant, essentially bankrupt cor-porations, for fear of the political ramifications of letting them die—then the Political Arena during these extended organizational death throes becomes significantly dysfunctional.

To summarize, we have argued that the confrontation form of the Political Arena may be functional or dysfunctional, or even neutral, depending on the circumstances. But when it is provoked by a change in a fundamental condi-tion of the organization, or by the breakdown in the established order of power, then it tends to be functional, if not at first, at least eventually, in a later flare-up. The shaky alliance too, may be functional or dysfunctional, although we suspect that those that are dysfunctional do not long endure. But neutral ones, by tending to endure, become dysfunctional. The functional shaky alliances tend to reflect natural, balanced, and irreconciliable forces on the organization—

[10]Fellini was apparently using the orchestra to make this point about the whole of Italian society vis-à-vis its government. But I tend to watch movies as an organization theorist, not a political scientist.

they are, in other words, inevitable if the organization is to perform its mission effectively. We believe that the form of Political Arena we called the politicized organization is usually dysfunctional, because its pervasive politics, although moderate, consumes so much energy. Often the organization is left completely paralyzed. As for the complete Political Arena, we see it as primarily dysfunctional, except where it serves to speed up the death of a spent organization.

To conclude this discussion, we have suggested that there may be a natural order among organizational configurations, akin to the natural order Darwin described among biological species, one that reflects states of and changes in the environment. In the world of organizations, politics seems to be a major force to promote necessary adaptation, in two ways. First, organizations, unlike biological species, can redesign themselves during their own lifetimes to better suit new conditions, and politics is what often encourages them to do so. In many cases, however, existing organizations are unable to make the necessary changes, and so adaptation must take place through death and displacement, as it does in the case of the biological species. Those best suited to the prevailing conditions survive, while the others die. And here politics plays its second role in adaptation, by helping to speed up the deaths of organizations no longer suited to their environments. In these regards, the Political Arena clearly has a functional role to play. But there is no denying that it also produces its share of aberrations.

ILLUSTRATIONS OF PARTIAL POLITICAL ARENAS

We have identified four basic forms of the Political Arena—confrontation, complete Political Arena, shaky alliance, and politicized organization. One of these—the complete Political Arena—was discussed at the outset, and was described as being the purest of the four and the least likely to occur or at least to sustain itself. Here, therefore, in closing this chapter by seeking to flesh out our description of the Political Arena, we focus on the other three—the partial forms.

In practice, the Political Arena can appear in an enormous number of variations. We are dealing here not with an orderly configuration of power, but with one that is essentially open-ended, ranging from moderate conflict between two centers of power to outright war among many, at the limit to anarchy. To flesh out our descriptions of the three partial forms of the Political Arena, therefore, we attempt no more than the presentation of various illustrations of each.

TAKEOVER AS CONFRONTATION POLITICAL ARENA Common in the life of organizations is the attempt by one group of influencers to seize control from another. The most dramatic example of *takeover* we have seen involved a powerful consensus of external influencers intent on bringing a strong-willed entrepreneur under control. His resistance led to a war between the coalitions, each dominated in its own way. This is the story of Hans Isbrandtsen, who ran his shipping company in direct contradiction to all of his competitors as well as to the wishes of the United States government. Both supported a policy of extensive subsidization of the U.S. Merchant Fleet (60 percent of total operating costs in 1960) coupled with support for a tight international cartel that set rates and carved up territories. So long as Isbrandtsen's firm remained profitable, he could pursue his strategy, retaining personal control of the Internal Coalition. But the outside forces were powerful, and when they finally managed to weaken its financial position, concurrent with a sudden breakdown in its own focus of power, they succeeded in taking it over, drawing its power out to the External Coalition. Perrow recounts the story:

> Hans Isbrandtsen and his company made money—not much, but enough to carry on the battle. Efficiency was their weapon in an industry where there was no incentive for it. They also took spectacular risks in political matters, staying within the law but running blockades (e.g., Taiwan's blockade of mainland China), to the annoyance of the State Department, suing the government for illegal practices, attacking the secretary of State in full-page ads, and the like. The U.S. government refused to give them business or to sell them surplus ships, and finally the Maritime Commission allowed a rate war to take place in the Pacific that was directed solely at Isbrandtsen. The weapon was a complex of rate changes and restrictions that was subsequently declared illegal by the Supreme Court, but not until the damage was done and the firm had left the Pacific. Goods were being shipped by Isbrandtsen and the cartel at 80 percent below established rates. Isbrandtsen paid out more simply to load and unload the cargo than it made in freight charges. During this rate war Hans Isbrandtsen died, and his son later agreed to join the cartel. The son applied for a government subsidy, which the government indicated it would be delighted to review. (1970, pp. 157–58)

The Isbrandtsen organization, an Autocracy from the looks of things, became a confrontation form of Political Arena because of its resistance to being taken over and rendered an Instrument of the cartel. Larçon and Reitter (1978, 1979) describe a Political Arena that emerged after formal takeover, because the members of the organization resisted consolidation of that takeover. The organization was a French subsidiary, which had a good deal of Autonomy from its American parent, producing home furniture with a strong tradition of quality and exclusivity. In this respect, it seemed more like a Missionary, coupled with certain elements of Autocracy and Meritocracy, than an Instrument. But after the parent firm was sold by family interests to a "finance-oriented, diversified company," managers were sent in to the French subsidiary to reorient it to mass production in the office furniture market, and to manage it with more formalized controls. These changes were, of course, resisted:

Such changes cannot be implemented in one day, especially when a whole social body is against it. Inside the firm, executives and employees were resisting change, outside the firm, media, dealers and former consumers were resisting change and image dilution. Corporate identity at that time was clearly schizophrenic and that, in turn, had undesirable effects on daily operations. (1978, p. 10)

The parent firm, of course, won out—"the French company progressively evolved toward a more professional and orthodox [i.e., bureaucratic] style of management and new internal values." But at a price. Years later, the firm was still experiencing difficulties, having "lost much of its core skills" (p. 11).

What we have here is a smooth takeover in the legal sense, followed by conflict in the consolidation of that legal takeover. Formal power was willingly ceded to a new external influencer. But much informal power remained in the System of Ideology, as well as that of Expertise. To render the organization its Instrument, the new external influencer had to destroy the ideology and limit the expertise, replacing them with bureaucratic controls, the one means by which that influencer could extend his formal power deep into the Internal Coalition. But that was resisted—by insiders as well as other external influencers—and so the organization was driven for a time to the confrontation form of the Political Arena configuration.

The takeovers so far discussed were essentially wars between the External and Internal Coalitions, the former trying to seize or consolidate control of the latter. The opposite case could, of course, be imagined as well—insiders seeking to take over control from dominant outsiders. And then there is the case where outsiders battle each other for control while insiders look on passively, hesitant to make any decisions until a winner emerges. In business, this can become rather formalized when it involves official tenders, proxy fights, and the like. Insiders in this situation can, of course, get involved—lining up with one side or resisting both by trying to encourage the widest possible distribution of the stock. Takeover can also occur exclusively within the Internal Coalition, for example, when the operating personnel mutany against the central authority, or when a group of young Turks executes a coup d'état. In one case, the takeover involves a change of configuration, in the other, only of the actors.

DIVIDED ORGANIZATION AS CONFRONTATION POLITICAL ARENA   It sometimes happens that an organization divides itself politically into two rival camps, perhaps because a changed condition pits reformers against an old guard, perhaps because an important group of influencers simply seeks the realignment of a coalition.

A common example of this occurs when two individuals who share the leadership—say two partners in a small business—have a falling out, conflicting over the strategic direction the organization should take. This divided authority splits the organization into two camps, as shown in Figure 23-4, one under each

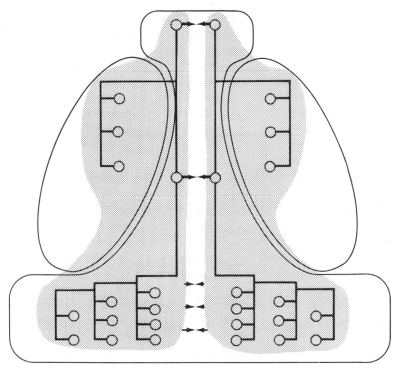

Figure 23–4. *The Divided Organization*

leader. The two may be able to reach a shaky alliance, as we shall see in examples later. But probably more common is the eruption of an intense battle for control, until one side dominates and imposes a new stability (or the organization is destroyed). As it is written in the Bible: "If a house be divided against itself, that house cannot stand" (Mark 3:25).

Our studies have uncovered a number of such divided houses, almost all unstable. Perhaps the most interesting, investigated by management students in France, involved the recent merger of three companies that produced a particular kind of candy. Three entrepreneurs, each one used to running his own company, suddenly found themselves sharing power, one the "président" concerned largely with external affairs, a second the "directeur général" concerned only with internal affairs (note that the CEO of the French corporation is usually called the "président–directeur général," or PDG), and the third the director of finance and administration. The marriage was never consummated, and by the time of the study the performance of the organization had deteriorated seriously. There was clearly the need to return to some central basis of authority, and, in fact, six months after the study, the "président" and the director of finance resigned. As Rumelt has noted, in a merged firm "resource allocation decisions may focus on 'which side of the house' gets supported, rather than on individual investment proposals," to the detriment of performance (1974, p. 152).[11]

An organization can also become divided along ideological or missionary lines, as we saw in the conflict over whether rehabilitation or custody should be the true mission of the prison. Mission is so central to the functioning of every organization that conflict over what it should be usually tears an organization apart, forcing virtually all the influencers to choose sides and form into rival camps. The CEO either takes a side himself (the conflict continuing if he is weak) or else tries to sit between the two camps in a kind of no man's land (another sign of his weakness).

Even when mission does not normally figure among the primary goals of an organization—in other words, when it has a weak System of Ideology—mission will nevertheless move into a position of prominence during such a conflict. Pursuit of other goals will be suspended as each side focusses on promoting its favored mission. Often, however, it is not just missions that are competing, but the fundamentally different power configurations that underlie each (and, of course, the influencers who stand to gain from one configuration or the other). Thus, in prisons experiencing the conflict mentioned above, the custodial mission called for the Instrument configuration, with power going to the administrators and external influencers (and the guards retaining considerable control over the prisoners), while the rehabilitation mission called for a Meritocracy configuration, with power going to the professional staff.

SOME HYBRIDS AS SHAKY ALLIANCES As noted earlier, sometimes different systems of influence come to coexist in balanced and rather enduring relationships, especially when each reflects some natural condition or need of the organization. In terms of our configurations, these are hybrids. Of course, such a hybrid need not always be conflictive. As noted earlier, Clark's distinctive colleges, combining features of Meritocracy and Missionary, seemed harmonious enough. Likewise, before it was taken over, the furniture company just described probably achieved a harmonious blend of ideology and expertise, with some personalized control as well—in a sense, it developed its own configuration. But many of these hybrids do in fact generate more conflict than the typical case of the purer configuration. They are shaky alliances, in which politics diminishes to a tolerable level, so that the organization can function, but remains present nevertheless, and ever ready to flare up.

We have come across a large number of examples of such shaky alliances, leading us to conclude that many organizations experience conflicting pressures that they cannot reconcile. It is presumably the fortunate ones that are able to favor one orientation—one system of influence, one mechanism of coordina-

---

[11]Rumelt was writing about the merger of two firms concentrated in different businesses, but our example suggests that the same problems can arise in the merger of firms in the same business, until a consummation of the merger is achieved.

tion—enabling them to achieve the consistency and harmony of a pure configuration.

The symphony orchestra, an Autocratic Meritocracy if you like, has served as our prime example of the functional hybrid. A similar hybrid, equally functional, might be found in various small organizations, in which the professionalism of the experts must coexist with the personal control of the owners —the small advertising agency, consulting or architectural firm, as well as the entrepreneurial high-technology company.

If the symphony orchestra has been our favorite example of the functional hybrid, then the school system, hospital, or university closely controlled by the government—the Dominated Meritocracy, if you like—has been our favorite example of the dysfunctional one. This hybrid is shown in Figure 23–5, with the professional operators and lower managers lined up in one camp, against the government, technostructure, and senior management in the other. (Of course, the senior managers could instead line up with the professionals, or the lower managers with the senior ones; somewhere along the line, the split must take place, with those managers at the margin perhaps sitting in the no man's land between the two camps; as noted in Chapter 22, that is often the fate of the CEO.)

This hybrid tends to arise whenever a would-be Meritocracy is dependent on a single external influencer for much of its support—as many public professional organizations are on government. As we saw in Chapter 22, such dependency may encourage the external influencer to try to exercise close control, which can result in more than usual centralization, formalization, and attention to the goal of economic efficiency at the expense of those of mission and professional excellence. As shown in Figure 23–5, the administrative pressures are exerted at two points: down the hierarchy, through line managers who seek to exercise direct supervision over the operators, and from the technostructure, through staff analysts who seek to impose standards on the work and outputs of the operators. Either way, the intention is the same: to usurp the prerogatives that the professionals of independent Meritocracies take for granted. The professionals in turn resist, as shown in Figure 23–5 primarily through their representatives (who are in fact the managers at the lower levels in the line hierarchy) and, perhaps, secondarily by unionizing and exerting pressures on the other camp via the External Coalition. Conflict ensues, so that the result is not only to partly machine bureaucratize a Professional Bureaucracy but also to politicize it. Outright confrontation is likely, or else the two camps will form a shaky alliance—in effect, a hybrid of Meritocracy and the Instrument—which, as we argued in Chapter 22, will probably prove less effective than the pure Meritocracy.

We see an attempt to create a similar hybrid, but approached from the opposite direction, when an organization structured as a Machine Bureaucracy, sensing the need to be innovative, sets up a project structure—in effect, a mini-Adhocracy—off in a corner. Often the graft will not take, because the

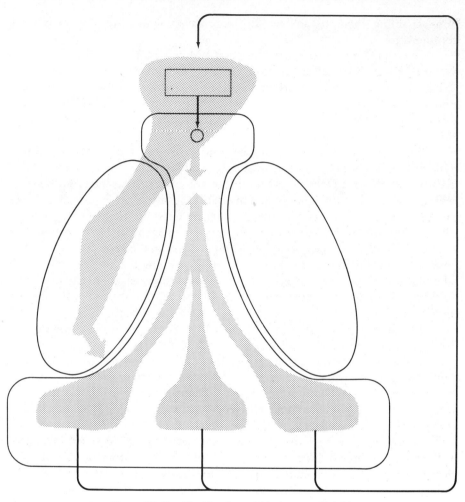

Figure 23–5. *The Dominated Meritocracy Hybrid*

bureaucratic controls of the larger organization tend to be pervasive, finding their way into the corners too. The controllers insist on measures of perfor-mance, the planners want plans, the personnel people insist on the standard procedures for the evaluation of applicants even for unconventional jobs. Machine Bureaucracy sweeps out Adhocracy. But the hybrid can emerge when the need for innovation is so great that the Adhocracy component is established on an equal footing with that of Machine Bureaucracy, so that neither can dominate the other. In other words, balance between the different systems of influence remains the key to sustaining a hybrid. Note that this hybrid does not intermingle the different systems of influence directly, as does the public professional organization discussed above. Rather, each is established in an independent, parallel structure, only loosely coupled with the other. On one side is the Adhocracy component, a Meritocracy in which expertise reigns for purposes of innovation; on the other is the Machine Bureaucracy component, an Instrument or Closed System dominated by authority in order to execute systematically the innovations of the Adhocracy.

Earlier we discussed the house divided against itself that cannot stand. Our findings here suggest that many such houses do indeed manage to stand, at least so long as their divisions are moderated (and, if they are not functional, so long as they are somehow propped up). Our final example of such a house serves to indicate that we have barely touched the surface of the hybrids that are possible in organizations. This house, a Canadian subsidiary studied by one of the McGill MBA group, manufactured furniture, but in quite a different way from the company discussed earlier. As shown in Figure 23-6, it consisted of a rather shaky set of alliances. Dominating the External Coalition was the U.S. parent. Within the firm, the chief executive controlled the staff groups, as well as the head of manufacturing, in a personal way. But none of these controlled the plant, which was run as the fiefdom of its own manager. Similarly, the sales force was run as the personal preserve of the sales manager. This meant four somewhat independent centers of power—three would-be Autocracies and a would-be Instrument. The arrangement hardly seems the epitome of viability, but it did function, perhaps because the organization was sustained by the technological know-how of its parent.

The large number of shaky alliances that we have encountered, with all kinds of curious and often contradictory distributions of power, suggests that all is not clean in the world of organizations. Compromise is often the order of the day. We have suggested that some of this compromise is necessary, dictated by the different conditions faced by an organization. But much is also dysfunctional, originating less in fundamental conditions than in uncorrected anomalies—in established centers or peripherial pockets of power that should be stronger or weaker than they are. These anomalies can give rise to Political Arenas that endure when they have some artificial means of support, but their ultimate effect is to weaken the organization and, eventually in some cases, to destroy it.

THE CONTROVERSIAL PUBLIC AGENCY AS POLITICIZED ORGANIZATION   Here we come to another anomaly, but of a very different sort. Conflict, rather than being restricted to the relationships between specific systems of influence, as in the hybrid, instead pervades all relationships, so that the whole organization appears as an anomaly in society. We discuss two examples of this politicized organization to complete this chapter, the first in the public sector, the second ostensibly in the private sector (although, as we shall see, that is one of the points of contention).

The politicized organization—one pervaded by moderate conflict—frequently appears in public agencies for at least two reasons. First, every agency of government, because of its public mandate and visible actions, as well as

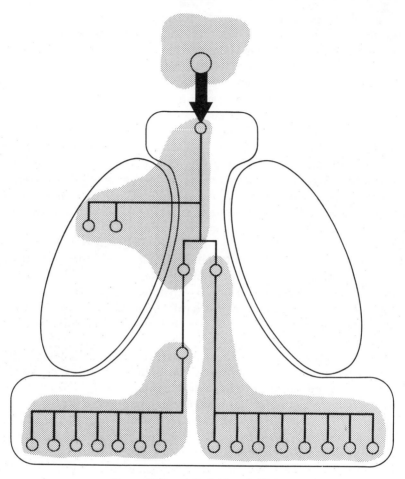

Figure 23-6. *A Shaky Set of Alliances*

the pervasive consequences of those actions, has a high potential for politics. When, all of this is coupled with a controversial mission—one that attracts many insistent external influencers with conflicting needs—then some form of Political Arena must be the expected result. (Of course, not all government agencies pursue controversial missions: the post office, for example, has a fairly straightforward one which elicits general agreement that it be pursued with the greatest possible efficiency. Hence, as we saw in Chapter 18, the post office can be an Instrument with a consensus-dominated External Coalition.) And second, the public agency can endure a state of pervasive politics because its support is guaranteed by the government. It need face no market test of effectiveness in order to survive; indeed the very disagreement about what goals it should pursue ensures that no one can possibly measure its overall performance.

The Tennessee Valley Authority as described by Selznick in 1949 seems to be one example of what we are calling the controversial public agency. Interestingly, one finds characteristics of all of our configurations in his description—of Meritocracy (in the type of work performed), of Missionary (in its ideological character), of Autocracy (in the power of certain of its leaders), of Instrument (in the alliance of external influencers that was able to displace certain of its official goals), and of Closed System (in its own attempts to coopt these influencers). Having to combine all of these characteristics, as the description suggests, caused the TVA to look much like what we have described as the politicized organization. (The implication is that as the complexity of the shaky alliance increases—specifically, as the number of centers of power which must accommodate each other increases—this form of Political Arena merges into the politicized organization form. Conflict spreads beyond specific points of contention to pervade the entire system.)

Despite the conflict, the TVA Selznick describes was apparently able to function. Perhaps this was the result of the firm foundations laid by its first leader. But other controversial public agencies sometimes become paralyzed by their conflicts. Earlier we saw the example of the New York City Board of Education. We often read of the same result in regulatory agencies. Ostensibly set up to regulate others, everyone ends up regulating them instead. As we shall see in Chapter 28, the regulatory agency can become so enmeshed in its own politics that it emerges as completely ineffective, the truly paralytic organization.[12]

The extent to which a public agency is driven toward the Political Arena configuration depends, of course, on the type of governmental system in which it finds itself. In the American pluralistic form of democracy, public agencies are apt to be more politicized than, say, those in a parliamentary form of government (let alone those in a dictatorship). Parliamentary democracy concentrates a great deal more power in the executive branch of government (assuming the governing party holds a majority of the seats in parliament), making it far easier to render the public agencies the Instruments of the government in power. The American system's check and balances, its relative absence of party discipline, and its encouragement of lobbying practices, all tend to divide the External Coalitions of the controversial public agencies, and to politicize their Internal Coalitions.

Indeed, one can describe the whole of American government as a kind of Political Arena (with pervasive, moderate conflict, in the form of the politicized organization). In contrast, majority government in the parliamentary system looks more like integrated Machine Bureaucracy—taking the form of the Instrument (of the people) or a Closed System (of the politicians and civil servants), depending on one's perspective, and cynicism—though hardly devoid of characteristics of the Political Arena as well. As a result, at least in this writer's

---

[12]Of course, it is those to be regulated who often have the most to benefit from the inactivity of the regulatory agency. So in that sense, paralysis renders it their Instrument!

opinion, Americans enjoy a more open system of government, but one more ridden with conflict and polarization and so less capable of acting decisively and in an integrated fashion.

We have alluded to governments reflecting the characteristics of our different power configurations at a number of points in our discussion. While this is a book on organization theory and not political science, it may nevertheless be worthwhile to pull these conclusions together. (Ours, after all, is increasingly a world of organization, in which even governments tend to look more like clusters of organizations than forums of elected representatives. The tendency may not be altogether encouraging, but it does indicate the role organization theory can play in helping us to understand the behavior of government.)

We have seen examples of our Autocracy configuration in the dictatorship, and even in the democratically elected government ruled personally by an all-powerful leader. The example of a de Gaulle in France suggests that conditions of crisis can bring on this configuration in democratic states. The Instrument, of course, appears in the form of the colony, ruled by the mother country. Also, the parliamentary government elected by a clear public consensus can be viewed as society's Instrument. Carried to its logical conclusion, the welfare state might be so described as well. In Chapter 19, we noted that the communist state—at least the independent ones that have grown beyond the cult of personality—seems to resemble rather closely our Closed System power configuration. We also saw important indications of this configuration in the governments of the West, notably the highly centralized ones, France being perhaps the best example. Cultural revolution, as experienced in China in the 1960s, was seen to reflect many of the characteristics of our Missionary configuration.

As we have just seen, the pluralist form of government used in the United States seems to resemble our Political Arena in many ways, at least in its pervasive, moderate form. This is clearly by design. Italy, in contrast, seems to have fallen into this configuration of power by default (much as postwar France did, before the crisis in Algeria brought de Gaulle to power). More generally, it seems evident that the Political Arena will be found in the breakdown of any form of government, under conditions typically described as anarchy or revolution. Anarchy in society resembles breakdown in the established order of power in the organization, while revolution corresponds to politically induced transition of power in a coalition or the configuration of an organization.

Of course, no modern government is devoid of the characteristics of the Political Arena, or, for that matter, those of the Closed System. Given the massive power, size, and bureaucratization of governments everywhere, all are to some degree impervious to external control (even by the politicians, let alone the citizens), yet at the same time permeated with conflict. Likewise, while we can think of no government that we would comfortably label Meritocracy (although, as we saw in Chapter 22, Young believes it is only a matter of time), all governments today, because of their need for expertise, reflect certain of its characteristics. If we consider the interplay of the six forces that underlie our configurations, in the wealthier nations at least, it appears that personalized leadership and ideological belief, not to mention direct control by those external influencers called the citizens, have been significantly displaced by the pervasive forces of bureaucracy, meritocracy, and politics. Perhaps we are being governed increasingly by a dysfunctional hybrid.

THE GIANT CORPORATION AS POLITICIZED ORGANIZATION   It is not, of course, only the controversial public agency that can take on the form of the politicized organization. Organizations in other spheres tend to exhibit similar characteristics, notably when their activities too are visible, consequential, and controversial. In the late 1960s, for example, universities and other institutions were seen as controversial, and so became politicized. But that was a rather short-lived phenomenon. More significant has been a slower but steadier politicization of the giant business corporation.

Let us pick up the history of the corporation where we left off in Chapter 19 on the Closed System power configuration. Largely unimpeded by external influencers and in some cases encouraged by their ability to dominate markets, certain corporations grew immensely large and their actions came to have increasingly significant impact on society. The traditional premise of corporate autonomy—Adam Smith's laissez-faire doctrine, that free markets would regulate corporate behavior—come increasingly into question. In its place grew the belief that the giant, widely held corporation was a system closed to external influence, an institution whose leaders—apparently self-selected and self-perpetuating—wielded an immense amount of power, social as well as economic. As Lodge wrote:

> It is now quite obvious that our large public corporations are not private property at all. The 1,500,000 shareholders of General Motors do not and cannot control, direct, or in any real sense be responsible for "their" company. . . . the reader may ask, if GM and the hundreds of other large corporations like it are not property, then what are they? The best we can say is that they are some sort of collective, floating in philosophic limbo, dangerously vulnerable to the charge of illegitimacy and to the charge that they are not amenable to community control. (1974, p. 65)

As we noted in Chapter 17, nature abhors a vacuum, and society most of all abhors a power vacuum. When exit is difficult, as Hirschman (1970) has noted, then voice will be raised to try to control behavior directly. In the case under discussion here many citizens have come to feel that they cannot escape the consequences of corporate actions, sometimes the actions of a single corporation (as in the closing of a plant or the marketing of a dangerous product), sometimes the actions of the collectivity of corporations (as in the promotion of questionable foods or the spoiling of the environment). So various citizens have tried to move into the power vacuum left by the retreating shareholders, to raise their voices to get the giant corporation to act in interests other than its own as a system.

The result has been that corporation after corporation has woken up to find an External Coalition no longer quite so passive as it used to be. Berle and Means, who first described in 1932 the transition in large corporations from a Dominated External Coalition to a Passive one, were also astute enough at that time to prophesize a later transition to a Divided External Coalition:

> On the one hand, the owners of passive property, [the shareholders] by surrendering control and responsibility over the active property, have surrendered the right that the corporation should be operated in their sole interest. . . . At the same time, the controlling groups [the management], by means of the extension of corporate powers, have in their own interest broken the bars of tradition which require that the corporation be operated solely for the benefit of the owners of passive property. Eliminating the sole interest of the passive owner, however, does not necessarily lay a basis for the alternative claim that the new powers should be used in the interest of the controlling groups. The latter have not presented, in acts or words any acceptable defense of the proposition that these powers should be so used. No tradition supports that proposition. The control groups have, rather, cleared the way for the claims of a group far wider than either the owners or the control. They have placed the community in a position to demand that the modern corporation serve not alone the owners or the control but all society. (1968, pp. 311–12)

Such demands have indeed come forward since Berle and Means wrote these words. The largest of the giants—the General Motors, the AT&Ts, the Exxons—have been attacked on all sides. Because the corporation has been perceived as responsible to no one, suddenly it becomes responsible to everyone. General Motors is challenged by Ralph Nader and his associates, first for ignoring safety issues and then because its board of directors is not perceived as representative enough; AT&T is accused by women and minority groups of prejudice in its personnel policies; Exxon is accused by the Canadian government of diverting crude destined for its Canadian subsidiary to its home market, and in the United States is regularly threatened, along with its six sisters, with antitrust and other government actions; and so it goes, ad infinitum. Where once the individual large corporation was free of public pressure unless it specifically misbehaved—stifled competition, endangered its employees, or whatever—today it is being challenged for virtually everything it tries to do, and, indeed, for not taking the initiative in the social sphere. Once there were only the owners' goals to attend to, later the systems goals. Today the corporation is being asked to respond to a confusing host of public goals, social as well as economic.

Ackerman (1975) describes some of the effects of the new social pressures on the giant corporation: increased complexity of managing the organization, including proliferation of nonfinancial reporting systems and realignment of the bases for evaluating executives; boards of directors drawn into issues of social responsibility; more ambiguous and difficult assignments for line managers at middle levels, resulting in greater tensions and pressures in their relationships both inside and outside the corporation; the blurring of responsibilities in the structure; and "a pronounced diffusion of effective control over operating decisions" (p. 326).

The implication is that all of this pressure has served not only to divide the External Coalition of the giant corporation but also to begin to politicize its Internal Coalition. For example, new external influencers have forged direct links with insiders, bypassing the System of Authority and encouraging them to attend to goals inconsistent with the formal ones sent down the hierarchy. The personnel manager becomes an internal lobbyist for hiring of people from minority groups; the factory manager living in the local community takes the case for the installation of pollution abatement equipment to headquarters; the pleas of consumerists get responded to in the research laboratories where the new products are designed. "Thus, for instance, instead of the research and medical staff of a pharmaceutical house asking of a possible new drug only can we sell it? will it pass the FDA standards? they might ask in addition, will it do something for medicine that existing drugs do not? enough to be worth the effort of development and marketing?" (Kaysen, 1967, p. 218). All of this introduces a host of new social influences into decision making, and brings on conflict with the traditional economic ones. The result can be constructive socially, but it also politicizes the Internal Coalition. As Macrae has noted:

> Big business corporations now face the difficulty that they are too large to inspire people to hunt together as a pack, so, behind many of their facades, the employees from just below the managing director to those around the shop steward are forming separate packs to hunt each other. (1976, p. 60)

In summary then, the giant corporation, despite its official status of private ownership, is coming to be viewed increasingly as a de facto public agency, one surrounded by a good deal of controversy. From its current state as a Closed System, we see the beginnings of "The politicization of the corporation," to use Blumberg's term (1971), its emergence as a Political Arena. With conflict of a relatively moderate nature pervading it, it takes the form that we called the politicized organization. And this may well prove to be an enduring form, since many giant corporations will no doubt be able to use their market and political powers to sustain the inefficiencies that politicization will inevitably bring. Increasingly, survival may come to depend more on how big a firm is, and who its executives know, than on how well it serves its customers. Perrow's description of how Consolidated Edison of New York circumvented its operating inefficiencies through its ability to coopt politicians is perhaps an indication of the things to come. "By buying security through political relationships, Con Ed has apparently not had to worry about its deficiencies" (1970,

p. 155). The "politicized corporation" may be here to stay, at least as long as the society that tolerates it itself can survive.[13]

To conclude, as organizations of all types—public, private, and those in between, not to mention government itself—grow larger and more powerful, the Political Arena becomes a more prevalent and more enduring power configuration, with some inevitable and in many ways unfortunate consequences for the societies that have spawned them.

---

[13]A major reflection of these tendencies in the literature of organization theory is what is called the "resource dependency" view, the most popular of the new topics in the field. But the focus is on how corporations do and should react to the pressures, how they can and might use political means to protect themselves as Closed Systems (as exemplified by the work of Pfeffer and Salancik [1978], discussed in Chapter 19). But when organizations come to sustain themselves politically, instead of functionally through pursuit of their missions, and thereby threaten society's interests, it becomes imperative that they be studied, and that prescriptions be developed, from a societal perspective. The premise at the root of so much comtemporary thinking about organizations, especially business organizations—of each one for itself—becomes seriously deficient. A broader social premise—that each organization is part of the system called society, and contributes directly by its actions to the determination of social goals—becomes necessary in organization theory.

24

Transitions Among
the Power Configurations

At the close of Chapter 16—our last one on the elements of power—we described the system of power and goals in and around the organization as being in a state of dynamic equilibrium. By this we meant that it tends to achieve steady state despite continual changes of low amplitude, interrupted by periodic and more disruptive changes of high amplitude. At that point in our discussion, we introduced our configurations of power as these steady states. We then proceeded to so describe each of our configurations, at least until the last chapter. There, in discussing the Political Arena, we reintroduced the aspect of dynamism into our discussion. First we described some forms of the Political Arena as unstable in the short run, and then we suggested that all of our configurations of power have to be viewed as unstable in the long run. Each remains stable only under the conditions that naturally support it, and destabilizes as soon as these conditions change, unless, of course, it is challenged arbitrarily first.

In fact, in each of the configurations are forces that can arise to change its conditions, and so to destroy it. As Perrow notes: "people tramp in and out [of organizations] with mud on their shoes that they bring in from the outside world. . . . Furthermore, the windows and doors are always open because the organization processes raw materials . . . Viewed in this light it is very hard to maintain control in an organization" (1970, p. 56). Indeed, as we shall soon see, some of the forces working to destroy each configuration arise from its very own nature. In other words, each configuration helps to sow the seeds of its own destruction. In the long run, therefore, all the configurations of power are unstable.

This brings us back to our description in Chapter 14 of organizational power as a pulsating phenomenon, "at times imploding or concentrating toward a center, at other times exploding or diffusing to the peripheries." As we noted, the cycles of low amplitude, usually brief in duration, do not threaten the steady state. In fact, by oscillating about a mean, they help to define it. They may be frequent and pervasive, but they do not induce significant change. They resemble the vibrations of a motor that from a distance appears to be stationary. More important are the cycles of high amplitude. These are the ones that destroy established systems of power and give rise to new ones, in other words, that effect *transitions* between and among the power configurations.

The analysis of these transitions is of particular interest to us here for at least two reasons. First, it introduces the dynamic aspect to what has been in this section (except for the last chapter) a rather static perspective. Second, analysis of the transitions enables us to study the patterns of interrelationships among the configurations, and so to learn how organizations evolve over time. We have devoloped the configurations to be used not simply as a typology, but as a framework to help build integrated theory. The configurations, in other words, have been designed to be played with, and one interesting game—a form of "lego" if you like—is to use them as building blocks to construct theories of organizational life cycles. And so, the analysis of organizational transitions helps us to flesh out and energize our discussion of the power configurations. It should also enable the reader to assess the usefulness of thinking about organizations in terms of configurations.

Our discussion is divided into two parts. The bulk of it is devoted to a description of the transitions *between* the configurations, considering each configuration in turn. Then we conclude the chapter with a description of transitions *among* the set of six configurations, presented in terms of a revised model of stages of organizational development.

Our discussion of the transitions between the configurations will follow a particular sequence. For each configuration, we shall first consider the conditions that draw an organization *to* it. These were in fact discussed in each of the preceding chapters, but their brief review at this point serves to put our discussion of transitions into context. Each condition is categorized, roughly, according to whether it is (a) *necessary* to bring on the configuration in question, in other words, is virtually a requirement for its existence; (b) *sufficient* to bring it on, in other words, can do so alone; (c) *facilitating*, in other words, helps to bring on the configuration without being either necessary or sufficient; and (d) *overriding*, in other words, capable of dominating most other conditions that would drive the organization toward another configuration (an overriding condition obviously being a strong form of sufficient condition). The reader may recall that these conditions were listed and so categorized for each of the configurations in Table 17-1, on pages 308–311.

Then, assuming the configuration is established, we ask ourselves how stable it is. We look at its purposes in the society of organizations (which were also listed in Table 17-1) and discuss its legitimacy in terms of these purposes and of its power arrangements. Ironically, in many cases we conclude that the stability of a configuration is inversely related to the perceived legitimacy of its power relationships. Some of the least legitimate configurations seem to have the greatest staying power, and vice versa.

Finally, we discuss the forces that drive an organization *from* the given configuration, and the transitions that these induce. We are particularly interested in which configurations are likely to succeed each one as it falters. Two sets of forces are discussed (and have also been summarized in Table 17-1 as the principle conditions weakening each configuration). *External* forces are independent of the configuration. They may or may not arise; if they do, they act to drive the organization toward another configuration. Inherent or *intrinsic* forces, of greater interest to us, are built right into the configuration. They arise from its very nature, and, unless external forces intervene, they eventually tend to bring it down, driving it toward particular transitions. It is in terms of these intrinsic forces that we see how each of the configurations sows the seeds of its own destruction (and, in some cases, of the destruction of the organization as well). The transitions effected by these intrinsic forces are considered the natural ones for each configuration, since, in the absence of external forces, they indicate where an organization with a given configuration is likely to go next.

Table 24-1 summarizes our conclusions on the transitions between the configurations in a six-by-six matrix. Each configuration is listed on each of the two dimensions, in a row as the origin of the transition ("From") and in a column as the result of it ("To"). Note that all thirty-six boxes are filled in. This means that the transition from every configuration to each of the others is discussed, as well as the transition to itself (the case of a change in power without change in configuration, as when the players switch but the favored means of influence remains the same). Thus we conclude that forces exist that can drive any configuration to any of the others or to a different form of itself. But most of these are external forces. We also conclude that in the absence of such forces the intrinsic forces eventually drive each of the configurations to specific transitions: for two of them, to one other specific configuration; for two others, to one other specific configuration or to a different form of itself; for one configuration, to any of four different configurations; and for the remaining configuration, to oblivion. We highlight these particular transitions—both in Table 24-1 and as propositions in the text—in boldface type because, as noted earlier, we consider them to be the most natural ones. It is these propositions as a set that we use to build our model of stages of organizational development at the end of the chapter.

TRANSITIONS TO AND FROM
THE INSTRUMENT

The Instrument emerges when power in the External Coalition of an organization is (a) focussed, (b) organized, and (c) speaks with a clear voice, that is, imposes clear, operational goals on the organization. All are necessary

TABLE 24-1. Transitions between the Power Configurations

Natural transitions are highlighted

From ＼ To	Instrument	Closed System	Autocracy
Instrument		**Success and growth, leading to diffusion of external influence and increased difficulty of surveillance (e.g.; dispersal of stock)** Also overregulation	Wresting of power from external influencer(s) by CEO, or replacement of CEO by external influencer; also crisis and appearance of strong-willed leader
Closed System	Rise of external dependency	**Stagnation, leading to replacement of leadership (often via coup d'etat) as form of renewal**	**Appearance of strong-willed leader, sometimes temporarily to effect necessary renewal before returning to Closed System** Also crises not caused by own inability to adapt
Autocracy	**Precariousness, or organization becoming established, leading to forced takeover or voluntary transfer of power to external influencer (i.e., separation of management from control; e.g., sale of small firm to conglomerate or passing of entrepreneurial power to heirs)** Also stabilization of the environment leading to takeover	**Departure of founding CEO or of strong leader from large organization (one with established administration);** also **completion of renewal of stagnating Closed System**	Replacement of one strong leader by another (probably outsider) typically in organization continuing to face conditions of Autocracy (e.g., small size; simple, stable environment)

Missionary	Takeover of organization and destruction of ideology	**Growth and/or aging of organization, leading to atrophy of ideology; rise of administration (Michels's Iron Law of Oligarchy), perhaps to further institutionalize mission or due to vulnerability of organization;** also goal displacement to members' needs, and overdoing ideology	Appearance of strong-willed leader (in some cases able to coerce loyal followers); crisis
Meritocracy	Rationalization of expertise in presence of focussed external influence, or transfer by dominant external influencer to new, simpler mission (e.g., to mass produce innovation of Adhocracy)	Rationalization of expertise in absence of external dependency; transfer by administrators to new, simpler mission; also possibly unionization of experts	Appearance of strong-willed leader able to transfer organization to new, simpler mission; crisis
Political Arena	**Resolution of conflict during transition from Autocracy to Instrument** Overpoliticization of IC in presence of strong external influencer; favorable tilting of balance in any shaky alliance involving Instrument; also resolution of conflict in any transition to Instrument	**Resolution of conflict during transition from Missionary, Instrument, or Autocracy to Closed System, or during renewal of Closed System** Overpoliticization of EC in presence of strong administration; favorable tilting of balance in any shaky alliance involving Closed System; also resolution of conflict in any transition to Closed System	**Renewal of politicized organization to save it** Overpoliticization of IC and EC (or EC) in presence of shrewd leader; favorable tilting of balance in any shaky alliance involving Autocracy; also resolution of conflict in any transition to Autocracy

TABLE 24-1. Transitions between the Power Configurations (continued)

Natural transitions are highlighted

From \ To	Missionary	Meritocracy	Political Arena
Instrument	Emergence of ideology to divert attention of insiders	Change in technology or technical system necessitating use of expert skills and knowledge (e.g., shift to rehabilitation orientation in prisons)	**Resistance of dominant influencer to challenge by administrators** or any others
Closed System	Emergence of strong ideology, perhaps reflecting disillusionment with bureaucratic controls and utilitarian norms (e.g., cultural revolution)	Change in technology or technical system necessitating use of expert skills and knowledge	**Accumulation of great power followed by its exploitation, leading to external challenges and internal conflicts, resulting in politicized organization** Also resistance by administrators to any challenge, especially resistance by senior management to renewal of **Closed System**, leading to confrontation
Autocracy	**Departure of charismatic leader followed by institutionalization of leader's beliefs into strong ideology**	**Organization of experts becoming established** Also change in technology or technical system necessitating use of expert skills and knowledge	**Conflict over succession, between different administrators or between insiders favoring ideology and outsiders intent on control; also resistance by leader to challenge from outsiders or administrators or experts or others; also attempt to function with divided personalized leadership; and overdoing personalized control (cult of leadership)**

Configuration			
Missionary	Replacement of one ideology by another (usually in enclave or else requiring spinoff of new organization; eventually perhaps back into original organization)	Introduction of status differences due to change in technology or technical system necessitating use of expert skills and knowledge	**Resistance of loyal members to destruction of ideology by administrators or others**
Meritocracy	Emergence of ideology taking organization to new, simpler mission	**Displacement of one body of expertise by another, usually to renew organization** Also shift of Adhocracy to stable environment (and Professional Bureaucracy form)	**Exploitation of expert power, through callousness of experts, leading to external challenges and internal conflicts, resulting in politicized organizations; resistance of established experts to renew Meritocracy; also resistance by experts to challenges of external influencers or others**
Political Arena	Favorable tilting of balance in any shaky alliance involving Missionary; also resolution of conflict in any transition to Missionary	**Resolution of conflict during transition from Autocracy to Meritocracy or during renewal of Meritocracy** Favorable tilting of balance in any shaky alliance involving Meritocracy; also resolution of conflict in any transition to Meritocracy	**Intensification of conflict of politicized organization (to complete Political Arena) before demise of organization** Also flare-up of shaky alliance (to confrontation); moderation of confrontation or of complete Political Arena (to shaky alliance or complete Political Arena); pervasion of Political Arena (to complete Political Arena)

See Table 17-1 on pages 308–311 for summary of conditions favoring and weakening each configuration.

conditions, none is sufficient. Any other condition that concentrates important bases of power in the External Coalition can bring on the first two of these conditions, and so is a facilitating condition. One is the existence of a critical dependency in the organization's environment, for example, the reliance on a single customer or supplier. Another is the presence of a key legal prerogative, focussed in the hands of influencers able to organize and exploit it to their advantage, as in the business firm closely held by its owners. The Instrument also tends to emerge when the external influencers of an organization form a consensus around a clear goal system, as in custody for prisons or efficiency for fire departments.

A number of other conditions, because they encourage the design of a Machine Bureaucracy structure within the Internal Coalition, can also facilitate the emergence of this configuration. One is an environment that is simple and stable, a second is a technical system that is simple and regulates the work of the operators, as in much of mass production, and a third is a work force that is unskilled. Under all of these conditions, the work of the organization can easily be understood and its outputs measured, and so its goals can be imposed in operational form by outsiders and then monitored by them. Sometimes an organization concerned with its precariousness will allow or even encourage itself to become an Instrument, slipping under the control of an external influencer in order to protect itself. An entrepreneur in trouble sells out to a conglomerate or contracts all of his firm's production to a major client, surrendering its independence to save his organization.

How stable is the Instrument? Let us first consider this in terms of its legitimacy and its purpose. Organizations attain a legitimacy in society by serving ends beyond themselves. All do to some extent, in the products they produce and the services they render. But society typically demands more than this—efficiency in the pursuit of mission, positive side benefits (externalities) to their actions, and an equitable distribution of their surpluses. The purpose of the Instrument configuration is to ensure that organizations serve their relevant (or at least dominant) constituencies in these ways, that what they do is determined by whom they are supposed to do it for. The Instrument, as we shall see, also serves as a means to attain efficiency under certain conditions and to help create necessary organizations when entrepreneurial initiative is not forthcoming.

The Instrument, then, means external control of the organization, and external control usually implies legitimate control. Thus, once established, this should be a rather stable configuration. Because the Instrument serves someone else, or better still, an external consensus, it cannot be accused of serving itself. Nevertheless, forces do arise to change it. In fact, as we shall soon see, despite its ostensible legitimacy, the Instrument emerges as one of the less stable configurations, an arrangement of power that can rather easily be changed.

As discussed earlier, the Instrument creates a continuous chain of power from the external influencer(s) through the CEO down the line hierarchy to the operators. But there is a weak link in this chain, the one between the external influencer(s) and the CEO. The key to this configuration is the capacity of the external influencer to maintain control while remaining outside the management processes of the organization. This he does through his ability to impose clear, operational goals on the management, which in turn is supposed to operationalize these goals in the hierarchy of authority. But this arrangement between External and Internal Coalition is vulnerable in a number of places.

The first vulnerability exists in the External Coalition. It involves the danger of dispersal of external influence, so that the External Coalition can no longer speak with one clear voice. One external influencer may face the challenge of another or of the diffusion of his power among many. Or, in the case of a consensus among a number of external influencers, there is the obvious threat of breakdown in the consensus, or, less obvious but perhaps more likely, breakdown in their ability to organize, so that they become passive vis-à-vis the management. The second vulnerabiltiy exists between the two coalitions, in the need for regular surveillance of the performance of the Internal Coalition. Any letup is an invitation for the insiders to pursue their own goals. Such surveillance takes energy, and outsiders are that because they have limited energy to devote to the organization. Sometimes they run out of available energy, other times they lose interest (as we saw earlier in the case of second-generation shareholders who have no desire to exercise control over their inheritances). And the third vulnerability, also between the two coalitions, is the danger of the emergence of nonoperational goals, which remove a key prerequisite for external control. Let us consider the various possible transitions from the Instrument in terms of these vulnerabilities.

In our opinion, **the natural transition for the Instrument is to the Closed System**. In other words, the forces intrinsic in itself, those that sow the seeds of its own destruction, drive it toward the Closed System.

External influencers render an organization their Instrument in part by establishing in it a Machine Bureaucracy structure—one characterized by a clear hierarchy of authority and pervaded by bureaucratic controls. In other words, thanks to the outsiders, the insiders become highly organized, with power in the Internal Coalition concentrated at the top of a hierarchy of authority. Now, few insiders are enamored with having to pursue goals imposed on them from the outside. So given half the chance, they will happily sieze the power from the outsiders. And, when they do, the obvious result is a Closed System, since it involves no change in the Internal Coalition. The system of bureaucratic control remains dominant and intact, with the senior managers—the ones likely to have led the resistance to external control—still in charge. A Closed System is, after all, nothing more than an Instrument free of external influence. The organization simply becomes the instrument of its administrators.

As suggested above, diffusion of external influence, breakdown of consensus or of the ability of outsiders to organize, lapses in external surveillance, all give the insiders more than half the chance they need to seize control of the organization. In effect, any reduction in external power encourages the rise of the Closed System. But reductions in external power do not only occur extrinsically, independent of the configuration of power. They are also encouraged by the very nature of the configuration, by factors intrinsic to itself. As an Instrument succeeds, it grows. Surveillance becomes more difficult, with increasing information needed to maintain control. External influencers become more numerous, and their ability to organize diminishes. In corporations, growth not only tends to disperse the stockholding directly, as we saw earlier, but also to increase the diversity of product lines, which reduces reliance on any one set of customers. In cooperatives, growth increases the membership, complicating the problems of organizing independently to control the management. Moreover, all kinds of evidence already discussed suggests that the administrators, delegated power as the trustees of the external influencers, often exploit that power to further these processes and so to weaken external control. Restricting information vital for external control is one obvious activity. Another is to engage in merger and acquisition activity which, as discussed in Chapter 19, can serve not only to disperse stockholding but also to reduce the information available to those stockholders who wish to exercise control.

Thus, in a variety of ways the Instrument naturally creates the conditions that rob the external influencers of their control and shifts it instead to the administrators, thereby effecting a transition to the Closed System. And, of course, **the natural resistance of the external influencers to loss of control may drive the organization to a confrontation form of Political Arena for a time during the transition, or even to the form of shaky alliance as the two sides share power during an interim period.**

Other transitions are, of course, possible too, although these are driven more by external forces than those inherent in the Instrument configuration itself. One is the transition of the Instrument to itself. One dominant influencer replaces another, keeping the configuration intact, as when a company is sold or a proxy fight results in the transfer of power from one major shareholder to another. Another is the transition to Autocracy, which can happen in at least two ways. On one hand, a strong CEO can wrest power from the dominant influencer(s), and then consolidates it around himself. On the other, the external influencer, intent on controlling the organization more closely than he can through the imposition of operational goals, or perhaps unable to control the organization, instead involves himself in the management of the organization directly so that he becomes in effect or in fact the chief executive officer. As he effectively moves into the Internal Coalition, an Instrument controlled externally becomes an Autocracy controlled internally. The players and even the distribution of power remain the same, but the means of control—and thus the configuration—changes.

Transitions to other configurations are certainly possible but probably less likely. A strong ideology can grow up within an Instrument, diverting the attention of the insiders to it and so sealing them off from external influence, giving rise to a Missionary. Jenkins (1977) describes how the full-time employees of the National Council of Churches seized control from the members (which were a number of Protestant denominations that sent representatives to its General Assembly). But contrary to what Michels's law would lead us to expect, they transformed the organization into a Missionary in pursuit of "radical" goals—"promoting activist efforts to bring about social change for the benefit of deprived groups" (p. 576).

Likewise, the need for expertise can arise in the Internal Coalition, bringing in experts who challenge the dominant external influencer(s). By rendering the organization's goals nonoperational, such expertise can drive an Instrument to Meritocracy. We saw this in prisons where the inside professionals succeeded in promoting the mission of rehabilitation, thereby seizing control from the external influencers who had formed a consensus around the operational goal (and mission) of custody. The Instrument can, of course, also revert to a Political Arena when the dominant external influencer is challenged by other influencers in the Internal or External Coalitions and resists, as is likely to happen in many of the transitions already discussed. (These transitionary forms of the Political Arena will be covered all together, in our discussion of that configuration.)

Of interest for each of the configurations is what happens when it is overdone, in other words, when its prime means or system of influence is overexploited by the key influencer(s). As we shall see repeatedly, rather than strengthening the configuration, such efforts serve to weaken it by transcending its natural state, sometimes driving it into a transition to another power configuration. In the case of the Instrument, the evidence suggests that too much external control—overregulation—drives it toward the Closed System.[1] Frank (1958–59) describes this phenomenon in the Soviet factory. We introduced his study in Chapter 7 (and mentioned it in Chapter 15), noting that too much government control pacified an ostensibly Dominated External Coalition. That control, from a multitude of government departments, consisted of a host of objectives and other constraints on the factory manager:

> Administrative superiors establish plans for the enterprise and send down countless directives to the manager to amplify, modify, or counteract plans and other prior directives. The directives typically concern type, quantity, quality, and assortment of production; amount of materials and labor to be used; wages to be paid; and production norms which workers are to achieve. It should be noted

---

[1] Note that this is different from the situation dscribed above, where the external influencer intent on controlling through personal means drives it to Autocracy. There the means of influence changed. Here the dominant influencer continues to control externally, through the imposition of operational goals and the like, but overdoes it.

that the standards. . . are always difficult to achieve relative to possibilities open to the enterprise. Frequently, they are mutually incompatible as well. . . .

Another set of standards may be grouped under the rubrics of priorities, campaigns, and socialist competition. . . . From time to time, more or less well-defined orders of priority are superimposed on already existing priorities, as well as on contractual and other arrangements to which existing standards have given rise. Similarly, the Communist Party frequently organizes campaigns aimed at encouraging enterprises to meet certain new standards or to meet old ones better; and it offers special awards for successful participation. (pp. 8–9)

Each standard, objective, or constraint may have been operational, but as a set they were not: no factory manager could possibly have satisfied all of them. And that, ironically, gave the manager a good deal of discretion. Since everyone knew the standards could not be met, a variety of clandestine behaviors were tolerated. One was "to provide for a safety factor," that is, to have the standards set generously and to accumulate organizational slack (for example, by stockpiling material). Another was to feign the meeting of standards, by simply lying about performance or by complying with the letter of a standard if not with its spirit (for example, meeting an output measure by reducing quality, in effect trading off one standard—less easily measured—for another). And a third was to use a system of "blat," or personal influence, to get around the constraints of the system. In some sense, because "the priority among standards [was] ambiguous" (p. 11), the managers had some freedom to select the ones they wished to pursue. And that drew a good deal of power from the External Coalition into the Internal Coalition:

> The existence of conflict among standards prevents [factory managers] from following rules alone, forces them to handle and decide each issue individually, and thus turns all members of the system, subordinates as well as superiors, into policy-makers. (p. 11)

As Frank's discussion suggests, at the limit overregulation drives the organization from Instrument toward Closed System: The Internal Coalition rejects the goal system as unworkable and pursues its own goals instead:

> Over many years, the Magnitogorsk Firm had violated its financial plan and the state laws. It had accumulated huge debts to suppliers because its funds were tied up in illegal capital construction and in supplying consumers' goods to its workers. It had given non-existent items as "security" for loans from the State Bank. Yet, although these conditions were exposed in a national magazine, the firm's director was still retained at his post, and in less than two years was given the second highest post in all Heavy Industry. The reason was clear: on the whole, his management had been successful. (Granick, quoted in Frank, p. 10)

TRANSITIONS TO AND FROM
THE CLOSED SYSTEM

The Closed System represents the takeover of an organization by its administrators—specifically its CEO and line managers aided by the analysts of its technostructure. The External Coalition is precluded from exerting influence, bureaucratic controls dominate the International Coalition, and the systems goals come to the fore. What draws the organization to such a configuration of power? What, in other words, pacifies the external influencers and puts power in the system of bureaucratic controls and, particularly, those who control it?

Since the Closed System shares with the Instrument a Bureaucratic IC, it also shares with it those characteristics that facilitate the emergence of such an Internal Coalition, namely an environment that is simple and stable, a technical system that is simple and regulating, and a work force that is unskilled.

But what distinguishes the Closed System from the Instrument? Clearly any characteristic that weakens the External Coalition does, such as the dispersal of external influencers, breakdown in external consensus, and so on. Perhaps most important as a facilitating condition, judging from the previous discussion, is maturation of the organization—namely, its aging and growth to large size. These diffuse external control, as noted earlier, and they also encourage machine bureaucratization (Mintzberg 1979a), sometimes at the expense of personal forms of control or established ideology.

What is the purpose of the Closed System? Why does society tolerate it? In part, no doubt, it does so because it has no choice. The Closed System may be dysfunctional in some ways, but it survives because it is organized where society is not. It imposes itself on society. (Indeed, all of society, especially communist society, comes to look increasingly like one or a set of Closed Systems out of control.) But that is not the entire story. This configuration too has its purpose. Specifically, by accelerating the process of institutionalization, often coupled with growth of the organization to large size, the Closed System enables missions to be pursued systematically and on a large scale. The price, of course, is loss of control of the organization to the administrators, who make many of the decisions to suit themselves.

In this regard, as noted in Chapter 19, the Closed System suffers from severe problems of legitimacy. It should, therefore, be one of the least stable of the power configurations. Here is the organization that serves itself first and often even has the audacity to take increasing control of its environment as well. The system is closed only to external influence; the object of the exercise in the Closed System is to import more energy than it exports so that its administrators can live comfortably off the surpluses.

Yet, ironically, in practice this seems to be one of the most stable configurations, because the organization has often been able to weave a nice neat cocoon around itself to keep out external influence. The organization is typically large, stable, and established, and most importantly has succeeded in pacifying or even controlling its external influencers. How then does the configuration get dislodged?

A variety of forces may arise to effect a transition to any of the other configurations. An important influencer may emerge in the External Coalition, perhaps because of some new dependency, and take it over as his Instrument. Or a strong willed CEO may appear and manage to consolidate power around himself, converting it to an Autocracy. Likewise, the advent of a new, complex technology or technical system may take power from the administrators and put it into the hands of a group of experts, driving the organization toward Meritocracy. Or a "cultural revolution" brought on by some factor—perhaps a disillusionment with excessive bureaucratic controls and utilitarian norms— may give rise to a strong ideology, which will cause the displacement of the systems goals by mission, and lead to a Missionary configuration.

But each of these transitions is brought on by forces external to the Closed System configuration itself. And any of these forces must be strong indeed to overcome the natural resistance of a system that is both closed to external influence and organized internally in a tight hierarchy of authority. In other words, the Closed System is typically a resilient configuration, one difficult to transform into an Instrument, Autocracy, Missionary, or Meritocracy. It easily fights off forces of external control, personal leadership, ideology, or expertise unless they happen to reflect a dramatic change in a condition of the organization.

But there is one force that the Closed System cannot easily fight off for it arises intrinsically, the natural outgrowth of its own characteristics. The seeds of the Closed System's destruction are sown in its own detachment from external influence. What ultimately undoes it is its exploitation of its own absolute power—it simply gets carried away. Since no natural forces exist to temper the power of the Closed System, its natural tendency is to overindulge itself. In other words, while the other configurations *can* overdo things, the Closed System seems *bound to*.

The process of exploitation cannot go on forever. At some point it must stop. As the system gets larger, more powerful, and more self-indulgent, two intrinsic forces arise to weaken it. In the External Coalition, the illegitimacy of its power distribution becomes increasingly evident, and various groups begin to marshall the energy needed to challenge it. In Hirschman's (1970) terms, as exit becomes less feasible—the organization's influence having become increasingly pervasive and inescapable—voice comes to be increasingly favored. And within the Internal Coalition, the insiders become increasingly greedy for the spoils—for larger and larger shares of the pie they consider their own. As a result, they tend increasingly to clash with each other.

Both of these forces dictate the natural transition for the Closed System. The different challenges from the outside not only divide the External Coalition but also give rise to war between the two coalitions as the insiders resist giving up any real power. And the conflicts within serve to politicize the Internal Coalition. In other words, the conflict tends to be pervasive. But it also tends to develop gradually. Hence we would expect it to be moderate, and enduring. Thus we conclude that **the Closed System is driven naturally over time toward the Political Arena configuration, in the form of the politicized organization** (which is characterized by moderate, pervasive, enduring conflict). This, of course, is exactly what we found at the end of the last chapter in the case of the giant business firm that becomes a politicized corporation because it is too important, too visible, and too controversial to be allowed to remain a Closed System.

There is one other challenge that appears to be intrinsic to this configuration, and so likely to occur. But it comes not to the power configuration itself but to its leaders. Closed Systems, having Machine Bureaucracy structures, are notoriously nonadaptive (Mintzberg 1979a, pp. 342–47). Over time they lose touch with their environments. "The more institutionalized power is within an organization, the more likely an organization will be out of phase with realities it faces" (Salancik and Pfeffer 1977, p. 19). And so, periodically, in order to sustain itself as a Closed System, the organization requires a form of renewal. To change its strategies, or perhaps just to clean out a stagnant administration, it must replace its leadership. And since the leaders sit on top of the hierarchy—the apex of power in this configuration—and are unlikely to replace themselves, they must be forced out. In other words, lacking a natural means to effect smooth succession of its leadership, **the Closed System naturally reverts to a confrontation form of the Political Arena periodically but briefly in order to renew itself.**

Often this renewal is accomplished through the game we have called young Turks. Certain insiders challenge the established leaders in order to replace them. Thus Zald and Berger see "a push to conspiracy in corporate hierarchical forms," reflected in coups, insurgencies, and mass movements (1978, p. 833). It is one type of conspiracy in particular, the coup d'état—a rapid change of the players while the structure remains intact—that would seem most likely to occur in the Closed System.

> . . . [coups] are not related to any underlying structural change. Coups in organization may have relatively few consequences below the elite level. The coup leads to a change in the chief executive and possibly to a few shifts down to the assistant vice-president level. Beyond that there is no necessary change. (pp. 836–37)

Once the new leaders are installed, they may take over the reins of power as these existed previously and so retain the configuration exactly as is. But when major changes must be made—for example, when key strategies have to be redesigned—bureaucratic procedures may have to be suspended and power concentrated personally in the hands of the chief executive to enable him to conceive and impose the changes in an integrated fashion, free of the constraining effect of standards. Once this is accomplished, the bureaucratic procedures can be reinstated (although this sometimes necessitates another change in leadership), and the organization is ready to function as before. In other words, as discussed in the *Structuring* book (p. 347), **the Closed System may have to revert temporarily to Autocracy** (and its structure from Machine Bureaucracy to Simple Structure) **after the confrontation form of Political Arena, in order to accomplish its renewal.**

Note that this temporary renewal may stave off what we see as the longer-term and more permanent transition of the Closed System configuration to the Political Arena. By adapting itself to changed conditions periodically, although remaining closed to direct external influence, the Closed System may gain itself reprieves from the sustained external pressures and internal conflicts that must eventually come. Eventually, however, self-renewal will not suffice, and we believe the Closed System will succumb once and for all to these more deeply rooted forces.

TRANSITIONS TO AND FROM
THE AUTOCRACY

Autocracy means domination by the chief executive officer: Control is embodied in personalized leadership. What brings this on? Youth seems to be a sufficient condition; at least at the very outset, most all organizations naturally assume the Autocracy configuration when they are created. Power is consolidated in the hands of their chief executive in order to get them going. Many in fact retain this configuration throughout their formative years, since it can take time to establish the bureaucratic procedures that displace personalized leadership. Indeed, as we noted in Chapter 20, power vested in the hands of the founding chief executive does not readily dissipate once the organization is established. That leader's ability to set the organization up on his terms, with his people, means that so long as he remains, sometimes well into the maturity of the organization, power may remain consolidated around him. Often the configuration will change only after the founding leader departs.

Small size is a facilitating condition, since it is far easier to retain full personal control of a small organization than a large one. Thus, when a founding leader does lose personal control while still in office, it is typically due to the fact that the organization has outgrown it. A simple, dynamic environment is likewise a facilitating condition, indeed generally a sufficient one. A simple environment, because it can easily be comprehended by one individual, encourages the centralization of power. And dynamism precludes the use of bureaucratic controls, enabling personalized ones to emerge as preeminent instead. With such controls around a central leader, the organization can respond quickly and flexibly to its unpredictable environment.

Some conditions are able to override most others to drive an organization to a particular power configuration. In other words, while they may not be necessary conditions for a given configuration, they are sufficient ones. Two of these apply to Autocracy, as noted in Chapter 20. One is strong leadership. Leadership capabilities alone—the power of one individual to control others through will and skill, or to attract them through what is called charisma—may be enough to produce Autocracy, even though all other characteristics point to Closed System, Political Arena, or whatever, as the natural configuration. A second such overriding condition is crisis. Faced with a threat to its survival, many an organization, no matter what its usual configuration of power will consolidate its power in the hands of its chief executive. Influencers in both coalitions rally around the leader, suspending their usual demands and their normal means of influence to enable him to act in a rapid and integrated manner to correct things.

How stable is Autocracy? Let us consider this first in terms of the legitimacy and purpose of the configuration. On one hand, society appears to impute a certain legitimacy to the Autocracy, specifically to the single, forceful leader who creates a new organization and then guides it through good times and bad. Such people, notably the business entrepreneurs, are the subjects of much of the folklore in management, especially in the United States. The prime purpose of Autocracy is to create new organizations, in order to render new services or provide new goals to society, also to see established organizations through times of crisis, and to enable small organizations to function effectively, particularly ones in simple but dynamic environments—organizations which tend to provide a steady stream of simple innovations. All of these purposes legitimize personalized leadership.

On the other hand, Autocracy is viewed as an anachronism in democratic society, a configuration of power out of keeping with the norms of the society that houses it. But its absence of democracy does not seem to undermine Autocracy, any more than its folklore sustains it.

What really threatens Autocracy is its basic precariousness. The Autocracy is wholly dependent on one individual—a single heart attack can literally wipe out its basis of coordination and control. Moreover as the personal preserve of one individual, other potential influencers lose interest in the organization. External ones look elsewhere while internal ones become passive. This means that no one may be there to worry about or protect the organization when it is threatened. Indeed, with its power so centralized, the threat often comes from the CEO himself, who loses touch with the environment yet has no one to convince him of the need to adapt, or to force him out. Finally, Autocracies are precarious simply because so many of them are small and vulnerable, young and so not firmly established, positioned in risky environments or simply face-to-face with crises of suvival. Thus, **perhaps the most natural and common transition for the Autocracy is to dissolution of the organization**—to disintegration rather than to another power configuration.

But when the organization does manage to survive, how long does its

Autocracy power configuration last? From what we have said above, Autocracies would seem to be mostly short-lived. Those that emerged because conditions of crisis or of strong leadership overrode more natural forces would be perpetually pulled toward other configurations by these forces. Moreover, the very essence of crisis is that resolution must be quick or the organization will die. So the period of Autocracy must be brief before another configuration is reinstated. When a strong leader overrides other conditions to establish Autocracy, he may have to resist a good many natural forces to sustain it. How long he can hang on is a function of how strong he proves to be, how able he is to consolidate power around himself.

Most Autocracies appear in the formative years of organizations. How long, then, are such periods? In some cases they can be very short—just long enough to build the facilities and hire the staff. Professional organizations, such as hospitals, hire people who are already trained in their basic skills. It takes them little time to settle into their work and assume their usual influence. In other words, the period of Autocracy need only be brief before Meritocracy establishes itself. Likewise, as we noted in the last chapter, organizations that from the outset experience irreconciliable forces that are natural and balanced tend to become shaky alliances very quickly, after only brief periods of Autocracy. Other organizations, however, can experience much longer periods of formation, especially when they must develop their own operating procedures and do not face balanced conflictive forces.

Two conditions do tend to sustain Autocracy naturally, namely, small size of the organization and simple, dynamic state of its environment. Both allow for and even encourage personalized leadership. Both however, by rendering the organization precarious, also expose it to destructive forces.

Given that a transition must be made—that an organization has outgrown its founder or at least his form of leadership, has resolved its crisis, has grown large or beyond its simple, dynamic environment—to what configuration does Autocracy tend to give way? Unlike the other configurations, here we must conclude that a variety of transitions are perfectly natural, inherent in the nature of the configuration itself. In particular, for the new organization that has become established—its founder having done his job—or the established one whose founder or strong-willed leader departs, we believe any one of four transitions to be natural.

First, **many Autocracies naturally become Instrument due to their inherent precariousness.** This precariousness causes their leaders, or those who inherit the mantle of leadership, to seek the protective umbrella of a strong external influencer. As an entrepreneur ages, for example, the precariousness of his organization may begin to bother him. In search of security, he sells his firm to a conglomerate, which quickly converts it to an Instrument. In other cases, it is after the entrepreneur departs that the Autocracy is converted to an Instrument, as the heirs who inherit the firm sell out. There is, of course, another way to reduce precariousness, although it can lead to the same transition. The entrepreneur steps aside and names a "professional" manager to run the organization more systematically (that is, bureaucratically), converting it into his own Instrument. Or his family does the same thing after the entrepreneur dies. Each of these cases reflects the same widespread phenomenon in the evolution of the business firm—the separation of ownership from management as the organization grows and ages. The same thing frequently happens in nonbusiness organizations: External influencers, perhaps those who commissioned the founding of the organization in the first place, consolidate their formal power after the founding chief executive moves on.

Of course, the transition to Instrument need not always be so smooth. Often it is involuntary, an external influencer seizing control of an Autocracy against the will of its leader. We saw a dramatic example of this in the story of Hans Isbrandtsen's shipping company. Again, in this example and in gerneral, it is Autocracy's inherent precariousness that makes it vulnerable to such takeover attempts. Being typically small, and perhaps also positioned in a risky environment, it likely has few resources to sustain itself in a conflict. Moreover, it has only one real influencer to fight back. And when an organization has reverted to Autocracy to deal with a crisis, then it is especially vulnerable to takeover.

Other, external conditions can drive an organization to the Instrument as well. When the environment stabilizes, for example, personalized control may become dysfunctional, and the organization may be ripe for takeover by an external influencer who can force in the required bureaucratic forms of control.

Another natural transition for the Autocracy is to the Missionary, as a result of charismatic leadership. Leaders of Autocracies are often highly charismatic individuals. When they move on, what they leave behind can get institutionalized, resulting in the Missionary power configuration. The legacy of the charismatic leader is a set of experiences, which can become an ideology. And it is these that give rise to the Missionary. In fact, we believe that Autocracy is a necessary prerequisite to the Missionary, that strong personalized leadership of a charismatic nature must exist before a strong ideology can form as the center of a power system. By the same token, however, the charismatic leader must move on before the pure Missionary configuration can emerge, that is, before power can become diffused throughout the Internal Coalition on the basis of the standardization of norms instead of being concentrated at its strategic apex.

We see these two configurations—the Instrument and the Missionary—as the most natural successors of the Autocracy, in other words, the ones that arise from conditions inherent in the Autocracy. One takes advantage of its precariousness, the other of its charismatic nature. Which way an Autocracy goes depends, presumably, on the strength of the belief system compared with the precariousness of the organization and the power and will of external influencers to exploit this. In fact, Autocracies separated from their charismatic leaders frequently experience conflict as their insiders, favoring a transition to the Missionary, resist attempts by outsiders to destroy the ideologies and take them over as their Instruments. **In general, the transition from Autocracy to Instrument is often accompanied by a brief period of Political Arena in the form of confrontation and/or shaky alliance.**

Two other transitions are also likely, but under more restricted conditions. **The Autocracy can naturally become a Closed System when it is already large and its administration established (although these are not the most natural occurrences in Autocracy).** When the ideology is weak and no strong external influencer stands ready to seize control, but a set of administrators do, then the power of the chief executive may get institutionalized in the administrative hierarchy instead. In effect, one obvious group of insiders are poised to take over, and naturally move into the large power vacuum left by a departing or weakening leader. Thus we have the consolidation of power by the bureaucrats and technocrats after the death of a Stalin or a Mao Tse-Tung repeated thousands of time on a smaller scale. But not too much smaller, because a precondition for the transition to the Closed System is the prior existence of a strong administration. In other words, conversion to the Closed System is natural only in the case of fairly large Autocracies, ones whose leaders were able to retain personal control *despite* large size. But, as we noted earlier, growth to such large size is not natural under Autocracy, since it is difficult for one leader to maintain personal control of a large organization. Hence, this transition to the Closed System must be considered a less natural one than those to the Instrument or the Missionary. In the typical Autocracy, which remains small, the administrative component never gets a chance to establish itself on a solid footing. And so the transition to one of these other configurations is more likely. Only later, as we shall see, when the administration gets a chance to grow under either of these other configurations, does the organization make a more natural transition to the Closed System.

When an Autocracy does indeed grow large, the tensions that arise naturally between the leader and the other administrators typically encourage the beginnings of the transition to Closed System even before the leader departs. As the organization grows and its leader ages, his personal control begins to give way to bureaucratic controls, and he gradually loses power to managers of the middle line and analysts of the technostructure. An entrepreneur, for example, may remain in formal charge of his firm until his death. But only by sharing his power with administrators, in a kind of shaky alliance, can he maintain the firm's viability as it grows large. The same thing seems to have been true of the leaders of some large American trade unions. The era of dominant leadership gradually gave way to that of the rule by the bureaucrats and technocrats, a process whose beginnings Wilensky (1961) has documented. Thus, **during the transition from Autocracy to Closed System, we would expect the appearance of the Political Arena, likely in the form of a shaky alliance between chief executive and administrators but possibly of confrontation between them as well.**

Finally, **an Autocracy can naturally become a Meritocracy when it arose merely to initiate an organization of experts.** As soon as the organization is on its feet—and, as discussed earlier, that can be soon indeed—the conversion to Meritocracy begins. Of course, any Autocracy can be driven toward Meritocracy when a new technology appears externally that forces the organization to disseminate substantial power to staff or operating experts. **And this transition is likely to involve a period of Political Arena as well, as experts oppose the established leader or else form a shaky alliance with him.**

What about an Autocracy making the transition to another Autocracy, as one dominant chief executive replaces another? This may seem like a natural transition for this configuration, since the existing structures favor personalized control. However, one thing no strong leader will tolerate is another strong leader. (The presence of two of them, as we saw in the last chapter, encourages confrontation, or at best a shaky alliance, both forms of the Political Arena.) Thus, when the leader of an Autocracy departs, his replacement is unlikely to be found in the Internal Coalition. This is particularly true of the small organization, where strong individuals have no place to hide. (And the big one, as we noted, is less likely to tolerate continuation of personalized leadership.) In fact, the tendency for "yes-men" to surround the chief executive of the Autocracy encourages a transition to another configuration once he passes on. They say "yes" to external control, or to his ideology, or to their own bureaucratic tendencies, finding, in effect, a new prop to support their own weaknesses. Should the organization in fact require continuation of Autocracy—because it is small, or still developing, or in need of remaining in a simple, dynamic niche in the environment—then its new leader will likely have to be found elsewhere.

Finally, what happens to the Autocracy whose leader overdoes personalized controls. This phenomenon, sometimes called "the cult of personality," can create so much fear and tension in the organization that the emergence of the Political Arena may be inevitable, if not during the tenure of the leader then as soon as he departs.

TRANSITIONS TO AND FROM THE MISSIONARY

The Missionary is characterized above all by loyalty to an ideology, the dedication of the members to a set of beliefs revolving primarily around the pursuit of mission. One set of conditions gives rise to such a confrontation—a mission that is clear, focussed, distinctive, and, above all, inspiring, at least to a set of people. These are necessary conditions, they are sufficient conditions, and they can be overriding conditions, causing organizations attracted to other configurations to emerge as Missionaries instead. The conditions that generally underlie such a mission—in other words, necessary conditions for the typical Missionary—are a distinguished history of the organization and charismatic leadership in its past.

Certain other conditions facilitate the emergence of this configuration, namely, small size of the organization, so that personal contact can be maintained between the members; middle age of the organization, since ideologies generally take time to form and tend to decay with age; simple environments and technical systems, so that no overriding need exists for expertise, which tends to violate the egalitarian norms of ideology; and volunteer membership, which reduces utilitarian pressures. But, as noted, the conditions of the mission can override others, so that Missionaries exist that are old and large, that operate in complex environments and with complex technical systems, and whose members are paid employees.

By its very nature, the Missionary appears to be a highly stable configuration, its behaviors being rooted in norms, beliefs, and traditions. As Hirschman notes, members who pay dearly to join—in the form of extensive socialization and indoctrination—do not easily give up their beliefs: They "will fight hard to prove that they were right after all in paying a high entrance fee" (1970, p. 93). In fact, however, like Autocracy, this tends to be a highly vulnerable configuration, subject to self-induced destructive forces to which it frequently yields. Often yielding means not just the destruction of the power configuration, but of the organization as well. This is one configuration that in many cases would rather die than switch. Thus, **one natural transition for the Missionary is to dissolution of the organization, due to its unwillingness to adapt to the utilitarian demands of the world around it.**

The problem for the Missionary, as discussed at length in Chapter 21, is to retain its ideology without losing complete touch with its environment, in other words, to differentiate itself in order to maintain its distinctiveness yet remain integrated with the rest of the world. That puts it on the knife edge between isolation and assimilation. On one side, Missionaries die because they seal themselves off rather than risk contamination of their ideologies; they simply run out of energy. Earlier we saw that the vast majority of communes have disappeared because they were unable to sustain their resources and to replace their members who left or died. On the other side, more open Missionaries develop links with the world around them that gradually tend to coopt them. Here, the organization may live on, but the ideology, and the power configuration, die.

The natural transition for those Missionaries that survive is to the Closed System, because their External Coalitions are so passive and their diffusion of internal power favors their central administrators. As Selznick (1952) points out, a major problem in this kind of organization is the need to maintain discipline without reverting to authority. So long as the beliefs and loyalties remain firm, ideology remains the dominant system of influence. But a number of forces naturally arise in the configuration to weaken it.

One is the need for administration. This configuration faces the constant threat that an inner circle—composed of administrators who believe themselves purer ideologically, or more worthy, or who are simply greedy for personal gain—will seize the power and institutionalize it in the System of Authority, driving the organization to the Closed System configuration. (Hence, overdoing it in this configuration—exploitation of ideological belief—tends to encourage transition to the Closed System.) Of course, a single leader may seize the power instead, and exercise it personally, giving rise to Autocracy. But with standardization already prevalent in the organization, we would expect the system of bureaucratic control to emerge as predominant. Standard norms are more easily converted to standard rules than to personal directives. A number of stories of transition from Missionary to Closed System in the literature attest to this, notably in Michels' (1915) description of his iron law of oligarchy.

Michels considers such a transition dysfunctional. Ironically, however, it is sometimes necessary in order to accomplish the organization's intended mission. The purpose of the Missionary is to change the norms of society, either directly or through changing its own members. Also this configuration adds inspiration to work, enabling organizations to pursue their missions with more enthusiasm and perhaps more effectiveness. In fact, the Missionary typically emerges to institutionalize the beliefs of its own charismatic leader—to spread the word, so to speak. But that process of institutionalization is often unable to go far enough, the organization in Missionary form being restricted in its size and its effectiveness. Ideology, in other words, may be no substitute for administrative effort in order to bring about widespread change. Many Missionaries are simply too small, too poor, or too pure, to diffuse their desired changes widely. Only when a fuller form of institutionalization takes place can the organization develop the size, wealth, security, and pragmatism necessary to bring about the desired change. The mission will certainly be pursued with less inspiration and less commitment, and probably less care as well, but it may be pursued more pervasively. In other words, Machine Bureaucracy may turn out to be the only structural form able to accomplish the ambitious mission set for the organization. And that requires a Closed System power configuration (or the Instrument, but that is less likely given the passivity of the External Coalition).

Time is another force that weakens ideology and naturally drives power to the administrators. Even if the administrators do not seek power actively, the aging of the organization may give it to them. It is difficult to sustain ideologic fervor over long periods of time, unless the mission is a very potent one, the traditions very strong, and the organization able to maintain a high rate of achievement. As an organization ages, the spirit tends to leave its ideology. Norms rigidify into procedures, beliefs into rules. The members come increasingly to view the organization as the means to serve themselves rather than viewing themselves as the means by which the organization serves some higher ideal. Growth can have the same effect, since it is difficult to replicate the spirit of a small group in a large one, where all the members cannot know each other personally. Large Missionaries try to split themselves into small enclaves to avoid this problem, but not all succeed, since it is that much more difficult to ensure loyalty to a single ideology across independent units.

As noted earlier, this transition from the Missionary to the Closed System is seen in a number of studies in the literature. We cited Michels's work earlier, in which he describes how the full-time administrators seized power from the volunteer members in European socialist parties and labor unions at the turn of the century. Some other studies document not so much a seizing of power by the select few as a turning inward by all, with ideals displaced by members' needs for personal gratification. The system comes to serve its insiders, and so emerges as a form of Closed System, as we noted earlier. Where once the mission was the raison d'être, or primary goal, later it became the means to serve the personal goals of the members.

We have already discussed a number of these studies in Chapter 21, for example, religious congregations or American Legion branches whose missions became the excuse to get together for social purposes—bingo in place of salvation. We also discussed those Israeli kibbutzim where materialism has displaced missionary zeal. Gussfield's (1957) description of the aging of the Woman's Christian Temperance Union shows the forces of both social need and administrative influence at work. Created as a reform movement to help the poor by promoting total abstenance from all alcoholic beverages, the Union underwent major transformation after the repeal of the prohibition amendment. Its doctrine became one of expressing "moral indignation toward contemporary American middle classes" (p. 323). Power came to reside in the hands of an "active minority" of the members who tended to perpetuate themselves in office. The national offices—full-time jobs without pay—tended to be restricted to women living near the headquarters whose availability was facilitated by their husbands' wealth.

Of course, not all Missionaries are transformed into Closed Systems. Other transitions occur too. Sometimes one leader is in fact able to seize the power, under conditions of crisis, and the Missionary becomes an Autocracy.[2] Given the high degree of loyalty of the members, they can be easily coerced by an autocrat who captures the leadership. Other times, a need for expertise arises in the organization, as it did in many of the kibbutzim, and power must be allocated disproportionately to certain skilled individuals, damaging the egalitarian norms necessary to sustain the Missionary. Meritocracy arises in its place.

A Missionary can become an Instrument too, when an external influencer is able to seize control of it and destroy its ideology by denying its traditions and beliefs. We saw an example of this earlier in the Larçon and Reitter story of the French furniture company. Another example appears in Jenkins's (1977) study of the National Council of Churches. Earlier we saw how the insiders seized control of the organization to put it on a missionary course. But the story did end there, for the congregation members "became more opposed to the [reform] programs as . . . reform became more visible and threatening to their economic and political interests" (p. 580). A war ensued between the external members

---

[2]Gussfield's description, cited above, shows characteristics of Autocracy as well.

and the internal reformers, which resulted in a reorganization of the General Assembly. More power was given to the lay members, and expansion of activist programs was curtailed. Eventually the General Assembly "ordered" the executives "to cease promoting broad national programs and to emphasize providing technical service for local programs" (p. 581), and changed the basis on which the Council was funded to ensure compliance.

Note that there was no instant transition to the Instrument configuration in either of these examples. Rather conflict ensued as the two sides fought a battle for control. In other words, the Missionary became a Political Arena for a time until it was converted to an Instrument. This suggests that **when its ideology is challenged, the resistance of its supporters drives the Missionary to the Political Arena for a time, in the form of a shaky alliance or confrontation.**

Jenkins's study also shows how one Missionary can transform itself into another. One of the most radical programs of the Council—affiliated with the Farm Workers Union—spun off and became a Missionary in its own right, supported financially by the more liberal denominations and church agencies. Here of course the ideology did not change, only the place where it was pursued. But we would expect a similar result when a new ideology threatens an old one: the commitment of most members to the existing beliefs should force the reformers to create a new organization, or at least a new enclave, to pursue their own beliefs independently (Leeds 1964). Only with time, perhaps, might they succeed in replacing the ideology of the whole organization.[3]

TRANSITIONS TO AND FROM THE MERITOCRACY

The purpose of the Meritocracy is to accomodate society's needs for complex skills and knowledge—either in standardized form, through Professional Bureaucracy, or in innovative form, through Adhocracy. This configuration arises when an organization's dependence on such skills and knowledge necessitates a major diffusion of power to its experts. One condition gives rise to this—a technology (that is, knowledge base, one element of what we have been calling the "environment") or technical system (the instruments of production or operations) that is complex in nature. This is a necessary condition, a sufficient condition, and a condition that can usually override almost any other to dictate the use of Meritocracy. The organization may be small or large, it may operate in an environment that is stable or dynamic—these things do not

---

[3]"In a study of ideological change in American Protestant seminaries, Adams (1968) found that larger proportions of faculty retire, die, or are fired, and are also hired just prior to or after a new ideological school is formed. He concluded that revitalization in theology rests on new faces, not on changing theology of already-present faculty" (McNeil and Thompson 1971, p. 633).

matter. Unless it is just being formed, the chances are that the organization will adopt the Meritocracy configuration in whole or at least in good part.

Because its dictating condition—a complex technology or technical system—tends to override most others and because this condition tends to remain intact over long periods of time, the Meritocracy itself may be the most stable of the six configurations of power. In essence, an organization dependent on expertise must inevitably reflect characteristics of Meritocracy. The presence of other conditions—say a dominant external influencer or a strong ideology—may give rise to other characteristics as well, but these must always accompany those of Meritocracy in a hybrid. Conversely, to try to impose Meritocracy on an organization lacking complex skills and knowledge is a futile exercise. As noted in the last chapter, the result is likely to be a Political Arena instead, as influencers try to hang on to power through artificial means, such as feigned expertise.

This suggests that the main way to dislodge Meritocracy is either to move the organization away from the mission that requires the expertise, or else to rationalize that expertise. A strong leader, or external influencer, or set of administrators, in order to consolidate their power, may try to move the organization to a simpler environment, where a mission can be pursued that requires no special expertise. The experts might even try to do this themselves when a strong organizational ideology that they believe in necessitates such a change in mission.

But changing missions is usually easier said than done. The only other sure way to change the configuration is to rationalize or "program" the skills and knowledge of the experts—in other words, to break them into simple component parts each of which can be taught quickly and easily with no prior training. This removes the basis of expert power, namely skills that can only be performed after years of training. Unskilled workers are then able to replace the experts, and power flows into the technostructure, to the analysts who do the programming. The Professional Internal Coalition becomes a Bureaucratic one, and the organization an Instrument, if there is a strong external influencer, otherwise a Closed System. Of course, rationalization can also so simplify the tasks that even bureaucratic controls become unnecessary, and Autocracy emerges instead if there is a strong leader or Missionary if the ideology is strong. And if, by chance, the rationalization of one body of expertise gives rise to another, or if another body of expertise stands ready to replace it, then one Meritocracy simply transforms itself into another.

Crozier (1964) claims that all expertise is susceptible to rationalization, that it is only a matter of time before a body of knowledge or skills becomes so programmed and the expert loses his basis of power. In his view, "experts have power only on the front line of progress—which means they have a constantly shifting and fragile power" (p. 165).

But Crozier was describing pockets of expertise in Machine Bureaucracies, such as that of the maintenance men in tobacco factories. That the experts have fragile power in Meritocracies—in organizations dominated by experts—seems doubtful. Hospitals, univeristies, and accounting firms have for decades exhibited a strengthening rather than a decline in their Systems of Expertise. Crozier's point about shifting power may have more justification, however. Individual tasks do get simplified in such organizations. But these are simply delegated to support people, or out of the organization altogether, while the experts get on with the perpetual inventory of more complex tasks awaiting their attention. This can happen so regularly that some Meritocracies seem to be in states of perpetual transition to new forms of themselves. However, such changes are usually gradual, so that the transition is not disruptive, indeed hardly evident. Only when a major change occurs, requiring a sudden displacement of one body of expertise by another, is the transition evident and disruptive, usually involving a good deal of conflict between different groups of experts.

What all this means is that while rationalization may be the most obvious way to dislodge the Meritocracy configuration, it is not an easy one, nor very natural. Even the changing of mission, while conceivable, is hardly natural. Given the power of the experts in this configuration, a change as important as this inevitably requires their concurrence. But why should they concur when their very power is rooted in the skills and expertise demanded by the existing mission. In the absence of their concurrence, a leader, external influencer, or set of administrators intent on changing the mission would literally have to fire all of them. (Something akin to this can, of course, happen when the owners of an Adhocracy convert it to a Machine Bureaucracy to mass produce one of its innovations.) In principal, as noted above, the experts might concur when the change of mission is necessitated by the presence of a strong ideology that they themselves support. But since ideology is rooted in mission in the first place, we should hardly expect it to necessitate a change in mission.

There is one situation in which change of mission is common, but that does not dislodge Meritocracy, only changes its form. As an Adhocracy and its experts age, and weary of years of turbulent environments and fluid working arrangements, a desire often arises on their part to settle down to a more stable structure, in which they can concentrate on a few standard skills instead of having to innovate all the time. So they change the nature of the mission and shift the organization to Professional Bureaucracy structure. But the power configuration remains Meritocracy, and the power of the experts is not reduced (see the *Structuring* book, p. 478).

Thus, the forces of rationalization and change of mission, which can conceivably destroy Meritocracy, are not inherent in its own makeup. Quite the contrary. So transition to the Instrument or Closed System, or even to Autocracy or Missionary, for these reasons, is hardly the natural one for the Meritocracy.

Does that mean that Meritocracy is the end of the line for the organization that requires expertise, its natural configuration forever more? Not quite. There is one set of forces that does threaten this configuration, forces inherent in its own makeup.

In certain ways, the Meritocracy is much like the Closed System. Specifically, both are arrangements of power whereby an elite set of insiders controls the organization to serve some of their own personal needs. In the Closed System, these insiders are the administrators; in the Meritocracy, they are the experts. But in terms of the forces working to destroy the configuration, this makes little difference. As in the Closed System, some insiders of the Meritocracy tend to get carried away with their own power. The power of the experts of this configuration can be near absolute—hardly constrained by administrative or external forces—and as Acton pointed out, "absolute power corrupts absolutely." We have already discussed callousness in professional organizations—the surgeon prepared to cut open anyone in sight, the professor who ignores his students for the glory of his research, the social worker intent on bringing power even to the people who don't want it. Overdoing it in Meritocracy means that the experts became so enamored with their expertise that nothing else matters, not the organization, not even its clients.

Some callousness is present in every Meritocracy. Usually it is contained by professional norms. Even when it gets out of hand, professional norms can often bring it back in line. But with no other constraining force, sometimes callousness can occur on a more permanent and pervasive basis, personal interest coming to dominate professional norms. Whether temporary or permanent, these excesses drive the Meritocracy to the Political Arena, just as does overindulgence by the insiders of the Closed System.

Callousness amounts to greed—people overwhelmed by the urge to serve themselves at the expense of others. As in the Closed System, greed within the Meritocracy pits insider influencers against each other. Increasingly intent on serving themselves, the experts come into more frequent conflict with one another, and political means of influence replace expertise as the basis for making choices. Thus, callousness, a force intrinsic to every Meritocracy, can drive it over the edge to the Political Arena.

It should be noted that Meritocracies are inevitably close to that edge. This is the most politicized of the configurations aside from the Political Arena itself, as noted in Chapter 22. The experts naturally engage each other in various political games—budgeting, empire building, strategic candidates, and so on. Constantly on the verge, it takes little—a reduction in resources, the introduction of a new technology, a rise in callousness—to tilt the organization toward the Political Arena.

In Adhocracy, where the experts are highly dependent on each other, having to work in temporary groups in highly fluid structures, the possibilities for political excesses are great. The line between constructive and destructive conflict—the former a necessary condition for every Adhocracy, the latter an underlying characteristic of the Political Arena—is never very wide. As for Professional Bureaucracy, because the experts work largely on their own, the lid can more easily be kept on political activity. *More* easily does not, however, mean easily, because flare-ups are common, as the professionals clash with each other over the allocation of resources or the gray areas in the pigeonholing process.

To all this we must add that the external influencers are constantly on the alert. The Meritocracy, like the Closed System, is typically visible and consequential. We described its External Coalition in Chapter 22 as barely passive, stopped short of being divided by the power of inside expertise. Again, little is needed to tip the balance. Sometimes a change in the environment suffices, or perhaps just the feeling by some external influencers that the time has come to exercise control. The factor most likely to activate the external influencers is the perception of growing callousness by the experts. But no matter what the cause, attempts by the external influencers to control the organization naturally evoke resistance from the experts, and that gives rise to war—hot or cold—between the two coalitions.

With intrinsic forces striving to politicize its Internal Coalition, divide its External Coalition, and/or create war between the two of them, the natural transition for the Meritocracy is to the Political Arena, sometimes temporarily in the form of confrontation (perhaps to renew itself), sometimes more permanently in the form of the politicized organization. In essence, what we have in the organization of experts is a continual struggle between the forces of expertise on one hand and those of politics on the other. Constantly on the verge, Meritocracies sometimes tip over to become Political Arenas.

This transition can be temporary. In fact, many of these temporary reversions to the confrontation form of Political Arena reflect attempts by the organization to renew itself, after major changes in its required body of expertise. Such changes typically bring various groups of experts into conflict with each other. Young Turks with new skills and knowledge seek to replace an old guard of experts, struggling to maintain its power.

In the federated form of Meritocracy—the Professional Bureaucracy— expertise changes from time to time, requiring professionals to displace each other in the pecking order. But most such changes are minor, involving conflict between only a few professionals, and so are not broadly disruptive. When such changes are major, however—involving many professionals in significant ways—the organization tends to become highly politicized during the transition. Established experts wedded to their standarized skills seldom give up without a fight. But once the confrontation is over, the organization typically settles down again to its calmer life of Meritocracy.[4]

In the collaborative form—Adhocracy—such shifts in expertise are more frequent and more significant, due to the dynamic nature of the environment. Indeed, Adhocracies seem to be designed to deal with major shifts in expert

---

[4]A graphic illustration of such a confrontation, involving the resistance to the introduction of a new form of treatment in a psychiatric hospital, can be found in Mintzberg, Raisinghani, and Theorêt (1976, pp. 268–70).

power on a regular basis, almost as a natural course of events (Galbraith 1973). As such, the organization seems to be cycling continually between Meritocracy and Political Arena, between what appears to be constructive and destructive conflict. But these periods of Political Arena evoked by major changes in expertise are truly destructive in neither form of Meritocracy, because they represent the most feasible and natural way for this configuration to renew itself. In the absence of strong authority, politics becomes the vehicle necessary to bring about the necessary changes. Much like the Closed System then, the Meritocracy renews itself by becoming a confrontation form of the Political Arena for a short time, as its insiders challenge each other. In this way, the Meritocracy makes a transition to a new form of itself.

The natural transition to the Political Arena can, however, also occur on a more permanent basis. Callousness by the experts increases beyond some reasonable level and the external influencers respond (or else external influence increases and the professionals respond by becoming more callous), and conflict pervades relationships in and around the organization. The conflict becomes moderate and endures—experts and outsiders alike not wishing to destroy the organization altogether—and so the form of Political Arena we called the politicized organization emerges.

This transition to a more permanent form of Political Arena can be considered, as noted, a natural one for the Meritocracy, because it arises from forces intrinsic to its own makeup. Many of the external forces, however, tend to provoke the same kind of transition. That is to say, even many of the forces that arise independently of the Meritocracy drive it, not toward another focussed configuration, but also toward the Political Arena. This can be explained by the tenacity of expertise. So long as the technology or technical system remains complex, the System of Expertise must remain strong in the organization. Thus, when some external force promotes another system of influence, it does not displace the System of Expertise so much as create opposition to it. An escalation of conflict is the likely result, since the experts do not generally like any other form of influence—external, personal, or bureaucratic control, even ideological control in many cases. At best, the conflict moderates into a form of shaky alliance. For example, the rise of a critical external dependency may bring a dominant external influencer on the scene who tries to convert the organization into his or her Instrument. The experts resist, and direct confrontation may ensue, or else the two may accommodate each other in a tense hybrid of Instrument and Meritocracy.[5]

To conclude, through either kind of destructive force—intrinsic or exter-

---

[5]In effect, whereas overregulation of the Instrument—meant to be regulated—converts it to a Closed System, overregulation of the Meritocracy—not meant to be so regulated—drives it to the Political Arena. And, as per our discussion in Chapter 22, unionization by the experts as a response to external control serves as a force to strengthen the hand of the administrators, encouraging the emergence of characteristics of the Closed System configuration, which may further complicate the hybrid and intensify the conflict.

nal—the Meritocracy is likely to be driven toward the Political Arena, in one form or another, at least so long as its basis of expertise remains intact.

TRANSITIONS TO AND FROM
THE POLITICAL ARENA

We have already discussed at some length in the last chapter the conditions pulling an organization toward the Political Arena, as well as its purposes in society and the stability of the different forms it takes. Here these need be reviewed only briefly.

What distinguishes the Political Arena from the other configurations is an organization captured in whole or in part by conflict. And what brings this on is conflicting demands imposed on it—either an important challenge to its existing order or important challenges between its existing influencers. This is a necessary condition, it is a sufficient condition, and it is a condition that will usually override others, turning any kind of organization into a Political Arena until the conflict is resolved.

Facilitating this can be a number of conditions—a fundamental change in an important condition of the organization, a breakdown in its established order of power, none to begin with, or a maladaptation to a previous change or breakdown. Each of these conditions encourages challenges from influencers to realign a coalition or change the configuration, although such challenges can also arise of their own accord.

If there is strong, direct resistance to the given challenge, conflict ensues, and the confrontation form of the Political Arena arises. The emergence of the Political Arena is also facilitated by the presence of balanced and irreconcilable forces on the organization, which encourages its appearance in the form of a shaky alliance, by a mission that is both visible and controversial, which tends to give rise to the form called the politicized organization, and by the severe weakening and perhaps imminent death of an organization, which can evoke what we called the complete Political Arena.

Because its prime system of influence is that of politics, which we defined in Chapter 13 as illegitimate power, the Political Arena emerges as the least legitimate of the six power configurations. It may sometimes be tolerated, but it is not esteemed, and the natural tendency is to try to terminate it as quickly as possible. When this proves impossible, attempts are at least made to disguise it, so that its presence is not obvious. Politics is not a respectable activity in this world of organizations, at least not outside of government legislatures. But then again, as we saw in Chapter 23, the Political Arena serves a number of important purposes in society, and from these it does derive a certain legitimacy: it induces necessary but resisted changes in organizational power, it enables certain necessary hybrids to function, and it sometimes speeds up the deaths of spent organizations and so helps to recycle their resources.

The stability of the Political Arena, as we saw, is largely a function of the form it takes. The intense Political Arena—in its complete form or contained, as confrontation—is highly unstable. It must resolve itself, moderate the intensity of its conflict, or destroy the organization. The moderate forms are more stable, however, although no form of Political Arena can be called highly stable. The shaky alliance is just that, an alliance that tends to flare up frequently in confrontation. But so long as its underlying forces remain in balance, these flare-ups amount to no more than vibrations about the mean, and the basic configuration remains intact. As for the politicized organization, with its pervasive, moderate conflict, as noted it may remain stable so long as it retains some artificial means to support it.

What are the natural transitions for the different forms of the Political Arena? What follows confrontation, the shaky alliance, the complete Political Arena, and the politicized organization?

This last question was, of course, discussed at length in Chapter 23, in the section on "Life Cycles of the Political Arena," and the results can be seen in Figure 23–2 on page 434. We can summarize those conclusions as follows: The confrontation form tends to lead either to full resolution of the conflict, or else to standoff if the conflict cannot be reconciled, in the form of a shaky alliance or perhaps the politicized organization, although intensification to the complete form of Political Arena is also possible. The shaky alliance tends to remain stable so long as its underlying forces remain in balance, although it will flare up in the form of confrontation periodically. When the balance tilts, a transition to a more focussed configuration becomes possible. The politicized organization tends to make an eventual transition to the complete form of Political Arena, although full resolution is a remote possibility as well, while the complete Political Arena usually results in the death of the organization although, again, full resolution may also be possible, or perhaps moderation to the politicized organization.

But which of these transitions should be considered natural? From what we have concluded so far, being captured by conflict cannot be considered a natural state of affairs for an organization, except under two conditions: first, that it has become conflictive during a natural transition from one of the focussed configuration to another, as when a confrontation or shaky alliance arises during the shift from, say, Instrument to Closed System; and second, that a form of Political Arena *is* the result of a natural transition from one of the other transitions, as when a Closed System or Meritocracy becomes a politicized organization. Let us focus on each of these in turn.

First, consider the situation where a Political Arena serves to induce a transition between two of the more focussed configurations, say between Autocracy and Meritocracy or Instrument and Closed System. Here, the Political Arena usually appears as a flare-up, involving the confrontation form or perhaps the complete form of Political Arena, although it may also appear in the form of shaky alliance if the transition takes place gradually. In this situation, what obviously follows the Political Arena—in other words its own transition—is the new focussed configuration of power. Thus, all of the other transitions so far discussed which are natural yet involve conflict must be considered natural transitions for the Political Arena as well. We have so far discussed eight such transitions, plus two others from focussed configurations to forms of the Political Arena itself (not to mention transitions between different forms of the Political Arena). These have been highlighted in the bold faced propositions in the text and the boxes of Table 24-1. Let us consider the conflict involved in each of these in turn:

* The Instrument makes its natural transition to the Closed System. For this to happen, the administrators must seize power from a dominant external influencer(s). This can certainly involve conflict, likely in the form of confrontation, although the change can also take place gradually and involve a kind of shaky alliance for a time.

* The Closed System makes its natural transition to the Political Arena itself (in the form of the politicized organization). Also, it renews itself naturally through periods of internal confrontation, in effect making a transition to a different state of itself.

* The Autocracy can make its natural transition to the Instrument, Closed System, Missionary, or Meritocracy. The transition to Missionary should be harmonious—without conflict—since it is widely supported by the insiders after a charismatic leader leaves. In fact, it is the attempt to force one of the other transitions that typically involves conflict, because the insiders who favor the Missionary (or others, for different reasons) resist. Often, it is the leader himself, still in office, who resists giving up personalized power. In any case, confrontation ensues, or perhaps a shaky alliance emerges during the transition. In particular, the attempt by an external influencer to take over the organization and render it his Instrument usually evokes the resistance of the leader or the other insiders who remain after he leaves; the attempt by administrators to institutionalize power in the form of the Closed System is usually resisted by the leader during his tenure; and the diffusion of the leader's power to the experts may be resisted by the founding leader himself or perhaps by the administrators after his departure.

* The Missionary makes its natural transition to the Closed System. Here the administrators seize the power for themselves, and destroy the ideology, or else members less committed to the ideology and intent on serving their own personal needs, do the same thing. No matter how this transition comes about, it is likely to provoke conflict, as members who remain loyal to the ideology resist its destruction. Brief confrontation or a longer period of shaky alliance is probably inevitable.

* Finally, the Meritocracy makes its natural transition to the Political Arena itself (in the form of the politicized organization). Also, like the Closed

System, it renews itself naturally through periods of internal confrontation, in effect making a transition to a different state of itself.

Drawing these conclusions together, we conclude overall that **the Political Arena, in the form of confrontation or shaky alliance, is likely to appear naturally in natural transitions from Autocracy to either Instrument, Closed System, or Meritocracy, and from Instrument or Missionary to Closed System, as well as in the natural renewals of the Closed System and the Meritocracy (transitions to different states of themselves).** That is not to say, of course, that the Political Arena is precluded from appearing during other transitions, which we have not labelled natural, those caused by external forces. All of the boxes of Table 24-1 are filled, meaning that any configuration can make a transition to any other, or to itself in another state. And virtually any of these transitions can involve conflict, driving the organization to the confrontation or shaky alliance form of Political Arena for a time.[6]

Only under particular conditions is an organization likely to avoid an intermediate stage of conflict during a transition—for example, when a specific change is long overdue and is widely supported, when an old center of power disintegrates quickly and its obvious successor takes over immediately, or, as noted, when a leader's beliefs naturally become an ideology upon his departure. More typically, however, the destruction of one configuration and its replacement by another (or another state of itself) takes time and involves friction, giving rise to a form of the Political Arena in the interim. Ideologies do not disappear overnight, experts do not give up without a fight, even when their skills have been rationalized, nor do administrators whose bureaucratic systems of control have become redundant. In other words, transitions from the Missionary, Meritocracy, or Closed System inevitably require a stage of Political Arena. And so too in many cases does transition from the Instrument or Autocracy, when the dominant external influencer or CEO is unwilling to step aside submissively. Our general conclusion is that the Political Arena can be shown in all of the transitions of Table 24-1, as a possible way station between the old and new configurations. Thus, the bottom row and right hand column of Table 24-1 could be filled with all kinds of possibilities; rather than cluttering up the table, for the most part we have just noted the general case.

So far we have discussed the Political Arena as it appears during the transition between two other power configurations. But some transitions begin or end with the Political Arena itself. What happens then? Sometimes a Political Arena in fact appears during what is intended to be another transition, but deflects that transition, so that the Political Arena becomes the end point. For example, a confrontation ends in a stalemate so that the transition is stopped in midstream

---

[6]Although, for convenience, we have ignored this point in the chapter so far, describing each transition as from the initial stable configuration to the final one.

and a shaky alliance form of Political Arena emerges instead. Or the confrontation pervades the organization, but moderates in intensity, leading to the politicized organization form of Political Arena.

Given the organization is faced with a stable form of the Political Arena configuration—shaky alliance or politicized organization—what transitions do we expect from that?

For the shaky alliance, so long as the different forces that underlie it remain in balance, we would expect it to remain intact. Periodic flare-ups will likely be common—amounting to temporary transitions to the confrontation form of Political Arena. But with the underlying forces in balance, we would expect a quick return to the shaky alliance. A change in one of the underlying forces, however, can tilt the balance and send the organization to one of the more focussed power configurations. Again, the possibilities are so numerous here that we need not clutter Table 24–1 by trying to list them.

The politicized organization, as we have seen, can emerge in the pattern of natural transitions between our five focussed configurations. Specifically, it naturally follows the Closed System and Meritocracy, once these configurations have collapsed due to the destructive forces intrinsic to themselves. These forces divide their External Coalitions, politicize their Internal Coalitions, and create conflict between the two. As conflict gradually pervades the entire power system, the politicized organization emerges. Our question here is: What happens next?

As we have already noted, because it consumes so much energy in conflict the politicized organization cannot support itself. And so it must be considered only as stable as its artificial means of support. Pull out its props, and down it goes. Of course, as we also noted, these props can be rather firmly implanted, a reflection of years of having been a powerful Closed System or Meritocracy configuration. But the props cannot last forever. Eventually the organization must use up its surplus resources, overexploit its monopoly position, exhaust its benefactor, or whatever. Then what? What becomes of the organization pervaded by conflict?

Resolution of some sort is, of course, possible. As noted in Chapter 23, faced with a threat to the survival of their organization, the influencers may back off completely and let a new, more focussed configuration emerge to save the organization. Since threat to survival is the ultimate crisis for an organization, and since, as we saw in Chapter 20, crisis conditions tend to give rise to Autocracy, this is the configuration we would expect to appear when the conflict of the politicized organization is suspended. The influencers put power in the hands of a single leader in order to save the organization, giving him a chance to initiate a major and comprehensive program of renewal.

There is another point to make about the resolution of the conflict of this form of Political Arena. The politicized organization amounts to an overdoing of conflict, since the conflict is both pervasive and enduring, seriously weakening the organization. And overdoing conflict, just as overdoing any of the other internal forms of influence, can cause a transition to another configuration of power. Which one might we expect? When the excessive conflict is restricted to the Internal Coalition, the external influencers may gain the upper hand, as the insiders destroy each other, sending the organization toward the Instrument. Alternatively, excessive conflict only in the External Coalition can strengthen the hands of the insiders and drive the organization toward one of the configurations which focusses power internally, for example, the Closed System. But to be a politicized organization means to experience conflict in both of the coalitions. And, as we noted in Chapter 20, if excessive conflict everywhere is able to strengthen anyone, that person is likely to be the chief executive officer, at least the one capable of exploiting extreme confusion to build a personal power base. So by this argument too, we would expect Autocracy to emerge. Thus, we conclude that **the politicized organization may be able to revert naturally to Autocracy in order to save itself through renewal.**

Such a transition can be natural because it reflects certain forces inherent in the politicized organization. But we suspect that it is not most likely to occur. An organization may be likely to resolve the intense conflict of the confrontation form of Political Arena, because that conflict is contained. But when the conflict pervades the entire power system, as it does in the politicized organization, our suspicion, mentioned in Chapter 23, is that the organization is unlikely to ever shake itself completely free of it.

A second transition from the politicized organization is, in our opinion therefore, more natural and more likely to occur. Rather than resolution of the conflict, we expect its eventual intensification. Self-interest turns into consumptive greed, and organizational process breaks down completely. In other words, as discussed in Chapter 23, **once an organization has been captured by the pervasive conflict of the politicized organization, the eventual and most natural transition of this configuration is to the complete form of the Political Arena, which is followed naturally by the death of the organization.** Thus we believe that the most natural transition for the politicized organization is not back to some more focussed configuration but on to the more intensive as well as pervasive form of the Political Arena, namely the Complete Political Arena. And the natural transition for this, as we have already seen, is to the demise of the organization. In other words, the politicized organization appears near the end of the line in the life of an organization rather than serving as a way station to some other stable and harmonious state. For example, it appears unlikely that may politicized corporations will ever revert to being Instruments, Closed Systems, or Autocracies. Having come to be viewed as significant, quasi-public institutions, which of their major groups of influencers will leave them alone? Once politicized in this pervasive way, therefore, an organization seems destined to remain so until its conflict finally destroys it altogether.

A REVISED MODEL OF STAGES OF
ORGANIZATIONAL DEVELOPMENT

So far in this chapter we have discussed transitions *between* the configurations, considering where each is driven when it disintegrates of its own accord or is subjected to external forces. Now we come to a more interesting issue, namely, how these transitions can string together to form patterns of change in power. In other words, now we consider common transitions *among* the power configurations.

The literature on patterns of transition among types of organizations is generally referred to as "stages of development" theory. Such theory assumes, as we have done in this chapter, that certain intrinsic forces drive organizations naturally from one type to another, in stages, as they age, grow, and elaborate their structures. Organizations are believed to spend most of their time in the steady state of one coherent type, interrupted periodically by the transition to a new type—frequently a disruptive process, involving a kind of organizational revolution.

As discussed at some length in the *Structuring* book (Mintzberg 1979a, pp. 241–48), the different writings on stages of organizational development—most of which focus specifically on transitions between various types of organizational structures—have shown a sharp convergence. Specifically, most describe all or parts of a three-stage sequence: in the terms of that book, from Simple Structure to Machine Bureaucracy to the Divisionalized Form.[7] No writer claims that this sequence is inevitable. Some in fact show that certain kinds of organizations tend to settle into certain stages and not move on, or even to break the sequence by skipping stages or reverting back to earlier ones. But the assumption underlying all stages of development theory is that certain patterns are more natural than others—in other words, driven by forces inherent in organizations themselves as they develop—and are therefore expected to be more common.

In the terms of this book, this three-stage sequence translates into: Autocracy followed perhaps by the Instrument and then probably by the Closed System (since Machine Bureaucracy can be found in either the Instrument or the Closed System, while, for reasons we have discussed in Chapter 19, the Divisionalized Form seems typically to be associated with the Closed System). We believe this to be a natural sequence, so far as it goes, but we also find it incomplete. It is consistent with most of what the research tells us about organizational structure, but includes little of what we have learned about organizational power. Also, it deals with the growth of organizations but tells us nothing

[7]Some of the more recent literature was noted to hint at a fourth stage, of matrix structure, or Adhocracy. But this conclusion remains speculative.

about their demise. It presents a life cycle that ends at maturity, as if old age and death were not part of the cycle of life. By using what we have learned about power in and around organizations, we can add to this conventional theory, describing a more complete picture of the life cycles of organizations. Hence, we refer to this as a revised model of the stages of organizational development.

If life cycles are believed to reflect the forces inherent in organizations as they develop, then the set of propositions we have introduced in this chapter which describe what we have called the "natural" transitions—those highlighted in boldfaced type and in certain of the boxes of Table 24-1—should serve as the basis for our revised model. In fact, to derive our model we need only connect the configurations according to these proportions. This we have done in Figure 24-1, which shows our full model. Hence, our discussion of this model to close this chapter and section of the book serves not only to propose another view of the stages of organizational development, but also to summarize much of what we have concluded in this chapter and, indeed, in our discussion of the seven that preceded it.

Underlying this model is our belief, supported by a number of the arguments already presented in this chapter, that the configurations tend to take their place at different stages in the lives of organizations, according to their own purposes. Autocracy often appears early—typically in the formative years—with the purpose of establishing the organization in the first place. But, being dependent on a single person, it tends also to be a short-lived configuration.

The Instrument and the Missionary tend to appear in earlier years as well, something akin to adolescence, during which growth is sustained and maturity is approached. But neither typically give birth to an organization. Both generally require that it first be established by a leader, in the case of Missionary, by a charismatic individual who establishes a strong system of beliefs. Both, however, stand ready, each in its own way, to take over from that leader, in order to institutionalize his innovation or beliefs. On the other hand, neither of these configurations tends to be able to sustain itself past some point of organizational development. The Instrument requires an organization that is small and malleable enough to accept direct external control, while the Missionary requires unquestioning loyalty to a mission. As organizations develop, they tend to become less malleable, and loyalties tend to atrophy.

The Closed System and Meritocracy were described as the most stable of the power configurations. Thus, they seem akin to the stage of maturity or adulthood. Both must be preceded by other configurations, which establish the organization, but once either of these configurations captures the organization, it seems able to sustain itself for a long period of time. While the purpose of the Closed System is to further institutionalize the organization's mission and especially to facilitate its pursuit on a large scale, the presence of this configuration also signals a deterioration in that mission and a growing displacement of external or societal goals by internal and self-serving ones. Much the same thing can be said for the Meritocracy, which exists for the purpose of institutionalizing some mission involving complex skills and knowledge, yet can partly displace the goals associated with that mission in favor of ones that serve the insiders.

Finally, we saw that the Political Arena appears at the end of the life cycle of an organization in two forms. First, as the politicized organization, it represents the state of decay, equivalent to old age. And then, in the form of the complete Political Arena, it carries an organization through its death throes, serving to dispose of its resources. Other forms of the Political Arena, however, appeared at other stages. The confrontation form and sometimes shaky alliances as well were seen as necessary to bring about many of the transitions between the stages, and also to renew stagnant Meritocracies and Closed Systems. As such, they resemble transitional periods in human lives, as in puberty, or mid-life crisis, or menopause.

In brief then, our model, as shown in Figure 24–1, suggests that organizations are typically born as Autocracies. Those that survive eventually tend to make a transition to either Instrument or Missionary, equivalent to a stage of adolescence, or rapid development, although some go directly to the maturity stage of Closed System or Meritocracy. The Instruments and those Missionaries that survive typically become Closed Systems eventually. (All of the transitions so far discussed, except Autocracy to Missionary, frequently involve an intermediate stage of Political Arena, in the form of confrontation and/or shaky alliance.) Closed Systems and Meritocracies tend to endure for considerable periods of time, in part because of their ability to renew themselves through the confrontation form of Political Arena (sometimes followed by a brief period of Autocracy in the case of the Closed System). But these configurations tend to politicize gradually, emerging eventually in the stage of organizational decline or demise as the form of Political Arena we called the politicized organization. And while an overall renewal of the organization is possible, through a regression to Autocracy—to begin a new life cycle—more likely the politicized organization is a dead end, leading ultimately, through the complete form of the Political Arena, to the death of the organization.

Let us now consider each of these stages in turn.

BIRTH OF THE ORGANIZATION   It is common for an organization to begin its life as an Autocracy, set up by one forceful leader. At least until it is established, external influencers tend to leave it alone. And the internal influencers, typically hired by that leader, tend to be loyal to him, with the result that the Autocracy form of power configuration may last throughout his tenure in office. Whether that actually happens, of course, depends on the nature of the organization. Those with many professionals sustain briefer periods of Autocracy than, say, those that operate with unskilled workers in simple, dynamic environments.

Some organizations are of course created to be Instruments. An individual intent on remaining outside the organization hires someone to establish it on his

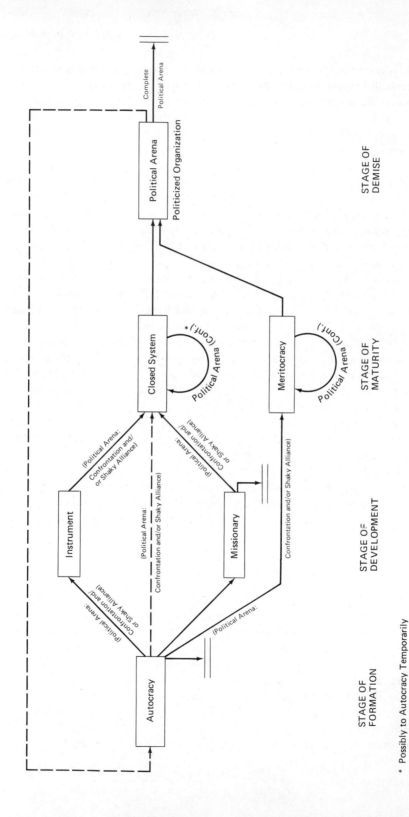

Figure 24-1. A Revised Model of Stages of Organizational Development

STAGE OF FORMATION   STAGE OF DEVELOPMENT   STAGE OF MATURITY   STAGE OF DEMISE

* Possibly to Autocracy Temporarily
= Signifies Demise of the Organization

behalf. But even here, the need for strong leadership at the outset—and the attraction of strong leaders to situations in which they can create organizations—usually gives rise to characteristics of Autocracy, for some time at least. (And this fact often makes it more convenient for those in need of an organization as their Instrument to take over one already established, rather than trying to have a new one created for them.)[8]

DEVELOPMENT OF THE ORGANIZATION   As noted earlier, Autocracies tend to be vulnerable, and many organizations die in that form. (Demise of the organization is shown in Figure 24–1 by two parallel lines.) But those that survive and outgrow their configuration naturally go any one of four ways.

Founding leaders tend to be charismatic ones. When they depart, therefore, there is a natural tendency for the remaining members to consolidate and institutionalize that charisma in the form of norms and traditions. In other words, the members coalesce around an ideology and effect a transition to the Missionary. (Or to put this the other way, the forces that give rise to ideological movements tend to be manifested first in the form of Autocracies under charismatic leaders; only when those leaders depart do the organizations emerge as the more egalitarian Missionaries.) The organization then settles down to the pursuit of the departed leader's mission. Left on their own, that is what is inclined to happen to many Autocracies after their founders leave. And so there need be no conflict in the transition, that is, no intermediate stage of Political Arena.

But most are not left on their own. Being vulnerable after the departure of their founders, or even during their founder's reign, they become prime candidates for takeover and fall prey to external influencers (or perhaps even actively seek the protection of one). Another strong leader may of course move in, maintaining the organization as an Autocracy. But because there is often the need to institutionalize procedures, especially after a period of rapid growth under personalized leadership, we would rather expect an external influencer to seize the power and render the organization his Instrument, nipping the ideology in the bud as he forces in bureaucratic controls to serve his interests. Figure 24–1 shows the possibility of Political Arena during this transition, since the insiders committed to the ideology or the chief executive intent on maintaining personal control will often resist the takeover. A confrontation might be expected, or perhaps a period of shaky alliance as leader and external influencer share power (as in the

---

[8]As noted in Chapter 22, some organizations begin their lives as federations, their administrative structures intended as the Instruments of their founding members. Where the board of the federation is significant compared with its administrative apparatus, this may indeed be what happens. But when the administrative apparatus becomes significant, and especially when the members become highly dependent on it, Autocracy may instead emerge in the formative period, followed by the Closed System as institutionalization sets in and the administration, created to achieve coordination among the members, consolidates its power over them, The flow of power reverses itself, and the federation comes to look increasingly like a top-down Divisionalized Form, with power focussed in the headquarters and then delegated to the subordinate divisions.

case of the conglomerate that retains for a time the entrepreneur of the company it buys). But once the transition is fully accomplished, the organization enters a steady state with power firmly lodged in the External Coalition.

Not all Autocracies become Missionaries or Instruments, however. Some become Closed Systems instead, as their administrators succeed the chief executive at the center of power. Dictatorships, for example, are often followed by bureaucratic regimes, as in the case of the Soviet Union after Stalin. And this example suggests the conditions under which the transition to the Closed System can override the more likely one to the Missionary or the Instrument: the established presence of an administrative apparatus, which usually means a large organization, probably operating in an environment that has become or is becoming stable. Thus, we see the same transition when an entrepreneur builds a sizable corporation or a union chief a large union. The leader cannot avoid setting up an administrative apparatus, with which he must share power in what is bound to become a shaky alliance during the transition, flaring up into confrontation periodically. And once the leader departs, unless the form of succession is clear, we would expect other confrontations. Different administrators may vie with each other for power at the top of the hierarchy. Or the administrators promoting bureaucractic controls may have to confront other influencers, for example, different insiders who wish to institutionalize the leader's beliefs in the form of ideology and convert the organization to a Missionary, or external influencers seeking to render the organization their Instrument, or perhaps even an insider seeking to take over the leadership and make the organization his Autocracy. Hence Figure 24-1 shows the possible occurrence of the Political Arena, in the form of shaky alliance or confrontation, during the transition from Autocracy to the Closed System power configuration.

Few Autocracies become Closed Systems directly, however, because most are small and lack the administrative apparatus required to take control of the organization. They are inclined to become Instruments or Missionaries instead, two configurations by which that apparatus can begin to grow (especially in the case of the Instrument, which encourages the establishment of bureaucratic procedures). Then later, as we shall see, as that apparatus is established, the transition to the Closed System tends to begin.

There is one other transition the Autocracy can make, which is a perfectly natural one under a special condition. In the presence of the need for expert skills and knowledge, it becomes a Meritocracy. As noted earlier, under this condition, the period of Autocracy is likely to be brief, since the experts can begin to take over much of the power once they have settled into place (especially in Professional Bureaucracy, where virtually from the outset the organization adopts standard programs already used in sister organizations). We might still expect a transitional period of Political Arena, however. Confrontation may appear between the chief executive in no rush to surrender power and the experts intent on taking over quickly. Or the two might even form a shaky alliance for a time. Either way, the period of conflict should be brief, and it should typically be less divisive than that during the transition from Autocracy to Closed System, or even Instrument, since the basis is clearly established for expert power.

MATURITY OF THE ORGANIZATION   So far our organizations typically began as Autocracies, and most of them have become either Missionaries or else Instruments if external influencers intervened, unless they were destined because of their need for expertise to become Meritocracies or managed to grow very large under personalized leadership and were diverted by their administrators to the Closed System configuration instead. What typically happens next to the Missionaries and the Instruments? In our view the answer is: Eventually the same thing that happened more directly to the Autocracies that grew large. Assuming they survive and develop, both Instruments and Missionaries are drawn increasingly to the Closed System configuration. Gradually, their procedures become routinized as formal standards, their administrators augment their own power, and their insiders come to think of the organization as serving themselves rather than some outsider or noble mission.

In the Instrument, the administrators, hired to implement the goals of the dominant influencer come increasingly to exploit for their own purposes their direct control of decision making. They even make efforts to pacify the External Coalition and especially its dominant influencer. These efforts are, of course, supported by the growth of the developing organization, which serves to diffuse external control and to make external surveillance increasingly difficult.

As for the Missionary, time can blunt the ideology, converting enthusiasm into obligation, traditions into dogmas, norms into rules. Excitement diminishes as unrealistic expectations are not met, or realistic ones are. As the organization develops, a mission that was once inspiring may become bland. Administrative influence, always a threat to the egalitarian nature of this configuration, grows as the ideology wanes, and helps to accelerate its demise. Status differences arise between insiders, reinforcing hierarchy, and self-interest displaces missionary zeal. Gradually the Missionary becomes a Closed System.

Of course, not all Missionaries survive long enough to make this transition. As noted earlier, all sit on the knife edge between isolation and assimilation. Those that assimilate and survive, rather than simply disintegrating into the world around them, tend to be driven quickly to the Closed System configuration. To be part of this world is to feel the pressures to machine bureaucratize the structure, and in the presence of a growing administration, free of external influence, that means a Closed System configuration. Only by remaining significantly apart, in order to sustain the unique characteristics of the ideology, can the pressures to formalize procedures, build hierarchy, and concentrate power at the top be resisted. Of the organizations that do isolate themselves as Missionaries, however, a good number run out of resources and members and die as Missionaries, maintaining their ideologies to the very end. Hence we show two parallel lines coming out of Missionary as well in Figure 24-1, to signify the demise of the organization as a natural consequence of this configuration. (Organizations as Instruments can of course die, too, but this is considered less likely, and not a natural consequence of the configuration, given the external support and protection available to the organization.) But even those Missionaries that isolate themselves and survive tend to make an eventual transition to the Closed System, as their members come to worry more about fulfilling their own needs than accomplishing the organization's mission.

Both these transitions—from Instrument or Missionary to Closed System—are likely to involve a form of the Political Arena. Either the administrators and the dominant external influencer or members supporting the ideology will engage each other in an intense confrontation, or else a shaky alliance will form during the transition, between administrative influence on one hand and external control or ideology on the other. Perhaps these two forms of Political Arena most often work in concert: From a tilt toward one configuration, there gradually builds up a balance of power until the tilt shifts toward the other, which provokes a confrontation that consolidates power in the hands of the administrators once and for all.

Thus our model has drawn us to the conclusion that, unless the presence of expertise evokes a Meritocracy configuration after the formative stage of Autocracy, organizations that survive and develop tend to become Closed Systems in their years of maturity. In fact, if we stop to think about it, the Meritocracy seems much like the Closed System, almost a variation of it (which is why it is shown in Figure 24-1 in parallel with it). Both seal the organization off from external influence and put the power in the hands of insiders who use much of it to serve themselves. In one case it is the administrators who gain the power, in the other it is the experts—which it is depends on how much expertise the organization requires—but the consequences are not so very different. Indeed, these two configurations were described earlier as the most stable of the six, it being difficult to displace the power of administrators or experts who firmly entrench themselves.

Hence we see this stage of maturity as being very enduring. Organizations are able to sustain themselves as Closed Systems or Meritocracies for long periods of time. This is so not only because of the capacity of the insiders to solidify their power, but also because each of these configurations—and these alone—exhibits a special capacity to renew itself after it stagnates. As shown by the loops under each in Figure 24-1, a common and natural transition for each is to a different and renewed state of itself, through the confrontation Political Arena. As significant changes in the need for expertise take place in the Meritocracy, new experts challenge established ones to displace them in the pecking order of power. Similarly in the Closed System, often only by displacing senior administrators as they lose touch with a changing environment, dulled by years of pursuing a given strategy with standardized procedures, is the organization able to renew and revitalize itself. Since the Closed System contains no natural means of succession, aside from the established leaders naming their own successors, politics becomes the natural means to displace the leadership, for example, through an organizational coup d'état by a group of young Turks. (And, should radical change in strategy be necessary after the displacement, the confrontation form of Political Arena may be followed by a brief period of Autocracy during which the new leader is able to make the necessary changes, unencumbered by bureaucratic procedures, before the organization settles down again to its life as a Closed System.)

The other configurations, at earlier stages of the life cycle, lack this capacity for natural self-renewal, for different reasons. The leader of Autocracy can also get out of touch, but the rest of the organization is generally so weak that it contains no one willing or able to displace him. In the Instrument, it is the separation of control from management (power from knowledge) that can often impede self-renewal, although the external influencer is certainly able to replace the CEO at will. As for the Missionary, since its ideology is sacrosanct, self-renewal is precluded. Stagnation in each of these cases, therefore, typically leads to the death of the organization (particularly for Autocracy and Missionary) or else to a necessary transition to another configuration. And so the period of Autocracy, Missionary, or Instrument tends to be short, equivalent to childhood in one case, adolescence in the other two, compared with that of the Closed System or Meritocracy, representing the stage of maturity.

DECLINE OF THE ORGANIZATION   Once organizations have reached the stage of Closed System or Meritocracy, they seldom die. They are simply too stable, too established, and, especially in the case of the Closed System, too powerful.[9] What they tend to do, sometimes only after very long periods of time, is make a transition to another power configuration. As noted earlier, Closed Systems have a habit of growing powerful and arrogant. Their internal influencers tend to get greedy, which brings them into conflict with one another over the spoils, thereby politicizing the Internal Coalition. And they eventually attract the attention of external influencers, who, by challenging the organization, divide the External Coalition and incite war between the two coalitions. Thus, in the natural course of events, the Closed System tends to give way gradually to the Political Arena, in the form of the politicized organization.

Much the same thing can happen to Meritocracy. The Internal Coalition is constantly on the verge of politicization. When many of the experts become callous, as can happen to people over whom there are few external controls, conflict increases. In the External Coalition, influencers stand constantly ready to challenge the absolute power of the insiders; they hesitate only because of the difficulty of doing so. But watching the organization growing influential yet remaining closed to external influence, and perceiving increasing callousness on the part of the experts, they eventually make the effort. Thus the Internal Coalition becomes politicized, the External Coalition divided, war ensues between the two coalitions, and the politicized organization tends to emerge, as it does in the case of the Closed System.

All the arrows of Figure 24–1 point toward the Political Arena, in this enduring form. Is this, therefore, the end of the line for the typical organization? In

---

[9]Certain forms of Adhocracy, notably Operating Adhocracy, uncertain of maintaining a steady stream of incoming projects, can be exceptions.

other words, can there be a return from pervasive politics? We have argued that, in general, the answer to this question should be no. The Political Arena should be viewed as the end of the line, in general although sometimes not in particular. Once an oganization has been captured by conflict—once it has attracted a variety of conflicting external influencers and its insiders have become used to pursuing their own needs through political games—then there may be no turning back. The politicized organization may survive for a long time, despite its inefficiencies—sustained by the position it established for itself as a Closed System or Meritocracy, perhaps propped up by an outside benefactor. As Pfeffer and Salancik note, "Large organizations, because they are interdependent with so many other organizations and with so many people, such as employees and investors, are supported by society long after they are able to satisfy demands efficiently" (1978, p. 131). But once that artificial support runs out, the organization must die. As its demise becomes imminent, the organization makes one last transition—to the complete form of Political Arena—before it finally burns itself out, as indicated by the parallel lines at the far right of Figure 24–1.

Some organizations, of course, do manage to pull themselves out of this state of conflict and renew themselves, like the legendary Phoenix that arises from its own ashes every five hundred years to begin a new cycle. Since the life cycle of the organization begins with Autocracy, since conflict almost to the point of demise represents the ultimate crises, and Autocracy resolves crisis, and since in the confusion of pervasive conflict the only one likely to seize power, if any one can, is the shrewd leader, then we would have to predict that renewal begins with Autocracy. A chief executive with near absolute power to effect change holds the greatest hope of restoring order and rebuilding the organization. This corresponds with our conclusion that overdoing politics tends to lead to Autocracy. The politicized organization certainly overdoes its politics, not in intensity but in pervasiveness and perhaps in duration as well.

Is this rebirth a good thing? Clearly rebirth is never quite so refreshing as birth. The mythical Phoenix may arise in the freshness of youth; the real organization does not. Legacies remain, which cannot help but influence behavior. The organization may be the wiser for its experiences, but it must also be the wearier. Perhaps it would have been better to let it die, enabling a truly fresh organization to replace it.

Our suspicion, however, as we noted, is that such rebirth is less common than gradual death. In fact, our belief that the Political Arena appears at the end of the organizational life cycle, and tends to sustain itself for long periods of time, seems to be supported by the increasing number of politicized organizations one finds in our developed societies. And this has profound social consequences.

RENEWING OUR WORLD OF ORGANIZATIONS   Increasingly, our giant organizations—private and public—seem to be surrounded and pervaded by moderate politics, as we saw at the close of the last chapter. All the aberrations of power seem to collect near the end of the life cycles of these once effective organizations. We have Meritocracies subject to government controls and corporations challenged by all kinds of pressure groups, both of which have become politicized, and, of course, all those government departments permeated by self-interests of every sort. We can appreciate the source of each of these pressures. Yet their effect is to cut deeply into the abilities of these organizations to serve society as they must—through the vigorous pursuit of their given missions.

Ironically, today all of the configurations of power are vulnerable except the Political Arena, in the form of the politicized organization. Autocracies tend to be small, and precarious in a world of giant organizations; moreover, they violate democratic principles. Missionaries are the most democratic of the configurations we know, but they are anachronisms in a world so obsessed with Machine Bureaucracy. It seems to be increasingly unfashionable to believe in something beyond service to oneself, except of course to the system itself—that of formal administration with its impersonal rules, regulations, and standards. Outsiders may create Instruments, but the pressures of the cult of administration take their organizations away from them. Power is driven to the administrators or, when there is expertise, to the experts. But absolute power corrupts absolutely, as Acton said, and as the insiders get greedier, external groups become alert and active. Conflict spreads. Society ends up with a glut of politicized organizations, able to sustain themselves, and each other, through illegitimate means. The problem is that many of these giant Political Arenas are aberrations, unable to serve the very purposes for which they were created.

The preferable solution is renewal, not of old organizations but their replacement by new ones. Only by constantly replenishing our stock of organizations can we maintain a vibrant society. Like people, organizations tend to follow life cycles. When these are interfered with—for example, by sustaining spent organizations beond their natural lives—the renewal of the species is endangered. The young never get a chance to be born, or at least to receive the support necessary to grow to maturity.

Yet this is exactly what is happening in our world of organizations. Giant organizations have learned how to sustain themselves artificially—through monopolizing markets, manipulating public opinion, exercising their power with other giant organizations. What is worse, giant governments seem intent on sustaining them—these once glorious institutions that, having been captured by conflict, will probably never serve us well again. Governments do so in part no doubt because of the power these organizations have over the politicians, and also because governments, too, consist of giant, politicized organizations, interdependent with the others. Moreover, governments fear the disruptions that the death of a giant organization can bring. No democratically elected government feels comfortable letting several hundred thousand automobile workers become unemployed, or forcing an established monopoly to face a new competitor. Yet preventing the natural deaths of too many spent organizations—the giant Political Arenas—can result in another death instead, that of the society that sustains them.

CYCLES IN THE LIVES OF ORGANIZATIONS We have developed in this section, a model which describes some natural life cycles of organizations. We must emphasize once more that only some organizations travel the paths laid out in it. An organization can stop at any point along them, or get diverted from any point to any other, shown ahead of it, behind it, or in parallel with it. In other words, any transition between the six configurations of power is possible. Which one occurs is dictated by a variety of forces that can arise, some of which are external to the configuration, and can override forces intrinsic to it. Conditions in the environment can change unexpectedly, influencers come and go, technological breakthroughs occur, and so on.

Our contention, however, is that these external forces are discontinuities that interrupt the natural flows of events, and that these natural flows are dictated by forces intrinsic to the configurations themselves. In other words, barring interruption, intrinsic forces tend to drive organizations along the paths indicated in the model. These paths become, therefore, the most natural ones for organizations to take as they develop, and so probably emerge as the most common. Three paths from birth to death are indicated in the model, suggesting three basic cycles of the lives of organizations.

* The *cycle of expertise*, common to professional organizations, begins with a brief period of Autocracy, followed, perhaps after some conflict in the form of confrontation or shaky alliance, by a long life of Meritocracy; this is interrupted by periods of confrontation as conflict flares up between the experts to renew the organization; the Meritocracy eventually falls prey to a pervasive form of Political Arena as conflict arises first in the Internal and then the External Coalition; this can eventually kill the organization unless Autocracy somehow emerges to restore it as a Meritocracy.

* The *cycle of ideology*, common especially to volunteer organizations, sees birth as Autocracy followed by a harmonious transition to the Missionary after the departure of a charismatic leader, as his beliefs are institutionalized in the form of an ideology; in time, the ideology weakens and, should the organization continue to survive, a second form of institutionalization takes place, with transition to the Closed System as norms become formalized; this transition may involve a good deal of conflict, in the form of confrontation or a shaky alliance; the Closed System may endure for a long period, interrupted by brief periods of confrontation, and sometimes Autocracy as well, as the organization seeks to adapt itself belatedly to changes in its environment; eventually the Closed System is likely to fall prey to the Political Arena, in the form of the politicized organization, as conflict typically arises internally and then spreads, pervading both coalitions as well as the relationships between them; the organization may be able to sustain itself in this form for a time until the conflict intensifies and the complete form of Political Arena brings its eventual demise, again unless Autocracy somehow manages to emerge to initiate a new cycle of life.

*   The *cycle of bureaucracy* common especially to private organizations, begins with what could be a fairly long period of growth as Autocracy; should the organization survive, this is followed by a takeover in the form of the Instrument, as the seeds of ideology are destroyed and behaviors are institutionalized as bureaucratic procedures; resistance to the takeover, however, typically drives the organization to confrontation or a shaky alliance during the transition; thereafter this cycle proceeds much as does the previous one: institutionalization continues to the point where external control itself is weakened and a second transition, involving the same sort of conflict, takes place to the Closed System (although, when the organization grows large under personalized leadership, the stage of Instrument may be bypassed); the Closed System tends to endure for a considerable period of time, sustained by brief periods of confrontation, sometimes followed by Autocracy, in which a stagnant organization renews itself; with no strong ideology in its past, the organization is even more likely than that of the last cycle to fall prey to the Political Arena, in the form of the politicized organization, conflict arising within the Internal Coalition as well as between the two coalitions over questions of legitimacy, and then spreading more quickly and more divisively than in the previous cycle; but because the organization likely has a firmer power base, it may be able to sustain itself longer in the form of politicized organization; since the likelihood of Autocracy emerging to initiate a new life cycle is less, due to more divisive politics and less of a legacy of ideology, the expected conclusion is an intensification of the conflict, followed by the death of the organization as a complete Political Arena.

Throughout this book, we have seen his last life cycle—particularly the first three quarters of it—as characteristic of the business firm. Indeed, our note on the displacement of mission as a goal by the systems goals (in Chapter 16), suggests that this has been the life cycle of the private sector as a whole, over the course of the last two centuries.

The business firm is typically given life by an entrepreneur, who runs it as his own personal domain. The firm, if successful, grows, and begins to adopt a more bureaucratic structure. Eventually the entrepreneur leaves, or is pushed out by his inability to maintain personal control, and so-called "professional management" takes over. Power at first tends to concentrate itself in the External Coalition, in the hands of the entrepreneur's heirs or of another party that takes the firm over. The Autocracy has become an Instrument. But as the firm continues to grow, stockholding tends to become increasingly diffused, with the result that the External Coalition becomes passive. The Instrument bcomes a Closed System. But that arrangement sustains itself only so long as the organization disturbs no important external influencers, or manages to control those that it does, and also manages to contain internal conflict. The problem is that, as a Closed System, the corporation tends to grow very large and influential and to seize a good deal of power in its environment. Eventually it attracts oursiders intent on influencing it, and also raises the expectations of its insiders, who come into increasing conflict with each other. The Closed System corporation begins to look like a Political Arena.

Will the giant corporation in fact become a Political Arena? Or will it be able to remain as a Closed System, or perhaps even revert to an Autocracy or to the Instrument of its owners or maybe even of the society that sustains it? Who should control the corporation? It is on the discussion of this question—around which a debate currently rages in the United States and elsewhere— that we shall conclude our study of power in and around organizations.

PART V

WHO SHOULD CONTROL
THE CORPORATION?

In whose interests ought the giant business corporation of today to be run? To what extent should it pursue public social goals as opposed to private economic ones? Who should control the corporation, and how, to ensure that it pursues one set of goals or another? Should the giant corporation be forced to revert to the status of Instrument, to pursue the goals of a particular outside group? Should it be encouraged to reinforce its tendencies toward a Closed System, free to pursue the systems goals of growth, control, efficiency, and survival? Or should it be allowed to become a Political Arena, to pursue a host of conflicting parochial goals?

We shall close this book with a discussion of this debate, for two reasons. First, the debate is a central one in the study of power in and around organizations, underlying directly or indirectly a good deal of the research. Because the issues involved in the debate can be conceptualized neatly in terms of our elements and configurations of power, a review of them here serves both to summarize and to illustrate the theory that has been presented in this book.

Second, the debate over who should control the corporation is a major one facing developed societies, and is far from over. If anything, it is increasing in intensity. The logic of the different positions seems to be becoming more and more submerged in the passions of political ideology. If our theory can be used to compare systematically the different positions being taken, and thereby to help clarify the issues and perhaps even to suggest some possible solutions, then our efforts in this closing section of the book will be worthwhile.

In the first chapter of this section, we review briefly some of the reasons for the debate and then describe a "conceptual horseshoe" that depicts eight positions taken as to who should control the giant American corporation.[1] Each of the next eight chapters then reviews one of these positions, while a final chapter summarizes my personal views as to possible resolutions of the debate.

[1]The American orientation in this section reflects (a) the literature to which I have been exposed, the bulk of it coming from the United States, and (b) my own cultural roots, since I am describing the society I know best (which is, more precisely, North American). References will, however, be made to the European situation where appropriate. In fact, the debate over who should control the corporation is strongly bounded by culture. It is probably fair to argue that the eight positions discussed in this section have proponents in all societies, but the nature of the debate and the emphasis given to different positions varies markedly from one society to another (as we shall see, for example, in Chapters 26 and 27).

25

A Conceptual Horseshoe

Why has the giant corporation come under attack? Why now? The reasons have appeared throughout this book. Essentially, this corporation is perceived in many quarters today as a Closed System of questionable legitimacy, with enormous economic, social, and political power. At one time the corporation was run for the benefit of specific owners, who clearly controlled it. Legitimacy was established by a chain of power that ran directly from those owners to the managers and then down the hierarchy. Furthermore, at that time, singly or collectively, the largest corporations did not wield the social power they do now. But as ownership became more and more dispersed, management assumed control. At the same time, increasing size enabled large corporations to dominate some of their external influencers—in certain cases, consumers, smaller suppliers, sometimes even government itself (in the form of a regulatory agency, for example). The Internal Coalition came to be viewed as too powerful, too detached from external control. A power vacuum was perceived in the External Coalition, and the issue became: Who would fill it? In this chapter we first develop more fully these arguments about changing conditions and power relationships, and then show who has tried to fill the power vacuum and how.

THE ORIGINS OF THE ATTACK
ON THE CORPORATION

Let us take a closer look at the emergence of the debate about who should control the corporation, in terms of four basic points.

1. Within the private sector, economic power has become highly concentrated. That the concentration of economic power in the United States has been increasing throughout this century seems irrefutable; so too does the thesis that this has resulted in the concentration of enormous influence in the hands of relatively few corporations. The "Fortune 500" for example—the five hundred largest American industrial corporations as ranked by *Fortune* magazine—accounted in 1973 for something of the order of two-thirds of the sales of all American industrial corporations, three-fourths of the employees, and four-fifths of the profits (Blumberg 1975, p. 24). A publication of the Organization for Economic Co-operation and Development (1979), entitled *Concentration and Competition Policy*, cites U.S. government figures to show that in 1976, the two hundred largest manufacturing corporations in the United States accounted for 44 percent of all value added by American manufacturing, up from 30 percent in 1947 (the fifty largest accounted for 24 percent, up from 17 percent). The top *one* hundred companies in 1976 accounted for more value added in 1976 then did the top *two* hundred in 1947—33.5 percent versus 30 percent (p. 84). Citing receipt figures, in order to compare across sectors, fifty U.S. manufacturing firms accounted for 36.5 percent of the total in 1974; two hundred of them accounted for 55 percent in that year. The figures for finance firms were comparable—35 percent and 51 percent—while those of the utilities were much higher—51 percent and 73 percent. Wholesaling and retailing showed lower concentration ratios—18 percent and 27 percent of the receipts for the fifty and two hundred largest firms—as did services—14 percent and 22 percent—with services the only sector that did not show an increase in concentration for 1968 to 1974 (p. 86).

But concentration ratios alone are insufficient to explain the contemporary attack on corporate power, because America has known a reasonably high level of corporate concentration for many years. "In 1870, the United States was a land of small family-owned businesses. By 1905, the large, publicly owned corporation dominated the economic scene" (Kristol 1975, p. 126). And that corporation was never very popular: "At least until the 1940's," it "had little political support among the American electorate" (Chandler 1977, p. 497). Kristol puts the conclusion more forcefully:

> . . . in no way did it seem to "fit" into the accepted ideology of the American democracy. No other institution in American history—not even slavery—has ever been so consistently unpopular as has the large corporation with the American public. It was controversial from the outset, and it has remained controversial to this day. (1975, p. 126)

Populism as a movement—"the constant fear and suspicion that power and/or authority . . . is being used to frustrate 'the will of the people' " (p. 127)—has always opposed big business. But two factors have combined more recently to raise the tone of the debate as never before.

2. The economic power of the private sector in general, and of individual giant corporations in particular, has had increasingly significant social consequences, while 3. public expectations about the economic and social behavior of business have risen in recent years. Increases in the impact of business actions on the social environment have combined with increases in what the public expects from business to change the entire perspective on the role of business in society.

Inadvertently as well as intentionally, the corporation has come to have a tremendous impact on society outside of the economic sphere. Laissez-faire capitalism, as described by Adam Smith in 1776, defined the corporation as a system closed to political influence because it was open to economic influence. That was the justification for leaving it alone. But Smith talked of tiny entrepreneurial enterprises, not the giant corporations that now dominate the economy.

> . . . both the Founding Fathers and Adam Smith would have been perplexed by the kind of capitalism we have in 1976. They could not have interpreted the domination of economic activity by large corporate bureaucracies as representing, in any sense, the working of a "system of natural liberty." Entrepreneurial capitalism, as they understood it, was mainly an individual—or at most, a family-affair. . . . The large, publicly-owned corporation of today which strives for immortality, which is committed to no line of business but rather (like an investment banker) seeks the best return on investment . . . such an institution would have troubled and puzzled them, just as it troubles and puzzles us. (Kristol, 1975, p. 125)

Size alone makes economic decisions social. When a plant employing thousands of workers is opened or closed, the impact on a community and on many lives is direct and consequential. As a result, the corporation gets caught in its own web of power; it cannot remain neutral. We can see this in the experience of Dow Chemical with the sale of napalm during the Vietnamese war. The transaction was economic, but so too was it social: to refuse to sell it was a political statement, as was the decision to sell it.

> . . . an organization known as the Medical Committee for Human Rights, which held shares in the company, requested inclusion in management's proxy statement of a proposition that "napalm shall not be sold to any buyer unless that buyer gives reasonable assurance that the substance will not be used on or against human beings." Its objection to such sale was based not only on "concerns for human life," but also on the adverse effect that the use of Dow's napalm in the Vietnamese war was having on the recruitment of able young men for company positions and on an unfavorable public reaction hurting the company's "global business." (Chamberlain 1973, p. 189).

Dow management fought the proposal, and the SEC ruled in its favor. But a U.S. Court of Appeals directed the SEC to reconsider the matter, noting that

The management of Dow Chemical Company is repeatedly quoted in sources which include the company's own publications as proclaiming that the decision to continue manufacturing and marketing napalm was made not *because* of business considerations, but *in spite* of them; that management in essence decided to pursue a course of activity which generated little profit for the shareholders and actively impaired the company's public relations and recruitment activities because management considered this action morally and politically desirable. (quoted in Chamberlain, p. 191)

Ironically, as Chamberlain points out, the company was "in effect arrogating to itself the power of deciding *moral* issues confronting the company, but denying to its shareholders the right to challenge the morality of its position" (pp. 190–91).

Externalities is the label given by economists to costs that are incurred by an organization but not charged to it, what we described in Chapter 4 as inadvertent byproducts of an organization's activities. Often the problem is that the costs cannot be incorporated into the organization's accounting system, because they cannot be measured and allocated. How to charge the corporation for the "cost" to the physical environment of its pollution, for the "cost" to workers of mental illness caused by a speeded-up assembly line.

The nub of the problem is that the growth of the corporation, and of a corporate way of life, has multiplied such externalities enormously. In the case of pollution, for example, Davis describes "the increasing load on our natural environment," with business "a substantial contributor to that load. The environment has been a *free good* that business could use as it wished" (1976, p. 18). The costs were borne by society. But as they became heavy, "society found itself with burdensome costs that it did not wish to bear" (p. 18). The issue, as Bell describes it, is one of "performance," specificallly a broadened definition of performance: "A feeling has begun to spread in the country that corporate performance has made the society uglier, dirtier, trashier, more polluted and noxious" (1971, p. 7). Other "costs" have been incurred more subtly, for example in the way people think: "violence, sex-role stereotypes, paranoia, and advertisements for junk foods are examples of ways business shapes the social behavior of American children" (Madden 1977, p. 76). But perhaps the major costs lie in the power of the private sector to divert society's resources and values toward economic ends—"the imbalance [that arises] between public goals and private goals" (Bell 1971, p. 14). As a student radical group of the 1960s commented:

To regard the various decisions of [the] elites as purely economic is short-sighted: their decisions affect in a momentous way the entire fabric of social life in America. . . . the ethical drug industry, for instance, spent more than $750 million on promotions in 1960, nearly four times the amount available to all American medical schools for their educational programs. The arts, too, are organized substantially according to their commercial appeal; aesthetic values are subordinated to exchange values, and writers swiftly learn to consider the commercial market as much as the humanistic marketplace of ideas. The tendency to over-production, to gluts of surplus commodities, encourages "market research" techniques to deliberately create pseudo-needs in consumers—we learn to buy "smart" things, regardless of their utility—and introduces wasteful "planned obsolescence" as a permanent feature of business strategy. While real social needs accumulate as rapidly as profits, it becomes evident that Money, instead of dignity of character, remains a pivotal American value and Profitability, instead of social use, a pivotal standard in determining priorities of resource allocation. (from "The Port Huron Statement," Students for a Democratic Society, quoted in Perrow 1972*b*, pp. 13–14)

As the story is repeated from one issue to another, the social actions of big business come to be viewed as pervasive. Epstein (1973, 1974) has categorized the dimensions of corporate power as follows:

- Economic—over prices, products, the distribution of scarce goods
- Social and cultural—over the character and performance of other social institutions, over mores, lifestyles such as the "cult of progress," conformity in work and consumption, the absence of democratic norms in bureaucracies embedded in democratic societies
- Technical—over the technology used in society, as in the impact of the automobile
- Environmental—over the use of natural resources, the development of different regions, etc.
- Political—over goverment policy making, as in the case of lobbying for trade barriers

Adding them all up, significant segments of the population come to feel swamped by corporate actions and corporate values—large numbers of workers by the assembly line, managers by the bureaucratic controls, consumers by advertising, naturalists by pollution, citizens by lobbying, all of them by the immense power of the system of private enterprise to make social choices for economic ends and thereby to shape societal values. The economic institution has become a dominant social force.

Hazel Henderson takes this argument to its logical conclusion, describing society as headed toward an "entropy state"—"an evolutionary cul-de-sac"—as "social and transaction costs equal or exceed society's productive capabilities" (1977, p. 3). She sees inflation, from one perspective, as "a multiple crisis of suboptimization—individuals, firms, and institutions simply attempt to 'externalize' costs from their own balance sheets and push them onto each other or around the system, onto the environment or onto future generations" (p. 4). Moreover, the costs of government coordination must increase in response, as must the "costs of cleaning up the mess and caring for the human casualties of unplanned technology—the dropouts, the unskilled, the addicts, or those who just cannot cope with the maze of urban life or deal with Big Brother bureaucracies and corporations" (p. 3). The service sector becomes the "social cost sector," with inflation "merely [masking] the decline of society" (p. 3).

While all of this has been happening, the expectations of the public of the economic and social behavior of business has been rising. Much of this can certainly be explained as a response to these problems. The writings of people like Bell and Henderson have made the public increasingly aware of externalities, resulting in a corresponding insistence that they be "internalized." More and more people want the corporation to pay all the costs of its own actions.

But rising expectations reflect other factors as well, some quite independent of the behavior of the corporations. Bell argues that as the "traditional sources of social support"—the small town, church, and family—"crumble in society," corporations and other kinds of organizations have taken their place, "and these inevitably become the arenas in which the demands for security, justice, and esteem are made" (1971, p. 23). Growing levels of education have also had an impact. The demands of society have become more sophisticated and, as a result of faster and more pervasive forms of communication, more articulate.

In Chapter 5, we noted that social norms naturally rise over time, that behavior acceptable yesterday are often questioned today and rejected tomorrow. Years ago the public worried about safety on the job, today it worries about the quality of working life, tomorrow it will likely worry about industrial democracy.[1] In line with Maslow's (1954) needs hierarchy theory, workers who once sought satisfaction of physiological and safety needs (many of the latter economic) now look to the corporation to satisfy belonging needs by what it does and status and self-actualization needs by the work it provides. The period immediately after World War II has been referred to as the only one during this century that was highly favorable to business. The explanation is simple. The corporation could satisfy the pent-up demand for goods, for things. But as people become saturated with goods, their obsession with material things diminished. "In a democratic republic such as ours . . . institutions are not supposed simply to be efficient at responding to people's transient desires, are not supposed to be simply *pandering* institutions" (Kristol 1975, p. 139).

That these rising expectations—whether caused by corporate behavior or not—failed to be met by corporations is reflected in a series of opinion pools. In 1966, 55 percent of the population expressed "a great deal of confidence" in the heads of large corporations; by 1975 that figure was down to 15 percent; in 1968, 70 percent of those polled thought that "business strikes a fair balance between profits and the public interest," in 1974 only 20 percent did. In a 1975 poll, big business came in last in terms of a "confidence" score (at 34 percent), just behind organized labor (38 percent) and well behind the executive branch of government (52 percent), the military (58 percent), education (67 percent),

[1] In America; Europeans already do.

and organized religion (68 percent) (Silk and Vogel 1976, pp. 21–22). Some of these figures recovered in subsequent years, but to nowhere near their previous levels. (For example, "a great deal of confidence" in the heads of large corporations rose to 23 percent in 1977 and then declined to 18 percent in 1979; *Public Opinion*, October-November 1979, p. 30).

In summary, with the social consequences of its economic power and with the rising public expectations around it, the giant corporation has emerged, in the words of Kristol, as a " 'quasi-public' institution" (1975, p. 138). And if so, then the obvious question becomes: Who is wielding all of that power? Who controls the corporation, decides what it does? And the answer has appeared quite clearly in this book.

4. The giant corporation is typically controlled by its own administrators, despite the absence of a fundamentally legitimate basis for their power. Were the corporation controlled by those upon whom it had an impact, there would be no issue of who should control it. What difference would concentration of power, increased social consequences, or rising expectations make if those who cared about the actions controlled them.

The problem is that with the dispersal of stockholding, the corporation has become more and more like a Closed System controlled by its own administrators, and to be viewed as such. We have already presented a good deal of evidence for this, for example, in Chapter 4 that by 1963, 85 percent of the two hundred largest American corporations appeared to be management controlled, and in Chapter 6 that less than 2 percent of all the directors of the Fortune 500 represented significant shareholdings. Then in Chapter 19 we discussed at length the emergence of the large corporation as a Closed System power configuration. To quote Cheit:

> It is now widely held. . .that there has been a mutiny of sorts, that the captain and officers of the ship have committed an act of disseisin by extending their authority far beyond mere matters of navigation. It is they, and not the persons having the underlying property interest, who are directing the voyage, altering the vessel, determining the character of the cargo, and distributing the profits and losses. (1964, p. 168)

Back in 1932, Berle and Means described the problem of legitimacy clearly. Commenting, as we noted in Chapter 19, on the "dissolution of the old atom of ownership into its component parts, control and beneficial ownership," the former in the hands of the nonpropertied management, they put the issue into an historical perspective:

> This dissolution of the atom of property destroys the very foundation on which the economic order of the past three centuries has rested. Private enterprise, which has molded economic life since the close of the middle ages, has been rooted in the institution of private property. . . . Private enterprise. . .has assumed an owner of the instruments of production with complete property rights over those in-

struments. . . . the organization under the system of private enterprise has rested upon the self-interest of the property owner—a self-interest held in check only by competition and the conditions of supply and demand. Such self-interest has long been regarded as the best guarantee of economic efficiency. It has been assumed that, if the individual is protected in the right both to use his own property as he sees fit and to receive the full fruits of its use, his desire for personal gain, for profits, can be relied upon as an effective incentive to his efficient use of any industrial property he may possess.

In the quasi-public corporation, such an assumption no longer holds. As we have seen, it is no longer the individual himself who uses his wealth. Those in control of that wealth, and therefore in a position to secure industrial efficiency and produce profits, are no longer, as owners, entitled to the bulk of such profits. Those who control the destinies of the typical modern corporation own so insignificant a fraction of the company's stock that the returns from running the corporation profitably accrue to them in only a very minor degree. The stockholders, on the other hand, to whom the profits of the corporation go, cannot be motivated by those profits to a more efficient use of the property, since they have surrendered all disposition of it to those in control of the enterprise. The explosion of the atom of property destroys the basis of the old assumption that the quest for profits will spur the owner of industrial property to its effective use. It consequently challenges the fundamental economic principle of individual initiative in industrial enterprise. It raises for reexamination the question of the motive force back of industry, and the ends for which the modern corporation can be or will be run. (1968, pp. 8–9)

Thus the legitimacy of managerial control—free of the direct influence of the owner, in many cases even of the directors, as we have seen—has come to be questioned. "Power without property" is the phrase used by Madden (1977, p. 65), "the appropriation of public authority by private rulers" is that of Dahl (1970b, p. 115).

"General Electric has repeatedly affirmed its objective of seeking 'the balanced best interests of all.' The difficulty is that just what constitutes such balance of interests is left to management's discretion to determine" (Chamberlain 1973, p. 186). "By what right does the self-perpetuating oligarchy that constitutes 'management' exercise its powers?" asks Kristol (1975, p. 138). "Why are private corporations and their executives the appropriate managers of the most powerful process ever created for mass acculturation of human beings?" asks Madden (1977, p. 77).

That ownership today is "simply a legal fiction," to use Bell's term (1971, p. 28), is no better illustrated than in the case cited earlier of Dow Chemical. Here, with the purchase of a share or two, a group of activists could tie up company, commission, and courts, all trying to decide on the rights of the "owners." The real point was not really whether the managers could do what they liked instead of being dictated to by the owners, not even "management's patently illegitimate claim of power to treat modern corporations with their vast resources as personal satrapies implementing personal political or moral predilections," to quote the opinion of the court (in Chamberlain 1973, p. 191). The real point was that ownership did not have any meaning. That is what made the whole proceeding seem so absurd. And that, ultimately, is what will bring the facade of external control down.

We have seen that the Closed System, free of external influence, tends to pursue what we have called the systems goals. Specifically, it seeks to survive and to attain an acceptable level of efficiency, thereafter to control its environment and, above all, to grow. These are the goals that serve the managers and analysts who control it. Externalities call for an *open* systems view of corporate power; the absence of external influence promotes a *closed* system. Issues that affect many people are decided upon by a few with particular interests. This leads commentators such as Blumberg to talk of "the failure of business leadership," which he sees as having been "unpardonably slow to respond" to "morally sound" demands (1971, pp. 1553, 1554). It leads, as we shall see later, a friend of business to point out that it has fought every progressive piece of American legislation of this century, from child labor laws on up (Levitt 1968). It leads a company like Dow Chemical, as well as the SEC and the courts, to tie themselves into knots trying to figure out what is a legitimate basis for corporate action.

These, then, are the reasons for the attack on big business—its concentration of power, vastly increased use of that power outside the economic sphere, rising expectations about the use of that power, and the growing realization of the absence of a basis of legitimacy in the exercise of that power.

What then are the proposed solutions?

THE POSITIONS AROUND A HORSESHOE

Thus the debate has arisen, and has heated up. Who should control the corporation? How to make it responsive to its constituencies? And there has been no shortage of proposals. The government stepped in early to "regulate it," with legislation such as the Interstate Commerce Act of 1887 to control the railroads and the Sherman Antitrust Act of 1890 to break up the giant trusts. Regulation has increased steadily ever since, at least until very recently. For others—special interest groups—this was ineffective; their approach was to "pressure it," to subject it to pressure campaigns to force changes in behavior. Ralph Nader, in particular, popularized this approach in the 1960s. Others took more extreme positions: in the depression of the 1930s, to "nationalize it" was thought to be one answer, in more recent years, to "democratize it." Formal power should be taken from the shareholders and given to the government, or to the workers, or to special groups of external influencers. There were extreme positions of another sort too. Milton Friedman has long argued to "restore it" to the real control of its traditional owners, the shareholders. And then there have been the rearguard actions to maintain its managerial control but make that control more responsive. "Induce it," said some, by rewarding it for pursuing social goals. "Trust it," said others, or at least "socialize it" to ensure that its existing managers were socially responsive. This view, called "noblesse oblige," has in fact existed for centuries. And finally, there were the few who said "ignore it" because they believed it paid to be socially responsible. To them, there was no conflict between social and economic goals.

Clearly, these proposals fall along the whole range of the political spectrum, from the nationalization of the corporation by the government at one extreme to its restoration to the control of its traditional owners at the other. Ironically, however, in managerial terms—from the perspective of the theory presented in this book—these two extreme positions are rather close together. Both call for the corporation to be treated as the Instrument of some external group with specific goals, in one case social, in the other economic. And if the extreme positions are so close to each other, then perhaps the moderate ones are the farthest from the extremes, and close to each other as well.

Translating this into graphical form, we come up with a "conceptual horseshoe." The different views of who should control the corporation, and how, are laid out along a continuum from left to right, but a continuum that doubles back on itself so that the extreme views appear together, farthest from the moderate ones. Figure 25-1 shows eight positions around our conceptual horseshoe. It seems to us that many of the participants in the debate over who should control the corporation place themselves at one of these eight points and then proceed to attach those on either side. These eight positions are as follows:

  *   At the extreme left (politically if not graphically) is the position taken by those who wish to "nationalize it." Essentially, they are calling for a return to the Instrument configuration, but this time with the government as the dominant member of the External Coalition, in order to impose social goals on the corporation.

  *   Next are those who wish to "democratize it," broaden its goal system by changing its formal power base. The proponents of "democratize it" assume two main postures. Some wish to broaden representation on the board of directors, calling in effect for a Divided External Coalition. We shall refer to this as *representative* democracy. Others prefer to broaden formal participation in internal decision making, the likely result of which would be a certain politicalization of the Internal Coalition. We shall refer to this as *participatory* democracy.

  *   Less extreme are those who call to "regulate it," that is, to have government play a more active and formal role as a counteracting power in the corporation's External Coalition by imposing more formal constraints on it. This, too, would encourage division of the External Coalition, which would likely

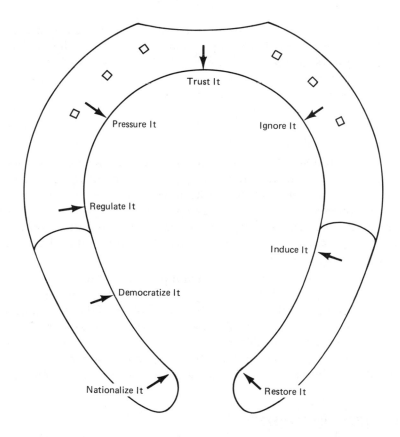

Figure 25–1. *A Conceptual Horseshoe ("horse" shoe courtesy of a Corsican mule, ©Henry Mintzberg, 1976)*

increase politicization of the Internal Coalition although both effects might be milder than in the case of democratization.

   *   Those who support the "pressure it" position believe that change is best brought about through pressure campaigns mounted by special interest groups and others. Essentially they favor the notion that a more active (and divided) External Coalition, with countervailing powers but in this case exercised informally, will make the corporation more responsive to social goals.

   *   The next position, called "trust it" is taken by those who believe that it is the moral duty—the "noblesse oblige"—of the management of the corporation to act responsibly, by which they mean to balance the pursuit of economic goals with social ones. This position is placed in the center of the horseshoe, furthest from the two extremes, because of that balance and because implicitly it stands for the status quo in the power system: managers will retain control of the corporation because they will exercise power responsibly.

    *   Shifting to the right side of the horseshoe, but remaining conceptually rather close to "trust it," we have the position taken by those who say "ignore it," because "it pays to be good." Here social goals are attended to because it is in the corporation's *economic* interest to do so. The difference between these two positions is subtle but significant: whereas the proponents of "trust it" implicitly accept a tradeoff between social and economic goals, those of "ignore it" see no conflict between the two. And again, not coincidentally, power remains in the hands of the management.

    *   Further to the right is the stand taken by those who say "induce it," that is, "pay it to be good" (or, from the corporation's point of view, "be good where it pays"). Proponents of this position recognize a real conflict between social and economic goals, and they come down clearly on the side of the economic ones. Only where it pays in economic terms to pursue social goals should the corporation do so. Now the goals of the corporation have shifted clearly in favor of its owners.

    *   Finally, at the extreme right, (again politically if not graphically), is the "restore it" position, taken by those who say that the corporation should be given back to its "rightful" owners, the shareholders. Like their colleagues on the extreme left, with whom they share the bottom of the horseshoe, the proponents of this position call for a return to the Instrument configuration. In this case, the owners will be restored to their previous dominance of the External Coalition, able to force the organization to pursue only economic goals.

THE POSITIONS IN CONTEXT

    Before discussing each position, it will be helpful to put them into different contexts relative to each other.

    *   First is the context of *conventional politics*, shown in Figure 25–2. In *The True Believer*, Eric Hofer defines conservative, liberal, skeptic, radical, and reactionary in terms of attitude towards the present, future, and past:

> The conservative doubts that the present can be bettered, and he tries to shape the future in the image of the present. He goes to the past for reassurance about the present... To the skeptic the present is the sum of all that has been and shall be.... The liberal sees the present as the legitimate offspring of the past and as constantly growing and developing toward an improved future: to damage the present is to maim the future....
>   The radical and the reactionary loathe the present. They see it as an aberration and a deformity. Both are ready to proceed ruthlessly and recklessly with the present, and both are hospitable to the idea of self-sacrifice. Wherein do they differ? Primarily in their view of the malleability of man's nature. The radical has a passionate faith in the infinite perfectibility of human nature. He believes

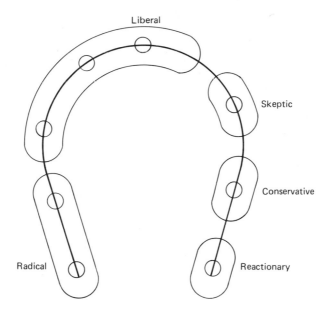

Figure 25-2. *The Positions by Conventional Political Stance*

that by changing man's environment and by perfecting a technique of soul forming, a society can be wrought that is wholly new and unprecedented. The reactionary does not believe that man has unfathomed potentialities for good in him. If a stable and healthy society is to be established, it must be patterned after the proven models of the past. He sees the future as a glorious restoration rather than an unprecedented innovation. (1966, pp. 70–71)

In these terms, we can label the two positions on the extreme left of the horseshoe as radical: "nationalize it" and "democratize it" are oriented towards the building of "wholly new and unprecedented" power structures. The position on the extreme right can be called reactionary—"a glorious restoration." These are the positions of the "true believers." The three positions at the center and center-left—"trust it," "pressure it," and "regulate it"—are essentially liberal—a constant "growing and developing toward an improved future." To the right of center, "ignore it" is the position of the skeptic—the present as the "sum of all that has been and shall be"—while "induce it," to its right, is essentially conservative: "the future [shaped] in the image of the present."

* Next is the context of the *goals favored* by each of the positions, shown in Figure 25-3. Here we see the symmetry of the horseshoe: the postures to the left favor the social goals, those to the right favor the economic goals, while "trust it" in the center seeks a balance between the two.[2]

---

[2]"Ignore it," to the right of "trust it," claims no conflict between economic and social goals, but proposes that social goals be pursued only because they serve economic ends.

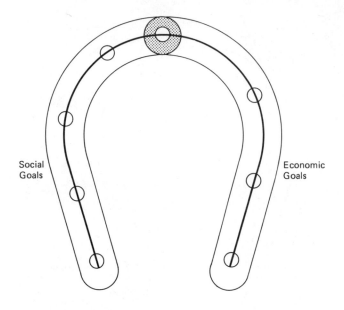

Figure 25–3. *The Positions by Goals Favored*

*   From the perspective of *different disciplines*, Figure 25–4 also exhibits a basic symmetry. Those positions to the left take a sociological perspective,

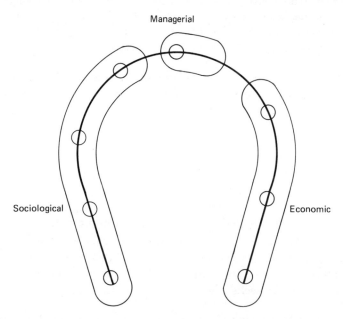

Figure 25–4. *The Positions by Disciplinary Perspective*

rooted in the need to challenge the control of the managers, to draw the corporation into social issues. Their view of the problem tends to be "get the bastards." The positions on the right take an economic perspective, rooted in the need to withdraw the corporation from the social fray. Their view of the problem is "how to keep the corporation private" (often in order "to keep the hoards at bay"). And in between, the perspective of "trust it" is essentially managerial. It claims, from the perspective of the manager: "What's the problem? We're nice guys who will take care of things through our good will."[3] In the context of the story of the goose that laid the golden eggs, the group on the left is concerned with who gets the eggs, that on the right with how many eggs there will be, and the one in the middle with the goose itself.

* Next is the perspective of *interpersonal relationships*, specifically of the presence of conflict or harmony in the pursuit of social and economic goals (Schneider and Lysgaard 1952). Now we begin to see the positions, as depicted in Figure 25-5, not along a two-end continuum, but around a closed loop.

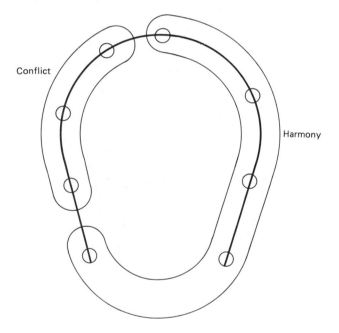

Figure 25-5. *The Positions by Interpersonal Relationships*

Three of the positions promote a perpetual state of interpersonal conflict in the organization in order to reconcile social and economic goals. "Democratize it" sets up conflicts between different factions represented either on the board of directors or in the Internal Coalition, while both "regulate it" and "pressure

[3]"Ignore it" also claims there is no problem, but in this case because economic forces resolve all conflict.

it" are based on the concept of "countervailing power" (Galbraith 1952). Both suggest, in other words, that the behavior of the corporation can be kept in check only if the power of the External Coalition is able to match that of the Internal Coalition. All of the other positions, both to the left and the right of these three, effectively make a case for interpersonal harmony, but for different reasons. The central position—"trust it"—promotes harmony by having the top managers reconcile the social and economic goals in their own heads (or, more to the point, in their own hearts). "Ignore it" does away with conflict completely, even within the hearts of the managers, by postulating a natural harmony between social and economic goals. And the other three, more extreme positions dispense with conflict by recognizing the need to pursue only one of these two sets of goals, economic in the case of "induce it" and "restore it," social in the case of "nationalize it."

*   Figure 25–6 depicts the positions in terms of the kind of solution, or

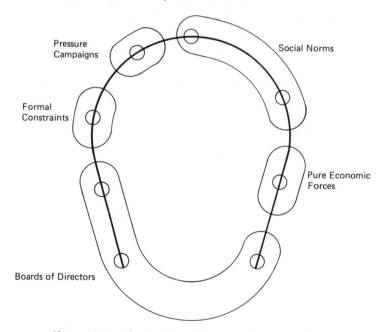

Figure 25–6.   *The Positions by External Means of Influence*

external means of influence, each proposes to the problem of corporate power. The positions nearest to the bottom of the horseshoe, that is, the extreme ones, seek to change the corporation by formal means. "Restore it," "nationalize it," and "democratize it," all call for changes in the formal governance of the corporation, specifically in the rules by which the members of its board of directors are selected.[4] "Regulate it" also uses a formal means of influence, but a

[4]In the case of "democratize it," this refers to representative democracy. Participatory democracy calls for formal changes in the way managers are chosen and authority is distributed in the Internal Coalition.

different one: it calls for government legislation that will impose formal constraints on the corporation. Continuing in a clockwise direction, "pressure it" relies on the informal pressure campaign as its external means of influence to solve the problem, while both "trust it" and "ignore it" are based on another external means of influence that is informal, the social norm. The belief is that the norms of society will bring about the necessary changes in corporate behavior. The process is more direct in the case of "trust it," the norms acting through the decision makers. It is indirect in the case of "ignore it," the norms acting implicitly to bring economic motives in line with social needs. Finally, "induce it" stands alone as precluding the need for any external means of influence to bring about the necessary changes. Here, the changes will come about exclusively through economic forces. Power has no role to play in changing corporate behavior.

* In Figure 25-7, we have the direct answer to *who* should control the corporation. Here we see most clearly the divergences between the various

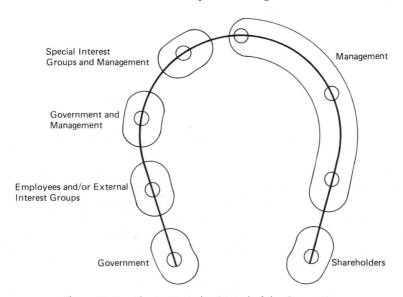

Special Interest
Groups and Management

Management

Government and
Management

Employees and/or External
Interest Groups

Government

Shareholders

Figure 25-7.   *The Positions by Control of the Corporation*

positions. "Restore it" claims that the shareholders should control the corporation; "nationalize it" presents the case for government; and "democratize it" proposes that the employees and/or various groups of external influencers control corporate behavior. "Regulate it" takes the implicit stand that government share control with the management, while "pressure it" proposes that this sharing be between special interest groups (and perhaps others) and the management. The three remaining positions all support control by the management. "Trust it" makes this case explicitly, while "ignore it" and "induce it" come to this conclusion implicitly, by favoring the status quo.

* Finally Figure 25-8 shows the *power configuration* implied by each

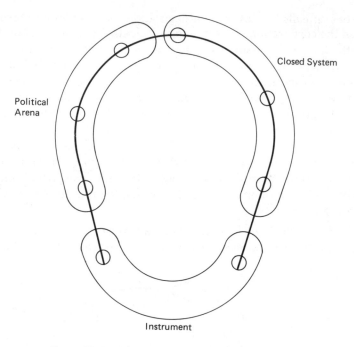

Figure 25-8. *The Positions by Power Configuration*

of the eight positions. Here especially we see the coming together of the two ends of the horseshoe: both extreme positions call for the Instrument, that is, an External Coalition dominated by a single group of influencers who can impose one clear set of goals on the organization. The two positions differ only in which influencer they would like to see as dominant and what goals they wish that influencer to impose. "Nationalize it" sees the corporation as government's Instrument in order to pursue social goals, while "restore it" sees it as the Instrument of the private shareholder in order to pursue economic goals. (Interestingly, as we shall see, some proponents of the position on the extreme right claim that any movement in the counterclockwise direction will inevitably result in a slide all the way around the horseshoe to the extreme left. They can imagine no stable power configuration other than the Instrument! Likewise a prime argument used for nationalization is that there is no other way to dislodge what is inevitably and effectively owner control. The ends see no middle ground!) In their encouragement of conflict (as shown in Figure 25-5), the three other positions on the left—"democratize it," "regulate it," and "pressure it"— implicitly encourage a Political Arena configuration, more or less. Each of the three remaining positions, in the center and on the moderate right, by accepting the status quo distribution of power, implicitly support the Closed System power configuration, at least in the sense that the administrators retain control of the corporation (although not necessarily that only the systems goals be pursued). "Trust it" postulates that the administrators can be relied upon to pursue social goals, without the need for direct forms of external influence (that is, other than social norms). So too, ostensibly, does "ignore it" (although we shall find that this position in fact collapses without the campaigns of "pressure it"). Indeed, we shall see that a popular argument of the proponents of "ignore it" is that "it pays to be good" because that is the only way to keep the External Coalition passive! And "induce it" too leaves the administrators in charge, since social goals need be pursued only to the extent that they are encouraged by economic incentives.[5]

Now that we have placed our eight positions around the horseshoe and in context, let us investigate each of them.

[5]Of course, "induce it" encourages society to use the corporation as its instrument to evoke social change. But not an Instrument as we defined that power configuration, in which the external control is direct. Here the corporation serves society by serving itself, much as Adam Smith's small enterprises were supposed to do.

26

"Nationalize It"

In reviewing the issue of "public responsibility and the businessman," Robert Ackerman notes that a view of the corporate world has emerged

> in which (a) the freely competitive marketplace has been replaced by oligopolistic managed markets, (b) the corporate manager is no longer responsive to stockholder interests and has in fact adopted non-profit maximizing goals and (c) the functions of business and government have become so interdependent that a businesslike separation of duties is no longer a near approximation of reality.... In general terms the problem arises as a result of corporate power. The solution involves a fundamental choice; that power may be abrogated in some way, or it may be controlled. (1973, p. 406)

If the mature corporation is, as Ackerman quotes John Kenneth Galbraith, "an arm of the state" (p. 409), then one obvious solution is simply to make it an *agent* of the state, in other words, to abrogate its power by nationalizing it. The argument of Berle and Means would seem to lead to the same conclusion:

> Few American enterprises, and no large corporations, can take the view that their plants, tools and organizations are their own, and that they can do what they please with their own.... Corporations are essentially political constructs. Their perpetual life, their capacity to accumulate tens of billions of assets, and to draw profit from their production and their sales, has made them part of the service of supply of the United States. Informally they are an adjunct of the state itself. (1968, p. xxvii)

If informally, why not formally?

NATIONALIZATION IN THEORY
AND IN PRACTICE

Nationalization is the "viewpoint that economic power must belong to the community and be removed from the tiny groups that still possess it" (Jenkins 1976, p. 13). In theory, nationalization retains the bureaucratic features of the Internal Coalition of the corporation. The bureaucracy merely becomes an Instrument of the state instead of a Closed System under the power of its own administrators. In other words, the state, as the new dominant influencer, would keep the existing control systems intact and merely replace one set of goals with another—social goals in place of systems goals. Presumably, the directors would also be changed, a new CEO, loyal to the government, might also be named, and the surpluses would be redistributed. In effect, a new program would be plugged into that computer known as the corporation.

At least this is how nationalization appears to its proponents—a convenient takeover of power at the top to redirect the efforts of the bureaucracy. Nice and neat. But the effects of nationalization in practice are rather more complex than that. For one thing, the new social goals are not so easily operationalized as the old ones of growth and profit. Improved employment, a clean environment, safe products, not to mention decisions taken with a view to supporting a host of existing government policies, are not easy goals to operationalize in a system of bureaucratic controls. Moreover, government may be less a single influencer that speaks with a clear voice than a plethora of ministries and agencies that pursue a variety of conflicting goals. Thus, as we saw in Frank's description of the Soviet factory, nationalization can result in such a cacophony of voices that the organization instead of being an Instrument, moves to a form of Political Arena, or even beyond to revert to a Closed System. Indeed, nationalization encourages the other external influencers intent on controlling corporate behavior to exert their influence on government itself, thereby further complicating the issue:"...the more actively government participates in the resolution of conflict over the firm the more likely it is that the contestants will shift their battleground from the firm level to the political level. 'Control' of the government may then become the means for establishing 'control' of the firm" (Papandreou 1952, p. 203).

NATIONALIZATION IN GENERAL
AND IN PARTICULAR

An interesting feature of the American debate on who should control the corporation is that nationalization is almost never expressed as a general position, at least not in the "overground" press. (This is less true in Canada, which has many nationalized utilities, a government chemical corporation, a government development corporation set up as a conglomerate to buy up private companies,[1] a government oil company, and a government-owned radio and television network, among many others. Nor is it true of Western Europe, where government ownership is much more widespread and the case for nationalizaton continues to be debated vigorously.) In the United States, the word nationalizaton is almost a taboo, even among the most liberal of commentators. None of the writers on the problems of corporate control—including those quoted at the outset of this chapter—endorses it as a solution. The political scientist Robert Dahl, clearly on the left of the U.S. political spectrum, comments on one solution to the problem of corporate power that ought *not* be seriously discussed: "...centralized, bureaucratic socialism has so little to be said for it that even socialists—democratic socialists, anyway—have virtually abandoned it" (1971). And George Cabot Lodge writes in the case of electric power:

> The need for federal intervention to plan the future of electric power seems plain. Regional power production jurisdictions should be planned, research on new technologies needs to be increased; technology and site decisions must be made. The problem is far too big and too national in scope to leave to a scattering of private companies.
>
> But this does not mean that these companies should be nationalized. That will be the inevitable result, however, unless more intelligent steps are taken soon. These companies must realize what government, and only government, can and must do: plan the allocation of resources and make the critical judgments of costs and benefits. To do this it must intervene with authority and coherence. (1974a, p.72)

Nationalization simply does not correspond with the prevailing ideology in America, which continues to view the holding of private property as a natural or absolute right. "Adam Smith treated property as a 'natural right' (following the teachings of Locke) and its protection as a 'law of nature'" (Berle and Means 1968, p. 299). But the ownership of property is no more an absolute right in the industrialized society than it is in the jungle. It is a possiblity, that is all, because of the mechanisms that exist in each. In one case, property can be accumulated privately because of the laws of the state—the rules of the game —and can be retained because of the presence of the state's law enforcement agencies; in the other case, it is physical prowess that enables an individual to accumulate and retain private property. In other words, the holding of property in society is bound up with our laws. Those laws, for example, give the individual the right to own land in the city, and shares in the corporation; they also deny the individual the right to own land in the parks, or shares in its wildlife.

And so new laws can change property rights. Government can, when it chooses, remove the right to own certain forms of property. One can debate the effects of nationalization, but one cannot deny the right of the government

[1]The latter recently took formal control of the former, and it also issued shares to the public making it a kind of hybrid government-private (widely held) firm.

to carry it out, that is, to convert private corporate property into collective public property, assuming just compensation (whatever that is). Nationalization violates no natural or social law. So the relevant questions really become (a) Can the government in a democratic society get away with nationalization, that is, will the people support it, and, more importantly, (b) Will nationalization in fact help matters?

The pragmatic answer to both questions appears to be, "in general, no; in particular, sometimes yes." For despite the *general* abhorrence for nationalization in the United States, the fact is that it comes up frequently as a *particular* solution to specific problems. Whenever a major corporation runs into serious difficulty, such as facing bankruptcy with the possible loss of thousands of jobs, massive government intervention, often including direct nationalization, inevitably comes up as an option. And sometimes that option is exercised. Travellers in the United States now ride on Amtrak; Tennessee residents have for years been getting their power from a government utility; indeed the U.S. Post Office was once a private enterprise. Few people challenge these arrangements. Yet the suggestion that other utilities—electric power companies, for example—be nationalized raises all sorts of hackles.

This is not to suggest that nationalization is generally good or efficient—that clearly depends on the circumstances—but merely that even in America, "nationalize it" is an acceptable posture, in particular if not in general. The fact is that the government does seem to get away with it, sometimes, that people do indeed support it, sometimes, probably that it even helps matters, sometimes.

NATIONALIZATION FOR WORSE AND FOR BETTER

What remains unacceptable in the United States is nationalization as a broad-based solution to the problem of corporate power. And in many respects for good reason. Large-scale nationalization—as examples from the other side of the Iron Curtain suggest—creates a monolithic society, which centralizes power, reduces dissent, and discourages adaptability. In addition, the conversion of the Closed System to the Instrument does not reduce Machine Bureaucracy. If anything, it increases it. And many of the social problems of the giant corporation stem from its bureaucratic nature. Moreover, as noted earlier social goals cannot easily be operationalized in the control systems of the Machine Bureaucracy, and so, despite the government's intentions, social goals still tend to get displaced by economic ones after nationalization.

As leader of the Labour Party in Britain, Harold Wilson offered the nationalization proposal as a way "to render accountable to the public the power of these 'increasingly anonymous, unidentifiable, often faceless, more often soulless corporations, national and multinational'" (quoted in Epstein, 1977, p. 285). But as Epstein points out his analysis, the social record of the nationalized enterprises in Britain has "not been conspicuously superior" to that of private firms "with regard to broader social issues such as consumer satisfaction with goods and services, labour relations, industrial democracy and workers' participation, and environmental protection" (p. 284). Epstein concludes that "public ownership *per se* does not resolve the issue of social responsibility" (p. 310). Even under government ownership—perhaps especially so—the Machine Bureaucracy remains faceless, soulless.[2]

Thus, Clive Jenkin's book *Power at the Top,* subtitled *A Critical Survey of the Nationalized Industries* [in Britain], makes for interesting reading. Introducing himself as committed to nationalization (as quoted earlier in the chapter), Jenkins documents all of its failures, yet attributes none to the inherent problems in nationalization itself: ". . .the nationalized industries can be seen to have become an instrument in maintaining the frozen class structure of British Society" (p. 21); "there has been a planned and purposeful counterrevolution which has resulted in the return of active adherents of the older property-possessing groups and their social attitudes to direct management power in the nationalized industries" (p. 22); British Petroleum has remained "a member of the oil consortium which has backed in turn every puppet premier and feudal king in the Middle East" (p. 34); "It may be said that nationalization has not so far lived up to the expectations [of greater worker participation] precisely because too much power is left in the hands of managements and not enough given to the workers" (quoting Hugh Gaitskell, p. 272). In making his case for the failure to reap the social benefits of nationalization, Jenkins in fact makes the case for the failure of nationalization to reap social benefits.

On the other hand, while nationalization may not solve the social problems, because ultimately it does not change the structure or functioning of the corporation very much, for the same reason the state-owned enterprise can sometimes function as effectively as the best of private ones, at least in an environment that respects and supports it. Thus, France has a highly successful automobile company called Renault, nationalized after the war. In Canada, among the most highly respected organizations in their industries on the continent are the provincially owned Hydro Quebec in energy and the federally owned Canadian National and Air Canada in transportation, and the Canadian Broadcasting Corporation and National Film Board in entertainment. (The first came about through nationalization of a number of healthy companies, the second of a number of bankrupt ones, and the rest were created as state-owned enterprises.) At the time of this writing, a comparison of the performance of these organizations with that of the three major American automobile manufacturers, many of the U.S. utilities, most of the American airlines and railroads, and much of the American media would make an impressive case for nationalization. In other words, there is more to performance and innovation than just ownership.

[2]At the time of this writing, Canadians could well appreciate this conclusion, since alongside articles in their newspapers of bribes to foreign politicians by executives of the private Lockheed Corporation of the United States appeared articles describing the same behavior by the executives of the government-owned Atomic Energy of Canada Ltd.

Indeed, the ineffectiveness of state-owned organizations in the United States may very well be a self-fulfilling prophecy (just as their effectiveness in cases elsewhere may be so as well). On the whole, Americans believe that government ownership leads to interference, politicization, and inefficiency. In part, this may reflect their own system of government, which, as we noted earlier, being based on the division of powers, tends to politicize government agencies more than does the parliamentary form of government, such as that used in Canada. But beyond that, perhaps American government organizations cannot help but produce according to their image of inefficiency because that image interferes with their ability to attract top talent and to overcome the ingrained resistance of their clients to dealing with government. Canadians suffer less from these biases—perhaps in part because government ownership has proven to be one reliable alternative to foreign domination of important sectors of the economy—and so have had a good deal of success with their state-owned enterprises.

What then are we to conclude about the role of "nationalize it." First, it is no answer to the problems of the social performance of the giant corporation. Nor, of course, is it to be preferred per se for economic efficiency, although we have tried to make the case that it can sometimes do quite well. But it is logically used under two conditions.

First is when a mission deemed necessary will not be provided, or at least not in a sufficient way, by the private sector. That is presumably why the United States has a government-owned Post Office, and why the bankruptcy of critical firms in the United States, in transportation for example, has sometimes led to their takeover by government. And that also explains a good deal of the state ownership in Canada as well. As noted, it proved the only reliable alternative to foreign domination of many sectors of the economy, which had been creating a number of problems in the country.

Second is when the activities of an industry are so intricately tied in to government policy that its organizations are best managed as direct arms of the government. That is one reason why the Canadian government has an oil company called Petrocan. (Another is, if course, to help reduce foreign ownership in that industry.) When, during an oil shortage, Exxon diverted to its American refineries Venezuelan crude destined for its Canadian subsidiary, the Canadian government could turn for help to Petrocan, the one source within itself that had intimate knowledge of this complex industry. Contracts were able to be negotiated quickly between the Canadian and Venezuelan governments, cutting out the foreign middleman.

To close this discussion, we note that it is not rhetoric that should determine the appropriate role for "nationalize it" among the eight positions, but the capacity of this position to deal with the problems at hand. "Nationalize it" should certainly not be embraced as a panacea for the problems of who should control the corporation, but neither should it be rejected out of hand as irrelevant.

27

"Democratize It"

A less extreme position, but still well on the left side of our conceptual horse-shoe—in other words, radical, at least in terms of the present debate in America—is the one that proposes formal devices to broaden the governance of the corporation. The corporation, to use the popular expression, should be democratized:

> The supporters of this position argue that big corporations are not only economic and social, but political units as well. Their activities should, therefore, fall under the same democratic controls as those of any political institution. Furthermore, the argument goes, democracy in the traditional political sphere alone is inadequate for the realization of a democratic social order . . . as long as most organizations with which the citizen comes into daily contact have authoritarian structures. Only if participative decision-making permeates business corporations is there any hope for a true and stable democracy. (Bergmann 1975, pp. 27–28)

Even for the executives, according to Jay, the corporation is not a place in which the citizen exercises free will:

> In the important part of their lives, their forty years of work, they have none of the freedoms that matter: no political freedom—the corporations rarely have the courage to risk the customer and community antagonisms which might be aroused by an executive who campaigned for a political party or ran for election on a party ticket; no freedom to publish—they cannot write newspaper or magazine articles without clearing them with the corporation . . . ; no freedom of speech—if they talked to the press about the incompetence of their board they would be

sacked . . .; no right of trial, and no judiciary which is independent of the executive—their career can be blighted and promotion stopped for utterly unjust reasons such as the personal whim of a hostile [superior]; and they have no sort of representation in the councils which decide how the firm shall be run, no say in its government, however much the decisions may affect their lives. (1970, pp. 26–27)

Today, according to law, the shareholders govern the corporation, through their directors, while the managers serve as their trustees. According to fact, however, as we have seen, with the stock widely held, the shareholders exercise no direct control. They relegate themselves to the role of suppliers of capital, while the managers control the corporation. This enables the proponents of "democratize it" to attack the corporation in two ways. They can accept the legal fiction and criticize the narrow base of control of the corporation, arguing that the shareholders must move over to make place for others affected by its actions. Or else they can criticize the reality by claiming that the managers' power is illegitimate and so must be subordinated to the power of others. In the following passage from a newspaper article entitled "Citizens of the Corporation," political scientist Robert Dahl combines these two points into a single argument:

Thus the government of the corporation denies citizenship to all affected parties except the stockholders—the one group that does not, will not, and probably cannot exercise their rights. It is reasonable to ask whether, and how, full citizenship in the government of the corportion might be granted to groups affected by its decisions who would be able to exercise their rights of citizenship more effectively than stockholders and more legitimately than present managements. (1971, p. 9)

How can the corporation be democratized? The answer is far from obvious. Saying "one person, one vote," for example, does not tell us which persons or what the votes will be about. So we need to break our question down into two others: What can be the means of democratization? And who can be involved in the process?

In this chapter, we shall discuss two basic means of democratization. The first focuses on the board of directors and involves the election of representatives to it. We call this *representative democracy*. The second is to establish direct involvement in internal decision making. We call it *participative democracy*. Note that the first means of democratization is formal and indirect—related to the official governance of the corporation—while the second, although still involving formal representation, goes beyond formal power to give influencers a direct say in the actual processes of the corporation.

In principal, any individual or group affected by the activities of the corporation can be involved in either form of democratization. That can mean owners, customers, suppliers, representatives of the public or of particular groups, managers, analysts, support staffers, operators. The problem is to determine who gets how much representation. Most proposals for democratization, however, involve two basic groups. On one hand, involvement focuses on the *employees*, in some cases all of them, in others, the "workers," which can mean the operators and possibly some of the staff and managerial personnel at lower levels in the hierarchy as well. The European debate over corporate democracy has focused on this group. On the other hand, involvement focuses on outside *interest groups* of one kind or another—consumers, minorities, environmentalists, representatives of the local community or of the "public interest," and so forth. The American debate over corporate democracy—at least, as it has begun to evolve—has tended to focus on these interest groups. In essence, one group involves the internal influencers, the other, the external influencers.

Combining the two means with the two groups gives us four basic forms of corporate democracy, which are shown in the two-by-two matrix of Table 27–1. At least these are forms of corporate democracy in theory. With one possible exception, they have hardly been attained—or even approached—in practice. That they are even attainable in the corporation remains a debatable point, as we shall see, although we shall also see that some have been closely approximated in other kinds of organizations.

TABLE 27–1.   Four Basic Forms of Corporate Democracy

| | | Groups Involved | |
		Internal Influencers (employees)	External Influencers (interest groups)
Focus of Attention	Board of Directors	Worker Representative Democracy (European style, e.g., "co-determination" or worker ownership)	Pluralistic Representative Democracy (American style, e.g., 'public interest" directors)
	Internal Decision Making Process	Worker Participatory Democracy (e.g., works councils)	Pluralistic Participatory Democracy (e.g., outsiders on new product committees)

What we are calling *worker representative democracy* has clearly received the most attention, being the focus of the European debate. It is also the form to have been most closely approximated, the workers of all but the smallest Yugoslavian firms owning them officially and filling all the seats on their boards of directors. Under so-called "co-determination," worker representative democracy has been half attained in the middle-sized and large German firms, worker representatives sharing the board seats with representatives of the stockholders.

What we can call *pluralistic representative democracy* has received much less overall attention, but has formed the basis of the emerging debate in America. There is no American corporation to our knowledge that in any way approaches this form of democracy, but the attempts to elect "public interest" directors or representatives of particular consumer or environmental groups to corporate boards reflect the spirit of it.

What constitutes the representative forms of corporate democracy— control of the board of directors—is at least easy to understand, if not to attain. What constitutes participative democracy is another story. As a result, the debates over this form have been more confusing and less fully developed, and few results have been forthcoming. *Worker participatory democracy* means worker control of decision making. The creation of works councils in certain European firms indicating slight moves in this direction. *Pluralistic participatory democracy* is probably the form of corporate democracy most difficult to define, since neither those involved nor the means of their involvement are clear. At least worker participatory democracy makes clear *who* is to be involved. All we know here is that a variety of external influencers are somehow to be included in internal decision making. An example of a step in this direction might be the appointment of representatives of consumer groups to a new product committee in a corporation.

Let us now look more closely at these four possible forms of corporate democracy.

REPRESENTATIVE DEMOCRACY OF THE CORPORATION

Those seeking to broaden the legal power base of the corporation have found the board of directors the obvious place to start, investing their efforts in the fight to have certain seats designated for specific groups. What they have been seeking is some kind of representative democracy in the corporation, where certain influencers will be able to elect their own representatives to the body that legally controls the corporation.

THE AMERICAN DEBATE: INTEREST GROUP REPRESENTATION The debate over representative democracy has taken a very different form in Europe and the United States. While the European proponents of "democratize it" have for some years been concerned primarily with opening up the board to the workers—in effect seeking a constitutional democracy of all the insiders—the American proponents of this position, far fewer in number, have in recent years been pursuing representation of outside interest groups such as consumers and minorities. Thus Robert Dahl, referring to the European proposal as "self-management," calls the American proposal "interest-group management": "Interest-group management seems much more in the American grain than self-management. It fits the American ethos and political culture, I think, to suppose that conflicting interests can and should be made to negotiate; therefore let all the parties at interest sit on the board of directors. It would be a very American thing to do" (1971, p. 9).

What might better be called interest group representation[1] has become an issue in the United States only quite recently, although there is at least one example that dates back seventy-five years. Six of the twenty-four members of the board of Prudential Insurance are selected by the Chief Justice of the Supreme Court of New Jersey, the company's state of incorporation, as public directors. This arrangement, instituted in the insurance companies of that state after an investigation of problems in the industry in 1906, has been found "quite workable" by the company, according to a Conference Board report (Bacon and Brown 1975, p. 48). Indeed, the New Jersey law calling for public directors was repealed in 1949, but the practice was reinstated in 1953 "at the instigation of Prudential management itself" (p. 48). Of course, the issue of representation is well-known to non-profit institutions such as universities and hospitals, which for years have had to deal with the problem of allocating seats on their boards to different constituencies. Indeed, as we saw in Chapter 7, some have achieved a kind of representative democracy, as in the case of Quebec hospitals whose board seats are formally allocated by provincial government legislation to representatives of the users, the local community, the clinical and nonclinical staff, and so on.

Interest group representation in the private sector really entered the American consciousness in 1970 with "Campaign GM." This was the attempt by a group of activist Washington lawyers, Ralph Nader among them, to force a number of changes in the governance of General Motors, most notably to elect "public-interest" directors. The group, interestingly enough, did not take the perhaps more obvious route of lobbying the government to enact legislation to broaden the legal power base of the corporation. Rather, it chose to work within the existing legal framework: it simply sought to activate the dormant shareholders of one corporation by the use of the proxy machinery.

The story of Campaign GM (Round I), as widely reported in the press, unfolded as follows: In June 1970, a group called the Project for Responsibility purchased twelve shares of General Motors stock (out of the quarter billion outstanding). As shareholders, they then requested that nine proposals related to corporate social responsibility be included in the proxy materials sent to the shareholders of the company before its annual general meeting. General Motors

---

[1]"Management" implying direct involvement in decision making.

contested the proposals before the Securities and Exchange Commission as not appropriate for shareholder vote. (An interesting insight by George Cabot Lodge is worth noting here in passing, one reminiscent of the Dow Chemical example discussed in Chapter 25. "Here we have an odd philosophical situation: the hired hands were asking the state to prevent private property owners from discussing how the hired hands should use and direct their property," [1972, p. 193]. Elsewhere, pointing out that the activists were in effect trying to "force shareholders to behave like owners and thus to legitimize corporations as private property," Lodge comments: ". . . it is a peculiar irony that James Roche, as GM chairman, branded such agitation as radical, as the machinations of 'an adversary culture. . . antagonistic to our American ideas of private property and individual responsibility.' In truth, of course, *GM is the radical*; Nader et alia were acting as conservatives, trying to bring the corporation back into ideological line" [1974a, p. 65].)

Under pressure from both the left and the right, the SEC rejected seven of the proposals but agreed to the inclusion of two of them: that a shareholders' committee for corporate responsibility be elected and that three "public directors" designated by Campaign GM be added to the board. (The rejected proposals concerned pollution, mass transportation, auto and employee safety, product warranties, and opportunities for minorities.) There then followed a vigorous campaign to solicit the proxy votes of the shareholders. The Project group concentrated its attention on institutions such as churches, universities, and pension funds, while the corporation undertook a massive public relations campaign to tell shareholders, as well as the general public, of its exemplary "Record of Progress" in automobile safety, air pollution control, mass transit, plant safety, and social welfare (Blumberg 1971, p. 1561). Furthermore, according to the Campaign GM lawyers, company people made calls to large shareholders and foundations, even to universities, "to the scholarship office, not the treasurer" (quoted in *The New York Times*, May 23, 1970). The results of the proxy contest surprised no one: the two proposals were supported by 6 percent and 7 percent of the shareholders, representing about 2.5 percent of the shares in both cases. As an attempt to broaden the legal power base of the corporation, Campaign GM was a failure. (It was in 1932 that Berle and Means first wrote that "the proxy machinery has. . . become one of the principal instruments not by which a stockholder exercises power over the management of the entreprise, but by which his power is separated from him" [1968, p. 129]).

But in another important way, as a pressure campaign, Campaign GM was a resounding success, a "decisive event in the politicalization of the corporation" (Blumberg, p. 1561). Shortly after the campaign General Motors voluntarily enacted changes that related not only to the proposals voted upon but also to some of those rejected by the SEC. (These will be discussed under "pressure it," which is where the *tactics* of Campaign GM really fall.) More importantly, Campaign GM invigorated the debate on the legitimacy of the power base of the American corporation.

It was not long after Campaign GM that proponents of "democratize it" began to call for changes, not in specific corporations within the context of their constitutions, but in the legislation that defined the constitutions of corporations in general. In January 1971, Ralph Nader called for the "popularization"[2] of the corporation:

> He suggested that in the large corporation, 5 of 20 directors should be elected directly by the public at large in a national election. The remaining 15 would be elected by shareholders under a proxy system that would permit the submission of management and opposition slates in a single corporate solicitation at corporate expense. He would accomplish this change through the mechanism of a federal incorporation statute, which would supersede, at least for large public corporations, the corporation laws of the various states. (Blumberg 1971, p. 1560)

A similar proposal came from Robert Townsend, once chief executive of Avis, that a federal law require "every corporation with assets of $1 billion or more to support the office of a public director to the tune of $1 million a year for staff. . . . He could attend all board meetings; 'all doors and files could be open to him,' and he would call a press conference twice a year 'to report on the state of the corporation and its effect on the public'" (Chamberlain 1973, p. 195).

In a paper written in 1974, Boston law professor Philip Blumberg notes that "The different reform proposals currently in vogue have a fundamental common objective. They seek to transform the large corporation into a public institution" (p. 114). Interest group representation would not simply broaden the perspective of the corporation; it would lead to a fundamental change in its power relationships: "The essence of special interest representation is that the representatives reflect the interest of the group selecting them, rather than the interests of the institution in whose governance they are participating" (p. 115).

Blumberg found that most of the efforts to seat other kinds of directors have used proxy proposals similar to those of Campaign GM, and that these have attracted only limited support, one receiving more than 9 percent of the votes cast but most of the others less than 3 percent. Of the various proposals, Blumberg found that the most serious involved the employees, but that American unions had not taken up the issue and that "the proposals are being advanced without grass-roots support." The proposals that have concerned consumers, suppliers, and dealers Blumberg refers to as "purely theoretical or symbolic," with little or no support, and those from environmentalists as "hard to take seriously . . . except as symbolic or quixotic gestures." Other proxy proposals have dealt with women, minority groups, "even" investment bankers.[3] Blumberg

---

[2]Nader has apparently also referred to "constitutionalizing" the corporation (Jones 1977b, p. 5).

[3]Blumberg notes that only about twenty American corporations have women directors. A more startling fact presented in his 1971 article is that, of California's sixty-seven largest corporations, not a single one of the 1,008 directors was black or Mexican-American, and only six were women, "most related to company executives" (p. 1584).

also discusses the proposals for directors who would act as trustees of the public at large, but downplays the idea because they would lack a clear constituency or appointing agency. Furthermore, "it is clear that the effectiveness of outside or public or professional directors will be severely limited so long as they are part time, not well compensated, and are not assisted by an independent staff" (although Townsend's proposal addresses these problems). Government directors, another possibility, "stirs little enthusiasm" (all quotations from 1974, pp. 117–21).

Blumberg concludes that while special interest representation and related proposals are "no more than topics for academic discussion in the U.S. . . . there are deep-seated underlying forces [notably worker alienation] that could conceivably make proposals of this nature . . . a matter of realistic concern in the future" (p. 134).

In the same volume, edited by Sethi (1974a) and entitled *The Unstable Ground: Corporate Social Policy in a Dynamic Society*, this issue is discussed by another law professor, Melvin Eisenberg, at the opposite end of the country (Berkeley) and, apparently, of the political spectrum as well. Eisenberg reviews some of the interest groups in question and concludes in each case that their interests would be better served by laws. For example, in the case of customers and suppliers, he questions whether they possess the skills required to make complex decisions and how they would be elected: "Are *all* customers and purchasers to have a voice in corporate affairs, or only small ones?" (p. 137). Eisenberg also notes the possibility of conflicts of interest, citing one writer on the resulting "political gangsterism that would destroy the efficiency of business management" (p. 138). He concludes that the associates are better off negotiating with the corporation as detached economic entities. This, of course, has also been the traditional stand of American labor, and Eisenberg believes that it should stay that way. He cites Professor Detlev Vagts that "Most American commentators find a system in which management and labor bargain as representatives of conflicting interests less likely to produce pressures and conflicts" (pp. 139–40). Eisenberg concludes that the major shareholders should control the boards of large corporations. In other words, he positions himself at "restore it."

Eisenberg's arguments are based on the traditional view of the corporation. He disregards the conflict between social and economic goals and turns a blind eye to the broader questions of power raised by the activists. For example, in discussing labor representation on the board, Eisenberg refers to the danger of short-run interests which "will often severely conflict with the long-run interests of the enterprise" (p. 139). As if these long-run interests are (a) given, (b) fixed, and (c) purely economic. In other words, to Eisenberg there is no question that the corporation has goals, and these are economic; the corporation is not a social institution. While Eisenberg endorses the view that "political gangsterism would destroy efficiency," others are trying to say that widespread representation would build social responsibility. Nevertheless, Eisenberg does raise some valid technical problems associated with broadening the legal power base of the corporation, notably those of election procedures and power distribution in the case of vaguely defined interest groups.

THE EUROPEAN DEBATE: WORKER REPRESENTATION   European attempts to broaden the legal power base of the corporation have proceeded along very different lines. There the focus has been on one special interest group—the employees. This, of course, eliminates the technical problems of elections and representation; as Eisenberg himself notes, "There is readily at hand a principle for allocating labor's votes—one per employee" (p. 139). As a result of this, as well as an earlier start and a weaker free enterprise ideology, European proponents of "democratize it" have had much greater success in broadening the representation on the corporate board.

In Europe, the issue of board representation has been treated as one of power and democracy, not one of efficiency. McNulty (1975) is one of the few to articulate this perspective in an American management publication. He argues that because management has been left "unaccountable to any effective constituency" (p. 579), it should be held responsible to the employees, those who possess a kind of property right in the corporation by virtue of their personal contribution to it. Management's legitimacy would then be democratic rather than autocratic. As in government, authority in the corporation would rest on the consent of the governed. Such a view "recognizes the legitimate interest of all employees in formulating corporate goals in terms analogous to Rousseau's general will" (p. 587).

Yugoslavia is the most advanced European nation in this regard, having used worker representation "as a means of legitimizing the retreat from a centralized to a market economy" (Strauss and Rosenstein 1970, p. 172). There, since the 1950s, business enterprises (except for tiny ones) are in effect owned by the workers themselves, who elect the managers: ". . . social ownership must not be confused with State ownership. . . . [In the latter], a business organization is the property of the society as a whole and is administered by a State Agency[;] in Yugoslavia the ownership right or, precisely, the right to management, rests with the workers of that organization" (Kralj 1976–77, p. 9).

In Western Europe, German law has traditionally been the most far-reaching,[4] although other governments have moved toward it and even the

[4]Strauss and Rosenstein suggest some reasons for German leadership on this issue:

> . . . managers saw it as a means of protecting their plants from Allied dismantling immediately after the war, unionists viewed it as a means of preventing the re-establishment of a management-controlled nationalist party, while Catholic liberals found it consistent with papal encyclicals. (Cynically, one might add that the SDP leaders may have perceived support of participation as a means of preserving their credentials as socialists while at the same time abandoning the class struggle and nationalization as political objectives.) (1970, p. 172).

German proponents of worker representation used the following slogan: "Capitalism = freedom − equality; communism = equality − freedom; codetermination = fraternity + freedom + equality" (Bergmann 1975, p. 29).

Common Market has considered laws of representative democracy for all of its member nations. "Co-determination" or "Mitbestimmung" in Germany can be traced back to 1834 when consultative works councils were first proposed, and 1881 when they were first instituted.[5] During World War I, all industrial corporations with more than fifty employees were required by law to have them. After the war, the constitution of the Weimar Republic called for "2 employee representatives (out of at least 6) on the supervisory boards [boards of directors in the American sense] of large corporations; and participation of the worker councils in personal and social, and consultation in economic matters" (Bergmann 1975, p. 20). This, however, did not satisfy the labor leaders, one of whom referred to the regulation as the "fig leaf of capitalism" (p. 20). A new law was passed in 1951 "after much trade union agitation," which gave the workers of the larger mining and steel companies equal representation with the shareholders (hence co-determintation), and this was broadened by a law passed in 1976 to apply to most large German corporations.

Essentially, as described by Agthe (1977), worker representatives on the supervisory board include, depending on the size of the corporation, two or three directors named by the unions, and four to seven elected by the employee delegates, themselves elected. The latter directors include blue-collar, "ordinary" white-collar, and "supervising or managing" white-collar representatives, according to their proportions in the firm, with a minimum of one of each, and all of them employees of the firm. The shareholders elect an equal number of representatives, although they "retain a certain, though minor, predominance because managing employee representatives are considered to be employer oriented" (p. 10).[6] (No member of what the Germans call the management board—a lower-level board similar to the American executive committee, except that its membership and terms of office are formalized and must include a labor (personnel) manager—can serve on the supervisory board.) Figure 27-1 shows a typical board for corporations with between ten and twenty thousand employees. A reading of some of the clauses of the 1976 law gives the impression of highly legalistic procedures, the formal governance of the German corporation having become somewhat like that of the nation-state.

According to a review of the European experience by Garson (1977), the German approach has become the model for other European nations, replacing what he calls the "voluntaristic" approach in Scandinavia and the "leftist-dominated" ones in France and Italy. The Swedes, in experiments carried out in Volvo and some other firms, emphasized voluntary "labor-management

[5]These were bodies by which the opinions of representatives elected by the workers could be heard by managers, although they were later given more tangible powers, as we shall see farther on in this chapter.

[6]The general act of 1976 went beyond that of 1951 (still applying to the coal and steel industries), which included no representative of the managers. Moreover, the 1976 act provides for a chairman—who can break tie votes—elected by a two-thirds vote of the directors, or failing that, his selection by the shareholder representatives. The 1951 act provides for a neutral chairman agreeable to both groups, and gives the worker representatives the power to elect the labor (personnel) manager.

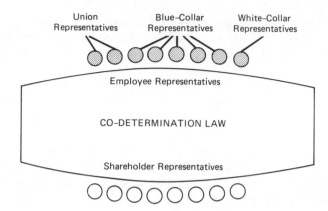

Figure 27-1. *Worker Representation on the Board, "Co-determination" (the 16-member board of directors for German firms with between 10,000 and 20,000 employees [from Agthe, 1977, p. 7])*

cooperation" in shop floor relations and communication with the higher management. But these experiments—claimed to be a necessary response to high absenteeism and labor shortage—did not spread, and reviews of them "show they tend to become encapsulated and stagnant because of unwillingness to democratize higher levels of the power structure of the enterprise" (p. 67). As a result, the unions came to support co-determination, and legislation in 1972 brought worker representatives onto corporate boards. Norway followed suit. In France and Italy, the left-wing unions traditionally opposed co-determination. They preferred confrontation with the management, not what they believed to be cooptation through the acceptance of managerial responsibilities in the context of the existing power system. Yet both nations have moved increasingly toward co-determination.[7] Finally, the European Economic Community itself discussed a law of co-determination, which provided "one-third worker representation, one-third shareholder representation, and one-third public members co-opted by both sides" (p. 72). But Garson believes that may well be the limit. "The compromise model hammered out by the EEC...may well prove to be the maximum extent of industrial democracy that will be attained in most European countries in this century" (p. 77). In fact, that law never went through, although new ones were being discussed as this book went to press.

THE EFFECTS OF REPRESENTATIVE DEMOCRACY ON THE FUNCTIONING OF THE CORPORATION   What effect does the addition of the representatives of con-

[7]Ironically, the American labor unions have traditionally taken a similar stand on co-determination, coming to it from a totally different political philosophy. They have always preferred the negotiation of equals to the cooperation of partners, in other words, a "contractual basis" of participation rather than a "legal basis" (Dachler and Wilpert 1978, p. 10). Does the European experience suggest that co-determination may be on its way to America despite that stand? The bargaining of his way onto the board of the Chrysler Corporation by the head of the autoworkers union may be indicative of things to come.

stituencies other than the shareholders or the management have on the corporation? The evidence for worker representation at least seems clear.

Bergmann (1975) summarizes the criticisms of co-determination as follows: ". . . it leads to a politicization of technical questions, increases bureaucratization, hampers entrepreneurial drive, dilutes responsibilities, delays decisions, and endangers the unity and flexibility of management," not to mention that it "is incompatible with the free market system and existing property rights" (p. 27). In the light of all this, it is interesting to find in Bergmann's analysis that the actual effects of co-determination have been minor and not harmful to the economic interests of the corporation. Bergmann sums up the German changes as having had "no revolutionary effect": "They did not bring about a New Society, nor have they led to socialism, nor have they fulfilled the hopes for true industrial democracy, nor have they changed significantly the working conditions of the individual worker" (p. 23).

In mining and steel, where the experience with co-determination has been the longest and the form of it the most advanced, voting splits have been rare, with financial and technical questions left to the management while the employee representatives have had more freedom of action in wage and welfare matters. In Bergmann's view, this has amounted to a check on management rather than joint management, and has not impaired managerial effectiveness. Furthermore, middle and lower management has been ignored, and paternalism has not disappeared (". . . now we have a joint employer-union paternalism" [p. 24]). The ordinary worker, aside from the few representatives among the thousands, is no better off and is apparently not even very interested in the issue. "Many workers in the steel industry are not even aware of co-determination" (p. 29).

These conclusions are supported widely. In a review of the studies of worker participation in at least eight countries in Europe, Asia, and the Middle East, Strauss and Rosenstein (1970) find that "in practice it has had only spotty success" (p. 171). In general, the worker's representatives have really been interested only in decisions that affect the workers directly, notably those of personnel and welfare.

> It has not brought power and influence to the ordinary worker; nor has it unleashed workers' creativity or even actively involved the leadership in making production decisions. The division of labor between decision-makers and those who carry out decisions has not been abolished. . . . Understandably, small changes in the formal structure at the top have not changed the meaning of the work at the bottom. (pp. 187–88)

Kralj (1976–77), in discussing the Yugoslav experience very much from the party line, claims that the workers are "directly involved" in decision making: "Decisions are no longer made at the top; they are only integrated and co-ordinated there, in the joint interest" (p. 13). Only!

One thing the empirical evidence makes clear is that representative democracy is most decidedly not participative democracy. Workers may sit on the boards, but that does not enable them to make the key decisions. In fact, worker representation seems to have the effect of *weakening* internal participation, by strengthening the hand of top management at the expense of other inside groups. Its effect has been "to bypass middle management, to weaken the staff function, and to inhibit the development of professionalism" (Strauss and Rosenstein 1970, p. 186; see also Bergmann 1975).

As we have seen throughout this book, when a constituency is dispersed, it becomes passive, and power focuses on those able to take command at some center of authority or communication. This is Michels's message when he writes: "Who says organization, says oligarchy" (1915, p. 401). As we saw in Chapter 19 in our discussion of the Closed System, the fact that an individual in a large system gets to choose a representative periodically does not bring him any closer to participation in decision making. This is shown symbolically in Figure 27–2: giving the worker the power to vote for someone way up above, whose influence must pass through all of the layers of the impersonal bureaucracy before it finally reaches him, understandably does not excite him. He remains remote from the real center of power. In fact, evidence from the laboratory of the social psychologist suggests that this form of democracy can serve in counterproductive ways (Mulder 1971): given differences in knowledge, the greater the participation, the greater the power differences between members! "More participation enabled the more powerful to use their influence more effectively" (p. 34).

One thing worker representation almost certainly does do—as we noted in our description of the German co-determination laws—is to force in more rules and regulations, more formalization. In other words, it drives the corporation closer to a structure of Machine Bureaucracy (Garson 1977, p. 75).[8] And that has the effect of robbing managers lower in the hierarchy of their power—of institutionalizing it, as discussed in the *Structuring* book—and concentrating more of it at the top of the hierarchy. These kinds of rules make the workers as a collectivity less subordinate to their immediate supervisors; they enable the workers, officially at least, to bypass their supervisors to reach the senior managers directly.

To summarize, while managers have been heard to express the fear that "democratize it" will "politicize it," the evidence seems to suggest, instead, that it "bureaucratizes it" and "centralizes it."

Ironically, there is evidence that representative democracy may not even solve the problem of social responsiveness, the issue that brought us to this discussion in the first place. Hoover et al. (1978) asked the top executives of thirty-two firms in Yugoslavia—all worker owned—and thirty-five in Peru—where worker representatives shared the seats on the board with shareholder representatives—to rank six sets of goals. "Social contribution" came out last

[8]Garson argues from this conclusion that representative democracy may serve to inhibit experimentation in workplace participation, rendering the experiments "exercises in sociotechnical engineering rather than . . . catalysts for or stepping stones toward broader democratization of the enterprise" (p. 76).

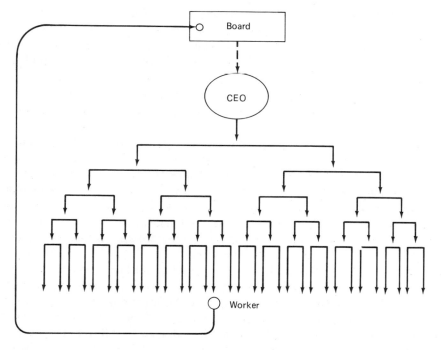

Figure 27–2. *Worker Representation as "Corporate Democracy" (after a fashion)*

by far in Peru, and second to last in Yugoslavia, behind, in order of ranking, production, economic development, technological leadership (these two tied in Yugoslavia), profitability (in Peru only, this was last in Yugoslavia), and employment. In other words, economic goals seem to remain foremost in the minds even of managers who report to worker-directors. And so, like "nationalize it," "democratize it" does not appear to offer a basic solution to the problem of social responsiveness. We must continue around our horseshoe, toward the right, in search of solutions.

One can, in fact imagine cases where representative democracy could aggravate the problem of social responsiveness. An all-worker board in a monopoly, for example, could lead to severe exploitation of the customers, as the worker-directors vote their colleagues even larger salary increases, unimpeded by market forces. Thus Goyder warns: ". . . the consumers' voice must be heard within the company wherever monopoly or oligopoly . . . has reduced or removed the consumers' first and natural protection of a competitive market" (quoted in Mitchell, 1976, p. 53). The danger of worker control of the board is that it can take the corporation farther into the confines of the Closed System power configuration, the only change being a larger share of the pie going to the workers themselves. Alternately, of course, an all-customer board could make life miserable for those workers who have no options, by cutting production costs at the expense of salaries or safety precautions. The all-government board, as we saw in "nationalize it," poses similar dangers.

All of this suggests that if there is to be representative democracy, no one group alone should be represented. Nor should there be a blanket formula for representation, as is dictated by the co-determination laws in Europe. Rather, the representation should be tailored to the situation—an approach known in management as "contingency theory." Industry is probably the most important factor here. We might expect, for example, a greater proportion of customer representatives on the boards of utilities, or of worker representatives on the boards of competitive mass production firms.

This leaves the technical problem of how to select the representatives. While, as noted earlier, a ready formula is available for selecting workers, since they are a well-defined constituency, none is evident for most other groups. Yet, as the example of Prudential Insurance on page 548 shows, such problems are never so complicated as they seem once they are approached with a constructive attitude and a little bit of imagination.

We have delayed the most important question for last. Given the evidence of its effects, why should we even bother to consider this form of "democratize it" further? Because there is other evidence, of different effects, which supports representative democracy even from a management and an economic perspective. German Chancellor Helmut Schmidt told a visiting British Commission charged with recommending proposals on industrial democracy that "the key to his country's post-war economic miracle was its sophisticated system of workers' participation" (quoted in Garson 1977, p. 63). While no one can prove this statement, it is certainly undisputable that co-determination cannot have done the German economy much harm. As even the *U.S. News and World Report* noted:

> To date, the European experience with co-determination has not borne out the worst predictions of its detractors. As one international labor expert in Geneva put it: "Co-determination has not prevented Germany from becoming Europe's leading industrial power and the wealthiest nation in Europe." (May 10, 1976)

How might representative democracy help economic efficiency? One possible answer relates to its form rather than its substance. Specifically, representative democracy gives an air of legitimacy to the governance of the corporation. Groups over which the corporation exercises power are given formal rights in the control of it. Worker control of the boards in Yugoslavia, for example, may not have democratized the daily workings of the firms, but at least it might have given the workers the feeling that they are working for themselves. What we are saying is that worker representative democracy may strengthen slightly the organization's internal ideology, and thereby drive it somewhat toward the Missionary configuration with a corresponding improvement in productivity. But as we shall see later, the improvements that can be attributed to this are likely to be small.

There have, however, been substantive benefits as well. Co-determination has opened channels of communication between workers and managers, which "has spurred employers to pay more attention to the human side of enterprise" and has made managers "somewhat less authoritarian" (Bergmann 1975, p. 23). Managers can more easily come to know the needs of the workers. For their part, German unions claim the benefits of "greater access to management information, considerable influence over working conditions and social and personnel policies, and a foothold aiding the spread of unionism into unorganized enterprises" (Garson 1977, p. 63). (This last point might best explain the German unions' support of co-determination.) Most importantly perhaps—and the factor that may best explain the relationship between co-determination and economic growth in Germany—is the sense of cooperation and understanding that this two-way flow of information between managers and workers can engender. Disputes that might otherwise spill into a public arena can sometimes be settled quietly in the boardroom.

American observers have, on the whole, been hostile to representative forms of corporate democracy, especially co-determination. From his own poll and one conducted by the *Harvard Business Review*, Krishnan (1974) finds that a majority of the American business executives surveyed

> . . .do not take the view that employees should have the right to participate, through the democratic process, in making organizational decisions. They do not even favor allowing employees direct input to the decision making process through direct access to the top policy making body or presentation of their viewpoints to the chief executive, except when the nature of the problem is such that the traditional managerial prerogatives will in no way be affected. (1974, p. 346)

A president of General Electric referred to co-determination as "meaning union usurption of managerial authority" (Jones 1977*b*, p. 5), while Peter Drucker, ignoring the other side of the power argument altogether, claims the new representatives

> . . .cannot function as board members. Their role is to represent this or that outside group, this or that special interest. Their role must be to make demands on top management and to push special projects, special needs, and special policies. They cannot be concerned with, or responsible for, the enterprise. Nor should they be expected to hold in confidence what they hear at board meetings; in fact their trust is not to the enterprise but to their constituents outside. (1973, pp. 630–31)

As if the corporation must always remain a system unto itself, closed to external influence.

Yet we have seen that representative democracy has relatively little impact on decision making, if anything strengthening the hand of top management and possibly even promoting greater harmony as well. So perhaps all of this resistance is misplaced, an unwillingness to adapt and face new realities. One wonders, for example, if the telephone company might not be better off to negotiate rates with its customers in the confines of its boardroom, rather than having to face them at public hearings every year.

Ultimately, representative democracy provides the corporation with the legitimacy it often lacks, yet seems to do little harm to the power of its senior managers or even to its Closed System nature. The main reason is simply that the board of directors is hardly the place to exercise close control of corporate decision making, especially, as we saw in Chapter 6, when the constituency represented there is widely dispersed. The board does have certain official powers, notably the appointment of the chief executive officer. But the directors do not manage the corporation, or more exactly, if they do they cease to represent those who elected them (as has happened in the case of the labor managers in Germany, according to Bergmann 1975, p. 24).

The problem is one of commitment and involvement. If the directors are full time, as noted above, they lose identification with their constituents. The director who spends all of his working hours in that capacity is no longer a worker, or a consumer, or whatever; he is a manager. That is his primary identification. And the director who is part time—who, for example, must spend most of his time working in the factory alongside those he represents—is no match for the manager when it comes to control of strategic decision making. As we noted in Chapter 6, the senior manager devotes all of his time to these matters. In the process, he hones the requisite skills—not only to make decisions but also to gather and assimilate the requisite information, to convince and negotiate, and so on. The part-time director, lacking the necessary time, information, and skills, cannot easily challenge the manager and so tends to be easily coopted by him.[9] Even in Yugoslavia, in the worker councils at the plant level, "the evidence suggests that management dominates the proceedings. It does most of the talking, initiates most of the action, and . . . is seen as exercising most influence within the council. Indeed the existence of the council seems to have made little difference in the perceived distribution of influence" (Strauss and Rosenstein 1970, p. 185).

As for the commitment and involvement of the constituents themselves, they are remote from their representatives. As we tried to show symbolically in Figure 27–2, the single worker among thousands who gets to elect a representative to sit on top of a hierarchy, the weight of which he eventually feels through many layers of managers, hardly considers himself in control of his destiny.

---

[9]The "professional" director—an individual who works full time, perhaps on behalf of some constituency, on just a few boards (few enough to become well informed about each, but not so few that he risks full cooptation)—may be a possible compromise solution. One possible danger, however, is the lack of identification with the constituency. (Can anyone who is not a worker properly represent workers?) Only time and experience with this option will tell.

The problem, as we shall see in the next section, is fundamentally one of structure, and cannot be resolved by the election of a few representatives.

That is presumably why study after study of workers in enterprises with representative democracy find them apathetic and disinterested, often even unaware of their "privilege." (In these ways they are no different from the shareholders of the widely held corporation.) In Germany, for example, "it has been found that although about three quarters of workers knew that co-determination had been introduced into their enterprise only half of the interviewed workers had any concrete ideas about the actual meaning of co-determination" (Archbold 1978, p. 58).[10] Child (1975) finds that even in such an egalitarian and socialistically minded society as Israel, in a plant employing only four hundred people, "Worker representatives are not able any more to keep in close contact with their constituents on the shop floor. In practice, these representatives tend to speak for a relatively small group of elite, older workers. Newer workers are not effectively represented" (p. 19). And Blumberg echoes the same conclusion in the case of customers:

> The desirability of adding consumer directors to the board receives little support from the history of the consumer-owned enterprises in the country, such as the mutual insurance companies owned by policyholders or the mutual savings banks owned by depositors. These consumer-owned companies invariably involve self-perpetuating boards and have not demonstrated a discernible degree of concern for consumers that differs from the attitudes of their stockholder-owned competitors. (1974, pp. 118–19)

In co-determination, the unions seem to have been the ones to move into the new directorships, converting would-be democratization of the Internal Coalition into representation for members of the External Coalition instead.[11] That shifts the power play to one between the oligarchies of union chiefs and managers, with the workers off to the side, little better off than before.

Thus, representative democracy may be a convenient way to broaden the legal power base of the corporation—the board, as we noted at the outset, is the most obvious place to begin—but in the final analysis it makes little difference in the actual distribution of power or in what decisions get made. That is why attention has turned somewhat to the possibilities for participatory democracy.

[10]Mulder claims that co-determination has been "promoted primarily by the intellectual" and that even the "Yugoslav laborers never asked for workers' self-government...but they received [it]...as a gift from the academicians" (1971, p. 35).

[11]Bergmann (1975, p. 29) notes that although only 31 percent of the total German work force was unionized, 70 percent of the 10,000 labor representatives on the boards of directors were union members. In iron and steel, 490 out of the 500 labor representatives and all of the 80 labor managers were union members. (But then again, so were more than half of the members of the German Parliament.)

PARTICIPATORY DEMOCRACY
OF THE CORPORATION

Let us consider first the participation of workers in the decision making of the corporation, since they already hold positions inside of it. Then let us turn to the participation of representatives of groups external to the corporation.

PARTICIPATION OF THE WORKERS IN DECISION MAKING   When the French talk of "auto-gestion," some of them at least seem to have in mind a grass-roots, internal democracy in which the workers would participate in decision making and would also elect the managers (who would then become more administrators than bosses). In this way, top-down hierarchy of authority would become bottom-up participatory democracy. Yet the proposals are generally vague, and we have come across no example of a large corporation—not even one owned by workers or a union[12]—that has achieved anything close to this.

Participatory democracy need not, of course, be an all or nothing arrangement. One can imagine partial forms of it, that would give the workers limited formal powers in decision making. For example, only specific decisions might be included, and over those, only the power to be consulted or to authorize and veto, as opposed to the actual choice. The works council is one example of partial participation already mentioned. Originally set up within German plants to allow management to consult workers' representatives on proposed actions, they gradually gained veto power over decisions related to working hours, vacation, schedules, various wage issues, vocational training, welfare programs, and accident policies. They also received the legal right to be consulted on actions leading to changes in worker assignments and jobs and to be informed on all major changes that could affect the workers (Bergmann 1975; Agthe 1977).

The evidence on the direct use of these powers, however, appears to be similar to what we saw earlier. The representatives tend to be uninformed and so the managers do the talking (75 percent in one study) and the initiating, the workers tending to show interest only in those issues that effect them directly in the short run (Mulder 1971). Nevertheless, the councils have obviously had their indirect influence—probably more so than the boards because of their proximity to the workers and their needs—primarily in serving to check implicitly some changes that management might have otherwise tried to make.

A far less ambitious form of participatory democracy—better referred to as "judicial" form in our view—is that discussed by Crozier (1964), where the workers have been able to force in rules, such as promotion by seniority, to delimit the power of managers over them. As Crozier describes it, the workers

[12]Agthe claims that in companies owned by the Federation of German Unions, "the union clearly has the upper hand. Co-determination changes nothing for the workers of such companies" (1977, p. 12).

end up being less at the mercy of arbitrary decisions by their supervisors, but at the expense of a structure that is more bureaucratic and centralized. The relationship between worker and supervisor becomes impersonal, while the decision-making power moves up the hierarchy, to a level where discretion can still be exercised. The lower-level managers lose power but the workers do not gain it. Both are locked into the same straitjacket. It is the top managers who come out ahead, just as they do in the case of representative democracy.

There is one other form of participation worth mentioning here, but only to ensure that it is not confused with democratization. That is so-called "participative management," which has been very popular in the United States and, as we saw earlier, in Sweden too for a time. In this case, management takes the initiative in involving workers in decision making. This is not democracy because democracy depends on no one's generosity; power is distributed constitutionally. In democracy, rights are not granted—nor can they be revoked—by certain individuals. They are defined within the legal system.

THE FUTILE SEARCH FOR WORKER PARTICIPATORY DEMOCRACY   Why has worker participative democracy attained so little real success? One could, of course, argue that it is simply too early to judge, that works councils barely represent a beginning. But there is reason to believe that true participatory democracy by the workers will never be attained because the problem lies in the nature of the work and the design of the structure, not in the distribution of power.

In the *Structuring* book, we described five basic configurations of structure (Mintzberg 1979a). Only two of these approach democratic ideals—Professional Bureaucracy and Adhocracy, the two forms of what we have called Meritocracy in this book. Both do so because the complexity of their work requires extensive delegation of decision-making power to experts, in one case who work alone, in the other who work and share power in groups. Figure 27–3 shows a symbolic representation of participatory democracy in Professional Bureaucracy, where a good deal of the power rests with individual professionals, from whom it flows up into the administrative structure. (See Figure 22–3 on page 394.) In the other three structural configurations—Simple Structure, Machine Bureaucracy, and the Divisionalized Form—because the work is relatively simple, no such extensive delegation is necessary. Quite the contrary, in fact. These structures need tight forms of coordination, ones that can only be achieved by an administrative apparatus, consisting of the chief executive, line managers, and/or staff analysts. This has been demonstrated even in laboratory experiments. Guetzkow and Simon (1954–55) found that when assigned simple, repetitive tasks, leaderless groups with flexible channels of communication tended naturally to organize themselves into hierarchies to structure their work, their communication flows, and their power relationships.

Now, were it democratization of Adhocracy or Professional Bureaucracy people wanted, there would be little problem. But that is not the issue. The

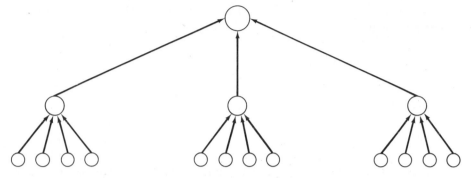

Figure 27–3. *Participatory Democracy in the Professional Bureaucracy*

proponents of participatory democracy are not lobbying for changes in universities or research laboratories. It is the giant mass producers they are after, in other words the Machine Bureaucracies (often grouped into Divisionalized Forms).[13] And these are precisely the organizations in which the need for tight administrative control and coordination is paramount. Here is where the efforts of thousands of workers producing single integrated products must be coordinated by technocratic standards. And participative democracy—in which, at the limit, everyone gets a shot at every decision—hardly encourages such coordination.

The myriad of decisions associated with producing an automobile at the Renault works on Ile Sequin near Paris cannot be made by autonomous work groups, each one doing as it pleases. The whole car must fit together by the end of the assembly line. These decisions require a highly sophisticated system of bureaucratic coordination. That is the main reason why automobile firms are structured into rigid hierarchies of authority. It is not because their managers lust for power (although lust for power some of them no doubt do). And that is why mass producers inevitably end up as oligarchies, not democracies, and why Kralj's comment that decisions in Yugoslavian enterprises "are no longer made at the top" but "only integrated and coordinated there" (1976–77, p. 13) is so amusing.

The need for such coordination precludes serious participatory democracy, restricting it to works councils that can veto specific kinds of decisions, ones that directly affect the mass of workers, not individual ones. This too is the reason why attention has been focused on representative democracy. From the workers' point of view, if democracy cannot be approached in substance, perhaps it can at least be achieved in form. Or, from the viewpoint of external

[13]A sixth structural configuration, discussed at length in this book but only hinted at in the one on structuring, is the Missionary. But it too is hardly the scene of the battle. Missionaries, as noted in Chapter 21, tend to be found in smaller organizations, not typically in mass production. Moreover their workers are highly motivated and already consider themselves involved. It is the large impersonal organization, mostly devoid of ideology and identification and characterized instead by alienation, that emerges as the prime battleground.

interest groups, perhaps the Machine Bureaucracies can be rendered society's Instruments, instead of being allowed to continue as Closed System. Blau and Scott describe the basic dilemma of the two forms of democracy. They do so in reference to what they call the commonweal organizations (such as fire departments), but their comments apply equally to the giant mass production corporations:

> The issue... is that of external democratic control—the public must possess the means of controlling the ends served by these organizations. While external democratic control is essential, the internal structure of these organizations is expected to be bureaucratic, governed by the criterion of efficiency, and not democratic.... (Internal democratic control by the membership might well be at the expense of efficiency and thus lessen the organization's ability to effect the democratic will of the community.) (1962, p. 55)

To add to the problem, ironically, representative democracy does not diminish the level of Machine Bureaucracy, the main block to participatory democracy—and the main reason for wanting it. Rather, it increases the level, making substantive participation even more elusive. As we have seen, the addition of worker directors through representative democracy—even the imposition of rules through what we have called judicial democracy—serves, at the expense of worker and client alike, to further centralize and formalize the structure. And these are the two chief characteristics of Machine Bureaucracy. Our large organizations seem to have us caught in a vicious circle.

PLURALISTIC PARTICIPATION IN DECISION MAKING   Of course, workers need not be the only group involved in decision making. Others—external influencers—can gain the right to participate as well. Thus, self-proclaimed "corporate activist" Philip Moore, Executive Director of the Project on Corporate Responsibility in the United States, commented in 1974:

> ... it is obvious why the thrust of any change must be in terms of structure—the way the corporations run. People have got to have access to decision making to express their concerns and to influence policies that affect their lives....
>
> What is required is a shift of accountability from management to the people affected by corporate decisions. We need a system of corporate governance by which affected people control decisions....
>
> We need a constitution that defines the internal process by which corporations work... (1974, pp. 53, 55)

Moore's proposals are rather vague on this point. But we can imagine at least two ways in which the internal decision processes of corporations could be made accessible to outsiders. One is what was earlier referred to as planting a representative, where a group of external influencers names one of its own people to a position inside the corporation. If the German steel workers can appoint the labor (personnel) managers, so too presumably could an American consumer group appoint product safety managers and conservation groups appoint environmental protection managers. Of course, creating and staffing such positions would neither ensure acceptance and cooperation by the other managers of the firm, nor guarantee against cooptation of the planted manager (as has in fact happened with the labor managers in Germany, according to Bergmann [1975]). But the overall influence on the social responsiveness of the corporation might be positive.

A second approach, perhaps more effective in this regard, would be the direct participation of representatives of external groups on certain decision-making committees in the corporation. This, of course, is hardly a new idea in the public sector, where task forces named to deal with social issues frequently involve representatives of affected groups along side civil servants. When the corporation must make a decision that will profoundly affect some outside groups, giving that group the legal right to participate in the decision-making process might make some sense. The law already recognizes such rights in the collective bargaining process, where management cannot impose wage settlements unilaterally but must instead share its decision-making powers with the representatives of the workers. And most observers today would agree that this has helped the managers as well as the workers. Rather than having to confront a powerful group publicly with a fait accompli, management can work out the conflicts before the decisions are made. Might not the same advantages accrue to the firm by extending this practice?

Given the increasing pressures from consumer and environmental groups, among others, it may in fact be in management's best interests to have representatives of such groups serve on the committees that reach certain decisions in the first place. Consumers could serve on certain new product committees, environmentalists and representatives of local communities on committees concerned with the design of new plants. This would certainly take more management time and effort in decision making, but it might lead to a great deal less time and effort devoted to the execution (and protection) of decisions already made. Indeed, not all such participation need result in the hard-nosed bargaining of labor-management relations, although that would not necessarily be a bad thing. One can also imagine committees of insiders and outsiders working harmoniously to develop more socially responsive corporate decisions.

These are only two possibilities. But they do suggest that with the application of a little effort and good will, the inner workings of the corporation could be opened up to the participation of outside groups, to the benefit of both sides. Again, we should not expect a great deal of interest group participation, nothing close to what could reasonably be called participatory democracy, for reasons already stated. The need for coordination of decision making will remain paramount if the corporation is to remain viable. But we should expect some useful changes.

To conclude, there are a great many ways to think about democratizing the corporation. Some involve representative democracy, others participatory democracy; some focus on a single "unenfranchised" group, namely the workers, others on a host of groups, such as consumers, environmentalists, and so on. All of the proposals to involve them pose problems, including who should be represented, in what numbers, by what means, chosen by whom, and ensured by what. "We now move to a community ethic, without that community being, as yet, wholly defined" (Bell 1971, p. 32). Some proposals raise problems of efficiency and the effective achievement of the corporation's mission. Any reasonable degree of participatory democracy, in particular, may prove incompatible with the kind of coordination most large corporations require. Certain changes can be pursued only so far until the corporation becomes a plague on everybody's house, client and worker and manager alike.

However, the opposite problem must be also recognized by the opponents of democratization: that the corporation as presently constituted is felt to be a plague on some houses, notably the powerless over whom the corporation has a great deal of power. As Kenneth Arrow has noted, "Authority is undoubtedly a necessity for successful achievement of an organization's goals, but it will have to be responsible either to some form of constitutionally planned review and exposure or to irregular and fluctuating tides of disobedience" (1974, p. 79). In our terms, the less "democratize it" succeeds, the more we shall see of "pressure it." Our discussion has suggested that feasible options do exist. While hardly achieving true democratization of the corporation, they can increase its legitimacy, give some power to those who see themselves as disenfranchised, and sometimes strengthen its social goals as well. Yet they do surprisingly little harm to the functioning of the corporation as an economic entity.

The search for democracy in our corporations is not just an incidental exercise. It is not, like many of the other positions around our horseshoe, a search simply to solve the problem of corporate social responsiveness. Nor does it represent some kind of subversion of free institutions. Quite the contrary. That search is a reflection of the fundamental belief that a society cannot call itself free if its most powerful institutions do not come under democratic controls. And so the search must go on, as Michels argued more than half a century ago:

> The peasant in the fable, when on his death-bed, tells his sons that a treasure is buried in the field. After the old man's death the sons dig everywhere in order to discover the treasure. They do not find it. But their indefatigable labour improves the soil and secures for them a comparative well-being. The treasure in the fable may well symbolize democracy. Democracy is a treasure which no one will ever discover by deliberate search. But in continuing our search, in labouring indefatigably to discover the indiscoverable, we shall perform a work which will have fertile results in the democratic sense. (1915, p. 405)

There shall have to be a lot more digging in the fields of "democratize it"!

28

"Regulate It"

In theory, regulating the corporation is about as simple as democratizing it is complex. Practice is, of course, another matter. But to the proponents of "regulate it," the corporation can be made responsive to social needs by having its decisions or actions subjected to the controls of a higher authority. Specifically, government imposes formal constraints on the corporation and backs them up with the power of the judicial system or of special regulatory agencies. These constraints are imposed from the outside, while the internal governance of the corporation, as well as its ownership, are left alone. Hence "regulate it" takes us an important step closer to the center of our horseshoe, leaving the politics of the more radical left behind.

THE EMERGING ROLE OF GOVERNMENT
IN THE REGULATION OF THE CORPORATION

Organizations have, of course, been regulated for as long as anyone cares to trace their history. The Code of Hammurabi, four thousand years ago, provided guidelines for Babylonian merchants and peddlers (Kast and Rosenzweig, 1974, p. 28), while regulations concerning products spread in Medieval Europe and proliferated during the Renaissance: "Between the thirteenth and sixteenth centuries, when this development reached its peak, all the major trades and industries were subject to detailed regulations. Rules in Barcelona in 1330, for instance, specified the exact number of rivets to be put in breastplates" (Nader 1980, p. 5).

American regulation as we know it really began in the late 1880s when antisocial actions of many industrialists—specifically the creation of trusts with enormous monopolistic powers—"created much public dissatisfaction with the business system" and led to the Interstate Commerce Act of 1887 and the Sherman Antitrust Act of 1890 (Kast and Rosenzweig 1974, p. 85). The latter in particular "set the groundwork for the view that the government should regulate business in the public interest" (p. 36). The depression of the 1930s gave birth to the theories of John Maynard Keynes, who "questioned the foundation of the classical economic doctrine of laissez faire, whereby the market mechanism and price system would automatically adjust to an equilibrium point for full utilization of resources and employment" (p. 37). Keynes had the Depression as his evidence that equilibrium could be reached despite massive unemployment. Hence he argued that "it was necessary . . . to have an external force provide the balancing mechanism—this force was the government" (p. 37). The result in America was the New Deal, which brought major government intervention in the economy. Essentially, the state emerged as the chief countervailing power to the corporation, "perhaps the major peacetime function of the federal government" (Galbraith 1952, p. 142). Since that time, government intervention in all aspects of economic activity increased rapidly, especially during World War II and the 1960s and early 1970s (although the pendulum did begin to swing back in some areas in the late 1970s):

> . . .social demands, which previously had been voiced in the press or on the streets, were gradually converted into regulations at local, state, and federal levels. Environmental protection legislation progressed particularly rapidly in this regard. Regulatory activity was also apparent in equal employment, occupational health and safety, consumer protection, solid waste disposal, and product safety, to name only a few. Some 28 pieces of legislation affecting consumer rights alone were passed from 1966 through 1973. (Ackerman 1975, p. 9)

With many of these pieces of legislation came new government regulatory agencies, so that today the giant corporation faces all kinds of government units probing into its affairs. For example, the *Catalog of Federal Regulations Affecting the Iron and Steel Industry*, published in 1976, "lists 5,600 regulations from twenty-seven different agencies that have some impact on the manufacture of steel," including environmental pollution, worker safety, worker civil rights, industrial relations, antitrust, foreign trade, taxes, energy conservation, and other areas (Madden 1977, p. 52).

In this discussion, we shall take a broad view of "regulate it," including under regulation any formal constraints imposed by government on the corporation to intervene in what it does.[1] Such intervention can take a wide variety of forms, covering a wide variety of issues. For example, "regulate it" is one

---

[1]The Random House Dictionary defines "regulation" as "a rule or order prescribed by authority, as to regulate conduct; a governing direction or law."

means by which "democratize it" is achieved, as we saw in our discussion of the development of co-determination in Germany.

Regulation is probably best suited to controlling externalities, at least where some attribution of cost can be made to specific industries or organizations. In other words, regulation is logically suited to making corporations pay the full costs of their actions, or at least forcing them to reduce those costs. As Edmunds notes, "business is going to reckon the long-run social costs of its decisions, either upon its own assumption or by regulation. A century of regulation tells us that" (1977, p. 43). Thus, if one of its assembly lines drives an automobile worker to mental breakdown, there are those prepared to argue that General Motors should be made to bear the costs of the hospitalization. And Daniel Bell "proposes a new form of what he calls 'total social accounting,' under which we would tot up the costs of a problem such as pollution, and charge each company for its share of causing it, almost like a sewer tax. This is presently done in West Germany, where companies are charged a fee for each ton of waste material they dump in the river Rhine" (from Henderson 1968, p. 84).

More recently, attention has also turned to questions of disclosure and personal liability. It is felt that corporations should be made to reveal more about their activities (e.g., Medawar 1976), for example, to allow access to information on the tests of their product and on their dealings with foreign governments. Others feel that legislation should be enacted to make members of the corporation more personally responsible for its behavior. For example, "there are signs that governmental pressure on directors will increase, that the directors will become more accountable to government than they are now," and that they may be more exposed to personal liability in the courts for neglect of their responsibility to monitor corporate activities (Bacon and Brown 1975, p. 9). More far-reaching are moves to increase the personal responsibility of employees for illegal actions they carry out on behalf of the corporation. While it is true in principle that "A dependent employee cannot escape liability by pleading that he acted in the name of or for the benefit of a corporation," (*Harvard Law Review*, 1979, p. 1259), in practice employees have often been able to hide within the intricacies of the bureaucracy. Traditionally, the corporation not the chemist has produced the dangerous drug, and so the charges have often been civil rather than criminal. "End limited liability" says Joseph Bower, by "the elimination of corporate anonymity" (1974, p. 206).

> Certainly the men who build roads that are unsafe and inadequate, who make drugs that kill, or aeroplanes that crash, ought to bear more individual responsibility for their decisions than is presently the case. (p. 206)

According to one observer, "business executives are honest until immersed in the formlessness of the modern corporation . . . they engage in unethical conduct only after shedding their individuality. Therefore . . . the fog of the 'persona ficta' legal status of the firm" should be cleared away, removing the "broad disclaimers of responsibility for unethical conduct" (Madden 1977, p. 74, referring to Christopher Stone). Ending limited liability would have a profound effect on the corporation, for it would break the chain of formal authority, making employees deep in the hierarchy personally responsible to the public at large.

Singer and Wooton (1976) put this into a broad perspective in their discussion of Albert Speer as manager of the German Third Reich's war production machine. At his Nuremberg trial, in sharp contrast to most of his colleagues, Speer "endorsed the concept of commitment to a 'higher moral authority' and thereby refused to disclaim responsibility for the consequences of his actions. Furthermore, he accepted full responsibility for actions of his associates even though he was not a 'direct' participant in many of their activities" (p. 96).[2] In America, in the past, "there have been few cases where individuals in organizations have been held personally responsible for actions of organizations in which they were employed—in most cases the organization as a collective body was assigned accountability" (p. 96). But recent trials related to bribery and illegal political contributions have begun to change that.

> The move today to make organizations more "socially responsible" is a move to implant the spirit of Nuremberg into the decision-making processes of those organizations. . . . The lesson from Nuremberg is that there is a tremendous potential for human and societal abuses when decision-making processes or organizations are shrouded in collective and moral neutrality. (p. 97)

THE POLITICS OF "REGULATE IT"

What distinguishes the proponents of "regulate it," at the limit, is their belief that only through government intervention can certain behaviors of the corporation be changed, so that more attention will be paid to social goals. As Hazel Henderson notes, for example, the attempts by corporations, as well as individuals and other organizations, to "'externalize' costs from their own balance sheets and push them" elsewhere "inevitably dictates" increasing governments regulation (1977, p. 4). Implicit—and often explicit—in this argument is the belief that corporate management, or at least some corporate managers, cannot be trusted to deal voluntarily with the social consequences of their decisions. And so they must be forced to.

An extreme rendition of this point of view—amounting to a severe attack on business ethics—is expressed by Tumin (1964). Basing his argument on "the

---

[2]There is an important contradiction here. Holding a manager personally responsible for the actions of one of his subordinates puts us right back into the hierarchy, and implicitly reintroduces limited liability for the employee. Ending limited liability will presumably have to mean that responsibility becomes related to knowledge, decision, and action, not position.

principle of least morality"—"'bad' conduct surely drives out 'good' conduct with predictable vigor and speed" (p. 127)—Tumin concludes that business behavior must "sink to that of the least moral participant":

> . . . business conduct is held to be successful when, through intense competition, one contestant secures maximum personal gain in scarce resources, to the detriment and loss of other contestants. While business ideology is not devoid of rules of "decent" conduct in this intense competitive process, such rules are not likely to be very effective if, as must always be expected, one of the contestants, seeking to maximize his chances for winning, departs from the rules. At that point, the other competitors must restrain or expel him from the game, or in self-defense, must be willing to employ the deviant tactics themselves. The temptation to follow the leader in this resort to deviant tactics is apparently very strong. . . .
>
> As a result, one may fairly say that what business stands for, ideologically insists upon, and tries to get adopted as general principles of conduct, run directly against and reduce the chances of evoking affection and love as principles of relationship, identification with an entreprise as a source of voluntary and conscientious labor, and a sense of significant membership in an organization arising out of effective participation in decision-making. . . .
>
> In promoting themes quite inimical to identification, affection and significant membership, business thereby and to that extent tends to bring out, standardize, and reward the most unsocialized impulses of man. (pp. 127, 130)

But one need not go this far to make a case for the regulation of business. The moderate can simply say that competition does not enable the well-intentioned manager to attend to certain social consequences of his decisions. It is, therefore, up to the government to change the rules so that all managers will attend to them on an equal footing. Consider, for example, the case of pollution. A corporate president may know that the exhausts from his factory are causing grave environmental damage. But the installation of pollution abatement equipment may be so expensive that by acting voluntarily, and alone, he might so weaken his firm's competitive position that it could face bankruptcy. He will be able to act as he feels he should only if the government forces all the firms in his industry to install that equipment.

Of course, the logical implication of this argument is that businessmen themselves should be in the forefront of the demand for certain government regulations. They should be lobbying the government with the slogan, "Help us to be more responsible." That would indicate a true concern for social needs, one that reflects their competitive realities. As Peter Drucker has noted:

> Where elimination of an impact requires a restriction, regulation is in the interest of business, and especially in the interest of responsible business. Otherwise it will be penalized as "irresponsible," while the unscrupulous, the greedy, the stupid, and the chiseler cash in. (1973, p. 335)

Some managers have, in fact, taken up this position. The president of Atlantic

Richfield oil company, for example, presented in 1975 his three basic rules for executives:

Rule (1): He should stick to his own competencies....

Rule (2): Within those competencies, become a prime mover for change at the rule-making level, whether it is in national government, regional areas, or states.

Rule (3): Don't fight to preserve the status quo, because there are plenty of others who will do that for you. Fight for constructive changes that will apply to all companies in your industry. In my area of competencies, this would mean that I should fight for the stiffest pollution control laws that are technically and economically feasible. (Bradshaw 1974, pp. 30–31)

And sometimes such words have been turned into actions: "...some months after botulism was found in cans of Bon Vivant soup, resulting in one well-publicized death, the National Canners Association asked the Federal Drug Administration to adopt stricter regulations for the industry" (Ackerman 1975, p. 26).

Unfortunately, however according to evidence presented by Theodore Levitt (1968) in a *Harvard Business Review* article entitled "Why Business Always Loses," that must have been a rare event indeed, brought on by an extreme situation. "Business has not really won or had its way in connection with even a single piece of proposed regulatory or social legislation in the last three-quarters of a century." Rather, "It has placed itself in the unedifying role of contending against legislation which the general public has viewed as liberating, progressive, and necessary. Business has been the perpetual ogre, the bad guy who is against good things" (pp. 82, 81). Levitt, a friend of business, recounts part of the "dismal record of American business's endless series of lost causes" — the Sherman Antitrust Act, the Federal Reserve Act, the Federal Trade Commission Act, the National Park Service Act, the Child Labor Acts, the Securities Exhange Act, the Wagner Act, the Fair Labor Standards Act of 1938, the Old Age and Survivors Insurance Benefits Act, the Federal Housing Acts, the Marshall Plan, the Aid to Dependent Children Act, the Federal Education Act, the Poverty Program, and Medicare. "The computer is programmed to cry wolf" (p. 83). Levitt strengthens his point by noting that much of this legislation has in fact been good for business. It has dissolved the giant trusts, enabled labor unions to emerge as responsible entities, forced disclosure of financial information to create a more honest and effective stock market. Indeed business would not exist without government intervention, even if only to guarantee the enforcement of contract law so that exchanges could be transacted with certainty (McNeil 1978, p. 71).

Yet business has always viewed regulation in almost every form as an encroachment on its freedom, on its right to act without formal constraint. And it continues to. A 1976 survey of 1,200 readers of the *Harvard Business Review* found them "least sanguine about increased governmental regulation: 64 % fear it would have a negative impact and 14 % say it would have none, while only 21 % feel it might be beneficial" (Brenner and Molander 1977, pp. 70–71). There seems little doubt that power factors underlie this stance of business, that managers are not prepared to encourage the opening up of the Closed System power configuration they have enjoyed for so long. How else, for example, could one explain the phenomenon of "associated interests," the notion that

> when a proposed government expansion appears to threaten the unrestricted freedom of certain businesses, it threatens all of business. It follows naturally that other businesses come to the defense of their oppressed brethren.
>
> The Pure Food and Drug Act is a good example. When the food and drug industries were clearly threatened with regulation, the machine tool industry was easily persuaded to denounce it. It felt an associated interest, or a communality of interest, with other businesses threatened by the government. (Levitt 1968, p. 84)

Thus, while the argument that competition impedes attention to social issues naturally evokes sympathy, the knee-jerk resistance of business to government regulations that would help businessmen to help themselves does not. Such resistance is viewed by much of the public as a last-ditch effort to sustain a power system of questionable legitimacy. Citing the results of a 1975 survey of public attitudes, a *Fortune* magazine writer concludes that "More and more people consider businessmen rapacious. . . .[Americans] increasingly believe that businessmen are greedy and indifferent to the human consequences of what they do. . . .'And they see government as the only one who can do something about it.' Thus 62 % want government regulation to be maintained at its current level or expanded" (Weaver 1977, pp. 189–90; quote by executive of advertising agency). Summarizing similar results in another study, Westlin concludes:

> . . .because of general public mistrust of institutional leaders and doubts about the willingness of most of them to renovate their own existing policies, the public looks to law to set minimum standards for business. It believes that the legislative and judicial processes, for all their weaknesses, offer the best available forums for weighing competing interests and setting fair balances. . .(1979, p. 16)

In other words, "regulate it" seems to be the posture of a good deal of the American population (the events of the late 1970s and early 1980s notwithstanding).

"Regulate it," therefore, would seem to have much to commend it. It helps businessmen to help themselves, or, barring that, it confronts business with the countervailing power of government; it can be used to transfer certain externalities back inside the corporation and to pin liability on the persons responsible for misdeeds; moreover, it seems relatively easy to effect and it has wide public support. But what regulation seems and what it is are two different things. "Regulate it" is no panacea for the problem of who should control the corporation, as we shall now see.

THE PROBLEMS WITH "REGULATE IT"

There are at least three major problems with "regulate it" as a means to elicit socially responsive behavior in the corporation.

First, "regulate it" only imposes formal constraints, that is, sets minimum (and usually crude) standards of acceptable behavior. Arrow notes that "it is hard to make regulation flexible enough to meet a wide variety of situations and yet simple enough to be enforceable" (1973, p. 310). This is hardly a devise to deal with nuance, with subtle problems requiring careful interpretation. Regulation is a blunt and clumsy instrument, a kind of meat cleaver rather than a scalpel. The best it can do is impose constraints that are standardized, formalized, and set at minimum level of performance.

As a device of government, regulation is supposed to apply equally to all firms. It cannot differentiate. It must be standardized, therefore, which renders it incapable of dealing with specific, individual problems. Regulation must also be explicit, sufficiently well defined, for example, to hold up in courts of law. It must be formalized, therefore, which renders it ineffective in dealing with issues of a judgmental nature.

Most importantly, regulation can only constrain unacceptable behavior, it cannot provoke desirable behavior. In other words, it is punative in nature, restricting corporate activity, rather than motivational in nature, encouraging social responsiveness. As Sethi puts it, the emphasis is placed on the "negative duties (the thou-shalt nots)," such as minimum pollution standards. "This has the effect of defining corporate responsibility as the lowest possible common denominator" (1975, p. 62). We see this clearly in the words of one of the best-known proponents of regulation, Franklin D. Roosevelt:

> Whenever...the lone wolf, the unethical competitor, the reckless promoter, the Ishmael of Insull whose hand is against every man's, declines to join in achieving an end recognized as being for the public welfare, and threatens to drag the industry back to a state of anarchy, the Government may properly be asked to apply restraint. (1968, p. 44)

The more recent examples of government regulation cited by Ackerman reflect this same orientation toward the *unacceptable*: in advertising, "such malpractices as deceptive use of research studies, unsubstantiated claims, inadequate disclosure, and deceptive television demonstrations" (p. 27); in safety, the reduction of textile mill noise level to 90 decibels; in personnel, the processing of claims by minority employees of discrimination; and so on.

Boling notes that "One may fully abide by the law and still remain unethical" (1978, p. 362). Solzhenitsyn articulates this point eloquently in the broadest perspective, and in the process provides us with the most scathing critique of "regulate it":

> One almost never sees voluntary self-restraint. Everybody operates at the extreme

limit of those legal frames. An oil company is legally blameless when it purchases an invention of a new type of energy in order to prevent its use. A food product manufacturer is legally blameless when he poisons his produce to make it last longer: after all, people are free not to buy it.

I have spent all my life under a communist regime and I will tell you that a society without any objective legal scale is a terrible one indeed. But a society with no other scale but the legal one is not quite worthy of man either. A society which is based on the letter of the law and never reaches any higher is taking very scarce advantage of the high level of human possibilities. The letter of the law is too cold and formal to have a beneficial influence on society. Whenever the tissue of life is woven of legalistic relations, there is an atmosphere of moral mediocrity, paralyzing man's noblest impulses.[3]

Second, "regulate it" tends to be applied slowly and conservatively. Government is typically reluctant to legislate—to inscribe the behavior it expects of corporations in the concrete form of statutes—until it is sure it fully understands the issue in question, and has the standardized means to deal with it. Furthermore, government is subject to corporate lobbying, which as we have seen is typically used to block or at least delay proposed regulations, often through "long and extensive court battles" (Davis 1976, p. 19). Thus, legislation supported by a good part of the population is often delayed by bureaucratic conservatism and political maneuvering. As a result, external influencers turn to other means to influence corporate behavior, as we shall soon see.

Third, "regulate it" is often difficult to enforce. Even when the regulations exist, enforcement does not always follow suit. Ackerman shows how effective regulation requires a learning process, which can involve a considerable period of time. In the case of water pollution control, for example, the first act, passed in 1956, resulted in only one court case in its fourteen years. A subsequent act of 1965 attempted to set systematic national standards, but seven years later, some states had still not complied with it. Only in 1972 was an act passed that "established the framework for a comprehensive network of standards and compliance procedures" (1975, p. 34).

But even after considerable learning, problems of enforcement frequently remain. Arrow (1974) discusses three kinds of formal intervention in corporate behavior—what he calls legal regulation, taxes, and legal liability (in civil law). For example, a pollution problem can be addressed, respectively, by setting standards to reduce emissions, by charging for emissions ("the violator pays for violations"), or by enabling those affected to sue for damages. Given an ability to measure the consequences of an action, taxation can be effective. It charges the corporation for the externality, and then leaves the decision of whether or not to continue the action, and incur the cost, to the corporation—or its customers. Civil legal liability functions in a related way, except that here the onus is on the private citizen to seek damages. This can be a costly procedure,

[3]Quoted in "Why the West has Succumbed to Cowardice," *The Montreal Star, News and Review,* June 10, 1978: B1.

and where many citizens suffer only minor damages, it may not pay any to exert the necessary effort to bring suit (although class action suits have changed this considerably).[4] In any event, "enforcement by continuous court action is a very expensive way of handling a repetitive situation" (p. 313). And so legal regulation is often resorted to. When the regulations are particularly complex and the ends sought less than precisely defined, the government will often be forced to set up an agency to regulate corporate behavior.

The regulatory agency often finds itself in the uncomfortable position of performing, at one and the same time, the legislative, executive, and judicial functions of government. That is to say, it may establish the regulations, enforce them, and judge and punish the offenders. This would seem to provide it with a great deal of power, but in fact there is much evidence that regulatory agencies are often ineffective. There are a number of reasons for this.

For one thing, because regulatory agencies typically lack an adequate definition of the public interest, they are unsure of what to do. Thus Leo Pellerzi, Assistant Attorney General of the U.S. Department of Justice, explains why he believes the record of the regulatory agencies "is dismal, to say the least" (1974, p. 177):

> In the approximately 1000 cases that I presided over in almost ten years as an administrative law judge, the "public interest" never meant anything of substance to me beyond the materially related interests of the parties that were before me. Among the parties, all represented by lawyers, were the principal motor carriers, all the class-one rail carriers in the United States, and most of the 500 largest corporations. Somewhere in that representation there should have been a discernable public interest looking at this thing called "corporate social responsibility." But it was never represented as such, and to the extent that there are open, pervasive hearings across the country, dealing with these large regulatory issues and involving hundreds of witnesses plus thousands of pages of testimony, the effect is to obscure much of the problem. (p. 177)

The record of regulatory agencies has also been dismal because of their small size given the complexity of the industries they are supposed to regulate. Regulation is expensive. But government budgets are limited. The common result is that the agencies are not equipped to understand the complexity of the issues they are supposed to regulate. In fact, the regulators often become dependent on the industry people for information, and so become coopted—regulated if you like—by these they were supposed to regulate.

And then there are all the problems of finding effective people to staff the regulatory agencies. Those foreign to the industry may know too little to be effective, while those experienced in it may know too much—notably that they will be returning to it in a few years and so see no compelling reason to make enemies. Fenn (1974), writing in the same volume as Pellerzi, describes the sloppy

[4]See our discussion of Olson's (1965, 1968) theory of collective action and of forces that reduce its effect in Chapter 7.

procedures often used in selecting regulators, with choices sometimes based on congressional influence, favors expected, industry pressures, or personnel problems ("where to put him?"). Of a number of appointments he analyzed, "11 were in the 'quality' file, five in the 'congressional must' group, seven in the 'personal friendship' box, two 'personnel problems' elsewhere, and two minority appointees" (p. 195).

In another article in the same volume, Katz (1974) describes the industry pressures on the regulatory agencies, noting particularly their ability to veto controversial appointments and to exploit the agencies to harass their competitors. And in another, Kohlmeier, who covered Washington for the *Wall Street Journal* for twelve years, while rejecting the notion that "regulators are venal men and women who can be bought by regulated industries" (p. 183) or who "have been captured by [them]" (p. 184), nevertheless concludes:

> ...the regulators were launched on stormy, uncharted seas with very little in the way of foul-weather gear. Congress provided them with no sure means of protecting their independence and is unlikely to do so. It gave them specified terms of office, usually five or seven years, but has never seriously considered giving regulators the lifetime tenure that the Founding Fathers deemed a necessary protection for federal judges....
>
> The public interest that the regulators are supposed to act for is too diverse and unorganized a force to make itself heard. Congress by and large ignores the agencies and presidents take the attitude that since the regulators owe them nothing, they will utilize the agencies for political patronage appointments and little more.
>
> The regulators thus are left with the only constituency available to them, and indeed the only protection that may be available: the regulated. (pp. 186–87)

And the regulated, of course, are only too willing to help, so that the result, despite Kohlmeier's claims, really is capture. A variety of cozy relationships develop between regulator and regulated.

For example: "The SEC, effective as it has been in ridding the stock market of manipulators, always has been and still is quite protective of the dominant 'private club' position of the New York Stock Exchange. The CAB has never allowed a new trunkline to enter the commercial aviation business since the board was created in 1938" (Kohlmeier, p. 189). "The Interstate Commerce Commission has been equally vigilant. Volotta...found that the number of truck carriers has persistently declined, despite more than 5000 applications per year for new certificates" (Pfeffer and Salancik 1978, p. 204). Another study noted that at its inception, the same Commission enabled the large railroads to enforce a previously shaky cartel, and at higher rates to boot (pp. 204, 206). So too "trucking firms are among the biggest supporters of continued regulation of trucking," and "estimates of the effects of regulation on prices in electric utilities, airlines, trucking, and natural gas have indicated that regulation either increases price or has no effect" (Pfeffer 1976, p. 43).

Clearly it is the largest firms in an industry that tend to capture the regulators. But even without capture, regulation produces a natural bias in favor of those firms. Only the large firms can afford the staff necessary to deal adequately with extensive regulation, such as that found in the iron and steel industry with its 5,600 regulations. Regulation may be costly, but so too is dealing with regulation: ". . . the regulating process . . . currently creates economies-of-scale in dealing with the government and thereby further encourages industrial concentration" (Kasper 1976, p. 295). The greatest cost of regulation may be the stifling effect it has on the small entrepreneurial firm.

Thus regulation is a blunt instrument, a slow, conservative means of control that sets only minimum standards which are difficult to enforce. It should come as no surprise, therefore, that the American government of late, under both Democratic and Republican administrations, has reacted against the myriad of regulations enacted during new deals, great societies, and so on. A housecleaning was certainly in order, to get rid of costly, ineffective, and inappropriate regulations.

But the whole story is not negative. Much regulation has not only worked, but has been indispensible. It is difficult, for example, to imagine dealing with the enormous problems of externalities without being able to use regulation. "Regulate it" may be no panacea, no automatic solution to the social problems created by the large corporation. But it is certainly one important position in the debate over who should control that corporation. That is why the pendulum will eventually swing back.

29

"Pressure It"

If "regulate it" cannot motivate the individual corporation to act beyond some base level of acceptable behavior, then "pressure it" is designed to do just that. Taking this position, interest groups and others bring specific pressure campaigns to bear on specific corporations, sometimes to stop one kind of behavior, other times to initiate another. The intention is to keep the corporation on its toes, quick to respond to needs other than its own as a Closed System. Thus speaks the patron saint of the pressure campaigners:

> I have a theory of power: That if it's going to be responsible, it has to be insecure; it has to have something to lose. That is why putting all economic power in the state would be disastrous, because it would not be insecure. If General Motors is sensitive at all, right now, with the tremendous dominant position it has, it comes from fear of losing something it has. (Ralph Nader, quoted in Ackerman 1973, p. 411)

"PRESSURE IT" IN CONTEXT

The "pressure it" position is shown to the right of "regulate it" on our horseshoe because regulation inherently assumes greater power over the corporation: it proceeds on the assumption that the government has the right to usurp the power of the corporation, through formal constraints. "Pressure it," in contrast, accepts the power of the corporate managers to make their own decisions; it then seeks to influence those decisions through informal pressures.

In this sense, "pressure it" is inherently less radical than "regulate it." The fact that its American advocates themselves tend to be more radical than those who advocate regulation does not change this conclusion; that fact merely indicates where the debate stands in the United States. Given the power of the corporations and the response of government to them (including the ineffectiveness of its regulatory agencies), Americans with somewhat radical views about corporate power have found that they can achieve more through pressure campaigns than through regulations. And so "pressure it" displaces "regulate it" in their priorities. In Europe, it should be noted, the debate is quite different, there "regulate it" appearing to have been more successful in controlling corporate behavior.

Typical of the line of reasoning that underlies the "pressure it" position is that of Chamberlain (1973). He argues that as the corporation grows, "it becomes increasingly difficult even to define its constituency, let alone represent it" (p. 196). Chamberlain thus rejects the positions at both ends of the horseshoe: "To continue to speak of the shareholders as the constituency is an historical lag" (p. 196), but it makes equally little sense to him to concentrate power in the hands of the government through nationalization. So Chamberlain concludes that management must play the central role in the power system, because of the need for coordination (as we argued at length in Chapter 27 on "democratize it"). But that must be an "insecure" management, one subject to the pressures of the one constituency Chamberlain is able to identify—"society at large." Thus, "with management in control, and recognizing the obligation to balance the interests of all—whatever its interpretation of the words—management at least becomes the recognized focal point on which pressures can be brought for change of social policy or redress of public grievance" (p. 197). And then Chamberlain clearly positions "pressure it" close to the center of our horseshoe:

> In a sense, [those pressures] legitimize management by the very fact that they address their grievances to it, within the existing institutional mechanisms. Management may feel indignant at being exposed to public criticism, but its indignation should be tempered by the realization that it is its exercise of discretion, not its authority, that is being questioned. (p. 199)

Chamberlain draws an analogy with the labor unions "which do not attempt to unseat the management with which they bargain, but only to influence its decisions" (p. 197). He is even careful to distinguish "pressure it" from "democratize it," arguing that a certain form of pressure "turns back . . . demands for broader participating roles; it requires no sharing of power. The government of the corporation remains firmly in place" (p. 199).[1]

Earlier, we made the point that "nationalize it" encourages interest groups

---

[1]Curious is the narrow context in which Chamberlain advocates "pressure it"—in proxy fights and at annual meetings, to convert such meetings "from ritual to public forum" (p. 196).

intent on changing the corporation to pressure the government. That is where the formal power over the nationalized corporation would lie. The same could of course be said of "regulate it"—the place to bring the pressures is on the regulators. "Pressure it," which in effect displaces "regulate it" (and "nationalize it"), encourages exactly the opposite response: groups intent on changing society (not just single corporations or even the private sector in general) are encouraged to pressure what seems to be society's most powerful institution, the large corporation. As Blumberg notes, "The state is regarded as the corporate state, and the corporation is a prime target" (1971, p. 1553). He elaborates:

> Increasingly, as the result of the search for a more vulnerable target, the corporation, rather than the political structure, has become the recipient of the political goals and pressures of various youth, anti-war, anti-pollution, anti-racist and consumer-oriented organizations.
>
> At a conference of social activists held at Carnegie Mellon University in April 1970, the keynote speaker, Professor Staughton Lynd, summarized: "Our inevitable enemy in the coming years is the corporation," and *Business Week* reported that "the underlying theme of the gathering was that the corporation is replacing the university and the government as the scapegoat of radical dissatisfaction with American society." (pp. 1557–58)

Milder but no less direct is the tone of the comments of Hazel Henderson (1968), who describes herself as "one of those strange creatures—an aroused citizen" (p. 77):

> . . .more and more citizens are beginning to turn to business in the realization that it has the power—and apparently the know-how—to solve the nation's pressing problems. In fact, many people have begun to see that it is often easier and more fruitful to bring about change by pressuring business leaders than by the more traditional method of pressuring lawmakers. (p. 78)

THE COMINGS AND GOINGS OF "PRESSURE IT"

"Pressure it" seems to be a fashionable position that comes and goes in waves. It came into prominence years ago with the rise of the labor unions, which developed the strike as their tool of pressure. Roosevelt also made use of it during the 1930s, to back up the regulations of the New Deal. World War II stimulated cooperation between government, business, and the unions, and the postwar period was also relatively free from pressure campaigns as the country adjusted to a peacetime economy. But social pressures "began anew during the 1960s, after a thirty-year hiatus and after the postwar structural transformation [to divisionalization] in the large corporation had been essentially completed" (Ackerman 1975, p. 3).

In that decade, a host of new pressure groups appeared, using a variety of new tactics, ranging from throwing sludge on the corporate carpets to smearing the corporation in the newspaper or in the law courts with class action suits. But whereas earlier, countervailing power was an important factor—the unions and government having to match the power of the corporation in order to change it—in the 1960s this was no longer the case. The giant corporation was repeatedly brought to its knees by the smallest of pressure groups. Campaign GM, whose budget probably amounted to a fraction of what that corporation would normally spend to develop a new windshield wiper, was able to evoke a significant response from this, the largest of the giants. In Chapter 27, it was noted that General Motors mounted an immense public relations campaign to meet the attack, and won the specific issue, garnering more than 97 percent of the proxy votes cast. But what seems more significant, not long after the vote the corporation initiated a whole series of changes that responded directly to many of the demands of the Campaign GM group. Blumberg lists them:

> • An appropriate interval after the Annual Meeting, General Motors designated 5 of its public directors as a Public Policy Committee to supervise the environmental and social impact of the company's operations.
>
> • In January, 1971, the General Motors' Board elected Dr. Leon J. L. Sullivan, as its first black director. . . .
>
> • In February, 1971, General Motors appointed a prominent authority on air pollution. . . as a vice president in charge of environmental activities.
>
> • Later in February, 1971, General Motors announced that it had obtained the services of a group of six distinguished American scientists. . . to advise it on technological and scientific matters "including in particular the effects of General Motors' operations and products upon the environment."
>
> • In March, 1971, General Motors appointed a black, Abraham S. Venable, as director of urban affairs. . . .
>
> In brief, the foregoing represents a series of remarkable developments arising after the conduct of Campaign GM Round I by a group of a few young people holding 12 shares of the 286,000,000 outstanding General Motors shares. It also represents a vigorous and imaginative response by General Motors to the political situation confronting it. (pp. 1561–62)

Thus, while Campaign GM clearly failed to "democratize it," in terms of "pressure it" it was an immense success. In other words, while no legal or constitutional changes were forced on the corporation, it itself responded to the external pressures. In fact, Campaign GM showed just how vulnerable the giant corporation can be when faced with a small but cleverly organized pressure campaign.[2] The corporation is simply too exposed, too vulnerable: ". . . a gold-

[2] It might be noted in passing that Dow Chemical, perhaps in response to the pressure campaign discussed in Chapter 25, eventually "ceased the manufacture of napalm and established an environmental testing advisory board to study possible environmental effects of new products" (Chamberlain 1973, p. 199).

fish has got to be good," says Allen (quoted in Dent 1959, p. 378). Having been a Closed System for so long, having grown so large, and having developed so much bureaucratic momentum, the corporation has simply not known how to cope with such external pressures. "As John Gunther . . . remarked of the automotive titans of Detroit, they resemble Japanese wrestlers, enormous but flabby, easily set quivering by a public-relations panic" (Long 1960, p. 205). Indeed, the point is made even more forcefully when Nader earlier acted against General Motors on his own, first with a book that condemned (and eventually destroyed) the Corvair, and then with his revelation that the corporation had hired detectives to investigate his private life. That revelation proved so embarrassing to General Motors that it appears to have served to reorient its whole attitude toward social responsibility.

Campaign GM was the brainchild of an increasingly common influencer, particularly of the late 1960s and early 1970s, the self-proclaimed "corporate activist." Taking Ralph Nader as their model, these individuals represent no specific constituency; rather they place themselves in the role of representing what they believe to be the public interest. Their demands are usually specific, as in Nader's first campaign for safer automobiles. But behind them is often the more ambitious goal of broadening the informal power base of the corporation. While "pressure it" is not the same as "regulate it" or "democratize it," it can nevertheless raise similar issues. Thus, shortly after Campaign GM ended, an article appeared in the *New York Times* stating that the issue was not what the corporation had or had not done, but "over who will have the power to make the decisions":

> What Campaign GM has done is raise the issue—the issue of big business and the public interest—and put giant General Motors on trial, on trial on the campuses, in the board rooms of the great foundations, and among the institutions, the banks and the churches that hold General Motors stock.
>
> The campaign may not have won many votes, but it may have captured the high moral ground and the fight may just be beginning.
>
> The issue has centered on pollution, but behind that is a question of power, the power of corporations to make decisions that affect the public.
>
> The guerrillas of Campaign GM say "all corporations must serve interests larger than their shareholders if the community and the corporations are to function effectively in the increasingly complex years ahead."[3]

Referring to 1970 as the year of "the corporate guerrilla fighter," Blumberg records Campaign GM–type proxy battles in at least seven other corporations, the presence of organized confrontations or disruptions at the annual meetings of seven major corporations; picketing, sit-ins, demonstrations and boycotts at five; bombings, sabotage, and burnings at eight. He notes the formation of public interest groups, with the corporation as the prime target, under such titles as

[3]"GM Campaign Goes Down to Defeat," *The Montreal Star,* May 23, 1970, from *The New York Times* service.

Industrial Areas Foundation, Council for Corporate Review, Public Interest Center, and so on. "The Public Affairs Council has published a twenty-eight-page directory of 'organizations dedicated to changing the private sector,' many of which are directing their activities at the corporations" (1971, p. 1552).

Such a pace could not continue, however, and as Ackerman notes, corporate activism declined in the early 1970s. "The novelty of expressing outrage at corporate malfeasance seemed to have waned and corporate legal staffs no longer reflected the air of panic that had been prevalent in the Dow Chemical and 'Campaign GM' proxy contests of 1968 and 1970" (1975, p. 8).

But "pressure it" continued, and continues. New waves come and go, while the long-term trend, at least in America, seems to be an increasing attention to this particular position.

The point, again expressed best in Hirschman's (1970) terms, is that as corporations have grown larger, those affected by their actions find their options for exit reduced, and so turn increasingly to voice. As Zald and Berger note, for example, "consumer protests increase as monopoly increases" (1978, p. 845). Olson's (1965, 1968) argument, discussed in Chapter 7, is that it does not pay any one influencer marginally effected by an action to mobilize an ad hoc group to change it. But Zald and Berger, as we also discussed in Chapter 7, suggest a counterargument: "The greater the associational density and the higher the proportion of organizational participants who are members of associations, the easier it is to mobilize" (p. 845). While it may not pay an individual to organize a group around one issue, he may find it worthwhile to devote all of his efforts to maintaining a permanent special interest group. Hence the emergence of the full-time "corporate activist." Ralph Nader's very raison d'être is activism. And with the presence of many such groups—which is what Zald and Berger mean by "high associational density"—activism becomes that much easier. This, in fact is what we have been seeing in the United States—the establishment of more and more permanent groups that stand ready to pressure the corporations. It is these that have become the most important countervailing power to the corporations.

"Pressure it" has not, however, been restricted to full-time activists with lofting "public interest" goals. Other groups, with more specific interests, have also raised their voices against the corporation. Black and women's groups have pressured AT&T to correct discriminatory pay scales, conservationist groups have disrupted the operations of strip mining companies to protest the defacing of the environment, church groups have confronted U.S. multinationals about their policies toward black workers in South Africa. An internal committee of the General Electric Company in 1970 reported "97 threats or demands having a potential impact on various functions or aspects of the corporation. They ranged from the dismemberment of large diversified firms to the provision of day-care centers to consumer boycotts and class action suits" (Ackerman 1975, p. 16). Ackerman presents his own inventory of social issues (pp. 17–28), categorized by business function: in manufacturing, degradation of the environment and health and safety in the workplace; in personnel administration, demands for equal opportunities by women and minority groups and, "less visible at the moment, but potentially of larger import" (p. 24), more sensitivity to individual needs and greater participation by managers and hourly employees alike; in product development, "consumerism" related to product safety and quality, disclosure of product specifications, the disposal of obsolete products and nonrecycled packages ("the solid-waste issue," p. 26); in selling and marketing, the practices of deceptive advertising and packaging, questionable selling habits, and the failure to honor warranties.

The "pressure it" position has also been adopted in some unexpected quarters. Governments reluctant to "regulate it" have sometimes resorted to the pressure campaign instead. In 1962, John F. Kennedy used his power to condemn U.S. Steel publicly for its price increases, and to threaten antitrust and other actions if it did not roll some of them back. In Campaign GM, the shareholders themselves—the owners of the firm—were brought into the pressure campaign, a traumatic experience for many churches and universities which had always signed their proxies automatically at the request of management.

> [Campaign GM]...shattered for all time the pattern of institutional neutrality under which the institutional shareholder, particularly the non-profit institution, automatically voted its shares for management. As a result of Campaign GM, American corporate electoral processes have become fundamentally changed. (Blumberg 1971, p. 1561)

Even the heads of corporations have found themselves engaged in pressure campaigns against one another:

> In 1946 and 1947...public pressure forced the Pennsylvania Railroad to begin replacing smoky, coal burning locomotives as part of the drive to clean up Pittsburgh's air. The Pennsy fought a rear-guard action to block a comprehensive smoke-control bill from becoming state law. Finally, some of Pittsburgh's most prominent business leaders threatened to take their freight-haulage business elsewhere if the railroad did not desist. The Pennsy gave up and began purchasing a spanking new fleet of diesel locomotives—an innovation that put the railroad several years ahead of its competition. (Henderson 1968, p. 83)

To conclude, "pressure it" has the advantage of being informal, flexible, and focussed, and, as such, has been highly successful. Given the shaky legitimacy of managerial authority, the giant corporate goldfish has proven reluctant to endure the exposure of the well-founded, well-organized pressure campaign. That is presumably why Brenner and Molander (1977) found in their poll of the factors causing higher ethical standards, in the opinion of *Harvard Business Review* readers, that those associated with "pressure it" came out on top, far ahead of those associated with "regulate it" or "trust it," as much as six to one in the case of certain forms of "pressure it" versus "trust it." (These results are reproduced in Table 29–1.)

TABLE 29-1. Effectiveness of "Pressure It," "Regulate It," and "Trust It" Factors as Perceived by Readers of the *Harvard Business Review*

Factors Causing Higher Ethical Standards	Percentage of Respondents Listing Factor
Public disclosure; publicity; media coverage; better communication	31%
Increased public concern; public awareness, consciousness, and scrutiny; better informed public; societal pressure	20%
Government regulation, legislation, and intervention; federal courts	10%
Education of business managers; increase in manager professionalism and education	9%
New social expectations for the role business is to play in society; young adults' attitudes; consumerism	5%
Business's greater sense of social responsibility and greater awareness of the implications of its acts; business responsiveness; corporate policy changes; top management emphasis on ethical action	5%
Other	20%

From Brenner and Molander 1977, p. 63.

However, compared to the positions to its left, "pressure it" is irregular and ad hoc, not grounded in any formal or permanent change in power relationship. (It was the current leaders of General Motors, after all, who got to choose who that black director would be.) Moreover, this position does not make consistent demands on the organization, nor does it make clear when the corporation should respond. Thus, when the president of Atlantic Richfield meets a corporate activist who tells him "We have changed the rules, and you are still playing the same old game," he can reasonably respond, "Well, if the game has been changed, no one has let us know about it. My company is still judged by its return on investment, its earning per share, and its growth track record" (Bradshaw 1974, p. 25). And compared to the positions to its right, "pressure it" is based on confrontation rather than cooperation, restricted to the view that the corporation has to be forced to change, not that it wants to change. Perhaps change can sometimes come about more effectively if the managers themselves take the initiative.

30

"Trust It"

From the point of view of social needs, must the corporation necessarily act irresponsibly? To elicit socially desirable behavior, must it be owned by the state, subjected to the democratic control of workers or outsiders, regulated by the government, or pressured by special interest groups? The next two positions around our horseshoe argue that it need not, but for different reasons. In this chapter, we discuss the first of these, "trust it," or more specifically, "trust the corporation to the goodwill of its managers." "Trust it" rests its case on the claim that social goals weigh heavily on the shoulders of corporate managers. These individuals attend to social goals *for their own sake*, because it is the proper thing to do, not because there are pressures from the left or incentives from the right.

"Trust it" has been placed in the center of our conceptual horseshoe because it postulates a natural balance between social and economic goals. The reconciliation between the two is made in the heads (or hearts) of responsible businessmen. And implicit in this position is that there need be no change in the power situation. The corporation can be trusted, even as a Closed System, because its leaders are prepared to respond voluntarily to society's needs, both social and economic.

VARIATIONS ON THE THEME OF "TRUST IT"

The first point we must make is that "trust it" could equally well have been labelled "socialize it." "Trust it" considers the position from the perspective of the managers looking out and from a *de*scriptive point of view. The managers can be trusted *by others* because they *are* responsible. "Socialize it" considers the position from the perspective of outsiders looking in at the corporation and from a *pre*scriptive point of view. The *managers themselves must* be socialized so that they can in fact be trusted.

"Trust it" or "socialize it" is as old as business itself. In America, "The personal dilemma for the businessman in the pre–Civil War era was the reconciliation of religious beliefs with economic opportunities. To seek riches for the sake of riches was a sin of avarice; instead one ought to be a steward for those in less fortunate circumstances" (Ackerman 1973, p. 402). In those days, "trust it" went under the heading of "noblesse oblige"—literally "nobility obliges"—which according to the Webster's Student Dictionary "used to denote the obligation of honorable and generous behavior associated with high rank or birth." Noblesse oblige is epitomized in the famous reply by George F. Baer, president of a U.S. railroad, to a request in 1902 that, as a "Christian gentleman," he should be more conciliatory with workers out on strike: "The rights and interests of the laboring man will be protected and cared for, not by labor agitators, but by the Christian men to whom God in his infinite wisdom has given control of the property interests of the country" (quoted in Harris 1938, p. 127).

Recently, this position seems to have developed renewed vigor, under the title "social responsibility." Now not only the leaders but all managers—indeed all employees—are to act responsibly. In fact, it is probably fair to conclude that since 1950 the American business community has been virtually obsessed with the issue of corporate social responsibility in one form or another. As Elbing (1970, p. 79) notes, citing references in each case, this issue has been discussed academically in universities, pragmatically by businessmen, politically by public representatives; it has been approached philosopically, biologically, psychologically, sociologically, economically, even aesthetically.

In part, the interest in "trust it" can be explained by the unprecedented success of American industry in achieving economic goals. The affluent society created by the corporation has taken material wealth for granted and so has become increasingly predisposed to worry about social goals. But there seems little doubt that the renewed interest in the issue also reflects the shaky legitimacy of the giant corporation's power base: it simply cannot remain so large and powerful and at the same time a system closed to direct external influence unless it itself actively responds to social needs.

Thus, "trust it" is the favored position of the "professional" manager, responsible not merely to his shareholders but to everyone. Here is the true peak coordinator, to use Papandreou's (1952) term, balancing all kinds of goals and needs of the society in which his firm operates. Drucker speaks for him:

> To maintain management as autonomous, and indeed as "private," is an essential need of society. It is essential for keeping society free. It is essential for keeping society performing... Yet to have a society of organizations with autonomous

managements, each a decision-maker in its own sphere, requires that managers, while private, also know themselves to be public. ...they are public in that they consciously, knowingly, openly, strive to make a public need into a private opportunity of their autonomous self-governing institution. (1973, pp. 810–11)

Perrow makes the same case, but with a touch of cynicism:

A host of respectable men have lately informed the American public that it labors under a misconception about business and businessmen. The greedy, selfish, entrepreneur with his "public be damned" point of view is no longer with us, the upright men tell us. "The tycoon is dead," *Fortune* magazine tells us in an advertisement. This nasty old capitalist has been replaced by the new corporate manager, with his new corporate conscience, his sense of public responsibility, and his foremost desire to serve the public good while serving also his board, his stockholders, and his customers. (1970, p. 101)

Large corporations, typically run by "professional" managers, feel compelled to justify their actions in social terms, even those clearly motivated by economic factors. Products are made to serve the clients, profits are earned to serve the economy, the corporation exists to serve all of society. Rhenman (1973) refers to these as "quasi-goals," noting the emphasis on emotive words such as innovative, in order to "enhance them with some lustre of social usefulness." (p. 116). He quotes an extreme example from Frederick Kappel, when he was President of AT&T:

We in business are doing more than earning profits. We are doing more than furnishing goods and services. We are producing more than material wealth. We are working to help build a political and social system different in important respects from any other the world has ever known. The lives of our heirs will depend in great measure on how successful we are. The countries of the world are watching our progress as a nation. The emerging nations of Asia and Africa are looking for models on which to fashion their own growth. Our whole Western society in all its aspects is engaged in a decisive struggle with the power of an alien philosophy, one that would destroy everything we value. The challenge to us is to demonstrate that the initiative of free men can continue to build strength for the future that will assure the prospect of freedom. (pp. 114–15)

All of this from the simple service of enabling people to talk to each other on the telephone!

The rhetoric notwithstanding, the fact of the matter is that on a day-to-day basis, the businessman can adopt a wide range of behaviors on the social issues he faces. Ackerman refers to this as a "zone of discretion," noting that until the expected behavior on new social issues is established by public norms and government regulations, managers have a wide latitude as to "how soon and in what way to respond" (p. 33). They can choose to lead public sentiment, just keep pace with it, or lag behind it, doing the necessary minimum. The choice exists,

Ackerman believes, because shareholders have shown little interest in the issue and competition is not always stringent. "For instance, a study of pollution control in the paper industry revealed wide variations in the level of effluent treatment. . . . Other studies have shown comparable variations among steel companies and public utilities in pollution control, coal companies in mine safety, and drug companies in a variety of social concerns" (p. 40).

Social responsibility presumably begins with at least keeping up, a posture Sethi describes as "bringing corporate behavior up to a level where it is congruent with the prevailing social norms, values, and expectations of performance" (1975, p. 62; see also 1979). Sethi refers to this posture itself as "social responsibility," to distinguish it from what he calls "social obligation" on one side—doing the bare minimum—and "social responsiveness," on the other, by which he means behavior that is anticipatory and preventative in nature. Sethi cites, as examples of the latter; accounting for corporate actions to outside groups and making information available to them; taking the lead in the development of pollution abatement equipment; granting financial support to philanthropical causes as well as to new, controversial groups; taking definite stands on issues of public concern; and avoiding meddling in politics. (How these last two behaviors are to be reconciled Sethi does not mention.)

Carried to its logical limit, social responsiveness postulates that "only business can do it": only corporations have the resources and/or the administrative skills to handle complex social problems. It follows, therefore, that "If we don't, who will?" Lodge summarizes this position as follows:

> There is a disposition to suppose that American business can solve the social and socio-technological problems of our time. The opinion is heard that if business wanted to, if it were "socially responsible," it could effectively address the problems which plague our major cities, such as poverty, housing, unemployment, transportation and education; it could wipe out the blight of pollution; it could even set about the establishment of a new world order through the workings of multinational enterprises. Business, it is said, is engaged in a war with the evils of our time, a war it must win. This view which is held oddly enough by governmental leaders, businessmen, liberals, conservatives and bomb-throwing extremists is a reflection of the traditional American myth that business is nearly omnipotent. (1972, p. 185)

Thus Haynes tells us that "private corporations possess most of the brains and muscles needed to save the world from self-destruction." The large international companies, in particular, are the "masters of the new technology," the possessors of "the innovative strengths," of "the capacity to engineer change," of "the requisite organizational and managerial skills," of "extraordinary financial power." "Clearly, if these capabilities are not employed—far more directly than they have to date—in the salvation of man from his many impending catastrophies, the world, as we know it, will end either with a whimper or a bang, but end it surely will" (1969, p. 8). And Peter Drucker (1973), while rejecting the extreme form of this position—what he calls "unlimited social responsibility" (p. 349), that business should set out to solve a multitude of social problems beyond its own mission—nevertheless endorses the general one: "The fact remains that in modern society there is no other leadership group but managers. If the managers of our major institutions, and especially of business, do not take responsibility for the common good, no one else can or will. Government is no longer capable . . ." (p. 375).

Thus we are urged to "trust it." But should we? Can we?

SHOULD IT BE TRUSTED?

"Trust it" in all of its forms discussed above has been the subject of sharp attacks, from the left as well as the right (sometimes on the same grounds). The attacks boil down to whether corporate managers should be trusted when they claim to pursue social goals, and if so, whether they have the personal capabilities to pursue these goals and whether they have the right to do so. And then, given all of this, the final attack questions whether they can in fact pursue these goals given the structures in which they must work.

First Attack: Social responsibility is all rhetoric, no action. The most elementary attack comes from those who simply do not trust the corporation. They view all the talk of social responsibility as a giant public relations campaign, all rhetoric and no action. The head can pronounce; the hands do not necessarily respond. Thus Cheit refers to the "Gospel of Social Responsibility," "designed to justify the power of managers over an ownerless system": ". . . managers must *say* that they are responsible, because they are *not*" (1964, p. 172, 165). And Chamberlain writes that "The most common corporate response to criticism of a deficient sense of social responsibility has been an augmented program of public relations" (1973, p. 9).

Second Attack: Businessmen lack the personal capabilities required to pursue social goals. Another, more far-reaching attack is that by the very nature of their training and experience, businessmen are ill-equipped to deal with social issues. Theodore Levitt argues this case:

> The more successful the large corporation executive is as professional manager and the higher his rank, the more he is asked to take a public stand on matters outside the area of his experience. It is, however, the unhappy irony of a world whose work increasingly gets done by specialists that the more successful a man is as a manager and the higher up he is in his organization, the less he is equipped to understand proposed changes in the external environment . . .
>
> For, say, 30 years, he has diligently dedicated his life to mastering the task of managing the internal environment of his company, but in the process he has automatically insulated himself from the world around him. . . . When he has read the newspapers during these years, rarely has he given the front page as much time

as the financial page. When he has read a magazine, it usually has been a trade journal or a general business magazine, not a public affairs journal. . . . When he has read lengthier public affairs articles, all too often he has read them in a business journal whose chauvinistic patter told him what the editors thought he wanted to hear. (1968, pp. 85)[1]

Others make a related case by claiming that the orientation of business organizations towards efficiency and control renders their leaders inadept at handling complex social problems, which require flexibility and political finesse. Harrington expresses this point of view:

> . . . when business methods are sincerely and honestly applied to urban problems, with very good intentions, they still inevitably lead to antisocial results. It is exactly when crass concerns are not paramount that the real problem—the inapplicability of business methods and priorities to the crisis of the cities—emerges most clearly. . . . What cities need are "uneconomic" allocations of resources. . . Businessmen, even at their most idealistic, are not prepared to act in a systematically unbusinesslike way. (quoted in Ackerman 1973, p. 414)

And *Fortune* magazine provides us with an excellent illustration of just this:

> A little over a year ago Boston's EG&G, Inc., set out to build up a small labor-intensive metal-fabricating subsidiary in the depressed Roxbury section, to be staffed and managed by Negroes. Today the plant is closed. EG&G President Bernard J. O'Keefe, 50, doubts that his high-technology systems company, which has sales of $120 million a year, will try again—"though I'll help the next guy who tries. The failure was the result of classic misconceptions," says O'Keefe. The company underestimated the time and money needed to establish the capitalist motivation in a culture to which it was alien. Federal officials gave less help than anticipated, and promised support from other businesses never materialized. Try as it would, O'Keefe says, EG&G was unable to turn up enough experienced black management: nor did it have much luck in convincing customers of the quality of its products. Perhaps the most important mistake, which O'Keefe says "almost foredoomed" the venture, was in the selection of the managers whom EG&G put in charge at Roxbury. "This kind of venture attracts the people who are 'socially committed,' and doing the job on their own time," says O'Keefe. "But not the people who are concerned about costs or meeting budgets." (May 1970, p. 74)

Third Attack: The corporation has no right to pursue social goals. In this, the most far-reaching argument against corporate social responsibility, the left and right join forces to attack the center. Their argument is a simple and appealing one: that corporation managers lack broad public legitimacy; at best they are appointed by private shareholders, more likely they are self-selected.

---

[1]Levitt does exempt the individual who reaches the top quickly, whether by birth, entrepreneurship, or luck. Not having "clawed his way arduously to the top" (p. 86), this individual, in Levitt's opinion, tends to be more liberal and better informed about social issues.

Therefore they have no right to pursue broad social goals, to impose *their* interpretation of the public good on society. "Who authorized them to do that?" asks Braybrooke (1967, p. 224). Critics from both sides agree that business should stick to its own business, which is the pursuit of economic goals, while the elected representatives, responsible directly to the people, should look after the social goals. In other words, public functions should not be exercised by private businessmen. "If we are to have rulers, let them be men of goodwill; but above all, let us join in choosing our rulers—and in ruling them" (Lewis 1959, p. 395).

Other critics ask what values will be imbedded in the "socially responsible" choices of businessmen. How much of business ideology—bigger is better, competition is good, material wealth leads to a better society, and other beliefs—will come along with these choices. Henderson, for example, asks what "hidden costs" will society have to pay for socially conscious behavior on the part of corporations:

> ...consider the statement of William M. Day, the president of Michigan Bell Telephone, when asked why his company wanted to adopt Detroit's Northern High School; the purpose, he said, is to provide aids designed "to help prepare the students for the business world. We think we can make a real difference in pupil attitudes."
> The issue raised by his statement is whether this is the basic purpose of public school educating. If corporations took over more of the task of educating our children, might they not pay more attention to this sort of education than to teaching art appreciation, poetry, literature, and music? (1968, p. 79)

Still other critics, attacking from the right as well as the left, ask to what extent business can be allowed to, or expected to, dominate society. "Business has enough power," so the argument goes (Davis 1973, p. 320[2]). In a paper entitled "The Dangers of Social Responsibility," Levitt (1958) comments that "its guilt-driven urge" has caused the modern corporation to reshape "not simply the economic but also the institutional, social, cultural, and political topography of society" (p. 44). He sees continuation of this trend as posing a serious threat to democracy:

> ...at the rate we are going, there is more than a contingent probability that, with all its resounding good intentions, business statesmanship may create the corporate equivalent of the unitary state. Its proliferating employee welfare programs, its serpentine involvement in community, government, charitable, and educational affairs, its prodigious currying of political and public favor through hundreds of peripheral preoccupations, all these well-intended but insidious con-

---

[2]Davis lists eight arguments in all against social responsibility, three of which fall under this third attack: "business has enough power," a lack of accountability, and "lack of broad support." We cover the other five elsewhere: business's role of "profit maximization," the "costs of social involvement," business's "lack of social skills," the "dilution of business's primary purpose," and "weakened international balance of payments."

trivances are greasing the rails for our collective descent into a social order that would be as repugnant to the corporations themselves as to their critics. (p. 44)

And then there are the pure economic arguments, from the right, that the function of business is economic, not social. Social responsibility means giving away the shareholders' money; it weakens the firm's competitive position and it dilutes the efforts of its managers, who are supposed to focus on economic productivity (Davis 1973). The best-known voice here is that of Milton Friedman:

> What does it mean to say that the corporate executive has a "social responsibility" in his capacity as businessman? If this statement is not pure rhetoric, it must mean that he is to act in some way that is not in the interest of his employers. For example, that he is to refrain from increasing the price of the product in order to contribute to the social objective of preventing inflation even though a price increase would be in the best interest of the corporation. Or that he is to make expenditures on reducing pollution beyond the amount that is in the best interests of the corporation or that is required by law in order to contribute to the social objective of improving the environment. Or that, at the expense of corporate profits, he is to hire "hard-core" unemployed instead of better-qualified available workmen to contribute to the social objective of reducing poverty.
>
> In each of these cases, the corporate executive would be spending someone else's money for a general social interest. Insofar as his actions in accord with his "social responsibility" reduce returns to stockholders, he is spending their money. Insofar as his actions raise the price to customers, he is spending the customers' money. Insofar as his actions lower the wages of some employees, he is spending their money. (1970, p. 33)

Finally there comes perhaps the most pointed criticism, from left as well as right: how are businessmen to determine what is socially responsible? To whom are they responsible: the whole of society? the customers? the industry? the employees? the managers' families? the corporation itself? What happens when responsibility to one means irresponsibility to another? Should profit be given up to help needy customers? How much profit? Is lobbying for a stronger merchant marine—so that it will be available in the event of war—a socially responsible activity on the part of a shipping company? Is the granting of funds to the American Medical Association to conduct research on the relationship between smoking and lung cancer a socially responsible thing for a tobacco company to do? Is resisting government intervention responsible? How about donating money to universities, with the stipulation that it be used for the schools of engineering and management?

Clearly social responsibility involves a host of complex and contradictory needs in a perpetual state of flux. It would seem to be an unwillingness to recognize this fully that leads writers such as Sethi to claim on one hand that corporations should take definite stands on issues of public concern and on the other hand that they should avoid meddling in politics. Sethi seems to be saying that corporations should get involved only in the "good" issues, as if we all know exactly what those are. Unfortunately, when we get right down to it, we do not, or, more exactly, each of us has his or her own opinion. As a result, sometimes the most well-meaning corporation is attacked for what it truly believed was responsible behavior while the most blatantly selfish act of another corporation, justified in the lofty terms of social responsibility, hardly gets noticed.

One of the sharpest voices from the left—outside the underground press— is that of Paul Goodman, who, in 1967, at the height of the Vietnam escalation, told a group of executives from the National Security Industrial Association (which includes some four hundred major corporations from industries such as aircraft, motors, electronics, and oil) meeting to discuss national goals:

> These goals indeed require research and experimentation of the highest sophistication, but not by you. You people are unfitted by your commitments, your experience, your customary methods, your recruitment, and your moral disposition. You are the military industrial complex of the United States, the most dangerous body of men at present in the world, for you not only implement our disastrous policies but are an overwhelming lobby for them, and you expand and rigidify the wrong use of brains, resources, and labor so that change becomes difficult. . . . But if we ask what *are* the technological needs and what ought to be researched in this coming period . . . the best service that you people could perform is rather rapidly to phase yourselves out, passing on your relevant knowledge to people better qualified, or reorganizing yourselves with entirely different sponsors and commitments, so that you learn to think and feel in a different way. (quoted in Eells and Walton 1974, pp. 248–49)

But the voices from the right can be no less shrill, heaping equal abuse on the would-be socially conscious businessman. In the following passage, Milton Friedman pulls out all of the stops, using many of the perjorative terms in the book of right-wing ideology:

> When I hear businessmen speak eloquently about the "social responsibilities of business in a free-enterprise system," I am reminded of the wonderful line about the Frenchman who discovered at the age of 70 that he had been speaking prose all his life. The businessmen believe that they are defending free enterprise when they declaim that business is not concerned "merely" with profit but also with promoting desirable "social" ends; that business has a "social conscience" and takes seriously its responsibilities for providing employment, eliminating discrimination, avoiding pollution and whatever else may be the catchwords of the contemporary crop of reformers. In fact they are—or would be if they or anyone else took them serious—preaching *pure and unadulterated socialism*. Businessmen who talk this way are unwilling *puppets* of the intellectual forces that have been *undermining* the basis of a *free* society these past decades. (1970, p. 33, italics added)

Thus, we seem to have an open and shut case against social responsibility, one beyond redemption. The words of businessmen cannot be trusted; not only are they ill-equipped to deal with social issues, but they have no business trying to do so. Let them stick to their own business, which is business itself.

But we have not yet finished with the case against social responsibility. Let us drive a few more nails in its coffin, by citing from the good deal of evidence that social responsibility cannot work, even if it should. Only when we have presented the full case against social responsibility will we be ready to show that not only must it work but that it indeed does.

CAN IT BE TRUSTED?

The *final attack* is the most devastating of all: not that "trust it" is a facade, nor that businessmen are unsuited to it, nor that they have no right to consider it, but that *social responsibility is not possible in the large corporation, given the nature of its structure and control systems.* Appropriate or not, "trust it," it is claimed, simply cannot and does not work. Proponents of social responsibility are dismissed as naive: corporations, by the nature of their activities, create the social problems. How can they solve them?

> If we all understood the basic ground rules of private enterprise a little better, we would realize that the large corporation is not a rain god, and that no amount of prayer or incantation will unleash its power. The spectacle of otherwise sophisticated people going on bended knee to companies and pleading with them to have the kind of conscience and moral sensibilities only rarely found in individuals is nothing less than laughable. (Henderson 1968, p. 81)

Henderson's conclusion receives strong support from a number of empirical studies. Some have even shown that corporations sincerely encouraged by their top managers to be socially responsible have difficulty being so. Let us begin with the evidence from surveys, which leaves little room for optimism, and then look at the more important evidence on how the very structure and control systems used by the large corporation discourages socially responsible behavior.

SURVEYS OF CORPORATE SOCIAL RESPONSIBILITY Surveys of the employees themselves on the social responsibility of their corporations have not been very encouraging. Brenner and Molander (1977) compared their survey of *Harvard Business Review* readers with one carried out fifteen years earlier and concluded: "Respondents are somewhat more cynical about the ethical conduct of their peers than they were" (p. 59). (And they hardly lacked cynicism to begin with, despite the finding that "Most respondents...have embraced [social responsibility] as a legitimate and achievable goal for business," p. 59.) Close to half the respondents agreed with the statement that "the American business executive tends not to apply the great ethical laws immediately to work. He is preoccupied chiefly with gain" (p. 62). On a question of change in ethical standards over time, 32 percent felt that the standards of 1976 were lower than those of 1951, while 27 percent felt they were higher (41 percent felt they were about the same). In a finer breakdown of these responses, 12 percent of the respondents felt standards to be "considerably" lower, only 5 percent to be "considerably" higher. And as noted in the table reproduced in the last chapter, only 5 percent listed social responsibility as a factor "influencing ethical standards," whereas 31 percent and 20 percent listed factors related to pressure campaigns, and 10 percent listed regulation.[3]

On some specific questions, 89 percent of the respondents felt it "acceptable" to pad an expense account by about $1,500 a year if the superior knew about it and said nothing; 55 percent would do nothing in the case of a shady deal between a pilots' association and an insurance company whose board they have just joined (as an inside director; as an outside director, 36 percent would do nothing); and 58 percent would pay a "consulting fee" to a foreign minister to gain a lucrative contract (although a full 91 percent believe the average executive would pay, a reflection of the "real magnitude of [the] cynicism," p. 65). Of the respondents, 43 percent attributed unethical practices to competition, and, more importantly as we shall see, 50 percent to superiors, who "often do not want to know how results are obtained, so long as one achieves the desired outcome" (p. 62). Brenner and Molander believe that two factors most likely explain these results: "ethical standards have declined from what they were or situations that once caused ethical discomfort have become accepted practice" (p. 59).

Other studies support these results, especially the ones pertaining to subordinate managers. Collins and Ganotis (1974) stress, as one of the most significant findings in their survey of attitudes of managers toward social responsibility, "a sense of futility concerning the ability of lower- and middle-level managers to effect corporate social policy and a perhaps related attitude that social goals can best be achieved by individuals working outside their companies. These attitudes were particularly strong among lower-level managers" (p. 306).[4] Another survey, conducted of managers within Pitney-Bowes, "a leader in [the] campaign for business ethics....reported that they do feel pressure to compromise personal ethics to achieve corporate goals"; similar results were obtained in Uniroyal (Madden 1977, p. 66). Even *Business Week* has concluded that "such pressures apparently exist widely in the business world" (quoted in Madden, p. 66). Finally, 64 percent of the business managers

---

[3]The general public has concurred in this rejection of "trust it." Only 15 percent of those polled in a 1977 survey agreed that "business tries to strike a fair balance between profits and interests of the public" (in 1968, 70 percent agreed; in 1973, 34 percent). Asked to choose between "trust it" and "regulate it," the public came down strongly for the latter (Westlin 1979, pp. 14, 16). In another poll, carried out in 1976, the "honesty and ethical standards" of business executives, were rated "very high" by 3 percent of the respondents, "high" by 17 percent, "average" by 58 percent, "low" by 16 percent, and "very low" by 4 percent (2 percent had no opinion). The figures for "professional and business" respondents were 2 percent, 22 percent, 55 percent, 14 percent, 6 percent (and 1 percent) respectively (Gallup 1978, pp. 838–40).

[4]More discouraging perhaps, they also found that the young managers experienced the lowest sense of personal responsibility for social problems and the weakest perception of the need for the corporation to involve itself in such problems. Apparently "trust it" was not their position.

surveyed by J. S. Bowman (1976) agreed with the statement that "Private managers feel under pressure to compromise personal standards to achieve organizational goals," that belief being "particularly prevalent in middle and lower management levels" (1976, p. 50). And 78 percent agreed with the statement: "I can conceive of a situation where you have good ethics running from top to bottom, but because of pressures from the top to achieve results, persons down the line compromise their beliefs" (p. 51).[5] One respondent wrote: "It is not people per se, but rather the structure of large organizations and the ruthless competition in them that develops unethical conduct" (p. 51).

THE PROBLEM OF STRUCTURE   Let us take this comment as our point of departure. There can be little doubt that competition from within or without influences the corporation's ability to be socially responsive. (It also provides an excuse not to be responsive, but that is another issue.) This is the point of Tumin's "principle of least morality," discussed in Chapter 28, that in a competitive situation, the least responsible members of the community set the tone for all of the others. But the results we have seen above may be better explained by problems inherent in the actual design of the large corporation. The organizational structures the corporation must use may drive social responsiveness and even social responsibility out of it. The corporation may be " 'trapped' in the business system that it has helped to create" (Chamberlain 1973, p. 4).

In his important paper, Daniel Bell (1971) describes modern industrial society as "a product of two 'new men,' the engineer and the economist, and of the concept which unites them—the concept of efficiency" (p. 9). This concept gave rise to "a distinct mode of life," which Bell calls the "economizing mode"—"the science of the best allocation of scarce resources among competing ends" (p. 10). Economizing meant "maximization," "optimization," "least cost." Underlying this was a concept of rationality, specifically "a rationality of *means*, a way of best satisfying a given end." The ends "were seen as multiple or varied, to be freely chosen by the members of society." But, much as we saw in our discussion of efficiency in Chapter 16, "the ends that 'became' given all involved the rising material output of goods. And other, traditional modes of life (the existence of artisan skills and crafts, the family hearth as a site of work) were sacrificed to the new system for the attainment of these economic ends" (p. 10). The new rationality and new goals needed "to be institutionalized in some renewable form of organization. That institution was the corporation" (p. 11).

The corporation, in other words, emerged as the rational tool to pursue economic goals. "The justification of the corporation no longer lay, primarily in the natural right of private property, but in its role as instrument for providing more and more goods to the people" (Bell, p. 7). And the key to the functioning of that tool was its structure—specifically what we have called Machine Bureaucracy. The economic goals plugged in at the top filtered down through a rationally designed hierarchy of ends and means, to emerge at the bottom in a

[5]Corresponding responses for public sector managers were similar but slightly lower.

form that allowed workers to carry out highly specific tasks designed according to the precepts of division of labor. These workers were impelled to put aside their personal goals and do as told in return for remuneration. To ensure that they did, the whole system was overlaid with a hierarchy of authority supported by an extensive network of formal controls. And to keep this whole system on its economic track, society created its own controls—a price system, competition, a stock market that measured results, that watched the corporation's well-known bottom line.

Now, what happens when the concept of social responsibility is introduced into all this. The evidence from the surveys cited above suggests an answer: Not much. The system is too tight.

Let us now turn to some more specific evidence, on the impact of structure on the social performance of the corporation. This evidence will explain why it is the lower-level managers who are the most pessimistic about social responsibility.

In principle, social goals can be plugged into the top instead of economic ones. Or else they can sneak in lower down, as "subordinates" ignore the demands of the hierachy and instead do what they believe is right. But a number of factors work against such social goals. External competition and the pressures to demonstrate economically effective performance are two obvious ones. Internal competition is another. According to Maccoby (1976), the pressure to get to the top of the hierarchy favors the "gamesmen" of the corporation, people to whom winning is all important. In Madden's summary, the work of these gamesmen "does little to satisfy or even stimulate what Maccoby calls the 'qualities of the heart': loyalty, a sense of humor, friendliness, compassion... Perhaps the key aspect of Maccoby's study is to note the decline since 1950 of an ideological or ethical basis for action among the generation of executives born in the 1930s... Winning...turns out to be...'the only thing'" (p. 68). And winning is measured in numbers, which, as we saw in Chapter 16, favors the economic goals over the social ones. To quote Bell, the system "measures only economic goals":

> Clean air, beautiful scenery, pure water, sunshine, to say nothing of the imponderables such as ease of meeting friends, satisfaction in work, etc.—they are "free goods" either because they are so abundant that there is little or no cost, or because they are not appropriable and saleable. Such free goods contribute greatly to our total welfare. But in our present accounting schemes, priced at zero, they add nothing to the economist's measure of wealth. Nor, when they disappear, do they show up as subtractions from wealth. (1971, p. 14)

Thus Madden concludes: "To repeat a key theme: the internal master of the executive is the bottom line, guarded relentlessly by the investment analyst" (p. 72).

Now what happens to the managers lower down, intent on performing in a socially responsible manner, when the numbers plugged in at the top of the system are economic? In fact, what happens from the top when the senior managers themselves try to plug in social goals alongside the economic ones?

ACKERMAN'S STUDY OF THE EFFECTS OF FINANCIAL CONTROLS ON SOCIAL RESPON-SIBILITY   These are the questions addressed by Robert Ackerman (1975) in an important book entitled *The Social Challenge to Business*. Ackerman looks at the effects on social responsibility of the Divisionalized Form—that structure, overlaid on Machine Bureaucracy, used overwhelmingly by America's largest corporations (Wrigley 1970; Rumelt 1974). His study was stimulated by the proposition that "the difficulty corporations were having in satisfying their social critics might lie precisely in the organizational innovations that had permitted them to cope effectively with diversification and competitive conditions" (p. vii).

Ackerman studied two firms in depth. He interviewed managers and specialists at different levels, analyzed documents, and investigated the functioning of their structures. He looked at planning, control, and budgeting systems, and he carried out "process research" studies "to understand as thoroughly as possible how specific decisions involving social issues were made" (p. x).

Ackerman begins with the premise that, although some "rascals inhabit the executive suite," most business leaders "would like to avoid doing what they believe to be irresponsible" (p. 4). This said, he puts the rhetoric of noblesse oblige aside and looks instead at how managerial and structural arrangements have affected social responsiveness. In other words, what interests Ackerman as a management theorist is how social goals do or do not get operationalized in the making of specific decisions:

> Some readers may dissent and remain firm in the conviction that the prime requirement for achieving corporate responsiveness is the ethical sensitization of top management. I hope to persuade such dissenters that even if ethical conversion were a prime requirement, it would not be sufficient in itself to provoke responsive behavior in the corporation. There is a substantial administrative task facing even the most converted executive. (p. 4)

In the Divisionalized Form, the divisions are fully responsible for operating their individual businesses while the headquarters controls them through systems that measure performance. In other words, the bottom line is transferred one peg down the hierarchy.

> Financial budgeting and control systems have become essential to the management of the divisionalized corporations.... [They] provides information that is relatively easy to understand and can be presented in comparable terms for all units year after year. Accounting reports are not immune to misinterpretation but they relieve the reviewer of the need to sift through and comprehend operating data from diverse businesses. Ironically, but perhaps inevitably, as large corporations become more complex, the gauges used to control them becomes simpler....
>
> Most important, financial controls are result-oriented. They monitor the actual and expected outcomes and not the process used to secure them. (p. 49)

And so the divisional managers, and sometimes their own subordinates in turn, are appraised—and rewarded—on the basis of their financial performance. Specifically, they "are encouraged to pay close attention to the near-term profitability of their units, be it a whole division or a single plant. The further tendency for managers to experience relatively short tenures in each assignment reinforces their efforts to meet the current budget, even though it may mean sacrifices in potential future benefits from the unit" (p. 50). In other words, even if the chief executive sings the praises of social responsibility, his subordinates march to the tune of economic performance. What they actually do is determined not by the words he utters but by the control systems he institutes.

The question becomes, what happens when a new social issue comes along? Ackerman believes that it poses three major dilemmas for the corporation:

(1) Social demands subvert corporate-division relationships.
(2) Financial control systems are ineffective in explaining and evaluating social responsiveness.
(3) The process for evaluating and rewarding managers is not designed to recognize performance in areas of social concern. (p. 52)

A new social issue—say concern about bias in hiring minorities—encourages top management to intervene in the decisions of the divisions, for two reasons. First, even local issues can have implications for the entire corporation (as, for example, when the company's name is identified with a charge of racial discrimination). And second, in a hierarchical organization it is the chief executive who is ultimately held responsible for its actions. But intervention violates the principle of divisional autonomy. And so the top manager falls on the horns of a dilemma. If he hesitates, "it is probable that social responsiveness will lag." The division managers have already made commitments to their short-term targets; they will take a "dim view" of having their energies diverted elsewhere. But if he acts, he upsets the system: ". . . he may diminish the extent to which he can hold the divisions accountable for achieving agreed upon financial results" (p. 54). In effect, the neat separation of powers designed for economic performance impedes social responsiveness.

Of course, if the costs and benefits of the social issue could be measured, the well-meaning executive at headquarters would simply plug them into the control system. Unfortunately, however, although some of the costs can be measured, typically few of the benefits can:

> What is the value to the corporation of, for instance, reducing noxious emissions into the atmosphere below the levels required by current law? There may be some fairly direct benefits in a rosier public image, a better bargaining position with government regulators seeking compliance at other plants, pride among managers that "we're one of the good guys," an attractive posture for recruiting on campus, a jump on meeting future regulations at today's prices; if good fortune abounds, perhaps even a process innovation that will increase yields. The list could be extended indefinitely. But what are these benefits worth? From the accountant's point

of view, they have the unfortunate characteristics of being largely intangible, un-assignable to the costs or organizational units creating them and occurring over an undeterminable future time period. (pp. 55–56)

Thus, even the chief executive at headquarters who wishes to incorporate social responsibility into his control system cannot easily do so. Ackerman touches the heart of his argument with the following comment:

> ...the financial reporting system may actually inhibit social responsiveness. By focusing on economic performance...such a system directs energy and resources to achieving results measured in financial terms. It is the only game in town, so to speak, at least the only one with an official scorecard. (p. 56)

In effect, the head may speak good intentions, but the arms and legs, where the actions take place, are wired to a different set of nerves, that of the operational goals.

And to switch metaphors, when the screws of financial performance are forever being tightened—as they are, increasingly, in the contemporary versions of these control systems—the division manager can lose much of his personal discretion to pursue social goals. "Relentless pressure for growth exerted on the organization through the financial reporting system diminishes the prospects for aggressive responses to social pressures at operating levels" (p. 57). Thus Joseph Bower, a colleague of Ackerman at the Harvard Business School where he wrote this book, cites a well-known case from 1961 of the effect of so turning the financial screws:

> The corporate management of [General Electric] required its executives to sign the so-called "directive 20.5" which explicitly forbade price fixing or any other violation of the antitrust laws. But a very severely managed system of reward and punishment that demanded yearly improvements in earnings, return, and market share, applied indiscriminately to all divisions, yielded a situation which was—at the very least—conducive to collusion in the oligopolistic and mature equipment markets. (1970, p. 193)

Bower's conclusion seems to make the point of this whole argument precisely:

> In short, the same forces in a diversified firm that tend to strip away economic fat and social tradition from the management of the enterprise tend also to strip away noneconomic aspects of all issues facing division managements, even those that are not remotely economic in character. The result is that while the planning process of the diversified firm may be highly efficient, there may be a tendency for them to be socially irresponsible. (p. 193)

WATERS'S "CATCH 20.5"   What of the ability of the manager lower down not even to act responsibly but merely to avoid acting irresponsibly. Here, too, the evidence is discouraging, as we saw in the polls cited earlier. This issue was, in fact, investigated directly by James Waters (1978), and reported in a paper entitled "Catch 20.5: Corporate Morality as an Organizational Phenomenon." Curious how such things as General Electric's directive 20.5 could go unheeded, Waters studied testimony of various U.S. congressional investigating committees into corporate wrongdoing and interviewed some of the managers involved. What was of interest to him was not "What was going on with those *people* to make them act that way?" but rather "What was going on in that *organization* that made people act that way?" (p. 5). Waters provides his answers in terms of seven "organizational blocks"—"aspects of organizations that may get in the way of the natural tendency of people to react against illegal and unethical practices" (p. 5):

- *Block 1: Strong role models*—socialization of new members into unethical practices already accepted in the organization; identification with mentors responsible for them.
- *Block 2: Strict line of command*—respect for the chain of authority; don't question the boss; fear of reprisal if one speaks out; even if one wishes to speak out, "to whom does he report the illegal goings-on?" (p. 7).[6]
- *Block 3: Task group cohesiveness*—being "members of the club," as one General Electric conspirator commented (p. 7).
- *Block 4: Ambiguity about priorities*—for example, General Electric's directive 20.5 "was often dominated by line-of-command directions to the contrary" (p. 8); here Waters cites Ackerman's findings that hard criteria tend to drive out soft: " 'Do this but make sure it doesn't keep you from meeting your profit objectives,' " hence "Catch 20.5" (p. 9).
- *Block 5: Separation of decisions*—having to work on the basis of a strategy imposed from above; having to work in an area in which certain unethical practices are the norm (e.g., kickbacks to get construction contracts in New York City).
- *Block 6: Division of work*—focussing on one's own specialized work and ignoring unethical practices elsewhere in the organization, or simply not having the "big picture" to know what is going on elsewhere despite suspicions, or being bypassed if one refuses to carry out an unethical act.
- *Block 7: Protection from outside intervention*—avoiding internal investigation of wrongdoing for fear of public exposure.

THE ROOT OF THE PROBLEM: STRUCTURE OR MANAGEMENT?   All of this indicates that the problems of getting "trust it" to work are inherent in the very conception of the corporation and in the design of the structure and control systems it uses. Machine Bureaucracy and especially the Divisionalized Form, by their very nature, seem to encourage people to behave in at best socially unrespon-

---

[6]Of course, the opposite can happen too, when subordinates, to protect themselves, shield their managers from information so that the latter do not know what is going on.

sive, at worst socially irresponsible ways. As Boling notes, citing the psychologist Piaget, "the types of individual morality derive from the types of social structures in which individuals are involved" (1978, p. 363).

Were social irresponsibility restricted to the fly-by-night operator—once the seller of patent medicines, later the school of dancing lessons, more recently the creator of pyramid selling arrangements—it would be manageable, so to speak. But it is not: specifically unethical acts continue to be pinned on the largest and most prestigious of corporations, in the recent past on General Motors, General Electric, Ford, Gulf, Lockheed, ITT, and many others. *Fortune* magazine, in an article entitled "How Lawless Are Big Companies?," concludes that "a surprising number of them have been involved in blatant illegalities" (Ross 1980, p. 57). Of 1,043 major corporations studied, 117 had been involved in one or more "serious crimes" within the United States during the 1970s—antitrust violations, kickbacks, bribing or illegal rebates, illegal political contributions, fraud, tax evasion. One recent chairman of the Securities and Exchange Commission writes: "There has been bribery, influence-peddling, and corruption on a scale I had never dreamed existed." And his words are echoed by another, in reference to charges of illegal practices against nine large corporations: "always there was direct involvement and participation by senior management officials" (quoted in Walton 1977, p. 3). How is anyone to "trust it"—to acknowledge all the ethical behavior that really does take place—when unethical behavior appears to be so rampant? "The moral canvas seems black indeed," writes Walton (p. 4). And the president of Cummings Engine received a standing ovation when he told a group of top executives "that we are 'losing our freedoms' not because of the appetite of some monster government, but because we (businessmen) 'have abused our freedoms when we had them'" (p. 3).

According to the evidence from the surveys, the problem seems to be getting worse, perhaps in good part because the Divisionalized Form of structure is becoming more pervasive and its control systems tighter. Remember too, from our discussion of Chapter 19, that this tends to strengthen the hand of the Internal Coalition at the expense of the External Coalition, making the corporation less and less responsive to external influence.

But the root of the problem may go much deeper than structure, at least if Singer and Wooton's study is any indication. It will be remembered that they analyzed Albert Speer's "administrative genius" as Minister of Armaments and War in Germany's Third Reich. Speer's organization was neither a Closed System nor a Machine Bureaucracy. It functioned as an Instrument of the state, and was designed as an Adhocracy. This was an "adaptive, problem-solving temporary organization" that used a "matrix system with project management" and relied on "industrial self-responsibility" and "collegial decision making" (1976, pp. 82–84). Speer, in fact, rallied against German bureaucracy. Yet all of this—"advanced, participative, and 'humanistic' "—was used "to promote the goals of one of the most inhumane societies in the history of mankind" (p. 80). The implication is that the root of the problem may be beyond structure, in the very concept of management itself: "It is not that managers are authoritarian themselves; rather . . . it may be that the process of management is authoritarian" (p. 100).

The "professional" manager is a "hired gun," so to speak, concerned with means not ends. But that very distinction may prove to be the problem, depersonalizing relationships and breeding socially irresponsible behavior. Speer said, "The people [who suffered] became abstractions to me, not human beings" (quoted on p. 82). The "professional" manager can become encapsulated, insulated from the consequences of his actions; like Speer, he can come to see challenges "as tasks to be performed, as functions to be organized . . . as power to be exercised" (p. 82). Singer and Wooton's message is that "many managers today are so caught up in the procedural demands of their work that they easily lose sight of the important end results of their activities" (pp. 98–99).

All in all, one is not very encouraged to "trust it"!

PROPOSALS TO "SOCIALIZE IT"

How to deal with the problem? How to "socialize it" so that it can be trusted? Ironically, a number of the proposed solutions ignore the structural roots of the problem. More bureaucratic procedures are proposed to solve the problem created by bureaucratic procedures—for example, codes of ethics, like General Electric's directive 20.5. Shades of the Latin American countries that have passed laws to insist that previous laws be respected. As Waters notes, "A mechanistic approach—such as having everybody sign a standard affidavit like GE's '20.5'—can impersonalize and desensitize the issue" (1978, p. 13). Even the industry-wide code of ethics, as Arrow notes, "however much it may be in the interest of all, is . . . not in the interest of any one firm. . . . it will be to the advantage of any one firm to cheat—in fact the more so, the more the other firms are sticking to it" (1973, p. 315).[7] In general, Waters believes that " 'battening down the hatches' can have exactly the opposite effect from the one intended. Increasing the clarity of the control procedures may enable the bad guys to navigate their way around the system more easily" (pp. 12–13).

There are, of course, other approaches. The chief executive who feels strongly about a social issue can force his subordinates to respond to his personal directives. In other words, he can throw out the "objective" system of bureaucratic control in favor of a "subjective" one of personal control. Personal control requires the CEO "perforce . . . to rely on his own judgement of how effectively his subordinates are managing social responsiveness" and "to pene-

---

[7] Arrow, nevertheless, endorses such codes "limited in their scope" (p. 316), basing his argument on the large size of many firms, with their diffuse external social pressures and their "internal pressures for acceptability and esteem," on the belief that it is in the best interests of those who obey the codes to enforce them, and on the likelihood that some employees will blow the whistle on violations in their own firms (p. 316). The evidence we have cited in this chapter supports just the opposite conclusion.

trate further into the hurly-burly of decisions at the operating levels" (Ackerman 1975, p. 59). But a curious paradox arises from using this approach, because it suggests that to evoke socially responsive behavior, the corporation must revert to Autocracy.[8] Furthermore, this approach is ad hoc, and tends to be applied superficially, so that the resulting changes are often minor and, to use Bower's term, "out of organizational context" (1974, p. 201). As we saw in the example cited earlier of the ghetto manufacturing venture, applied out of organizational context, social issues have little hope of being taken seriously. Thus, relying on personal control is at best a fleeting solution to a complex problem. The organizations in question are simply too large for that kind of management on a regular basis. Many issues compete for the attention of their chief executives; it is only a matter of time before they must move on to other ones. Those goals that fail to get implanted firmly in the system of bureaucratic control tend to get lost.

Thus, to cite more systematic research on the urban issue, one study of ghetto manufacturing ventures in three firms "found that the project received support at the behest of the chief executive but lacked both the organizational and analytical accommodations accorded other new ventures." Another, a survey of 247 large corporations, "noted that *ad hoc* organizational arrangements were devised to cope with urban programs. The task was almost always assigned to an urban affairs committee or specialist or to personnel or public relations staff groups. The assignment was typically more ambiguous and tentative than usual in a large corporation, not the sort of job that a career conscious executive would necessarily welcome" (Ackerman 1973, p. 418).

There is another possible solution, implicit in Bower's finding that "The best records in the race relations area are those of single-product companies whose strong top managements are deeply involved in the business" (1970, p. 193). Not only are the managements naturally involved, but because such firms are typically not divisionalized (Wrigley 1970; Rumelt 1974), they have less need for the financial control systems that cause so many of the problems. Of course, these are not the corporations that dominate the Fortune 500 (again, Wrigley 1970 and Rumelt 1974). The battle over who should control the corporation revolves less around them than around the divisionalized giants. The implication, then, is clear: to reduce diversification and concomitant divisionalization. In other words, as we shall soon see, we may have to "restore it" in order to "trust it."

Ackerman (1975) proposes a different solution, a kind of mixed compromise, based on a pattern he observed to work in his research. This pattern proceeded through three phases, as described below:

[8]And, perhaps, aristocracy: Levitt (1968) finds, as noted in the first footnote of this chapter, that ". . . a more liberal posture is characteristic mostly of high-level businessmen who reached their positions in *other* ways than the slow and arduous, 30-year, promotion-by-promotion path" (p. 86). They were either born there, as in the case of the Rockefeller brothers, started out as entrepreneurs, as in the case of Norton Simon, or were signalled out as protégés early in their careers, as in the case of Charles Percy (pp. 86–88).

PHASE I: POLICY   The issue emerged at first as a concern of the chief executive. His job was to build up a political base for the issue in the organization, to drive it into the corporate consciousness. In effect, pressure on the External Coalition had to be converted into pressure on the Internal Coalition. But at this point, there was no corporate action: no government regulation required response, no pressure groups forced the organization to act, and the organization still lacked the skills to act.

PHASE II: LEARNING   The first action, generally at the behest of the chief executive, was the addition to the headquarters staff of specialists on the issue. But their role was a difficult one, since the line managers generally denied them support. But at least the specialists made the line managers conscious of the issue, at time raising organizational hackles. Gradually they built up expertise on the issue, and began to develop support when the line managers had to call upon them to help resolve related social problems.

PHASE III: COMMITMENT   Finally the focus shifted to the operating line management, where action could readily be taken. Ackerman found that responsibility for the issue became "firmly lodged" there, and performance on the issue was measured and rewarded within the formal control system. However, the transition from Phase II and III tended to be "traumatic," set off by a social demand—such as a pollution complaint or an employee discrimination charge. That transition involved friction between an intervening headquarters and a resisting division. It also entailed a good deal of inherent chaos: ". . . imagine seven levels of management, from the president to a first-line supervisor, located in four cities attempting to coordinate response to a delicate employee controversy" (1975, p. 78). But the division managers eventually learned that the issue was important, that they were responsible for acting on it, and that they would be left alone if they did. A significant component of successful resolution, however, was incorporation of the issue into the corporation's formal control system: ". . . division managers . . . tended to see the familiar budgeting and reporting format as preferable to the ad hoc surveillance that had existed previously" (p. 79). And so "supplementary reporting and auditing practices tended to proliferate at division levels" as "criteria used in performance evaluation at division levels began to incorporate responsiveness to . . . social demand[s]." The headquarters' "specialist concentrated less on initiating response and more on managing the reporting system and analyzing division programs," while " the chief executive . . . tended to place emphasis on reviewing division plans and evaluating results" (p. 80).

Ackerman presents this pattern as a model to be followed by the divisionalized corporation. He found that by its use, "the strengths of the divisionalized organization were ultimately applied to social responsiveness rather than being subverted by it" (p. 80).

Such an approach should certainly be encouraged where it can work. But in at least two ways it falls far short of satisfying the opponents of "trust it." First, as Ackerman's description makes clear, a prerequisite for dealing with social issues in this way is the presence of measures that can be incorporated into the formal control system. But as noted earlier, even in a quotation by Ackerman himself, for many of the most sensitive social issues, effective measures simply do not exist. So the corporation is reduced to preselecting the social issues to which it will respond, according to the measures available, or else to operationalizing certain social goals in trivial ways (for example, measuring product safety by counting the number of customer complaints received in the mail). And second, Ackerman's description also makes clear that "trust it" cannot be trusted alone. The fact is that he makes an excellent case for "pressure it," by showing that only after specific outside pressures does the corporation respond to social issues:

> In my observation the transition to Phase III was consistently accompanied by one or more incidents that traumatized portions of the organization. . . . the shock of being enmeshed in a highly visible situation that could have unpleasant consequences sparked the realization that the social demand and the corporation's reaction to it was of direct and immediate significance to [the operating manager]. It could not be avoided or left to others. . . . is trauma inevitable? It is readily acknowledged that more peaceful means of effecting change may be available; in time, managers may know enough about how to employ them effectively in the large corporation. But, I suggest that under current circumstances, trauma is highly probable. (pp. 304–5)

Ackerman in fact helps us to put some of our different postures into perspective by suggesting that there exists a predictable "social issue life cycle" (which we introduced back in Chapter 5). At first the issue is "unthought of or unthinkable." Indeed sanctions are often applied to those who dare to raise it. The issue then goes through stages of " increasing awareness, expectations, demands for action and ultimately enforcement." At the end of all this— probably a matter of decades—the issue "may cease to be a matter of active public concern. New standards of behavior may then have become so ingrained in the normal conduct of affairs that to behave otherwise would bring the social and economic sanctions formerly reserved for the contrary behavior" (all quotations from p. 31).

As shown in Figure 30–1, in our terms this translates into the following sequence: "Pressure it" comes first, as special interest groups challenge specific organizations in order to change their behaviors as well as to raise the general consciousness of the public. "Regulate it" follows, as public sentiment forces the government to impose formal constraints on the corporation. And the end comes with "trust it," as the issue becomes accepted as a social norm, perhaps to the point of where it no longer even need be reflected in the formal control system

"Pressure It" ➡ "Regulate It" ➡ "Trust It"

Figure 30–1. *A Pattern Among the Positions (based on the findings of Ackerman, 1975)*

of the corporation.[9] Note the location of "trust it": at the end of the sequence. This suggests that corporate behavior lags behind social sentiment. The corporation is not responsive or even, as defined earlier, responsible; it is reactive.

"TRUSTING IT"

Earlier we promised that after driving nails all around the coffin of social responsibility, we would conclude that not only must it work but that it indeed does. The coffin may be sealed, but the spirit manages to escape. Given all this negative evidence, how can we salvage this position? How can we possibly "trust it"?

The task of salvaging is in fact quite a simple one, based on two fundamental points usually forgotten in the attacks on social responsibility. The first, mentioned at the outset of our discussion in Chapter 25, is that **the strategic decisions of large organizations inevitably involve social as well economic consequences, inextricably intertwined** (e.g., Pfiffner 1960; Mintzberg, Raisinghani, and Théorêt 1976). That is what renders the arguments of Friedman, and their echoes from the left, so utterly false. The neat distinction between private economic goals and public social goals, which sounds so good in theory, simply does not hold up in reality. Every time the large corporation makes an important decision—to introduce a new product line, to locate a plant, to close down a division—it generates all kinds of social consequences. As we noted in Chapter 25, size alone makes economic decisions social. And as we commented there with respect to Dow Chemical's experiences with napalm, the large corporation cannot remain neutral when it makes strategic decisions. In other words, there is no such things as a purely economic strategic decision in big business. Every one is also social (or, if you prefer, political): ". . . the corporation is a social world, with social obligations to its members, as well as an economizing instrument competitively providing goods at least cost to an economic world of consumers" (Bell 1971, p. 24). Only a conceptual ostrich, with his head deeply buried in economic theory, could possibly use the distinction between economic and social goals to dismiss social responsibility.

This is not to suggest that we must embrace social responsibility as the

[9]To quote Ackerman: ". . . a final rather mild transition to a fourth phase may ensue. It is probable that eventually the measurement system and the associated link to performance appraisal will be found superfluous and eventually discarded. The reason lies not in the fact that continued action on the issue is unnecessary, but rather that the process for responding to it has been so institutionalized that separate accounting has little usefulness" (1975, p. 81).

solution to all our problems. It is nonsense to believe that business can solve the ills of society. It is also risky to allow business to use its resources without restraint in the social sphere, whether that be to support political candidates or to dictate implicitly how nonprofit institutions spend their money. But where business is involved in the issue to begin with, where it possesses "authority in the area and should...have it," that is where social responsibility comes in, as Drucker finally concludes (1973, p. 50). Thinking back on our discussion, a variety of places appropriate for social responsibility come to mind. Where formal regulations are necessary but cannot work, for example, where business creates externalities that cannot be measured and attributed to it. Where regulation could work if only business would cooperate to help enact sensible legislation. Where existing legislation needs compliance with its spirit as well as its letter. Where the corporation can fool its customers or suppliers or the government through its superior knowledge. Where employees need the freedom to blow the whistle on their superiors for the sake of the common good. Wherever a choice must be made—in the selection of products and services, for example—that can tilt the balance toward what is useful to society instead of what is useless or destructive. These are the places where we must expect responsible behavior: "...social responsibility is not telling society what is good for society but responding to what society tells the firm the society wants and expects from it" (Waters 1977, p. 44). The question is one of basic ethics.

But can the businessman be socially responsible, or ethical, in these areas? All the evidence notwithstanding, the answer is that of course he can. Our second point, as Ackerman shows, is that **there is always some zone of discretion in strategic decision making.** Contemporary control systems may reduce it drastically, but, as the saying goes, where there's a will, there's a way. That is presumably what prompted 77 percent of Brenner and Molander's respondents to reject the statement that "every business is in effect 'trapped' in the business system it helped to create, and can do remarkably little about the social problems of our time" (1977, p. 68).

There seems little doubt that social responsibility in large corporations could be an awful lot better. But it could be one hell of a lot worse too. We have no idea of the depths to which we can drop (although Singer and Wooton's description of Speers "administrative genius" provides some indication). It is our ethics that keep us from falling any lower. In other words, if we cannot trust our corporate managers, then we are in serious trouble. Those ethics need not only define a base level of social responsibility; they can also bring us up from where we are. We must, in Water's words "tap into the tremendous reservoir of energy that exists among employees" in organizations, "unblock [their] natural ethical instincts" (1978, p. 13). These are what must counter the forces pulling us down. Faced with a choice on Wednesday at 11:02 A.M., to decide how high to build that smokestack, what can counter the pressures of the financial controls is the manager's nagging sense of social responsibility, that there can be more important things in life than growth and profit.

To dismiss social responsibility is to allow corporate behavior to drop to the lowest common denominator, propped up only by external controls, by regulations and pressures and the like. It is to give credence to the voices of gloom, such as those of Tumin. Instead, we would do better to remember that of Solzhenitsyn: "...a society with no other scale but the legal one is not quite worthy of man... A society which is based on the letter of the law and never reaches any higher is scarcely taking advantage of the high level of human possibilities." We must reverse a long-term trend toward bureaucratic impersonality and utilitarianism—toward squeezing ideals, beliefs, feelings, and the sense of mission and purpose out of our organizations. Solzhenitsyn has experienced the natural finale to that trend. We are heading in that same direction, driven by bureaucracy—no matter that it be private as well as public. The pace of that trend is slowed only by social responsibility. But social responsibility can also reverse that trend.

To conclude, we cannot only "trust it"; we cannot "trust it" to do what is unsuited to it; we cannot "trust it" without "pressuring it" and "regulating it" and perhaps even "restoring it." But we had better realize that we are also obligated in good measure to "trust it." Without responsible and ethical people in important places, our society is worth nothing.

31

"Ignore It"
(Because "It Pays to Be Good")

Continuing around to the right on our horseshoe, the next position also holds that corporations need not act irresponsibly, but for a different reason. Proponents of this position postulate that the economic and social goals of the corporation coincide because "it pays to be good." This is sometimes referred to as "enlightened self-interest"—what Keim describes as "an objective effort to rationalize corporate social investment" (1978, p. 33)—although, as we shall soon see, some of its proponents are less "objective" and "enlightened" than others.

One of the clearest statements of this position, that the businessman "does well by doing good," comes from the second Henry Ford, who claimed in 1970 that the successful companies during the rest of this century will be those able to "get a jump on the competition" by being socially responsive: "There is no longer anything to reconcile, if there ever was, between the social conscience and the profit motive. Improving the quality of life...is nothing more than another step in the evolutionary process of taking a more far-sighted view of return on investment" (quoted in Ackerman 1973, p. 413).

And, not incidentally, if there is no conflict between economic and social goals, then it stands to reason that the corporation should be left alone as a Closed System: the positions to the left and right on the horseshoe that call for change are misguided because there is nothing to worry about. "Ignore it" is the implication: the managers can remain in charge because their behavior has to be socially responsible.

"Ignore it" is fundamentally different from, and slightly to the right of, "trust it." For while the proponents of "trust it" call on the corporation to change its behavior voluntarily, because "to be good" is the right thing to do, those of "ignore it" expect it to be good for its own self-interest, because it will pay to do so. The distinction may be subtle, but it is important. Here, not ethics but economics is the motivating force; social needs just fall conveniently into place. And yet, as we shall soon see, many a true believer in "trust it" hides behind the banner of "ignore it." The argument that "it pays to be good" provides these people with a means to ward off the attacks from the right that businessmen have no business pursuing social goals. Even Milton Friedman must admit that they have every right to do so if it can be shown to pay economically. As if socially responsible behavior needs an excuse in the corporation!

ARGUMENTS IN FAVOR OF "IGNORING IT"

Two fundamental perspectives must be distinguished in discussing the "ignore it" position. The "micro" perspective holds that the individual corporation will benefit directly from its own socially responsible actions, that there will be a specific payoff to it. The "macro," or collective, perspective holds that corporations in general will benefit, that while there may be no direct, immediate payoff, to specific firms, in the long run the whole business community will benefit indirectly from socially responsible behavior.

With this in mind, we can distinguish three basic arguments used to justify this position, one micro, one spanning both perspectives, and one macro.

THE DIRECT REWARDS ARGUMENT   The most direct argument focuses on the relationship between specific socially responsible behaviors and economic performance. A classic example is that between worker satisfaction and productivity (e.g., Likert 1961). "Treat them well, get them involved, and you'll make more money," we were told by a generation of industrial psychologists in the 1960s. Seldom did they say, "Treat them well because they are human beings like yourself," or "Get them involved because how else can we call this society democratic," although there never seemed any doubt, to this observer at least, that this was the hidden agenda. In the ways of business, everything had to be justified on economic grounds. In any event, research cast doubt on the basic proposition (at least in general [Fiedler 1966]), and so the proponents of worker participation have had to fall back on the more honest positions of "trust it" or "pressure it," or, increasingly in recent years, especially in Europe, "democratize it."[1] Learned, Dooley, and Katz provide a number of other examples of direct rewards for particular social actions (or losses for antisocial ones):

[1]In the eyes of some observers (e.g., Perrow 1974), "participative" management has also served the interests of the managers of the Closed System power configuration by providing a surrogate for democratizing the corporation without changing the basic power relationships. As we saw in Chapter 27, some observers believe that it was the gaining of popularity of this argument that caused the shift in the Swedish debate from participative management to co-determination.

• A supplier refuses to exploit his advantage during a sellers' market and thereby retains the loyalty (and continued business) of customers when conditions change to those of a buyers' market.

• A firm that employs handicapped persons discovers that they are actually more productive, hard-working, loyal, and so on than the nonhandicapped persons normally employed.

• A customer is dealt with unfairly and thereafter refuses to deal with the supplier in question. Other firms, learning of the situation, also refuse to deal with the supplier because "he has shown he cannot be trusted."

• A firm allows its salesmen to disseminate misleading information about its competitors' products. This invites open retaliation by competing salesmen (who perhaps prove even more effective in their use of this technique). (1959, p. 116)

THE SOUND INVESTMENT ARGUMENT   The second argument for "ignore it," really coming from its left on the horseshoe, builds on the premise that "social responsibility is a *sound investment*." Here the case is more general. Social responsibility pays off, it is claimed, in a better image for the firm, more positive relationships with its associates, indeed a healthier and more stable society in which to do business. For example, "crime will decrease with the consequence that less money will be spent to protect property, and less taxes will have to be paid to support police forces. The argument can be extended in all directions showing that a better society produces a better environment for business" (Davis 1973, p. 313).

But there can be direct payoffs too: the responsible firm will find it easier to attract customers, its employees will be more loyal, it will get better cooperation from the local community. Drucker (1973) aruges that both direct and indirect benefits can accrue from "solving the social problem." He cites the case of Julius Rosenwald, the builder of Sears, Roebuck, who financed the County Farm Agent program to help the American farmer out of his "poverty, ignorance, and isolation." This program raised the farmer's productivity and, as a result, expanded Sear's markets and profits. The company became the "farmer's friend" (p. 338). Similarly, "operators of phosphate strip mines in Florida have found that after mining they can convert the land to homesites on lakes, resulting in better land than it was originally—all with a profit" (Davis 1973, p. 317).

It is perhaps Bowman who develops the "sound investment" argument most fully, and literally. In a paper entitled "Corporate Social Responsibility and the Investor," Bowman (1973) proposes the hypothesis that through the effect of a "neo-invisible hand," the market price of a company's stock is affected by its social behavior. He attacks two "myths" in his paper, "that corporate social responsibility is dependent on either the noblesse oblige of the manager or the laws of the government," and "that corporate social responsibility is in fundamental conflict with investor interests" (p. 42). That is, he specifically rejects both the "trust it" and "regulate it" positions—at least in their pure forms— in favor of "ignore it." Bowman argues that the neo-invisible hand is supplied by the "viable coalition" of the corporation's constituents—its owners, employees, customers, the government, and so on. In some cases, a firm pays directly for irresponsible behavior. Bowman cites the example of the Dutch firm whose operations were struck by unions all over Europe angry about the disruptive effects to one local community of a proposed plant shutdown, and that of a French firm whose new plant could not start up for six months because the local town found the pollution levels unacceptable. Because these firms were not socially responsible, Bowman argues, they encountered costly pressure campaigns. (Bowman is, of course, implicitly making a strong case for "pressure it" too.)

But it is in the response of the investment community to social behavior that Bowman most forcefully presents his case that "it pays to be good": ". . . the market's perception of corporate responsibility may affect the price of the stock and, therefore, the investor's return. . . In addition to this direct effect, the price of the stock will have subsequent effects on the cost of capital to the growing company and ultimately on its earnings" (p. 33). In other words, Bowman introduces the stock market as the vehicle by which the indirect benefits of social responsibility are converted into direct ones. Bowman then presents a variety of arguments to make his point:

* ". . . many institutional investors now argue that the corporation which is not responsive to corporate social responsibility will be a more risky investment" (p. 34)

* To the extent that investors worry about social issues and as a result refuse to hold the stock of corporations perceived as socially irresponsible, the market for their stock thins and price falls (in effect, making the hypothesized relationship between social behavior and stock price a self-fulfilling prophecy); Bowman finds considerable evidence that an increasing number of investors are acting in this way, notably churches, universities, and individual holders of the so-called "clean" mutual funds, those intent on investing in "social benefactors" (p. 37).

* To the extent that investment portfolios are diversified, actions by individual corporations which benefit the corporate sector as a whole—for example, by improving the environment—also benefit the individual investor (an argument from Wallich and McGowan 1970).

Bowman presents his case in a straightforward manner, fully in the spirit of "ignore it." But a little scratching of the "sound investment" arguments of others often uncovers proponents of "trust it," trying to justify their beliefs in self-interest terms. In an earlier era, the arguments were religious and personal: "Be good or you will go to hell"—literally! Again, responsible behavior was not proposed as an end in itself—not a question of trust, or ethics, or even devotion—but the logical result of a self-interest calculation. Ethical behavior paid off, if not in this life, then at least in the next. Today, of course, the case has to be made in economic terms (during this life), although it remains fundamentally the same. The gates of the treasury in this world, if not those of the heavens in the next, will open to those who are socially responsible.

But using the "ignore it" arguments to justify what is essentially a "trust it" position can sometimes lead to curious logic, as is evident in the famous *A. B. Smith* vs. *V. Barlow et al.* court case. Here one company's donation of $1,500 to Princeton University was challenged by some of its shareholders, which forced it to justify the action in a court of law. State Supreme Court Justice J. Jacobs summarized in his opinion some of the testimony of the company executives and their influential supporters:

> Mr. Hubert F. O'Brien, the president of the company, testified that he considered the contribution to be a sound investment, that the public expects corporations to aid philanthropic and benevolent institutions, that they obtain good will in the community by so doing, and that their charitable donations create favorable environment for their business operations. In addition, he expressed the thought that in contributing to liberal arts institutions, corporations were furthering their self-interest in assuring the free flow of properly trained personnel for administrative and other corporate employment. Mr. Frank W. Abrams, chairman of the board of the Standard Oil Company of New Jersey, testified...that it was not "good business" to disappoint "this reasonable and justified public expectation"... Mr. Irving S. Olds, former chairman of the board of the United States Steel Corporation, pointed out that corporations have a self-interest in the maintenance of liberal education as the bulwark of good government. (*Atlantic Reporter*, 1953, p. 582)

While the judges found in favor of the company, the court in effect struck down "trust it." Reflecting what is essentially the perspective of the right side of the horseshoe, the court—in this case and others—forced businessmen to justify their actions in terms of self-interest. And, ironically, such justification plays directly into the hands of the activists on the left side of the horseshoe, who claim that all businessmen ever talk about is their own self-interest. The point is developed eloquently by John Desmond Glover, and is worth quoting at length:

> It is surprising and ironical, that, to judge by what businessmen often *say*, one would think that they, too, agree that the nature of business corporations is exactly and precisely what critics say it is; namely, that the corporation has no other purpose, and recognizes no other criterion of decision except profits, and that it pursues these profits just as single-mindedly and irresponsibly as it can....
>
> For many purposes of the law, the business corporation is conceived to be the very same bloodless, heartless, opportunisitc, selfishly calculating entity depicted by its critics....
>
> ...a *seemingly* charitable act can be justified if it can be shown that it was *really* motivated only by the ulterior intent of furthering the corporation's own interest in a calculated way....

In the inverted morality of corporations—as laid down for them by the law—any act in which there enters a thought of charity or philanthrophy, or any imponderable feelings of business responsibility and obligation, is not the kind of thing corporations can be expected ordinarily to do. . . .

This concept of the business corporation in law, and the rule which flows from it, results in corporation lawyers cooking up, for formal resolutions to be adopted by boards of directors, the most far-fetched kinds of reasons to rationalize as calculating acts for gain what were simply normal acts of people trying to exercise ordinary judgment. In fact, the rule *drives* lawyers to insist upon the invention of elaborate ulterior reasons for decisions which are actually made on the basis of ordinary, common-sense judgments. Corporations are compelled, for the record, to malign their own motives. (1954, pp. 328, 331, 333–35)

THE "THEM" ARGUMENT   The third argument in support of "ignore it"— always general and indirect in its promised benefits, coming from the right side of the horseshoe, and a little less "enlightened" in its self-interest—claims: "If we're not good, *they* will move in." In other words, "Be good or else!" Thus, Ackerman refers to the "fear of reprisal," the feeling by businessmen that they are vulnerable to attack from the left and so had better keep their noses clean. "The danger may be 'the fire next time' or a form of legal sanction more damaging to business interests in the long run than some measure of current sacrifice or self-regulation" (1973, p. 412). One needs only glance over to the left side of the horseshoe to understand the dangers: first pressure campaigns from special interest groups, then regulations from the government, beyond that democratization or even outright nationalization. Thus speaks the retired chief executive of Northern Illinois Gas Company in calling for corporations to broaden the representation on their boards of directors:

> The time has come for a hard-nosed, get-tough approach. With rising public concern over the alleged concentration and selfishness and coziness of corporate power, we had better work fast and hard at putting our houses in order, before the government assumes the job. (Chandler 1975, p. 82)

Here, it should be noted, social responsibility becomes a pure political tool, a means to maintain the features of a given system of power. This is how to keep the External Coalitions of giant corporations passive and to maintain them as Closed Systems, with their managers firmly in charge. "The clock is running out on free enterprise," says the chief executive of General Motors. "If we in business want to remain as free as we still are to respond to the desires of our customers, rather than to those of government regulators, we are going to have to fulfill the businessman's first, last, and always responsibility: the responsibility to satisfy these customers—today, right now, not tomorrow" (Murphy 1976, p. 11).

The trouble with this third argument for "ignore it," rooted as it is in the preservation of an existing—and to many observers questionable—distribution of power, is that it tends to encourage general pronouncements instead of concrete actions (unless, of course, "they" actually deliver with pressure campaigns). This seems to come out most clearly in the report of the fifty-fourth "American Assembly" (1978), a meeting of a lot of influential friends of the corporation. Entitled "Corporate Governance in America," the report presents the "them" argument in its preamble: ". . . if private initiatives fail, the issues of corporate governance are important enough that government will have to address them" (p. 5). The report then proposes a series of recommendations, in general always for social responsibility, in particular always for the preservation of the status quo of power. For example:

* Shareholders, as "the undisputed owners of the corporation," "should exercise [their] power" to "sensitize management and directors to social as well as economic issues" (p. 5).

* "Employees should be regarded as a crucial part of the constituency of the corporation" but their "interests will be better served by various means, such as collective bargaining, direct communications, and participative management approaches rather than by direct employee representation on boards of directors" (p. 6).

* "Managers must be made more aware of their various publics. . . Corporations can and should improve their responsiveness to emerging social and ethical questions" (p. 6).

* "Boards should continue to be the central focus in improving the way corporations are governed," and while candidates for directorships "should be recommended for the diversity of their substantive experience," they "should not be chosen to represent specific constituency interests" (pp. 6, 7). And, "rather than permanent staff of their own, directors should have free access to corporate staff" (p. 7).

* Concerning regulation: "We should continue to encourage private initiative by corporations and self-regulation by industry groups" (p. 9).

So much for the horseshoe; the American Assembly's corporate horse will have to ride on a single nail! That, however, just might prove painful.

EVIDENCE FOR AND AGAINST "IGNORING IT"

There is no shortage of rhetoric in the literature on "who should control the corporation." What it lacks is empirical evidence to show the effects of the different positions on the social and economic ends actually pursued by corporations. Each position raises not only questions of values and power, but also ones of facts and effectiveness. Does nationalization really reduce economic efficiency? Indeed, does it even increase social responsiveness? Do pressure campaigns produce real social progress or only corporate turmoil? Does democratization of the board of directors make any difference, either to corporate behavior or influencer participation? Does the corporate talk of social responsibility really get manifested in corporate action? Where we have systematic evidence, as in the case of these last two questions, the results are eye-opening, and change the whole tenor of the debate.

BOWMAN AND HAIRE'S STUDY OF PROSE AND PROFITS   In this regard, we have the beginnings of some evidence on "it pays to be good." Among the most interesting studies is one in which Bowman teamed up with Haire (1975, 1976) to test his hypothesis that some kind of neo-invisible hand aligns society's interests with those of the shareholders.

Bowman and Haire used an ingenious research methodology. They performed a line-by-line content analysis of the 1973 annual reports of eighty-two food processing companies in order to ascertain the percent of total prose devoted to issues of corporate social responibility. This figure was then used as a surrogate for actual company concern and activity, which they related to company performance. The researchers were quick to address the obvious question that arises, "that talk is cheap" (1975, p. 50). They took a list of fourteen companies that had been identified by the editor of *Business & Society* "as being outstandingly responsible firms," and matched each with another firm in the industry, randomly selected, of approximately the same size. A content analysis of the annual reports of the twenty-eight firms found the percentage of prose content on corporate social responsibility (CSR) to average 4.8 percent for the "premier" firms, 1.7 percent for the "neutral" ones, a difference that was statistically significant at the 2 percent level.[2]

Returning to the eighty-two food companies, Bowman and Haire found their main hypothesis supported at the 2 percent level as well. In other words, those firms mentioning CSR performed significantly better than those that did not (14.7 percent median return on equity [ROE] vs. 10.2 percent over the preceding five year period[3]).

But a breakdown of the data provides a more interesting result. As can be seen in Figure 31-1, firms that never mentioned CSR at all exhibited the weakest performance, those that mentioned it the least (0.1–8 percent of the prose of the annual report) performed best, while those with the most CSR prose (more than 16 percent of that in the annual reports) exhibited performance only slightly better than the first group (12.3 percent ROE vs. 10.2 percent, compared with 17.1 percent for the second group). In other words, the relationship between the two factors had an inverted U-shape. (Note that fifty-one of the eighty-two

[2]The authors also present data comparing the mention of international activity with Standard and Poor's rating of actual international activity, by which they substantiate the use of the prose of the annual report as "a reasonable surrogate for real activity" (1976, p. 15).

[3]The means were 14.3 percent and 9.1 percent respectively.

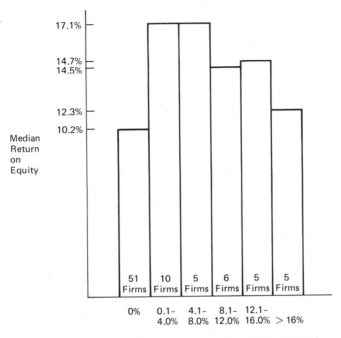

Median
Return
on
Equity

17.1%

14.7%
14.5%

12.3%

10.2%

| 51 Firms | 10 Firms | 5 Firms | 6 Firms | 5 Firms | 5 Firms |

| 0% | 0.1– 4.0% | 4.1– 8.0% | 8.1– 12.0% | 12.1– 16.0% | > 16% |

Percentage of Prose on Corporate Social Responsibility in
the Annual Reports of 82 Food Processing Companies

Figure 31–1. *Prose and Profits (based on figures from the study by Bowman and Haire, 1975)*

firms surveyed—almost two-thirds of them—fell into the first category, with no prose at all, a point we shall return to.)

Bowman and Haire explain this finding as follows: Social responsibility is costly. It means, in effect, the absorption of "positive externalities," that is, the incurring of costs for which there are no direct benefits (such as the hiring disadvantaged workers and absorbing the cost of having to train them). The stock market, however, is willing to reward such behavior—in effect, to create benefits for the firm. But only to a point. Beyond that, it is unwilling to absorb the costs. In other words, it pays to be good, but not too good.

But that is not quite the right conclusion to draw from these findings. As some of Bowman's examples cited earlier indicate, the real point seems to be not that social responsibility rewards the corporation, but that social irresponsibility penalizes it. It is not that "it pays to be good"; rather, apparently, "it costs to be bad." It also costs to be very good—what Sethi calls social responsiveness, being "anticipatory and preventative" rather than adaptive (1975, p. 63). "Don't stand out from the crowd," seems to be Bowman and Haire's real message; do no more than is expected. They say it themselves: ". . . the mean really is golden" (1975, p. 57). In Sethi's terms, the appropriate position is not even social responsibility but only "social obligation."

And then one is still left with the nagging problem of causation, of explaining what causes what in the relationship Bowman and Haire found between social responsibility and profits. Especially for the poor performers. While it seems reasonable to conclude that it costs to be very good, should we also accept that it costs to be bad? Is it not equally possible that poor economic performers cannot afford social responsibility, at least in the short run? As Drucker notes, "...in order to 'do good,' a business must first 'do well'" (1973, p. 345).[4] Indeed, from what we found out in the last chapter, is it not likely that the poor performers may tend to act irresponsibly in order to try to catch up? Were these suspicions true, the corporation could interpret the Bowman and Haire findings in the exact opposite way they intended: it does not pay to be too good, and if one is weak, it may even pay to be bad. Obviously their data say nothing about irresponsible behavior, but the absence of prose in the annual report could just as well mean irresponsible behavior as minimally acceptable behavior. All of this takes us a long way with some prose in an annual report, but it is fun to speculate.[5]

OTHER STUDIES OF SOCIAL RESPONSIBILITY AND PERFORMANCE   Other studies, for the most part, seem consistent with these findings. For example, Bowman and Haire (1975) refer to a study in the pulp and paper industry called "Is Pollution Profitable?" in which the researchers took a list of companies carefully ranked on an index of pollution control and then ranked them on different performance measures. The correlations between the two measures were all positive, and, under certain conditions, significant. When Bowman and Haire further broke down the sample, they again found the assymetrical inverted U-shaped relationship. In other words, the average firms on the pollution index performed best economically, while the lowest performed worst. Dent (1959), too, found a similar relationship between the propensity of managers to express public service as a goal and the performance of their firms in terms of rate of growth.

Alexander and Buchholz (1978) provide corroborating evidence of a sort. They cite two contradictory studies. One showed that fourteen firms with "good social responsibility credentials" (probably the same firms Bowman and Haire used in their test of the CSR measure) outperformed stock market averages

---

[4]He adds, "and indeed 'do very well,'" to which the reader of Bowman and Haire's findings might respond, "but in that case, not very good."

[5]Bowman does recognize the problem of causation, noting three possible explanations for the relationship between performance and social behavior: "Good investments require good company management, and good management is responsible, worldly, and modern, and these traits are evidenced by concern about and involvement in the general social / economic problems of our times; profitable and successful companies have sufficient resources so they can allocate a portion of social concerns, thus evidencing the power and flexibility of their resources; and corporate activities and expenditures for social concern at an adequate level are really in the self-interest of the firm..." (1973, p. 33).

during a six-month period. The other, of forty-five and fifty firms rated respectively by businessmen and students on "their perceived degree of social responsibility," found a negative correlation between these ratings and stock market performance during a twelve-month period. Then, in their own study of forty firms, Alexander and Buchholz found no significant correlation between stock market performance (or stock risk levels) over a five-year period and social responsibility ratings by students and businessmen. But these results should not be surprising given the U-shaped nature of the curve.[6]

SOCIAL RESPONSIBILITY AS A FUNCTION OF SIZE   There is one other finding in some of the research that is of interest, namely on the relationship between the size of the firm and its social behavior. Some studies have postulated that big firms, being more vulnerable, must be more socially responsive.[7] Thus Lentz and Tschirgi (1963), in an earlier content analysis of annual reports, found support for this (although, like Bowman and Haire, they found that few annual reports had any "ethical content" at all, only 52 of 219; such content tended to be associated with firms dealing directly with household consumers and the general public as well as those that were closely regulated). Buehler and Shetty (1976) found support for this, too, in a questionnaire study that surveyed the establishment of specialized social responsibility positions and the like. But both research teams admittedly studied only large firms in the first place.

The opposite perspective comes from Keim (1978), who argues that small firms, being committed to specific, identifiable communities, not only must be more responsive to their needs, but also have more to gain from being so, since the benefits are more localized. Shades of Bower's finding, cited in the last chapter, about the better social performance of the single-product companies, "whose strong top managements are deeply involved in the business" (1970, p. 193). Keim found that "in 1970 and 1971, firms with total assets in the five to ten million dollar range were considerably more generous in terms of percentage of net income given to philanthropic causes than were larger firms" (p. 37).

---

[6]Sturdivant and Ginter (1977) found that groups of companies scoring both best and honorable mention in a social responsibility survey significantly outperformed a group scoring worst, another finding consistent with that of Bowman and Haire. Of interest to researchers in this study is that the firms were found to differ on their response rates to the questionnaires sent them. The two former groups averaged seven and six responses per firm respectively, the latter, three. Returning researchers' questionnaires is also a socially responsible activity! So much for the use of questionnaires to survey attitudes on social responsibility.

[7]The suggestion has also been made (by Wallich and McGowen 1970, elaborated by Keim 1978, and mentioned in the review of Bowman's arguments) that the holder of the diversified portfolio—and that must include the largest corporations, which are mostly diversified in one way or another—has more to gain from broad socially responsible activity. That is because its effects are more likely to diffuse back to the various businesses it owns. But this argument would seem better suited to a communist economy—organized as one giant diversified firm—than one of private corporations in which the GNP has passed the $1 trillion mark.

Keim in fact probably makes the strongest argument of all for "ignore it," at least in this limited context, by showing that indirect benefits become direct when the firm relates to one identifiable community on a personal basis. The one-plant, small-town company simply cannot afford a bad reputation locally, and gains directly from benefits that accrue to the community. "A contribution to the local hospital improves medical service for the firm's employees"; moreover, better health care facilities may make it "easier to attract new employees to the community and to retain existing workers" (pp. 37, 38). The giant, diversified corporation, with its operations in many communities run by what have been called "executive birds of passage" is less committed to any single place, not to mention any single industry or group of customers. That should lead it to take a more detached perspective, which may mean a less socially responsible one. In a sense, because the constituency of the diversified giant is everyone, it is no one. What better incentive for rhetoric to replace action—the national public relations campaign instead of the local pollution control program.

In this regard, it is of interest to consider how social responsibility has been studied in firms of different size. While the studies of the big firms found that the "responsible" ones used more prose in their annual reports, impressed the editor of a national magazine, replied appropriately in a questionnaire, or created yet another slot in the bureaucracy—this one programmed to make everyone else responsible—the one study we have of small firms found that they actually put more cash on the table. We are back to the point made in the last chapter about the institution of more bureaucratic procedures to deal with the problems created by bureaucratic procedures, except that here it is the researchers who get caught up in the system, by using what are essentially bureaucratic research methodologies—that is, standardized, impersonal ones. How to measure the true social responsibility of a Beatrice Foods, with its four hundred some odd divisions? How to decide whether or not the three quarters of a million General Motors employees act responsibly? In the public mind, one scandal can cancel years of honest efforts on the part of thousands of employees. So too can a good public relations campaign encourage the public to forget about years of interminable irresponsibility. And if the researcher cannot even measure real social responsibility in the large firm, how are its top managers to ensure it, let alone think about it?

The point is that commitment—simple involvement on a *personal* basis—would seem to be at the root of true social responsibility. And this observer at least believes that the discouraging evidence presented in the last chapter reflects the limited possibilities for such commitment in the large, diversified firm. Is not the personalized control implicit in the commitment to a local community a far stronger basis on which to build social responsibility than the impersonalized control implicit in the publication of a list of bad guys in a national magazine? In other words, might we not conclude that the only way we can "ignore it" is to "restore it" (by "reducing it")?

SHOULD WE "IGNORE IT"?

To conclude, "ignore it" because "it pays to be good" would seem to hold some promise for the firm committed in a personalized way to some identifiable community (of customers, local citizens, or whomever). But, again, the debate does not revolve around these firms (probably for this reason); it focusses on the giant firms that are diversified, divisionalized, dispersed, and detached.

With regard to these firms, the case for "ignore it" is not very strong. The "direct rewards" argument does have some support, but it is limited to certain specific behaviors. Indeed, some other socially desirable behaviors—for example, improving the quality of work or encouraging the participation of workers— sometimes show opposite results, namely "direct penalties."[8] The "them" argument—social responsibility or else—seems to encourage, not constructive change, but retrenchment back to the status quo. As for the main argument— social responsibility as a "sound investment"—it, too, seems to rest on shaky ground. Even if we were to accept that prose becomes practice and that behavior affects profits and not vice versa, the effect of this argument is to encourage average behavior, while maintaining the Closed System power configuration. There seem to be much more in this argument for the manager inside than the citizen outside.

Indeed, the evidence presented by Bowman and Haire and others provides ammunition for the activists. First, it shows that management is most responsive to direct threats of loss—not to fear of "them" but to actions by "them." These studies tell us that pressure campaigns raise the cost of socially irresponsible behavior. Nothing gets through to corporate managers better than such campaigns, as we saw in the results of Campaign GM as well as in Bowman's own examples. In other words, "ignore it" means nothing without "pressure it." Second, this evidence makes the case for being average, in a world where, according to the surveys discussed in Chapters 25 and 30, average has not been good enough. Through opinion polls, the majority of American citizens—even businessmen themselves—have been saying that they expect far more responsible behavior from the large corporations. It is interesting that the firms in the Bowman and Haire study that said nothing about social responsibility in their annual reports—those least socially responsible by their measure—still managed 10.2 percent ROE, enough (at the time of their study) to remain viable. And these constituted the vast majority of firms in their study. Are we to accept these researchers' surrogate measure and conclude that the vast majority of food processing firms in America do not even live up to average expectations?

All in all the evidence on "ignore it" leads us to exactly the opposite conclusion of Bowman and Haire: that it cannot be ignored because it pays not to be good enough.

[8]Some of the mixed results of the quality of working life programs are discussed in the *Structuring* book (Mintzberg 1979*a*, pp. 76–78). Fiedler (1966) discusses some conditions under which participation does not pay.

32

"Induce It"
("Pay It to Be Good")

To the right of "ignore it" stand those uncomfortable with positions that encourage the corporation to take it upon itself to respond to social issues. To them, the introduction of social goals into business decision making simply confuses the issue. The only responsibility of business is to pursue economic goals as vigorously as it can.

There are two positions on the far right side of our horseshoe, close to each other philosophically but different in what they propose. "Induce it" concentrates on incentives to business, and implicitly accepts the status quo of the Closed System power configuration, while "restore it," farthest to the right, calls for fundamental changes in the makeup of the large corporation. Looking the other way, "induce it" resembles "ignore it" in its acceptance of the power status quo, but differs in the importance it places on social goals. To the proponents of "ignore it," social goals are pursued directly, because they enable the corporation to attain its desired economic goals; to the proponents of "induce it," social goals are not pursued at all, only social programs, when they enable the corporation to satisfy its economic goals. The corporation should mind its own economic business, responding to social needs only when there is direct economic gain from doing so. If society wishes to enlist the corporation in its pursuit of social goals, then it must offer the corporation economic inducements. So whereas "ignore it" tells the corporation "it pays to be good," "induce it" tells society to "pay it to be good," and tells the corporation to "be good only where it pays."

Goldston, whose firm, Eastern Gas and Fuel Associates, has provided extensive assistance in rehabilitating apartments in Boston's Roxbury ghetto, argues that business is better qualified than government to find solutions to many urban problems provided (a) it is adequately controlled, and (b) given economic incentives to do so. For him the "military-industrial complex" is a model which can be applied to other national needs, for instance through an "educational-industrial" complex. His major premise is that once government has decided on the goals, social problems can be converted into economic opportunities which business can deal with in a manner that has proven to be highly effective. However, economic carrots—guarantees, tax benefits, subsidies, management contracts, etc.—are necessary to justify business participation and to form the basis for measurement and public control. (Ackerman 1973, pp. 413-14)

WHEN TO "INDUCE IT"

There is a good reason why "induce it" faces "regulate it" on the opposite side of the horseshoe. For while one penalized the corporation for what it does do—in other words, charges it for its negative externalities—the other rewards it for doing what it would not otherwise do—in a sense, pays it for positive externalities. In fact, the two positions are often substitutable: pollution can be alleviated by introducing penalties for the damage done or by offering incentives for the improvements rendered.

However, as noted in Chapter 29, when a negative externality can be attributed directly to a corporation, "regulate it" would seem to be the obvious position. One wonders how a government could justify paying a corporation to stop causing specific harm. Were government to get into the habit of doing things like this, corporations would be encouraged to engage in a kind of blackmail, threatening to pollute, for example, unless they were rewarded for not doing so. (A Canadian provincial government once granted an American subsidiary a large sum of money to relocate its plant within its boundaries because the firm threatened to leave and take its jobs with it. By the same token, Canadian federal governments continually complain about being short-changed on jobs in the Canada-U.S. auto pact, yet continue to offer large incentives to U.S. automobile companies for the "privilege" of having them set up plants in Canada. What we have in these examples is a perverse form of "induce it": "pay it to be nice," not good!) Clearly it is the corporation—or more exactly its customers—that should pick up the bill for any attributable damage caused by the production and consumption of its products.

"Induce it" would seem to be the logical position where social problems exist which cannot be attributed directly to specific corporations, yet require for solution the skills and knowledge that corporations have to offer. As noted above, the renovation of slum dwellings in the city core may be an example.

In other words, this is where the "only business can do it" argument belongs. When the claim is true (and business has not "done it to us" in the first place, so to speak), then business should be encouraged to do it, but not as a favor to society. By inducing it, government makes use of the market mechanism to satisfy social needs, and at the same time minimizes the proliferation of its own bureaucracy.

Although "induce it" is basically a position of the right, and a popular one there, it has proponents on the left too, some corporate activists among them. They see this position as an important means of keeping the corporation in its place, that is, in the economic sphere. If society wants something from business, then let the relationship be clear, contractual, and purely economic, so that corporate values cannot creep into social issues. Thus we find Hazel Henderson making one of the strongest pleas for "induce it":

> Fundamentally, a corporation is like a computer in that it is programmed in the language of dollars and cents. Once we understand this, we are then in a position, if we decide that we do want the corporation to participate in solving public problems, to establish ground rules to permit it to do so...
>
> ...government incentives are the most direct method of stimulating private business to perform public chores, and of course this has been accepted practice for years—as, for example, in purchasing complicated military and space hardware.
>
> ...this trend toward more government-industry cooperation is rapidly expanding into a host of other areas, such as housing, and especially education and training of dropouts from our public school systems. This need not necessarily be a bad thing. On the contrary, it is probably the most satisfactory way to handle our central needs so long as a duly elected government body, at whatever level, or some accountable public agency writes the contract, sets the performance standards and general specifications, and pays the bill at the agreed-on price (1968, pp. 81–82)

In some ways, "induce it" is the least ideological of the eight positions. It cares not for the needs of society, nor does it fight the ideologic battles of free enterprise. It merely postulates the corporation to be an economic instrument, as Henderson says, "a computer...programmed in the language of dollars and cents." Does that mean the corporation is "amoral"?

THE "AMORAL" CORPORATION?

In a paper entitled "On the Amoral Organization," Bower states:

> The argument of this paper is that the large organization is amoral. It is, perhaps, the most important technological invention of our time, but it is only a tool and it has no intent. If we are not satisfied with the results of the legal personalization

we call the corporation, we must change the guidelines provided for the managers who use the tool, or change the managers. (1974, p. 179)

But is this conclusion justified? Can an institution such as the corporation be free of morals or values? Elbing (1970) argues in contrast that the corporation is "a basic source of individual values rather than just a depository of them" (p. 82). He elaborates:

> A firm, because it is a social system as well as an economic-technical system, has profound social influence on its members and upon the larger society—that is, beyond its economic influence....
> Because the firm functions as a social system, and because the businessman has a key role in that social system, it is logically impossible to construe his behavior as falling outside the moral realm, that is, as being amoral.... [The businessman's] choice is necessarily in the *moral* realm, to be evaluated as such. (p. 88)

And what does such an evaluation reveal? Bower's own evaluation is quite clear. The essence of his argument—like that of his colleague Ackerman, in fact the source of it—is that the formal control systems of the large corporation as well as the various indoctrination techniques it uses, such as job transfer practices, force it to favor short-run economic goals. Moreover, Bower contends that the corporation, particularly the one with a divisionalized structure, tends to exhibit a distinct kind of "anti-social" behavior: ". . . because the individual is measured by his short-run efficiency within the firm, and screened by the firm from the societal effects of his behavior, management behavior is biased in a potentially anti-social, or as I have argued, amoral fashion" (p. 210).

But that doesn't sound amoral at all. Bower seems to be making a stronger case for the organization obsessed with economics than for the amoral one. And that, of course, is the point we developed at length in the chapter on "trust it," that its structure and control systems drive the large corporation to act socially unresponsively if not actually irresponsibly. A related point was developed in Chapter 16, where we argued that the seemingly value-free "criterion of efficiency" is in fact a concept laden with value. The computer is programmed in the language of numbers—performance measures—and these inevitably turn out to be economic.

INDUCEMENT IN TERMS OF ECONOMIC MORALITY

Thus, while it may sound reasonable in theory to claim that society need merely turn a few incentive levers to make better use of its economic instruments, in practice business is the instrument only of those who can play *its* game, which means expressing their needs in clear, operational terms—economic ones. And that seems to contain the essence of the arguments for and against "induce it."

On one hand, where the solutions to social problems can be defined clearly and tied directly to economic rewards, society can unleash the power of the corporations on them. On the other hand, society and its governments must find another approach where solutions cannot be expressed in terms of neat, tangible criteria, nor where there is the danger of an economic morality filtering into solutions that must at their roots be social. As we saw in Chapter 30 in our discussion of corporate attempts to solve the U.S. urban crisis and of Albert Speer's management during the Third Reich, the "hired gun"—the "professional" manager and his large organization as well—tends to be impersonal, detached, not the person or institution with the finesse needed to handle complex and delicate social problems.

To conclude, "induce it" seems to hold some promise as a position, but its application is limited. It is best used where a social problem is not caused by identifiable corporations in the first place, where the business community possesses the specific skills and knowledge necessary to deal with the problem, where solutions can be clearly defined and tied to tangible economic rewards, and where the danger is minimal that an economic morality will deflect social needs from being met in a social way. For other social problems—a great many in contemporary society—"induce it" is not the logical place to be.

33

"Restore It"

The final position, on the far right of our horseshoe and strongly doctrinaire in character, seeks a fundamental change of the corporation's power configuration. It rejects all social goals in favor of the economic ones for the corporation, and again sees it as an Instrument, in this case of its owners. It is on this last point that change is proposed, for the proponents of this position believe that to the extent that the owners lost control, the corporation lost its legitimacy. Thus, they believe that the corporation should be restored to its former status, that is, returned to its "rightful" owners—the shareholders. Whereas the proponents of "induce it" implicitly accept power in the hands of the managers, those of "restore it" are convinced that the only way to ensure the unrelenting pursuit of economic goals—and to them that means the maximization of profit—is to put control back into the hands of those to whom profit means the most.

In our terms, power in the hands of the owners, with the specific goal of profit maximization, would switch the corporation from a Closed System power configuration to an Instrument of external control. In this sense, "restore it" is close to "nationalize it," at the other end of the horseshoe and of the political spectrum. The two share the same fundamental diagnosis—that self-selected managers have no right to impose *their* interpretation of goals on the corporation. And they share the implication of that diagnosis—that the External Coalition must be shifted from the passive to the dominated form. Where they differ is on who that dominating influencer should be and what goals he or she should impose on the corporation.

MILTON FRIEDMAN'S FORM
OF "RESTORE IT"

The proponents of "restore it" are not many—corporate managers hardly among them[1]—but they are outspoken. These are individuals strongly committed to an ideology, "true believers" in Hofer's terms (1966). The foundation of their ideology was laid by Adam Smith, prophetically in the year that the foundation was laid for the American Revolution. In this century, their house was built—or more exactly refurnished—by Milton Friedman. Thus wrote Adam Smith in 1776:

> . . .every individual necessarily labours to render the annual revenue of the society as great as he can. He generally, indeed, neither intends to promote the public interest, nor knows how much he is promoting it. . . .he intends only his own gain, and he is in this, as in many other cases, led by an invisible hand to promote an end which was no part of his intention. Nor is it always the worse for the society that it was no part of it. By pursuing his own interest he frequently promotes that of the society more effectually than when he really intends to promote it. I have never known much good done by those who affected to trade for the public good. It is an affectation, indeed, not very common among merchants, and very few words need be employed in dissuading them from it. (1937, p. 423)

And thus writes Milton Friedman today:

> In a free-enterprise, private-property system, a corporate executive is an employee of the owners of the business. He has direct responsibility to his employers. That responsibility is to conduct the business in accordance with their desires, which generally will be to make as much money as possible while conforming to the basic rules of the society, both those embodied in law and those embodied in ethical custom.
>
> . . .in a free society. . ."there is one and only one social responsibility of business—to use its resources and engage in activities designed to increase its profits so long as it stays within the rules of the game, which is to say, engages in open and free competition without deception or fraud." (1970, pp. 33, 126; quoting from 1962, p. 133)

Smith was essentially making a case for "ignore it," but in economic instead of social terms. He argued, in effect, that the independent businessman could be ignored because by pursuing economic goals as vigorously as possible, he was serving social ends. Friedman accepts that premise, pleading with the businessman to do just that in contemporary terms: to serve the economic goals of the owners so that society can be served by a vigorous private sector

---

[1]The Brenner and Molander survey of *Harvard Business Review* readers found that only 28 percent "endorsed the traditional dictum that 'the social responsibility of business is to "stick to business"'" (1977, p. 68).

(and pleading more vigorously with government to leave him alone to do it). While Smith was legitimizing the world of small business he saw around him— trading for the "public good" being an "affectation. . .not very common among merchants"—Friedman finds a different world and so takes a more prescriptive posture, what we call "restore it." The "affectation" seems prevalent to him, and so he feels compelled to rail against it. Ironically, therefore, he must stand foursquare against "ignore it," saying in effect: "We cannot ignore it if it cannot ignore (or be allowed to ignore) social goals."

What disturbs Friedman is that sometime between the 1770s and the 1970s something went wrong on the way to the market. Managers tended to displace owners in the determination of corporate goals, and governments interfered with the free exchange of goods in the marketplace. In essence, a shift began away from the position on the right side of our horseshoe. Earlier we saw the vehemence with which Friedman attacks the proponents of social responsibility, which he calls a "fundamentally subversive doctrine," promoted by business-men who serve as "unwitting puppets of the intellectual forces that have been undermining the basis of a free society these past decades" (1970, pp. 126, 33). Now we see the source of his concern: Friedman believes that this represents the start of an unstoppable skid around the horseshoe, that any shift away from the position on the extreme right will inevitably lead to that on the extreme left. Thus, in the opening chapter of his book *Capitalism and Freedom*, Fried-man (1962) discusses "The Relationship between Economic Freedom and Political Freedom" as an either/or choice between only two possibilities—traditional capitalism and socialism as practiced in Eastern Europe. The absence of the former must lead to the latter.

> The preservation and expansion of freedom are today threatened from two direc-tions. The one threat is obvious and clear. It is the external threat coming from the evil men in the Kremlin who promise to bury us. The other threat is far more subtle. It is the internal threat coming from men of good intentions and good will who wish to reform us. Impatient with the slowness of persuasion and example to achieve the great social changes they envision, they are anxious to use the power of the state to achieve their ends and confident of their own ability to do so. Yet if they gained the power, they would fail to achieve their immediate aims and, in addition, would produce a collective state from which they would recoil in horror and of which they would be among the first victims. (p. 201)

In our terms, Friedman recognizes only two positions on the horseshoe, those at the extremes—"restore it" and "nationalize it." Hayek has made the same point precisely: Management control "would not long be left uncon-trolled. . . .if the management is supposed to serve wider public interests, it becomes merely a logical consequence of this conception that the appointed representatives of the public interest should control the management" (1960, p. 107). In other words, "restore it" or else!

The problem of who should control the corporation, therefore, becomes a war between two ideologies, in Friedman's terms, between "subversive...socialism" and "free" enterprise. In this world of black and white, there can be no middle ground, no moderate position on the horseshoe between the black of "nationalize it" and the white of "restore it," none of the gray of "trust it." Either the owners will control the corporation or else the government will. And so "restore it" becomes the obvious solution: it is imperative that ways be found to anchor the corporation on the right side of the horseshoe, the only place where "free" enterprise is safe. Power must be restored to the owners, with whom it resided in the days of Adam Smith, and social responsibility must be eliminated so that profits can be maximized.

But how is this to be done? Ironically, most of the proposals call for government intervention, to change the rules. Unrestrained free enterprise has encouraged the rise of giant corporations and has contributed to the dispersal and weakening of their ownership, and now government intervention must resolve the related problems![2] Among the proposals to "restore it" are provisions for new voting procedures to give the shareholders more effective control of the board of directors and changes in the tax laws to return all corporate profits to the shareholders, so that they can decide what they wish to do with them.[3]

CRITICISMS OF FRIEDMAN'S "RESTORE IT" POSITION FROM THE PERSPECTIVE OF ORGANIZATION THEORY

"Restore it" as described above rests on three sets of assumptions— technical, economic, and political. Each contains its own fallacies.

TECHNICAL ASSUMPTIONS: THE FALLACY OF SHAREHOLDER CONTROL   Among the technical assumptions of this position are (a) that shareholders will be willing

---

[2]Friedman would not likely endorse this statement in principle. Yet his arguments, while on one hand denying it, on the other hand support it. He believes, for example, that the tax system, by encouraging corporations to retain their earnings, has contributed to the problem (1962, p. 130). Yet, by agreeing that the Sherman antitrust laws did constitute a reasonable intervention by government in the private sector (p. 199), he joins other observers in attributing at least part of the problem to corporate behavior itself.

[3]Most of Friedman's own proposals, like the latter, call for changes in government, not corporations, usually involving a reduction in its interventionist role. In fact, Friedman says surprisingly little about corporate behavior itself, although he acknowledges what are to him certain problems (such as the pursuit of social responsibility). This, presumably, reflects his perspective as an economist, just as our own discussion centering on problems in corporate behavior and in changing the corporation itself reflect ours as a management or organization theorist. This will be especially evident in the critique that follows.

to control the corporation formally, (b) that they in fact can, and (c) that such control will make a difference.

Every trend of stock ownership during this century seems to refute the first two assumptions. We have seen that shareholders increasingly see their role as suppliers of capital in search of a stable return; if they do not find it in one place, then they simply move on to another. By and large, shareholders have found it easier to change their stock than the behavior of the large corporation. In effect, a free market does exist in stock ownership, and it serves to detach ownership from control.

Indeed, it is a fitting irony that this shareholder behavior may be attributable directly to the kind of economic theory Friedman espouses, in the words of Hirschman, who makes this point, to "the economist's bias in favor of exit and against voice" (1970, p. 17). Conventional economics has always told us that if you do not like it, you don't speak up, you get out. For example, "economists have refused to consider that the discontented consumer might be anything but dumbly faithful or outright traitorous (to the firm he used to do business with)" (p. 31). How then can economists complain about shareholders who leave when they are unhappy instead of staying around to try and change things; that is exactly the kind of behavior they have endorsed (for consumers and workers, if not shareholders) for a century!

What causes this problem is, of course, the dispersal of stockholding. (We have already seen that closely held corporations are in fact controlled by their owners, but that these number few among the Fortune 500.) Olson's analysis (1965, 1968), discussed earlier, shows that when power is distributed widely among the members of a large group, it pays no one of them to exercise it. They prefer to remain passive. That is the basic problem, for which no workable solution seems to have come along. Some have proposed "cumulative voting" as a solution—that shareholders be able to concentrate all of their votes on single directorships, instead of having to spread them across a whole slate. But in the 273 companies that instituted the system (most because of state requirements) surveyed by The Conference Board, "very few stockholders use the privilege even when it is available.... With almost no exceptions, management slates have been elected regularly by overwhelming majorities" (Bacon 1973, pp. 6, 8).[4]

We did note, in discussing Ralph Nader and related phenomena, one condition under which the Olson argument breaks down: when full-time organizers or permanent organizations exist to mobilize a dispersed constituency. Some observers, such as Eisenberg (1974) and Dooley (1969), have indeed drawn attention to one such group: the institutional investors. The mutual funds, pension plans, trust departments, insurance companies, and the like, now own enough stock on behalf of their clients and contain enough technical sophistication to be able to exercise a good deal of direct formal control over most of

---

[4]Nevertheless, "managements have been opposed to cumulative voting" (Chamberlain 1973, p. 187), in Bacon's as well as Chamberlain's opinion because they believe it would lead some directors to represent minority interests and thereby disrupt the functioning of the board.

the large corporations.[5] But they have shied away from doing so, preferring the convenient role of supplier of capital, outside the External Coalition, to the controversial and demanding one of owner, inside of it. Perhaps they have been restrained by the fear of discovering how much economic power they really can wield, although Eisenberg suggests other reasons:

> Generally speaking, the institutional investors take the position that their primary obligation lies to their own beneficiaries (using this term in its broadest sense to include shareholders in investment companies), not to their fellow shareholders in portfolio companies; that their staffs have neither the time nor the skill to oversee management; and that a company that requires a management change will normally be an unsound investment, so that the institutional investor should switch out as quickly as possible rather than stay in and try to accomplish the change. (1974, pp. 146–47)

The last of the technical assumptions—that formal shareholder control, specifically through the board of directors, will really make a difference—has been addressed at length in Chapter 6. We have seen that most directors lack the time and the information necessary to exercise close control of the management. At best, they name the chief executive; after that, they leave the making of specific decisions to him. We have also seen, however, that when one director represents concentrated ownership, he generally makes the effort to inform himself and can generally dictate the goals that guide the managers' decisions. But that ten or twenty directors who represent millions of small shareholders will do so has never been demonstrated. Thus, "restore it" no more provides the solution to the absence of formal external control than does the representative form of "democratize it," and perhaps even "nationalize it," and for the same reason. Even if the shareholders or the workers or perhaps even the government could seize effective control of the board, they would not necessarily be able to control the decisions of the management.

ECONOMIC ASSUMPTIONS: THE FALLACY OF FREE MARKETS   A second set of assumptions rests on the conventional views of economic theory. At the limit, this postulates the existence of free markets and full competition, unlimited entry, open information, consumer sovereignty, labor mobility, and so on. The debate over whether or not all of this is mythology has raged long and hard, and both sides have scored points. Evidence can be found in industrial societies of both extremes, from the competitive grain merchant to the monopolistic power utility. One point, however, favors the sceptics: the larger the corporation, the more it can manipulate the market.

[5]Dooley, for example, argued back in 1969 that the trust departments of major banks could gain board representation in many corporations if they so wished. He cited as evidence a 1968 report of the Subcommittee on Domestic Finance (Committee on Banking and Currency, U.S. House of Representatives) entitled "Commercial Banks and Their Trust Activities: Emerging Influence on the American Economy."

In 1776, Adam Smith wrote: "It is not from the benevolence of the butcher, the brewer, or the baker, that we expect our dinner, but from their regard to their own interest. We address ourselves, not to their humanity but to their self-love, and never talk to them of our own necessities but of their advantages" (1937, p. 14). But Smith did not have in mind Swift & Co., Anheuser-Busch, and ITT Continental Baking Co. One wonders what he would write today in the light of the immense size and market power of America's largest corporations, a General Motors for example with annual revenues in excess of the Gross National Product of a great many nations and a work force not far from one million people. How would Smith have responded to the massive use of advertising expenditures to restrict entry into an industry, the forming of cartels, the trading relationships among the divisions of the conglomerate firm? How would he have reacted to the following events, hardly atypical of the behavior of today's giant corporations:

> It was to the notion of community need that ITT appealed in 1971 when it sought to prevent the Justice Department from divesting it of Hartford Fire Insurance. The company lawyers said, in effect: "Don't visit that old·idea of competition on us. The public interest requires ITT to be big and strong at home so that it can withstand the blows of Allende in Chile, Castro in Cuba, and the Japanese in general. Before you apply the antitrust laws to us, the Secretary of the Treasury, the Secretary of Commerce, and the Council of Economic Advisers should meet to decide what, in the light of our balance-of-payments problems and domestic economic difficulties, the national interest is. (Lodge 1974a, p. 66)

Lodge notes that "effective shareholder democracy," what we call "restore it," "might work in small companies" (p. 66). But again, that is not the issue, either for Friedman or for his critics. All of the fuss is about the giant corporations. Ralph Nader is after General Motors, not Luigi's Body Shop. He attacks it not only because of its immense power to influence markets, but also because there is no foreseeable way to restore purely competitive conditions, as Smith's butcher, brewer, and baker experienced them (at least in our fantasies). Friedman is certainly consistent in attacking behavior such as that attributed to ITT above, and in decrying all other efforts by large corporations to interfere with free competition. But notwithstanding the nostalgia for markets gone by (if in fact they ever existed), times have changed. We now have technology that requires a $1 billion investment to bring certain types of chemical complexes on line. We have governments granting multibillion dollar contracts for defense equipment. Corporations have grown immensely large feeding on such technology, contracts, and markets. The thought of returning to arm's length competitive markets—of corporations coming and going like Adam Smith's brewers—while perhaps desirable, must be seen as an illusion in many sectors of the economy. As Hazel Henderson (1977) notes, referring to the "golden goose" model—"that the private, 'free market' sector of the economy generates the wealth" that supports the rest of society (p. 6):

> . . . this golden goose has been on a government life-support system ever since the Employment Act of 1946, when Keynesian macro-economic management tools were instituted to give it transfusions and pump up demand for its products, if necessary, by printing money. Today the golden goose model of our economy conceals the extent to which private profits are won by incurring public costs. (p. 7)

As for the assumptions of the sovereignty of the consumer and the mobility of the worker, again something went wrong on the way to the market. Friedman asserts: "The political principle that underlies the market mechanism is unanimity. In an ideal free market resting on private property, no individual can coerce any other, all cooperation is voluntary, all parties to such cooperation benefit or they need not participate" (1970, p. 126). But does that principle apply in the world of giant corporations?

When the corporation knows more than its clients do—a Ford knowing something about its gas tanks that its buyers do not—then there is room for deception (Arrow 1973, p. 307). Arrow refers to as "empirically shaky" the assumption of the "defenders of unrestricted profit maximization . . . that the consumer is well informed or at least that he becomes so by his own experience, in repeated purchases, or by information about what has happened to other people like him" (p. 309). A good deal of advertising can only be described as purely manipulative in nature, that is, designed not to inform but to *affect*—to create emotional need or dependency. To the extent that this kind of advertising works—expressly as it is designed to—then to use Friedman's terms, it coerces the consumer and evokes involuntarily cooperation, thereby distorting consumer sovereignty. Thus Braybrooke (1967) attacks the statement by corporations that "We only give the public what it wants," arguing that "the corporations have had a good deal to do with instilling these wants in the public." There is, for example, "the systematic abuse of sexual interests, so that people have their wants for automobiles and all sorts of other things seriously mixed up with their sexual desires. . . . How often do members of the public get a chance to think quietly in a sustained way about what they might want out of life?" (p. 230).

As for the mobility of the worker, to argue that he cannot be coerced by the large hierarchical organization—that he can always change jobs—is a little bit like saying that if the tree does not like the soil where it is rooted, it is free to move on. The employee makes a financial and an emotional commitment to a community and a job. He may have roots in a one-factory town; he may have skills unique to the company that trained him; he may be locked into his firm by virtue of an immobile pension plan. The decision to change jobs is hardly a casual one to the average employee. It is, in fact, an ironic twist of conventional economic theory that the worker is the one who typically stays put, thus rendering false the assumption of labor mobility, while the shareholder is the mobile one, thus spoiling the case for owner control!

Edward Carr, in his interesting little book *What is History?*, provides us with good words to conclude this discussion of the fallacy of free markets:

[Since the depression of the 1930s] nobody, except a few Rip Van Winkles of the nineteenth century, believes in [the classical] economic laws... Today economics has become either a series of theoretical mathematical equations, or a practical study of how some people push others around. The change is mainly a product of the transition from individual to large-scale capitalism. So long as the individual entrepreneur and merchant predominated, nobody seemed in control of the economy or capable of influencing it in any significant way; and the illusion of impersonal laws and processes was preserved.... But with the transition from a *laissez-faire* economy to a managed economy (whether a managed capitalist economy or a socialist economy, whether the management is done by large-scale capitalist, and nominally private, concerns or by the state), this illusion is dissolved. It becomes clear that certain people are taking certain decisions for certain ends; and that these decisions set our economic course for us. (1961, p. 187)

POLITICAL ASSUMPTIONS: THE FALLACY OF ISOLATED ECONOMICS GOALS AND OF ENTERPRISE AS PRIVATE   The final set of assumptions underlying Friedman's "restore it" position are also ideologic in nature, but more implicit. These are the essentially political assumptions that the corporation is amoral, society's instrument for providing goods and services, and, more broadly, that a society is "free" and "democratic" so long as its leaders are elected by universal suffrage and do not interfere with the activities of businessmen.

At the basis of Friedman's argument is the assumption of a sharp distinction between social and economic goals, the one to be pursued by elected leaders, the other by private businessmen. But like so much of conventional economic theory, this distinction ignores the reality in favor of tidy conceptualization. We noted earlier that social and economic consequences are inextricably intertwined in the strategic decisions of large corporations, yet that these organizations cannot be described as amoral at all, but as vehicles of an economic morality. The effect on social needs is clear, and has already been discussed. In effect, Friedman ignores some of the fundamental arguments that underlie the attack on the giant corporation. We shall look at three in particular: (a) that some of the means used by the giant corporation contribute to undesirable ends in society, (b) that society cannot achieve the required balance between social and economic goals so long as its most powerful sector attends only to economic goals, and (c) that a society cannot be considered fully democratic so long as its most powerful institutions themselves are not run in a democratic manner.

The first argument proceeds as follows: In the world of corporate activity, means and ends interact. The corporation is not just a machine that ingests resources at one end and discharges products and services at the other, with a certain level of efficiency. All along the way, and at both ends, all kinds of social events take place, with both positive and negative consequences for the society at large. Jobs get created and rivers get polluted, cities get built and workers get injured, some individuals rise to their full potential and others waste their talents. In other words, the "firm necessarily produces two products: [its] economic goods and services... and... the social effect on people involved in the production, distribution, and consumption of those goods and services inside the firm as well as in the community in which the firm operates" (Elbing 1970, p. 82). As a result, "we can no longer measure the influence of business solely in terms of economic well-being and national wealth" (p. 83).

Some of these social "externalities" can be measured in economic terms, with the result that the corporation can be penalized or induced financially to respond to society's wishes. But many cannot, so that society must find means that do not work through the profit mechanism to elicit the desired behaviors. If the corporation is to be an Instrument, say the critics of "restore it," then let it be the Instrument of all those affected by its actions. Not only its economic ends but also its social means must be brought under societal control. Thus speaks one corporate activist: ". . . if society determines that the economic function previously delegated to corporations is no longer serving society, then society has the right and obligation to reexamine that function and, if necessary, to revoke the delegation of authority and redefine the function" (Moore 1974, p. 50).

The second criticism of the political assumptions focusses not on specific behaviors of the single corporation but on the influence of the whole corporate collectivity. When Adam Smith wrote that the pursuit of self-interest promotes the "public interest," he had something very special in mind, as does Milton Friedman today—society's economic goals. Social goals were to be left to another sector. But to many of today's critics, that neat division of labor has proved inequitable; the cards are stacked in favor of the private sector. The public sector may be large, but it too is heavily influenced by the power of business and its economic goals.[6] As a result, the economic goals of society are believed to dominate the social ones. How much of its resources ought society to devote to material pursuits? How much efficiency does it need, and at what social price? These choices—if they can, indeed, be choices—should, all would agree, be left to the public and its elected representatives. But economic values and corporate power are hardly neutral factors in these choices:

> In theory the public asserts control through government. Legislation proscribes or prescribes certain kinds of corporate activity, and the courts enforce those mandates. But, in fact, several key elements of this form of public legitimacy have broken down. One is the disproportionate power that corporations have to influence the elections of officials, as well as the course of legislation. McGovern's fund-raising theme is a simple example. He needed one million people to contribute $25 each, while Nixon needed 25 people to contribute $1 million each. The second is the way that corporations can fight full implementation of previously watered-down legislation. Corporations can spend years fighting off the filing of an anti-trust complaint, much less its prosecution. Corporations can outspend in tax

[6]A number of years ago, in an analysis of the activities of the Canadian federal government in terms of five national goals, I found that the great majority of departments, including the most powerful, were devoted exclusively or primarily to the pursuit of the goal of economic development (Mintzberg 1974).

deductible money, the U.S. attorney's office that is trying to enforce a federal environmental law . . . And . . . corporations have a disproportionate influence on public attitudes through advertising and public relations effort. (Moore, pp. 51–52)

How then can we talk of the amoral corporation or of the one which merely minds its own economic business when the economic morality of business can be so persuasive? The "amoral" corporation is accused of producing the one-dimensional society in which economic goals override humanitarian ones. Thus speaks Kenneth Arrow in a moderate voice:

> Profit maximization . . . tends to point away from the expression of altruistic motives. Altruistic motives are motives whose gratification is just as legitimate as selfish motives, and the expression of those motives is something we probably wish to encourage. A profit-maximizing, self-centered form of economic behavior does not provide any room for the expression of such motives. (1973, p. 306)

"Restore it" would, by reason of this argument, take society one step back toward the jungle from which it has just begun to escape. If corporations are indeed so powerful, then it is argued that they must be changed if society is to be changed:

> . . . I think it is fair to say that every important social and political movement in this country must at some point focus on the corporate institution. And the reason is simple. Corporations are powerful: they are where the action is: it's corporate products that pollute or don't work; it's corporate jobs that are not available to blacks or women. Corporations use an impersonal language with terms like efficiency, profit, and mass production that belie a lack of human concerns. . . . For any social change to be effective, the corporation has to be committed to that change. All the good laws, the good cases, the good ideas, and the good people are never felt by the beneficiaries of all that goodness until the corporations are committed to implementing those good things. (Moore 1974, p. 48)

In effect, Moore is saying that "only business can do it," although he believes that it will not do it of its own accord.

The final political criticism of Friedman's "restore it" is perhaps the most fundamental of all: Why the owners? If the power of the giant corporation is to be legitimized, why should it be concentrated in one group of influencers, especially that one. What is the justification for shareholder control, especially in the absence of vigorous competition. Such control would only restrict the enormous benefits of corporate power to one already privileged group, and in the process reinforce society's economic goals, to which the critics believe far too much attention has been paid already. Besides, property is not an absolute right in society: in a fundamental sense, the shareholders no more "own" the giant corporation than do the secretaries or the customers. As noted earlier, it is society's laws that have defined one kind of ownership, and society's institutions—judicial system, police forces, and so on—that have protected it. That same society has every right to change the definition of ownership if it so chooses.

Many of the laws pertaining to the giant corporation developed before it did. Maybe now is the time to make laws suited to what it has become. Lawyers such as Berle believe that society needs a new definition of property to correspond to the new power of the corporation. And he has seen it coming. Writing in 1952 about a "quiet translation" of U.S. constitutional law from the field of political to that of economic rights, he remarked: "The emerging principle appears to be that the corporation, itself a creation of the state, is as subject to constitutional limitations which limit action as is the state itself" (quoted in Berle and Means 1968, p. xvii). And so the question of who should "own" or "control" the corporation remains fundamentally open to social choice. Ultimately, it will be decided by people's contemporary needs, not by their conventional theories.

Who then should control the corporation? Conventional economic theory sees ownership as the reward of endeavor. He who exerted the energy to build the empire should own it. That is an appealing argument, to reward success. But how about the builder's son: Should he own the corporation because he happened to be born into the right family? How about the stock market operator who did something clever one day? Should one clever stunt count for more than forty years of sweat in the foundry? Bell finds it "politically and morally unthinkable that [the lives of the workers] should be at the mercy of a financial speculator," an "in-and-out" person with no commitment to the corporation. "True owners are involved directly and psychologically in the fate of an enterprise; and this description better fits the employees of the corporation, not its stockholders" (1971, p. 29). What about the government, which also contributed to building the corporation? As Berle notes, "Corporations derive their profits...increasingly from techniques resulting from state expenditures of taxpayers' money. In this sense, the American state is an investor in practically every substantial enterprise" (in Berle and Means 1968, p. xvi).

The fact is that ownership had a different meaning in the days of Adam Smith. Smith described one kind of democracy, where power would be distributed among many. He had in mind the many small proprietorships of his day, built and controlled personally by independent entrepreneurs, not Power Corporation or Imperial Oil (the actual names of two major Canadian corporations). Who should control Imperial Oil, Canada's largest petroleum company: the management of its American parent, Exxon? Exxon's millions of shareholders? The Canadian employees? The Canadian people? Their government? Precedent notwithstanding, the answer is far from obvious. But one thing is clear. Adam Smith's ideas cannot be transplanted wholesale into the twentieth century, when two hundred corporations control three-fifths of all the manufacturing assets of the United States. Of the largest of these Blumberg writes:

General Motors from many points of view can be regarded as a political or quasi-governmental institution. With 1969 sales of $24.295 billion...with 793,924 employees, economically dependent on it with annual wages of almost $7 billion and with an international production of 7.2 million cars and trucks in 1969, the decision of General Motors with respect to capital investment, plant locations and closings, employment, price and wage policies represent decisions of vast implications for the countries, communities and individuals involved. The concentration in the major industrial companies of such formidable economic power, affecting so many persons and communities, has been described by observers including Kingman Brewster and others as constituting private governments and it has been suggested that constitutional concepts developed with respect to traditional governmental processes might well be extended to the leviathans of industry. (1971, pp. 1563–64)

Should such concentrated power, outside of markets that can be called fully competitive, be subjected to the control only of those who happen to buy the stock? Indeed, at least one writer is prepared to make the case that the owners are the group *least* in need of formal power within the corporation, that the trading associates and others are the real disenfranchised ones:

> Of all those standing in relation to the large corporation, the shareholder is least subject to its power.... Shareholder democracy, so-called, is misconceived because the shareholders are not the governed of the corporation whose consent must be sought... Their interests are protected if financial information is made available, fraud and over-reaching are prevented, and a market is maintained in which their shares may be sold. A priori there is no reason for them to have any voice, direct or representational, in prices, wages, and investment.
>
> A more spacious conception of "membership," and one closer to the facts of corporate life, would include all those having a relation of sufficient intimacy with the corporation or subject to its power in a sufficiently specialized way. (Chaynes, quoted in Eisenberg 1974, p. 136)

Increasingly, the debate over who should control the corporation is addressing fundamental questions of democracy. What is that word to mean in highly developed societies? Should it be restricted to formal government, or broadened to encompass any institution that has an important influence on the citizen's daily life? Can a society be called democratic if its citizens must spend one-third of their awake hours in organizations which are not democratic, in which they are "subordinates" to other people, ultimately to a handful of self-selected managers at the top? Can democracy be preserved when a diminishing number of these organizations dominate the economic activities of the society, and, according to some, its social activities as well?[7]

---

[7]Many of these arguments could, of course, be made against other large organizations as well—independent institutions as well as agencies of the state. Indeed, we have already done so, for example at the end of Chapter 19, and we intend to do so again in later publications. The ultimate problem in our view is that of detached and impersonal bureaucracy, public *or* private—what we called the Closed System power configuration. That is why Friedman's argument that an unimpeded marketplace and absolute owner control is preferable to government ownership falls on deaf ears in our case.

To conclude this critique, Friedman's form of "restore it" rests on some rather shaky assumptions, some technical, but the most important ones economic and political. These assumptions have hardly been investigated by the proponents of this position, who seem blind to the changes that have taken place in America during this century and to the changing basis of the debate over who should control the corporation. Theirs appear to be voices crying in the wilderness of time gone by. "Restore it" may make some sense for the small firm in a competitive environment—which typically does not need to be restored in any event. But it seems quaint in a world of giant corporations, managed economies, and dispersed shareholders, not to mention one in which the collective power of the corporations is coming under increasing scrutiny, in which the distribution between economic and social goals is being readdressed, and in which some fundamental questions are being raised about the role of the corporation in a society that claims to be democratic. The voices of this age are demanding fundamental changes in the giant corporation, changes that "restoring it" to shareholder control cannot render.

OTHER WAYS TO "RESTORE IT"

We have seen throughout these chapters indications of alternate ways to "restore it," ways that may help correct some of the fundamental problems.

In a widely accepted book entitled *Markets and Hierarchies*, Williamson (1975) argues that corporations have grown large and have diversified as a response to inefficiencies in capital markets—to idiosyncratic knowledge, opportunistic behaviors, and so on. In essence, he argues that hierarchies have proven superior to markets in the allocation of capital across industries. And the same could be said for control: Headquarters' control of performance represents an improvement over that by passive boards of directors. The implication is that the giant corporation has solved an economic and a managerial problem.

Yet what we have seen in this section of the book, and in the *Structuring* book (Mintzberg 1979a, pp. 414–30), is that these new giant divisionalized corporations pose some very serious problems for society—in the ways in which their control systems make them behave and in the power they are able to wield in both the economic and social spheres. And this power has given rise to comparable, countervailing powers in both labor and government. As a result, our societies have become ones of monolithic organizations, systems of nonhuman proportion.

Rather than applaud the problems the giant corporations have corrected, we might do well to address the far more serious ones they have created. And then "restore it" would deal with ways to return to a perhaps more human scale.

"Restore its institutions" where possible would seem to be one possibility. If capital markets are inefficient, we might do better to find ways to make them efficient. If boards are passive, then we should find ways to activate them. On this latter point, we do have proposals—to hold directors legally responsible for carrying out their duties and to provide them with adequate compensation and with independent staffs to ensure that they can. Directors selected by the corporate managers and paid at their discretion can hardly be expected to exercise independent judgment. Thus, one SEC chairman has proposed "that all directors except one be independent outsiders with no financial, familial, or other attachments to management. The only insider would be the chief executive, and he would *not* serve as chairman" (in Smith 1978, p. 153). But that raises the question of how the directors are to be chosen, which leads to the conclusion that this form of "restore it" would have to be coupled with some form of "democratize it."

The real implication of much of what we have seen is to try to "reduce it" where possible. Perhaps one way to "reduce it" is to "devolve its activities," the so-called devolution model calling for the contracting out to smaller firms of a good many of the services now performed within the corporation. Extending this proposal to vertical integration, firms would be asked to trade with their suppliers and customers instead of ingesting them, thereby opening up competition considerably. Whole networks of smaller firms could then carry out particular business, instead of fewer giant, centrally controlled ones. The construction industry has operated in this manner for years, and that is how NASA produced its hardware to go to the moon.

Supporting the "reduce it" posture in order to make it more competitive, Kaysen argues that "it is in fact possible to move much further than we have in this direction, without either significant loss in the over-all effectiveness of business performance or the erection of an elaborate apparatus of control" (1959, p. 211). But he is pessimistic about America's willingness to embark on such a course. As Kristol puts it, "break it up" sentiments have existed for a century, with little effect: ". . . the effort is by now routine, and largely pointless" (1975, p. 129). How will a society break up the giant institutions that now so dominate it? Of course, as we saw earlier in this chapter, there are good reasons why certain business operations must be large. But only certain ones, in specific manufacturing sectors. And we have no convincing evidence that corporations need be diversified—at least not from society's perspective—and much that they should not be. "Divest it" of all but its basic business would seem to be a posture well worth serious consideration.

To conclude, "restore it" is the nostalgic position on our horseshoe, a return to the glorious past of our fantasies with none of the associated problems—neither today's nor yesterday's. "Restore it" is also the most ambitious position of the eight, because it seeks to reverse powerful social and economic trends. A classical economist's view of "restore it" has been presented and rejected and then we have proposed some of our own nostalgia in its place, ours probably no more attainable than his. But we must try to do better—whether by pushing forward to something new or reverting backward to the best of the past—because what we have now is not good enough.

34

A Personal View
(or "If the Shoe Fits...")

Who should control the corporation? We have seen that it can be nationalized by the state, democratized by a variety of influencers, regulated by the government, pressured by special interest groups, trusted to the goodwill of its managers, ignored when it pays to be socially responsible, induced by financial incentives, or restored to the control of its official owners. I can hardly claim to have held my personal views in check while discussing these different positions around the horseshoe. But now, in this proverbial last chapter, I exercise my right as author to at least make these views explicit, pulling together the various opinions I have implicitly (and not always knowingly) slipped into the last eight chapters, in the form of a personal statement of who should control the corporation. I do this, I might add, with some trepidation. The trouble with prescription is that one never knows how things are going to work out in practice. How much nicer to be a descriptive theorist, to explain things as they are found. Ultimately, we shall have to develop our solutions through trial and error. Nevertheless I present here what I, personally, think are the directions most worth pursuing, at least at this point in time.

THE POSITIONS AS A PORTFOLIO   While, like everyone else, I have my favorite positions—which I shall soon get to—my strongest belief is that we are best off treating the various positions around the horseshoe as a *portfolio*, a kit of available tools. In other words, we should be prepared to draw on any and all of them (with one exception that I shall get to in due course) as different needs arise. "If the shoe fits," as the saying goes, then the corporation should be expected to "wear it." This may seem like an unwillingness on my part to take a stand. I think not. Mine is a stand for pluralism and eclecticism. We need the institution called the corporation, but we need it subjected to a variety of controlling forces. No single one will suffice in the society I believe most of us wish to live in, a society that seeks to be as democratic as possible, yet productive. The positions on the extreme left or right, for example, both lead to limited, narrow perspectives, ultimately to a society controlled by few instead of many. The same is true of the position in the center, which leaves ultimate power in the hands of a few top managers and maintains the corporation as a Closed System. Yet can anyone argue that these positions must never be relied upon, that governments, shareholders, or managers should have no power?

Theories called "contingency" have underlain the approach of this book and, indeed, all the books in this series: rather than having to select between plausible but conflicting theories that purport to describe the same phenomenon, we can accept each, in its own context. Not, as we saw in Chapter 15 for example, maximization of one goal *or* sequential attention to many, but both, depending on whether the External Coalition is dominated or divided. The same approach makes sense for the positions around our horseshoe. Not which force should always control the corporation, but which one when. The size of the corporation, the competition and concentration in its industry, its externalities and the dangers they pose to society, the importance of its mission in society and the relationship of that mission to public policy, these and many other factors will indicate what positions make the most sense in a particular case.

This is not to imply that the different positions do not represent fundamentally different values. Clearly they do, and clearly individuals with particular ideological orientations will have reason to favor some over the others, as do I. But I maintain that even the most ideologically committed individual—so long as he or she appreciates the realities of power in and around organizations—will see the need to mix the positions to deal with the problem of who should control the large corporation. The mix may vary, but not the concept of treating the positions as a portfolio.

Boulding (1968) takes an approach close to this in his argument that society must seek a balance between exchange systems, integrative systems, and threat systems. Broadly speaking, these represent the right, middle, and left sides of our horseshoe. We can do without none of these perspectives. Corporations are and will remain economic institutions, charged with providing most of our goods and many of our services. Yet they require socially responsible leaders. And they must be controlled by social and political forces beyond themselves. With this in mind, let me present my views of how a contemporary industrial, or perhaps postindustrial, society should draw on the positions around the horseshoe.

FIRST, "TRUST IT," OR AT LEAST "SOCIALIZE IT." The place to begin, in my view, is with "trust it," because if we cannot trust the good will of our managers, then we are surely in trouble. Three facts place "trust it" front and center in my portfolio, whether we like it or not. First, as large corporations—particularly the prevalent type we have called Machine Bureaucracy—are now run, and must be run if we are to insist on a certain level of efficiency, their managers must retain a great deal of power to make decisions. As we have seen, no degree of external pressure, regulation, even shareholder control, democratization, or nationalization, will change that fact. Second, as we have also seen, every important decision of the large corporation generates social as well as economic consequences, inextricably intertwined. That is why we cannot rely exclusively on the positions on the right side of the horseshoe. Corporations are economic institutions, but there is no sense in pretending that they are not also social ones. And third, again as we have seen, social goals remain in large part nonoperational. That is why we cannot rely exclusively on the positions well over to the left side of the horseshoe, nationalization or representative democracy for example, positions that assume that new goals can be plugged into the corporate computer merely by changing the directors. To the extent that the new goals are ill defined, these positions will have little effect on social behavior, and we shall be forced to fall back on those nearer the center in any event.

In other words, managers simply have a great deal of discretion, discretion not only to ignore social needs but also to subvert regulations and norms and get away with it. We are kidding ourselves if we believe we can dismiss the phenomenon called social responsibility. We saw in Chapter 30 a number of good reasons why it should not work, and why it is working increasingly badly. Yet we also saw that it still does work, because it maintains a base level of morality below which we still have a long way to fall.

There is perhaps no more important priority than to prop up social responsibility, in other words, to "socialize it." Indeed, if the evidence of Chapter 30 on the increasing influence of formal control systems is correct, then we shall need more attention to social responsibility, not less. As external influence becomes more difficult—as corporations, and all large institutions become more closed and more bureaucratic—social responsibility becomes our main hope for improved social behavior. In essence, we need moral people in high places, and we should put nothing ahead of trying to get them there.

In my opinion, it is the chief executive who must set the tone for socially responsible behavior, not by his pronouncements but by his own actions. It is events—what we have called "sagas"—that underlie an ideology, and what the corporation needs now above all is an ideology of social responsibility. Let the chief executive, for example, reward someone within the system who blows the whistle on illegitimate behavior. Let him refuse to allow the production of products of questionable utility. Let him surround himself with responsible executives, not just any gamesmen who can make it to the top. Then perhaps we can watch corporate behavior change, watch an ideology of social responsibility permeate the hierarchy.

"Trust it" is in good part a self-fulfilling prophecy. If we act as if corporate managers are evil bastards who cannot be trusted, then that is surely how they shall behave. On the other hand, if we appeal to their sense of social responsibility—as decent human beings with important responsibilities, among whose ranks angels and bastards are distributed as everywhere else—then from most at least we may expect responsible if not angelic behavior. As we quoted Waters in Chapter 30, let us "tap into the tremendous reservoir of energy that exists among employees" (1978, p. 13). I have, I hope, shown that the corporations are *ours*—everyone's—not just those of their official owners. As such, their leaders are *our* leaders, and we should expect from them no less than we expect of our leaders in other sectors of society. And as the pressures of managing the corporations become greater—and they have, and will continue to—the corporations will require greater leaders, ultimately more socially responsible and responsive ones. In other words, we *must* believe in social responsibility, in "trust it." We have no other choice.

Yet, we cannot *only* believe in "trust it." The role of this position in our portfolio must be limited to where it can do the most good. And that, in my opinion, is within the corporation's own sphere of operations. The logical posture for "trust it" is the insistence on responsible behavior in the corporation's own areas of expertise, not in trying to solve problems in other areas. Getting its own house in order will be more than enough for the corporation—to solve the problems it creates, to consider the social consequences of its own actions beyond what regulations, pressure campaigns, and financial inducements force it to do. Where the corporation has the most discretion is where it must act most responsibly: where economic forces can most easily subvert social needs, where externalities are significant yet unattributable, where the managers know a good deal more than their clients or employees and so can easily exploit them. Let the corporation first ensure that its employees are treated well, that in so far as possible they can work with dignity, that its products are useful and effective and are promoted fairly and honestly, with respect shown to those who buy them, that its production facilities are clean and safe, interfering minimally with those who must live near them. More fundamentally, let the corporation select its mission in the first place as one that will contribute constructively to society, rather than allowing itself to offer any legal product or service that can make money. Many judgements are involved here, but judgements are at the root of ethics, and exercising judgement is the first skill of the effective manager.

Social responsibility has no place outside the sphere of operations of the corporation. Managers are citizens and can act as such in any sphere. But in the name of the corporation, and using its power and resources, managers have no business acting outside of their own business. For causes "good" or "bad." How are we to know when the corporation is acting selfishly and when altruistically? General social issues are sensitive ones, best left free of the influence of the enormously powerful corporate sector of the society, with its economic orientation.

Few people today believe the corporation can or should solve social problems such as the urban crisis. But many, for example, believe it should donate to charity. I am increasingly convinced it should not. Friedman's arguments are pervasive here. Who are corporate managers to decide on the allocation of funds to quasi-public institutions? Corporate values cannot help but get mixed up in noncorporate issues. If there are surpluses to be distributed—and corporate donations to charity suggest there are—then let some independent body allocate them. Let, for example, every corporation be taxed some given percentage of its profits for local charities, hospitals, universities, and so on (or, better still, let its own trade associations set standard levels of giving, perhaps related to profits), and then let autonomous groups, free of corporate and, preferably, government control, distribute these funds (a practice that already exists in France in a limited form).

A stickier issue concerns the socially responsible stand forcing the regulation of corporations themselves. In my opinion, the appropriate stand is primarily one of abstention. It is up to the public, not the corporations, to decide how corporations should be regulated. Lobbying is a fine concept when the sides are balanced. In matters affecting the corporation, they often are not. Too much economic power is concentrated on one side. The most responsible stand for the corporation is to keep out of political and social debates. The notion of the corporation as society's economic instrument collapses as soon as that instrument uses its enormous power to affect social legislation. Let citizens, not institutions, decide on priorities. The corporation's role should be restricted to an honest assessment of the means of regulation—of suggesting what will and will not achieve what the public wants.

Of course, I have no illusions about this. Corporations will hardly stand by watching powers being taken away from them. As we saw clearly in Chapter 28, corporate resistance to regulation has been ubiquitous throughout this century, from child labor laws on up. Yet these efforts have served only to alienate the public; a cooperative, socially responsible stand might ultimately have better served the interests of the corporations, possibly resulting in fewer and more reasonable regulations in place of excessive ones imposed over their threatened dead bodies. As we also noted in that chapter, corporations are sometimes better off to *en*courage rather than *dis*courage government regulation, as the one means to protect themselves from the unscrupulous operators among them. (But abstention may still be the better stand, even in these cases. Let the public decide when it wants to regulate, not the corporations.) Likewise, the socially responsible attitude to existing regulation is compliance with the spirit and not just the letter of the rules (indeed, when they are ill conceived, the spirit instead of the letter). It should not be forgotten that regulations ultimately represent the wishes of the public at large.

Not being able *only* to trust the corporation means not just a limited perspective on social responsibility but also the need to complement "trust it" with other positions around the horseshoe.

THEN, "PRESSURE IT," CEASELESSLY.   After making such a strong pitch to trust the corporation, it may seem strange to turn around now and argue for external pressure on the corporation. These two approaches seem contradictory. Do we trust it or not? I'm inclined to answer "Yes, but . . . ." We need a two-sided effort: if you like, a pat on the head and a kick in the rear, maintenance activity to prop up what we like about the corporation, and change activity to challenge what disturbs us. We need social responsibility, but as we saw earlier, too many forces interfere with it—competition, bureaucratic control system, the cult of efficiency, and so on. "Power," to quote Acton one last time, "tends to corrupt; absolute power corrupts absolutely." "Trust it" rests on the premise of a Closed System power configuration; without a countervailing force, it will tend to corrupt the corporation.

This need for two sides explains why I have been somewhat dichotomous in this section of the book, on one hand supporting the managers of corporations, on the other hand challenging them. I, too, am pulled two ways, as a professor of management policy on one hand, sympathetic to their needs, as a citizen on the other, concerned about the consequences of their power. Managers need discretion to manage the corporation, for the sake of accomplishing its missing efficiently. Yet many abuse that discretion, at a high cost to society. Of course, I am not alone in favoring this dichotomy of forces. As noted in Chapter 29, Ralph Nader has said that if the corporation is "going to be responsible, it has to be insecure; it has to have something to lose" (quoted in Ackerman 1973, p. 411). And Jacobsen (1966, p. 90) notes in more formal language the tension between "relatively autonomous bureaucracy" and "bureaucracy which is under control of the environment wherein it functions," essentially the distinction between our Closed System and our Instrument. The first can be committed, can take initiative, but it tends to go its own way. The second lacks that intrinsic drive, but at least it can be directed. We need both in today's corporation; it is acceptable neither as a pure Closed System nor as a pure Instrument.

I fully recognize the implications of this in terms of the theory I presented earlier—a hybrid configuration which will likely increase conflict. But at this point in the development of the giant corporation, I believe we have no other choice. The corporation will serve us best if it exists in a field of social forces—internal ones pushing out, constrained by various external ones pushing in, together defining in a dynamic way where we as a society wish it to be at given points in time.

Thus there is a need for a countervailing force to internal power. But which should it be? Should we nationalize it or restore it, democratize it or regulate it, or perhaps pressure it? I shall eventually discuss the place of all five of these positions. But heading the list, in my opinion, must be "pressure it."

There are a number of reasons for this, which I shall get to in due course. But the one I wish to emphasize at the outset is that the pressure campaign underlies the success of all the other positions. We have seen this throughout our discussion, beginning as far back as Chapter 5. It usually takes a pressure campaign to bring about regulation, the attack on antisocial behavior in one corporation bringing to light the need to control such behavior in all corporations. The pressure campaign has also been used to focus attention on the problem of corporate governance, and so to promote not only the "democratize it" position but even the "restore it" position. Indeed, what if not a pressure campaign is the media blitz by Milton Friedman to promote shareholder control of the corporation. We saw in Chapter 31 that a case—albeit a limited one—could be made for "ignore it." But we also saw that that case rests clearly on the position of "pressure it," since without the pressure campaign—without pressure groups to make the corporation pay for its transgressions—the argument that "it pays to be good" collapses. Indeed, "pressure it" even supports "trust it," providing the proponents of the latter (under the guises of "ignore it") with their most powerful ammunition: "If we are not responsible...." Without the threat from "them"—namely those behind the pressure campaigns—how can responsible managers hope to keep irresponsible ones in check? Thus we have the results of the survey discussed in Chapter 29 that even corporate managers admit that "pressure it" plays a far greater role in causing higher ethical standards than either "regulate it" or "trust it."

"Pressure it" thus emerges from our discussion as a critical position, one whose absence would dramatically reduce the responsiveness of the corporation to social needs. The pressure campaign is used to change social norms and to initiate formal constraints—regulations and the like—but it also serves to correct deviations from accepted social norms and to foil attempts to circumvent existing constraints. In other words, it not only changes the corporation, it also polices it. Indeed, it is in the pressure campaign that the pluralist and populist traditions are best manifested, the notions that our institutions must be subjected to a multiplicity of forces and that any center of power should be considered suspect. In my view, these are the main ways in which we sustain the level of democracy that we have achieved. One could make the case that "pressure it" represents the most significant difference between Western and Eastern "democracies." The communist states have either "nationalized it" or "democratized it"; they "regulate it," "induce it," sometimes perhaps even "trust it"; in their own way, they sometimes "ignore it," and they continually discuss "restoring it." But so long as they do not "pressure it," the socialist corporation will remain far less responsive than its Western counterpart, the one under constant attack from a host of pressure groups. Give me one Ralph Nader to all those banks of government accountants.

What makes the pressure campaign so successful is its flexibility and its focus. All it takes is a group committed to a reasonable cause, a bit of imagination, and a bureaucratic but sensitive corporation. Consider what Ralph Nader has been able to extract from General Motors. The possibilities for attack on these grounds are limitless, almost as limitless as the vulnerability of the corporation concerned about its image as a Closed System. Of course, such powers can be abused. But in general, an attack can be sustained only if it touches a popular nerve—in other words, only if it uncovers an issue, particular or general, over which there is widespread public concern.

Obviously, I think "pressure it" is an important position on the horseshoe—alongside "trust it," *the* important position. But it is no panacea as a countervailing power to managerial influence. The pressure campaign is ad hoc and irregular—like the social norm, often vague and inconsistent. It leaves the power of response in the hands of the corporate managers, which is sometimes not appropriate. General Motors broadened the representation on its board of directors after Campaign GM, but it was the established executives and directors who decided who the new ones would be.

Thus, "pressure it" is a critical position, essential to balance external control with managerial prerogative. It is the second most important position in my portfolio, far ahead of the third. But it is one that must, nevertheless, sometimes be superceded by that third, and by others.

AFTER THAT, TRY TO "DEMOCRATIZE IT."   "Democratize it" is the most radical position which I shall support strongly, putting it third in my own portfolio of priorities. But I shall argue that this position is radical only in the context of the rather conservative debate in America about who should control the corporation. In terms of basic values—especially American values—corporate democracy is not a radical idea at all.

The calls to "democratize it" do not rest on any alien or subversive doctrine, but on the simple fact that if the word "democracy" is to have any real meaning, it must apply to the citizen's everyday life. Increasingly, ours is a world of organizations, a world in which not so much government per se but formal organizations—public and private and those in between—regulate the lives of the citizen. In this world, democratic or popular control of the state itself as a totality—that is, the election of political leaders—means less than democratic control of organizations, of all types. What is the use of controlling the legislature if the legislature cannot control the police force or the post office. And what is the use even of controlling public institutions if we cannot control the private ones where they impinge on us, every day—in the work we do, the images we see on television, the cleanliness of our rivers, the reliability of our products. Democracy matters where it affects us directly, and it is so affecting us increasingly through the actions of corporations. It affects us as employees, as clients, as neighbors, even as shareholders who, like the Soviet citizen, can vote for no more than the single slate of candidates hand picked by the incumbents. How can a society call itself democratic when many of its most powerful institutions—two hundred of them controlling most of its manufacturing assets, one of them employing close to one million people—are systems closed to governance from the outside and run as rigid hierarchies of authority on the inside?

Adam Smith had a form of democracy in mind when he wrote of his invisible hand. The butcher, the brewer, and the baker were to serve society as free men, independent of close government control. But the tables have turned since then. What was then a case for democracy becomes now a case for oligarchy. Smith's was an economy of shopkeepers and small entrepreneurs. Ours is one of giant institutions. To maintain these free of formal external control is to free only a small number of people who sit at their apexes. Everyone else sits below, within a rigid hierarchy of authority, subject to the control of a "superior."

Is that what the writers of the American constitution had in mind as democracy? I think not. In fact, I believe the concept of control used in the contemporary American corporation is the alien doctrine. Certain forms of "democratize it" are to my mind much closer to the basic American ideology—to populist, pluralist democracy. If the New England town council, then why not the corporation?

In getting down to specifics, I should say that I have no illusions about having the answer. The issue is extremely complicated, and, as we saw in Chapter 27, attempts to "democratize it" have often backfired. Changes must be made carefully so as not, on one hand, to reduce democracy in the name of creating it, and, on the other, to achieve it at the expense of destroying the corporation's capacity to accomplish its basic mission. But experimentation must continue until a formula is found guaranteeing a reasonable degree of popular control together with a reasonable level of operating efficiency.

We have discussed two basic ways to democratize it—broadening representation on the board of directors and encouraging direct participation in decision making. Representative democracy is easier achieved than participative democracy, although as we saw in Chapter 27, it makes less of a difference in how the corporation functions. But it should be pursued for one fundamental reason. Today's widely held corporation rests on a basis of governance that is fundamentally illegitimate. The shareholders have lost control of the board of directors, and no one—save the managers, who select the directors—have replaced them. This situation is simply unacceptable—no matter how socially responsible the managers—and should be changed as soon as possible.

Given the relative impotence of the board, that change will be more one of form than of substance. We have seen repeatedly in this book that a seat on the board buys little direct control of corporate decision making. But form is important here, because representative democracy will at least give the corporation a new legitimacy. Indeed, as noted in Chapter 27, it cannot help but benefit the managers themselves, who would give up little in return for a more secure base on which to manage (probably gaining, in the bargain, a reduction in pressure campaigns).

Germany has found one way to do this, achieving a form of representative democracy by mixing ostensible worker-directors with ostensible shareholder ones. Different proposals have emerged in the United States, to represent all kinds of external interest groups—minorities, consumers, and so on. Most of these proposals have been deemed unworkable. Yet it is amazing how quickly things become workable in the United States when Americans put their minds to it. I find it telling that the one case of public directors I came across in the literature—that of the New Jersey insurance companies, discussed in Chapter 27, where the Chief Justice of the State Supreme Court names the public directors—is not only "quite workable" (Bacon and Brown 1975, p. 48) in the opinion of the management of the largest of these companies, but was even supported by the companies when the state wanted to terminate it. Perhaps the companies liked the idea of having a base of legitimacy; the arrangement probably made no difference as to how they were managed anyway.

The logical way to proceed, in my opinion, is to try to design a mixed and balanced board—a pluralist one—including representatives of the workers, consumers, local and other communities significantly influenced by corporate actions, the shareholders (where true representatives can be found, otherwise members of investment agencies), and so on. Exclusive worker representation— as in Yugoslavia—is, in my opinion, ill advised, at least as industries become more oligopolistic, less competitive. Where competition is assured, worker control of the board—essentially the establishment of the organization as a form of cooperative—might be worth investigating in places. But for most of the large corporations, such worker control would enhance the Closed System configuration and could encourage exploitation of consumers and the public at large through self-serving decisions. On the other hand, some worker representation would give those with the greatest personal involvement in the corporation— the people who spend a third of their awake hours there—a stake in its governance. Such representation might also help to strengthen organizational ideology—to make the corporation a little less utilitarian, a little more missionary—evoking a greater and a healthier identification of the worker with his or her place of work.

Corporate constitutions, probably embedded in law, would have to designate which groups were to get how many seats and how each director was to be elected. Representation would presumably vary according to the industry in question—for example, a greater proportion of consumer representatives might be desirable on the boards of energy utilities, perhaps a greater proportion of worker representatives where competition is stronger, and so on.

With regard to this, three conditions are, to my mind, imperative. First, the corporation—or more exactly the corporate managers—should have no control whatsoever of the election procedures, any more than does the incumbent government in a democratic state. Second, not only must the directors be free of the managers, but they must also be legally responsible to carry out their duties of control conscientiously. Lawsuits against directors for deriliction of their duties are no more abhorrent than are comparable suits against physicians. And nothing will improve the performance of directors faster. Third, to resolve the dilemma of directors either lacking the time to become informed or becoming coopted when they get too involved, I think it necessary that a system of professional directorships emerge, where individuals work on a full-time basis to represent certain groups on corporate boards—on few enough boards to get to know each corporation well but many enough to be able to maintain a certain independence from each. To work effectively, such a system will require mandatory support from the corporation—a substantial salary for the directors, a small independent staff, and the legal right to access any employee of the corporation confidentially. It is this last power that would probably have the greatest impact, providing the employees with a much needed alternate channel of communication, to bypass the hierarchy of authority. Truly independent directors would inevitably emerge as the ombudsmen that corporate employees (not to mention clients and others) now so badly need.

Participative democracy is, however, another story. I think it desirable in principle, but far more difficult to achieve in practice, given the need to maintain a certain level of effectiveness. As I have argued repeatedly, most large corporations are organized as Machine Bureaucracies (or clusters of them in the Divisionalized Form) because of their size and their technical systems. In other words, they require tight, formalized and centralized structures to accomplish their missions efficiently. Workers have no power not because their foremen or bosses further up are power-hungry devils, but because that is how functional, inexpensive products can be made to come off the end of the assembly line. Not every assembler in Volvo can decide where he would like to bolt on the fenders. Only one person does that, and he sits in an engineering office. And he in turn takes his cue from a designer, whose work is in turn integrated with many others across and up the hierarchy. That is why participative democracy in Machine Bureaucracy (not in Meritocracy, where a high degree of it naturally exists, due to the complexity of the work), while a worthy goal, is not one to be aspired to, at least not until we see a far greater degree of automation.[1]

Yet there are certain constructive steps that can be taken toward participative democracy. Members of affected communities can, for example, be included in certain corporate decision processes—customers on new product design task forces, local community people on plant design teams, employees on committees dealing with job conditions (as is mandated by law for the German works councils). In many cases, it will be in the corporation's own interest to include them. As noted earlier, it is often far better to negotiate quietly with an influencer beforehand than to face his pressure campaign to block a decision already taken. The precedent has already been set in collective bargaining with the workers.

Another significant step toward participative democracy would be taken—indirectly at least—if governments and courts would move decisively

---

[1] As we discussed earlier in this book and at greater length in the *Structuring* book (Mintzberg 1979a, pp. 264–66, 458–59), by substituting skilled for unskilled workers, automation drives Machine Bureaucracy toward Adhocracy.

to end the notion of the limited liability of the employee. Watch what happens to participation and to authoritarianism as soon as the individual is held as accountable for his actions inside the corporation as out. Why should an individual cease to be a citizen when he serves as an employee? This change—so logical, so overdue (in practice if not legally)—would make a world of difference in the social behavior of the corporation.

To conclude, we cannot expect revolution from "democratize it." Indeed, if the experience to date is any indication, managers have far less to fear from democratization than from pressure campaigns (which means they should probably favor the former to reduce the latter). Nevertheless, we can expect constructive changes. But no matter the result, in any society dominated by its formal organizations, the issue of organizational democracy is a critical one. At least so long as it wishes to call itself "democratic." For that reason alone, I believe we shall be hearing a great deal more of "democratize it."

THEN, ONLY WHERE SPECIFICALLY APPROPRIATE, "REGULATE IT" AND "INDUCE IT." The remaining positions on the horseshoe have less utility for me, although they still belong in the portfolio. Facing each other on the moderate left and right are "regulate it" and "induce it," in a sense, mirror images of each other. Both call on the government to act, in one case to reduce or limit a certain behavior, in the other to encourage it. As noted in Chapter 32, while in principle the two are substitutable, in practice they should not be. It makes no sense to pay someone to stop hitting you on the head, or polluting your garden—at least not in a free society—any more than it makes sense to force someone to solve problems he has not caused. In other words, there are appropriate places for regulations and for inducements.

"Induce it" is appropriate for social problems the corporation has not created but has the capability to help solve. This, not "trust it," is the logical place for issues of social responsibility outside the corporations own sphere of operations. That is to say, while corporations should not voluntarily involve themselves in broader social issues, they should be induced to participate where they can help. When "only business can do it," then it is up to government to lure it in with financial incentives. By getting involved only on that basis, the corporation keeps its participation clean. No one can accuse it of trying to influence public policy.

The basis of corporate involvement must be defined precisely, and tied directly to financial rewards. Clearly no one wants to encourage graft—illegal overpayment for services—but neither should altruism be encouraged—society getting more than it paid for. For it can end up paying in other ways—through the infusion of the corporation's economic values into issues that must be decided on the basis of social values. In other words, "induce it" works best where the corporation really can play the role of society's economic instrument, rendering a specific service in return for fair remuneration.

"Regulate it" is more appropriate where the corporation did it to us in the first place, or might soon. In the case of regulation, we charge the organization for what it did, or control it so that it stops, or doesn't start.

Regulation is an indispensable tool for some problems and an inappropriate one for many others. It belongs where the power of the corporation can be abused—where power based on resources, privileged knowledge, or the absence of competition, can be used to exploit the weak. In the perfect world—the world where "trust it" really works—regulations would not be needed. Social responsibility would more than suffice. But there are bastards among the angels, and they, unfortunately must be forced up to some minimal level of behavior.

Regulation also belongs, and works best, where negative externalities— behaviors or their consequences deemed antisocial—can be identified with specific corporations. Like the nickle company that creates acid rain, or the electrical utility that overcharges its customers, or the food or toy manufacturer that promotes products to children who cannot realize their questionable worth.

But regulation is a clumsy instrument, especially where it requires a good deal of interpretation. And so must be used prudently. It is usually costly and inflexible (because it requires government legislation, sometimes followed by the establishment of bureaucracy); it is difficult to do effectively (for various reasons discussed in Chapter 28, a prime one being the location of the necessary information in the corporations to be regulated); and, in any event, it sets only minimum standards of behavior. Government cannot be the watchdog of all corporate behavior—indeed only of a rather small part of it. Otherwise we risk bringing the functioning of the corporations to a complete halt. Or, more likely and perhaps a greater threat to society and its capacity to adapt, we risk damaging small business—which can least afford to respond to a myriad of regulations—at the expense of big. This may one day prove to have been the greatest cost of regulation.

Yet, ironically, the best way for businessmen to stop overregulation by government may be not to fight regulation, but to cooperate with it. Government, and the public behind it, tend to overreact when they feel they cannot trust businessmen. To ensure sensible regulation, responsible businessmen must help the government design it to ensure that it is effective. A point worth repeating is that certain regulations cannot but help the responsible businessman, putting him on an equal footing with his less scrupulous competitors.

OCCASIONALLY, SELECTIVELY, "NATIONALIZE IT" AND "RESTORE IT" (BUT NOT IN FRIEDMAN'S WAY).   I see "nationalize it" and "restore it" as extreme positions reserved for extreme problems. If "pressure it" is a kind of scalpel, and "regulate it" a cleaver, then "nationalize it" and "restore it" are guillotines. This is not to argue that the head should never be lopped off the corporate body. There are times when it must. But we should not go around doing so indiscriminately. We hardly require a reign of terror to correct our problems!

In some sense, both these positions stand as alternatives to "democratize it." That is to say, each is a kind of democratization, after a fashion. "Nationalize it" offers state control, that is control by everyone, at least in principle. That is why the communist states call themselves "democracies." The problem, as we have seen, is that control by everyone—the ultimate case of dispersed influence—means control by no one, except the administrators at the center, sitting atop ever more remote hierarchies, (whether these be in the corporation or the government). With pervasive nationalization, we end up with the whole economy as a Closed System power configuration, closed to the influence of customers, employees, and the public at large. That would be a step away from the kind of grass-roots democracy I believe is so necessary. The right to elect public officials every few years who then oversee gigantic, impenetrable institutions that dominate our daily lives is not my idea of democracy. Moreover, large-scale nationalization mixes up priorities, treating the corporation as an agent of government policy instead of an instrument to produce goods and services, subject to the norms of social responsibility.

For its part, "restore it" offers so-called shareholder democracy. But with millions of dispersed shareholders, that too ends up in the Closed System configuration. Or, where there are few, shareholder democracy means political oligarchy. And were it even achievable one way or the other, large-scale shareholder control would, in contrast to nationalization, tilt priorities too far in the other direction, making it even more difficult for corporations to fulfill their social obligations.

That is why, of the three forms, I have come out strongly in favor of "democratize it." Though still far from adequate, it offers the widest and most flexible form of governance—the closest to a pluralist form of corporate democracy. In general.

But in particular we cannot dismiss either of these two extreme positions. There are times when we should "nationalize it"—and indeed do—notably when private enterprise cannot provide a necessary mission, at least in a sufficient way, and when the activities of an industry are intricately tied in to government policy. For example, Canada needs a state-owned corporation to develop knowledge and establish a state presence in the complex and sensitive petroleum industry. World events have taught us that the seven sisters—even, I should say especially, in the form of Canadian subsidiaries—will not take care of our national interests.

As for "restore it," I do not believe Milton Friedman's proposals adopted wholesale will solve any problems. They will only aggrevate those of political control and social responsibility, strengthening oligarchical tendencies in our society and further tilting the imbalance of economic goals over social ones. Like Friedman, I find dominant state control of industry and other institutions abhorrent. But unlike him, I do not see "restore it" as the only protection against "nationalize it." As I have tried to show in this section of the book, the beginning of the rotation around the horseshoe from the far right need not result in an unstoppable skid to the far left. Positions do exist at intermediate points, ones in fact more desirable than those at the extremes. My response to Friedman is, "a pox on both your houses." Neither "nationalize it" nor "restore it" work as general solutions because both encourage detached, impersonal bureaucracy. That is the real problem, whether public or private.[2]

But there are other forms of "restore it" well worth considering, although these are unrelated to shareholder control per se. We have seen a good deal of evidence in this book (and in the previous one on *Structuring*) of the problems generated by the size of corporations and by their diversification.[3] Big means machine bureaucratic, and that means oligarchic, locking people into rigid authoritarian systems. As for diversification, that all too often means interference with free market mechanisms. Williamson's arguments (1975), that hierarchies have proved better than markets at moving capital around, and the equivalent arguments that headquarters have proved better than boards at control of the management, make a great case for state ownership, do they not. Moreover, we have seen a good deal of evidence that the bigger, more bureaucratic, and more diversified the corporation, the *less* socially responsible it tends to be. Ackerman's research (1975)—showing that the control systems used by diversified firms drive out social goals—is indeed sobering. Put this together with the evidence we have seen on the apparent decline in corporate social responsibility—in a period when corporations have been growing ever larger and especially more diversified—and we have great cause for concern.

If capital markets are inefficient, then let us fix them up, instead of creating antisocial hierarchies in their place. If boards of directors do not function effectively, then let us improve them, instead of displacing them with yet another level of bureaucratic control. Earlier, in the context of corporate democratization, I discussed some ideas for strengthening the board of directors. But these changes can be made without democratization; indeed they are easily made. In my opinion, top priority should be given to holding directors legally responsible for the conscientious performance of their control functions, and then, to enable them to perform these functions, as noted earlier they should be provided with adequate compensation, independent staffs, and confidential access to employees within the firm.

And finally we must ask some central questions: Are corporations too big? Are they too diversified? As noted in Chapter 33, corporations in some industries must certainly be large. But can all bigness—in hospitals, unions, schools, and every other institution in society, no less than in the corporations—be justified in terms of economies of scale? I think not. I think our obsession with the size of our organizations has more to do with the ambitions of managers and politicians than it does with the laws of economics. All too often, size seems to be used to counter these "laws"—to exploit established position or sheer political influence in order to sustain less than optimally efficient operations.

[2]"Who Should Control the Large Organization?"—with little change in the text—would have been a title of this section equally in keeping with my beliefs.

[3]Some of the points raised below and subsequently, are discussed at greater length on pages 333–47 and 414–30 of the *Structuring* book.

A giant power game has been taking place in our society over the course of this century, one that has left us with too many overgrown, insensitive monoliths. As we saw at the outset of this discussion, Hazel Henderson puts this argument in the broadest context, arguing that "we are proceeding apace toward an evolutionary cul-de-sac" which she calls the "entropy state"—an unmanageable society where "the social and transactional costs equal or exceed the society's productive capabilities" (1977, p. 3). Essentially these are the costs generated by our giant institutions—the costs of administering them and their externalities and the whole social system that supports them, not to mention the costs "in human maladjustment, community disruption, and environmental depletion" (p. 3). Society pays, and must eventually collapse under the weight of these expenditures.

What about diversification? What does it do for society? We have seen evidence in this book and the *Structuring* one that conglomerate diversification may not only cost the citizen in terms of corporate social responsibility but also the shareholder in terms of market flexibility and economic performance. Moreover, conglomerate diversification, by reducing the level of the knowledge of the shareholder (where consolidated reports are provided in place of ones on individual businesses) and by dispersing shareholding, has made the corporation more of a Closed System. And it has contributed significantly to the creation of these monoliths, which seriously threaten free markets and populist democracy.

What if we balkanized the conglomerates? Does a Beatrice Foods with 397 distinct businesses (Martin 1976) provide us with a better stock market or more social responsibility than 397 distinct corporations? Even vertical integration may sometimes introduce inefficiencies into markets. What is wrong with an economy consisting of networks of smaller firms that trade with each other in the marketplace, instead of an economy of a few giant corporations that control transactions through integrated hierarchies?

What all of this comes down to is two alternate forms of "restore it" worth considering in the portfolio. One is "reduce it" outright, the other is to have it "divest itself" (which will, obviously, reduce it). Small may not necessarily be beautiful, but it can certainly be more humane, and more competitive, in many cases, more efficient as well. We have seen evidence on a number of occasions in this book that the focussed corporation—the one that knows intimately, from the chief executive on down, its products, its markets, its customers, and its local community—tends to be more socially responsible and, under at least some conditions, more productive as well. And it poses less of a threat to our democratic institutions. Commitment seems to be an important ingredient in performance—commitment to something tangible, something human, not just some abstract numbers on a bottom line. Commitment is generated not by formal systems of control, but by human interaction, not by communication in the form of marketing research reports or public relations programs, but in the form of face-to-face contact with customers and citizens.

This brings us back to the link between goal and mission, and to the issue of organizational ideology, as discussed in Chapter 11. The contemporary corporation is badly in need of an injection of such ideology—of personal belief in mission, of caring about products produced and services rendered.

I guard no illusions about accomplishing these changes. While boards of directors could be strengthened immediately—with some minor legislation—"reduce it" and "divest itself" will not happen quickly nor easily, if at all. How can a society of giant institutions act to break them up? And yet, somehow, serious attention should be given to these two positions, to reducing the corporation to the most effective economic and, where possible, human scale, and to having it divest itself of all but its basic business. My own feeling is that what blocks social responsibility (not to mention economic performance in some cases) in today's corporation are its own intrinsic conditions—notably its size and its diversification. Perhaps we shall never be able to "trust it" until we find the means to "reduce it" and to have it "divest itself."

FINALLY, ABOVE ALL, DON'T "IGNORE IT."   I leave one of the eight positions out of the portfolio, because it contradicts the others. The one thing I do not believe we can afford to do is "ignore it." (Even the proponents of "ignore it" make a case for "pressure it," as we have seen.) Everything I have seen convinces me that the current situation is unacceptable, and is becoming worse. The surveys we have reviewed suggest that a large majority of the American population shares these concerns. We can perhaps ignore it in the case of the organization committed to an identifiable community. But, for one last time, the debate is not about control of these firms, which tend to be small.[4]

The large corporation cannot remain a Closed System, one apparently less and less inclined to attend to its social obligations. Changes must be made, but carefully so as not to make the situation worse than it now is. That is why I reject the extreme positions on the horseshoe as general solutions. The proposal to "restore it" to shareholder control is not a solution, but an inevitable way to aggrevate the problems we now face. Few in our society are prepared to allow the corporation to revert to the Instrument of the wealthy. It has become a quasi-public institution for good. Occasionally we may wish to "nationalize it," but in general we must be careful of this position too. It represents a different way to aggrevate the problems we now face. We have no need for ever larger, more remote Closed Systems. Yet the pressures for state control, if not outright nationalization, are strong. "Regulate it" and "induce it" are forms of this, and they should be used only in limited circumstances, where they work effectively and there is no alternative. But monolithic control—by the state or an oligarchy of owners or of managers—can really be countered only by the use of other, intermediate positions on the horseshoe.

[4]And the "ignore it" position in certain forms, as we saw in Chapter 31, may do some good by encouraging socially responsible behavior, even if for the wrong reason. But it is the external posture of "ignore it"—to be taken by the larger society—that I reject.

The debate over who should control the corporation has moved around the horseshoe over the course of this century, beginning on the right and shifting toward the left. It is imperative that it now be anchored near the middle, away from the extremes. "Democratize it" is not really an extreme. We must find ways to achieve this without destroying the corporation's effectiveness, for the strength of our society lies in the pluralistic nature of its democracy. And we should never cease to "pressure it," for that is our most flexible device to control it. Yet we do not wish it to become a complete Political Arena. And so, above all else, we must find ways to "trust it," even if that requires us to "reduce it" and to have it "divest itself" of some of its operations. Our challenge is to find ways to distribute the power in and around our organizations so that they will remain responsive, vital, and effective.

Bibliography

ACKERMAN, R. W., "Public Responsibility and the Businessman: A Review of the Literature," in *Top Management*, ed. B. Taylor and K. Macmillan. New York: Longman, 1973. Copyright © 1971 by President and Fellows of Harvard College. Used with permission of the Harvard Business School.

_____, *The Social Challenge to Business*. Cambridge, Mass.: Harvard University Press, 1975. Reprinted by permission.

ACKOFF, R. L., *A Concept of Corporate Planning*. New York: John Wiley, 1970.

ADAMS, R. L., "The Process of Ideological Change in American Protestant Seminaries." Unpublished dissertation, Vanderbilt University, 1968; cited in McNeil and Thompson, 1971.

AGERSNAP, F., "Organization and Environment: An Analysis of Goals," in *Behavioral Approaches to Modern Management*, Vol. 1, ed. W. Goldberg. Gothenburg: Studies in Business Administration, 1970.

AGTHE, K. E., "Mitbestimmung: Report on a Social Experiment," *Business Horizons*, February 1977, pp. 5–14. Copyright © 1977, by the Foundation for the School of Business at Indiana University. Reprinted with permission.

ALEXANDER, G. J. AND R. A. BUCHHOLZ, "Corporate Social Responsibility and Stock Market Performance," *Academy of Management Journal*, 1978, pp. 479–86.

ALLEN, T. S., AND S. I. COHEN, "Information Flow in Research and Development Laboratories," *Administrative Science Quarterly*, 1969, pp. 12–19.

ALLISON, G. T., *Essence of Decision: Explaining the Cuban Missile Crisis*. Boston: Little, Brown, 1971. Copyright © 1971 by Graham T. Allison. Reprinted by permission of the publisher.

AMERICAN ASSEMBLY, *Corporate Governance in America*. Fifty-fourth meeting, 1978.

ANSOFF, H. I., *Corporate Strategy*. New York: McGraw-Hill, 1965.

ANTHONY, R. N., "The Trouble with Profit Maximization," *Harvard Business Review*, November-December 1960, pp. 126–34.

ARCHBOLD, S., "Dimensions of Participation," *Journal of General Management*, Spring 1976, pp. 52–66.

ARROW, K. J., "Social Responsibility and Economic Efficiency," *Public Policy*, 1973, pp. 303–17.

————, *The Limits of Organization*. New York: Norton, 1974.

ASTLEY, W. G., R. AXELSSON, R. J. BUTLER, D. J. HICKSON AND D. C. WILSON, "Decision Making: Theory III," Working Paper, University of Bradford Management Centre, 1980. Used with permission.

ATLANTIC REPORTER, "A. P. Smith Manufacturing Company v. Barlow," Second Series, Vol. 98 A.2d. St. Paul, Minn.: West, 1953.

BACON, J., *Corporate Directorship Practices: Membership and Committees of the Board*. New York: The Conference Board and the American Society of Corporate Secretaries, Inc., 1973.

————, AND J. K. BROWN, *Corporate Directorship Practices: Role, Selection and Legal Status of the Board*. New York: The Conference Board and the American Society of Corporate Secretaries, Inc., 1975.

BALDRIDGE, J. V., D. V. CURTIS, G. ECKER AND G. RILEY, *Policy Making and Effective Leadership*. San Francisco: Jossey-Bass, 1978.

BALKE, W. M., K. R. HAMMOND, AND G. D. MEYER, "An Alternate Approach to Labor-Management Relations," *Administrative Science Quarterly*, 1973, pp. 311–27.

BARNARD, C. I., *The Functions of the Executive*. Cambridge, Mass.: Harvard University Press, 1938.

BARON, P. A., AND P. M. SWEEZY, *Monopoly Capital: An Essay on the American Economic and Social Order*. New York: Modern Reader Paperbacks, 1966.

BAUMOL, W. J., *Business Behavior, Value and Growth*. New York: Macmillan, 1959.

BECKER, S. W., AND D. M. NEUHAUSER, *The Efficient Organization*. New York: Elsevier, 1975.

BELL, D., "The Corporation and Society in the 1970s," *The Public Interest*, 1971, pp. 5–32.

BERGMANN, A. E., "Industrial Democracy in Germany—The Battle for Power," *Journal of General Management*, Summer 1975, pp. 20–29.

BERLE, A. A., JR., "The Corporation in a Democratic Society," in *Management and Corporations 1985*, eds. M. Anshen and G. L. Bach. New York: McGraw-Hill, 1960.

————, AND G. C. MEANS, *The Modern Corporation and Private Property, rev. ed.* New York: Harcourt, Brace & World, 1968. Copyright 1982 by Macmillan Publishing Co., Inc., renewed 1960 by Adolph A. Berle, Jr., and Gardiner C. Means.

BERLINER, J. S., "A Problem in Soviet Business Administration," *Administrative Science Quarterly*, 1965, pp. 86–101.

BERLSON, B., AND G. A. STEINER, *Human Behavior: An Inventory of Scientific Propositions*, New York: Harcourt, Brace & World, 1964.

BEYER, J. M., AND T. M. LODAHL, "A Comparative Study of Patterns of Influence in United States and English Universities," *Administrative Science Quarterly*, 1976, pp. 104–29.

BIDWELL, C. E., "The School as a Formal Organization," in *The Handbook of Organizations*, ed. J. G. March. Chicago: Rand McNally, 1965.

BLAU, P. M., *The Dynamics of Bureaucracy*. Chicago: University of Chicago Press, 1963.

————, AND W. R. SCOTT, *Formal Organizations: A Comparative Approach*. San Francisco: Chandler, 1962.

BLUMBERG, P. I., "The Politicalization of the Corporation," *The Business Lawyer*, 1971, pp. 1551–87. Copyright © 1971 by the American Bar Association. All rights reserved. Reprinted with the permission of the American Bar Association and its Section of Corporation, Banking and Business Law.

————, "Reflections on Proposals for Corporate Reform Through Changes in the Composition of the Board of Directors: 'Special Interest' or 'Public' Directors," in *The Unstable Ground: Corporate Social Policy in a Dynamic Society*, ed. S. P. Sethi. Los Angeles: Melville, 1974.

————, *The Megacorporation in American Society: The Scope of Corporate Power*. Englewood Cliffs, N.J.: Prentice-Hall, 1975.

BOLING, T. E., "The Management Ethics 'Crisis': An Organizational Perspective," *Academy of Management Review*, 1978, pp. 360–65.

BOULDING, K. E., *Conflict and Defense*. New York: Harper & Row, 1962.

————, "The Ethics of Rational Decision," *Management Science*, 1966, pp. B161–69.

————, *Beyond Economics: Essays on Society, Religion, and Ethics*. Ann Arbor: University of Michigan Press, 1968.

BOULTON, W. R., "The Nature and Format of Director Information Flows: An Exploratory Study." Unpublished doctoral dissertation, Graduate School of Business Administration, Harvard University, 1977.

————, "The Evolving Board: A Look at the Board's Changing Roles and Information Needs," *Academy of Management Review*, 1978, pp. 827–36.

BOWER, J. L., "Planning Within the Firm," *The American Economic Review: Papers and Proceedings of the 82nd Annual Meeting*, May 1970, pp. 186–94.

————, "On the Amoral Organization: An Inquiry into the Social and Political Consequences of Efficiency," in *The Corporate Society*, ed. R. Marris, New York: Wiley, 1974. Used with permission.

BOWMAN, E. H., "Corporate Social Responsibility and the Investor," *Journal of Contemporary Business*, Winter 1973, pp. 21–43.

————, "Some Reflections on Corporate Strategy and Corporate Governance," *International Studies of Management and Organization*, Winter 1979, pp. 100–107.

————, AND M. HAIRE, "A Strategic Posture Toward Corporate Social Responsibility," *California Management Review*, Winter 1975, pp. 49–58.

————, "Social Impact Disclosure and Corporate Annual Reports," *Accounting, Organizations and Society*, 1976, pp. 11–21.

BOWMAN, J. S., "Managerial Ethics in Business and Government," *Business Horizons*, October 1976, pp. 48–54.

BRADSHAW, T. F., "Corporate Social Reform: An Executive's Viewpoint," in *The Unstable Ground: Corporate Social Policy in a Dynamic Society*, ed. S. P. Sethi. Los Angeles: Melville, 1974.

BRAGER, G., "Commitment and Conflict in a Normative Organization," *American Sociological Review*, 1969, pp. 482–91.

BRAYBROOKE, D., "Skepticism of Wants, and Certain Subversive Effects of Corporations on American Values," in *Human Values and Economic Policy*, ed. S. Hook. New York: New York University Press, 1967.

BRENNER, S. N., AND E. A. MOLANDER, "Is the Ethics of Business Changing?" *Harvard Business Review,* January-February 1977, pp. 57–71. Copyright © 1977 by the President and Fellows of Harvard College; all rights reserved.

BROWN, C. C., AND E. E. SMITH, eds., *The Director Looks at His Job.* New York: Columbia University Press, 1957.

BRUCKNER, D. J. R., "The Sovereignty of Big Business," *The Montreal Star,* January 19, 1972, p. 11.

BUCK, V. E., "A Model for Viewing an Organization as a System of Constraints," in *Approaches to Organizational Design,* ed. J. D. Thompson. Pittsburgh, Pa.: University of Pittsburgh Press, 1966.

BUCKLEY, J. W., "The Empirical Approach and MIS Design," *Organizational Dynamics,* Winter 1972, pp. 19–30.

BUEHLER, V. M., AND Y. K. SHETTY, "Managerial Response to Social Responsibility Challenge," *Academy of Management Journal,* 1976, pp. 66–78.

BURNS, T., "Micropolitics: Mechanisms of Institutional Change," *Administrative Science Quarterly,* 1961–62, pp. 257–81.

———, AND G. M. STALKER, *The Management of Innovation,* 2nd ed. London: Tavistock, 1966.

BUTLER, R. J., D. J. HICKSON, D. C. WILSON, AND R. AXELSSON, "Organizational Power, Politicking and Paralysis," *Organization and Administrative Sciences,* Winter 1977–78, pp. 45–59.

CARR, E. H., *What is History?* St. Paul, Minn.: Vintage Books, 1961.

CARTER, E. E., "The Behavioral Theory of the Firm and Top Level Corporate Decisions," *Administrative Science Quarterly,* 1971, pp. 413–28.

CARTWRIGHT, D., "Influence, Leadership, and Control," in *Handbook of Organizations,* ed. J. G. March. Chicago: Rand-McNally, 1965.

CHAMBERLAIN, N. W., *The Firm: Micro-Economic Planning and Action.* New York: McGraw-Hill, 1962.

———, *The Limits of Corporate Responsibility.* New York: Basic Books, 1973. Used with permission.

CHANDLER, A. D., *Strategy and Structure.* Cambridge, Mass.: MIT Press, 1962.

———, *The Visible Hand: The Managerial Revolution in American Business.* Cambridge, Mass.: Harvard University Press, 1977.

CHANDLER, M., "It's Time to Clean up the Boardroom," *Harvard Business Review,* September-October 1975, pp. 73–82.

CHEIT, E. F., "The New Place of Business: Why Managers Cultivate Social Responsibility," in *The Business Establishment,* ed. E. F. Cheit. New York: John Wiley, 1964.

CHILD, J., "Industrial Participation in Israel: A Personal Impression." Working Paper, The University of Aston Management Centre, 1975. Used with permission.

CLARK, B. R., *The Distinctive College.* Chicago: Aldine, 1970.

———, "The Organizational Saga in Higher Education," *Administrative Science Quarterly,* 1972, pp. 178–84.

CLENDENIN, W. D., "Company Presidents Look at the Board of Directors," *California Management Review,* Spring 1972, pp. 60–66.

COHEN, M. D., AND J. G. MARCH, *Leadership and Ambiguity: The American College President.* New York: McGraw-Hill, 1974.

————, "Decisions, Presidents, and Status," in *Ambiguity and Choice in Organizations,* ed. J. G. March and J. P. Olsen. Bergen, Norway: Universitetsforlaget, 1976.

————, AND J. P. OLSEN, "People, Problems, Solutions and the Ambiguity of Relevance," in *Ambiguity and Choice in Organizations,* ed. J. G. March and J. P. Olsen. Bergen, Norway: Universitetsforlaget, 1976.

COLLINS, J. W., AND C. G. GANOTIS, "Managerial Attitudes Toward Corporate Social Responsibility," in *The Unstable Ground: Corporate Social Policy in a Dynamic Society,* ed. S. P. Sethi. Los Angeles: Melville, 1974.

CONSTAS, H., "The USSR—From Charismatic Sect to Bureaucratic Society," *Administrative Science Quarterly,* 1961-62, pp. 282-98.

CRESSEY, D. R., "Achievement of an Unstated Organizational Goal: An Observation of Prisons," *The Pacific Sociological Review,* Fall 1958, pp. 43-49.

CROZIER, M., *The Bureaucratic Phenomenon.* Chicago: University of Chicago Press, 1964. Used with permission.

————, "Why is France Blocked?" in *Organizations of the Future: Interaction with the External Environment,* ed. H. J. Leavitt, L. Pinfield, and E. J. Webb. New York: Praeger, 1974. Used with permission.

————, AND E. FRIEDBERG, *L'acteur et le système.* Paris: Editions du Seuil, 1977.

CUMMINGS, L. L., AND A. M. ELSALMI, "Empirical Research on the Bases and Correlates of Managerial Motivation: A Review of the Literature," *Psychological Bulletin,* 1968, pp. 127-44.

CYERT, R. M., AND J. G. MARCH, *A Behavioral Theory of the Firm.* Englewood Cliffs, N.J.: Prentice-Hall, 1963.

————, H. A. SIMON, AND D. B. TROW, "Observation of a Business Decision," *Journal of Business,* 1956, pp. 237-48.

DACHLER, H. P., AND B. WILPERT, "Conceptual Dimensions and Boundaries of Participation in Organizations: A Critical Evaluation," *Administrative Science Quarterly,* 1978, pp. 1-39.

DAHL, R. A., "The Concept of Power," *Behavioral Science,* 1957, pp. 201-15.

————, *Who Governs? Democracy and Power in an American City.* New Haven, Conn.: Yale University Press, 1961.

————, "After the Revolution? Authority in a Good Society," New Haven, Conn.: Yale University Press, 1970b.

————, "Citizens of the Corporation," *The Montreal Star,* May 3, 1971, p. 9.

DALTON, M., *Men Who Manage.* New York: John Wiley, 1959.

DAVIS, K., "The Case For and Against Business Assumption of Social Responsibilities," *Academy of Management Journal,* 1973, pp. 312-22.

————, "Social Responsibility is Inevitable," *California Management Review,* Fall 1976, pp. 14-20.

DEAN, J., *Managerial Economics.* Englewood Cliffs, N.J.: Prentice-Hall, 1951.

DEARBORN, D. C., AND H. A. SIMON, "Selective Perception: A Note on the Departmental Identifications of Executives," *Sociometry,* 1958, pp. 140-44.

DEMERATH, N. J., III, AND V. THIESSEN, "On Spitting Against the Wind: Organizational Precariousness and American Irreligion," *American Journal of Sociology,* 1966, pp. 674-87.

DENT, J. K., "Organizational Correlates of the Goals of Business Managements," *Person-*

nel Psychology, 1959, pp. 365–93.

DEUTSCH, K. W., "On the Concepts of Politics and Power," in *Internal Politics and Foreign Policy,* ed. J. N. Rosenau, rev. ed. New York: Free Press, 1969.

DILL, W. R., "Business Organizations," in *Handbook of Organizations,* ed. J. G. March. Chicago: Rand-McNally, 1965.

DOKTOR, R., AND D. M. BLOOM, "Selective Lateralization of Cognitive Style Related to Occupation as Determined by EEG Alpha Asymmetry," *Psychophysiology,* 1977, pp. 385–87.

DONALDSON, G., "Financial Goals: Management vs. Stockholders," *Harvard Business Review,* May–June 1963, pp. 116–29.

DOOLEY, P. C., "The Interlocking Directorate," *The American Economic Review,* 1969, pp. 314–23.

DRUCKER, P. F., *Management: Tasks, Responsibilities, Practices.* New York: Harper & Row, 1973.

EDMUNDS, S. W., "Unifying Concepts in Social Responsibility," *Academy of Management Review,* 1977, pp. 38–45.

EDWARDS, J. P., "Strategy Formulation as a Stylistic Process," *International Studies of Management and Organization,* Summer 1977, pp. 13–27.

EELLS, R., AND C. WALTON, *The Conceptual Foundations of Business,* 3rd ed. Homewood, Ill.: Irwin, 1974.

EILON, S., "Goals and Constraints," *The Journal of Management Studies,* 1971, pp. 292–303.

EISENBERG, M. A., "Voting Membership in Publicly Held Corporations," in *The Unstable Ground: Corporate Social Policy in a Dynamic Society,* ed. S. P. Sethi. Los Angeles: Melville, 1974.

ELBING, A. O., "The Value Issue of Business: The Responsibility of the Businessman," *Academy of Management Journal,* 1970, pp. 79–89.

ENGLAND, G. W., "Personal Value Systems of American Managers," *Academy of Management Journal,* 1967, pp. 53–68.

EOYANG, C. K., "Differentiation and Integration in Communist China." Working Paper, Graduate School of Business, Stanford University, 1972.

EPSTEIN, E. M., "Dimensions of Corporate Power: Part I," *California Management Review,* Winter 1973, pp. 9–23.

———, "Dimensions of Corporate Power: Part II," *California Management Review,* Summer 1974, pp. 32–47.

———, "The Social Role of Business Enterprise in Britain: An American Perspective: Part II," *The Journal of Management Studies,* 1977, pp. 281–316.

ESTES, R. M., "The Emerging Solution to Corporate Governance," *Harvard Business Review,* November–December 1977, pp. 20–26, 164.

ETZIONI, A., "Authority Structure and Organizational Effectiveness," *Administrative Science Quarterly,* 1959, pp. 43–67.

———, *A Comparative Analysis of Complex Organizations.* New York: Free Press, 1961.

———, *Modern Organizations.* Englewood Cliffs, N.J.: Prentice-Hall, 1964.

EVERS, F. T., J. M. BOHLEN, AND R. D. WARREN, "The Relationships of Selected Size and Structure Indicators in Economic Organizations," *Administrative Science Quarterly,* 1976, pp. 326–42.

FELDMAN, J., AND H. E. KANTER, "Organizational Decision Making," in *Handbook of Organizations*, ed. J. G. March. Chicago: Rand-McNally, 1965.

FENN, D. H., JR., "Dilemmas for the Regulator," in *The Unstable Ground: Corporate Social Policy in a Dynamic Society*, ed. S. P. Sethi. Los Angeles: Melville, 1974.

FIEDLER, F. E., "The Contingency Model: A Theory of Leadership Effectiveness," in *Basic Studies in Social Psychology*, ed. H. Proshansky and B. Seidenberg. New York: Holt, Rinehart, & Winston, 1966.

FINDLAY, M. C., III, AND E. F. WILLIAMS, "Capital Allocation and the Nature of Ownership Equities," *Financial Management*, Summer 1972, pp. 68–76.

FOLLETT, M. P., "Constructive Conflict," in *Dynamic Administration: The Collected Papers of Mary Parker Follett*, ed. H. C. Metcalf and L. Urwick. New York: Harper & Row, 1942.

FRANK, A. G., "Goal Ambiguity and Conflicting Standards: An Approach to the Study of Organization," *Human Organization*, Winter 1958–59, pp. 8–13. Reproduced by permission of the Society for Applied Anthropology.

FRENCH, J. R. P., JR., AND B. RAVEN, "The Bases of Social Power," in *Studies in Social Power*, ed. D. Cartwright, pp. 150–67. Ann Arbor: Institute for Social Research, University of Michigan, 1959.

FRIEDMAN, M., *Capitalism and Freedom*. Chicago: University of Chicago Press, 1962.

———, "A Friedman Doctrine: The Social Responsibility of Business Is to Increase Its Profits," *The New York Times Magazine*, September 13, 1970, pp. 32, 33, 122, 124, 126.

GALBRAITH, J. K., *American Capitalism: The Concept of Countervailing Power*. Boston: Houghton Mifflin, 1952.

———, *The New Industrial State*. Boston: Houghton Mifflin, 1967.

GALBRAITH, J. R., *Designing Complex Organizations*. Reading, Mass.: Addison-Wesley, 1973.

GALLUP, G. H., *The Gallup Poll: Public Opinion, 1972–1977*. Wilmington, Del.: American Institute of Public Opinion, 1978.

GAMSON, W. A., "A Theory of Coalition Formation," *American Sociological Review*, 1961, pp. 373–82.

GARSON, G. D., "The Codetermination Model of Workers' Participation: Where is it Leading?" *Sloan Management Review*, 1977, pp. 63–78.

GEORGIOU, P., "The Goal Paradigm and Notes Towards a Counter Paradigm," *Administrative Science Quarterly*, 1973, pp. 291–310.

GLOVER, J. D., *The Attack on Big Business*. Boston: Division of Research, Graduate School of Business Administration, Harvard University, 1954.

GOFFMAN, E., "The Characteristics of Total Institutions," in *Complex Organizations: A Sociological Reader*, ed. E. Etzioni, pp. 312–40. New York: Holt, Rinehart & Winston, 1961.

GORDON, R. A., *Business Leadership in the Large Corporation*. Washington, D.C.: Brookings Institution, 1945.

GORE, W. T., "Administrative Decision Making in Federal Field Offices," *Public Administration Review*, 1956, pp. 281–91.

GOSSELIN, R., "A Study of the Interdependence of Medical Specialists in Quebec Teaching Hospitals," Ph.D. thesis, McGill University, 1978.

GOULDNER, A. W., "Cosmopolitans and Locals: Toward an Analysis of Latent Social Roles," *Administrative Science Quarterly*, 1957–58, pp. 281–306.

———, "Organizational Analysis," in *Sociology Today*, ed. R. K. Merton, L. Broom, and L. S. Cottrell, Jr., pp. 400–428. New York: Basic Books, 1959.

GROSS, E., "Universities as Organizations: A Research Approach," *American Sociological Review*, 1968, pp. 518–44.

———, "The Definition of Organizational Goals," *British Journal of Sociology*, 1969, pp. 277–94.

GUETZKOW, H., "Communications in Organizations," in *Handbook of Organizations*, ed. J. G. March. Chicago: Rand–McNally, 1965.

———, AND H. A. SIMON, "The Impact of Certain Communication Nets Upon Organization and Performance in Task-Oriented Groups," *Management Science*, 1954–55, pp. 233–50.

GUSSFIELD, J. R., "The Problem of Generations in an Organizational Structure," *Social Forces*, 1957, pp. 323–30.

GUSTAVSEN, B., "Redefining the Role of the Board," *Journal of General Management*, Spring 1975, pp. 35–44.

HALBERSTAM, D., *The Best and the Brightest*. New York: Random House, 1972.

HALL, R. H., *Organizations: Structure and Process*. Englewood Cliffs, N.J.: Prentice-Hall, 1972.

HAMBLIN, R. L., "Leadership and Crises," *Sociometry*, 1958, pp. 322–35.

HAMMOND, J. S., III, "The Roles of the Manager and Management Scientist in Successful Implementation," *Sloan Management Review*, Winter 1974, pp. 1–24.

HARRIS, H., *American Labor*. New Haven, Conn.: Yale University Press, 1938.

Harvard Law Review, "Developments in the Law—Corporate Crime: Regulating Corporate Behavior Through Criminal Sanctions," 1979, pp. 1227–1845.

HAYEK, F. A., "The Corporation in a Democratic Society: In Whose Interest Ought it and Will it Be Run?" in *Management and Corporations 1985*, ed. M. Anshen and G. L. Bach. New York: McGraw-Hill, 1960.

HAYNES, E., "Executives Wanted: Innovators and Risk Takers Only Should Apply," *Columbia Journal of World Business*, May-June, 1969, pp. 7–12.

HENDERSON, H., "Should Business Tackle Society's Problems?" *Harvard Business Review*, July-August 1968, pp. 77–85. Copyright © 1968 by the President and Fellows of Harvard College; all rights reserved.

———, "Unrestrained Growth Baits the Hook of Inflation," *Planning Review*, March 1977, pp. 3–7, 12, 28.

HEYDEBRAND, W. V., "Autonomy, Complexity, and Non-Bureaucratic Coordination in Professional Organizations," in *Comparative Organizations*, ed. W. V. Heydebrand, pp. 158–89. Englewood Cliffs, N.J.: Prentice-Hall, 1973.

HICKSON, D. J., R. J., BUTLER, R., AXELSSON, AND D. WILSON, "Decisive Coalitions." Paper presented to International Conference on Coordination and Control of Group and Organizational Performance, Munich, West Germany, 1976.

———, C. A. LEE, R. E. SCHNECK, AND J. M. PENNINGS, "A Strategic Contingencies' Theory of Intraorganizational Power," *Administrative Science Quarterly*, 1971, pp. 216–29.

HILL, W., "The Goal Formation Process in Complex Organizations," *The Journal of Management Studies*, 1969, pp. 198–208.

HILLS, F. S., AND T. A. MAHONEY, "University Budgets and Organizational Decision Making," *Administrative Science Quarterly*, 1978, pp. 454–65.

HININGS, C. R., D. J. HICKSON, J. M. PENNINGS, AND R. E. SCHNECK, "Structural Conditions of Intraorganizational Power," *Administrative Science Quarterly*, 1974, pp. 22–44. Used with permission.

HIRSCHMAN, A. O., *Exit, Voice, and Loyalty: Responses to Decline in Firms, Organizations, and States*. Cambridge, Mass.: Harvard University Press, 1970.

HOFER, E., *The True Believer*. New York: Harper & Row, 1966.

HOLDAWAY, E. A., J. F. NEWBERRY, D. J. HICKSON, AND R. P. HERON, "Dimensions of Organizations in Complex Societies: The Educational Sector," *Administrative Science Quarterly*, 1975, pp. 37–58.

HOOVER, J. D., R. M. TROUB, C. J. WHITEHEAD, AND L. G. FLORES, "Social Performance Goals in the Peruvian and the Yugoslav Worker Participation Systems," in *Proceedings of the National Meeting of the Academy of Management*, 1978, pp. 241–45.

HUNT, J. W., *The Restless Organization*. Sydney, Australia, Wiley International, 1972.

HUYSMANS, J. H. B. M., *The Implementation of Operations Research*. New York: Wiley-Interscience, 1970.

IJURI, Y., R. K. JAEDICKE, AND K. E. KNIGHT, "The Effects of Accounting Alternatives on Management Decisions," in *Information for Decision Making*, ed. A. Rappaport, pp. 421–35. Englewood Cliffs, N.J.: Prentice-Hall, 1970.

IZRAELI, D. N., "The Middle Manager and the Tactics of Power Expansion: A Case Study," *Sloan Management Review*, Winter 1975, pp. 57–70.

JACOBS, D., "Dependency and Vulnerability: An Exchange Approach to the Control of Organizations," *Administrative Science Quarterly*, 1974, pp. 45–59.

JACOBSEN, K. D., "Public Administration Under Pressure: The Role of the Expert in the Modernization of Traditional Agriculture," *Scandinavian Political Studies*, 1966, pp. 59–93.

JAY, A., *Management and Machiavelli*. New York: Penguin, 1970.

JENKINS, C., *Power at the Top*. Westport, Conn.: Greenwood Press, 1976.

——————, "Radical Transformation of Organizational Goals," *Administrative Science Quarterly*, 1977, pp. 568–86.

JONSSON, S., AND R. LUNDIN, "Role and Function of Myths for Planning: A Case of Local Government." Working Paper FE-rapport 52, University of Gothenburg, 1975. Used with permission.

KANTER, R. M., *Men and Women of the Corporation*. New York: Basic Books, 1977. Used with permission.

KAPLAN, A., *The Conduct of Inquiry: Methodology for the Behavioral Sciences*. New York: Chandler, 1964.

KASPER, D. M., "Competition and Regulation: Public Policy Considerations for Controlling Corporations," in *Proceedings of the National Meeting of the Academy of Management*, 1976, pp. 291–95.

KAST, F. E., AND J. E. ROSENZWEIG, *Organization and Management: A Systems Approach*, 2nd ed. New York: McGraw-Hill, 1974.

KATZ, D., AND R. L. KAHN, *The Social Psychology of Organizations*. New York: John Wiley, 1966.

KATZ, R. N., "Business Impact on Regulatory Agencies," in *The Unstable Ground: Corporate Social Policy in a Dynamic Society*, ed. S. P. Sethi. Los Angeles: Melville, 1974.

KAYSEN, C., "The Corporation: How Much Power? What Scope?" in *The Corporation in Modern Society*, ed. E. S. Mason. Cambridge, Mass.: Harvard University Press, 1959.

————, "The Business Corporation as a Creator of Values," in *Human Values and Economic Policy*, ed. S. Hook, pp. 209–23. New York: New York University Press, 1967.

KEIM, G. D., "Corporate Social Responsibility: An Assessment of the Enlightened Self-Interest Model," *Academy of Management Review*, 1978, pp. 32–39.

KHANDWALLA, P. N., "Organizational Design for Change," *Learning Systems, Conceptual Reading 5*. New Delhi, India: 1976. Used with permission.

————, *The Design of Organizations*. New York: Harcourt, Brace, Jovanovich, 1977. Used with permission.

KIPNIS, D., "The Powerholder," in *Perspectives on Social Power*, ed. J. T. Tedeschi, pp. 82–122. Chicago: Aldine, 1974.

KOENIG, T., R. GOGEL, AND J. SONQUIST, "Models of the Significance of Interlocking Corporate Directorships," *American Journal of Economics and Sociology*, 1979, pp. 173–86.

KOHLMEIER, L. M., JR., "Effective Regulation on the Public Interest," in *The Unstable Ground: Corporate Social Policy in a Dynamic Society*, ed. S. P. Sethi. Los Angeles: Melville, 1974.

KRALJ, J., "Is There a Role for Managers?" *Journal of General Management*, Winter 1976–77, pp. 7–16.

KRISHNAN, R., "Democratic Participation in Decision Making by Employees in American Corporations," *Academy of Management Journal*, 1974, pp. 339–47.

KRISTOL, I., "On Corporate Capitalism in America," *The Public Interest*, Fall 1975, pp. 124–41.

LAAKSONEN, O. J., "The Power Structure of Chinese Enterprises," *International Studies of Management and Organization*, Spring 1977, pp. 71–90.

LARCON, J.-P., AND R. REITTER, "Corporate Identity and Societal Strategy." Paper presented to seminar on *Societal Strategy and the Business Firm*, European Institute for Advanced Studies in Management, Brussels, 1978. Used with permission.

————, *Structures de pouroir et identité de l'enterprise*. Millan, France: Les éditions Fernand Nathan, 1979.

LEARNED, E. P., A. R. DOOLEY, AND R. L. KATZ, "Personal Values and Business Decisions," *Harvard Business Review*, March-April 1959, pp. 111–20.

LEEDS, R., "The Absorption of Protest: A Working Paper," in *New Perspectives in Organizational Research*, ed. W. W. Cooper, H. J. Leavitt, and M. W. Shelly II. New York: John Wiley, 1964.

LENTZ, A., AND H. TSCHIRGI, "The Ethical Content of Annual Reports," *The Journal of Business*, 1963, pp. 387–93.

LEVINE, J. H., "The Sphere of Influence," *American Sociological Review*, 1972, pp. 14–27.

LEVITT, T., "The Dangers of Social Responsibility," *Harvard Business Review*, September-October 1958, pp. 41–50.

————, "Why Business Always Loses," *Harvard Business Review*, March-April 1968, pp. 81–89. Copyright © 1968 by the President and Fellows of Harvard College; all rights reserved.

LEWIN, A. Y., AND C. WOLF, "The Theory of Organizational Slack: A Critical Review." Paper presented at the Twentieth Conference, The Institute of Management Sciences, Tel Aviv, 1973.

LEWIS, B. W., "Power Blocs and the Operation of Economic Forces: Economics by Admonition," *The American Economic Review*, Papers and Proceedings of the Seventy-first Meeting of the American Economic Association, 1959, pp. 384–98.

LEYS, W. A., "The Value Framework of Decision-Making," in *Concepts and Issues in Administrative Behavior*, ed. S. Mailick and E. H. Van Ness. Englewood Cliffs, N.J.: Prentice-Hall, 1962.

LIKERT, R., *New Patterns of Management*. New York: McGraw-Hill, 1961.

LINDBLOM, C. E., *The Intelligence of Democracy*. New York: Free Press, 1965.

———, *The Policy-Making Process*. New York: Prentice-Hall, 1968.

LITTERER, J. A., *The Analysis of Organizations*. New York: John Wiley, 1965; rev. ed. 1973.

LODGE, G. C., "The Utility of Ideology for Environmental Analysis," in *Formal Planning Systems*, ed. R. F. Vancil. Conference for Planning Executives, Harvard Business School, 1972.

———, "Business and the Changing Society," *Harvard Business Review*, March-April 1974*a*, pp. 59–72. Copyright © 1974 by the President and Fellows of Harvard College; all rights reserved.

———, *The New American Ideology*. New York: Knopf, 1975.

LONG, N. E., "The Corporation, Its Satellites, and the Local Community," in *The Corporation in Modern Society*, ed. E. S. Mason. Cambridge, Mass.: Harvard University Press, 1960.

LOURENÇO, S. V., AND J. C. GLIDEWELL, "A Dialectical Analysis of Organizational Conflict," *Administrative Science Quarterly*, 1975, pp. 489–508.

LOVING, R. JR., "Raymond Mason Needs More Than Optimism Now," *Fortune* (November 1975) pp. 120ff.

MACCOBY, M., *The Gamesman*. New York: Simon & Schuster, 1976.

MACE, M. L., *Directors: Myth and Reality*. Boston: Division of Research, Harvard Business School, 1971. Used with permission.

MACRAE, N., "The Coming Entrepreneurial Revolution: A Survey," *The Economist*, December 25, 1976, pp. 41–44, 53–65.

MADDEN, C., "Forces Which Influence Ethical Behavior," in *The Ethics of Corporate Conduct*, ed. C. Walton, pp. 31–78. Englewood Cliffs, N.J.: Prentice-Hall, 1977.

MANIHA, J., AND C. PERROW, "The Reluctant Organization and the Aggressive Environment," *Administrative Science Quarterly*, 1965–66, pp. 238–57.

MARCH, J. G., AND J. P. OLSEN, *Ambiguity and Choice in Organizations*. Bergen, Norway: Universitetsforlaget, 1976.

———, AND P. J. ROMELAER, "Position and Presence in the Drift of Decisions," in *Ambiguity and Choice in Organizations*, eds. J. G. March and J. P. Olsen. Bergen, Norway: Universitetsforlaget, 1976.

———, AND H. A. SIMON, *Organizations*. New York: John Wiley, 1958.

MARTIN, L. C., "How Beatrice Foods Sneaked Up on $5 Billion," *Fortune*, April 1976, pp. 118–21, 124, 126, 129.

MARTIN, N. H., AND J. H. SIMS, "The Problem of Power," in *Industrial Man: Businessmen and Business Organizations*, eds. W. L. Warner and N. H. Martin. New York: Harper, 1959.

MASLOW, A. H., *Motivation and Personality*. New York: Harper & Row, 1954.

McCALL, M. W., JR. "Power, Authority, and Influence," in *Organizational Behavior*, ed. S. Kerr. Columbus, Ohio: Grid, 1979.

McCLEERY, R. H., *Policy Change in Prison Management*. East Lansing, Mich.: Michigan State University, 1957.

McCLELLAND, D. C., "The Two Faces of Power," *Journal of International Affairs*, 1970, pp. 29–47.

———, AND D. H. BURNHAM, "Power is the Great Motivator," *Harvard Business Review*, March-April 1976, pp. 100–110.

McDONALD, J., "How the Man at the Top Avoids Crises," *Fortune*, January 1970*a*, pp. 121–22, 152, 154–56.

McNEIL, K., "Understanding Organizational Power: Building on the Weberian Legacy," *Administrative Science Quarterly*, 1978, pp. 65–90.

———, AND J. B. THOMPSON, "The Regeneration of Social Organizations," *American Sociological Review*, 1971, pp 624–37.

McNULTY, M. S., "A Question of Managerial Legitimacy," *Academy of Management Journal*, 1975, pp. 579–88.

MEAD, M., "From the Stone Age to the Twentieth Century," in *Development and Society: The Dynamics of Economic Change*, ed. D. E. Novack and R. Lekachman. New York: St. Martin's Press, 1964.

MECHANIC, D., "Sources of Power of Lower Participants in Complex Organizations," *Administrative Science Quarterly*, 1962, pp. 349–64.

MEDAWAR, C., "The Social Audit: A Political View," *Accounting, Organizations and Society*, 1976, pp. 389–94.

MERTON, R. K., *Social Theory and Social Structures*. New York: Free Press, 1957.

MICHELS, R., *Political Parties, a Sociological Study of the Oligarchical Tendencies of Modern Democracy*. New York: Free Press, 1915. [Translated from the Italian]

MILLER, D., AND P. FRIESEN, "Archetypes of Organizational Transition," *Administrative Science Quarterly*, 1980, pp. 268–99.

MILLER, D., AND H. MINTZBERG, "The Case for Configuration." Working Paper, McGill University, 1980.

MILLER, G. A., "The Magic Number Seven, Plus or Minus Two: Some Limits on Our Capacity for Processing Information," *The Psychological Review*, 1956, pp. 81–97.

MINTZBERG, H., *The Nature of Managerial Work*. New York: Harper & Row, 1973. Reissued in "The Theory of Management Policy Series," Englewood Cliffs, N.J.: Prentice-Hall, 1980.

———, "A National Goals Hierarchy," *Optimum*, 1974, pp. 5–16.

———, "Patterns in Strategy Formation," *Management Science*, 1978, pp. 934–48.

———, *The Structuring of Organizations: A Synthesis of the Research*. Englewood Cliffs, N.J.: Prentice-Hall, 1979*a*.

———, "Beyond Implementation: An Analysis of the Resistance to Policy Analysis," in *Operational Research '78*, ed. K. B. Haley. Amsterdam, Netherlands: North Holland. 1979*b*.

———, "Organizational Power and Goals," in *Strategic Management: A New View of Business Policy and Planning*, eds. D. E. Schendel and C. W. Hofer. Boston: Little, Brown, 1979c.

———, D. Raisinghani, and A. Théorêt, "The Structure of 'Unstructured' Decision Processes," *Administrative Science Quarterly*, 1976, pp. 246–75.

———, and J. A. Waters, "Tracking Strategy in an Entrepreneurial Firm," *Academy of Management Journal*, forthcoming.

Mitchell, J., "Management and the Consumer Movement," *Journal of General Management*, Summer 1976, pp. 46–54.

Mohr, L. B., "The Concept of Organizational Goals," *The American Political Science Review*, 1973, pp. 470–81.

Monsen, R. J., "Ownership and Management: The Effect of Separation on Performance," *Business Horizons*, August 1969, pp. 45–52.

———, J. S. Chiu, and D. E. Cooley, "The Effect of Separation of Ownership and Control on the Performance of the Large Firm," *Quarterly Journal of Economics*, 1968, pp. 435–51.

———, and A. Downs, "A Theory of Large Managerial Firms," *The Journal of Political Economy*, 1965, pp. 221–36.

Moore, P. W., "Corporate Social Reform: An Activist's Viewpoint," in *The Unstable Ground: Corporate Social Policy in a Dynamic Society*, ed. S. P. Sethi. Los Angeles: Melville, 1974.

Moyer, R. C., "Berle and Means Revisited: The Conglomerate Merger," *Business and Society*, Spring 1970, pp. 20–29.

Mulder, M., "Power Equalization through Participation?" *Administrative Science Quarterly*, 1971, pp. 31–38.

Mumford, E., and A. Pettigrew, *Implementing Strategic Decisions*. New York: Longman, 1975.

Murphy, T. A., "Businessman, Heal Thyself," *Newsweek* column "My Turn," December 20, 1976, p. 11.

Nader, L., "Power and Continuity." Paper presented to the Conference on the Exercise of Power in Complex Organizations, Wenner-Gren Foundation, 1980.

National Industrial Conference Board, *Corporate Directorship Practices*. Studies in Business Policy, November 12, 1967.

Nelson, R. L., *Merger Movements in American Industry 1895–1956*. Princeton, N.J.: Princeton University Press, 1959.

Neustadt, R. E., *Presidential Power: The Politics of Leadership*. Mentor, 1964.

Niv, A., "Survival of Social Innovation: The Case of Communes." Working Paper, The Jerusalem Institute of Management, 1978.

Normann, R., and E. Rhenman, *Formulation of Goals and Measurement of Effectiveness in the Public Administration*. Stockholm: Scandinavian Institutes for Administrative Research, 1975. Used with permission.

Olson, M., Jr., *The Logic of Collective Action: Public Goods and the Theory of Groups*. Cambridge, Mass.: Harvard University Press, 1965.

———, "A Theory of Groups and Organizations," in *Economic Theories of International Politics*, ed. B. M. Russett. Chicago: Markham, 1968.

OLTON, C. S., *Artisans for Independence: Philadelphia Mechanics and the American Revolution.* Syracuse, N.Y.: Syracuse University Press, 1975.

ORGANIZATION FOR ECONOMIC CO-OPERATION AND DEVELOPMENT, *Concentration and Competition Policy.* Paris: OECD, 1979.

ORNSTEIN, M. D., "Assessing the Meaning of Corporate Interlocks: Canadian Evidence," *Social Science Research,* 1980, pp. 287-306.

OUCHI, W. G., *Theory Z: How American Business Can Meet the Japanese Challenge.* Reading, Mass.: Addison-Wesley, 1981.

———, AND A. M. JAEGER, "Type Z Organization: Stability in the Midst of Mobility," *Academy of Management Review,* 1978, pp. 305-14.

———, AND J. B. JOHNSON, "Types of Organizational Control and Their Relationship to Emotional Well Being," *Administrative Science Quarterly,* 1978, pp. 293-317.

PALMER, D. A., *"Broken Ties: Some Political and Interorganizational Determinants of Interlocking Directorates Among Large American Corporations."* Paper presented at the Annual Meetings of the American Sociological Association, 1980.

PAPANDREOU, A. G., "Some Basic Problems in the Theory of the Firm," in *A Survey of Contemporary Economics,* Vol. 2, ed. B. F. Haley. Homewood, Ill.: Irwin, 1952.

PARKINSON, C. N., *Parkinson's Law, and Other Studies in Administration.* Boston: Houghton Mifflin, 1957.

PARSONS, T., *Structure and Process in Modern Societies.* New York: Free Press, 1960.

PATCHEN, M., "The Locus and Basis of Influence on Organizational Decisions," *Organizational Behavior and Human Performance,* 1974, pp. 195-221.

PELLERZI, L. M., "A Conceptual View of the Regulatory Process," in *The Unstable Ground: Corporate Social Policy in a Dynamic Society,* ed. S. P. Sethi. Los Angeles: Melville, 1974.

PERROW, C., "The Analysis of Goals in Complex Organizations," *American Sociological Review,* 1961, pp. 854-66.

———, *Organizational Analysis: A Sociological View.* New York: Wadsworth, 1970. Reprinted by permission of the publisher, Brooks/Cole Publishing Co., Monterey, Calif.

———, *Complex Organizations: A Critical Essay.* Glenview, Ill.: Scott, Foresman, 1972a.

———, "Is Business Really Changing?" *Organizational Dynamics,* Summer 1974, pp. 31-44.

PETER, L. J., AND R. HULL, *The Peter Principle.* New York: Morrow, 1969.

PETTIGREW, A. M., "Information Control as a Power Resource," *Sociology,* 1972, pp. 187-204.

———, *The Politics of Organizational Decision-Making.* London: Tavistock, 1973. Used with permission.

PFEFFER, J., "Size and Composition of Corporate Boards of Directors: The Organization and Its Environment," *Administrative Science Quarterly,* 1972, pp. 218-28.

———, "Size, Composition, and Function of Hospital Boards of Directors: A Study of Organization-Environment Linkage," *Administrative Science Quarterly,* 1973, pp. 349-64.

———, "Beyond Management and the Worker: The Institutional Function of Management," *Academy of Management Review,* 1976, pp. 36-46.

————, AND G. R. SALANCIK, "Organizational Decision Making as a Political Process: The Case of a University Budget," *Administrative Science Quarterly*, 1974, pp. 135–51.

————, "Organization Design: The Case for a Coalitional Model of Organization," *Organizational Dynamics*, Autumn 1977, pp. 15–29.

————, *The External Control of Organizations: A Resource Dependence Perspective*. New York: Harper & Row, 1978.

PFIFFNER, J. M., "Administrative Rationality," *Public Administration Review*, 1960, pp. 125–32.

————, AND F. SHERWOOD, *Administrative Organization*. Englewood Cliffs, N.J.: Prentice-Hall, 1960.

PIRSIG, R. M., *Zen and the Art of Motorcycle Maintenance: An Inquiry into Values*. New York: Bantam, 1974.

PONDY, L. R., "Effects of Size, Complexity and Ownership on Administrative Intensity," *Administrative Science Quarterly*, 1969, pp. 47–60.

PUGH, D. S., D. J. HICKSON, C. R. HININGS, AND C. TURNER, "Dimensions of Organizational Structure," *Administrative Science Quarterly*, 1968, pp. 65–105.

————, "The Context of Organization Structures," *Administrative Science Quarterly*, 1969, pp. 91–114.

REID, S. R., *Mergers, Managers, and the Economy*. New York: McGraw-Hill, 1968.

REIMANN, B. C., "On the Dimensions of Bureaucratic Structure: An Empirical Reappraisal," *Administrative Science Quarterly*, 1973, pp. 462–76.

RHENMAN, E., *Organization Theory for Long-Range Planning*. New York: John Wiley, 1973.

RICE, G. H., JR., AND D. W. BISHOPRICK, *Conceptual Models of Organization*. New York: Appleton-Century-Crofts, 1971.

RICHARDS, M. D., *Organizational Goal Structures*. St. Paul, Minn.: West, 1978.

RIDGWAY, V. F., "Dysfunctional Consequences of Performance Measurements," *Administrative Science Quarterly*, 1956, pp. 240–47.

RIESER, C., "The Chief Shows Them How at Indian Head," *Fortune*, May 1962, pp. 129–31, 160–68.

RIKER, W. H., *The Theory of Political Coalitions*. New Haven, Conn.: Yale University Press, 1962.

ROGERS, D., *110 Livingston Street: Politics and Bureaucracy in the New York City School System*. New York: Random House, 1968.

ROOSEVELT, F. D., "Economic Individualism and the Public Weal," in *Management and Society*, ed. L. H. Peters. Encino, Calif.: Dickenson, 1968.

ROSNER, M., "Principle Types and Problems of Direct Democracy in the Kibbutz." Working Paper, Social Research Center on the Kibbutz, Givat Haviva, Israel, 1969.

ROSS, I., "How Lawless are the Big Companies?" *Fortune*, December 1, 1980, pp. 56–64.

ROSSEL, R. D., "Autonomy in Bureaucracies," *Administrative Science Quarterly*, 1971, pp. 308–14.

RUMELT, R. P., *Strategy, Structure, and Economic Performance*. Boston: Division of Research, Graduate School of Business Administration, Harvard University, 1974.

RUSSELL, B., *Power: A New Social Analysis*. London: George Allen & Unwin, 1938.

SALANCIK, G. R., AND J. PFEFFER, "The Bases for Use of Power in Organizational Decision Making: The Case of a University," *Administrative Science Quarterly*, 1974, pp. 453–73.

―――, "Who Gets Power—and How They Hold on to It: A Strategic-Contingency Model of Power," *Organizational Dynamics*, Winter 1977, pp. 3–21.

SALES, A., "The Firm and the Control of its Environment," *International Studies of Management and Organization*, 1972, pp. 230–57.

SAMPSON, A., *The Sovereign State of ITT*. New York: Stein & Day, 1973.

SAMUEL, Y., AND B. F. MANNHEIM, "A Multidimensional Approach Toward a Typology of Bureaucracy," *Administrative Science Quarterly*, 1970, pp. 216–28.

SAUNDERS, C. B., "Setting Organizational Objectives," *Journal of Business Policy*, Summer 1973, pp. 13–20.

SCHEFF, T. J., "Control over Policy by Attendants in a Mental Hospital," *Journal of Health and Human Behavior*, 1961, pp. 93–105.

SCHEIN, E. H., "Organizational Socialization and the Profession of Management," *Industrial Management Review*, Winter 1968, pp. 1–16.

―――, AND J. S. OTT, "The Legitimacy of Organizational Influence," *American Journal of Sociology*, 1961–62, pp. 682–89.

SCHELLING, T. C., "Bargaining, Communication, and Limited War," *Journal of Conflict Revolution*, 1957, pp. 19–36.

SCHIFF, M., AND A. Y. LEWIN, "The Impact of People on Budgets," *The Accounting Review*, 1970, pp. 259–68.

SCHNEIDER, L, AND S. LYSGAARD, "'Deficiency' and 'Conflict' Thinking in Industrial Sociology," *American Journal of Economics and Sociology*, 1952, pp. 49–61.

SCOTT, B. R., "The New Industrial State: Old Myths and New Realities," *Harvard Business Review*, March-April 1973, pp. 133–48.

SELZNICK, A., "An Approach to a Theory of Bureaucracy," *American Sociological Review*, 1943, pp. 47–54.

―――, "Foundations of the Theory of Organization," *American Sociological Review*, 1948, pp. 25–35.

―――, *The Organizational Weapon: A Study of Bolshevik Strategy and Tactics*. New York: McGraw-Hill, 1952.

―――, *Leadership in Administration: A Sociological Interpretation*. New York: Harper & Row, 1957.

―――, *TVA and the Grass Roots*, 2nd ed. Berkeley: University of California Press, 1966. [First published in 1949]

SETHI, S. P., ed., *The Unstable Ground: Corporate Social Policy in a Dynamic Society*. Los Angeles: Melville, 1974. Copyright © 1975. Reprinted by permission of John Wiley & Sons, Inc.

―――, "Dimensions of Corporate Social Performance: An Analytical Framework," *California Management Review*, Spring 1975, pp. 58–64.

―――, "A Conceptual Framework for Environmental Analysis of Social Issues and Evaluation of Business Response Patterns," *Academy of Management Review*, 1979, pp. 63–74.

SIAR, *Annual Report 1973*. Stockholm: Scandinavian Institutes for Administrative Research, 1973.

SILK, L., AND D. VOGEL, *Ethics and Profits: The Crisis of Confidence in American Business.* New York: Simon & Schuster, 1976.

SILLS, D. L., *The Volunteers.* New York: Free Press, 1957.

SIMON, H. A., *Administrative Behavior,* 2nd ed. New York: Macmillan, 1957.

————, "On the Concept of Organizational Goal," *Administrative Science Quarterly,* 1964, pp. 1–22.

————, AND A. C. STEDRY, "Psychology and Economics," in *The Handbook of Social Psychology,* 2nd ed., ed. G. Lindzey and E. Aronson. Reading, Mass.: Addison-Wesley, 1968.

SINGER, E. A., AND L. M. WOOTON, "The Triumph and Failure of Albert Speer's Administrative Genius: Implications for Current Management Theory and Practice," *Journal of Applied Behavioral Science,* 1976, pp. 79–103.

SMITH, A., *An Inquiry into the Nature and Causes of the Wealth of Nations.* New York: Modern Library, 1937. [First published in 1776]

SMITH, L., "The Boardroom is Becoming a Different Scene," *Fortune,* May 8, 1978, pp. 150–54, 158, 162, 168.

SOELBERG, P., "Structure of Individual Goals: Implications for Organizations Theory," in *The Psychology of Management Decision,* ed. G. Fisk. Lund, Sweden: Gleerup, 1967.

————, "Unprogrammed Decision Making," *Industrial Management Review,* Spring, 1967, pp. 19–29.

STAGNER, R., "The Analysis of Conflict," in *The Dimensions of Human Conflict,* ed. R. Stagner. Detroit: Wayne State University Press, 1967.

STARBUCK, W. H., "Organizational Growth and Development," in *Handbook of Organizations,* ed. J. G. March. Chicago: Rand-McNally, 1965.

STARR, M. K., *Management: A Modern Approach.* New York: Harcourt, Brace, Jovanovich, 1971.

STEDRY, A. C., *Budget Control and Cost Behavior.* Englewood Cliffs, N.J.: Prentice-Hall, 1960.

STERBA, R. L. A., "Clandestine Management in the Imperial Chinese Bureaucracy," *Academy of Management Review,* 1978, pp. 69–78.

STIGLER, G. J., "Review of P. S. Samuelson's Foundations of Economic Analysis," *Journal of the American Statistical Association,* 1948, pp. 603–5.

STRAUSS, G., "Tactics of Lateral Relationships: The Purchasing Agent," *Administrative Science Quarterly,* 1962–63, pp. 161–86.

————, "Workflow Frictions, Interfunctional Rivalry, and Professionalism: A Case Study of Purchasing Agents," *Human Organization,* 1964, pp. 137–49.

————, AND E. ROSENSTEIN, "Workers Participation: A Critical View," *Industrial Relations,* 1970, pp. 197–214.

STURDIVANT, F. D., AND J. L. GINTER, "Corporate Social Responsiveness: Management Attitudes and Economic Performance," *California Management Review,* Spring 1977, pp. 30–39.

STYMNE, B., *Values and Processes: A Systems Study of Effectiveness in Three Organizations.* Stockholm: Scandinavian Institutes for Administrative Research, 1972. Used with permission.

————, "A Behavioral Theory of Strategy Formulation." Working Paper, Stockholm

School of Economics, 1975. Used with permission.

SUKEL, W. M., "Third Sector Organizations: A Needed Look at the Artistic-Cultural Organization," *Academy of Management Review*, 1978, pp. 348–54.

SWANSON, G. E., "An Organizational Analysis of Collectivities," *American Sociological Review*, 1971, pp. 607–24.

TAGIURI, R., "Value Orientations and the Relationship of Managers and Scientists," *Administrative Science Quarterly*, 1965, pp. 39–51.

TANNENBAUM, A. S., "Unions," in *Handbook of Organizations*, ed. J. G. March. Chicago: Rand-McNally, 1965.

————, AND R. L. KATZ, "Organizational Control Structure," *Human Relations*, 1957, pp. 127–40.

TERKEL, S., *Working*. New York: Pantheon Books, a Division of Random House, Inc., 1972. Used with permission.

THOENIG, J. C., AND E. FRIEDBERG, "The Power of the Field Staff: The Case of the Ministry of Public Works, Urban Affairs and Housing in France," in *The Management of Change in Government*, ed. A. F. Leemans. The Hague: Martinus Nijoff, 1976.

THOMPSON, J. D., *Organizations in Action*. New York: McGraw-Hill, 1967.

————, AND A. TRUDEN, "Strategies, Structures and Processes of Organizational Decision," in *Readings in Managerial Psychology*, ed. H. J. Leavitt and L. R. Pondy. Chicago: University of Chicago Press, 1964.

TUMIN, M., "Business as a Social System," *Behavioral Science*, 1964, pp. 120–30.

UDY, S. H., JR., *Organization of Work*. New Haven, Conn.: HRAF Press, 1959.

VICKERS, G., *The Art of Judgment: A Study of Policy Making*. New York: Basic Books, 1965.

WALLICH, H., AND J. J. MCGOWAN, "Stockholder Interest and the Corporation's Role in Social Policy," in *A New Rationale for Corporate Social Policy*, pp. 39–59. New York: Committee for Economic Development, 1970.

WALTERS, K. D., "Corporate Social Responsibility and Political Ideology," *California Management Review*, Spring 1977, pp. 40–51.

WALTON, C., ed., *The Ethics of Corporate Conduct*. Englewood Cliffs, N.J.: Prentice-Hall, 1977.

WARNER, W. K., AND A. E. HAVENS, "Goal Displacement and the Intangibility of Organizational Goals," *Administrative Science Quarterly*, 1968, pp. 539–55.

WARRINER, C. K., "The Problem of Organizational Purpose," *Sociological Quarterly*, 1965, pp. 139–46.

WATERS, J. A., "Catch 20.5: Corporate Morality as an Organizational Phenomenon," *Organizational Dynamics*, Spring 1978, pp. 3–19.

WEAVER, P. H., "Corporations Are Defending Themselves with the Wrong Weapon," *Fortune*, June 1977, pp. 186–96.

WEBER, M., "The Three Types of Legitimate Rule," trans. H. Gerth, in *A Sociological Reader on Complex Organizations*, 2nd ed., ed. A. Etzioni. New York: Holt, Rinehart, & Winston, 1969, pp. 6–15.

WESTLIN, A. F., "Good Marks but Some Areas of Doubt," *Business Week*, May 14, 1979, pp. 14, 16.

WILDAVSKY, A. B., "Budgeting as a Political Process" in *International Encyclopedia of the Social Sciences*, Vol. 2, ed. D. L. Sills. New York: Crowell, Collier, Macmillan, 1968.

WILENSKY, H. L., "The Trade Union as Bureaucracy," in *Complex Organizations: A Sociological Reader*, pp. 221–34, ed. A. Etzioni. New York: Holt, Rinehart & Winston, 1961.

WILLIAMSON, O. E., "A Model of Rational Managerial Behavior," in *A Behavioral Theory of the Firm*, ed. R. M. Cyert and J. G. March, pp. 237–52. Englewood Cliffs, N.J.: Prentice-Hall, 1963.

———, *The Economics of Discretionary Behavior: Managerial Objectives in a Theory of the Firm*. Englewood Cliffs, N.J.: Prentice-Hall, 1964.

———, *Markets and Hierarchies: Analysis and Anti-trust Implications*. New York: Free Press, 1975.

WORTHY, J. C., *Big Business and Free Men*. New York: Harper & Row, 1959.

WRIGLEY, L., "Diversification and Divisional Autonomy." DBA thesis Graduate School of Business Administration, Harvard University, 1970.

YOUNG, M., *The Rise of the Meritocracy: 1870–2033*. New York: Random House, 1959.

ZALD, M. N., "Power Balance and Staff Conflict in Correctional Institutions," *Administrative Science Quarterly*, 1962–63, pp. 22–48.

———, "Comparative Analysis and Measurement of Organizational Goals: The Case of Correctional Institutions for Delinquents," *The Sociological Quarterly*, 1963, pp. 206–30.

———, "Who Shall Rule? A Political Analysis of Succession in a Large Welfare Organization," *Pacific Sociological Review*, 1965, pp. 52–60.

———, "Urban Differentiation, Characteristics of Boards of Directors, and Organizational Effectiveness," *American Journal of Sociology*, 1967–68, pp. 261–72.

———, "The Power and Functions of Boards of Directors: A Theoretical Synthesis," *American Journal of Sociology*, 1969, pp. 97–111.

———, AND M. A. BERGER, "Social Movements in Organizations: Coup d'Etat, Insurgency, and Mass Movements," *American Journal of Sociology*, 1978, pp. 823–61.

ZALEZNIK, A., AND M. F. R. KETS DE VRIES, *Power and the Corporate Mind*. Boston: Houghton Mifflin, 1975.

Index